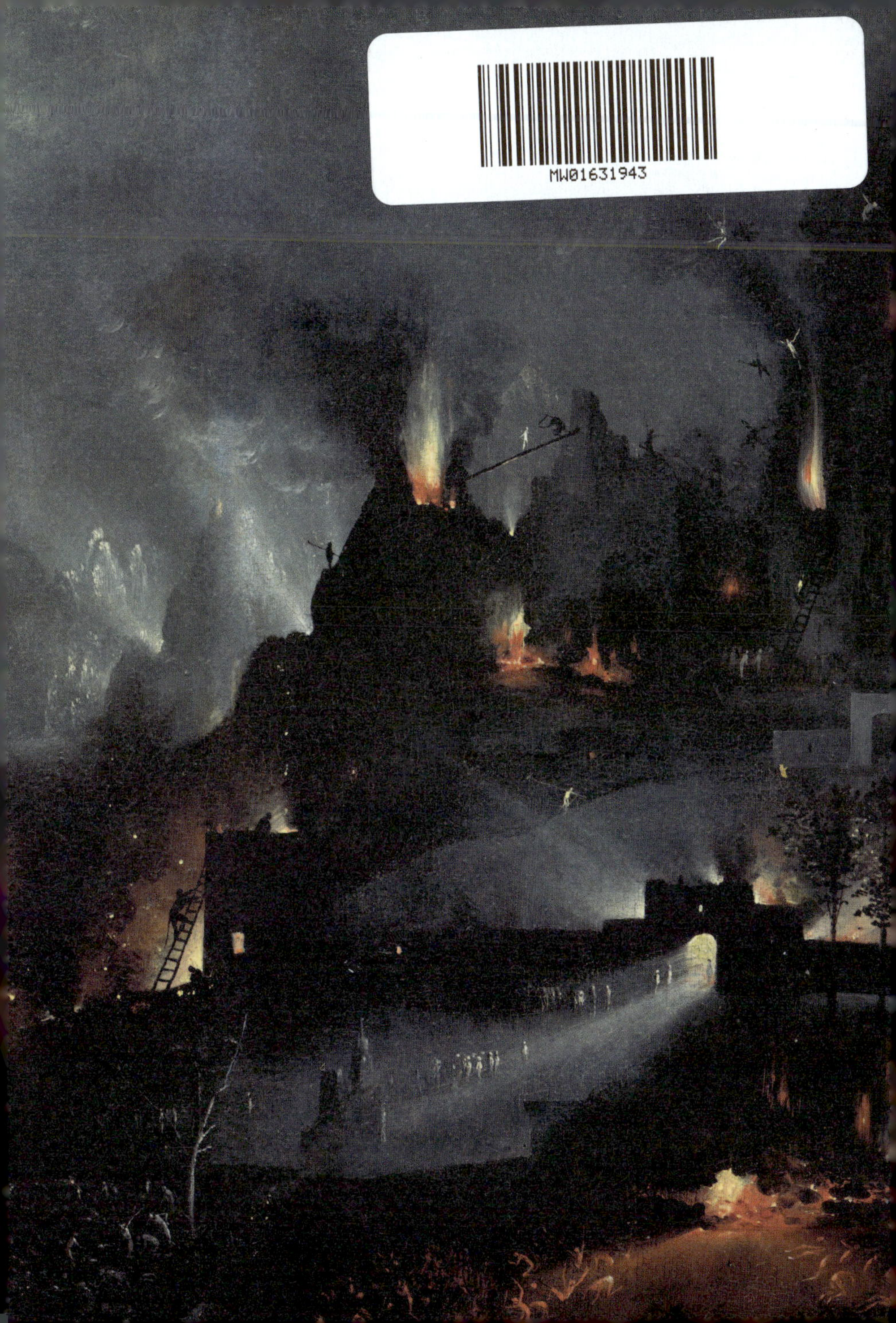

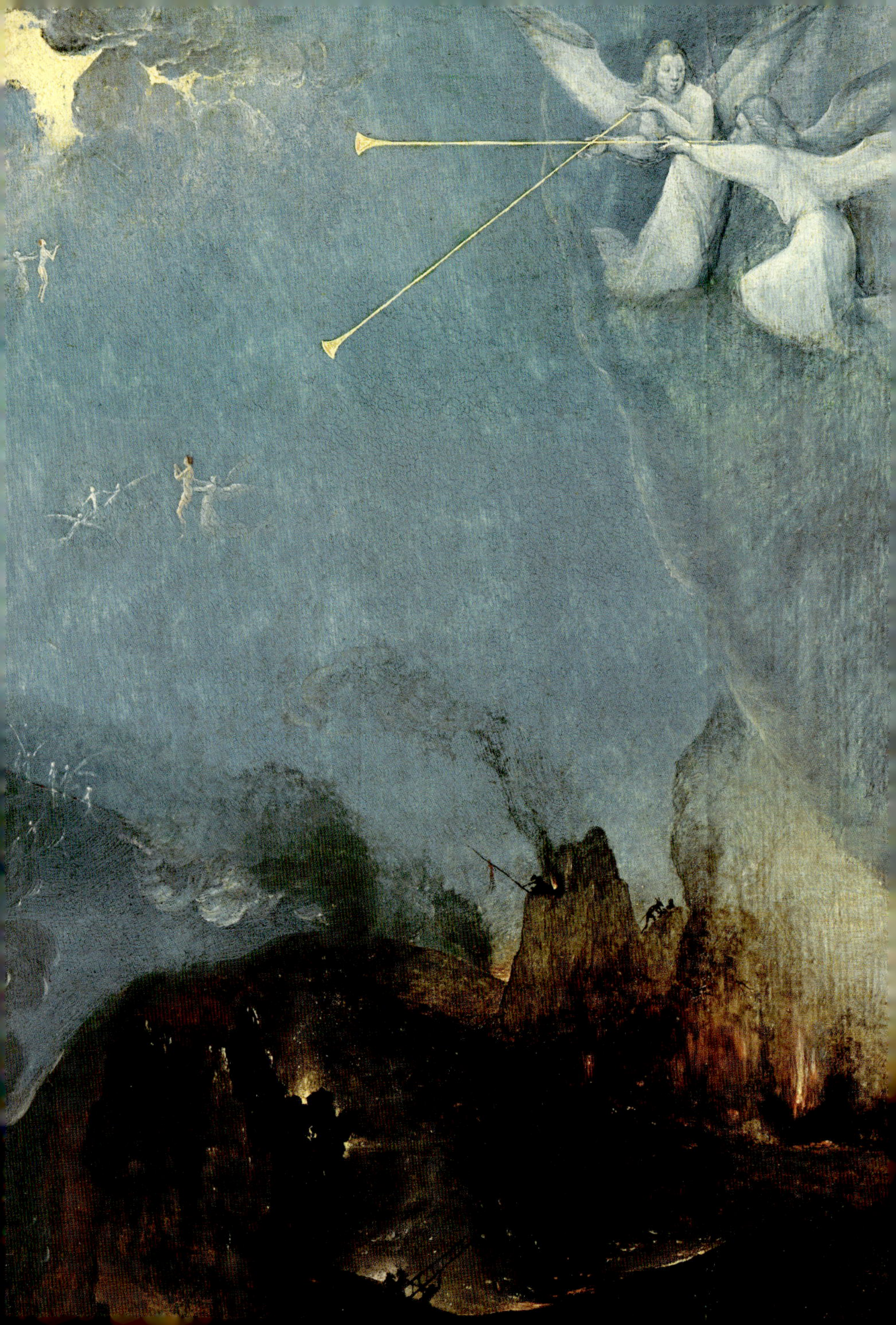

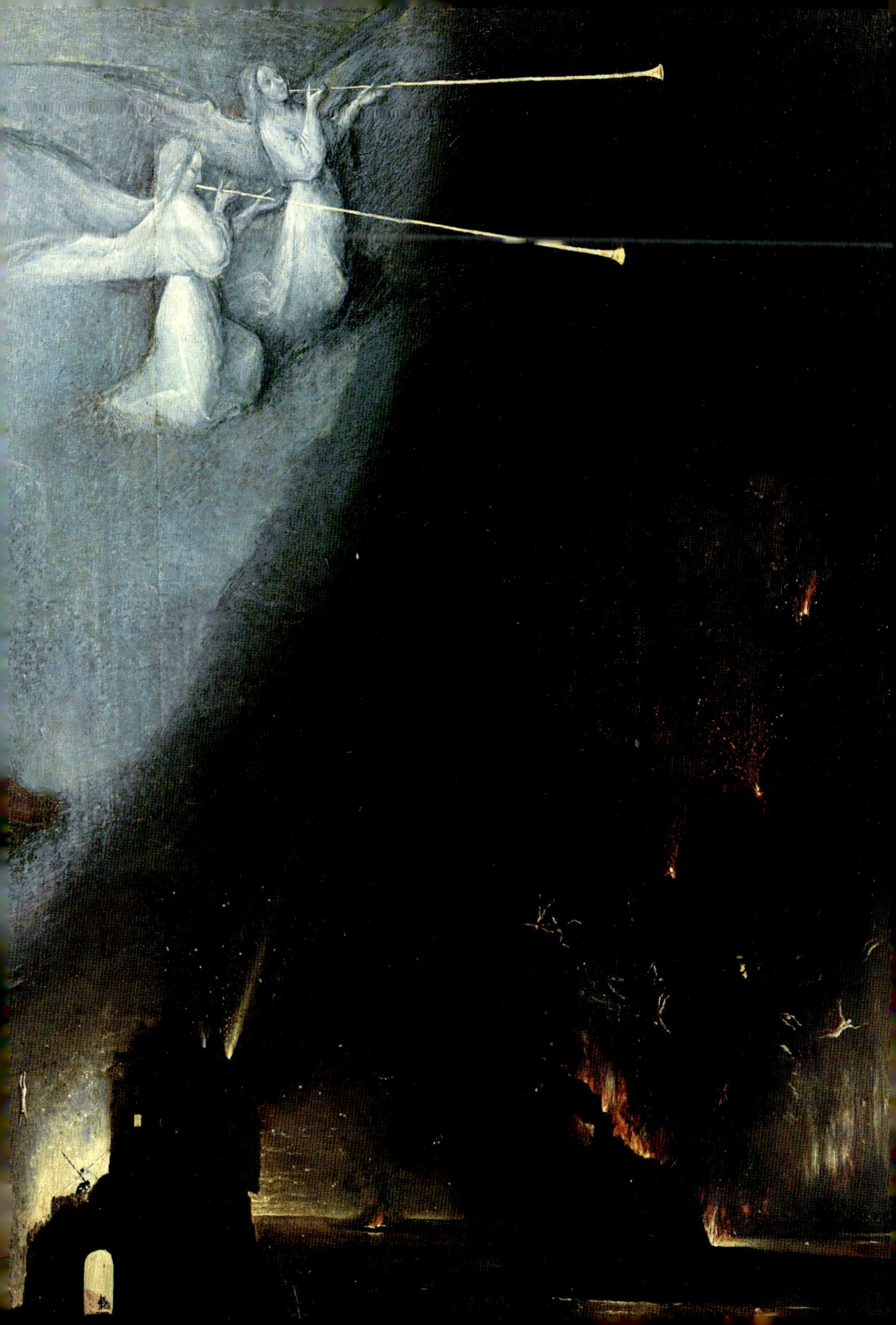

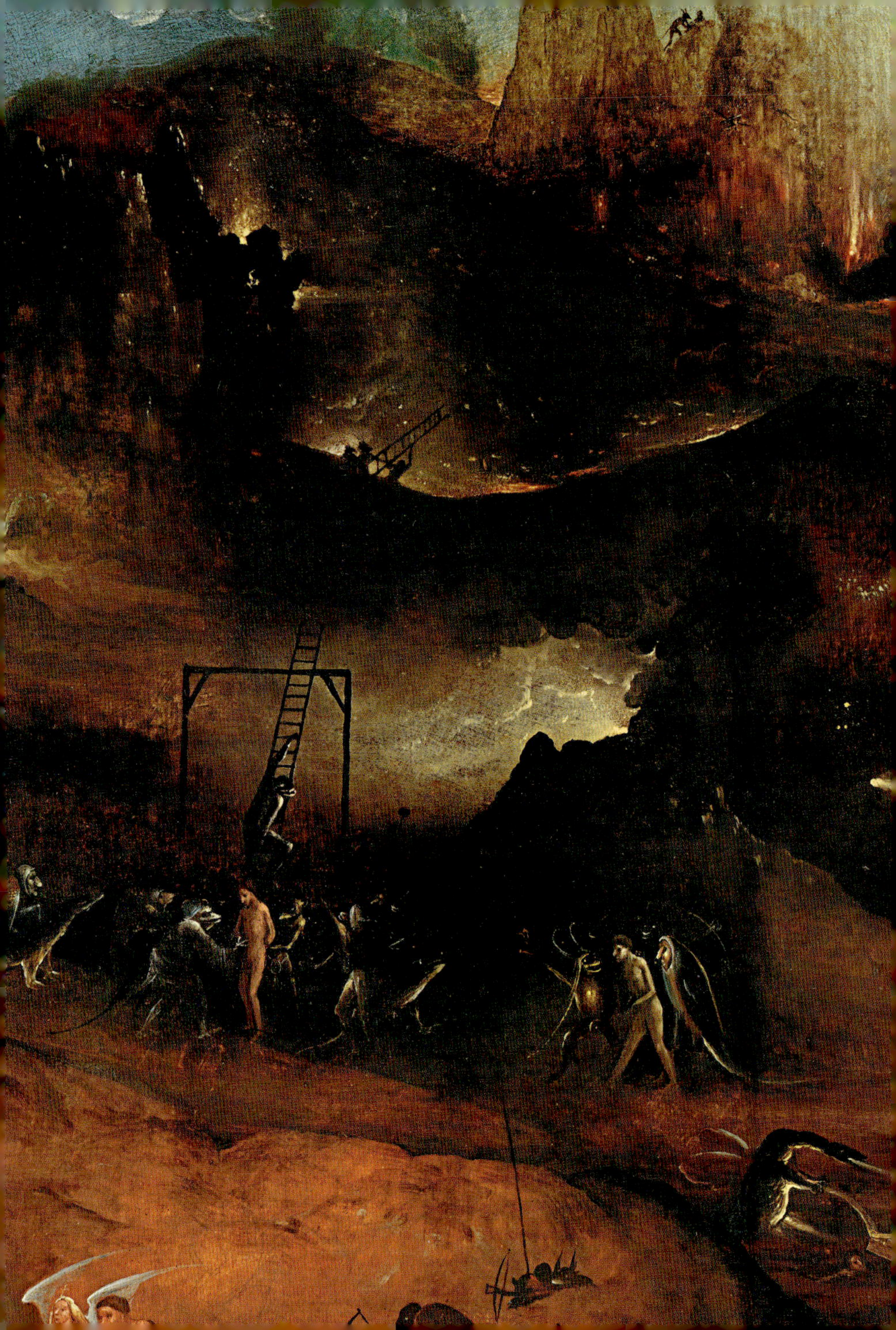

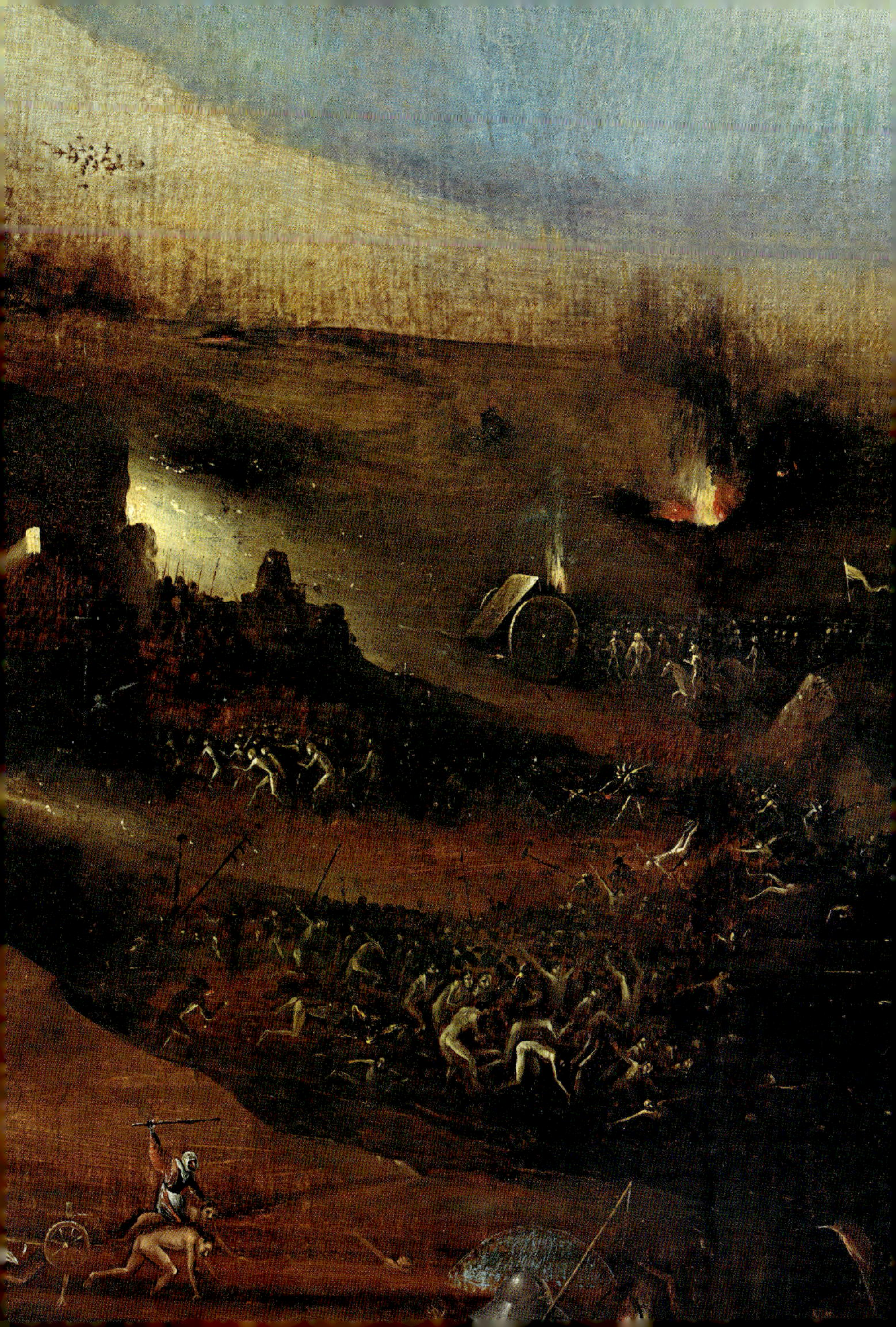

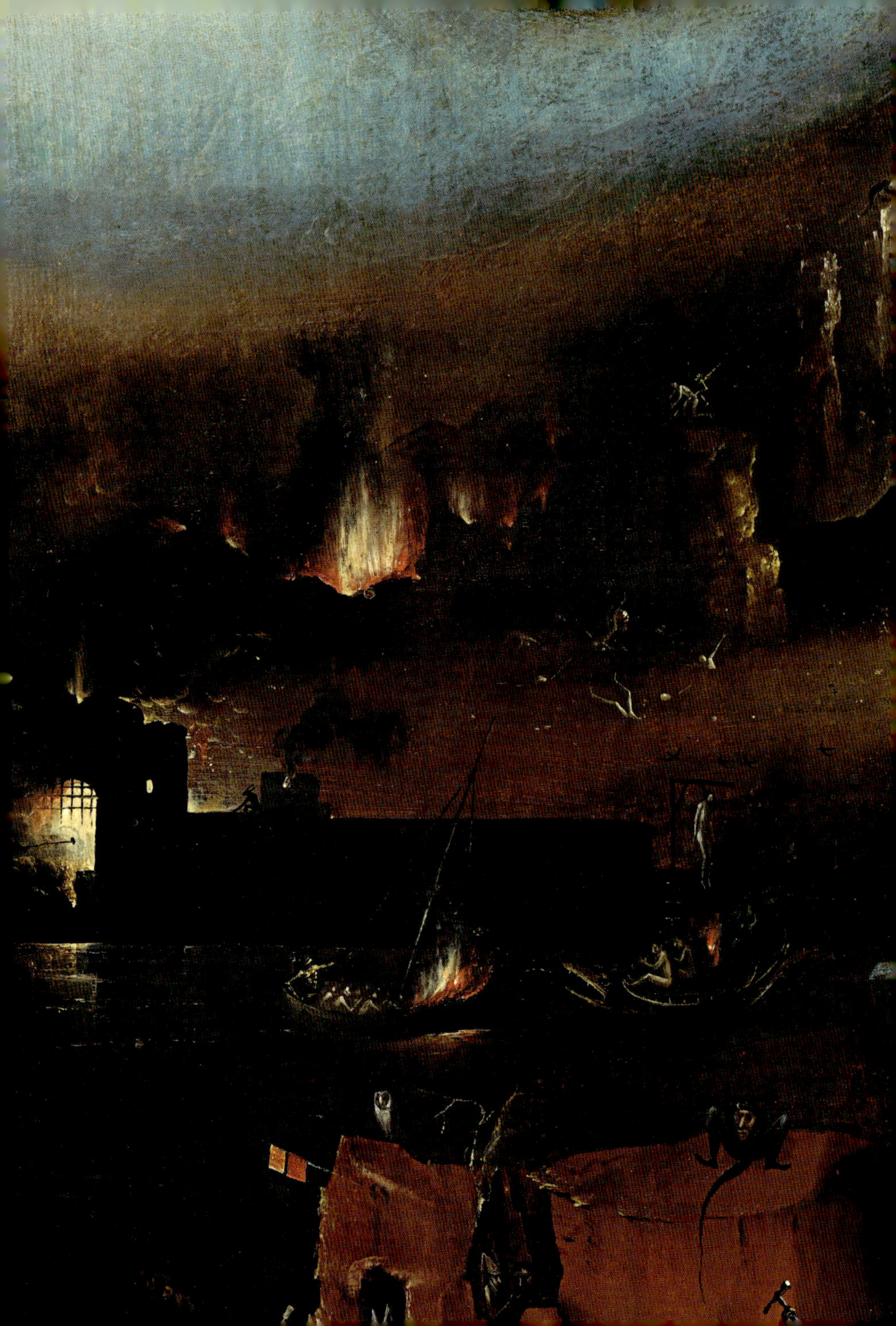

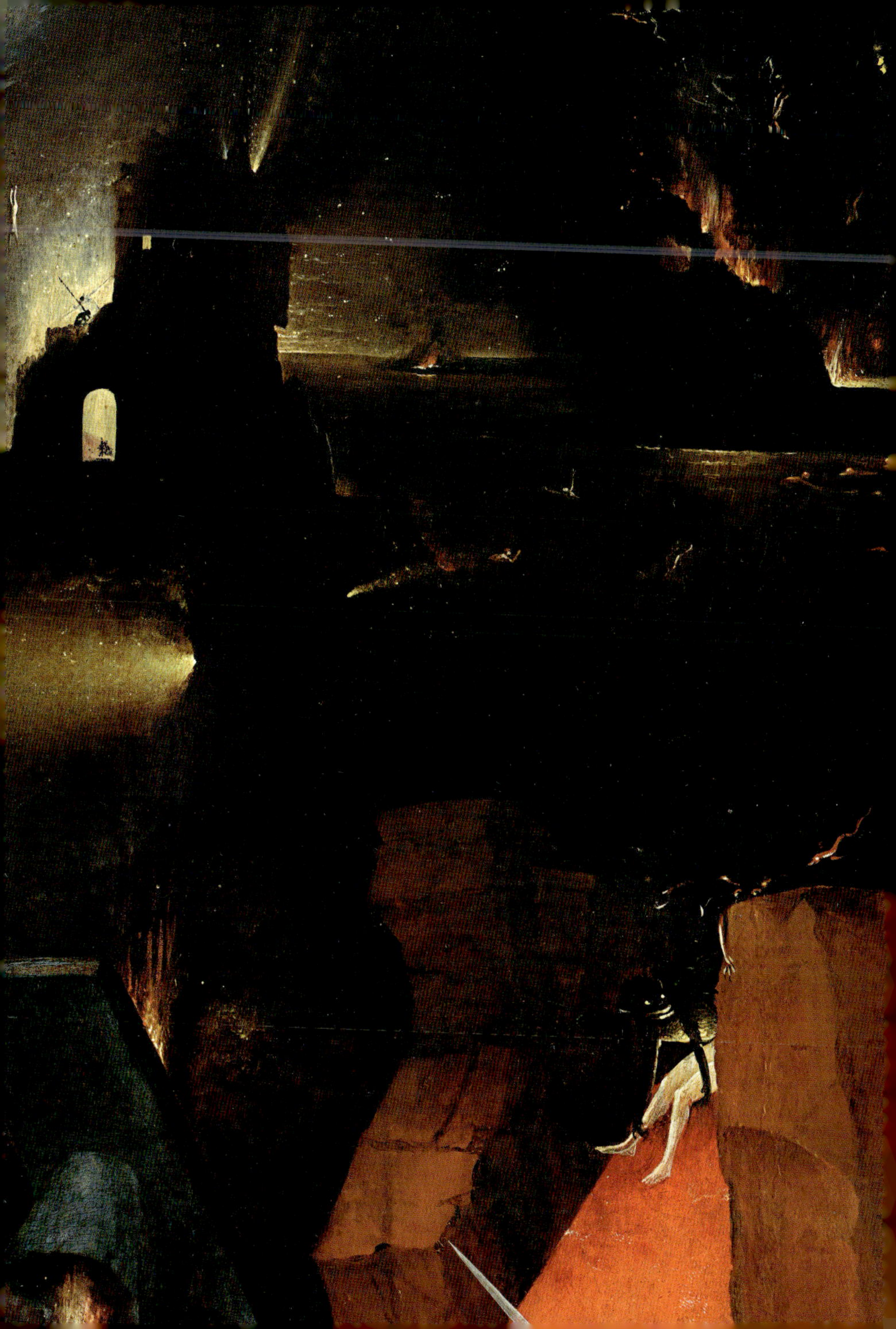

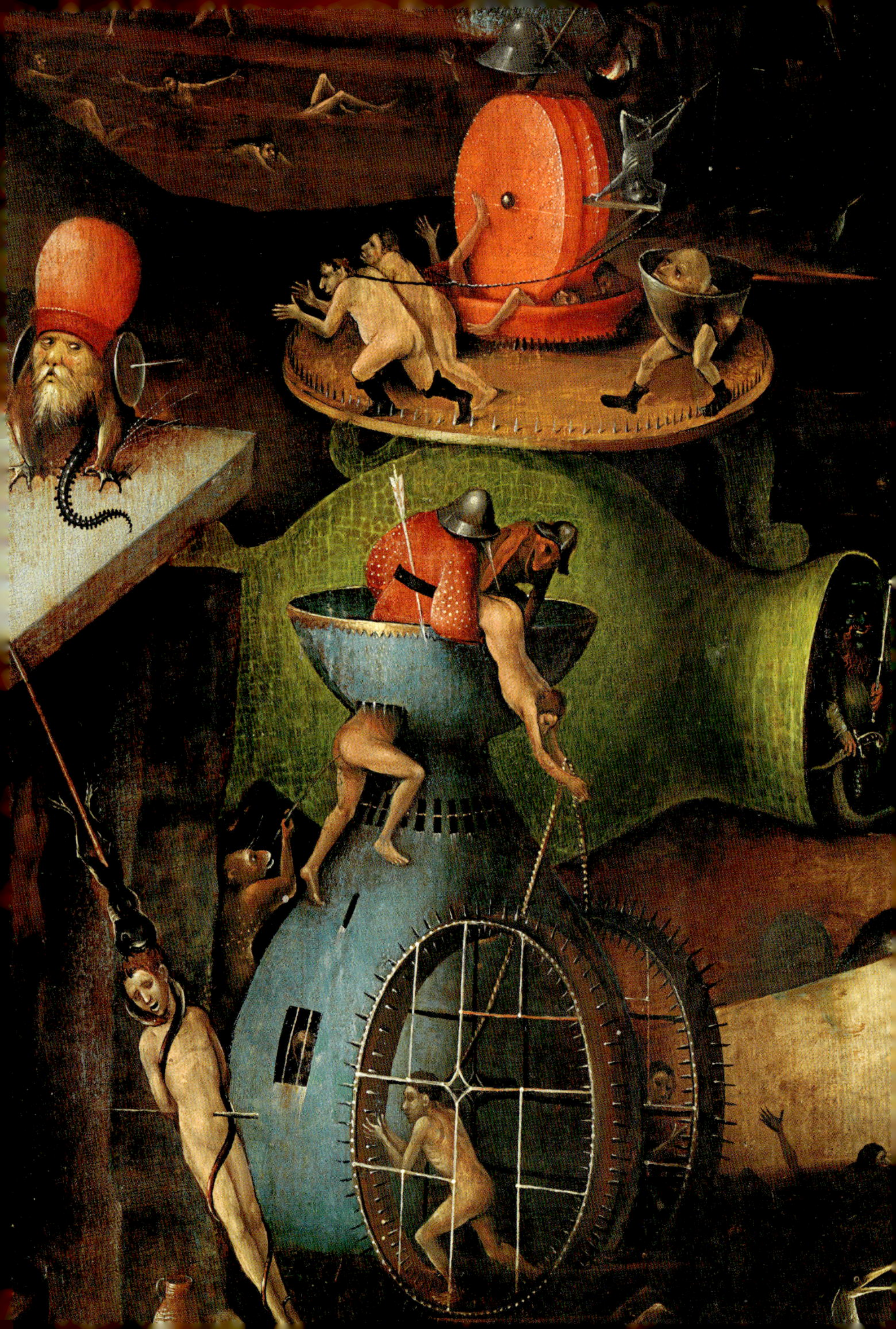

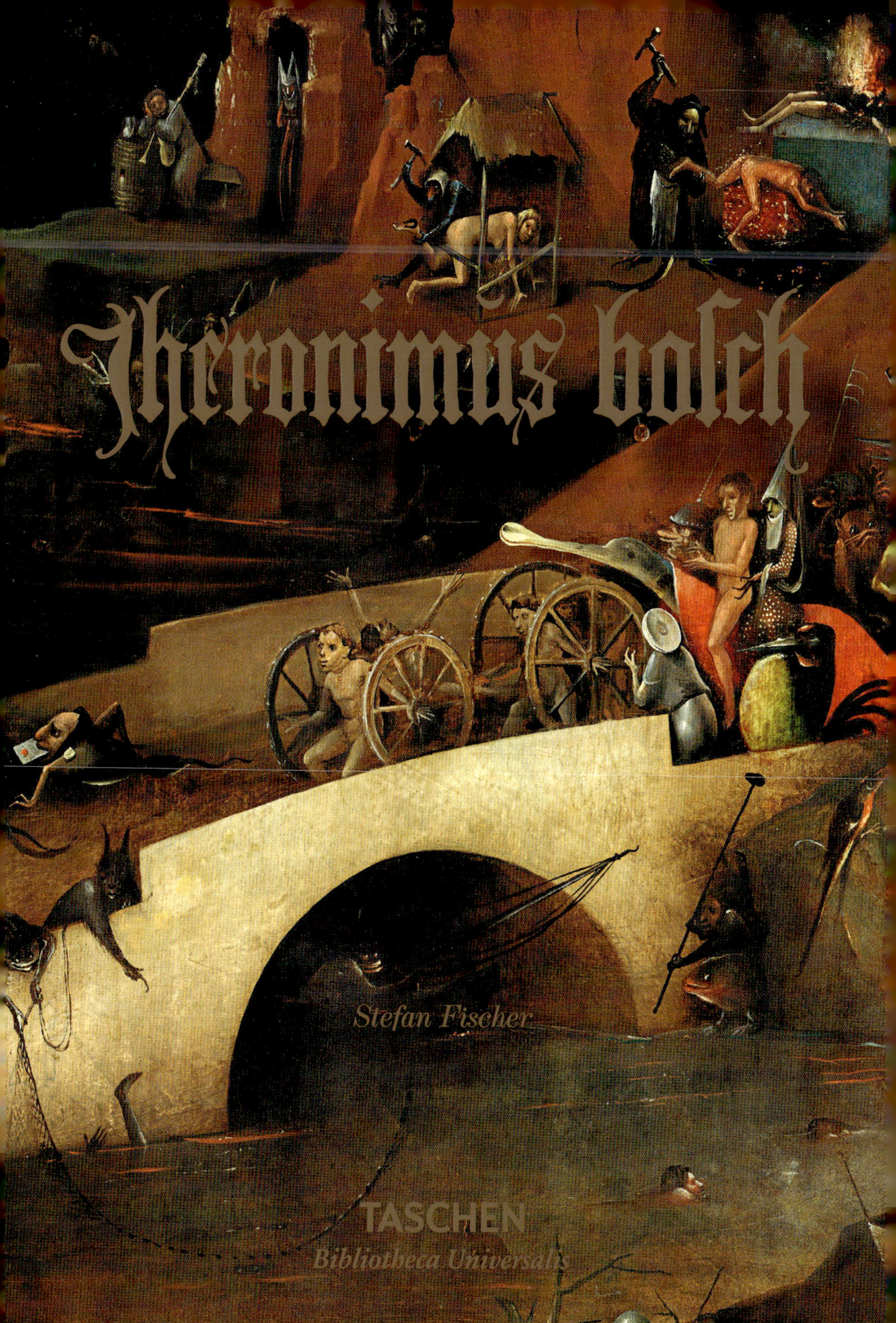
Jheronimus bosch
Stefan Fischer
TASCHEN
Bibliotheca Universalis

Contents

Perspectives on Bosch
12

I.
Family origins and first works
1474–1487
18

II.
Social and artistic ascent
1488–1501
34

III.
In the labyrinth of images: *The Temptation of St Anthony*
c. 1502
96

IV.
Nuptial art: *The Garden of Earthly Delights*
c. 1503
140

V.
Art for the king: *The Last Judgement*
c. 1506
222

VI.
Exemplum docet: Late works
1504–1516
256

Epilogue: An enigmatic bequest
332

Catalogue of paintings
338

Catalogue of drawings
430

Documentary sources on Bosch's life and work — 478
Bibliography — 490
Index — 509

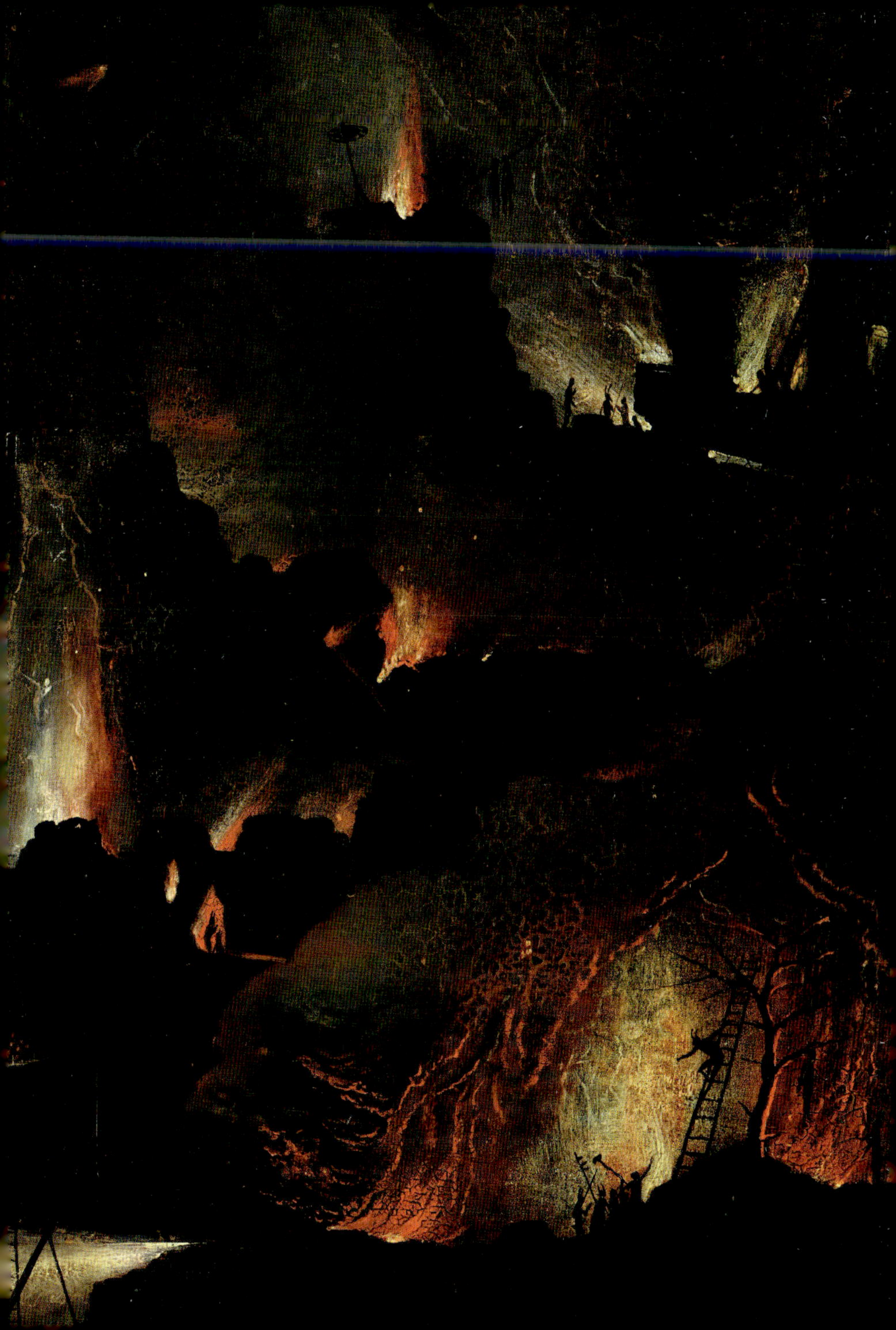

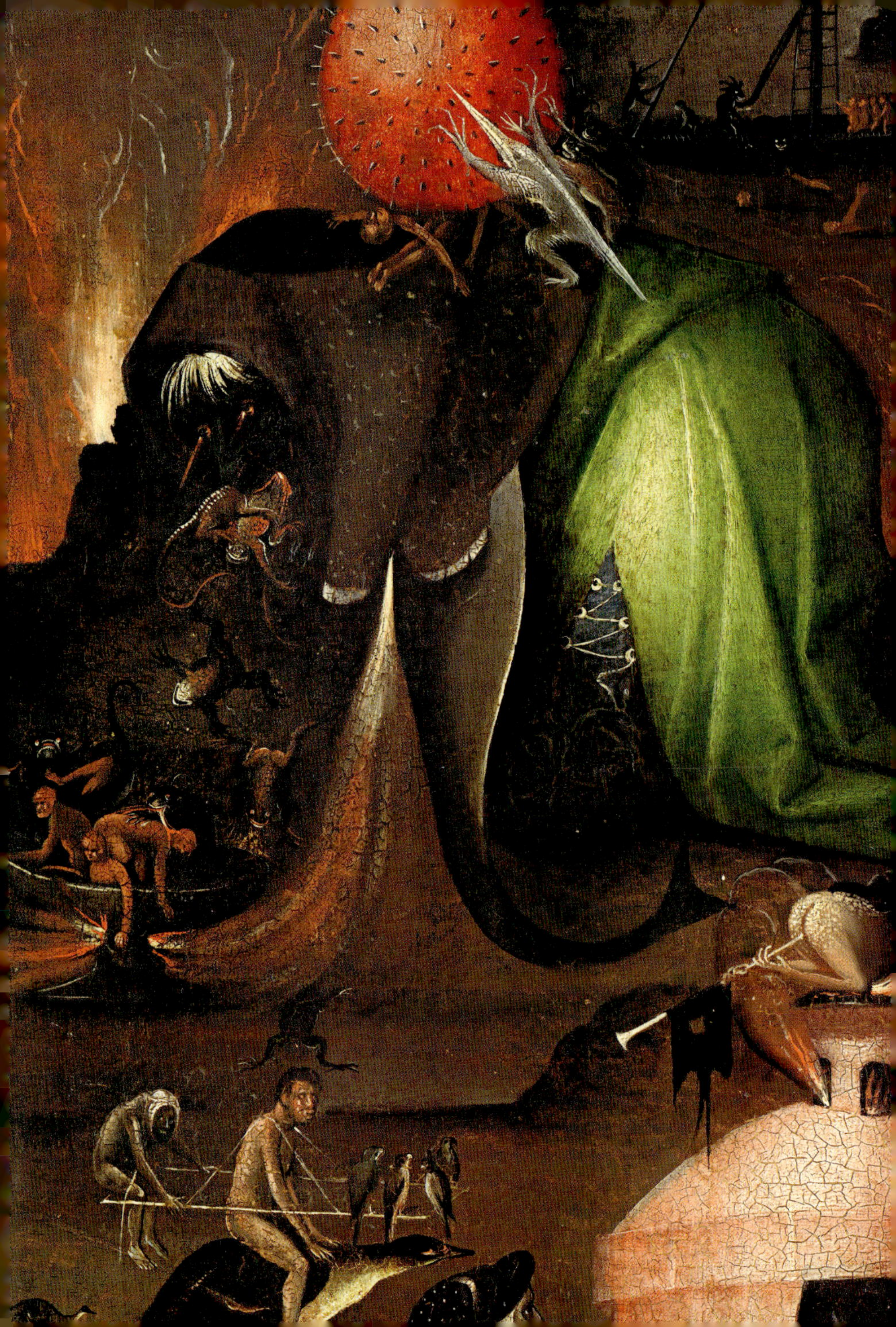

Perspectives on Bosch

In an era described as Late Gothic by some and as Early Renaissance by others, in which art strove increasingly towards harmony and brilliance, illusionism and monumentality, the Netherlandish artist Hieronymus Bosch (1450–1516) followed a very different path. With his innovative pictures, often populated by grotesque figures, of a religious or nature, the artist from 's-Hertogenbosch falls properly neither into the Flemish panel-painting of the 15th century nor into the Renaissance style that spread north of the Alps in the course of the 16th century. Albrecht Dürer (1471–1528) held the emphatically Renaissance view that an artist "should take care that he does not make something impossible, does not distort Nature, unless it be his task to make a picture of a dream. In such a picture he may mix all things together" (*Vier Bücher von Menschlicher Proportion*, 1528, in: Albrecht Dürer, *Schriftlicher Nachlass,* vol. 3, p. 283). In Dürer's book, in other words, Bosch – who was not concerned with the idealising portrayal of nature – fell into the category of a painter of dreams. And this was exactly how Bosch would be seen for centuries right up to the present: as a fantastical visionary, a visual chronicler of dreams and nightmares and the painter *par excellence* of Hell and its demons – subjects frequently connoted in negative ways as 'unnatural', just as was implied in Dürer's words.

The earliest defence of Bosch's art against such narrow definition was mounted by the Spanish scholar Felipe de Guevara (*c.* 1500–1563), who grew up in Flanders. In his *Comentarios de la Pintura* (Commentaries on Painting, *c.* 1560), Guevara criticised his Spanish countrymen for the fact that "any monstrosities that go beyond the limits of nature that they see in painting they attribute to Hieronymus Bosch and thus make him the inventor of monsters and chimeras", and insisted that it was "an error of judgement" to view the Netherlandish artist solely as a painter of devils (Guevara 1560, p. 41; cited here and below from Snyder 1973, pp. 28–30; here p. 28). The complexity and powerfully innovative nature of Bosch's oeuvre – which often overtaxed the viewer then as now – was also recognised by Fra José de Sigüenza (1544–1606), the second major Spanish writer on Bosch, when he expressed his amazement "that a single mind can imagine so many things" (Sigüenza 1605, p. 841; cited here and below from Snyder 1973, pp. 34–41; here p. 41).

For a long time very little was known about Bosch's life. When Carl Justi re-introduced Hieronymus Bosch to modern art history in 1889 with the remark that "we must content ourselves with a single testimony, albeit the most important one: his paintings, if we are to make any suppositions at all about the inner man" (Justi 1889, p. 122), a number of art historians were all too willing to follow his suggestion. Perhaps inspired too by the individuality and enigmatic nature of Bosch's pictorial inventions, a series of highly speculative interpretations of Bosch's psychology and the ideas behind his works have been proposed over the years. Many have wanted to see Bosch as an outlaw, an avant-gardist, a heretic or a conspirator. From today's perspective, these rather astonishing flights of intellectual fancy can now definitively be dismissed as misconstructions: no Cathars, Rosicrucians, astrologists or alchemists are to be found in any of Bosch's works, nor in the environment in which he lived or among his patrons. Neither was Bosch a social outsider: on the contrary, his steep career trajectory soon carried him into the ranks of the civic elite of 's-Hertogenbosch, as organised within the religiously oriented Brotherhood of Our Blessed Lady, while his richly inventive works delighted several princely patrons as well.

Within the pictorial traditions and concepts of art in the late Middle Ages, two terms in particular are key to understanding what was distinctive about Bosch's art: the grotesque (Kayser 1960, Stark 1977, Blank 1975) and the drollery, variously referred to in the contemporary vernacular as *grillen*, *drollen* or *capricco* (Vandenbroeck 1987b, Raupp 1986, Kanz 2002). These were collective terms for a 'lower-brow' style and for 'lower-brow' art forms that were sometimes fantastical, sometimes genre-like, moral and satirical, and which offered artists the freedom to astonish and impress the viewer with their inventions. Bosch took up this drollery tradition, already firmly established in the borders of illuminated manuscripts, architectural stone-carving and wood-carving, and transferred it to panel painting. What is unusual is that many of his themes had absolutely no source in established pictorial tradition but can be found only in contemporary texts: Bosch, in other words, was treating them in painting probably for the very first time.

For Bosch, these 'lower-brow' art forms opened up entirely new ways of representing human moral shortcomings and of holding up a mirror to the viewer. Sigüenza, who was himself considered an innovative preacher, recognised this when he described Bosch's works as "painted satires on the sins and ravings of man" (Sigüenza 1605, p. 837; cited here from Snyder 1973, p. 35). Pictures with a moralising content served not just as an admonishment to the viewer with an eye on the life to come, but also as a useful aid – conveyed through the stylistic means of parody and the grotesque – to living a good life in the here and now. The use of parody and the grotesque in the art of this period was only legitimised by their moral utility. Bosch here shows himself to be an erudite artist, even if not in the sense of Renaissance humanism: his art is Christian humanist teaching and testifies to his detailed knowledge – certainly not acquired solely through self-study – of the

Bible, the lives of the saints and medieval (animal) symbolism. This knowledge enabled him to imbue his pictorial themes with an intellectual dimension and to select and combine pictorial details in such a way that he arrived at unique iconographical inventions.

The grotesque as a vehicle of moral satire was a distinctive form of artistic expression that strongly developed in the visual arts and poetry over the course of the 15th century. Bosch not only made it his personal trademark but played a decisive role in enabling it to establish itself as an enduring stylistic trend and genre. In his seminal publication *Das Groteske*, Kayser writes thus of the works of Bosch and Pieter Bruegel the Elder (*c.* 1525/30–1569): "We feel the same way before their visions of Hell and the abyss as before the paintings and drawings of Goya" (Kayser 1960, p. 13). This unbroken lineage can surely be traced all the way to modernism. The grotesque and the hybrid remain universal principles that ensure Bosch's popularity beyond the boundaries of culture and language right up to today.

We must also pay tribute to Bosch's significance with regard to the development of genre and landscape painting. The artist was an accurate observer of his surroundings, and many of his paintings show objects and activities from everyday life that are equally of interest to European ethnologists. He also excelled in the 'high-brow' sphere of sacred art, infusing his representations of Christ and the saints with a new intensity. He showed himself to be artistically and intellectually in step with the pre-Reformation discourse, in so far as he portrayed the saints less in their traditional role as patron saints, and more as model exempla: what speaks out from these pictures is not a 'superstitious' faith but an educated morality rooted in Christian writings.

Alongside the discussion of Bosch's life and the interpretation of his oeuvre, this book also attempts to offer an insight into his workshop practice, that is to say, into both the material and the intellectual processes by which his ideas were translated into paintings, in the course of which we shall be drawing upon a wealth of comparisons with other works both inside and outside the genre of panel painting.

Pages 12, 17
The Last Judgement (details)
Right inner wing: **Hell**, *c.* 1506
(see ill. pp. 254/255)

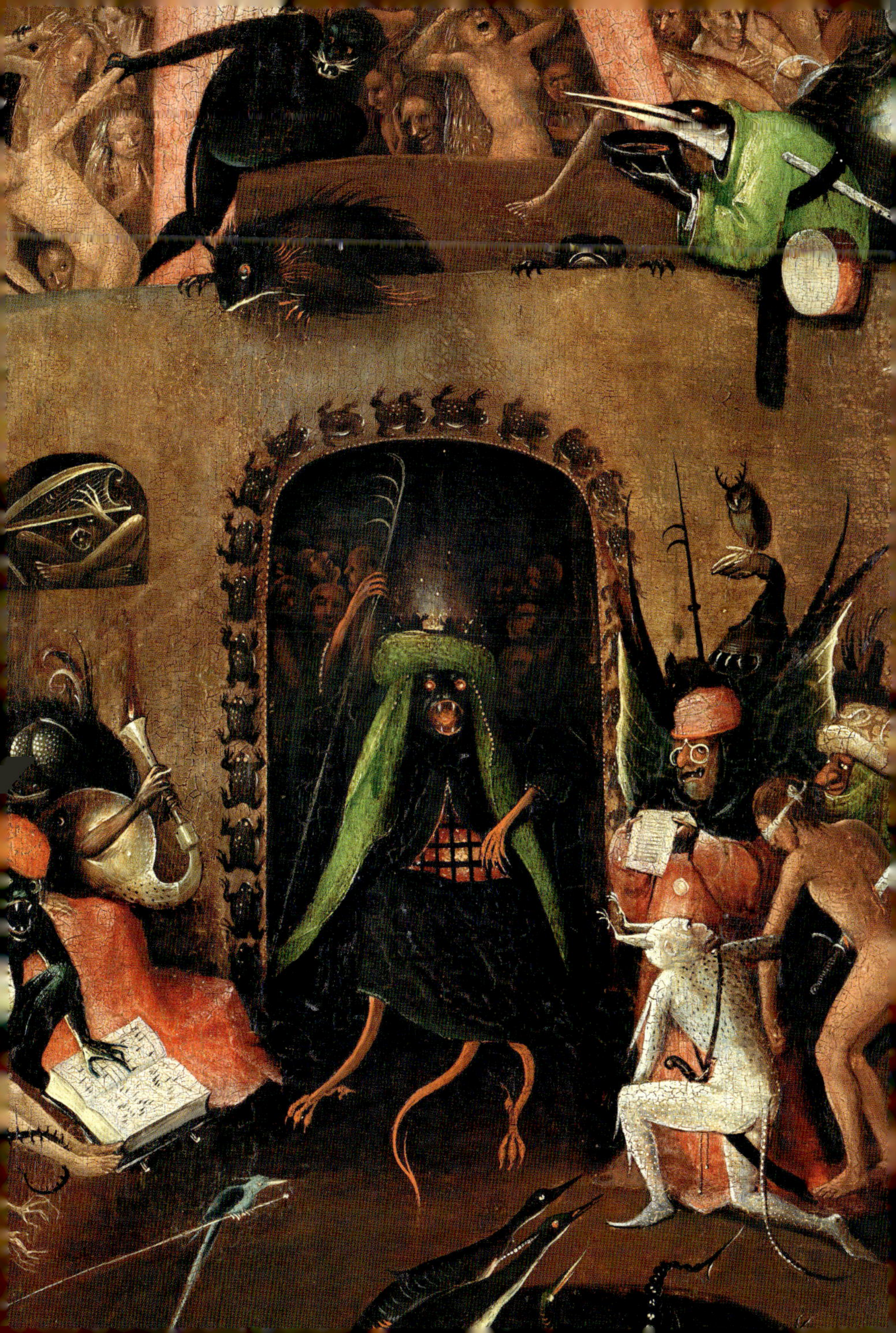

I.

Family origins and first works

1474–1487

"Bosch is a complete visionary... His oeuvre, having emerged out of oblivion, calls into question the very foundations of the art of painting."

ANDRÉ BRETON, 1957

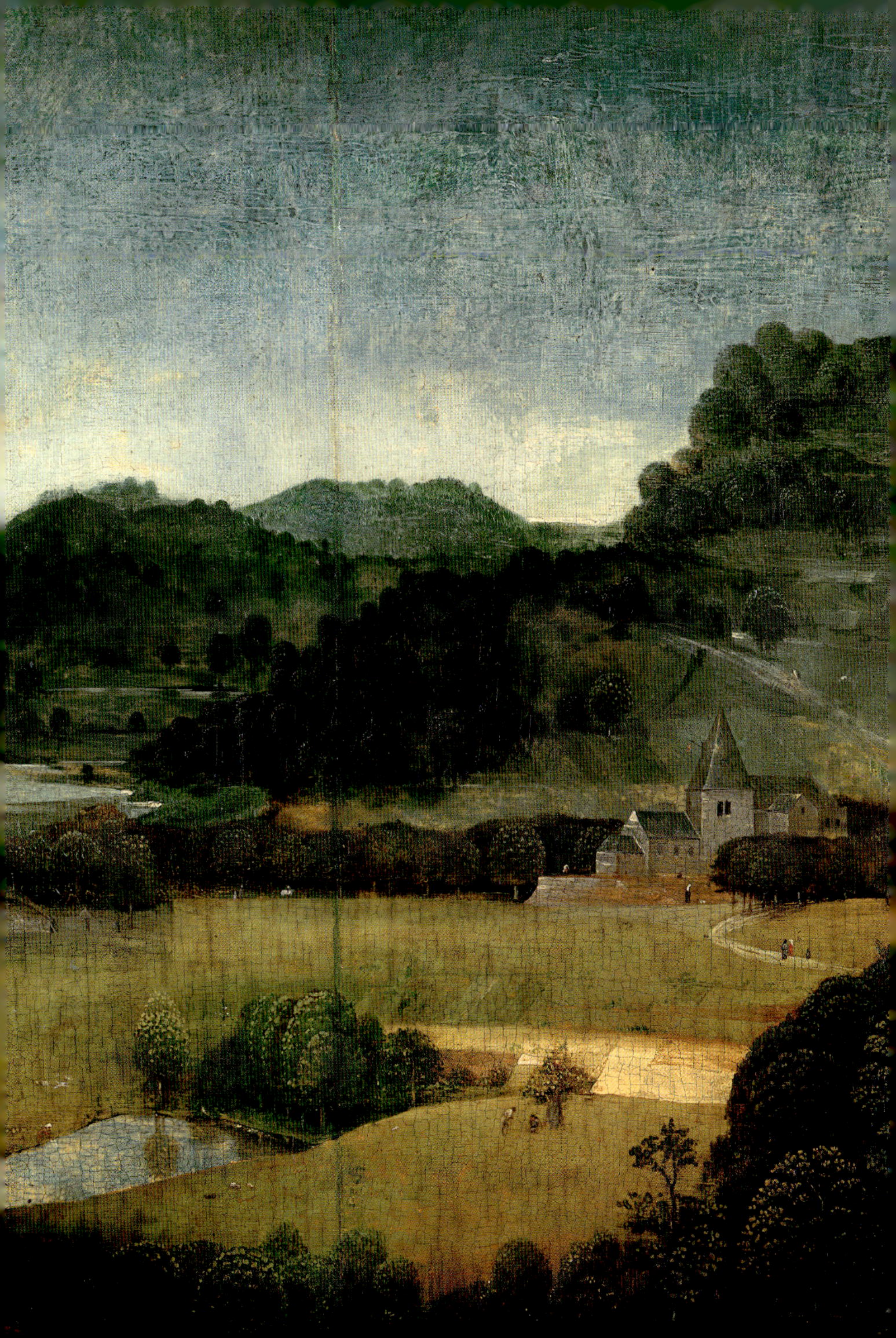

The desire to form an image of an artist's person is rarely felt as strongly as in the case of Hieronymus Bosch. According to the Humanist, poet and painter Dominicus Lampsonius (1532–1599) in his preface to a set of 23 portrait engravings of famous Netherlandish painters (*Pictorium aliquot celebrium Germaniae inferioris effigies*), which reflects Renaissance thinking, a handsome artist must surely produce a handsome painting, whereas a gloomy and discordant picture can only be the work of an ill-tempered, melancholy individual. Speaking directly to Bosch, Lampsonius also wondered whether the reason why his infernal and monstrous creatures looked so real was because he was reproducing them from first-hand experience of the Underworld: "What is meant by that astonished eye of yours, Hieronymus Bosch, or that pallor in your face? As if you had seen ghosts, the spectres of Erebus, flittering in front of you. I could believe that the caves of greedy Pluto and the houses of Tartarus lay open to you, seeing as your hand could paint so well whatever the lowest hollows of Avernus contain." (trans. from the Latin by Daniel Hadas for the Courtauld Institute of Art project *Picturing the Netherlandish Canon* [*Hondius Pictorium*, pl. 15]). Lampsonius's Latin text is reproduced beneath a portrait of Bosch (p. 23) engraved by Cornelis Cort (1533–1578) after an untraced original. Like the other presumed portraits of the artist (Gerlach 1988, van Dijck 2001b), it shows a gaunt man with an almost ascetic air, who fits the picture of a painter of religious or darkly fanatical subjects, and whose image may therefore equally well be an idealised representation.

Irrespective of the fidelity to life of these portraits and the authenticity of such psychograms, which were regularly devised over the years that followed, the study of the numerous documentary sources relating to Bosch's life has so far revealed nothing in itself extraordinary, nor anything to explain the extraordinary character of his art (Tolnay, Cinotti, Gerlach, van Dijck, Vandenbroeck, Vink; Gorissen 1973, pp. 1134–1138). For all his later international celebrity and the lasting influence of his pictorial inventions, sources show that Bosch remained closely tied to his birthplace, where he spent most, if not all, of his life: nothing in the surviving records testifies that he lived anywhere else. As Jheronimus van Aken, he grew up in 's-Hertogenbosch as part of the van Aken family of painters, whose significance extended no further than the local area. Almost no works have come down to us from other artists in the family, who are documented primarily in official records. The van Akens had settled in 's-Hertogenbosch, in the north

Page 19
Detail from: **St Jerome in the Wilderness (St Jerome in Penitence)**, *c.* 1485–1490
(see ill. p. *29*)

Page 21
Crucifixion with Saints and Donor, *c.* 1485–1490
Oil on panel (oak), 74.7 x 61 cm / 29½ x 24 in. Brussels, Musées royaux des Beaux-Arts de Belgique

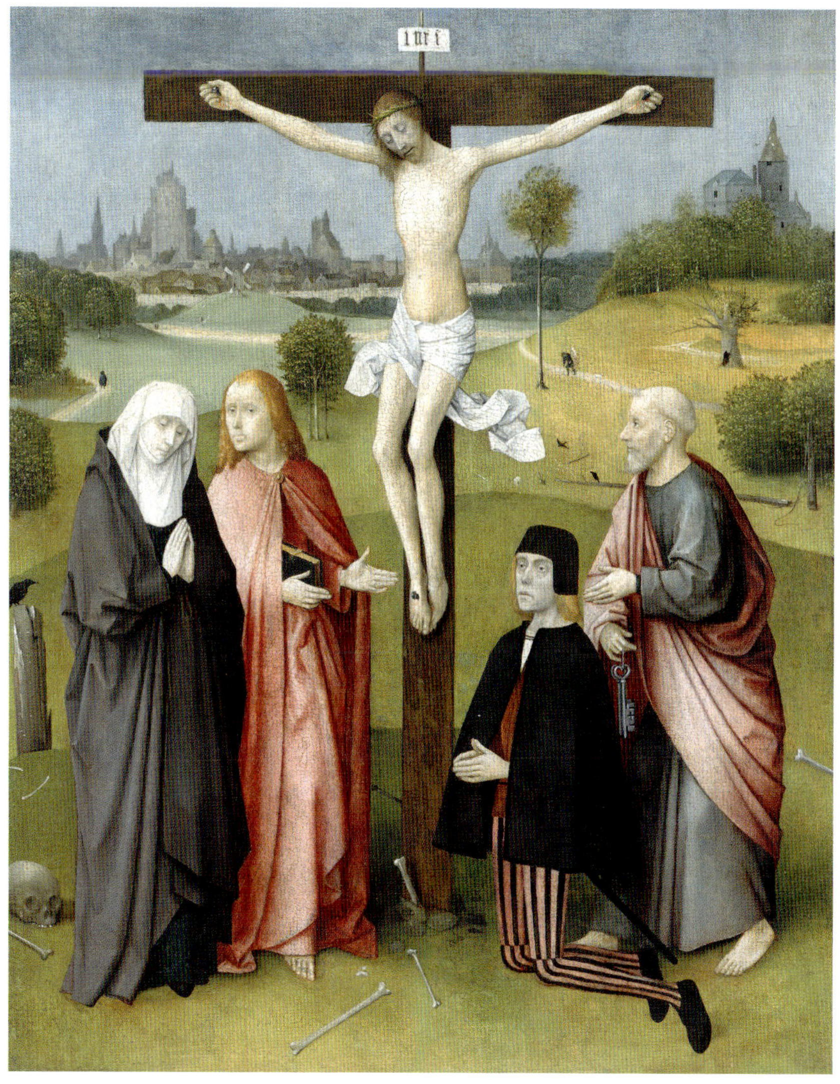
inri

of the Duchy of Brabant, in 1427 at the latest. Prior to this date, the family is documented between 1404 and 1422 in Nijmegen, 25 miles away in the neighbouring Duchy of Guelders. Nijmegen was important at this period from an art-historical perspective as the home of the three Limbourg brothers, the famous miniaturists (b. between 1375 and 1385, all three d. 1416), and their uncle Jan Maelwael (d. 1415), who was instrumental in introducing his nephews to aristocratic patrons in France, where he himself was active. Why the van Akens relocated is unclear, but for several family members, at least, this decision would prove to be the right one.

Johannes (Jan) Thomaszoon van Aken (*c.* 1380–1454) may be considered the founder of the family of painters and of the van Aken workshop in 's-Hertogenbosch (van Dijck 2001a, pp. 14–20, 141–157). He had five sons, all of whom became painters: Thomas (*c.* 1407–1462), Jan (*c.* 1413–1471), Hubert (1415–1463), Goessen (*c.* 1418–1467) and Antonius (*c.* 1420–1478), the last of these later becoming the father of Hieronymus Bosch. The surviving records indicate that Bosch's grandfather had been the leading painter in 's-Hertogenbosch before the middle of the 15th century. In the accounting year 1430/31 – whose beginning and end fell on 24 June – he and his wife became members of the city's most important society, the Illustrious Brotherhood of Our Blessed Lady (*Illustre Lieve Vrouwe Broederschap*), which brought together the intellectual, clerical, financial and political elite of 's-Hertogenbosch. In 1431/32 Jan Thomaszoon van Aken carried out work on a monstrance and a niche housing a statue of St Anne, as well as gilding and embellishing processional robes and accoutrements for the fraternity. Four years later he repaired the gold chandelier that had fallen down; he was also handsomely paid for a fabric painting of St Mary of Egypt. Probably destined for the Brotherhood's chapel, the painting – executed on the fragile medium of unprepared cloth – is one of the many such works that have not survived the centuries. Jan Thomas van Aken also received further commissions for executing and cleaning paintings for the 's-Hertogenbosch Tafel van de Heilige Geest (Table of the Holy Spirit) alms-house. In the church of Sint-Jan in 's-Hertogenbosch, where many of the vault decorations remain as yet anonymous, the Bacx choir features a most interesting wall painting – attributed to a member of the van Aken workshop – of a *Crucifixion with Donors* (p. 27), which is close in several aspects of its layout to Bosch's later *Crucifixion with Saints and Donor* (p. 21, Cat. 1). The donor has been identified as Willem Jacobs van Wijck, also known as van der Wyel, who appears in red to the left of the cross (van Dijck 2001a, p. 18 ff.). His first wife Katharina van Driel, who died in 1444, is depicted opposite, accompanied by an inscription calling for remembrance of her soul. She is followed by the donor's second wife and daughters. The mural was painted shortly after 1452, the year in which the donor's eldest son took his vows (he appears behind his father already dressed as a Franciscan friar in a grey habit and sporting a tonsure), and before one of Willem's daughters from his second marriage entered the convent of St Bridget as a nun. It is therefore just possible that the commission was carried out by Bosch's grandfather, Jan Thomas van Aken, who died in 1454. Another possible candidate is his son Goessen van Aken, one of Bosch's uncles: Goessen is the only one of the five van Aken brothers documented as active as a painter for the above-mentioned institutions and for Sint-Jan's church between 1438 and 1451, and thus before the execution of the *Crucifixion* wall painting (van Dijck 2001a, pp. 25–26 and 149–156). It would, then, be fact to say that over the course of the 15th century, the van Aken "painter dynasty" achieved a certain artistic status and by the second generation – which included Bosch's father – was living in solid financial and social circumstances. In 1460/61 two of Bosch's uncles, Thomas and Jan van Aken, took part in the annual Passion Play performed by the *passiebloem* (passion flower) guild of rhetoricians, which was closely associated with the Brotherhood of Our Blessed Lady, to which most of the van Akens belonged. From 1462 onwards, Bosch's father Antonius van Aken, of whose artistic activities we know almost nothing, was living with his family on the east side of the marketplace alongside numerous other craftsmen – a butcher, a pewterer and a *lakenscheerder* (a cloth-cutter or cloth merchant) – in a small to medium-sized stone-built house (today number 29).

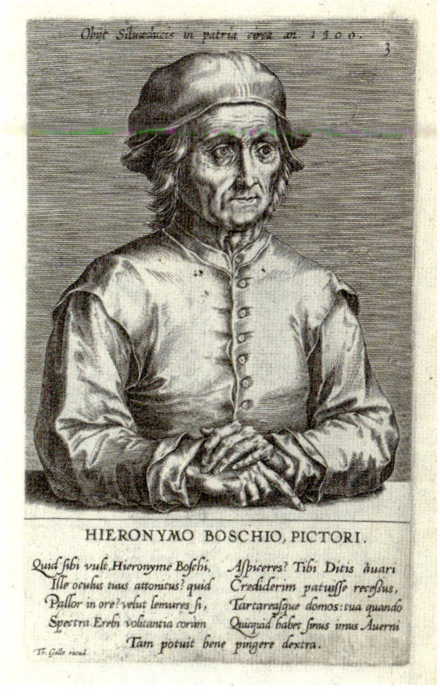

It was here that Jheronimus, familiarly known as Jeroen or Joen and later famous as Hieronymus Bosch, grew up as the fourth of five children, and as the third son, of Antonius van Aken and Aleid van der Mynnen (*c.* 1430–between 1455 and 1476). Practically nothing is known of his first twenty years, though we may assume they were dramatically marked by one event: the devastating fire that ravaged 's-Hertogenbosch on 13 June 1463,

Cornelis Cort, **Hieronymus Bosch**, *c.* 1572
from: Dominicus Lampsonius, *Pictorium aliquot celebrium Germaniae inferioris effigies*, Antwerp 1572, fol. 3
Copper engraving, 20.8 x 12.3 cm / 8¼ x 4⅞ in. Rotterdam, Museum Boijmans Van Beuningen

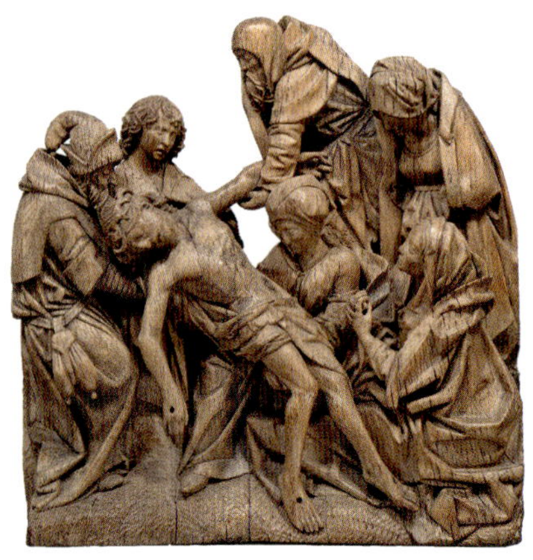

destroying the parental home in its path. There are, however, a number of documents that shed some light on his person and also convey an idea of his social, cultural and intellectual environment. The name Hieronymus first appears in a deed of 5 April 1474, in which he, his brothers and his father officially consent to the leasing of land by his sister Katharina. This is evidence that Hieronymus must have already reached a relative majority, in other words the age of at least 18, but not necessarily 24, which in the 15th century had not yet become the official age of adulthood. Bosch's birth can therefore be narrowed down to between 1450 and 1456. The up-and-coming painter is probably first documented in an artistic context in 1475/76, when he appears as a member of the paternal workshop. His father Antonius van Aken, accompanied by his sons, went with the two provosts and other members of the Brotherhood of Our Blessed Lady to the wine shop of Jan Maess, where they had a meeting with the highly regarded Utrecht sculptor Adriaen van Wesel (*c.* 1417–between 1490 and 1499). Their discussion centred upon the design of a new altarpiece that was to replace the one destroyed in the fire of 1463, together with the terms and conditions of the contract. The Brotherhood spent the lavish sum of 25 stuivers (= 1¼ guilders) on the food and drink with which the deal was sealed in the usual fashion (Unverfehrt 2003, p. 56). Van Wesel delivered the altarpiece – at this stage still without a surround – in 1477 as per his contract (pp. 24, 38) and was paid an additional bonus of 36 guilders over and above the hefty fee of 350 guilders already agreed, because his customers were so pleased with his work. The decision to commission the altarpiece from van Wesel represented a major step towards bringing high-quality art to 's-Hertogenbosch. How highly the sculptor's carved altarpieces were prized can be seen from the fact that, for a larger example, executed for Delft some ten years later, he was paid 1,000 guilders – 15 to 20 times as much as a master craftsman earned in an entire year.

Adriaen van Wesel, **The Deposition**, 1477
Fragment of altarpiece for the Brotherhood of Our Blessed Lady, Wood, 49.5 x 49.5 cm / 19½ x 19½ in.
Berlin, Staatliche Museen, Bode-Museum, Skulpturensammlung

Marriage as a door-opener

How long and to what extent Bosch was active in his father's workshop, whether he travelled as a journeyman in the years up to 1480 – at that time not yet an obligatory part of an artist's training or pursued a higher education, are matters we can only guess at. We do, however, know that Bosch's life took a decisive turn with his marriage to Aleid van der Mervenne (*c.* 1450–1522/23), the daughter of a wealthy merchant and patrician and thus a member of a higher social class than his own. This marriage must have taken place at some point between 24 July 1480 and 15 June 1481, since documents bearing these dates respectively show the pair to be not yet married and then as man and wife. It was during exactly this period that Bosch moved out of the parental home, having sold his share to his eldest brother Goessen (d. 1495). (As the eldest son, Goessen took over his father's house and workshop and the title of master.) Bosch then moved into the house of his wife and set up a workshop there. From now on he was an independent painter and is described in documents as *maelre*, *maelder*, *scilder* or *pictor*, but never as the term then used to signify "master". It was normal practice, and indeed a stipulation of the various guilds and the municipal council, that marriage should coincide with setting up a home and opening a workshop. Aleid was at least the same age as her husband, since her name appears in the record of a commercial transaction as early as 1471. Along with estates in the country, she brought into the marriage the town house Inden Salvatoer, which the couple moved into no later than 1483 (Vink 2001a, p. 90; van Dijck 2001a, pp. 46–47). Bosch now, therefore, not only had his own property, but one that stood on the marketplace and near the Town Hall. His contemporaries would only find themselves in a position to afford their own homes after 1500, and even then only in less desirable districts (Vink 2001a, pp. 30–35). Of this building, now Markt 61, only the side walls and cellar are still standing, with the cellar vaults accessible to the public. Through Aleid, whose parents had died several years earlier, Bosch not only improved his financial status, being now the owner of a house and land, but also his position within society. The van der Mervenne family, also known as Brants, were enterprising merchants (van Dijck 2001a, pp. 45 and 88). Aleid's grandfather had been a notary, lawyer and the 's-Hertogenbosch town clerk, and her close relatives included a steward, a canon and prior, several nuns, a priest and a university student.

While his forebears and brothers were first and foremost debtors, through his marriage Bosch became the recipient of payments, both in cash and in kind. Between 1481 and 1483 the couple sold shares in a farm and two parcels of land that lay a little way outside 's-Hertogenbosch, probably to raise funds to set up the workshop and their household. Following the death of her brother Goyaert, in July 1484 Aleid inherited the country estate of Ten Roedeken in the parish of Oirschot, near Eindhoven, 15 miles south of

’s-Hertogenbosch. This farm also brought the couple further revenue, to which Bosch was granted usufruct for life (van Dijck 2001a, p. 173).

At the very same time that Hieronymus Bosch became an independent painter and a full citizen, his path crossed those of two representatives of princely families who would facilitate his rise to the rank of Europe’s most famous artists: the not yet three-year-old Philip the Handsome (1478–1506), son of Maximilian I of Habsburg, and Engelbert II of Nassau (1451–1504), uncle of Henry III of Nassau-Breda (1483–1538). Both came to ’s-Hertogenbosch in May 1481, when the chivalric Order of the Golden Fleece – headed by the Habsburgs since the fall of the Burgundian Empire a few years earlier – met there for the first and only time.

First works

The earliest firm evidence of Hieronymus Bosch’s activity as a painter dates from a time when he had already turned thirty. *Crucifixion with Saints and Donor* (p. 21, Cat. 1), which was probably produced in the late 1480s, is considered to be his earliest surviving work. In line with representational tradition, it shows the Crucifixion as a donor picture in which the intercession by the saints on the donor’s behalf unfolds in a hierarchical manner. At the bottom of the hierarchy, to the lower right, is the donor kneeling at Christ’s feet with his hands folded in prayer, dressed in red-and-white striped hose, a white shirt, red doublet, black cape and black cap. Standing close behind him is his patron saint, St Peter, with the keys to the gates of Heaven, who gestures towards the donor with his left hand as he looks across to the two saints on the opposite side of the Cross, recommending his ward to them. St John the Apostle, Christ’s beloved disciple (John 19:25–26), standing next to the Cross in red robes, passes on the plea for intercession with a confidential air and a calm gesture to the Virgin standing beside him. With her eyes closed in meditation and her head inclined, Christ’s mother has already begun to pray, in order to intercede with her Son on behalf of the picture’s donor. The artist has placed the figural group very close to the front of the picture. Various symbols of death are scattered round about, including bones, a skull, tree stumps and carrion birds, probably crows, all of which allude to Golgotha, the Hill of the Skull. In the background, a gently rolling green landscape traversed by paths and walkers – some of them exceptionally small – leads the eye to the horizon, where a city, seemingly of Bosch’s era, is seen in silhouette. A number of trees in the middle ground serve either to interrupt or frame the view. Visual accents are provided by a complex of buildings on the right edge of the composition and a post mill on the left.

Although we know nothing of the location for which the *Crucifixion with Saints and Donor* was originally conceived and its specific function within that context, we can be sure that, with its portrayal of intercession, it fulfilled the primary function of religious images: to secure the salvation of the donor's soul and, with it, a place in Paradise. Paintings of this kind were consequently often part of a larger-scale endowment that included the regular celebration of requiem masses. The donor was evidently a public official who wielded administrative and law-enforcing powers, as indicated by his style of dress and the sword protruding from beneath his short cape. Bosch probably looked back in his *Crucifixion* to the wall painting of the same subject executed by the van Aken family workshop (p. 27), as a number of authors have suggested (Tolnay 1965, p. 11; van Dijck 2001a, pp. 17–20). Characteristic features of the present panel that are also found in the earlier mural include the softness of the internal contours, the restrained gestures and facial expressions of the figures, the Virgin's pose and certain details of the representation of Christ, such as the inclination of the head at a 45-degree angle, the position of the hands with the thumbs uppermost, and the arrangement of the feet and toes, which do not overlap but fuse to form an almond-shaped outline. The *Crucifixion* is one of the most conventional works in Bosch's oeuvre and reveals his 's-Hertogenbosch roots. It not only testifies to the fact that he took up and used local compositions; it also allows us a first glimpse of what distinguished his personal style from that of the other painters of his day, in particular those in the Low Countries. The ultimate yardstick for comparison in this regard is Rogier van der Weyden (1399/1400–1464), for his works exerted a profound influence upon artists across the whole of central Europe. One of van der Weyden's very widely known Crucifixion compositions probably also served as a basis for the van Aken *Crucifixion* and thus indirectly for Bosch. If we compare these two last works with Rogier's treatment of the theme in Vienna (p. 31), we can see that all three paintings show an emaciated, almost beardless Christ, with head drooping to the left, and thin extremities and legs that

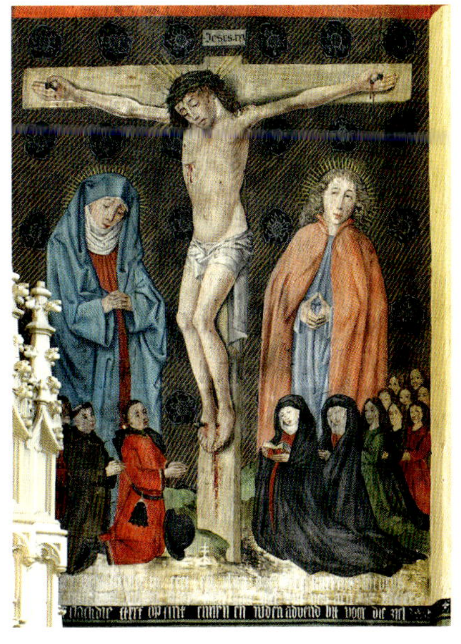

Johannes Thomaszoon van Aken or Goessen van Aken
Crucifixion with Donors, *c.* 1453/54
Wall painting, 's-Hertogenbosch, Sint-Jan, Bacx choir

bend, at the knee, to the left. Bosch's *Crucifixion*, however, is both far less illusionistic in its overall treatment and emotionally far less intense: his painting technique employs fewer internal contours in rendering the muscles and a soft, dissolving outline, while the saints are statue-like and none of those present exhibits any outward show of emotion at Christ's death on the Cross. Christ, likewise, appears as a less dramatic figure: the head is only slightly inclined and the loin-cloth flutters less vehemently. Nor do we find Bosch's saints shedding any of the tears seen in some of Rogier's paintings. This restrained dramaturgy and monumentality are characteristics found throughout the Bosch oeuvre: they are fundamental traits of his personal style.

Bosch's recourse to a model for his *Crucifixion* typifies the copying through which apprentices learned their trade, and also the traditional workshop practice of adapting concrete designs. An artist's ability to vary an existing work and to use it for a new composition were seen as signs of his quality and independence. Which other elements of Bosch's art were sourced from the repertoire of the van Aken workshop(s) has yet to be established. The family of painters might well have assembled a substantial body of figural and compositional designs over the generations. Bosch could have found further inspiration in the stone and wood carvings inside Sint-Jan's, such as those on the choir stalls, in the illuminated manuscripts housed in convent libraries (p. 46), in the work of Adriaen van Wesel and in many other examples now unknown.

Studies of the iconography of Hieronymus Bosch's works have revealed the huge breadth and variety of the visual media upon which he drew. Some of these exhibit no more than an analogous relationship with his works, while others clearly provided models and sources of inspiration. In addition to the abovementioned works, these also included engravings and woodcuts. Beyond this, however, many of Bosch's pictorial themes have no tradition in the visual arts at all. They are to be found, rather, in contemporary literary sources. Bosch was, not least, a keen-eyed observer of the world around him: the genre-like "realism" of everyday objects and patterns of behaviour in many of his pictures (Cat. 7, Cat. 10, Cat. 11, Cat. 17, Cat. 18, Cat. 20) makes them a source of delight for cultural historians, folklorists and ethnologists (Marijnissen 1987; essays in Koldeweij/Vermet/Kooij 2001). In the *Hell* panel of the *Garden of Earthly Delights* (Cat. 11.4), the schematic outlines of buildings can be seen rising in the distant background. They are bathed in a fiery glow that tinges the surface of the waters red. Streams of people, accompanied by devils or demons, become lost to sight in the darkness and through their own diminutive scale. Has the painter here processed his impressions of the blaze that

St Jerome in the Wilderness (St Jerome in Penitence), *c.* 1485–1490
Oil on panel (oak), 80.1 x 60.6 cm / 31½ x 23⅞ in. Ghent, Museum voor Schone Kunsten

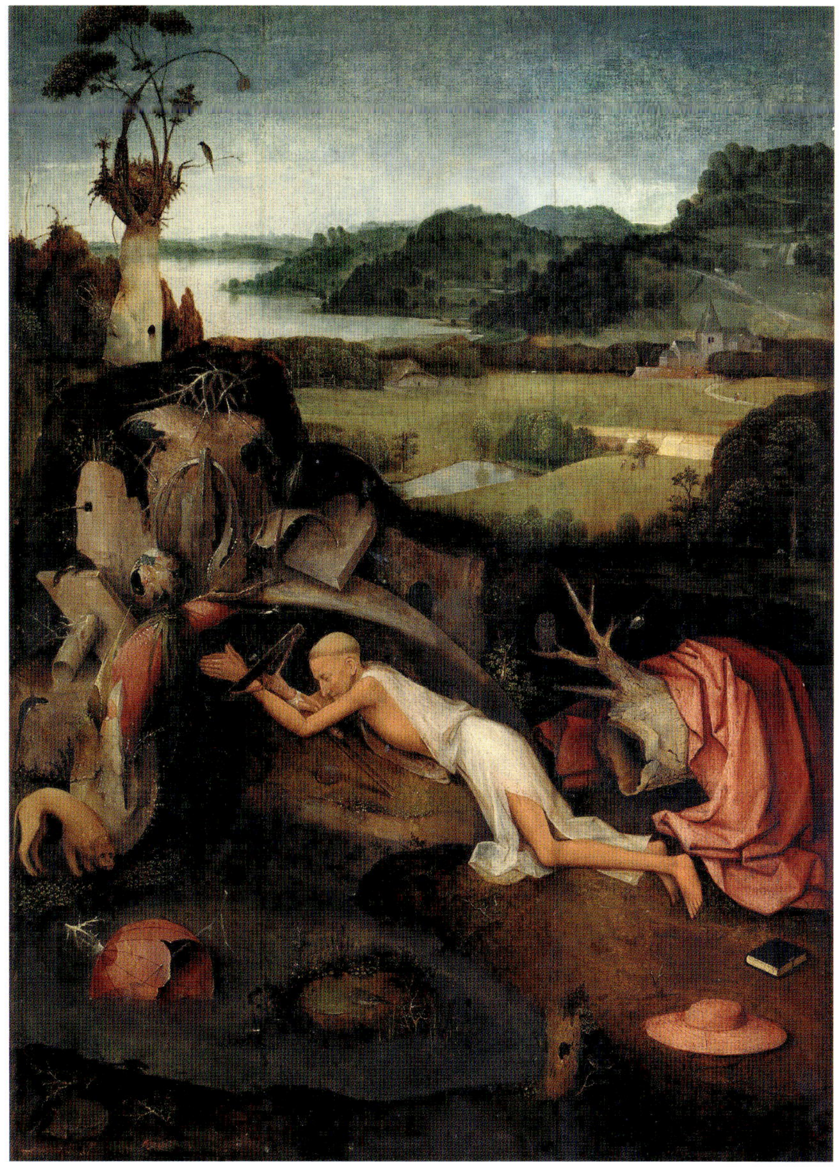

swept through 's-Hertogenbosch in 1463? Whatever the case, such a depiction would also demand a particular mastery of brush and palette.

Bosch did not build up his paintings in exquisitely fine layers of glaze on top of precise underdrawing in the manner of other 15th-century artists, but employed his own, highly distinctive technique, one that he ultimately developed himself (rather than learning it from another artist), and which suited the variety and multi-figural wealth of his pictures. His handling of paint was both economical and flexible, and consisted of the application of one or just a few thin layers with brushstrokes in different directions (e.g. pp. 134, 139, 290, 303) and with impasto, *alla prima* heightening and highlights (e.g. pp. 105, 123, 265, 266). His palette ranges very widely between pure grisaille (Cat. 10.1 and 10.2; Cat. 11.1), works employing tonal gradation (Cat. 20), and vibrantly coloured paintings (Cat. 6.2–6.4, Cat. 10.3–10.5, Cat. 13.3–13.5). His underdrawing is also variable, consisting for the most part of relatively wide, slightly transparent brushstrokes of fluctuating strength, but occasionally employing thin, regular lines and hatching (*inter alia* Filedt Kok 1972/73, Koreny 2002/03, Spronk 2011). This often shimmers through the paint layer (Cat. 5, Cat. 10, Cat. 12, Cat. 17, Cat. 19) and is found in the main figures, architectural elements and interiors. In amorphous parts of the picture, such as the landscape, it is usually absent. Within Bosch's oeuvre there are works with extensive underdrawing (Cat. 15, Cat. 17.5) and works with very little (Cat. 11, Cat. 14, Cat. 16); and the amount of underdrawing can indeed vary within individual works, from panel to panel, or from area to area (e.g. Cat. 10).

Alongside the practical aspects of design and technical execution, the creation of a work of art naturally includes an intellectual dimension. Bosch would not have been able to acquire his wealth of knowledge – which embraced biblical themes and the lives of the saints, bestiaries and typology, morality tales and devices of pictorial rhetoric and even elements of mysticism – through purely private study or at a grammar school or university. The best place to acquire such learning would have been the monasteries and convents of the reform-oriented Dominicans, Carthusians and Crosiers, and the Brethren of the Common Life in 's-Hertogenbosch, whose libraries – as was common practice – were accessible not just to the clergy but also to the various groups of lay people closely associated with the religious life. These last included tertiaries, who were attached to a religious order, semi-religious groups who voluntarily adopted a monastic style of life, and devout individuals. It was even possible for such readers to take books out on loan. In view of Bosch's personal and general circumstances, it is not only conceivable but indeed plausible that he lived for a while as a lay brother in one of these monasteries and, in this capacity, decorated it with paintings. He would then also have received regular religious instruction and might even have taken the opportunity to pursue guided study. In this way Bosch would have been

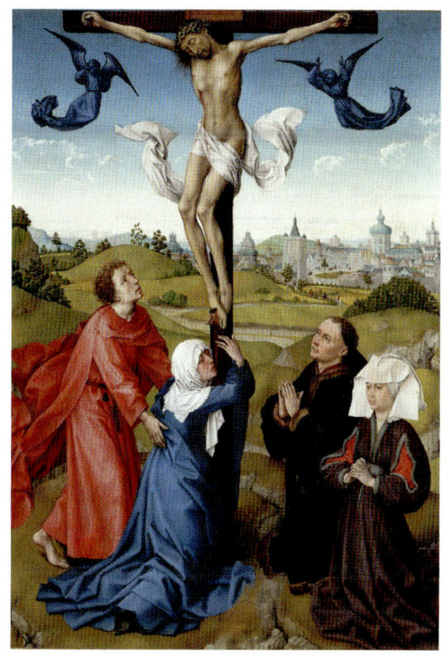

not only meaningfully employed but also provided with board and lodging. Demand on the services of the van Akens was probably not always so overwhelming that all the family members were needed all the time. Given such a scenario, we can begin to understand why Bosch's treatment of his pictorial themes is so steeped in intellectual thought and why he chooses their details so carefully. In his oeuvre, just as in the above-mentioned orders and religious communities, representations of the saints as ascetics or hermits play an important role, whereas the Virgin is almost entirely absent. Early works in this category include *St Jerome* (Cat. 2) and *St John the Baptist* (p. 37, Cat. 3.1) and its pendant *St John on Patmos* (p. 45, Cat. 3.2). These exhibit almost none of the features of traditional representations of patron saints, but may be seen as devotional images of model exempla with an emphatically didactic character.

St Jerome as model

One of Bosch's early works is *St Jerome* (p. 29, Cat. 2), whose iconography is rooted in a long tradition combining events from Jerome's legend with motifs found in his historical writings and letters. In Bosch's panel Jerome is portrayed not as a widely travelled man of the church and outstanding scholar, but as an ascetic. The attributes characterising him as a cardinal – cloak, hat and book – are lying near his feet. Surprisingly, the saint is not shown castigating himself with a rock in a crouching or kneeling position, as was the usual convention (cf. Cat. 12.2), but prostrate on the ground, a pose that places particular emphasis on his humility and absolute surrender to Christ. The tombstone above the saint's head indicates that the mortification of his flesh has left him in a state close to death (Marijnissen 1987, p. 211; Fischer 2009, p. 212). His devotion is further underlined by the

Rogier van der Weyden, **Crucifixion**, *c.* 1440–1442
Central panel of the Crucifixion altarpiece. Oil on panel, 96 x 69 cm / 37¾ x 27⅛ in.
Vienna, Kunsthistorisches Museum, Gemäldegalerie

way in which he clasps the crucifix to him as he prays. We may interpret this to read that the saint has both literally and metaphorically thrown himself at the feet of Christ in the shape of the crucifix. This, certainly, was how Jerome (347–419/20) expressed it himself in a letter written to his protégée Eustochium in AD 384: "Helpless, I cast myself at the feet of Jesus, I watered them with my tears, I wiped them with my hair" (*Ad Eustochium de custodia virginitatis* 22, 7). Drawing on this and on other clear references to religious texts, Ruppel (1988) offers an altogether unusual, iconographically innovative interpretation of the St Jerome theme. In the mystic language of exegetic treatises of the High and Late Middle Ages, the cave-like cleft in the rock in which Jerome is lying symbolises the wound in Christ's side, in which man finds shelter like a bird in an eyrie. The red in the left side of the cleft is the colour of Christ's wounds, and is symbolically crowned by the thorn bushes on top of the rock. Another explanation for St Jerome's prostrate pose is therefore that he is, as it were, reclining within the wound in Christ's side. The saint thereby embraces the crucifix in his arms and has his eyes closed in inner contemplation. This motif of visionary contact with the body of Christ is characteristic of mystical texts. Nor is it coincidental that, to the right of this scene, Jerome's cloak is draped over the hollow stump of a fallen tree: an owl, symbolising Evil and its temptations, is perched on one of the tree's withered branches, while beneath another branch there hangs a great tit, itself a symbol of the soul, and probably the owl's prey. The two birds stand for physical and spiritual death as a result of sin, which Jerome is striving to avoid through fasting, abstinence and prayer.

Allegorical interpretations of this kind are based on those found in medieval bestiaries, in which the habits and traits of animals were assigned a moral significance. From a Christian perspective, the owl stands in a negative light both as a nocturnal hunter and in view of its use as a lure for songbirds, which could then be trapped with birdlime. The owl is one of Bosch's trademarks: it appears in many of his drawings (Cat. D2–Cat. D5) and paintings (Cat. 2, Cat. 4, Cat. 6.3, Cat. 10.3, Cat. 11, Cat. 12.2, Cat. 13.1, Cat. 14, Cat. 17.1, Cat. 20.3). The lion on the opposing, left side of the composition is another of St Jerome's attributes: according to legend, it became the saint's faithful companion after Jerome extracted a thorn from its paw. It is far from naturalistic in appearance and may be understood in heraldic terms as an identifying characteristic. Below the lion, at the extreme lower right corner we find a fox curled up beside a rooster. These two animals are normally bitter enemies: the fox embodies all the cunning of Evil, whereas the cockerel usually symbolises Christian vigilance (cf. Cat. D1v and Cat. D3r, and Cat. 13 and Cat. 22), although it can also represent the untamed male sexual drive. If we take into account the nest in the top left corner, the words of Matthew 8:20 come to mind: "And Jesus said to him [a scribe who wished to become his follower], 'Foxes have holes and birds of the air have nests, but the Son of Man has nowhere to lay His head.'" This biblical verse, here translated into pictorial form, once again illuminates the situation in which St Jerome entrusts himself to Christ. The background is a landscape with a 15th-century character, similar to that in the *Crucifixion* (Cat. 1) and containing a number of buildings, perhaps a church or monastery, in addition to a path, travellers and a couple resting beneath some trees. Compared with Bosch's later landscapes, with their menacing details and marginal motifs, this scenery appears positively idyllic.

While many of Bosch's surviving works cannot be precisely dated, the artist produced a number of others that are both documented and dated but have not come down to us. The earliest commission known to us only from archival sources was awarded to Bosch in 1487 and related to work to be carried out for the Tafel van de Heilige Geest municipal alms-house (van Dijck 2001a, p. 174; Kappelhof 1980). Bosch was to provide a new wall-hanging, probably a sort of cloth painting, for the assembly hall, and to create a decorative mount for a set of antlers – tasks for which he was paid less than two Rhenish guilders. This kind of work was common, and would not have stretched Bosch's abilities. His subsequent documented but no longer extant commissions were all carried out for the Brotherhood of Our Blessed Lady and were awarded to him only after he had become a member. This took place at some point within the accounting period of 1486/87, when Bosch became one of several thousand external, ordinary members. Just one year later, however, he would be accepted into the elite and clerical inner circle of the "sworn brothers", as they were known, a step that undoubtedly marked a new chapter of his life as a citizen and as a painter.

II.

Social and artistic ascent

1488–1501

"He knew that he had a great talent for painting and that people would have considered him... a painter who ranked behind Dürer, Michelangelo, Raphael and others, and so he embarked upon a new road, one on which he left the others behind..."

JOSÉ DE SIGÜENZA, 1605

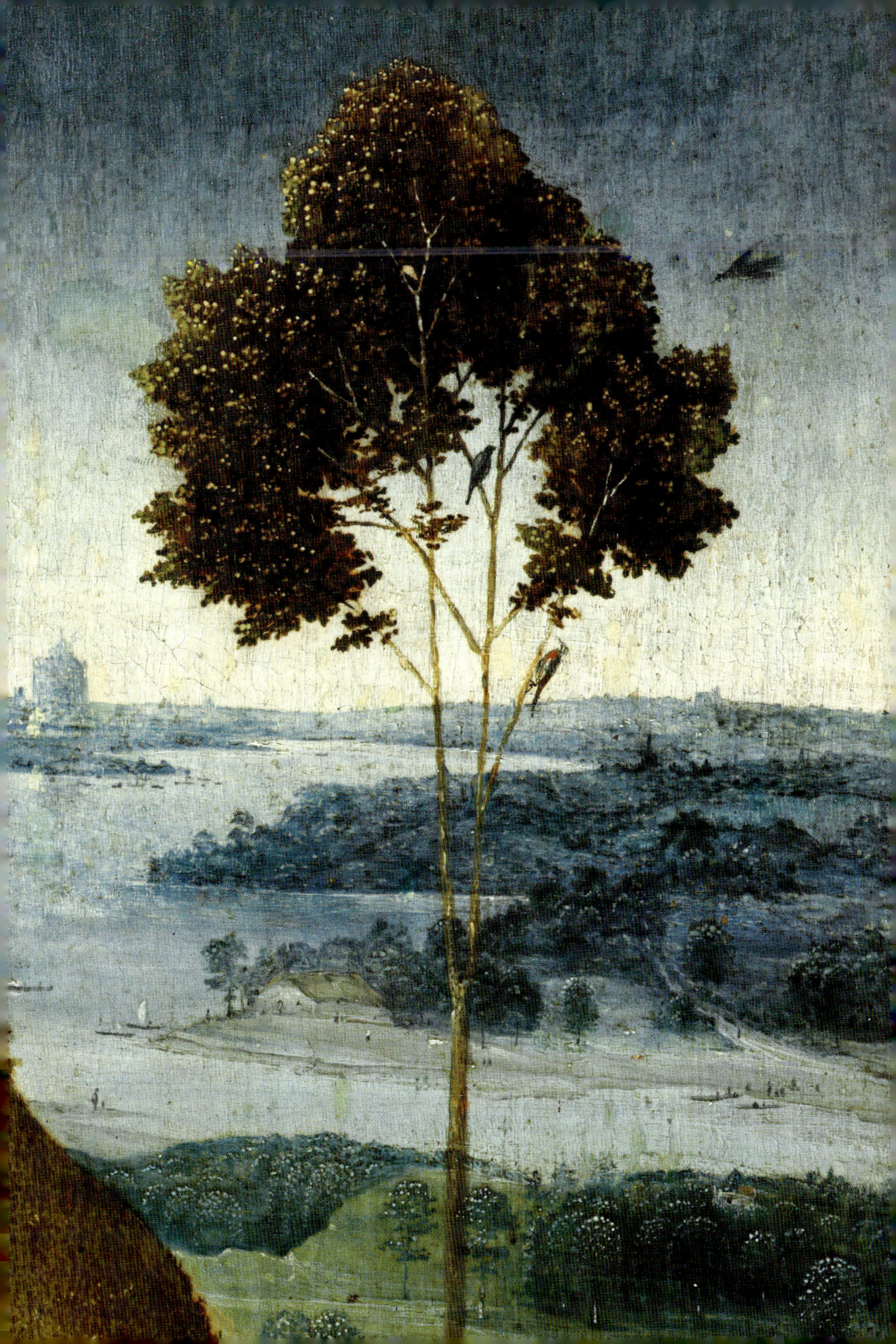

By comparison with Antwerp, with its thriving seaport, and the cities of Ghent, Bruges and Brussels, where life was shaped by the courts of the Habsburg Dukes of Burgundy as well as by commerce, late-medieval 's-Hertogenbosch must be described as provincial. Then as now, however, it served as a regional centre for North Brabant: it lived from transit trade and exported primarily cloth and metal goods to Holland, Antwerp and Bergen-op-Zoom. The general economic expansion and population growth marking the second half of the 15th century extended also to 's-Hertogenbosch; and it profited from Antwerp's rise to the position of leading centre of international trade, a development encouraged by Maximilian I of Habsburg (1459–1519), King of the Romans and later Holy Roman Emperor. During this golden age the population of 's-Hertogenbosch more than doubled, rising in the last quarter of the 15th and first quarter of the 16th century from around 11,000 to 24,000. This made it one of the largest cities in the Low Countries. This heyday was not, however, without its symptoms of a growth crisis: in 1473 the craft guilds stormed the council chamber to protest against the controlling power of the patricians and the burden of taxes imposed by the current Duke of Burgundy, Charles the Bold (b. 1433). Charles's death in 1477 was followed by a period of stagnation between 1482 and 1496, as Maximilian – who had acquired a claim to Burgundy through his marriage to Charles's daughter Mary in 1477 – fought with France and the cities of Flanders over the question of succession. As a result of this conflict, Bosch's home town found itself in a key military position vis-à-vis the renegade Duchy of Guelders, the former native province of the van Akens. By around 1500 's-Hertogenbosch had become a prosperous bourgeois and aristocratic centre of commerce of strategic and administrative importance, with a distinctively clerical culture to which Hieronymus Bosch owed a great deal.

The Brotherhood of Our Blessed Lady

The fact that Bosch was admitted to the elite and clerical inner circle of "sworn brothers" of the Brotherhood of Our Blessed Lady is something that requires an expla-

Page 35
Detail from: **St John on Patmos**, after 1488
Right inner wing of the two small shutters of a carved altarpiece
for the Brotherhood of Our Blessed Lady
(see ill. p. 45)

Page 37
St John the Baptist (in Meditation), after 1488
Left inner wing of the two small shutters of a carved altarpiece
for the Brotherhood of Our Blessed Lady
Oil on panel (oak), 49 x 40.5 cm / 19¼ x 16 in.
Madrid, Fundación Lázaro Galdiano

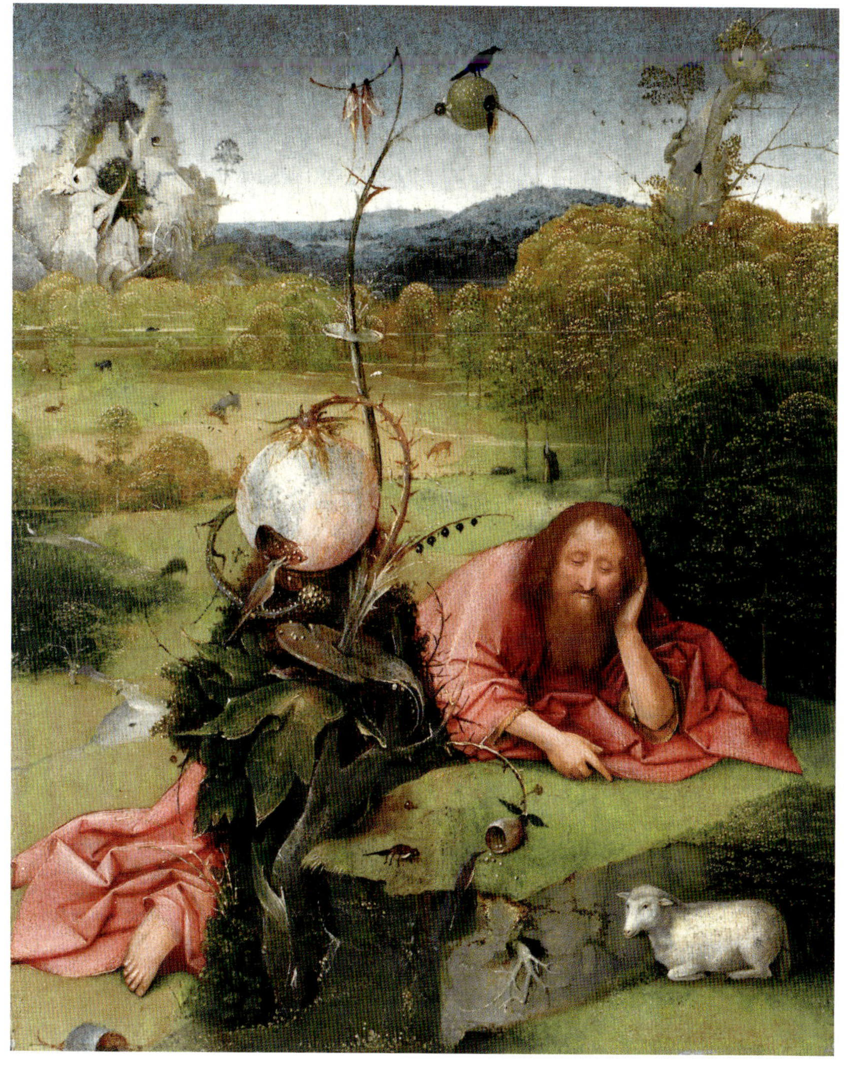

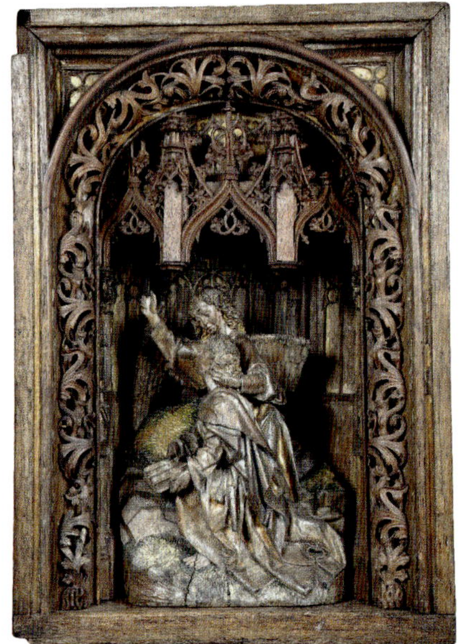

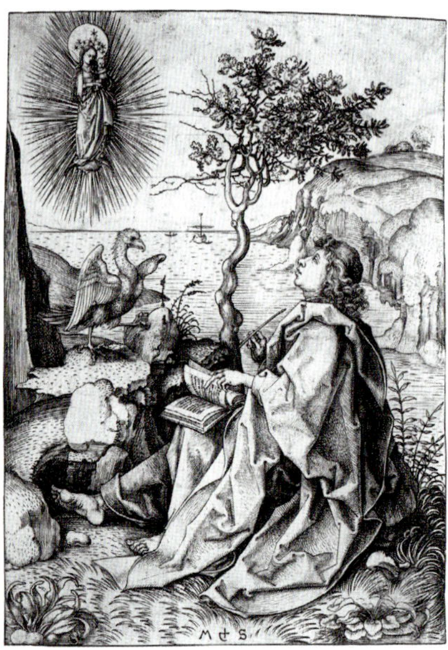

Adriaen van Wesel, **St John the Evangelist on Patmos**, 1477
Wing of altarpiece for the Brotherhood of Our Blessed Lady. Wood, 86.5 x 61.6 cm / 34 x 24¼ in.
's-Hertogenbosch, Brotherhoodof Our Blessed Lady, Museum Het Zwanenbroedershuis

Martin Schongauer, **St John on Patmos**, *c.* 1475–1480
Copper engraving, 16.0 x 11.3–11.4 cm / 6¼ x 4½ in. Berlin, Staatliche Museen, Kupferstichkabinett

nation. Members of the van Aken family had regularly worked for the Brotherhood over the years. In most cases they had also been ordinary members (van Dijck 2001a; Fischer 2009, p. 25), but had not advanced to the inner circle. Bosch himself had to meet two criteria: firstly, he had to dispose of his own land and/or buildings (a condition fulfilled by the property brought into their marriage by his wife), and secondly he had to have privileged clerical status, for which it was sufficient to take minor orders or simply the tonsure (van Dijck 2001a, p. 42; van Dijck 1973, p. 69). Bosch's tonsure involved cutting off just a small section of his hair and – as in the case of the donors of the painting *Ecce Homo with Saints and Donors* (Cat. 21) – would have been almost, if not entirely, invisible. Clerical status of this sort allowed the painter to marry and to live an outwardly civilian life, while at the same time giving him access to the Brotherhood's educational resources.

Compared with other elitist fraternities of that time, the Brotherhood of Our Blessed Lady (which exists to this day) was strongly clerical in its orientation (van Dijck 1973;

Fischer 2009, p. 23 ff.). It was founded in 1318 for "*clerici et scolares*", clerics and students. Membership grew rapidly from 1380 onwards, when a statue of the Virgin found in Sint-Jan's church started working regular miracles. This led in turn to a structural reorganisation: a disctinction was now made between external members, whose ranks eventually swelled to several thousand, and an inner circle of a few dozen sworn brothers, who were all members of the clergy. These last were not only required to wear the tonsure but had to swear to uphold the statutes of the Brotherhood and to live in or near 's-Hertogenbosch. The last condition could only be waived in the case of members of the upper aristocracy or senior clergy, who could be sworn brothers without actually having their residence in or in the vicinity of the city.

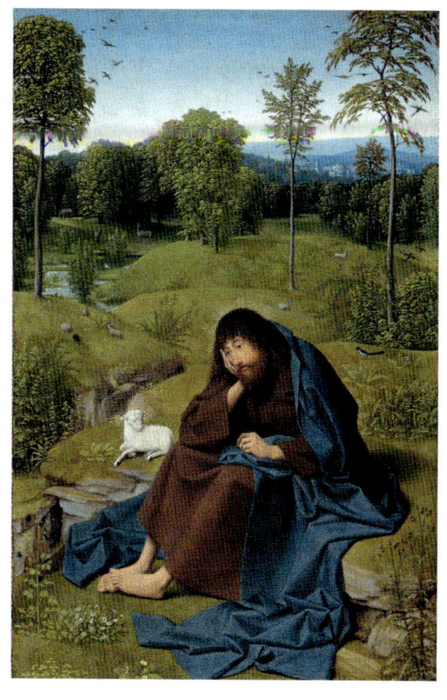

The total number of sworn brothers was around 60, of whom more than a third were already priests when they were admitted. Indeed, priests made up about half of the sworn brothers overall, while another fifth were *magister*, in other words theologians, lawyers and doctors who had studied at a university. The only exceptions to the rule stipulating that all sworn members had to belong to the clergy were the two or three so-called "swan brothers" – high-ranking honorary members representing the civic authorities or the Duke of Brabant's administration. Sworn brothers who did not come from the families of aristocrats, patricians and prosperous merchants making up 's-Hertogenbosch's social elite, had earned their place through education or other qualifications. In the period around 1500, sworn membership was, exceptionally, extended to individuals working in the sphere of the arts, such as architect Jan Heyns (d. 1516), musician Simon van Couderborch – and painter Hieronymus Bosch.

As a sworn brother, Bosch became part of an environment that would shape his life. The Brotherhood imposed a rigorous religious programme upon its members and, at the

Geertgen tot Sint Jans, **St John the Baptist**, *c.* 1490
Oil on panel, 42 x 28 cm / 16 ½ x 11 in. Berlin, Staatliche Museen, Gemäldegalerie

same time, held a visible and dignified position within the civic community. The brothers had to go to Mass twice a week: on Tuesdays to sing "the vespers of Our Blessed Lady with trebles", and on Wednesdays for "Lauds, assisted by servers and intoners who are dressed in official gowns and caps" (*Regulations*, fol. 3r). On Fridays (or, if that was impossible, on another day of the week), the sworn brothers were supposed to fast or do a good deed. They met at least once every six weeks for a ceremonial dinner, which Bosch hosted on three occasions, each separated by a gap of ten to eleven years. The first such occasion was in 1488/89, shortly after he was sworn in, the second in 1498, and the last in 1510. The icon of the Virgin was paraded during an annual procession, which was followed by a banquet for the members of the municipal council, guilds and monasteries, with entertainment provided by singers, musicians and actors. The sworn brothers wore a special set of ceremonial robes for these formal occasions. The Brotherhood celebrated Masses for the saints on all Marian feast days and several others besides. It also held 29 benefice and votive Masses and vigils for the dead and made donations of bread to the poor. The Brotherhood granted indulgences and had two provosts (*proosten*), a deacon (*dekan*) responsible for liturgy and choral prayers, and its own confessor. Other duties related to the running of the Brotherhood were assumed by non-clerics and, in some cases, outsiders: these dealt, for example, with deaths, finances, singing, housekeeping and cleaning (by Beguines). The Brotherhood of Our Blessed Lady enjoyed close links with the Brethren of the Common Life and in particular with the Dominicans, probably the most important monastic order in 's-Hertogenbosch, and likewise with the *passiebloem* guild of rhetoricians.

Outside the bounds of 's-Hertogenbosch, the Brotherhood also maintained a network of contacts with the civic, upper aristocratic and clerical elites in the Low Countries, which reached also as far as Cologne – a network that, around 1500, was growing ever more extensive (van Dijck 1973, pp. 79–87, 96–98 and 412–418). There was, accordingly, a recognition that the decoration and furnishings in the Brotherhood's chapel (today the sacristy) in Sint-Jan's ought to be upgraded. Immediately after joining, Bosch was commissioned by the Brotherhood to produce two *St John* panels (Cat. 3) for the chapel's existing altarpiece. They were to form the small wings that could be closed over the carved reliefs as shutters. The two patron saints of Sint-Jan's were chosen as their motifs: St John the Evangelist and St John the Baptist.

St John the Baptist

Bosch's *St John the Baptist* (p. 37, Cat. 3.1) reclines across the full width of the panel in the foreground of a landscape. Robed in the red of the Passion, with his head propped in his left hand and his eyes closed, he points towards the Lamb of God, symbol of Christ, with the index finger of his right hand: "'Behold! The Lamb of God who takes away the sins of the world!'" (John 1:29). The lamb is tucked into the lower right corner, where it is screened from the bizarre surrounding landscape by the edge of the grassy bank on which St John is lying. In meditating upon his position within the history of Salvation, in which – as the last prophet – he prepared the way for Christ, the Baptist has assumed a pose and expression that at first sight appear melancholy, but may be understood to convey his recognition of and surrender to the Divine Plan. A hair shirt can be glimpsed beneath his sleeves: a familiar attribute testifying to the Baptist's ascetic lifestyle. As X-rays and stylistic analysis have revealed, the donor who originally appeared in the foreground directly in front of St John was painted over by Bosch either before or soon after the panel's completion. The relatively large and bizarre plant seen rising in the same spot mostly follows the contours of this donor figure, who is kneeling in prayer, angled towards the right-hand foreground, and dressed in a fashion typifying the educated civic elite. The exotic plant is a pictorial invention: while it draws upon elements of naturally occurring flora, these are hard to identify. It bears three large fruits that resemble pomegranates in that their interiors are full of seeds. The pomegranate is considered a symbol of fertility and natural abundance, of loving kindness, immortality and the spiritual blessings of the Church. In Bosch's oeuvre, on the other hand, unnatural fruits and plants carry negative associations; in the central panel of the *Garden of Earthly Delights* (Cat. 11.3), in the *Temptation of St Anthony* (Cat. 10.4) and in *The Haywain* (Cat. 20.2), they stand for nature growing unchecked: a metaphor of the sinner who does not control his instincts and senses.

In *St John the Baptist*, a bird is assigned to each of the three fruits. Near the bottom of the panel, a dark bird is pecking at the open fruit lying on the grassy bank. Not far away, another bird (supplementary to the principal three) lies dead, its legs extending rigidly in front of it. Halfway up the plant, a bird with colourful feathers is gorging itself upon a large whitish fruit with accents of yellows and blues. At the top, silhouetted against the sky, a third bird is perched on an unpunctured fruit. If we interpret the three living birds as symbolising the soul, we may assume that the lowest one is in a state of sin, the middle one in a state of succumbing through the senses to temptation by evil, and the one at the top in the state of enlightenment and proximity to God. A comparable tripartite arrangement, in this case embodied by three hermits, can be found in *St Christopher* (Cat. 7; see p. 78).

The image of the soul's journey towards salvation as a process of three or four ascending steps was invoked by the profoundly influential Netherlandish mystic John of Ruysbroeck (1293–1381) and his pupils and followers, and likewise by the Observant mendicant orders who formed the backbone of the monastic Reform movement, to describe the protracted mystical process of redressing the deformed soul. The Franciscan Jan Brugman (*c.* 1400–1473) – a popular preacher whose writings are still well-known in the Netherlands

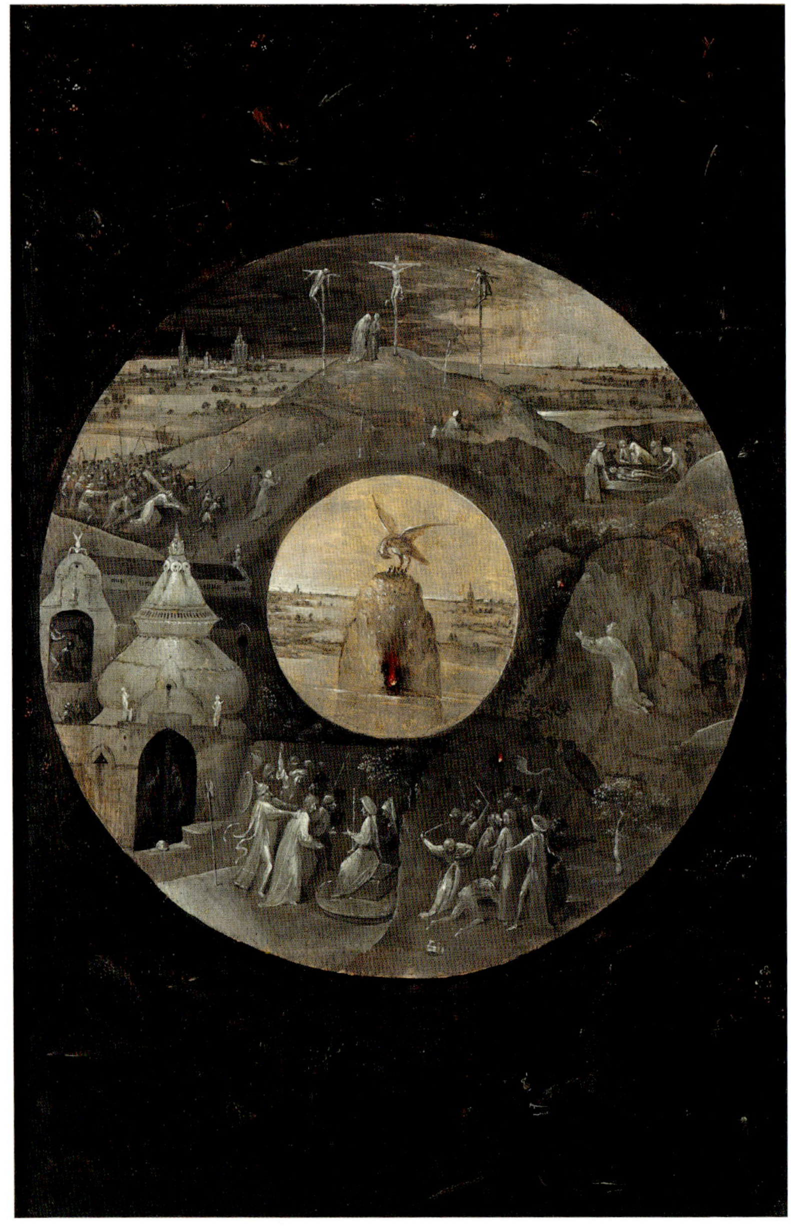

today and who also had links with 's-Hertogenbosch – took the relationship between the lily and thorns as the starting point for a three-step visual metaphor: "The first is the lily beneath the thorns, the second the lily among the thorns, the third the lily above the thorns" (Brugman, *Onuitgegeven Sermoenen*, sermon 19). The constants are the lily and the thorns, while their relationship to one another is variable. These three images can be interpreted individually and in mutual comparison, and are explained in allegorical terms by Brugman as follows: the first lily represents the sinner who is pure only on the outside. The second illustrates the constant battle against sin and the desires of the flesh. The third lily represents the state of the blessed few, who have risen above all temptation and subdued their nature. In this last context Brugman cites the positive exempla of the first and most important saints, including the Virgin (who as a "lily above the thorns" was also the emblem of the 's-Hertogenbosch Brotherhood of Our Blessed Lady), the two Johns and St Stephen. Bosch evidently drew on this type of three-step imagery from writings or sermons and used it as a model in his painting for similar metaphors of the ascent of the soul (Fischer 2009, pp. 332–337).

There are other respects in which Bosch's *St John the Baptist* clearly differs from other treatments of the theme. In the *St John the Baptist* (p. 39) by Geertgen tot Sint Jans (*c.* 1460/65–before 1495), the most important Dutch painter of his day, the saint may be portrayed in a similar fashion, but the landscape is completely different in conception: the woods in the background enclose a gentle landscape of meadows and trees, a *hortus conclusus* that seems almost paradisiacal with its pond, gambolling hares, deer and birds. Bosch, on the other hand, scatters his landscape with menacing signs, such as the bizarre rock formations in the background and the two bears, one about to devour a slain deer. Like the hermits in his other pictures, Bosch's St John lives in the *woestijn* or *woestenie* (desert, wilderness), as it is regularly described in Netherlandish legends of the saints. The landscape in Bosch's panel implicitly continues beyond the edges of the picture and is thereby equated with the world: attacks by lions, bears and wolves illustrate the dangers lying in wait for the soul in this earthly life. Life in the world is as hazardous for the soul as is uncivilised nature for the traveller. Bosch shows the world in its material, physical dimension as a potential cause of suffering, whereas the spiritual dimension recommends itself as a refuge of safety and constancy, solace and joy.

The Eye of God with Scenes from the Passion, after 1488
Right outer wing of the two small shutters of a carved altarpiece for the Brotherhood of Our Blessed Lady
Oil on panel (oak), 63 x 43.3 cm / 24¾ x 17 in. (exterior tondo: ∅ 39 cm / 15⅜ in.)
Berlin, Staatliche Museen, Gemäldegalerie

St John and the art of painting devils

The second altar wing painting, *St John on Patmos* (p. 45, Cat. 3.2.1), shows the author of *Revelation*, also equated with St John the Evangelist and Apostle, recording the visions he received during his exile on this Aegean island. Through the agency of an angel, St John sees the Woman of the Apocalypse, who was traditionally interpreted as the Virgin (Rev. 12:1–5). Bosch's composition is structured along a diagonal leading from lower right to upper left: the pictorial elements ascend in hierarchical order from the material to the invisible, in other words from the barren earth with the Devil at John's back, through the saint himself, then through the intermediary of the sky-blue angel up to the Mother of God enthroned on a crescent moon in the clouds. This visual axis originally extended beyond the panel to the miracle-working icon of the Virgin that stood at the very top of the altarpiece. At the same time, however, the composition is also laid out as a triangle with St John in the centre, the angel at the apex, and the eagle and the devil as adversaries at the lower corners. While no single work has so far been identified as Bosch's obvious model, his painting exhibits various analogies with other representations of the subject. It also resembles Martin Schongauer's (*c.* 1445/50–1491) engraving of *St John on Patmos* (p. 38) in its composition and motifs.

The true artistic value of Bosch's *St John on Patmos* lies more specifically in its handling of details. While St John receives his vision, the eagle, his symbolic creature, stands guard over the little pot of ink that the saint needs to write down the Book of Revelation. As man's antagonist, the Devil longs to seize St John's writing implements as a way of sabotaging the Divine Plan for Salvation. This devil scene is a typical feature of traditional Netherlandish representations of the *St John* theme; but Bosch uses it innovatively in allegorising the Devil. By illustrating the Netherlandish figure of speech "to have short arms" in a literal fashion, he at once signals to us that the Devil cannot possibly succeed in his scheming (cf. Röhrich 1973, vol. 1, *Arm*, p. 99), because he is quite simply unable to get his hands on the inkpot. The fire on his head symbolises both his infernal origins and the burning desire that is consuming his being. His body is made up of several parts that carry negative associations with Hell, sin and folly. He has the legs and tail of a gecko, a primarily nocturnal variety of lizard (Asmus/Grosshans 1998, p. 158), and therefore shuns the light of day or, in allegorical terms, the light of divine inspiration. His spectacles underline his focus upon the physical, sensual world (Fischer 2009, p. 325). His gaze is fixed upon the spot on the ground where the writing utensils are lying, and without

St John on Patmos, after 1488
Right inner wing of the two small shutters of a carved altarpiece for the Brotherhood of Our Blessed Lady
Oil on panel (oak), 63 x 43.3 cm / 24¾ x 17 in. Berlin, Staatliche Museen, Gemäldegalerie

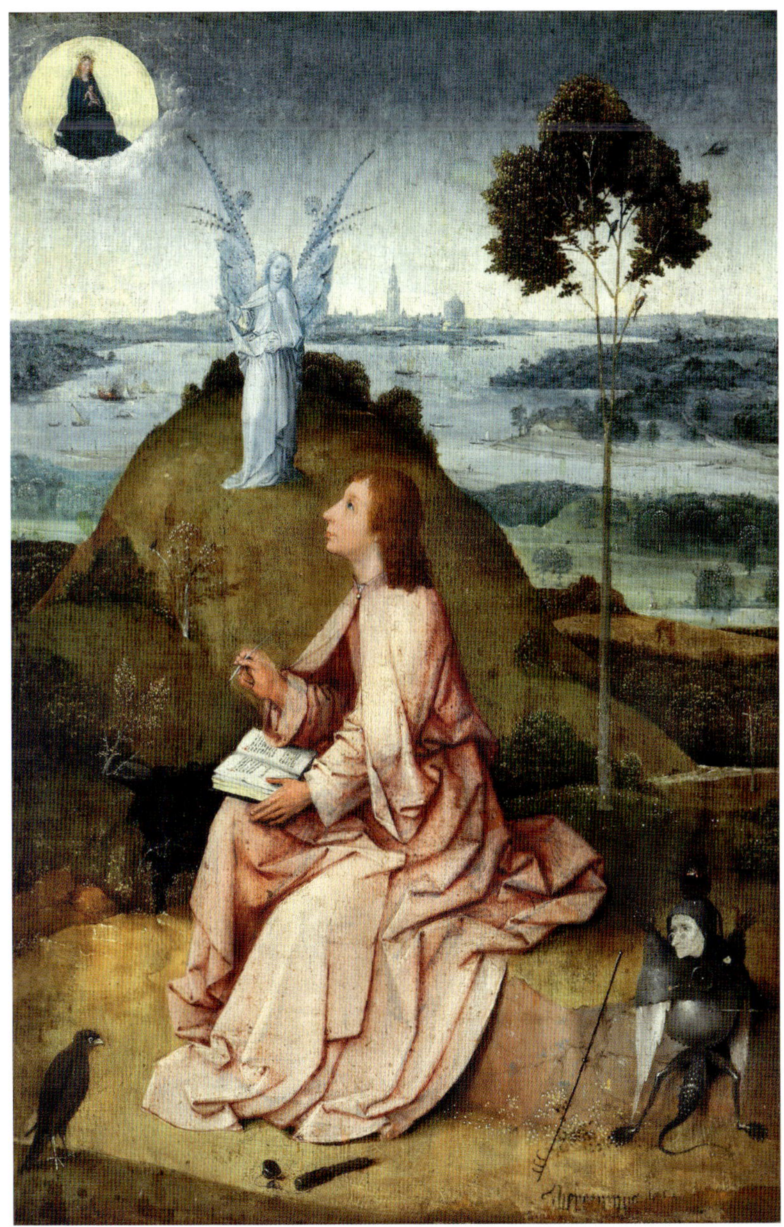

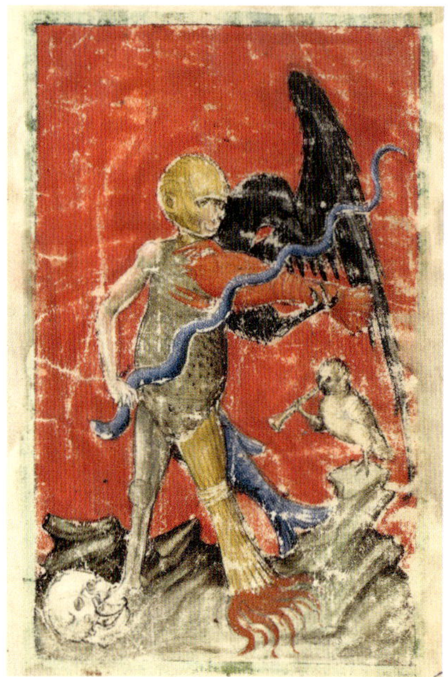

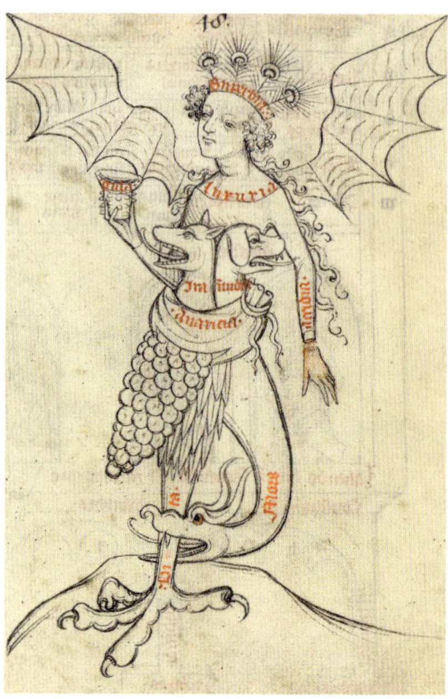

Anonymous artist, **Elemental Chaos**, *c.* 1420
from: *Aurora Consurgens*, fol. 1r (detail). Watercolor on parchment, 20.5 x 14 cm / 8 x 5½ in.
Zurich, Zentralbibliothek, Ms. Rhenoviensis 172

Anonymous artist, **Siebenlasterweib ("Woman of Seven Vices")**, *c.* 1414
from: the Metten *Biblia pauperum*, fol. 95r (detail). Pen and ink on parchment, 48.5 x 35 cm / 19 x 13¾ in.
Munich, Staatsbibliothek, clm. 8201

which St John would be unable to record the text of Revelation. The Devil's hooded cape is hard to interpret, as it was an item of clothing worn not only by monks but also by certain lay persons.

The scene with the eagle and the Devil is more than just an anecdotal battle over St John's inkpot. The Devil is an exemplum of blindness. As if in a drollery, he is a figure of contrast, elucidating the main theme either through parody or through negativity. This is also clear from the pictorial layout: the Devil stands on the shady side behind St John's back, incapable of seeing the apparition in the sky. In compositional terms he is separated from the rest of the picture by the verticals of the tree trunk, the border of St John's cloak, the writing utensils and the *crauwel* leaning beside him. The *crauwel* was a long pronged kitchen implement used in the preparation of meat; it often featured in representations of devils as an instrument of capture and torture, used to handle the damned like pieces of meat – as they were indeed described in some textual sources.

Such hybrid creatures in Bosch's oeuvre have their forerunners primarily in spiritual texts; but secular literature supplies a model in its occasional descriptions of mixed beings. These evolved, probably in the 12th century, out of moralising Christian interpretations of the *Ars poetica*, the epistle on the art of poetry by the Roman poet Horace (65–8 BC). Horace opens his letter by expressing his view that uniting the upper half of a beautiful woman to the bottom half of an ugly fish was – metaphorically speaking – the opposite of successful poetry (Klemm 1993/94). The hybrid creatures of the late Middle Ages were, typically, composed of various human and animal limbs and parts, all having a symbolic significance. A case in point is the *Siebenlasterweib* (the "Woman of Seven Vices") in the Metten *Biblia pauperum* of 1414 (p. 46), in which each limb represents a sin. In most representations of hybrid beings the disharmony of their parts betokened the absence of natural or divine order. This allegorical aspect of mixed creatures could even be used to inject a note of comic parody into compositions (p. 46).

Hybrid beings were already part of the artistic repertoire in Bosch's home town even before he embarked on his career. Bosch's concept of the Devil has its starting-point here. Only rarely does he paint the relatively uniform, "classic" type of devil with the usual features of cloven hoofs or claws, dark fur, long ears and an ugly grimace. Bosch's devils have the character of hybrid creatures whose physical components or attributes point plainly, as mentioned above, to certain vices. They define themselves not only as the infernal counterparts of angels, but also as the opposite of the virtues: they punish the poor souls of sinners, and at the same time embody these sins, rendering them visible to the viewer. Bosch lays bare these examples of human misconduct in situations and objects taken from everyday life. Just as the lives of the saints are relocated in his paintings to his own 15th-century context through the buildings, fashions, landscape and daily objects among which they appear, so Bosch's devils to a certain extent also assume familiar traits. A further characteristic of these sin-devils is that they are represented not simply as hideous and stupid in nature, but as tending towards the ridiculous. As viewers, we are consequently able to distance ourselves from both the sins and the devils confronting us, rather than feel unduly afraid at the sight of them. Last but not least, the principle of the hybrid creature provides the painter with fresh scope for invention since it functions in the same way as the rhetorical device of the neologism in poetry: both can be deployed to surprise the viewer or the reader/listener in ever new ways. With *St John on Patmos* the artist's pride in his creation probably also makes itself felt in the signature in the lower right corner of the panel. The picture is signed not van Aken but Bosch, as an abbreviation for 's-Hertogenbosch, indicating the painter's identification with his birthplace and addressed to those who have arrived from other parts.

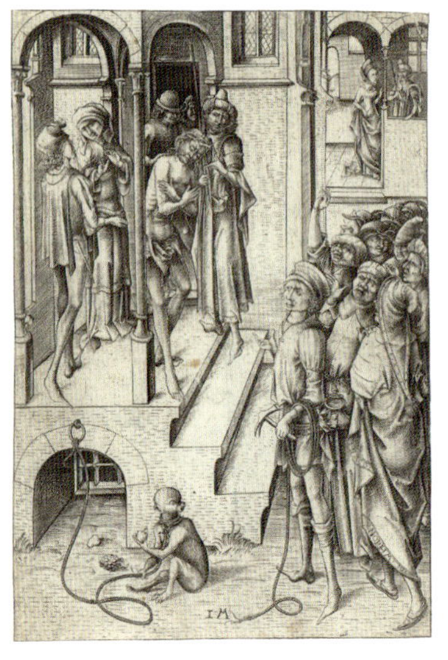

The grisaille exterior of the *St John on Patmos* shutter shows a remarkable representation of *The Eye of God with Scenes from the Passion* (p. 42, Cat. 3.2.2); its pendant on the opposite *St John the Baptist* shutter has not survived, but conceivably took up the theme of the life of the Baptist or the life of Christ. The portrait-format picture is essentially filled by a stylised eye made up of an inner circle and an outer ring. In the pale circle at the centre we see a pelican standing over its nest, which is perched on top of a rock surrounded by water and a sweeping landscape. According to the *Physiologus*, a text widely known in the Middle Ages and which presented animals and plants in an allegorical relationship to events of the Bible, the pelican was said to restore its chicks to life – having killed them itself – by feeding them with its own blood. The pelican is thus a symbol of Christ's sacrifice and the self-sacrificing love of God. The surrounding ring shows the Passion of Christ in scenes laid out in clockwise order. These start on the far right with Christ on the Mount of Olives, and continue with his Arrest (in which Judas delivers his treacherous kiss and a furious Peter draws his sword against Malchus), Christ before Pilate, the Flagellation (with Christ bound to a column), the Crowning with Thorns, the Road to Calvary, the Crucifixion, and lastly the Entombment at upper right. At the highest point of the composition, the three crosses atop the Mount of Calvary rise above the horizon and link Heaven and Earth. The circle may be understood as the earth or the world. In the Crucifixion scene darkness has spread across the left half of the sky (Mark 15:33). Lower down on the central vertical axis, directly aligned with the Crucifixion, the pelican spreads its wings like the arms of the cross.

Israhel van Meckenem the Younger, **Ecce Homo**, 1475–1485
Copper engraving, 20.9 x 14.5 cm / 8¼ x 5¾ in. Amsterdam, Rijksmuseum

Page 49
Ecce Homo with Donors, *c.* 1490–1495
Oil on panel (oak), 71.1 x 60.5 cm / 28 x 23¾ in.
Frankfurt am Main, Städel Museum
Inscriptions: "Ecce Homo" – "Behold the man!"
"Crucifige eum" – "Crucify him!"
"Salva nos xp [=Christ]e redemptor" – "Save us, Christ the Redeemer!"

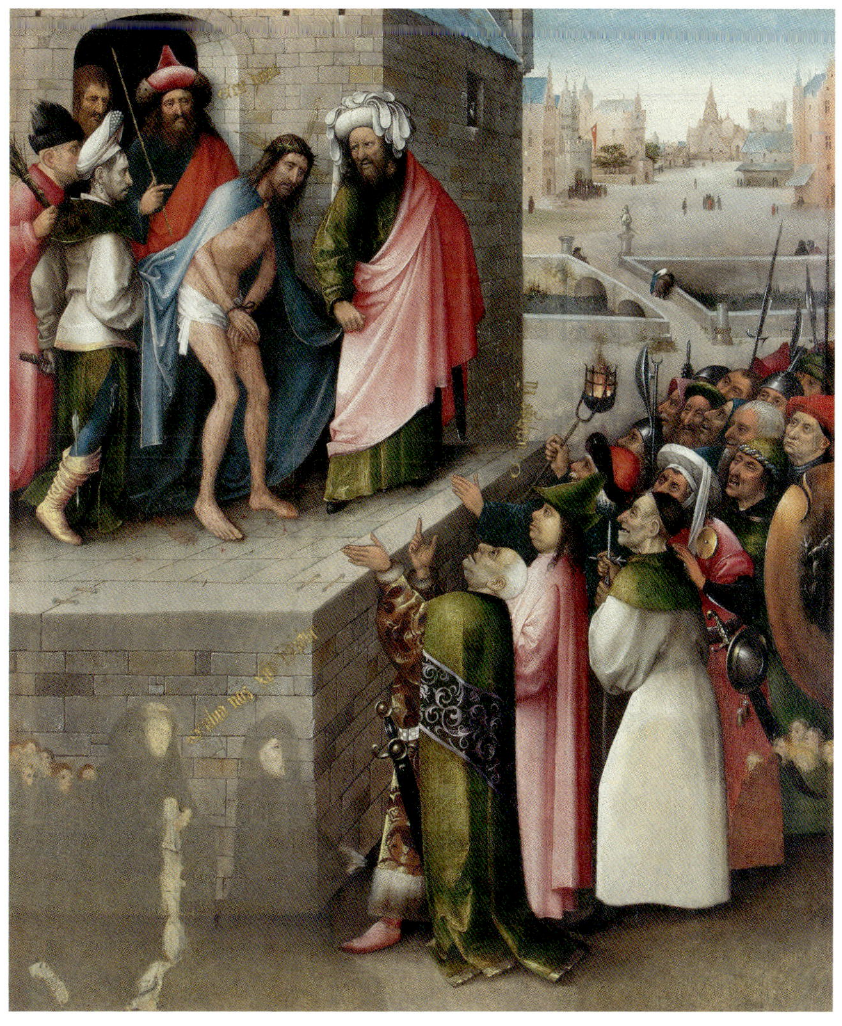

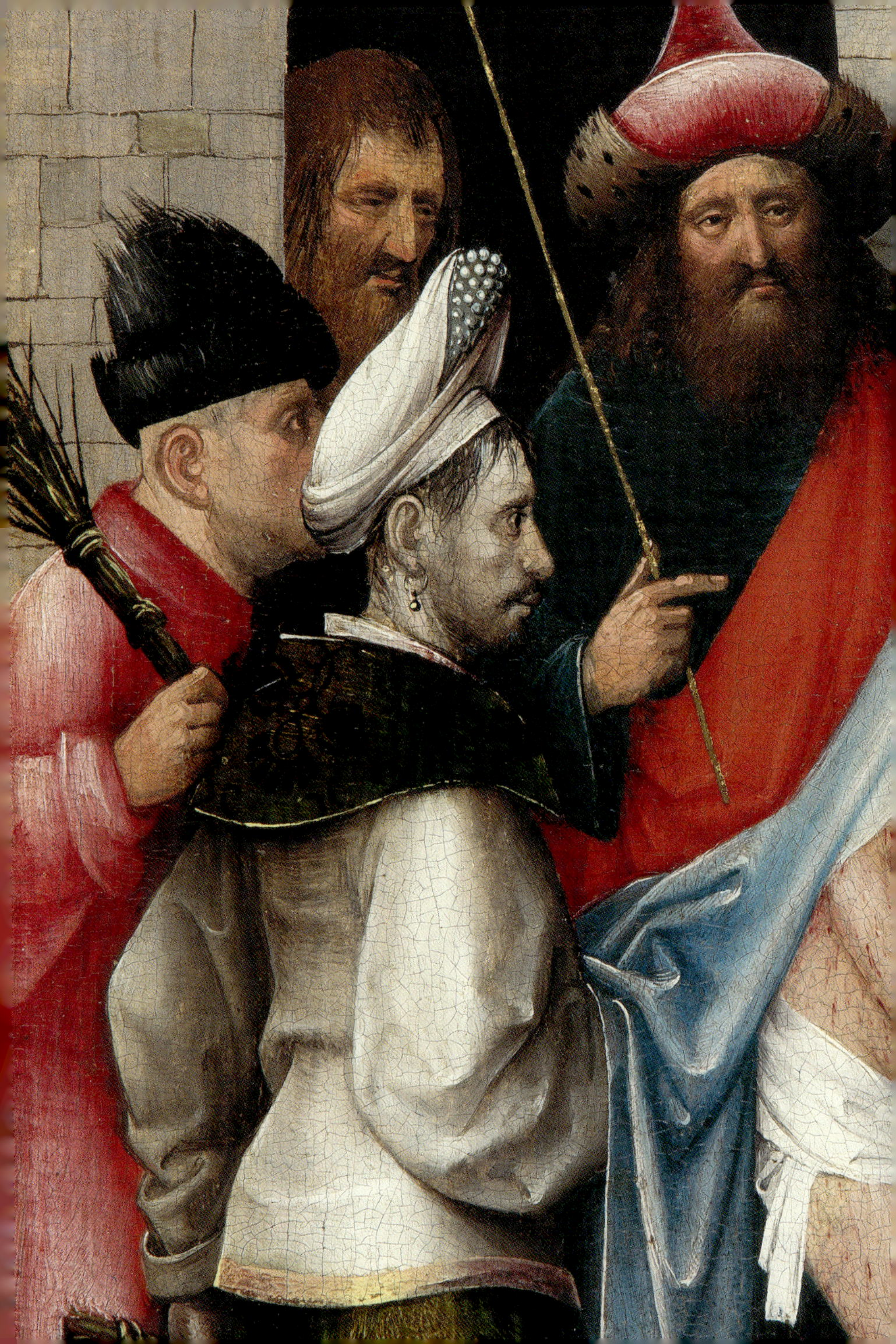

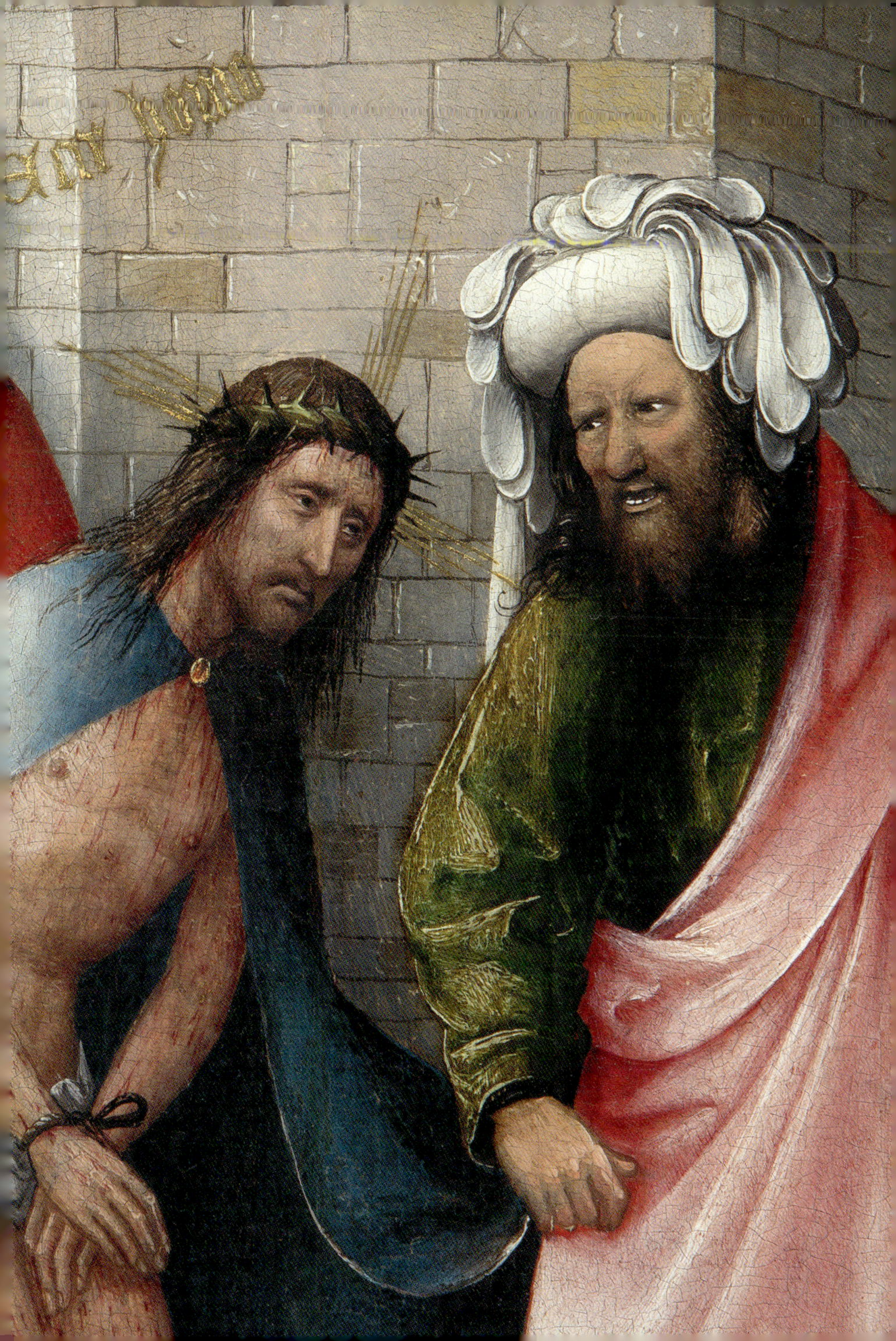

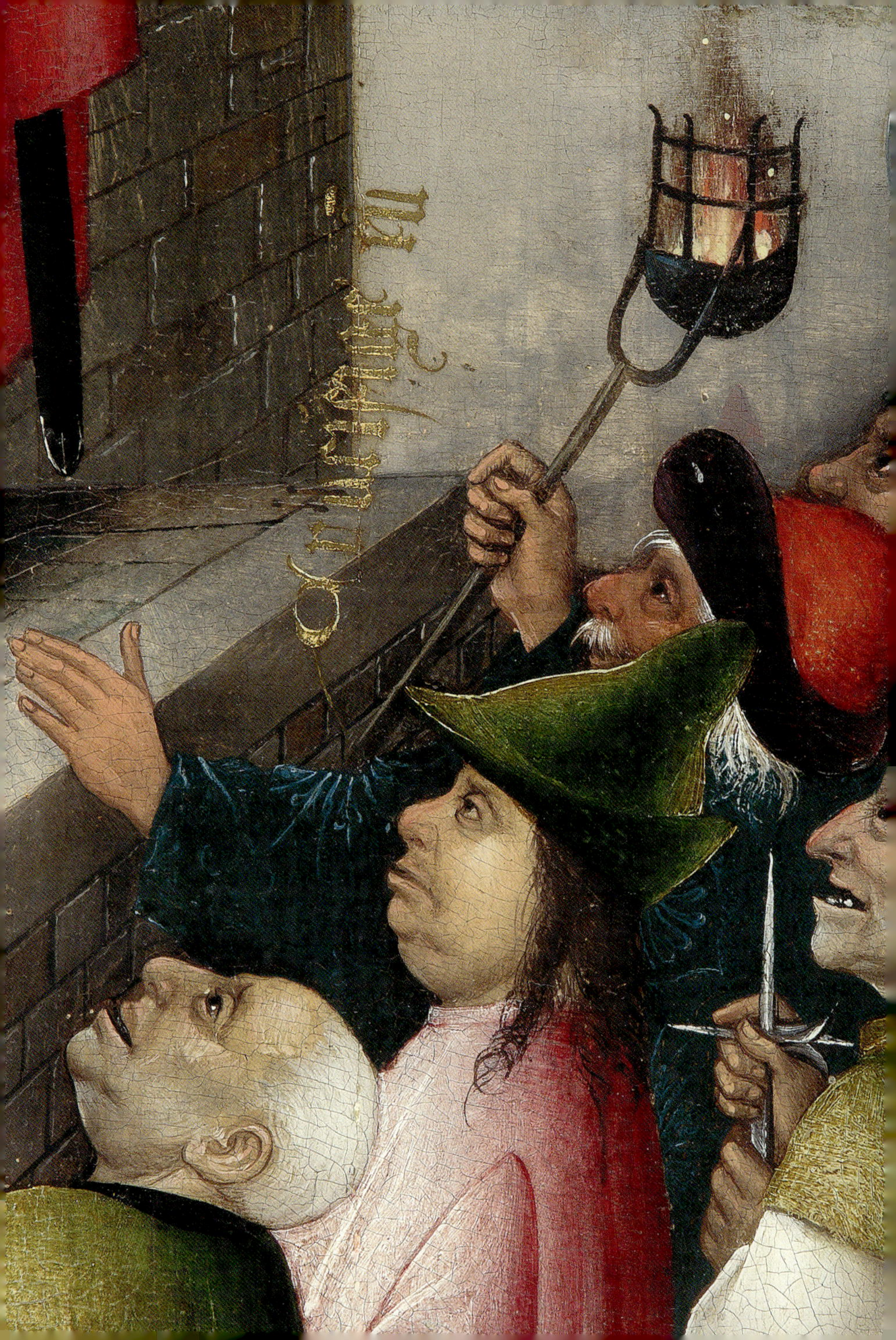

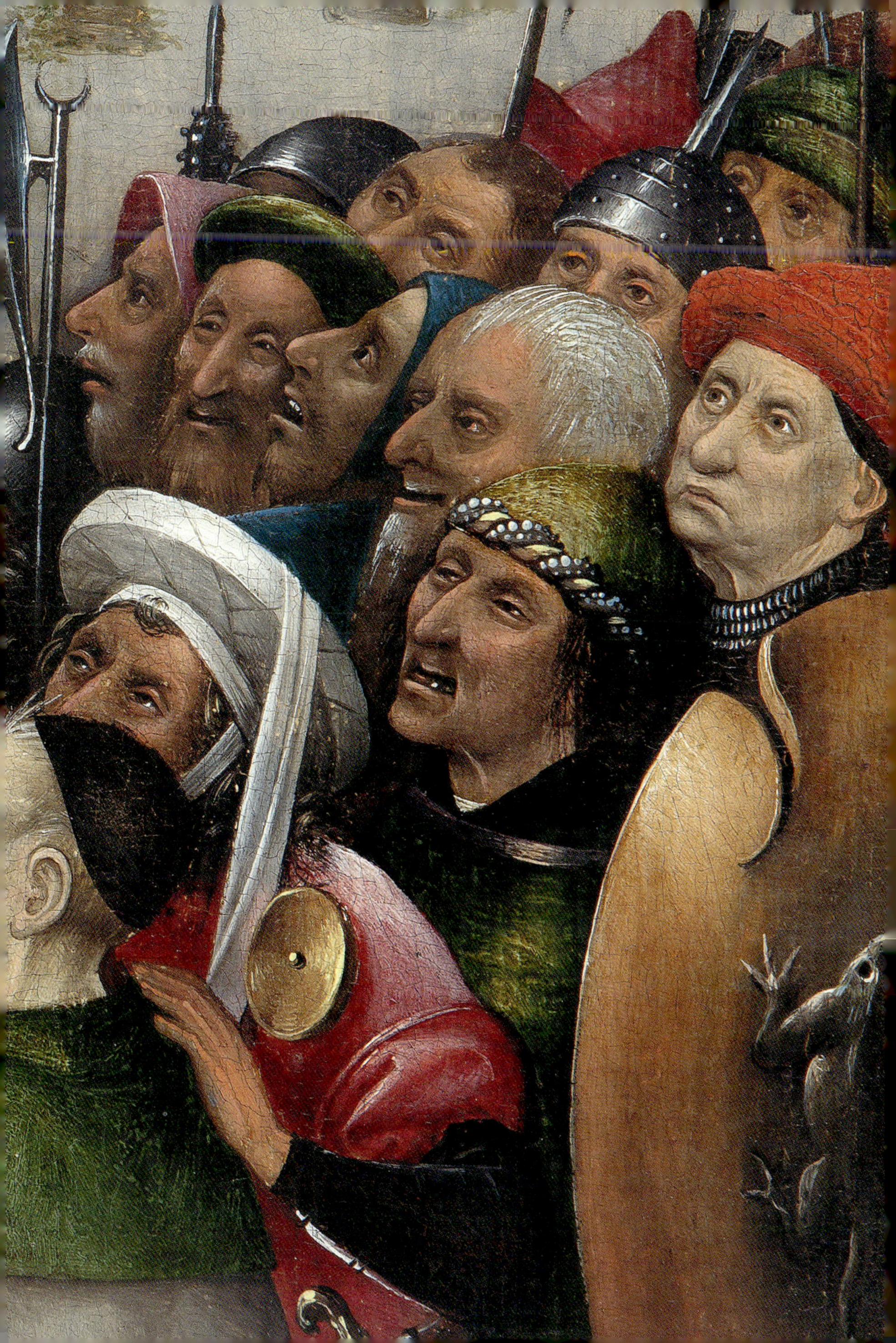

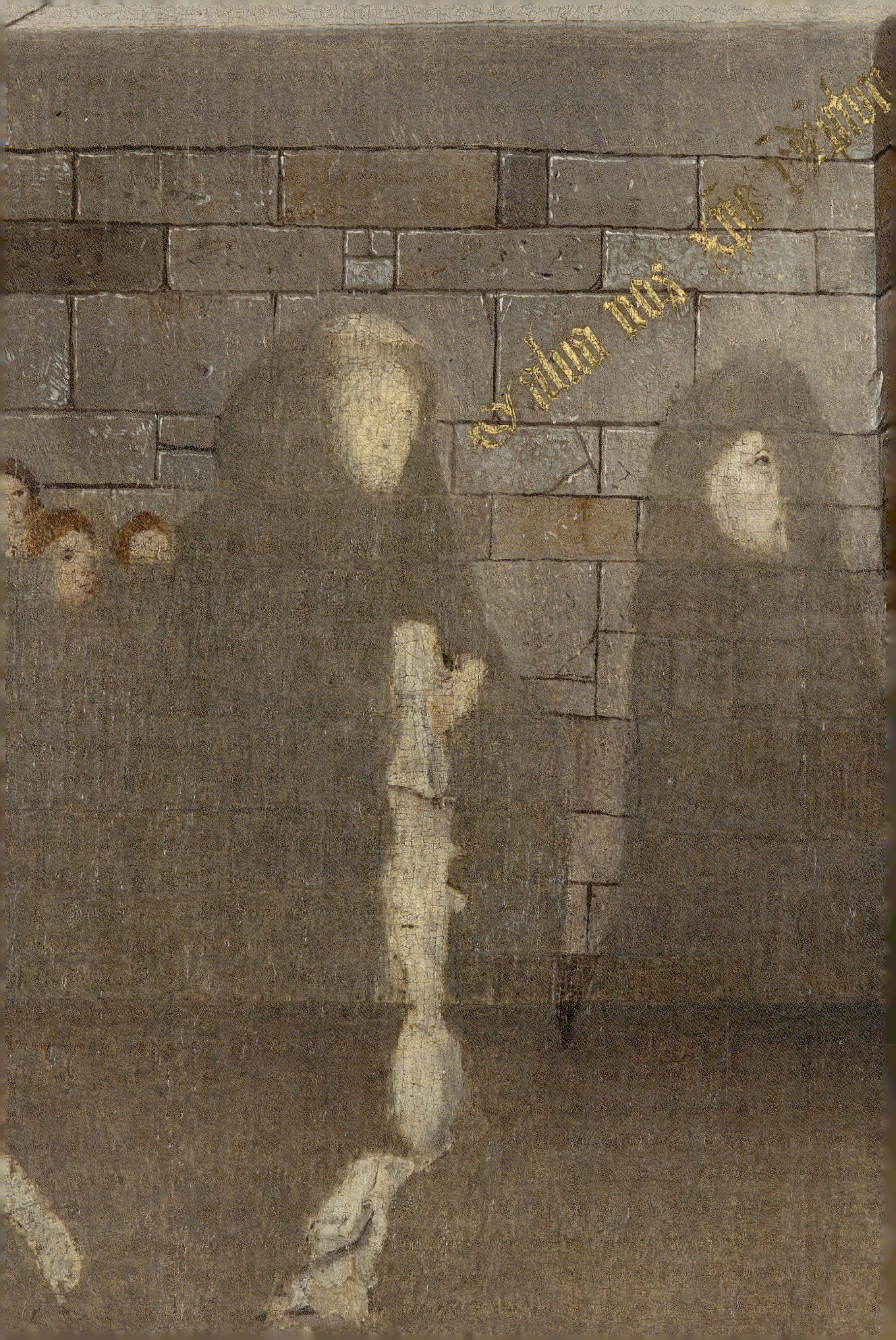
Salva nos

Surrounding the circular "eye" on all sides is a black surface representing the darkness, where a few barely discernible demons pursue their evil practices. Two stags shine palely through towards the lower left, and further left we can detect a porcupine and a cockerel, both of which also appear in the *Garden of Earthly Delights* (Cat. 11) and the *Last Judgement* (Cat. 13). A helmeted man carrying a ladder on his shoulder can be made out at the upper left, a harp on the right, and a carriage at the lower right. Birds and various fish monsters are scattered across the surface, along with dabs of white and pink paint that recall flowers. *The Eye of God with Scenes from the Passion* is a vivid illustration of the polarity between Good and Evil, between the light of divine knowledge at the centre and the darkness of ignorance at the periphery.

The fact that Bosch was commissioned to paint the two shutters for the Brotherhood's altarpiece in Sint-Jan's church directly after he had become a sworn member suggests that his tonsure and property holdings were insufficient on their own to earn him admission to the ranks of the 's-Hertogenbosch elite: he must also have been of particular use to them. As a general rule, the Brotherhood rewarded artists who had carried out specific services on its behalf only *after* the event, by waiving the membership fee, granting them free admission and occasionally even allowing them into the circle of the sworn members. Work carried out for a devout association was paid for with membership of the same. Architect Jan Heyns was only granted sworn membership in 1495/96, about a year after the completion of the works that he had supervised on the Brotherhood's chapel (Vink 2001a, p. 96). We know that the manuscript illuminator and panel painter Gerard David (*c.* 1460–1523) only joined the elite Bruges fraternity of Onze-Lieve-Vrouw van den Drogen Boom, made up chiefly of nobles and wealthy citizens, after he had successfully established himself in his profession.

When Bosch joined the Brotherhood in 's-Hertogenbosch, however, he evidently did not yet have any comparable artistic achievements to his name. Yet he may have been considered talented and a suitable choice for commissions. The fact that he was well-versed in theology may have been a point in his favour: this was something that the Brotherhood, with its Christian focus, would have expected from any painter within its fold. For Bosch himself the advantages of membership were not in the first instance material, but lay in the fact that the Brotherhood's contacts with high-ranking individuals in other regions of Europe opened up a wider field of potential customers. The Brotherhood of Our Blessed

Pages 50/51, 52/53, 54
Details from: **Ecce Homo with Donors**, *c.* 1490–1495
Inscriptions: "Ecce Homo" – "Behold the man!"
"Crucifige eum" – "Crucify him!"
"Salva nos xp [=Christ]e redemptor" – "Save us, Christ the Redeemer!"

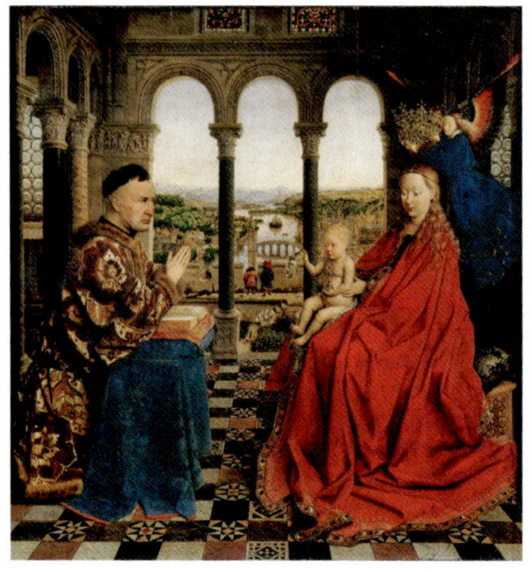

Lady was the institution that brought to 's-Hertogenbosch high-quality artworks by painters and sculptors of super-regional and even international renown. In 1456/57, for example, "Meester Rogier tot Brussel" – i. e. Rogier van der Weyden – had supplied the Brotherhood with a design for a painting of the Virgin.

Work continued apace on the completion and decoration of the Brotherhood's chapel in Sint-Jan's church, for the altarpiece of which Bosch had executed the two *St John* panels. Bosch's next commission for the Brotherhood, awarded in 1491/92, involved making a new panel carrying the names of sworn members, both living and dead. Van Wesel's carved altarpiece was installed in the almost completed chapel in 1493 (van Dijck 1973, p. 127); and in 1493/94 Bosch supplied a design for a stained-glass window at the Brotherhood's request. It seems that he painted the full-scale design on a couple of old bed-sheets (*een paer aulder slaeplakens*) and monitored its execution by the glass painter Willem Lombart. While these commissions earned him little or no income, Bosch built up his fortune by other means. A sign of his prosperity can be seen in the sales of wood from his country estates, which in 1492 and 1494 brought in 51 and 56 guilders, respectively, sums sufficient in themselves to cover the annual costs of running a two-person household.

Ecce Homo

Somewhere in the middle of the 1490s Bosch painted the *Ecce Homo* (p. 49, Cat. 4) now in Frankfurt am Main. The patron was a member of the social elite, as also represented in the ranks of the Brotherhood. Whether he was indeed a fellow member, however, can no longer be clarified, since the donor figures were scraped off and overpainted and were only uncovered during the panel's most recent restoration, in 1983. The donor couple and their seven sons – one of them a Dominican monk – and six daughters are now only visible as shadowy figures. The pictorial theme is taken from

Jan van Eyck, **Madonna of Chancellor Rolin**, *c.* 1435
Oil on panel, 66 x 62 cm / 26 x 24⅜ in. Paris, Musée du Louvre

Page 57
Detail from: **Ecce Homo with Donors**, *c.* 1490–1495 (see ill. p. 49)

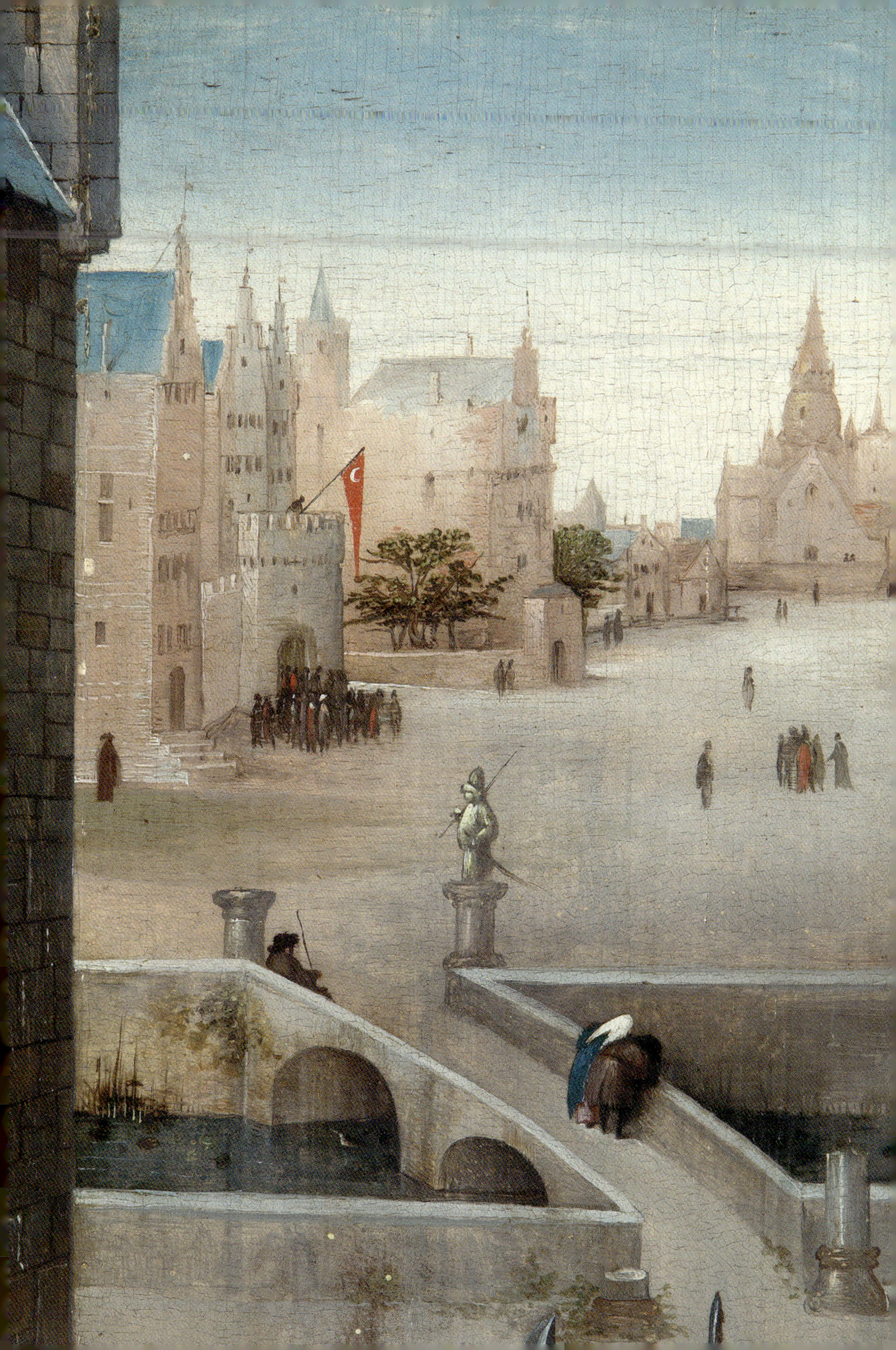

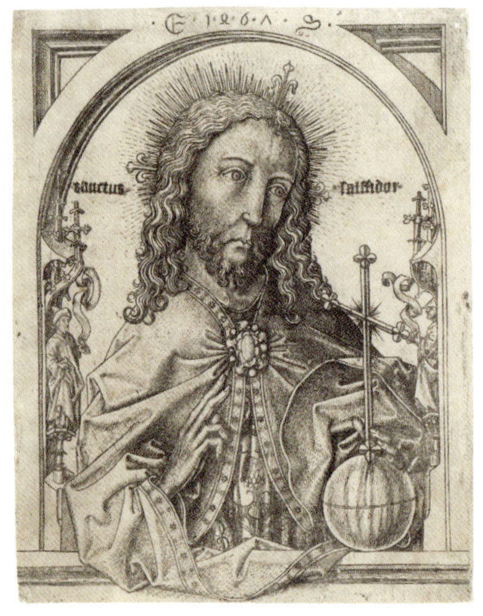

the Gospels (Matthew 27:11–26; Mark 15:2–15; Luke 23:2–7, 13–25; John 18:28–19:16). Jesus, beaten and crowned with thorns, is paraded in front of the palace by the Roman governor Pontius Pilate, who invites the assembled crowd to choose whether he should execute Jesus or Barabbas. Standing on a raised podium beneath the arch of a doorway on the left, robed in black and red and holding his staff of office in his hand, Pilate presents Jesus – the optical focus of the picture – to the hungry mob. The humiliated, bleeding and bowed Christ is escorted by a pale-faced guard in a turban on the right and a smartly dressed accomplice on the left, both holding and leading him by the folds of his blue cape. The ensuing dialogue can also be read in three inscriptions in gold lettering, which the artist has incorporated within the panel. Pilate announces "*Ecce Homo*" ("Behold the Man!"), in response to which the colourful crowd, clothed in fantastical costumes, clamours "*Crucifige eum*" ("Crucify him!"). Directly beneath Christ, the father and eldest son of the donor family pray:"*Salva nos xp*[=Christ]*e redemptor*" ("Save us, Christ the Redeemer"). The juxtaposition of image and inscriptions makes plain the eschatological orientation of the work: *Ecce Homo* expresses the fervent plea that God will deliver the souls of the donor and his family on the Day of Judgement, and thus secure them all a place in Paradise.

In compositional terms, Bosch's *Ecce Homo* is related to a woodcut of the same subject (p. 48) by Israhel van Meckenem the Younger (*c.* 1440–1503), an important engraver active in Bocholt in Westphalia, only about 62 miles from 's-Hertogenbosch. Bosch's treatment of the landscape is distinctly different, however, from that of earlier artists. Here, too, the landscape appears as an ambivalent "world" with bizarre and menacing elements.

Master ES, **The Holy Saviour (sanctus salffidor)**, 1467
Copper engraving, 14.7 x 11.7 cm / 5¾ x 4⅝ in.
Braunschweig, Herzog Anton Ulrich-Museum, Kunstmuseum des Landes Niedersachsen

Page 59
Christ Mocked (The Crowning with Thorns), *c.* 1495
Oil on panel (oak), 73.5 x 59.1 cm / 28⅞ x 23¼ in. London, National Gallery

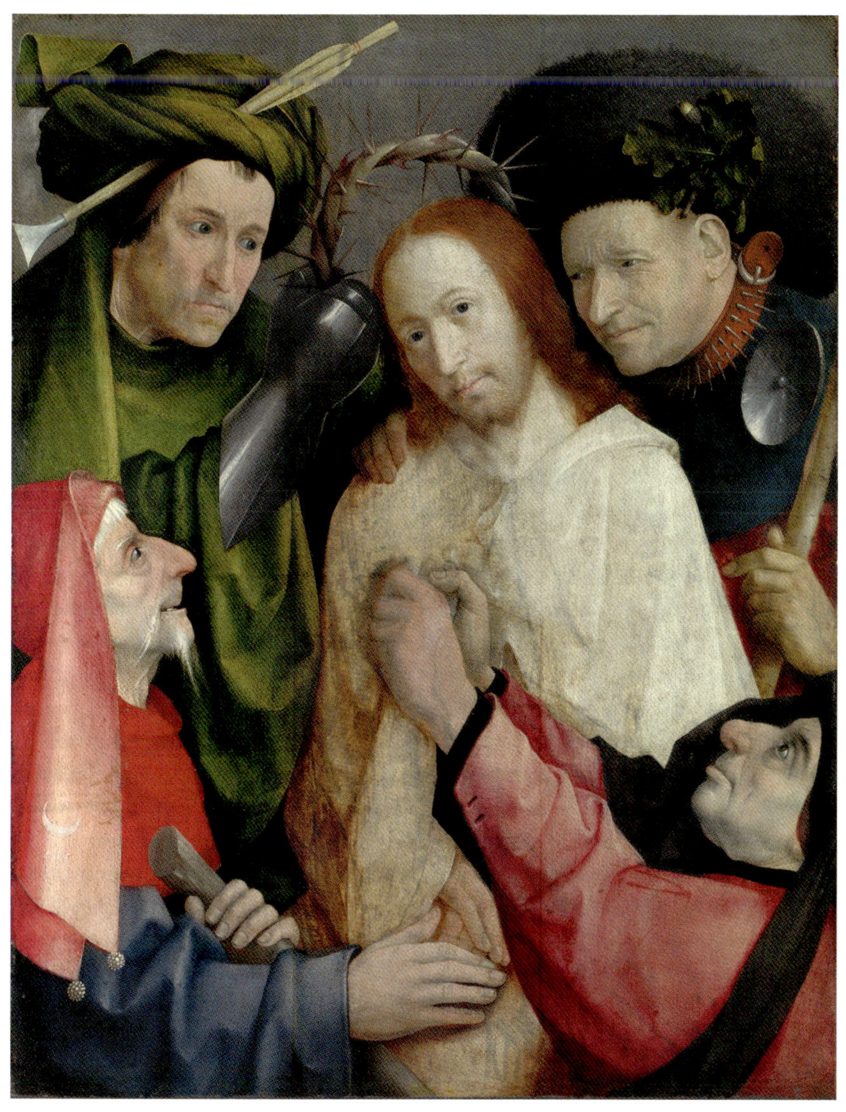

us to experience the ideal of humanity he embodies. Christ in the centre thereby appears in polarising opposition to the periphery, where the four guards – the upper two seen in three-quarter view, the lower two in profile – fix their piercing gaze upon Him from their respective corners. They clearly stand for traits of character and behaviour that depart from the central and ideal yardstick embodied by Christ: spiritual instability, misplaced faith, sinfulness and blindness. Thus, they illustrate deviations from the norm of divine likeness. Their physiognomy, poses, facial expressions and gestures, in combination with their clothing, pieces of armour and weapons, give the picture – so still at its centre – an aggression and intensity that renders Christ's psychological, rather than physical, torment clearly palpable. In a skilful staging of the duality of sin and Redemption, the only part of the composition that we experience as tranquil is the area around Christ's head and shoulders. The viewer is prompted by this polarity to reflect upon sin and evil on the one hand, and upon the Passion and Redemption on the other. Bosch's compositional stage-management also extends to his choice of palette: the four guards are characterised by large areas of contrasting colours (green/red/blue) and absolute values (black/white). These contrasts harmoniously resolve into muted, warm hues in the figure of Christ at the centre of the picture. Optical dissonances give way to stillness. Only Christ's black eyes add an incisive note. Given the current notion of Bosch as a painter of the grotesque, the sensitivity and naturalism of *Christ Mocked (The Crowning with Thorns)* come as a surprise. Its finely gradated areas of light and shade and differentiated treatment of flesh tones are also captivating. In the course of painting, Bosch actually toned down the aggression of the guards vis-à-vis the underdrawing and made their gestures and facial expressions more lifelike; their weapons also appear less menacing in the finished panel than in the underdrawing (Spronk 2011).

The faces of Bosch's guards can be situated within a late medieval tradition that drew on both theories of physiognomy and the visual arts. In 14th-century manuscript illumination ugly physiognomies in Passion scenes still tended to be somewhat coarse and stereotypical; from around 1400 onwards, however, they became a regular feature of panel painting north of the Alps, where they were couched in a violent and brutal pictorial language intended to profoundly disturb the viewer (Suckale 1990, pp. 27–28). In the second half of the 15th century artists began representing these physiognomic heads as half-length figures, a format that brought them into powerfully magnified close-up. In conjunction with the general tendency in art towards monumentalisation (even more pronounced after 1500) and the increasingly large dimensions in which artists were working, this served to reinforce their impact. In *Christ Mocked (The Crowning with Thorns)*, however, Bosch's realistic concept of ugly physiognomies does not exhibit the Renaissance trend towards caricatural exaggeration seen, for example, in the 1494 drawing of grotesque

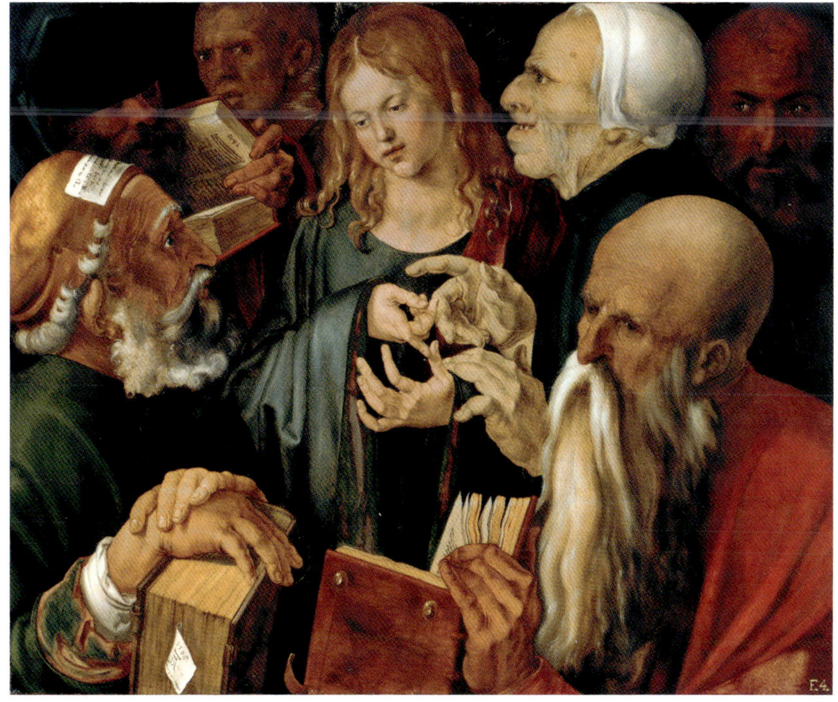

Albrecht Dürer, **Christ Among the Doctors**, 1506
Oil on panel, 64.3 x 80.3 cm / 25⅜ x 31⅝ in. Madrid, Thyssen-Bornemisza Collection

heads by Leonardo da Vinci (1452–1519) and in Dürer's 1506 *Christ Among the Doctors* (p. 63). This caricatural tradition is reflected in the *Christ Carrying the Cross* (Cat. 29) now in Ghent, a panel that, in my view, can on no account be attributed to the master himself, but is probably the work of an Antwerp-based follower.

A first masterpiece: *Adoration of the Magi*

One of Bosch's most appealing works is the well-preserved *Adoration of the Magi* (pp. 66/67, Cat. 6), executed *c.* 1496/97 for the Antwerp donor couple Peeter Scheyve (d. 1506) and his wife Agnes de Gramme (d. 1497 or 1500). The donors may have been put in touch with Bosch via the Brotherhood of Our Blessed Lady, whose regional contacts were shortly to gain for the Bosch workshop the commission for the *Triptych with Sts Job, Anthony and Jerome* (Cat. 22). Both in its competence as regards colour and technical execution and in the complexity of its iconography, elaborated in the finest detail, Bosch's early *Adoration* triptych is a dazzling work. The Antwerp commission offered an ideal opportunity for Bosch to impress a clientele with higher demands and expectations than were to be found in 's-Hertogenbosch, and to make his name known to a much wider public. The signature "jheronimus bosch" on the central panel thus serves both as a seal of quality and a mark of origin.

The port of Antwerp, with its advantageous location on the River Scheldt and its imperial privileges, was at that time Europe's most important centre of commerce. Over the course of the 16th century it also became the multiplier for Bosch's pictorial inventions. Judged in terms of the number of copies and variants that were made of this triptych over the following decades (cf. Cat. 24), the *Adoration of the Magi* is one of the 's-Hertogenbosch artist's most successful creations – if indeed not *the* most successful painting he ever produced. The triptych is based on the story of the Wise Men from the East as told in Matthew 2:"And behold, the star which they had seen in the East went before them, till it came and stood over where the young Child was. When they saw the star, they rejoiced with exceedingly great joy. And when they had come into the house, they saw the young Child with Mary His mother, and fell down and worshipped Him. And when they had opened their treasures, they presented gifts to Him: gold, frankincense, and myrrh." (Matthew 2: 9–11) In late Antiquity and over the course of the Middle Ages, this meeting was embroidered in legendary fashion with reference to other biblical passages and sources, to become at length the Adoration of the Magi.

The three kings are assembled in front of the dilapidated barn in the foreground and are worshipping the Child. The Virgin, in robes of deep blue, is seated on the right as the *sedes sapientiae* (Seat of Wisdom) and presents the naked Infant on a white cloth on her

Mass of St Gregory with Scenes from the Passion and Donor's Family, *c.* 1496/97
Outer wings of: **Adoration of the Magi with Donors**
Oil on panel (oak), 146.7 x 42.3 cm / 57¾ x 16½ in. (wings, including frame)
Madrid, Museo Nacional del Prado

Pages 66/67
Adoration of the Magi with Donors, *c.* 1496/97
Oil on panel (oak), 146.7 x 84 cm / 57¾ x 33 in. (central panel),
146.7 x 42.3 cm / 57¾ x 16½ in. (wings, including frame)
Madrid, Museo Nacional del Prado
Left inner wing: **St Peter with Male Donor**
Central panel: **Adoration of the Magi**
Right inner wing: **St Agnes with Female Donor**

Pages 68/69
Detail from: **Adoration of the Magi with Donors**, *c.* 1496/97
Central panel: **Adoration of the Magi** (see ill. pp. 66/67)

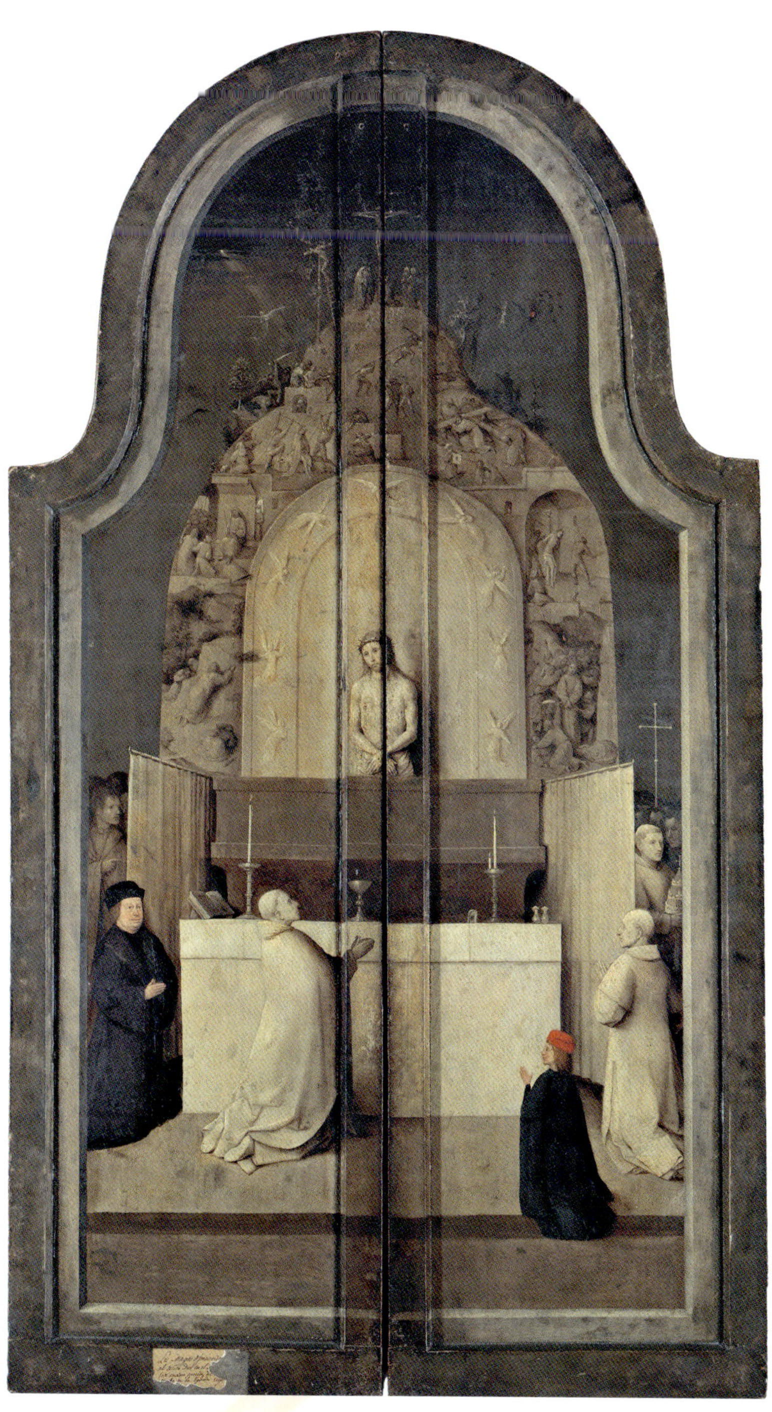

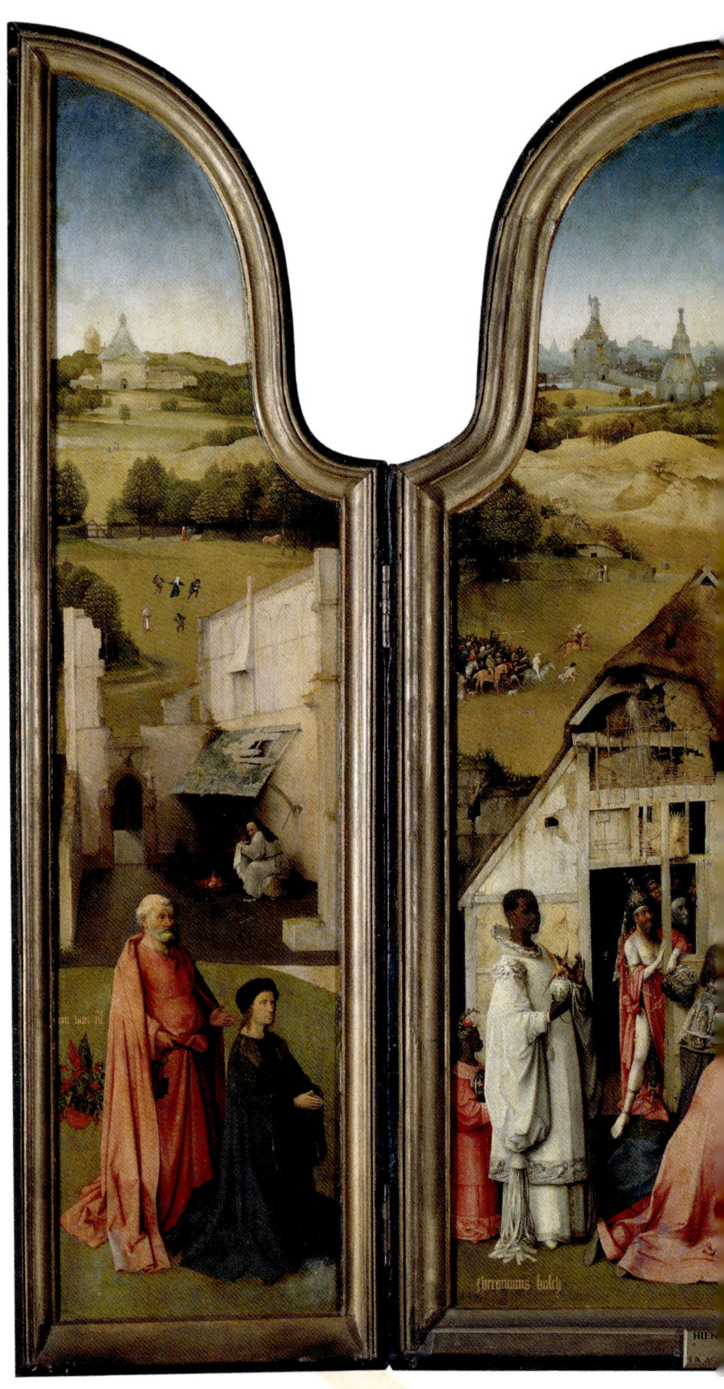
jheronimus bosch

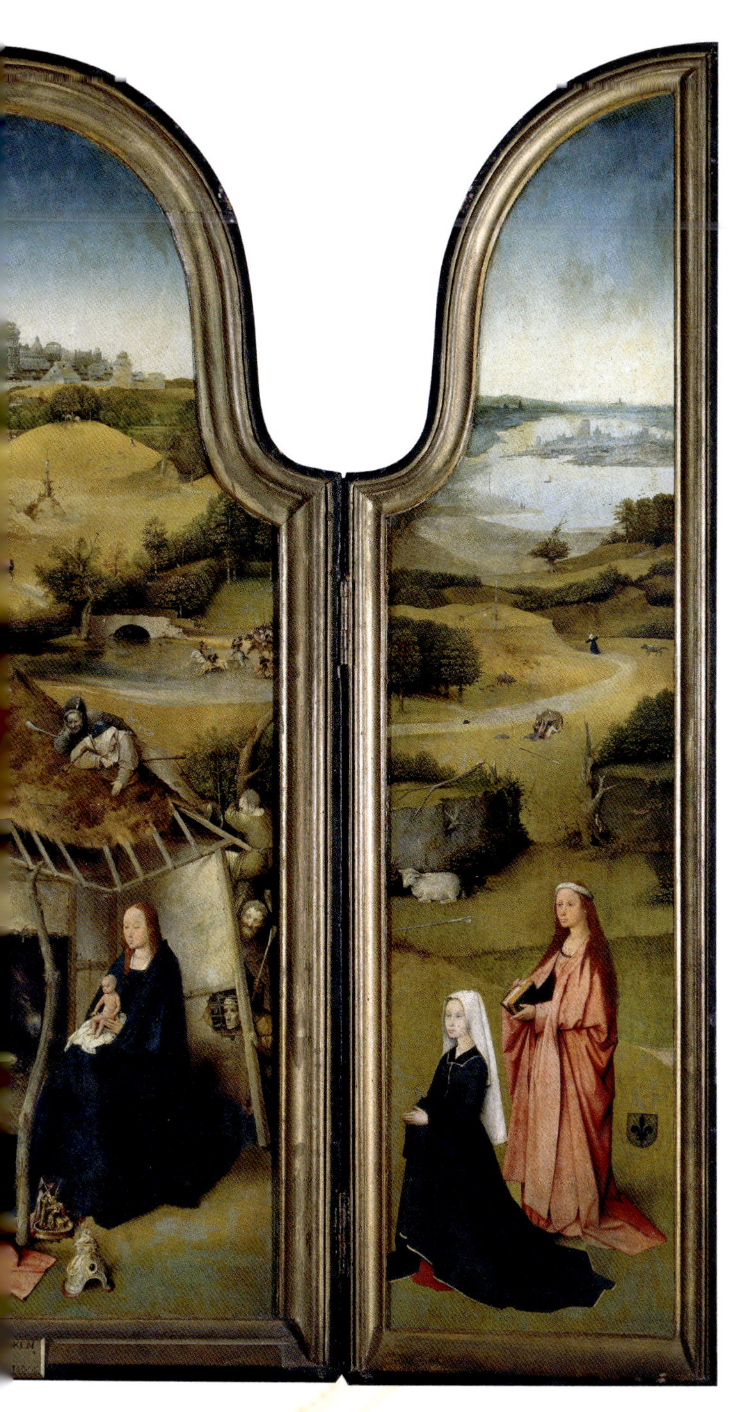

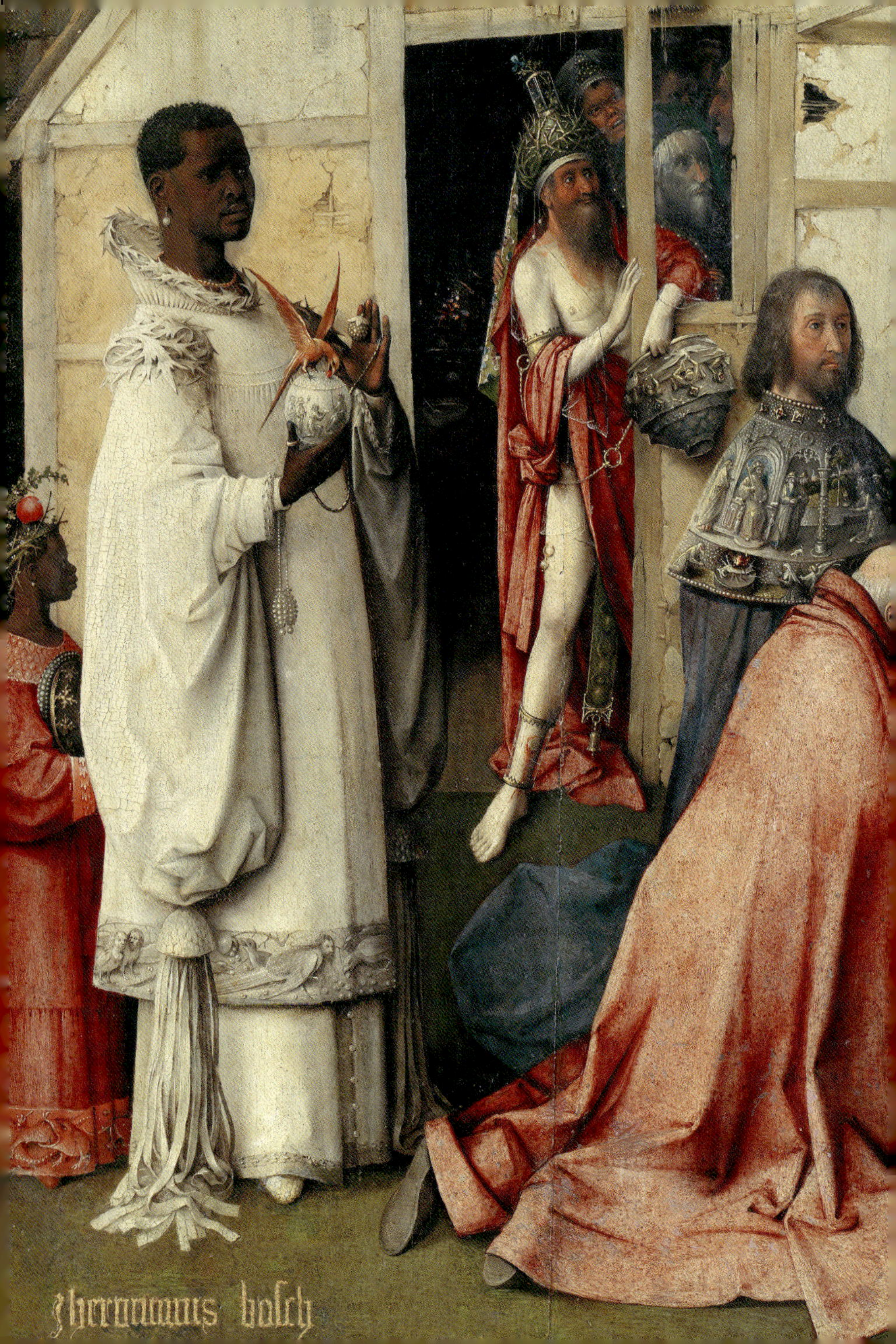
jheronimus bosch

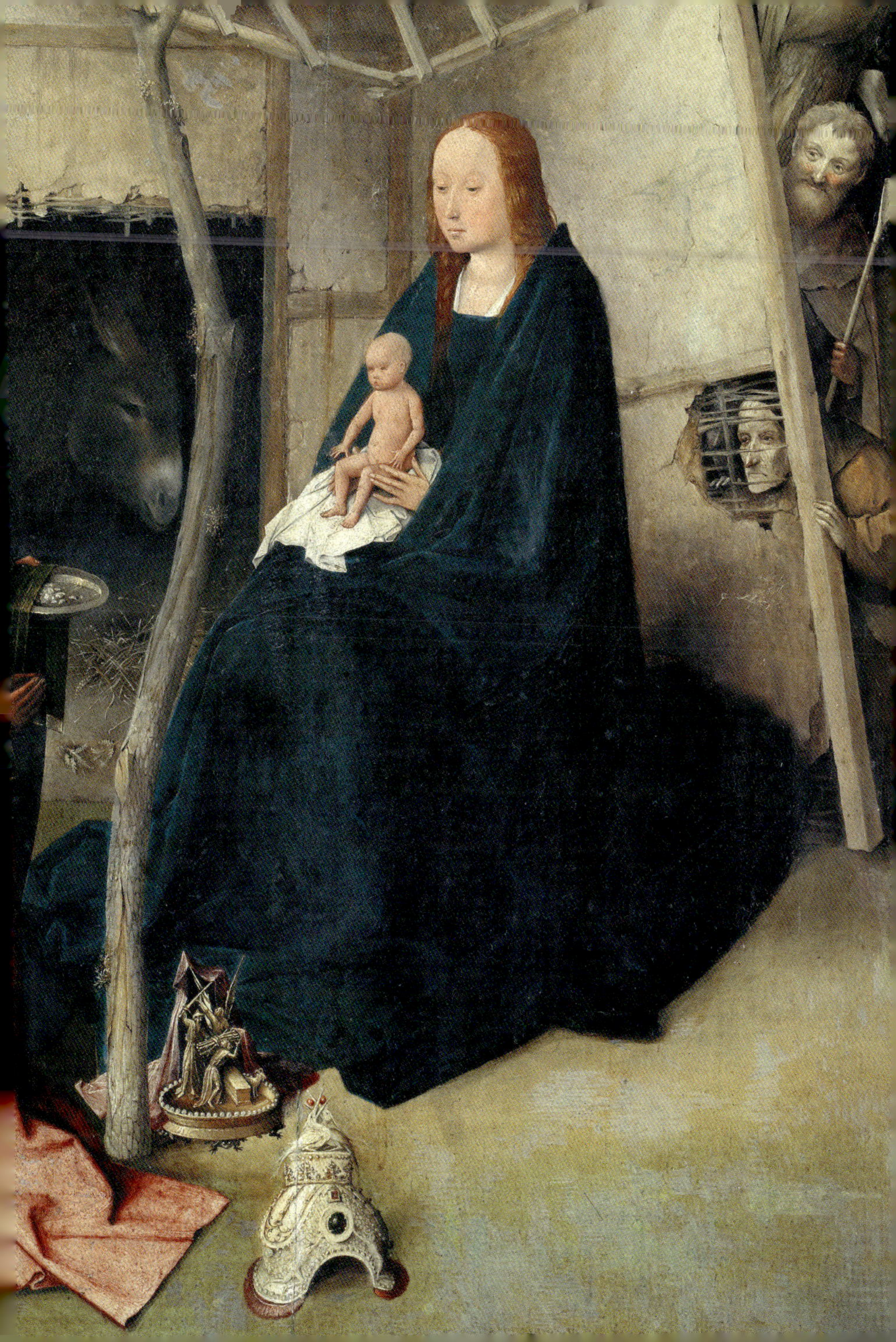

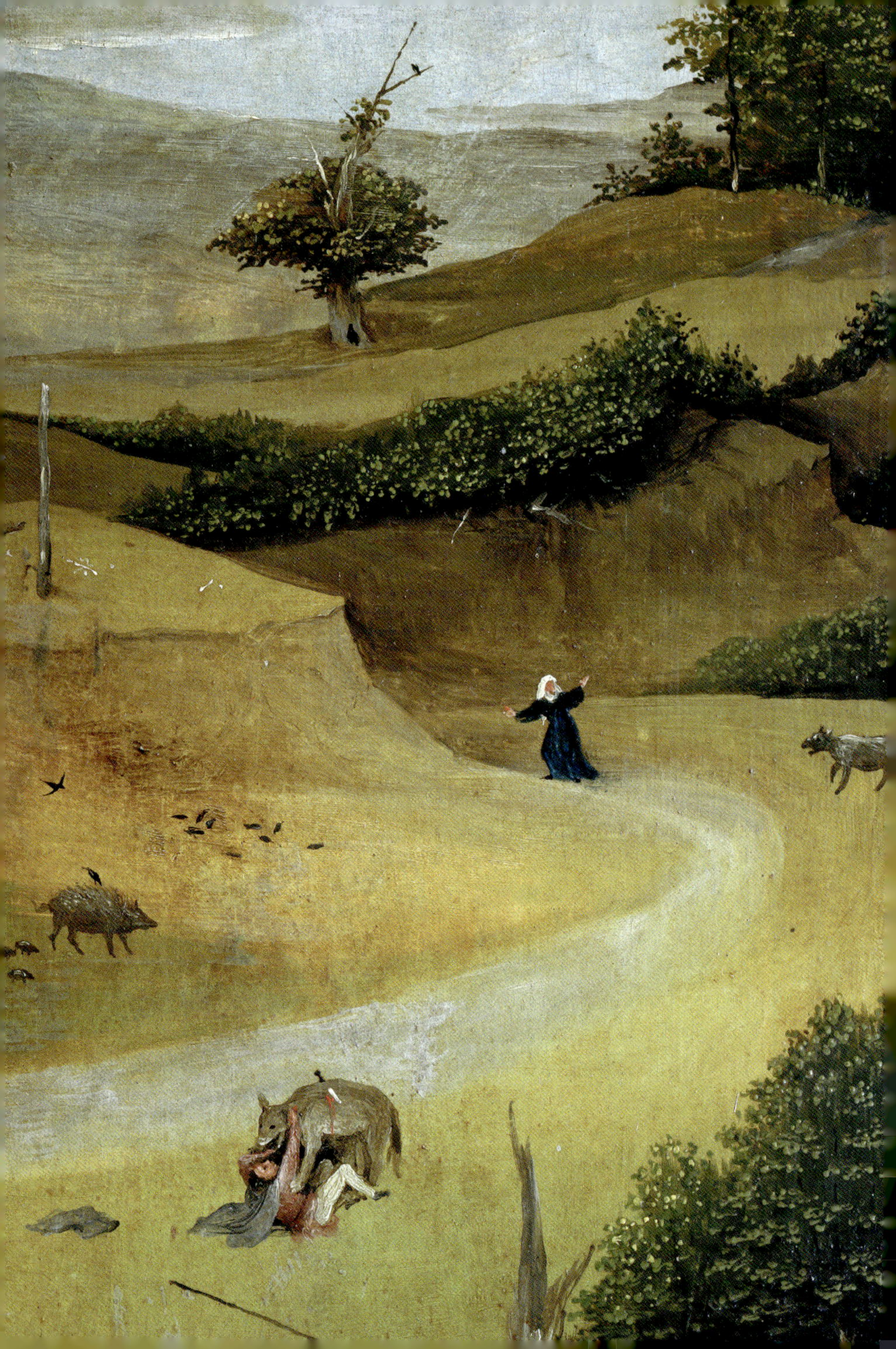

lap, her body serving as his throne. The eldest king kneels directly in front of the Virgin and Child. He is wearing a plain cloak of pale red, of the kind that Bosch otherwise chose for hermit saints such as St Jerome (Cat. 2), and is seen in *profil perdu*. The ring of white hair encircling his bald head like a tonsure testifies to his advanced years and so characterises him as a sage, just as the grey hair worn by *The Pedlar* (Cat. 17.1), for example, articulates his maturity and embrace of God. A second, bearded king in his middle years kneels behind the eldest king and is partially obscured by him. Dressed in robes of bluish grey, he presents his gift on a platter. The embroidered cape around his shoulders, resembling a mozetta, is decorated with figural scenes in grisaille enriched with yellows and blues, showing the Queen of Sheba's visit to Solomon – a scene traditionally considered an Old Testament prefiguration of the Adoration of the Magi. While the attributes of the eldest king paint him in the most positive light of the three Magi, the second king appears more splendid and less humble, and the third, black king is characterised in a predominantly negative fashion. This may seem surprising at first sight, but can be explained by the fact that, however firmly implanted in and around Cologne, the veneration of the Magi was by no means established everywhere. The third king stands a little apart from the main scene. Identified by his skin colour as a stranger from a distant land, he is also associated through some of his other attributes with the sin of lust. Not only does he represent youth, an age associated with a proclivity towards lasciviousness, but the hem of his cloak features a decoration with a pair of male and female siren birds, plus a single male siren bird surrounded by four birds pecking at seeds or fruits, all of which stand for lust. His page wears a green branch with a large red fruit on his head, and a robe trimmed with a border showing fish-like monsters, of which one is swallowing a smaller one, recalling the proverb "Big fish eat little fish". Black king and pageboy thus illustrate life as it operates in the natural world, ruled by the senses and base instincts and prone to sin. The virginal white of the third king's robes must in this case be interpreted as ironic or, alternatively, as signifying that the king has deliberately vanquished the sin inherent in him. The black king is nonetheless also linked to the other Magi by a positive attribute: the grisaille representation, on the spherical vessel in his hand, of Abner's visit to David – equivalent to the Queen of Sheba's visit to Solomon depicted on the cape of the middle king. These two episodes from the Old Testament look forward in typological fashion to the adoration of the Christ Child by the Magi and the presentation of their gifts.

As a group, the three kings can be said to illustrate a progression leading from left to right towards Christ, with each more important and closer to Christ than the one before.

Detail from: **Adoration of the Magi with Donors**, *c.* 1496/97
Right inner wing: **St Agnes with Female Donor** (see ill. pp. 66/67)

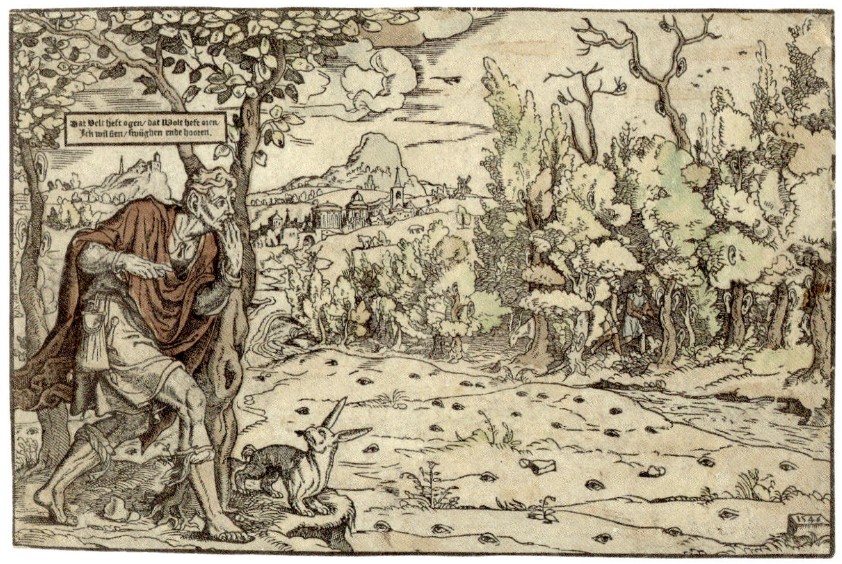

Netherlandish artist, **The Field Has Eyes, the Wood Ears**, 1546
Woodcut, 21,7 x 34,4 cm / 8½ x 13½ in. Berlin, Staatliche Museen, Kupferstichkabinett

Pages 74/75
Detail from: **Adoration of the Magi with Donors**, *c.* 1496/97
Central panel: **Adoration of the Magi** (see ill. pp. 66/67)

The enactment of the *Imitatio Christi* culminates in the eldest king, whose red draperies reveal more than conceal a small gilded sculptural group of the Sacrifice of Isaac, itself a typological forerunner of the Eucharist. The main scene takes place in front of a half-timbered stable in a picturesque state of dilapidation. A number of figures, clearly cast in negative roles, are gathered inside. Their leader, who stands on the threshold, has been identified by commentators as the Antichrist (e.g. Brand Philip 1953, Higgs Strickland 2007). This figure has a number of features that may be interpreted as distortions of those associated with Christ: a crown with a lattice of thorns on his head and a wound on his shin. He is half naked, half clothed in a red cloak that suggests both the Passion and a royal mantle. He is also holding, in his right hand, a tiered crown that recalls the tiara worn by the pope. Behind him, members of his retinue are peering out through a window. The Antichrist, so it was thought, would appear shortly before the Last Judgement in a shape that was not precisely known. As Christ's opponent, he would seek to lead humankind astray.In this way the entire composition is lent an eschatological orientation.

Another striking feature is the shepherds on the roof and peering round the side of the stable on the right, whose behaviour seems morally dubious (Raupp 1986, p. 201). On the two inner wings, separated from the events on the central panel and at the same time included within them, are the two donors, accompanied by their respective saints, St Peter and St Agnes. The foreground of the left inner wing is clearly demarcated at the back by walls and a small gateway arch, in front of which Joseph is to be seen, washing swaddling clothes. On the right the foreground is likewise sealed off, in this case by two grassy banks with a gap between them, in front of which a lamb – a symbol of Agnes as well as Christ – has found shelter and rest. The foreground is thus an enclosed space, a *hortus conclusus* for saints and donors. Beyond, the middle distance is a spacious landscape containing a wide variety of vegetation in greens and greenish browns, and dotted with figures and individual buildings. It extends to the harbour and city in the background. On the left, peasants are dancing in the open fields, demonstrating both worldly pleasure and ignorance of the advent of Christ (Raupp 1986, pp. 200–201).

The pictorial motif of a couple recurs in more or less the centre of each of the three panels (pp. 66/67). On the left inner wing the man and woman are standing with their backs to the viewer in front of a fence. In the central panel, the pair have changed sides and the man now stands on the woman's left (an unusual arrangement for this period). They have turned towards a shadowy inn with a dovecot and the sign of a swan hanging outside – features that announce it as a brothel (cf. Cat. 17.1). On the right inner wing the man and woman are being attacked by two wolves as they pass beneath a gallows. In each of their appearances from left to right, in other words, the state of their body and soul successively worsens. Bosch has here employed the principle of the three-step metaphor, as also seen in *St Jerome* (Cat. 2) and *St Christopher* (Cat. 7). In the present case, a parallel can be drawn with a passage in a treatise by Jan van Leeuwen (d. 1378), the most important pupil of John of Ruysbroeck. Van Leeuwen's works were primarily addressed to clerics and those living a semi-religious life, but were also intended for a lay readership. Writing in the style of a sermon, van Leeuwen uses the example of a wolf's attack on a sheep as the vehicle for a four-step process of spiritual exegesis (Leeuwen, *Bloemlezing*, p. 30). He describes four different versions of the attack, each progressively more ferocious, and expounds them in allegorical terms. In the first attack the wolf gets only a mouthful of wool; in the second it pins the sheep to the ground; in the third it bites into the sheep's coat; and in the fourth it rips out the sheep's entrails. The wolf embodies the principle of Evil, while the sheep stands for the faithful flock and the vulnerable soul. In Bosch's altarpiece, the couple as such remains the same: the progression from good to evil is conveyed via the different settings in which they appear and the change in their relationship with each other. The three scenes unfold along a more or less straight axis that descends

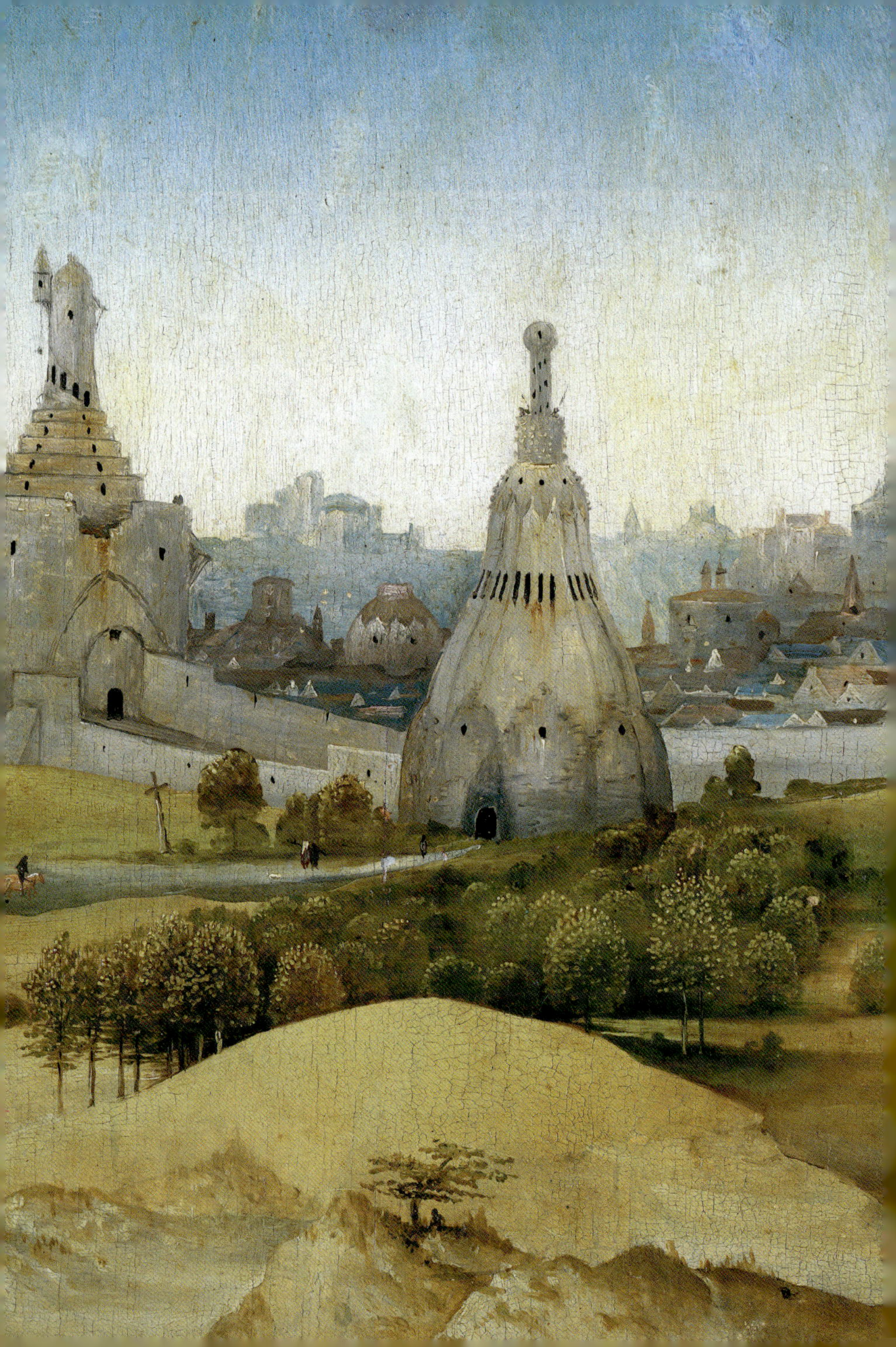

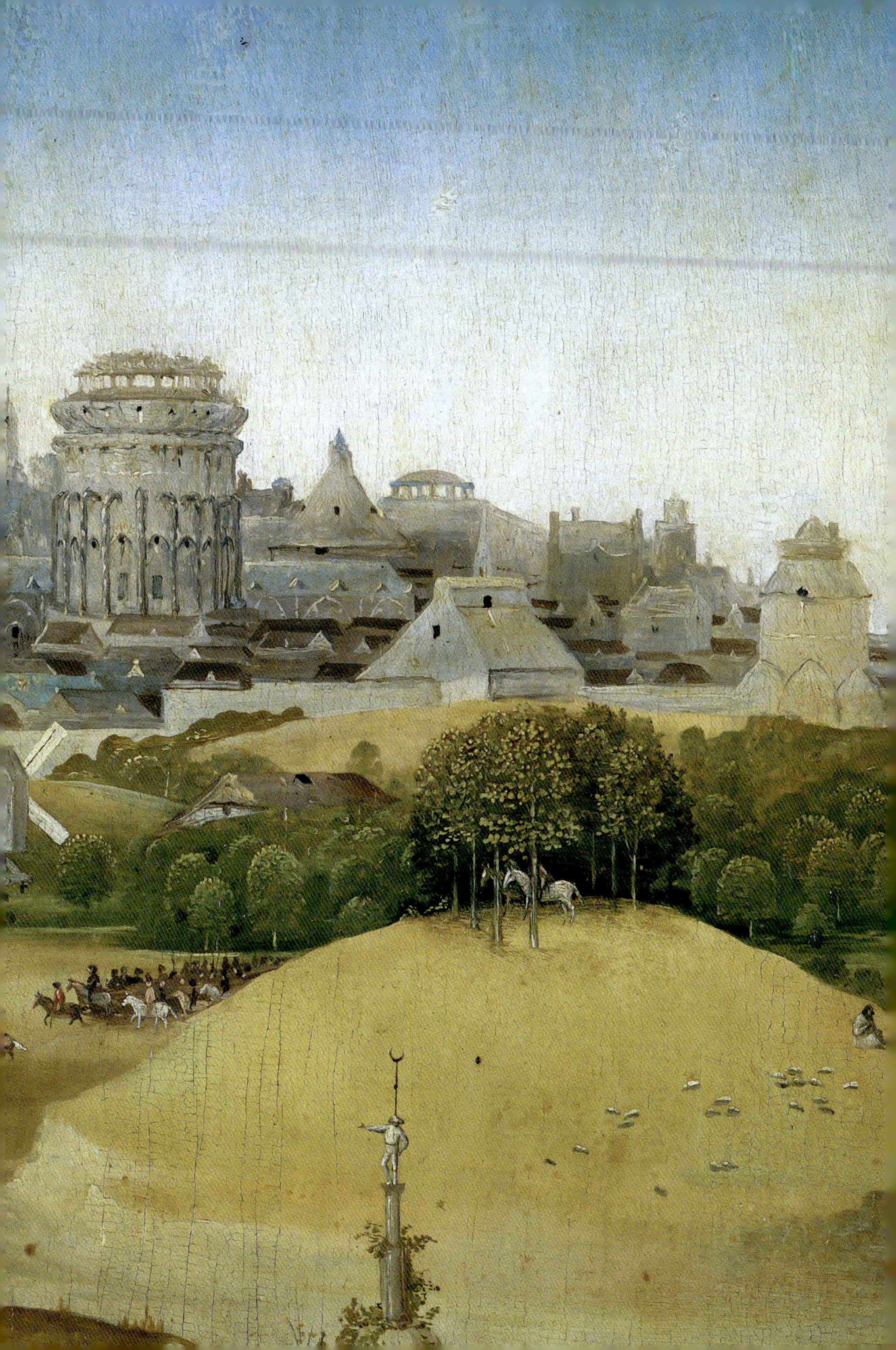

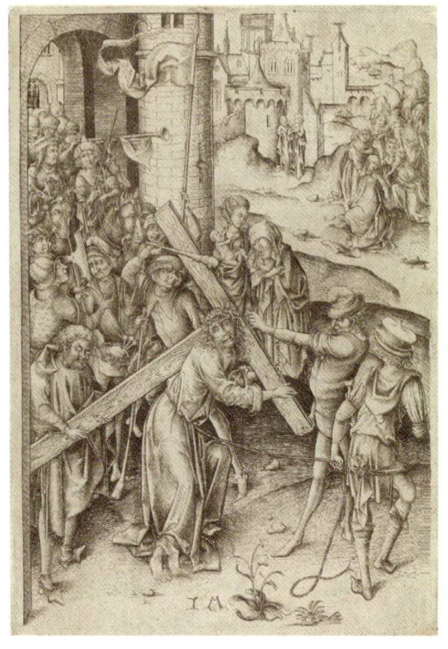

slightly towards the right. In each wing, furthermore, the scene is located near the centre of the panel.

In contrast to his predecessors, Bosch does not idealise the landscape in his compositions, but portrays it as the place of asceticism and spiritual struggle where men and women, having been expelled from Paradise, must grapple with sin and mortality. The triptych allows the viewer to pass through the still unredeemed world on a visual pilgrimage across its interior, and there perhaps to find spiritual guidance to God. The journey, and in particular the idea that human life was a pilgrimage, was a familiar theme in the late Middle Ages as a means of conveying the existential dimension of man's status. The details of the panels would undoubtedly only have disclosed themselves to the viewer in the course of extensive study and meditation. What they also reveal, however, is the intellectual sophistication with which Bosch, as the creator of the triptych, set about the design and conception of his work. The finished altarpiece would undoubtedly have appealed to its donors and their contemporaries from an aesthetic point of view, on account of its multi-figural composition, its proximity to nature and its many other demonstrations of artistic skill. First and foremost, however, it is a memorial picture and a liturgical work designed to stand on an altar: the sacrament of Communion would be celebrated directly in front of it, and the Body of Christ thus consumed under the eyes of the Infant Christ in the foreground. The link with bread as the Body of Christ is established by the sheaves of corn hanging from the gable and bearing small discs reminiscent of communion wafers, and by the Mass of St Gregory depicted on the exterior shutters (the face usually presented by the altarpiece in its own day, when the

Israhel van Meckenem the Younger, **Christ Carrying the Cross**, *c.* 1480
Copper engraving, 21.2 x 14.6 cm / 8⅜ x 5¾ in. London, The British Museum

Page 77
Large Christ Carrying the Cross, *c.* 1500
Oil on panel (oak), 150 x 103 cm / 59 x 40½ in.
Madrid, Palacio Real (properly speaking: Monasterio de San Lorenzo de El Escorial)

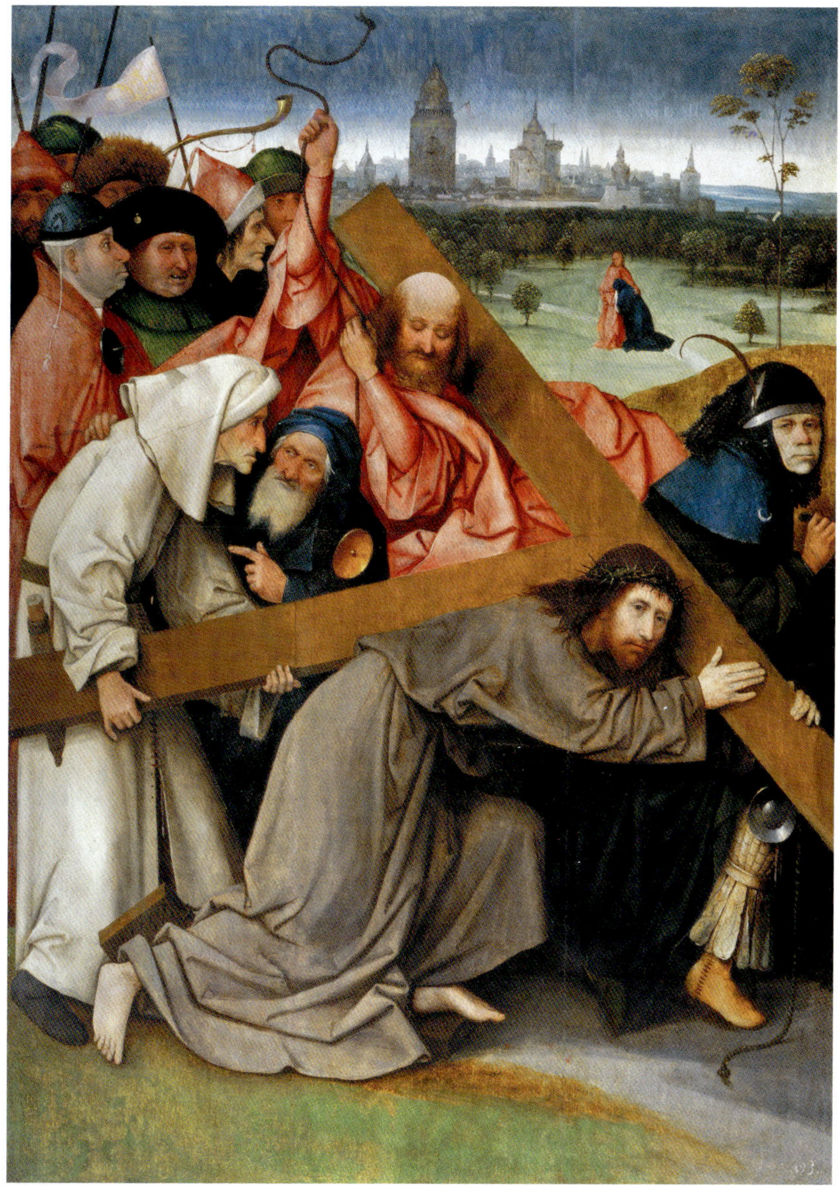

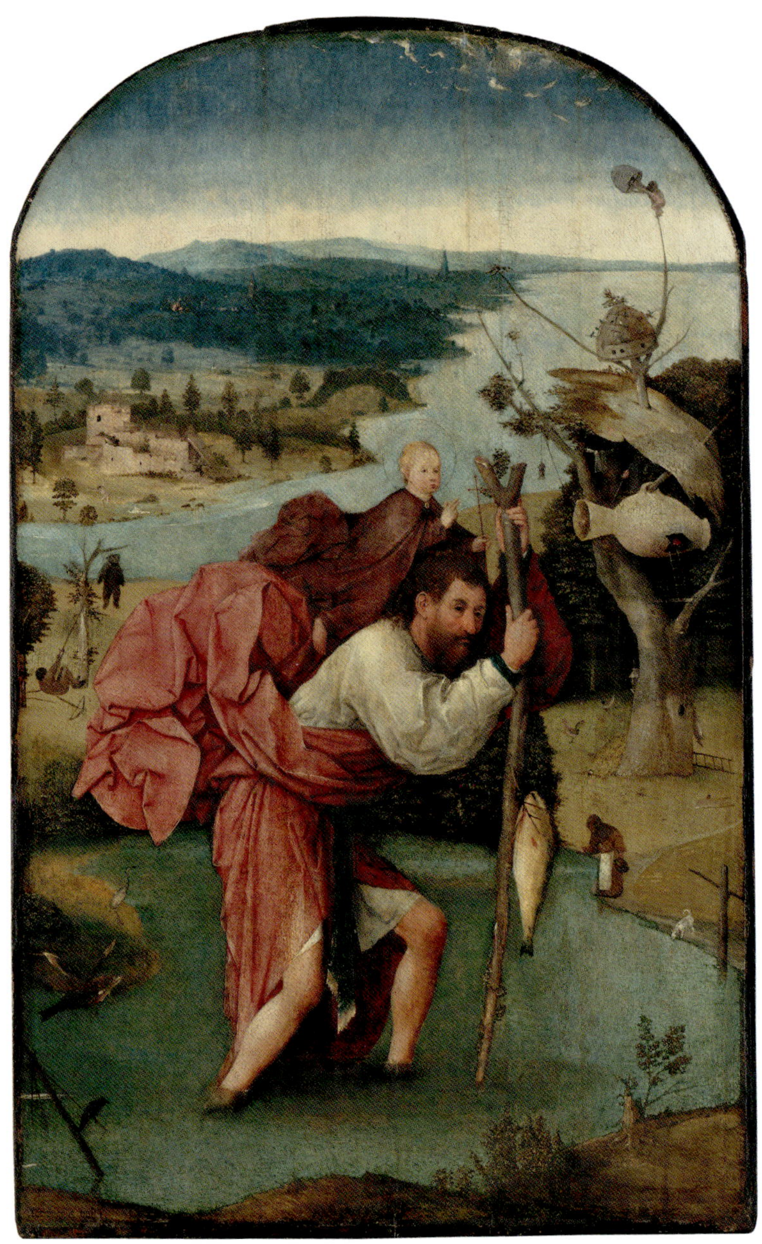

wings were more often closed than open), in which the figure of Christ appears to Pope Gregory as he celebrates Mass.

The Passion of Christ in the upper portion of the *Mass of St Gregory* (p. 65) is laid out in a completely different manner from the Passion scenes on the exterior of *St John on Patmos* (Cat. 3.2.2). The chronology of events unfolds in a zigzag sequence ascending from left to right. Starting at the lower left with Christ on the Mount of Olives, it continues directly opposite on the right with the Arrest of Christ and Peter's outburst of rage against Malchus, then crosses back to the scene of Christ before Pilate, in which Pilate's wife can be seen emerging from behind his throne. Next on the right we see the Flagellation with Christ bound to a column, then the Crowning with Thorns on the left, the Road to Calvary with St Veronica on the right and, at the top, the Crucifixion. An angel in prayer hovers to the left of the three crosses; Judas has hanged himself from a tree on the right, and the Devil is fetching the soul of the bad thief. All of these scenes are adapted to the shape of the two panels, with their arched and curving tops. Together, they constitute a picture within the picture of the *Mass of St Gregory*.

Bosch employs assistants

The Boston *Ecce Homo* triptych (Cat. 21) testifies to the fact that, by 1499 at the latest, Bosch was employing at least one assistant in his workshop – something only to be expected in the case of an established and celebrated artist such as himself. Whoever it was who executed the work in a compilation technique that drew upon the Frankfurt version of the same subject (p. 49, Cat. 4), it is clear that Bosch was now famous and wealthy enough to have others do the painting for him. It is nonetheless surprising that he should have entrusted the Boston *Ecce Homo* to his workshop, since it was commissioned by Peter van Os (*c.* 1467/69–1542), a sworn member of the Brotherhood of Our Blessed Lady and one of 's-Hertogenbosch's four town clerks, in other words by a high-ranking patron who held an important office within the civic administration. The figure of St Peter, the donor's patron saint, is largely copied from the St Peter on the left inner wing of the *Adoration of the Magi* (pp. 66/67, Cat. 6.2). The drapery folds across his shoulder and chest and around the hem of his robes at ground level are identical, for example. The proportions of Bosch's St Peter (Cat. 6.2) are more elongated, however. On the exterior shutters, van Os's father-in-law, Vranck van Langhel (also Franco van Langel, *c.* 1440–1497), appears with his sons on the left and his wife and their daughters

St Christopher, *c.* 1495–1500
Oil on panel (oak), 113 x 71.5 cm / 44½ x 28⅛ in.
Rotterdam, Museum Boijmans Van Beuningen

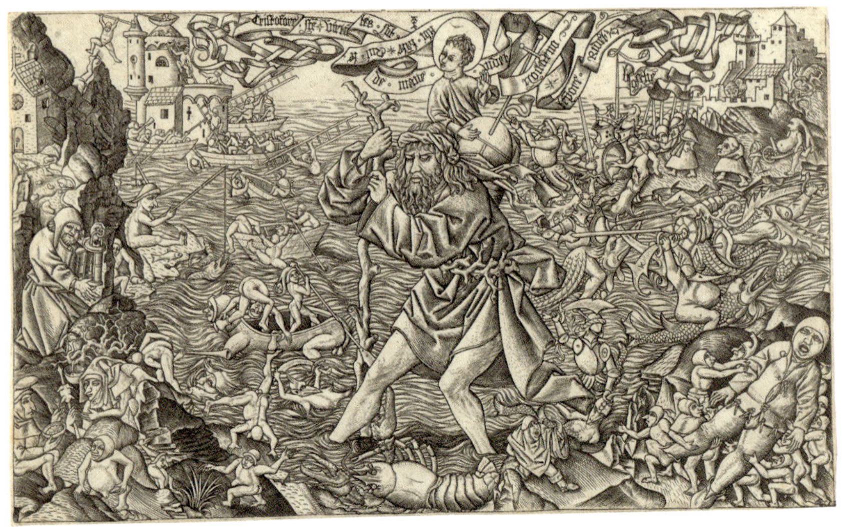

Alart Du Hamel, **St Christopher**, *c.* 1500–1504
Copper engraving, 19.9 x 33.4 cm / 7⅞ x 13⅛ in. Amsterdam, Rijksmuseum

on the right. Van Langhel, like Peter van Os on the interior, is wearing the lily badge of the Brotherhood of Our Blessed Lady. The first was made a sworn member in 1466, the second in 1496/97. As notaries, both men had the rank of secular clerics. Van Langhel was the notary before whom Hieronymus Bosch and his wife had settled some important legal matters in 1481.

It is likely that Bosch delegated the *Ecce Homo* commission to his workshop because he was away for all or part of the period of the triptych's production. There are two clues pointing to his absence. Firstly, although Bosch took his turn as usual at hosting a dinner for the Brotherhood in the accounting year 1498/99 (which ran from June to June), probably on 28 December 1498 (van Dijck 1973, p. 182), the meal was held not in his own house but in that of the apothecary Wouter van der Rullen, brother-in-law of the deceased Vranck van Langhel, many times provost of the Brotherhood and superintendent of Sint-Jan's. Secondly, on 17 May 1498 Bosch awarded *potestas monendi* – extensive power of attorney over his financial affairs – to three individuals, Gerardus de Heessel, Johannes 's-Greven and Victor vander Moelen, in front of civic representatives (van Dijck 2001a, p. 73). Between 1498/99 and 1506 Bosch is mentioned only incidentally and indirectly in records. On the other hand he also executed a large number of commissions during these years, meaning that he cannot have been absent all the time. On top of this, sworn members of the Brotherhood of Our Blessed Lady were required to live in or around 's-Hertogenbosch, a rule that could only be waived on important grounds.

We cannot establish today, of course, the nature of the personal relationship between Bosch and van Os. The Brotherhood would have offered ample social occasions for the two men to broach, discuss and shake hands on a commission, in particular during its regular communal meals. The formal procedure of the meal was one of the many things laid down in the *Regulations* of the Brotherhood of Our Blessed Lady published in 1518. From these it is clear that the Brotherhood's religious orientation was not just a devout framework but also fostered moderation and discipline at the level of social behaviour (*Regulations*, fol. 6v):"In order that this rule should foster *inter alia* fraternal love between members, all sworn brothers living in the city shall meet together every six weeks and on the four main feast days and they shall eat together in truthfulness, calm and good cheer. During this meal, the *Benedicite* [Daniel 3:57–88] and *Oratio* shall be sung by trebles, and likewise a joyful ode or hymn between every course. And after the meal the *Miserere mei Deus* [Psalm 51] and *De profundis* [Psalm 130] shall be read for the departed. And so that the meal should not turn into an unreasonable quarrel, it is forbidden for any man to drink more than half a jug of wine throughout the entire meal." Even so, the food normally rose above normal fare and traditionally consisted of beef and carrots seasoned with select spices, including ginger, pepper and saffron. On special occasions the meal extended in aristocratic style to several courses with poultry, a dozen types of fish, nuts and fruits, and on 28 December every year two swans were served (Unverfehrt 2003, pp. 58–63).

Bosch's earnings as a landowner and a painter meant that, from 1498 at the latest, he was one of the wealthiest citizens in 's-Hertogenbosch (Blondé/Vlieghe 1989). This can be deduced from the amounts he paid in rates and taxes. These included a regular tax representing a percentage of the estimated rental value of his property holdings, and the special *ruitergeld* tax levied at irregular intervals to fund the war against the Duchy of Guelders, which was calculated on the basis of his entire fortune and all his properties. Over the course of the years Bosch's contributions ranged from 3 to 15 Rhenish guilders, indicating that the artist found himself at various times among the top ten, six and on occasions even one per cent of 's-Hertogenbosch's richest citizens. In financial terms he was thus in the same class as many of his sworn brothers.

The *Large Christ Carrying the Cross* (p. 77, Cat. 8) was probably painted in the period around 1500. It adheres in essence to representational tradition, which was based on the Gospels (Matt. 27:32; Mark 15:21; Luke 23:26) and embellished with details from psalms and other accounts. Christ, clad in a greyish brown robe, is dragging his Cross along the road to Calvary. He has turned his face to look calmly out at the viewer. His suffering is not communicated through his facial expression or gestures, but symbolically through the weight of the Cross, the jostling crowd behind him and the boards spiked with nails around his ankles. A helmeted soldier wearing an indifferent expression pulls Christ along by a cord. The centre of the picture is dominated by a figure holding a rope high in the air, either because he is pulling it up or because he is about to bring it down on Christ. In other paintings this action is performed by a soldier, but in Bosch's painting, the man's pale red robes, full beard and shiny bald pate are all typical attributes of St Peter and in this context seem likely to be an error, since the Apostle does not appear at all in the context of Christ Carrying the Cross. Simon of Cyrene, dressed all in white, helps carry the foot of the Cross, as he has been ordered to do by a bearded man. Behind Christ, the accompanying throng takes up almost the entire upper left quarter of the picture. The figures are unusually large for Bosch and are clearly arranged one behind the other, conveying an impression of depth. Perpendicular to the group around Christ moving across the foreground, an implicit axis leads the eye to the middle ground, where the Virgin and St John are visible through a gap that has opened up as if by chance. Their silent participation in the events of the Passion is revealed in their pose, each turning to the other, while the jostling soldiers are placed in the foreground. This principle of inversion – that is, of portraying Good on a small scale and Evil on a large scale and with multiple figures – is a fundamental constant in Bosch's art.

The composition probably derives from an engraving of *Christ Carrying the Cross* by Israhel van Meckenem the Younger (p. 76). Here too, a soldier stands behind Christ with his right arm raised, in this case gripping a club rather than a rope. Further parallels between the painting by Bosch and the print by van Meckenem can be seen in the bowed posture of Christ's body and his upright head looking towards the viewer, and the looming crowd pushing forwards in a ruck. The sorrowing Virgin is supported in Bosch's panel by St John and additionally in van Meckenem's print by her female companions. The monumentality of the figures and composition in Bosch's *Christ Carrying the Cross* is found nowhere else in his oeuvre.

Directly dependent upon the *Large Christ Carrying the Cross* in terms of its motifs and composition is the *Small Christ Carrying the Cross* (p. 91, Cat. 9), which was executed as the left inner wing of a triptych whose central panel and right wing have not survived. The panel can be dated to approximately the first decade after 1500. The Calvary procession is structured in a very similar fashion, but is much more crowded and is seen from a higher viewpoint, so that the figures are stacked one above rather than one behind the other. The hooded figure of Simon of Cyrene – here in red and blue instead of white – recurs on the left. The figure with the rope and attributes of St Peter in the *Large Christ Carrying the Cross* is cited by Bosch, or one of his assistants, in a central position to the right of Christ and behind him (p. 77). The axis of his body and hence also of his arm is angled slightly more towards the right than in the first version. Marching ahead of the Cross is a soldier in a white tunic with a shield slung across his back. The shield bears the image of a toad – a symbol of sin and evil – seen belly up. At the bottom of the tall and narrow panel, which has in fact also been cut down at the top, the foreground is occupied by two figural groups. On the left is the bad thief, bound with a rope and surrounded by four soldiers, of whom one, at the far left, looks out at the viewer. This is something normally reserved for a real person – a donor or the artist himself. On the far right a priest in the guise of a Franciscan friar is hearing the confession of the good thief, who is securely bound and held by a soldier leaning against a slender, very tall, leafless tree. Behind the soldier a man dressed in red is looking up at the top of the tree, which is no longer visible since the semi-circular top of the panel has been sawn off. The ends of a rope can still be seen hanging down, however: this allows us to conclude that the tree originally supported a gallows wheel, as frequently seen in the background of Bosch's paintings (e.g. Cat. 6.4, Cat. 10.3, Cat. 17.1, Cat. 18, Cat. 20), and prominently, too, at the right edge of the *Way to Calvary* (Vienna, Kunsthistorisches Museum) by Pieter Bruegel the Elder. The motif of the two groups around the good and bad thieves is found on the right outer wing of the Lisbon *Temptation of St Anthony* (p. 117, Cat. 10.2).

In a formal analogy to the Cross being carried on the inside, the remarkable exterior of the panel (p. 84, Cat. 92) shows the Christ Child holding a toy windmill, a whirligig. It is possible that the opposite exterior shutter of the triptych originally showed the Infant St John, likewise holding a whirligig, as a pendant to the Infant Christ. The Messiah and the last prophet would thus have acted out a sort of joust with their respective windmills over their status in the history of Salvation (cf. p. 87). Despite the playful, light-hearted nature of this boyish game, its serious underlying significance would have rendered it suitably dignified as the exterior face for a Passion. Bosch elsewhere portrayed only the children of donors in a positive manner. In other contexts they carry negative connotations of sin and ignorance or folly, as, on the right outer wing of the *Temptation of St Anthony* (p. 117, Cat. 10.2), where a child is also shown holding a whirligig, on the right outer wing of the *Last Judgement* (p. 253, Cat. 13.2), and in the Gluttony scene on the panel of *The Seven Deadly Sins and the Four Last Things* (pp. 308/309, Cat. 15; see also the entry on Cat. 9). Overall, given that the *Small Christ Carrying the Cross* includes free variations on pictorial motifs found in the *Large Christ Carrying the Cross* and the Lisbon *Temptation of St Anthony*, the panel may be considered wholly or extensively the work of Bosch himself, with limited assistance of his workshop. The exterior in particular testifies once again to the inventiveness and independence of thought that enabled the 's-Hertogenbosch artist to find ingenious analogies to the triptych's interior without falling back on conventional saint and Passion iconography.

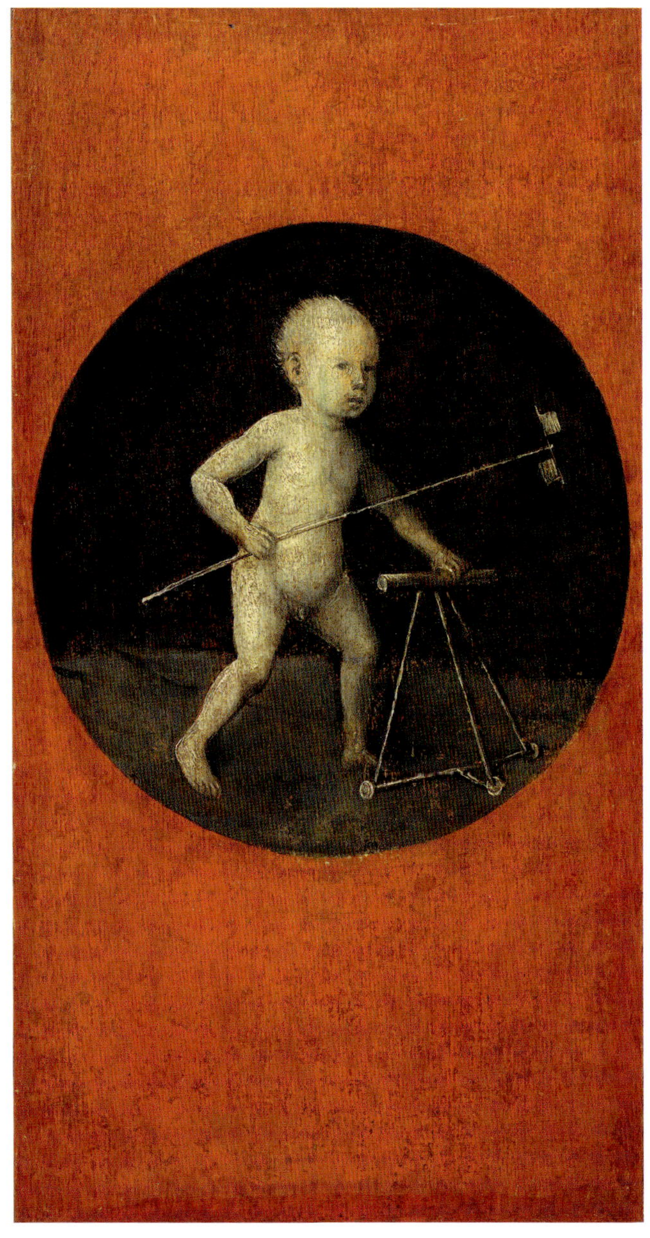

We have so far examined the role of landscape and the dualistic structure of Bosch's compositions in his rendering of the antagonistic forces of good and evil as these are to be found in his painted representations of the Passion and various saints. We gain an even clearer insight into the practical and intellectual processes by which his works were created, however, from some of his drawings. This fragile medium is able to tell us more about practices in Bosch's workshop than are his panel paintings. We can learn much about the relationship between pictorial theme, main figure or main scene and subsidiary motifs from Bosch's drawings, both those constituting specimen designs (Cat. D1, Cat. D7, Cat. D9) and those that appear, in a certain sense, to stand alone (Cat. D2, Cat. D3). The eight drawings here confidently attributed to Bosch (Cat. D1–Cat. D8) are executed in a technique that is a little sketch-like in nature and which is typically characterised by dashed and broken contours and the use of airy hatching to model sculptural forms. The hatching becomes denser towards the heart of the shadow, partly through cross-hatching, but it is also broken up by highlights. Bosch thereby succeeds in capturing effects of light in an almost impressionistic manner. All his drawings are executed in pen and ink; silverpoint or metalpoint were rarely still in use by 1500, and black and red chalk had yet to become widely established. Bosch's drawing technique allowed him to outline his motifs rapidly and clearly in a manner that was at once sketch-like, atmospheric and three-dimensional, and with an economy that also lightened the task of executing the large numbers of figures to be found in most of his paintings. This sparing approach to drawing and underdrawing had its counterpart in Bosch's rational *alla prima* manner of painting. Even though the pictorial motifs are executed in no more detail than necessary, they are in most cases easy to recognise – a quality indispensable to the efficacy of their symbolism. In Bosch's works the significance of the pictorial elements provides the basis of the process of pictorial invention. This is illustrated in the case of a symbolic creature found in four Bosch drawings and in the majority of his paintings: the owl, and more specifically *Athene noctua*, the little owl.

The silent owl that says much

The Nest of Owls (p. 442/443, Cat. D2) shows the bare crown of a crooked deciduous tree, probably an ancient oak, which is home to three owls, most likely little owls. A hole in the trunk serves the smallest as a nest. Nearby, though as yet unheeded, are four

Christ Child with Walking Frame and Whirligig, c. 1502–1510
Outer wing of: **Small Christ Carrying the Cross**
Oil on panel (oak), 57.2 x 32 cm / 22½ x 12½ in. (cut down by a quadrant at the top and minimally along the bottom, originally c. 77–80 cm / 30–31 ½ in. high; exterior tondo: ∅ c. 30 cm / 11 ¾ in.)
Vienna, Kunsthistorisches Museum

songbirds (magpies? jays?). One is perched on a branch on the right and stares down at a spider in its web. On the left, between a gallows wheel and the distant view of a small town in the background, a group of riders is passing through a valley. Further right the hillside is dotted with a wayside cross, a windmill, a settlement and probably a few people. All of these are tiny, finely drawn details. Although the drawing may look at first sight like a study of little owls in their natural habitat and in their usual nesting site, it is not in fact a detailed naturalistic reproduction of the kind seen in Dürer's *Little Owl* of 1508, and certainly not a nature idyll. The sheet is, rather, an exercise or a specimen for painting. Even if the owl is here not obviously presented as a symbol of Evil, it may well carry a moral significance reference when given the contemporary allegorical tradition as understood from the *Physiologus* and mediaeval bestiaries. At least one owl is hiding in the darkness of the tree cavity, and songbirds are perched or flying round about as if nothing were amiss. Elsewhere in Bosch's oeuvre (see Cat. 2, Cat. 11, Cat. 12.2, Cat. 13.1, Cat. 17.1, Cat. 20.3), songbirds appearing near owls symbolise innocent souls who are permitting themselves to be led astray by the seductive power of Evil. This idea is supported by the spider in its web, likewise awaiting its prey (Dittrich 2005, p. 405).

The Wood Has Ears, the Field Eyes (p. 444, Cat. D3r) is an allegorical drawing based on a most unusual concept. When the inscription on the front and the figural studies on the back are also taken into account, the sheet sheds much light on the significance of subsidiary motifs and their function within the overall context of a composition. The front of the sheet shows a gnarled tree of medium size with an owl sitting in its hollow trunk. Four birds are perched on its leafless crown and a fox and a cockerel are lying between the roots at its foot. Seven open eyes are evenly arranged in two rows across the meadow in the foreground. The tree, which stands in a grove of more than half a dozen slender leafy saplings, sprouts two ears, one on either side. Bosch has based his drawing on the proverb "The wood has ears, the field eyes", a saying that can be found in Latin literature of the High Middle Ages and which later passed into vernacular use. In a Netherlandish woodcut of 1546 (p. 72), regularly discussed in the literature, the proverb is illustrated as a full-scale landscape, within which the admonishing eyes and ears are seen in the middle ground and right-hand background. A figure in the left foreground, with whom the viewer can identify, puts his fingers to his lips in a meaningful gesture and points with his other hand to the panorama opening up in front of the viewer. The inscription "*Dat Velt heft ogen/Dat wolt heft oren/Ick wil sien/swijghen ende horen*" ("The field has eyes, the wood has ears, I will see, be silent and listen") explains the literal visualisation. Around 1530–1545 the Antwerp merchant and *rederijker* (rhetorician) Cornelis Crul (*c.* 1500–1550) adapted the same proverb in his moral and satirical poem *Mont toe, borse toe* ("Mouth shut, purse shut"), in which he delivers a warning: whether out of doors or at home, it is impossible for us to pass unnot-

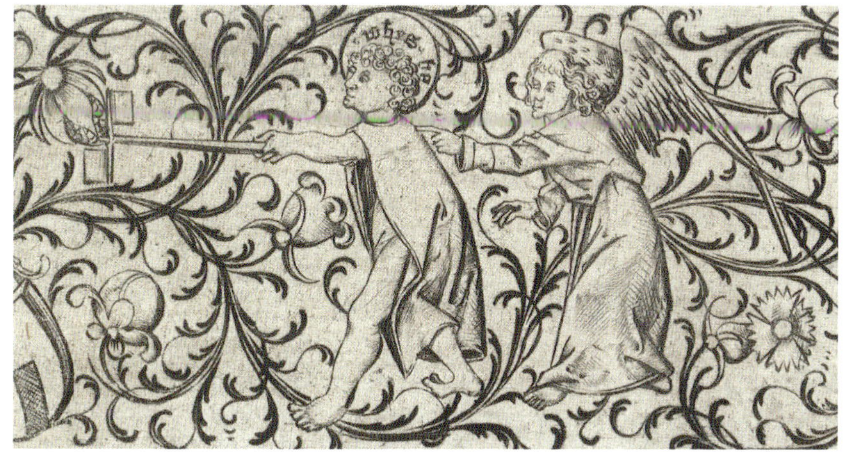

Israhel van Meckenem the Younger, **Christ and St John as children, jousting with windmills** (detail), c. 1470–1500
Engraving, 34 x 157 cm / 13 ⅜ x 61 ¾ in. London, The British Museum, inv. 1842, 0806.39

iced because we are under constant surveillance by mice, spiders, snakes, swallows, magpies and other birds. For "the field has already opened its eyes, all the woods and forests unfold their ears; you cannot speak, for they would hear it" (Bax 1956, pp. 172–173). To avoid possible calumny, we must curb our tongues, something that will also ultimately serve to preserve our wealth. As with the implication of our own expression, "Speech is silver, silence is golden", Crul sagely advises us to be careful what we say.

Bosch's drawing substantially predates both the woodcut and the poem and contains neither a human figure nor an explanatory caption. But the proverb at the heart of his image is complemented by two scenes that function in a similar fashion: the owl with the birds and the fox with the cockerel. These two motifs appear several times within Bosch's oeuvre; but they were in general use in his period, and can be considered familiar topoi. They were generally intelligible, at least among the educated elite, and were therefore useful as commentaries and exempla. They were designed to warn the viewer against Evil and the consequences of careless action. As a nocturnal bird, the owl in the centre of the image carries negative connotations and symbolises spiritual blindness and folly, the temptation of Evil, along with uncleanliness and wantonness (Vandenbroeck 1989; Bambeck 1987). The significance of the other birds is harder to ascertain. Painted in a negative light in the poem by Cornelis Crul, they can also carry a positive meaning, in so far as they represent free souls seeking to draw closer to God. In Bosch's drawing two birds on the left are flapping their wings; one of them has its beak open and seems to be turning on the owl in a hostile manner. This action is emphasised by the line of shading that descends from the branch on which the bird is perched to the right edge of the hollow in which the owl is sitting. A third bird perches on the end of a branch to the right, while a fourth is perhaps busy feeding.

In the relationship between the cockerel and the fox the latter appears as the aggressor. The fox traditionally had a bad reputation as an animal that stole poultry, lived in a den and ruined the Lord's vineyards (Song of Songs 2:15); and it was considered to symbolise hypocrites, heretics and Evil with its sly and cunning ways. In all contexts other than representations of fools, on the other hand, the cockerel was a symbol of vigilance, the good priest and teacher and the proclaimer of the Gospel, who announces morning while it is still night (Bambeck 1987, pp. 43–48; de Bruyn 2001a, p. 446). Owl and fox may thus be interpreted in a negative light as aggressors; while the four small birds and the cockerel are under attack, in danger and victims. In order to reinforce the message and communicate it even more urgently to the viewer, the aggressors look directly out of the picture, just as the eyes in the field and the ears in the wood are turned in our direction. The endangered birds exemplify three different states of peril: the victim condemned to death (the cockerel), innocent unconcern (the birds at the top), and vigilance and readiness for defence (the bird with its beak open). The combination of dead and flourishing vegetation in the drawing also makes a clear statement. Dead nature, to which the owl and the fox are assigned, points to death through sin. But flourishing nature, here linked with the critical senses, is equated with a good and new life that is pleasing to God, and with divine grace.

The figural studies on the verso (p. 445, Cat. D3v) show that the back of the drawing was used as an exercise sheet by Bosch's workshop. They have been executed by a number of different hands and include several attempts to copy – in simple outline and without interior contours – the figure (drawn at lower left by Bosch) of the crippled beggar on crutches and with a dog perched on top of his hooded head. The little dog appears three times in the lower right of the sheet, while the beggar's head in profile and the hand with the begging bowl can be seen at upper left.

A sentence in Latin, written at the start of the 16th century in an abbreviated form on the front of the sheet, can be deciphered to read *Miserrimi quippe est ingenii semper uti inventis et nunquam inveniendis*, which may be translated as:"For poor is the mind that always uses the ideas of others and invents none of its own." This commentary very probably has its source in the 13th-century treatise *De disciplina scholarium* (On the Education of Scholars) by Pseudo-Boethius and was relatively well known as a quotation or paraphrase (Vandenbroeck 1981). Unlike other inscriptions on Bosch's paintings and drawings, which complement or define the pictorial subject, this sentence may effectively be understood to reveal a workshop secret. It testifies to a healthy self-respect on the part of the artist since Bosch gives this general theoretical definition of what constitutes artistic talent an exemplary practical demonstration on the sheet below. He invents and innovates by complementing his visual illustration of the proverb with the two other scenes discussed above: the tree with the owl in the hollow trunk and the birds above, and the fox and cockerel among its roots. Art, that is to say, lies in finding and combining these topoi. The inscription can therefore be read as the standard that Bosch set for his own work: that the artist should be capable of inventing something new within the context of each commission and thus of fully satisfying the requirements of his patron. *The Wood Has Ears, the Field Eyes* is thus revealed as Bosch's most complex drawing, one whose allegorical intention – more pronounced than in the *Nest of Owls* – is conveyed by various analogous or related pictorial motifs. It represents a particular sort of specimen sheet for Bosch's workshop assistants, namely a visual lesson in artistic theory, delivered in a drawing that demonstrates, in an exemplary fashion, the inventive selection and organisation of pictorial motifs and thus the intellectual facet of the creative process. Bosch's oeuvre and creativity were devoted not to perfecting a pictorial tradition, but to developing a theme through the art of combination, resulting in iconographic inventions and innovations.

St Christopher as a grotesque

A good example of this can be seen in the painting *St Christopher* (p. 78, Cat. 7). Precisely when the panel was produced, for whom, and for what function and context have yet to be ascertained. It is clear, however, that the panel has been flattened off at the top and that it originally had a semi-circular arch, allowing us to conclude that it was probably the central panel of a triptych. Its main figure and overall layout have similarities with a woodcut printed in Basel and dated around 1490. The composition can be seen as a sort of preliminary exercise for the large triptychs of the following years; at the same time it marks an important point within the evolution of the theme, as Bosch breaks clearly from tradition and develops his *St Christopher* in an entirely new way. The lower half of the composition and the centre of its foreground are occupied by the main figure of St Christopher, carrying the Christ Child on his shoulders. Both are portrayed in conventional fashion and adhere to a pictorial tradition that was shaped by medieval accounts of the lives of the saints, in turn significantly indebted to the *Golden Legend*, a Latin anthology of lives of the saints compiled by Jacobus de Voragine (*c.* 1230–1298) and published around 1263–1273. According to this tradition, St Christopher wished to offer his services to the greatest and most powerful lord. Having served a king and then the Devil, he set off in search of Christ. On the way he encountered a hermit, who gave him the directions he needed. The hermit consequently became the most important subsidiary figure in artistic representations of *St Christopher*. He appears as an attribute of the "holy giant" in the present panel; but the context of their connection is largely alienating. The hermit was traditionally portrayed with a beard, wearing a monk's habit and carrying a lantern. He would be positioned in front of or inside a chapel or cave, sometimes near a tree-house. In Bosch's painting, the hermit is located as usual on a level with St Christopher's head and with the Christ Child on the giant's shoulders, but he is looking out of the mouth of an outsize jug that is suspended horizontally from an almost leafless tree and accessed at the other end by a ladder. The hermit's lantern is hanging from a rope slung over a branch above him. Higher up the tree an enormous roof of thatch extends over both hermit and jug. Archaeological finds in 's-Hertogenbosch show that the jug depicted by Bosch was based on imported wares from Siegburg, near Cologne. The hole in its side makes it likely that Bosch has depicted a so-called "starling pot": these pots featured a removable section on one side and were hung up as nesting boxes under the eaves or in trees, either as a way of collecting bird's eggs for food or for catching young starlings and teaching them to "talk" (Marijnissen 1987, p. 405). The jug may thus allude to the vice of gluttony (*gula*), particularly since it is emphasised by its unnatural magnification. The plucked chicken on a spit directly above the jug is also a symbol of gluttony. The dovecot above the thatched roof at the crown of the tree alludes to another vice, namely lust. The hermit is thus surrounded by sin, but not actively engaged in it. In Bosch's painting figures, plants and objects that are to be understood as lying geographically, spiritually or ethically on the "border of Christianity" are frequently represented in larger-than-life proportions, in the same way that unnatural size was a feature of exotic tales of "heathen" lands. Bosch employed the inversion of size relationships as a sign of a world turned upside down, as seen on the central panel of the *Garden of Earthly Delights* (Cat. 11.3), where it marks the reversal of the divine order of Creation. In a system of perspective where size equals importance, giant proportions reinforce the symbolic significance of the magnified object upon which humankind has become dependent and around which it now revolves.

To the viewer's surprise, two other hermits are also portrayed in the vicinity of the tree. One, completely naked but for his hood, has climbed right to the end of a bare, narrow branch, which is bending under his weight, and is reaching into a beehive. This scene recalls the fourth parable in the *Barlaam and Josaphat* text (a Byzantine story about these two saints), which describes how a man in a tree hanging over an abyss is so busy eating honey that he forgets his precarious situation and ends by tumbling into Hell. A third hermit, this time with positive connotations, stands on the right bank of the river

Small Christ Carrying the Cross, *c.* 1502–1510
Oil on panel (oak), 57.2 x 32 cm / 22½ x 12½ in. (cut down by a quadrant at the top and minimally along the bottom, originally c. 77–80 cm / 30–31 ½ in. high; exterior tondo: ∅ c. 30 cm / 11 ¾ in.)
Vienna, Kunsthistorisches Museum

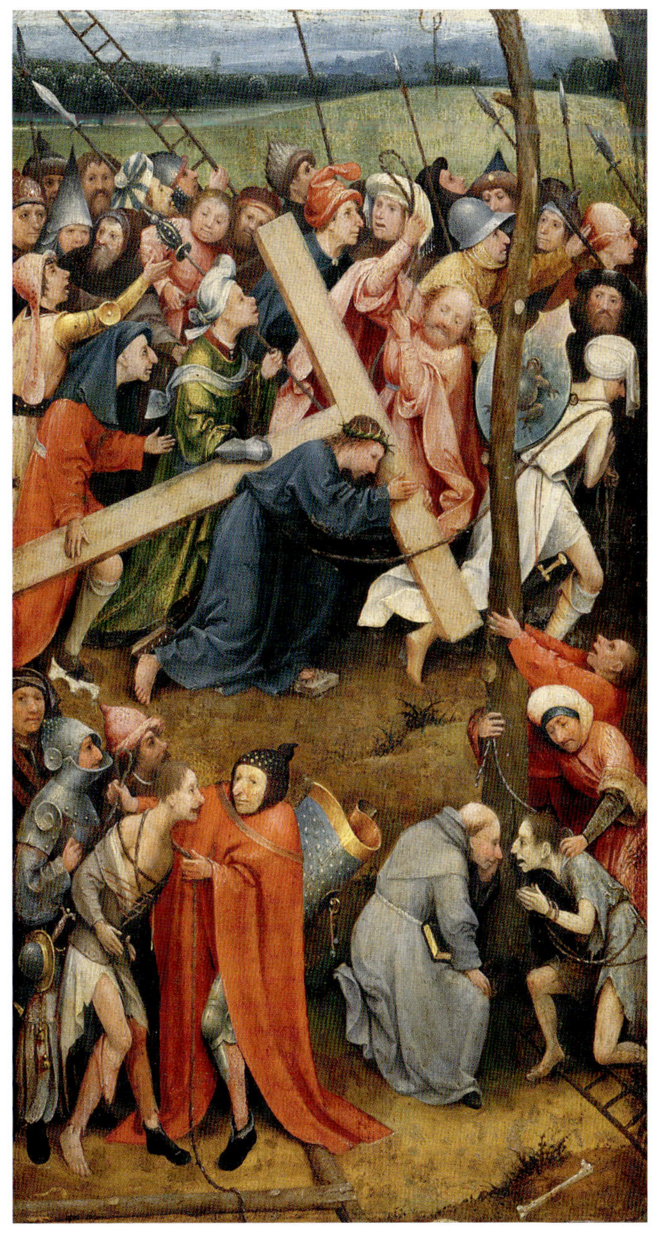

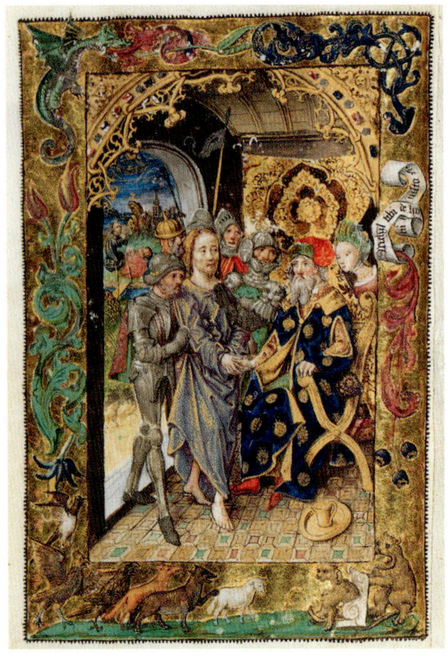

facing St Christopher. Wearing a white apron over his habit, holding a jug in his left hand and reaching forward with his right, he looks down as if in thought or meditation. A small white dog is drinking from the river further to the right, next to a post or a fence that is cut off by the edge of the panel so that it resembles a cross. In this context the jug and the act of drinking can be interpreted as symbols of quenching one's thirst at the eternally satiating fountain of Christ, and the jug itself as a symbol of the fragile body that serves as the container of the soul and is strengthened by turning to Christ.

Bosch has incorporated further scenes, some with positive, others with negative connotations, on the left riverbank. Our eye is struck first of all by a hunter who is hoisting a bear with a rope around its neck up over the branch of a tree. The bear is traditionally a symbol of the forces of Evil and of a variety of vices, chief among them lust (*luxuria*), wrath (*ira*) and sloth (*acedia*). It is also frequently portrayed trying to reach the honey inside a beehive. It embodies instinctual man, as also illustrated by the naked hermit climbing up to the beehive. Bosch has explicitly formulated the theme of temptation in depicting the hermit: just as a bear who steals honey will get stung by angry bees, so the sinner driven only by his physical needs will be punished by the Devil. The bear-slayer, on the other hand, illustrates the topos of the Soldier of Christ. This was newly topical around 1500, on account of the *Enchiridion militis christiani* (Handbook of the Christian Soldier, printed in 1503) by Erasmus of Rotterdam (*c.* 1467–1536) and alluded to by Bosch in the still-life of weapons and pieces of armour appearing in the foreground of the sin of Avarice in his painting *The Seven Deadly Sins and the Four Last Things* (Cat. 15). The Christian soldier (cf. Job 7:1) battles daily against the World, the Flesh and the Devil. In Bosch's *St Christopher*, the Devil is represented by the dragon (on

Netherlandish artist, **Christ before Pilate**, *c.* 1475
from: *Hours of Sophia of Bylant*, fol. 20v (detail) Parchment, 23.3 x 16.6 cm / 9¼ x 6½ in.
Cologne, Wallraf-Richartz-Museum & Fondation Corboud, Graphische Sammlung

the far side of the river) and also by the bear, the desires of the Flesh by the bear and the two hermits in the giant jug and the tree, and the temptations of the World by the giant jug, beehive and dovecot.

Two details that also deserve mention are the mast of a sunken ship and the flying fish in the lower left corner, both symbols of the perils of seafaring that are regularly illustrated in representations of St Christopher. Many of the pictorial motifs within the composition can be read as pairs of opposites. The hermit on the river bank is the antithesis of the hermit on the bare branch. The flying fish is a pendant to the dead fish hanging from St Christopher's staff (a symbol of spiritual nourishment and Christ's sacrifice on the Cross). The giant jug is opposed to the normal-sized one held by the hermit beside the river. The chicken on a spit is an effective reversal of the vigilant cockerels at the foot of the tall tree. The picture challenges the viewer to use the God-given sense of sight in order to arrive at greater understanding, as recommended in a 14th-century version of the legendary life of St Christopher: "Wherefore he gave the five senses to every man that he might recognise what evil or good he has done in his life, so that he might do good and leave off evil" ("*dar umb hat er die fumf sin / einem ieglichen menschen geben, / daz er erchen an seinem leben / waz bös oder guot sei getan, / daz guot er tue vnd daz bös lan*"; Schönbach 1874, p. 86, lines 36–40). The unreal element of the outsized jug serves as a signal, in the manner of the so-called drolleries in illuminated manuscripts, inviting us to reflect upon the picture and to interpret the symbols and exempla it contains.

In Bosch's panel St Christopher has found in Christ the ideal master for whom he had been searching; and he adopts the Christian virtues of humility and temperance. Christopher's stooped pose corresponds to that of *Christ carrying the Cross* (Cat. 8) and of *St*

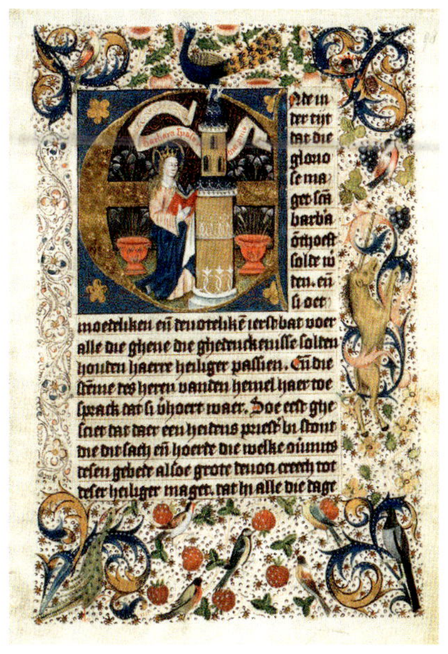

Anonymous artist at convent of St Bridget at Koudewater, near 's-Hertogenbosch
St Barbara, *c.* 1480
from: *The Life of St Barbara*, fol. 98r. Parchment, 24.6 x 17.3 cm / 9⅝ x 6¾ in.
The Hague, Koninklijke Bibliotheek, 133 B 13

James (Cat. 13.1). Studying and understanding the subsidiary elements of the composition enables the viewer in turn to recognise St Christopher as a model. If Bosch's composition is interpreted in this fashion, St Christopher's function shifts from patron saint to model of true piety. There was popular belief at the time that simply looking at an image of St Christopher was enough to protect one, at least for that day, from a "bad" death, i. e. from a sudden death that did not allow time for the last rites. As an intercessor with Christ, St Christopher was also believed to offer safety in foreign lands, provide protection against enemies and the perils of the sea, and relieve the burden of debt. He was the patron saint of travellers, merchants and goods carriers.

In the increasingly illusionistic, mimetic representations of St Christopher in panel painting at the end of the 15th century, his figure grows more monumental and sculptural and claims ever more of the picture space. Bosch's painting is probably among the first in a series of innovative *St Christopher* representations and diableries to be produced in the 16th century (Unverfehrt 1980), including – relatively early on – examples by Alart Du Hamel (*c.* 1450–*c.* 1506; p. 80) and the Master of Frankfurt (1460–1515) active in Antwerp.

Drolleries

The reciprocal relationships between motifs from sacred and profane or, more accurately, "high-brow" and "low-brow" thematic spheres within Bosch's oeuvre, motivated by considerations of form and content, allude – whether in their role, function or imagery – to drolleries. This connection between Bosch's works and drolleries has regularly been made in the literature, but without pursing the comparison in depth and considering its ultimate significance. The term *drôlerie* began to be used in the late 1500s in France as a collective name to refer to bawdily comic and grotesque figural or scenic representations. The corresponding German and Netherlandish terms *drollen* and *grillen* were applied more widely to prints and panel paintings, for example, by Pieter Bruegel the Elder and Hieronymus Bosch (cf. Raupp 1986, pp. 307 and 309–310). Drolleries had their origins in the subsidiary decorative details of church façades and interiors, such as stone capitals and wooden choir stalls, and in the marginalia of illuminated manuscripts. The earliest drolleries have been identified in the exempla offered in Dominican and Franciscan sermons (Randall 1957, 1966). After their initial flowering in the early 14th century, drolleries saw a major revival in the second half of the 15th century.

The names of the sculptors who carved drolleries on the choir stalls in Breda, Hoogstraten and 's-Hertogenbosch in Brabant have largely been forgotten. In the sphere of manuscript illumination, on the other hand, drolleries can be directly assigned to celebrated miniaturists such as Jean Pucelle (*c.* 1300–*c.* 1334), who worked for the French court, and the Flemish artists Willem van Vrelant (d. around 1481/82), Lieven van Lathem

(d. 1493), as also to the anonymous Master of Mary of Burgundy, all of whom decorated books for high-ranking patrons in the Netherlands in the third quarter of the 15th century.

Bosch's works make use of a number of motifs and themes that are more or less identical to those found in drolleries. In first place among the various types of drollery motif are representations of grotesque individuals whose bodies remain entirely human but whose gestures and poses show a complete lack of restraint and inhibition. These include mime artists of all kinds (such as acrobats, climbers, musicians, dancers) as well as people rudely sticking out their tongues or baring their backsides. Genre-like depictions of representative members of society with a tendency towards a particular vice make up another category of motif, and one also found in Bosch (cf. Cat. 15, Cat. 20), along with proverbs and sayings, fools and various motifs of the world turned upside down. The foregoing categories show people in comic, ridiculous or absurd situations or activities; but there is another type of drollery motif consisting of grotesque anatomies. These include "head-footers" (trunkless cephalopods consisting of a head on legs, probably inspired by similar figures from Antiquity), heads, masks and bodies of distorted proportions. Another category can be titled "the beast in man" or "man as beast", and comprises illustrations of fables or of animals behaving like humans, animals associated with specific vices, such as monkeys, dogs and pigs, and animals symbolising negative human traits or experiences, such as the owl and the fox (p. 92). One last category comprises figures of a monstrous nature: traditional hybrids of man and beast familiar since Antiquity (e.g. centaurs, siren birds and siren fishes) and mythological creatures (e.g. unicorns [p. 93], dragons and griffins). To these may be added the mixed creatures freely invented by the artist.

The existence and, indeed, the major evolution of drolleries within the sphere of religious art can be explained by the fact that the monstrous and the grotesque serve to illustrate sin and Evil and are thus part of this world and equally of the Divine Plan of Salvation. Hieronymus Bosch takes up this great tradition of visual art, previously tucked away in the margins of illuminated manuscripts and in the carved decoration of choir stalls and capitals, and transfers it to panel painting. Drolleries granted him a certain artistic freedom, in so far as he could choose from a wealth of pictorial motifs and then modify and combine his selected elements both with each other and with his main motif. The principle of creating hybrids out of several creatures also allowed him to construct entirely new figures.

III.

In the labyrinth of images: *The Temptation of St Anthony*

c. 1502

"For the first and perhaps for the only time, an artist had succeeded in giving concrete and tangible shape to the fears that had haunted the minds of man in the Middle Ages. It was an achievement which was perhaps only possible at this very moment of time when the old ideas were still vigorous while the modern spirit had provided the artist with methods to represent what he saw."

ERNST H. GOMBRICH, 1950

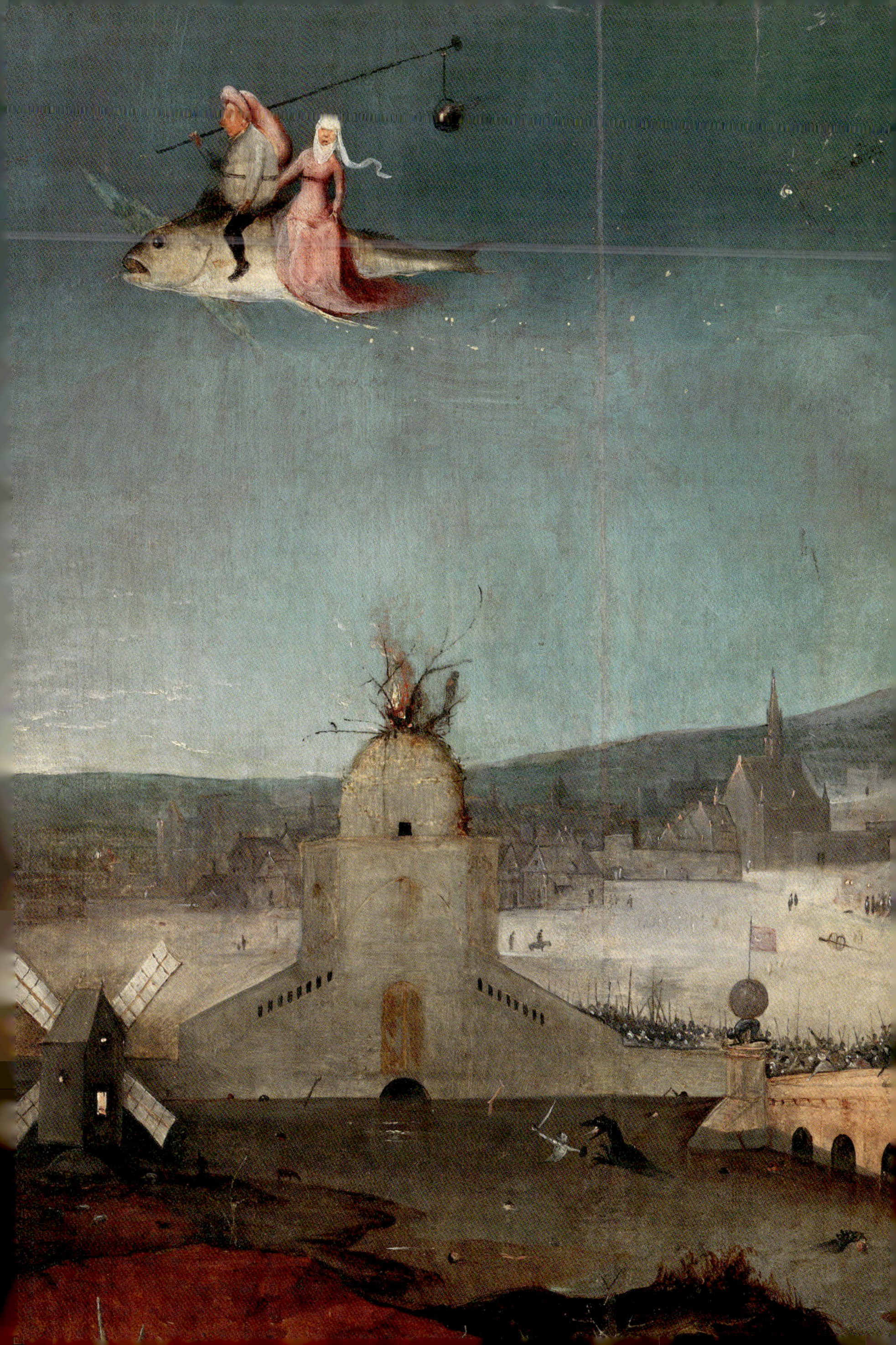

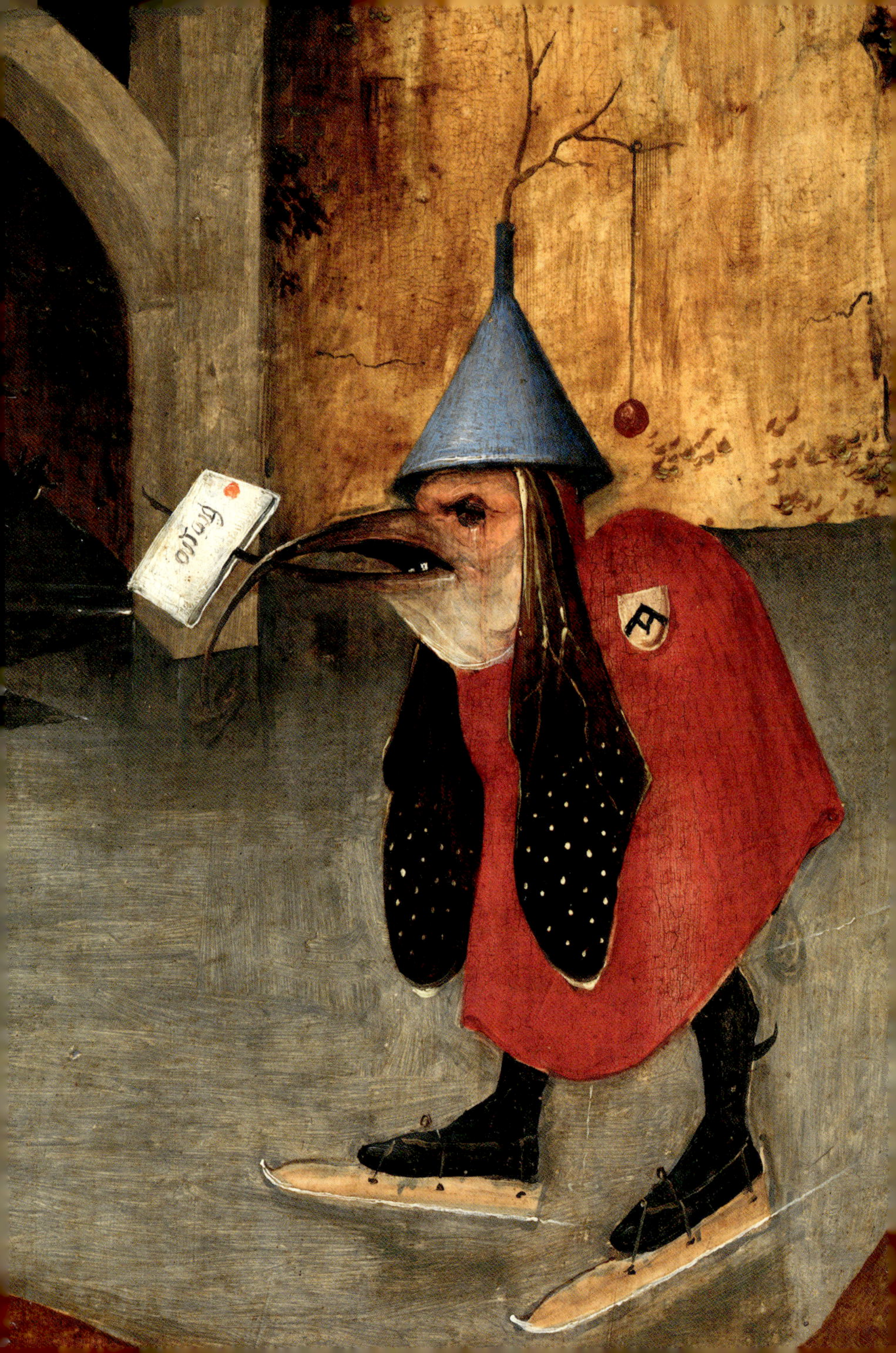

The *Temptation of St Anthony* (pp. 118/119, Cat. 10), produced in the years around 1502 and today in Lisbon, is the first of Bosch's large triptychs to employ drolleries to such a degree that the main figure almost disappears within the crowd of subsidiaries. A substantial proportion of the pictorial surface is occupied by grotesque motifs. Within Bosch's oeuvre the outstanding importance of the *St Anthony* theme in general, and of this triptych in particular, is undisputed. The patron of the work, its intended function and the occasion on which it was commissioned are unknown; but documentary sources dating from 1504 onwards indicate that various members of the Spanish and Netherlandish aristocracy bought and collected *St Anthony* paintings, sometimes in lavish versions and for large sums of money (see entry on Cat. 10). The representations of St Anthony in a number of other works by Bosch and his workshop (Cat. 12, Cat. 14, Cat. 22) are clearly based on this *Temptation of St Anthony* triptych; while the number of copies and imitations produced by Bosch's followers up to around 1650 is almost countless (Unverfehrt 1980). The earliest biography of St Anthony (251/52–356), who came to be considered the first hermit and the father of monasticism, was written in Greek by Athanasius of Alexandria (*c.* 298–373). Later pictorial tradition was usually based on the popular short versions of St Anthony's life found in the *Golden Legend* and in a German text, *Der Heiligen Leben* (Lives of the Saints, *c.* 1400), with artists often depicting St Anthony visiting the hermit Paul of Thebes (p. 101). This meeting is missing in Bosch. Looking more closely at the individual scenes within his *St Anthony*, it is apparent that he has consulted either the Latin or the vernacular edition of the *Vitas patrum* ("Lives of the [Desert] Fathers"; correctly speaking *Vitae patrum*) as his source for the St Anthony legend (Fischer 2009, pp. 308–323).

The second half of the 15th century saw a final phase of intense activity both in the monastic sphere, with new monasteries being founded and existing ones reformed, and more generally in the sphere of scribes and copyists engaged in the production of books. This resulted in the much wider availability of copies of the *Vitas patrum*, especially in its Netherlandish version (*Vader boeck, Leven der heiligen vaderen*). Bosch would have had access to the collection of legends of the saints through local religious bodies. The *Vitas patrum* was a prescribed text in reformed Dominican monasteries, for example; and it is therefore likely that a copy would have been available in the Order's large community in 's-Hertogenbosch. Among the few documented holdings of the libraries in 's-Hertogenbosch, moreover, are a manuscript copy of the *Vitae patrum* from around 1450, belonging to the Brethren of the Common Life and housed in its Gregoriushuis premises, and a 1478

Pages 97, 98
Detail from: **Temptation of St Anthony**, *c.* 1502
Right inner wing: **St Anthony in Meditation**
Left inner wing: **St Anthony Accused by Devils** (see ill. pp. 118/119)

Latin edition of the *Vitas patrum*, printed in Nuremberg and belonging to the Wilhelmite Order. Anthologies of lives of the saints were found not just in the libraries of monastic orders and religious communities, however, but also in the palaces of the aristocracy. The audiences for whom Bosch's *St Anthony* pictures were possibly intended could, then, also have been familiar with the details of the saint's legend. The Netherlandish Nassau family, for example, owned a French edition, the *Vie des anciens saints pères hermites*.

Bosch's triptych (Cat. 10) shows St Anthony in the three most important chapters of his life, presented chronologically from left to right across the three interior panels. Thus we see him embarking on his life as a hermit (left), at the height of his persecution by devils (central panel), and conquering their temptations to arrive at inner peace (right). In contrast to what we find in some works contemporary with Bosch's triptych and treating related themes – for example in *St Anthony with Donor* (p. 101) by the Cologne Master of the Holy Kinship (The Younger) of *c.* 1500 – where, within a continuous narrative, the main figure appears repeatedly as the events of his life unfold, Bosch reduces the number of St Anthony figures to four and groups the many episodes in his eventful life around them. This layout makes it more difficult, however, to identify the individual subsidiary figures and scenes.

On the left inner wing (Cat. 10.3) two Anthonite monks are supporting or carrying St Anthony, identified as a hermit by his habit. They are assisted by a third man, an agricultural worker who has often been interpreted as a self-portrait of Bosch. St Anthony has lost consciousness after being attacked by the Devil. This main scene is sandwiched between the two halves of a second scene. At the very top of the panel we find St Anthony, lying back in ecstatic prayer, being carried through the air by demons or devils; and at the bottom he is discovered in the group of devils under the bridge. This main scene shows an event that took place relatively late in the life of St Anthony (Athanasius 1924, Ch. 65): early one afternoon St Anthony fell into an ecstasy while meditating and saw himself being borne aloft by angels. His way was suddenly blocked, however, by devils demanding that he reckon up the sins of his youth: for these, they claimed, he was still accountable. St Anthony's mid-air struggle with these devils became a popular subject in visual art: it is found, for example, in the engravings of Martin Schongauer (p. 110) and Lucas Cranach the Elder (*c.* 1475–1553; p. 110).

In line with the principle of the world turned upside down, the elements of Bosch's painting descend into chaos; in the sky (pp. 120/121) St Anthony is surrounded by a wolf devil, a demon knight with a fish for a lance or battering ram, a flying sailing-boat with a naked manikin looking out from between his own legs, an upside-down jug with arms gripping a scythe and further flying fish. At the bottom of the panel, St Anthony's diabolical prosecutors are squatting in the shadow of the bridge and are already reading out

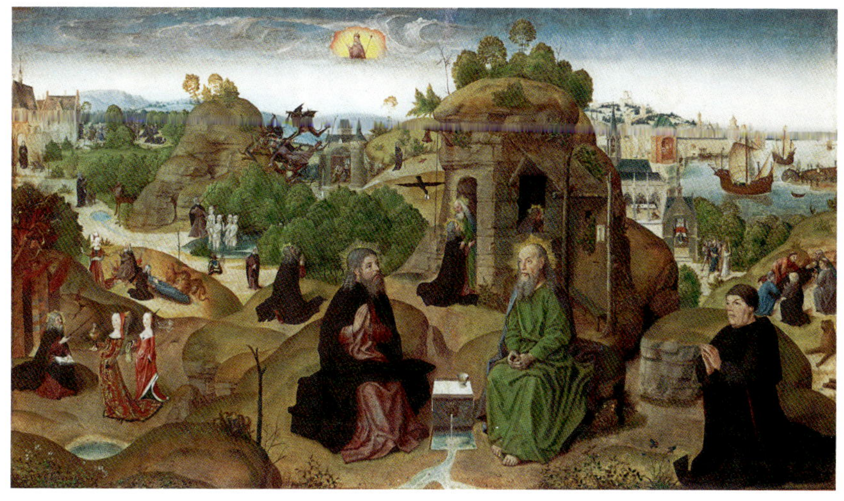

Master of the Holy Kinship (the Younger), **Legend of St Anthony**, *c.* 1500
Oil on panel, 103.2 x 190.1 cm / 40⅝ x 74¾ in.
Munich, Bayerische Staatsgemäldesammlungen – Alte Pinakothek

Pages 102/103
Detail from: **Temptation of St Anthony**, *c.* 1502
Central panel: **The Temptation of St Anthony** (see ill. pp. 118/119)

the charges against him, while a hunchbacked, bird-shaped messenger devil is crossing the ice to deliver a second document (p. 98). This last bears the inscription *protio*, in all probability an abbreviation of *protestatio* (Massing 1994), identifying it as an indictment. The devils are diabolical in the strictest sense: accusers and slanderers who sow discord among humanity.

Bosch has depicted the messenger devil as wearing ice-skates. These were a popular metaphor in literature and visual art in the late Middle Ages and early Renaissance. Writers of the 16th century described the world as "skating on ice" to signify that it had gone astray and was on the wrong course. This is an allusion to the carelessness of those who slip on thin ice and fall through into the water. The saying "*Ic sta op een krakend ijs*" ("I'm standing on cracking ice") carried a similar meaning (Massing 1994). These figures of speech were not confined solely to the local vernacular, however. A Latin proverb from the 12th century warns: "*Qui currit glaciem, se non monstrat sapientem*" ("He who crosses the ice does not show himself wise").

The symbolism of the leafless, withered branch protruding from the inverted funnel that the messenger devil wears on his head can be explained by passages in the Bible,

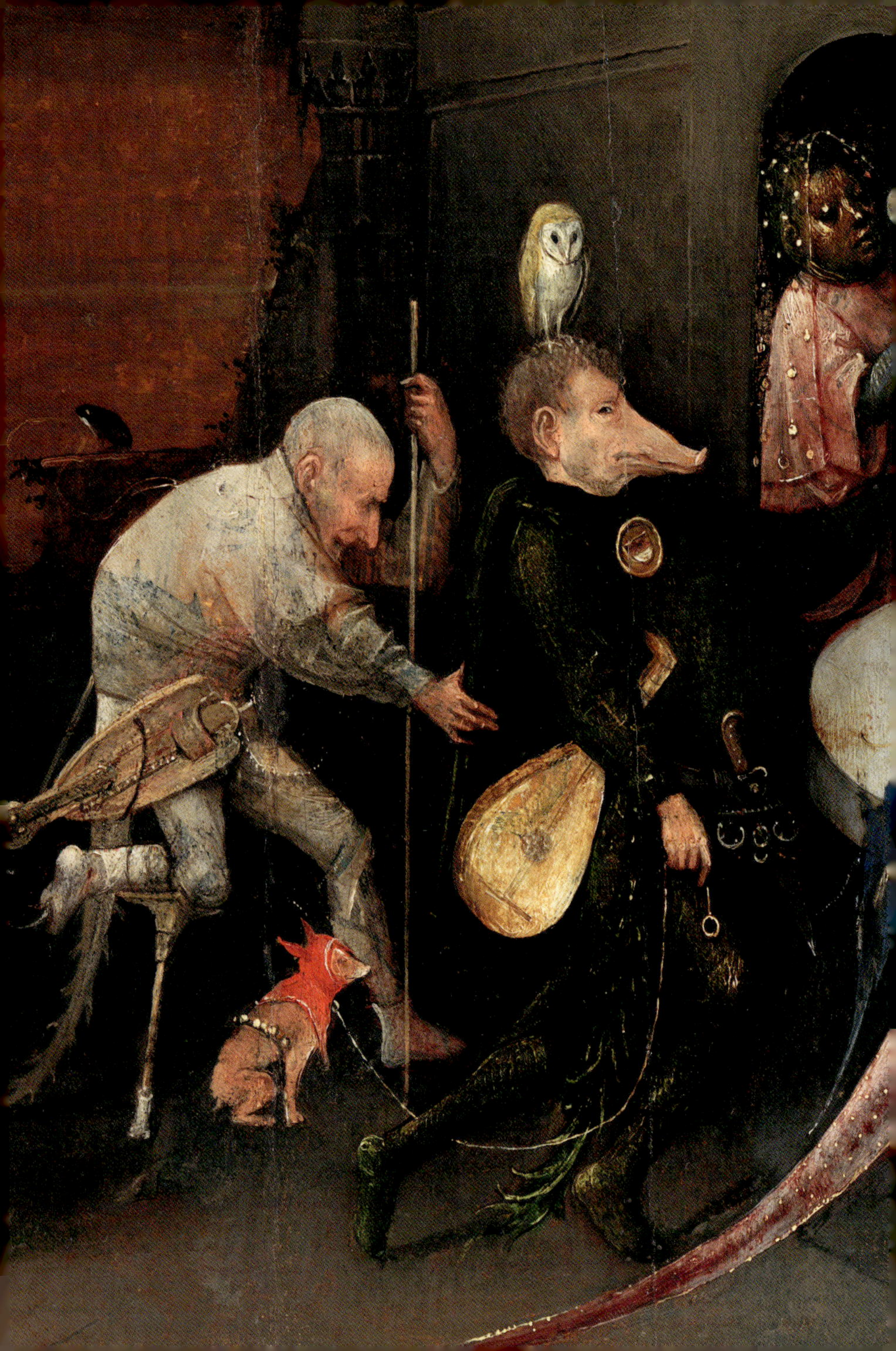

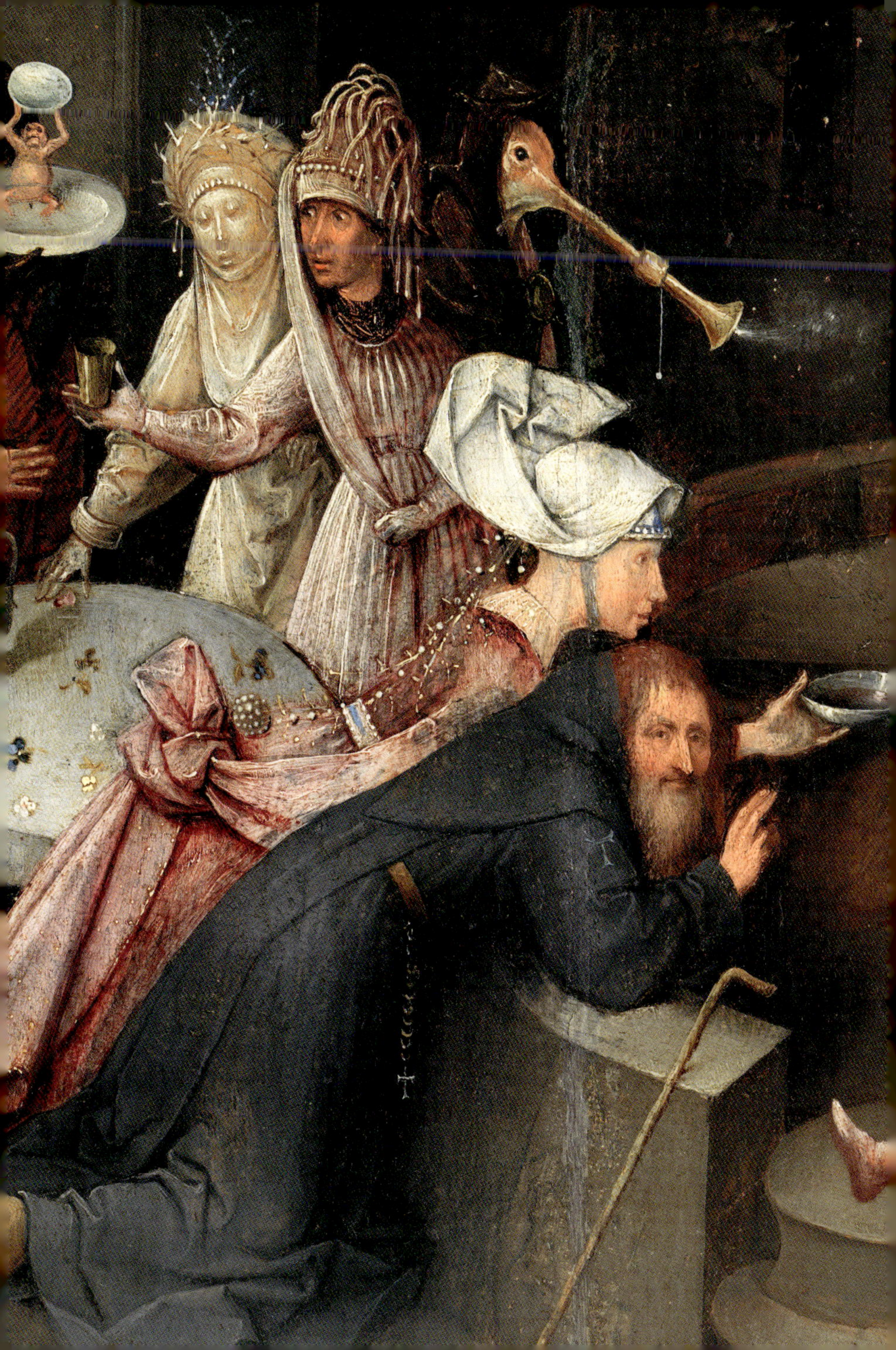

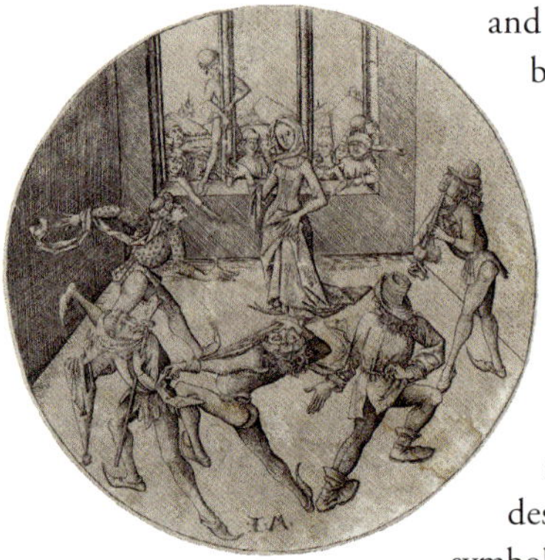

and even more precisely by a metaphor employed by Jan Brugman in a sermon: "*Soe moet ghi ghebenedijt werden niet van mi, Janneken Brugmans, een arm dorre twijchken, die verdroghet bin vander fonteinen der gracien*" ("So shall you not be blessed by me, Johnnie Brugman, a poor withered twig, in whom the fountain of Grace has dried up"; Brugman, *Verspreide Sermoenen*, Sermon 13, line 452 ff.). That this spiritual "withering" is caused by man's carnal desires is made clear both through the red ball (a symbol of fertility and virility) hanging on a string from the branch, and through the funnel (a symbol of intemperance, as in the notion of getting "tanked up", i. e. getting drunk; Bax 1983, p. 89, note 3).

Bosch has embellished the landscape on this left inner wing with further details. Above the main group, for example, a kneeling giant has taken on the shape of a tavern (pp. 124/125). The giant is a frequent motif in accounts of the life of St Anthony (e. g. *Vitas patrum*, Ch. 23 and 66); in such accounts, however, he is described as standing so tall that he reaches the clouds, and as stopping souls in the form of birds from ascending to heaven. The tavern or inn exhibits all the dubious characteristics typically associated with these sinful establishments in Bosch's paintings: as such, it represents a diabolical trap for human souls. Below the giant-tavern, a false bishop is pointing his companions – unlikely members of the clergy – towards its entrance. On the opposite, left edge of the panel (p. 123), a large, apparently stranded fish in an armoured vehicle, with the legs of a grasshopper and an aggressive-looking tail, is swallowing a smaller fish. This motif illustrates the saying "Big fish eat little fish" and recalls the words placed in the mouth of St Anthony in Chapter 85 of the *Vitas patrum*: "Fishes, if they remain long on dry land, die. And so monks lose their strength if they loiter among you and spend their time with you".

Many symbols of the path and the journey are scattered throughout the landscape. The bridge is a symbol of the passage from one stage of life or consciousness to another. One path leads directly to the right towards the central panel, while another winds away

Israhel van Meckenem the Younger, **Morris Dancers**, *c.* 1475
Copper engraving, ∅ 17.4 cm / 6⅞ in. Berlin, Staatliche Museen, Kupferstichkabinett

Page 105
Detail from: **Temptation of St Anthony**, *c.* 1502
Central panel: **The Temptation of St Anthony** (see ill. pp. 118/119)

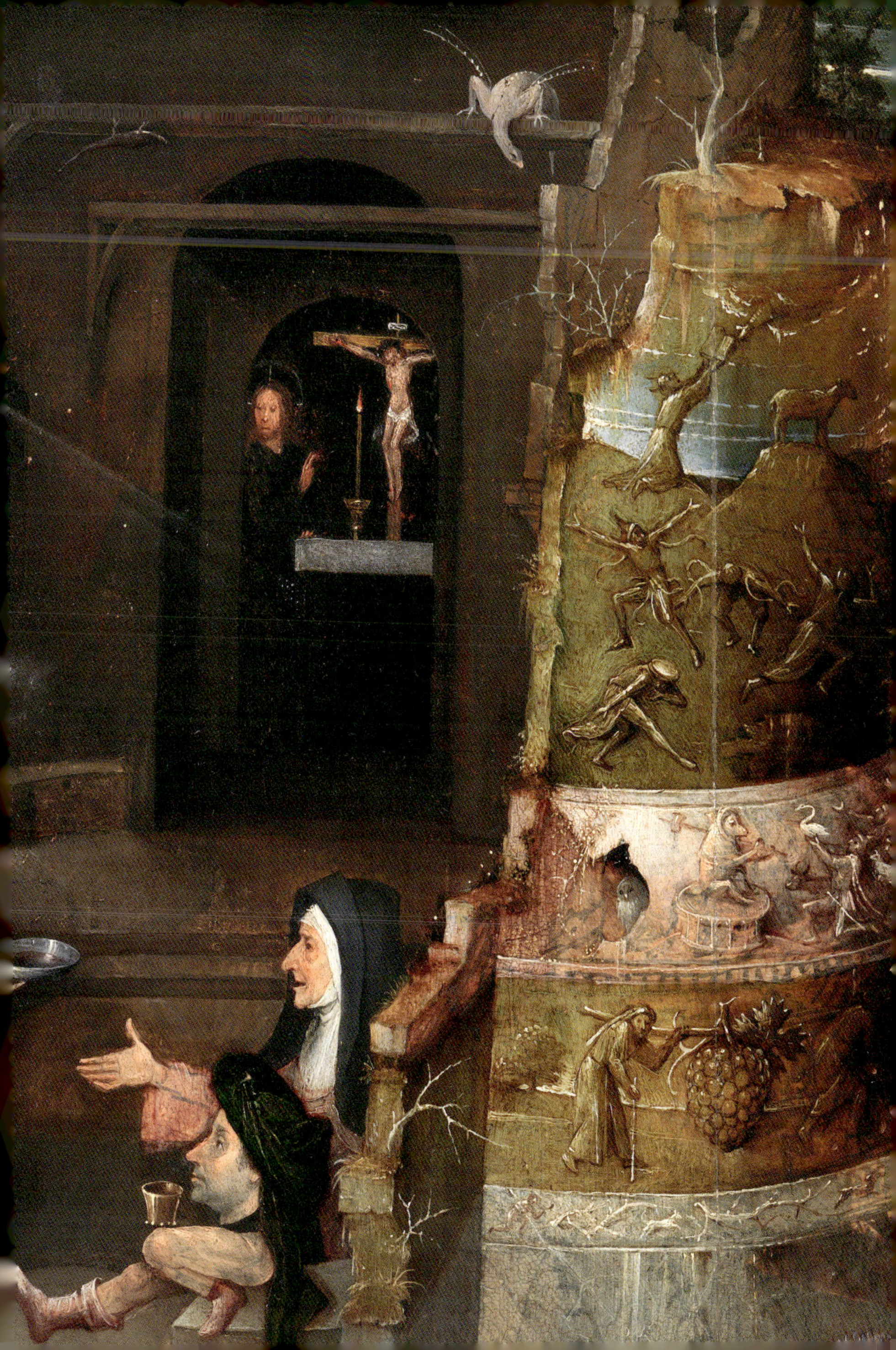

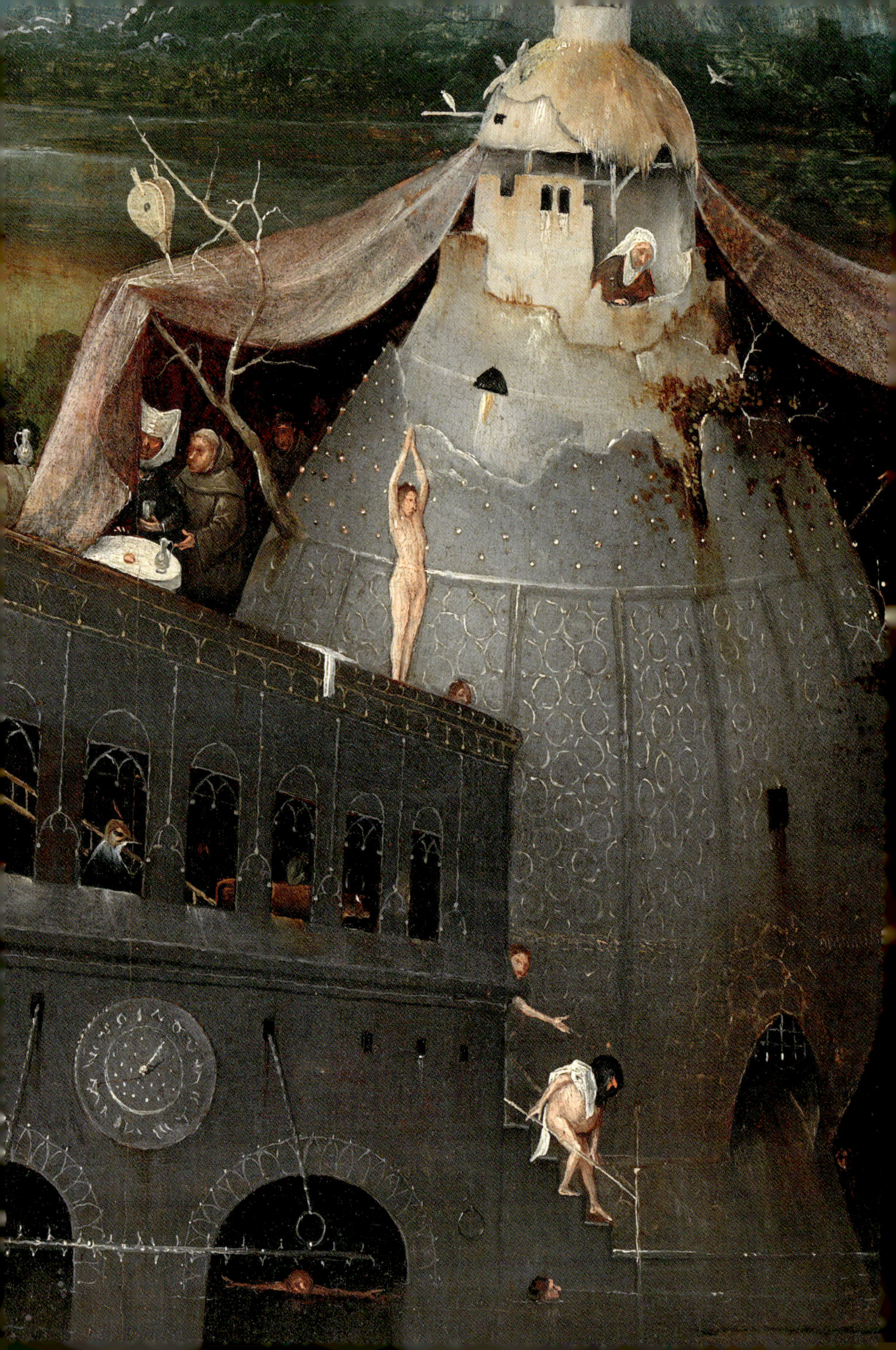

to the top left, eventually vanishing into the depths of the picture. "Swallowing" motifs appear twice on the left edge of the panel. They are a reference less to the sin of gluttony than to the bad end prepared for humankind by the forces of Evil. The idea was widespread that the entrance to Hell was a yawning chasm. The notion of the journey recurs in the sailing boats disappearing over the horizon and the beacon on the mountain top to the right. St Anthony is battling here less against specific sins and dangers to body and soul than over his departure from this worldly life. He has to make the decision between two options: on the one hand death and eternal damnation, on the other the immortality of the soul. Passive and helpless, he does not yet seem to have found his weapons in this fight.

St Anthony finds protection in the Lord

The central panel (Cat. 10.4) shows St Anthony at the height of his battle with the demons, who appear in large numbers and in densely knit groups around the saint. In contrast, however, to the *Temptation of St Anthony* on one of the wings of the celebrated altarpiece produced by Matthias Grünewald (*c.* 1470/80–after 1529?) for the Anthonite hospice in Isenheim (p. 109), these demons do not physically attack the saint. Although St Anthony serves as a model in both paintings for the fight against the forces of Evil, in Bosch's case the saint is doing battle with images assaulting him in his mind, whereas Grünewald's demons torment the saint's body. Bosch's representation is based on Chapter 9 of the *Vitas patrum* Life of St Anthony, where the saint declares that the sign of the cross and faith in the Lord are "a wall of safety" (cf. the Alemannic *Vitas patrum*, "[…] *so ist mir sin zeichen des heiligen crúces ein mur vnd ein schirme vor úwerem gewalt*", Williams 1996, p. 16; and the Latin version – "*Signum enim crucis et fides ad Dominum, inexpugnabilis nobis murus est*", Migne, PL 73, 132B).

In the centre of Bosch's painting, the bearded St Anthony is kneeling in front of the ruined remains of a fortified tower, inhabited by beasts of all kinds. He is looking out at the viewer with his right hand raised in blessing. The line established by the contour of his back leads our eye to the right and to the figure of Christ, likewise in blessing, standing in a sort of apse beneath an arch in the shell of the ruined tower, beside an altar bearing a crucifix. St Anthony is not only aligned physically towards Christ but sees him as a vision and emulates his form in so far as he transmits the gesture of blessing to the viewer. St Anthony has now armed himself, with the invincible weapon of Jesus Christ, for the fight against Evil. The link between Bosch's composition and the *Vitas patrum* text originally

Detail from: **Temptation of St Anthony**, *c.* 1502
Central panel: **The Temptation of St Anthony** (see ill. pp. 118/119)

extended even further: laid out to the left of the ruin in the underdrawing is a tent with demons (Lisbon 1972, n. p.; Venice 1992, p. 59; van Schoute/Verboomen 2000, p. 180), an allusion to Psalm 27:3, cited by St Anthony shortly before the above-mentioned passage: "*Si consistant aduersum me castra, non timebit cor meum*" ("Though a camp be set against me, my heart shall not be afraid") – in which *castra* signifies a military encampment. The tower is infused with further meaning through the decorations in trompe l'oeil relief on its exterior (p. 105). At the very top, to the right of the apparition of Christ bringing enlightenment, we see Moses on top of the mountain, receiving from God the tablets of the law with the Ten Commandments (Deut. 10:1–11). This transfer can be understood as prefiguring the descent of the Holy Spirit, and the ascents of Mount Sinai by Moses and his meetings with God as representing mystical ascension. In the foreground, the Israelites, shown dancing around the Golden Calf, are depicted in exaggerated fashion as beribboned Morris men (cf. p. 104). Below, we are given another example of idolatry, namely the veneration of an ape. The decoration concludes at the bottom with the scouts returning from Canaan carrying an enormous cluster of grapes (Numbers 13:23), a typological reference to, among other things, the delivery of the Ten Commandments and the Crucifixion.

By way of contrast to the apparition of Christ at the altar, the Devil is holding a parody of holy Mass around St Anthony, complete with sermon, music, Communion and almsgiving (pp. 102/03, 105). Bosch shows the Devil's efforts to tempt St Anthony first with a silver dish and then with a quantity of gold (*Vitas patrum*, Ch. 11 and 12). These lures are being paraded in front of the hermit monk by unlikely-looking beggars: a woman with a serpentine tail is offering the silver dish to a nun, while the gold here takes the form of the goblet resting on the knee of a torso-less nobleman in an old-fashioned Burgundian hat. On the left, at St Anthony's feet, a blind beggar – identified as such by his black beaver hat – has set out an amputated leg as a means of attracting alms. The figures of these beggars allude to St Anthony's admonishment that man should feed himself through the work of his own hands. Begging had acquired such a bad reputation in the 15th century that a ducal decree was issued, ordering the genuinely needy to identify themselves with a mark. Whatever the case, the other beggars in the picture are revealed by their hybrid appearance as illusions conjured by the Devil.

The position of St Anthony, with the female demon kneeling behind him, bears a resemblance to the arrangement of the two figures in *The Tiburtine Sibyl showing Emperor Augustus a Vision*, a scene found on the wing of the altarpiece carved by Adriaen van Wesel for the Brotherhood of Our Blessed Lady. The theme of the vision is also the same, but the positive connotations of van Wesel's Tiburtine Sibyl have become wholly negative in the figure of Bosch's female demon. Bosch had been thoroughly familiar with van Wesel's altarpiece since his journeyman days, and its character as an artistic model here becomes clear. Further parodies follow to the left of St Anthony, where a company dressed as nobles are indulging in some sort of meal (p. 102/03). This is probably another travesty of the Mass, as wine is being drunk and a white egg reminiscent of the Host is being raised demonstratively aloft by a pink frog-like mini-demon on a silver platter, held up in turn by a servant.

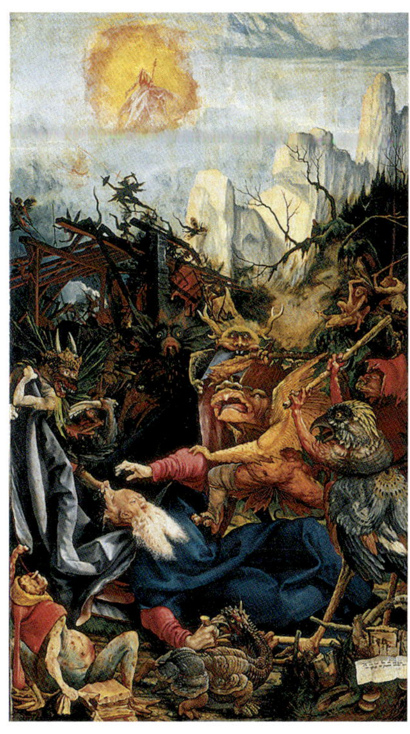

The company also includes a monster with a nose in the shape of a buisine (a herald's trumpet), a musician with a pig's snout and a lute, and a hurdy-gurdy player with one leg on a crutch. All three are secular musical instruments which in Bosch's day were associated with sensual pleasure and thus stood in sharp contrast to instruments used for edifying sacred music. In the three figures on the right side of the platform, it is possible that Bosch has portrayed the two heathen philosophers – or parsons (*Pfaffen*), as they are contemptuously called in the Alemannic version – mentioned in chapters 72 and 80 of the *Vitas patrum* (p. 92). The main figure seems to be performing a Mass, as it has a priest's tonsure, wears a sort of chasuble and holds a large book, from which it is straining to read with the aid of spectacles and its left index finger. A pig's snout identifies the figure as immoral and false. Meanwhile, his entrails are spilling out of his back below his ribs: an unmistakable sign of transience and death.

The inversions and parodies even of holy objects and figures, as seen here in Bosch's painting, are frequently to be found in medieval didactic treatises. In his quite widely read *Tafel van den Kersten Ghelove* (Table of Christian Faith; *c.* 1400), for example, Dirc van Delf (*c.* 1365–1404), chaplain at the court of the Governor of the Netherlands in The Hague, used the image of the body as a temple to show how gluttons worship their

Matthias Grünewald, **Temptation of St Anthony**, 1512–1516
Wing of the Isenheim Altar. Oil on panel, 265 x 139 cm / 104⅜ x 54¾ in.
Colmar, Musée d'Unterlinden

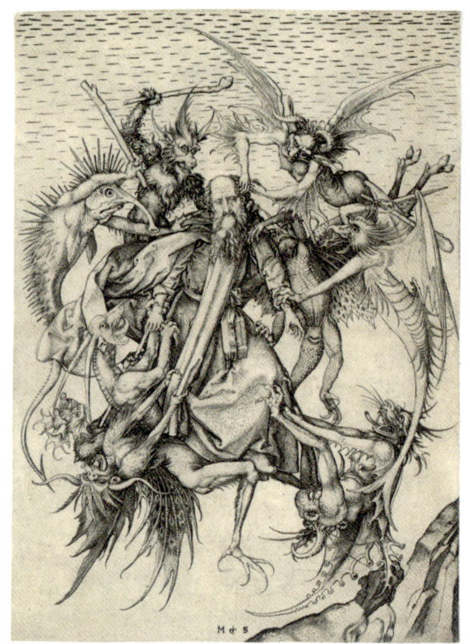

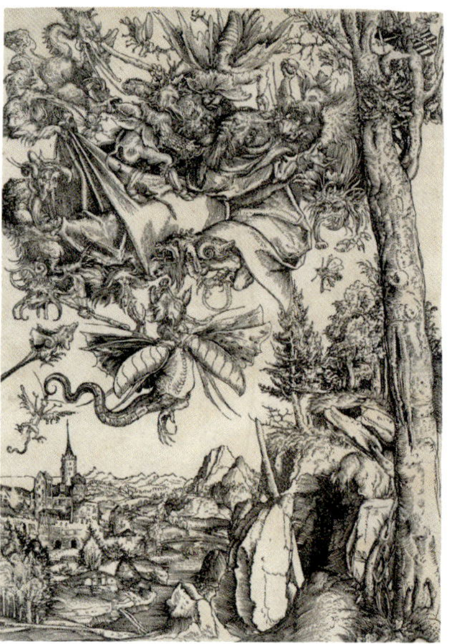

Martin Schongauer, **Temptation of St Anthony**, *c.* 1480
Copper engraving, 21.2 x 23.0 cm / 8⅜ x 9 in. Berlin, Staatliche Museen, Kupferstichkabinett

Lucas Cranach the Elder, **Temptation of St Anthony**, 1506
Woodcut, 40.0 x 26.8 cm / 15¾ x 10½ in. Berlin, Staatliche Museen, Kupferstichkabinett

stomachs. He presented this worship as a sort of failed and misguided imitation of the Eucharistic Mass: "The other is gluttony, when someone worships his own stomach: the temple is the kitchen, the altar the dining table, the deacon the head cook, the Sacrifice of the Mass boiled and roasted, the singing of the choir the bickering, squabbling and slandering during a quarrel" (for the original Dutch text, see Delf, *Kersten Ghelove*, vol. II, ch. XXXII, p. 209).

In the lower left corner, behind St Anthony and on an extension of Christ's line of sight, we see a representation of Wrath in the grey manikin sitting in a basket suspended from a branch, near a giant red fruit and several monsters (p. 89). This figure has his mouth wide open and brandishes a sword menacingly above his head, resembling the exemplum of Wrath (*ira*) in *The Seven Deadly Sins and the Four Last Things* (pp. 308/309, Cat. 15). Wrath here presents a contrast to the humility of Christ and St Anthony.

Midway up the central panel on the left, a strange-looking judge or bailiff is approaching the company around the table. He has a hollow tree-trunk on his shoulders and holds a *doornstocksken* – a rod or staff of office – in his metal gauntlet (p. 128). He also carries a bow and is accompanied by two armoured dogs, identifying him as a hunter. The pale "head-footer" demon shot by an arrow, being led along like a prisoner, is one he has apparently caught in the process of killing the pig that was the traditional attribute of St Anthony. Below, the other armed demons drag the beast along. An instrument of execution is also visible: a gallows wheel on top of a pole, still bearing parts of a corpse. There is also a crow.

The figures in the bipartite metallic building to the right of the ruined tower are characterised as idlers and libertines (p. 106). The egg-shaped tower is crowned with a dovecot; on the roof of the left half of the complex, two monks appear beside a lady at a circular table and beneath a withered branch; demonic figures inhabit the gloomy main wing, and swimmers take to the brackish waters. Another party of demons has congregated in the shallows on the lower right side of the central panel, some on mounts that include a giant rat (p. 121) and a jug on legs, others in bizarre boats (pp. 132/133). These demons are difficult to interpret either in the context of the legend of St Anthony or in more general iconographic terms. The riders are characterised as nobles and as such present a contrast to the hermit and his simple life. In the far background of the central panel Bosch demonstrates his ability to deploy fire and flames on an apocalyptic scale: demons are burning down a village, including all its churches (pp. 126/127). This representation corresponds to chapter 82 of the *Vitas patrum*, which describes how St Anthony received a vision of churches being plundered and despoiled by the Arians.

The central panel places greater demands upon the viewer's visual and cognitive faculties than do the two wings. The main figure of St Anthony is considerably smaller in scale, and there are many pictorial elements to distract the eye. Several lines nevertheless converge in his figure, his face lies at the absolute centre of the panel, and his commanding gaze seeks out that of the viewer.

St Anthony overcomes deceptive illusions

On the right inner wing (Cat. 10.5) Bosch shows St Anthony sitting quietly on a grassy bank with the Scriptures open in his hands. He does not allow himself to be distracted by the apparitions all around him and has found inner peace. In contrast to what we find in the other two interior panels, neither his body nor his gaze is angled towards an object within the composition. To his left, in the foreground, a pot-bellied "head-footer" and three naked men are grouped around a table. One of the men, lying underneath the table, is being run through with a blade by a devil. To the left of St Anthony (p. 139) a naked woman is looking out of a split and hollow tree-trunk that is draped with a red cloth. The tree-trunk stands for the female genitalia – an allusion later employed by

Johann Wolfgang von Goethe (1749–1832) in his play *Faust* (1808), for example, in the Walpurgis Night scene in Part I:"Mephistopheles: I had a wild dream some time back; / I saw a tree with a great big crack, / It had a gaping hole inside – / I like a hole that's nice and wide. / The Old Witch: You and your cloven hoof, Sir Knight / Are very welcome here tonight. / A hole like that need a big stopper, / So you can plug it good and proper!" (lines 4136–4143; cited here from *Faust: A Tragedy in Two Parts*, translated by John R. Williams, 1999, p. 133). The woman, who places one hand on her lower abdomen, which is covered by a barely visible veil, is the incarnation of Lust. She gazes down at a devil who is holding a fish out to her. Behind the tree, an old woman with a striking headdress and blue cloak is pouring liquid from a jug into a bowl held up by a devil. In this context she is probably a procuress. Bosch has here represented one of the many attempts by the Devil – as described in chapters 5, 19 and 23 of the *Vitas patrum* – to tempt St Anthony away from his life of devotion by parading before him, often all too blatantly, the seductive charms of women. The couple dressed in the style of the middle classes, flying through the air on the back of a fish leaving a trail of sparks behind it, may also be understood as an allusion to base instincts and sexual desire.

In the background of the right panel war is breaking out around a city. This may be a reference to the disputes at the time between Christians in the Arian conflict, and thus also to the secular plotting and scheming between individuals, from which St Anthony distanced himself. Alternatively, it may simply be a reference to the "troops of soldiers" described in Chapter 23 of the *Vitas patrum* as one of the Devil's many guises. The duel between the swordsman and the black dragon in the waters of the moat outside the city walls once again embodies the battle between Good and Evil. St Anthony seems unaffected by all the activities going on around him. He has attained a state in which the inner beauty of a soul that has turned to God triumphs over the visible beauty of the body and of images. Whether the Devil appears to St Anthony as an accuser, an adversary or a seducer, his attacks on the saintly hermit's eyes and ears prove powerless.

Just as in his *St Christopher* (p. 78, Cat. 7), in the *Temptation of St Anthony* triptych Bosch has portrayed the saint as a model of right conduct in the footsteps of Christ. This is underlined by analogies between the triptych's central panel and the two Passion scenes on the exterior of its shutters (p. 117, Cat. 10.1/2). On the left outer wing, Christ – unlike Peter in the foreground – puts up no resistance to his arrest, but merely drops to his knees. Likewise, in the triptych's central panel St Anthony kneels with no show of resistance towards the demons. On the right outer wing, near the figure of Christ carrying his

Detail from: **Temptation of St Anthony**, *c.* 1502
Central panel: **The Temptation of St Anthony** (see ill. pp. 118/119)

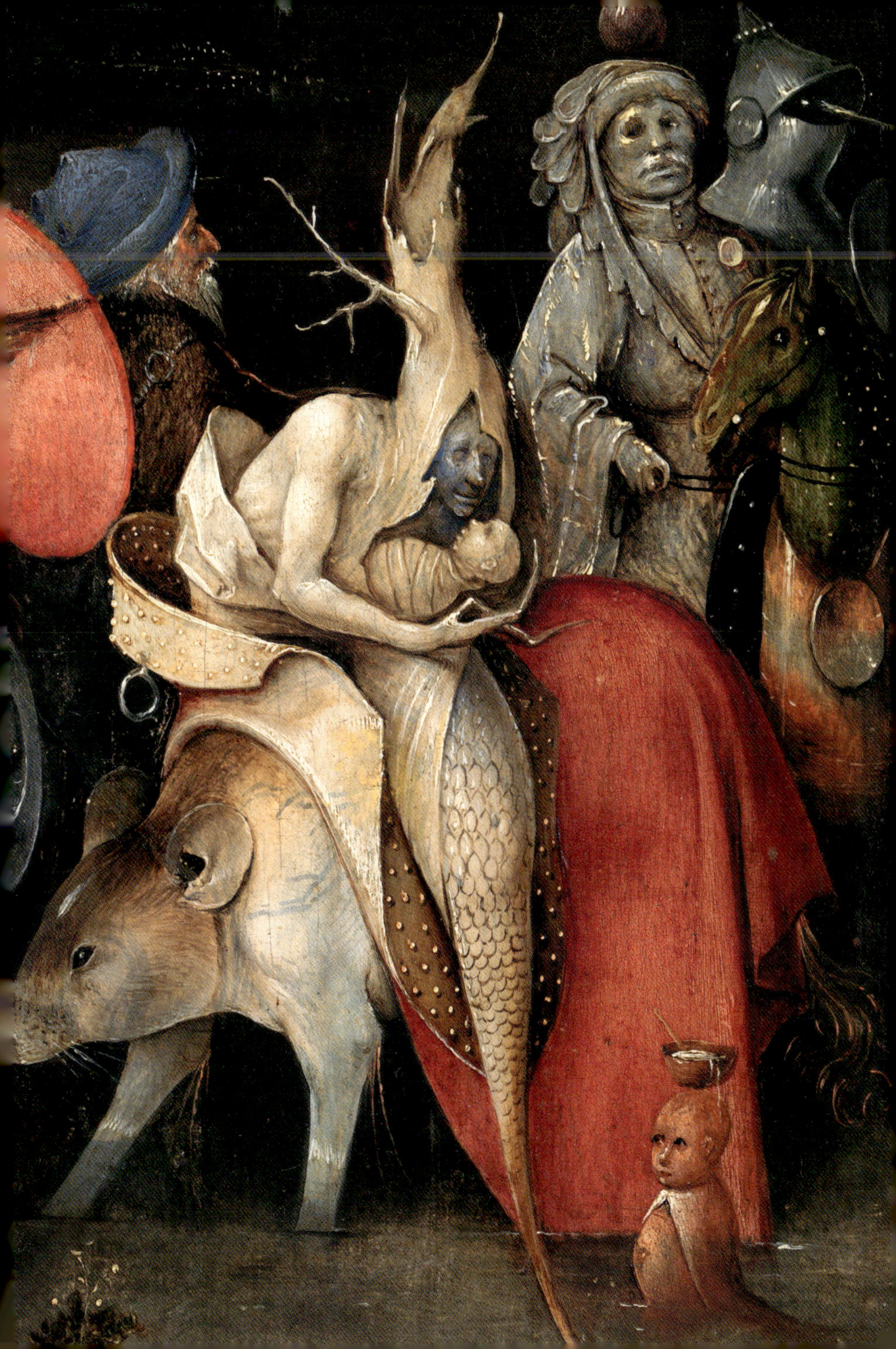

cross, St Veronica holds up the cloth with which Christ has wiped the sweat from his face and which now bears its imprint. In the vision experienced by St Anthony in the central panel, Christ appears next to the Crucifix, in other words next to his own likeness.

St Anthony, like St Christopher, ranked among the saints most widely venerated by all classes in the 15th and early 16th centuries. He was believed to offer protection against the forces of nature, such as fire and lightning, and against sickness. But he was also feared as an avenger: at his own discretion he could inflict or take away the dreaded St Anthony's fire, an often fatal disease that we now know as ergotism, caused by poisoning from rye ergot and accompanied by severe symptoms. Around 1500, however, the image of St Anthony underwent a slight but perceptible shift: in line with the demands of the reform movement within the Church, he was now viewed first and foremost as an examplar of Christian behaviour, and only secondarily as a patron saint. Bosch embraces this paradigm change in his *Temptation of St Anthony* triptych. His own interpretation is based on a solid study of the available biographies of St Anthony and the repertoire of drollery motifs. In his *History of the Order of St Jerome* (1605), José de Sigüenza – monk, preacher, librarian at the Escorial palace and confidant of Philip II (1527–1598) – interpreted the St Anthony portrayed by Bosch, or rather his followers, as a model intended to inspire and strengthen the resolve of the individual. Sigüenza discusses these paintings in terms of the legend of St Anthony, whereby he credits the artist with lending compositional and artistic expression to the saint's confrontation with his visions of temptation. Thus we see "the prince of hermits, with his serene, devout, contemplative face, his soul calm and full of peace [...] surrounded by the endless fantasies and monsters that the Arch-Fiend creates in order to confuse, worry, and disturb that pious soul and his steadfast love. For this purpose [the artist] conjures up animals, wild chimeras, monsters, conflagrations, images of death, screams, threats, vipers, lions, dragons and horrible birds of so many kinds that one must admire him for his ability to give shape to so many ideas. And all of this he did in order to prove that a soul that is supported by the grace of God and elevated by His hand to a like way of life cannot at all be dislodged or diverted from its goal even though, in the imagination and to the outer and inner eye, the Devil depicts that which can excite laughter or vain delight or anger or other inordinate passions." (Sigüenza 1605, p. 838; cited here from Snyder 1973, pp. 36–37).

Bosch's *Temptation of St Anthony* thus serves not simply to commemorate the life of the saint, but as a means of distinguishing and assessing, classifying and judging forms of conduct, ideas and perceptions. Speaking to his followers, St Anthony sought to encourage them with reminders of the grace of God and the Devil's lack of all authority. Citing an incident in the Gospel in which demons begged Christ to send them into a herd of pigs, Anthony concluded:"But if they had power not even against swine, much less have they any over men formed in the image of God" (Chapter 29). By turning to the divine, the godly and the holy within him- or herself, the devout viewer finds the yardstick against which right and wrong behaviour may be gauged. St Anthony also provides an explanation for the parody and metamorphosis characterising diabolical illusions: "For when they come they approach us in a form corresponding to the state in which they discover us, and adapt their delusions to the condition of mind in which they find us" (Chapter 42). By this same token, the demons become a mirror that can lead to greater understanding of the self. It is not always possible to distinguish reality from these phantasms; but in most cases Evil appears as surreal, hybrid, ugly, base and ridiculous, although sometimes, too, as overly beautiful or ideal. Bosch here encourages a discerning way of seeing, in as far as he deploys several types of image, each correspondingly different in its origin, relationship to reality and valence. An image may be apparition, representation, imagination or illusion. Thus: we see the true Christ as a vision embedded in a pictorial account of the historical life of St Anthony; then the reliefs as pictures-within-a-picture with their positive and negative exempla; and last but not least, the seemingly overwhelming apparitions of the Devil, which are not created beings and whose physical manifestation has no reality but instead consists of deceptive illusions. All that is real about them is their immaterial existence as forces of Evil.

It has yet to be established whether Bosch's *Temptation of St Anthony* triptych was destined for a secular patron or for a member of the clergy. Its spiritual and moral dimension is married, for the viewer, with the delights of its rich and multi-figural painting, as Sigüenza acknowledged with great feeling: "[Bosch] made variations on this theme so many times and with such invention that it arouses admiration in me that he could find so much to deal with, and it makes me stop to consider my own misery and weakness and how far I am from that perfection when I become upset and lose my composure because of unimportant trifles, as when I lose my solitude, my silence, my shelter, and even my patience. And all the ingenuity of the Devil and Hell could accomplish so little in deceiving this saint that I feel the Lord is just as ready to help me as him, if I would only have the courage to go out and do battle" (Sigüenza 1605, p. 838; cited here from Snyder 1993, p. 37).

The Arrest of Christ, *c.* 1502
Left outer wing of: **Temptation of St Anthony**
Oil on panel (oak), 131.5 x 53 cm / 51¾ x 20¾ in. Lisbon, Museu Nacional de Arte Antiga

Christ Carrying the Cross, *c.* 1502
Right outer wing of: **Temptation of St Anthony**
Oil on panel (oak), 131.5 x 53 cm / 51¾ x 20¾ in. Lisbon, Museu Nacional de Arte Antiga

Pages 118/119
Temptation of St Anthony, *c.* 1502
Oil on panel (oak), 131.5 x 119 cm / 51¾ x 46¾ in. (central panel), 131.5 x 53 cm / 51¾ x 20¾ in. (wings)
Lisbon, Museu Nacional de Arte Antiga
Left inner wing: **St Anthony Accused by Devils**
Central panel: **The Temptation of St Anthony**
Right inner wing: **St Anthony in Meditation**

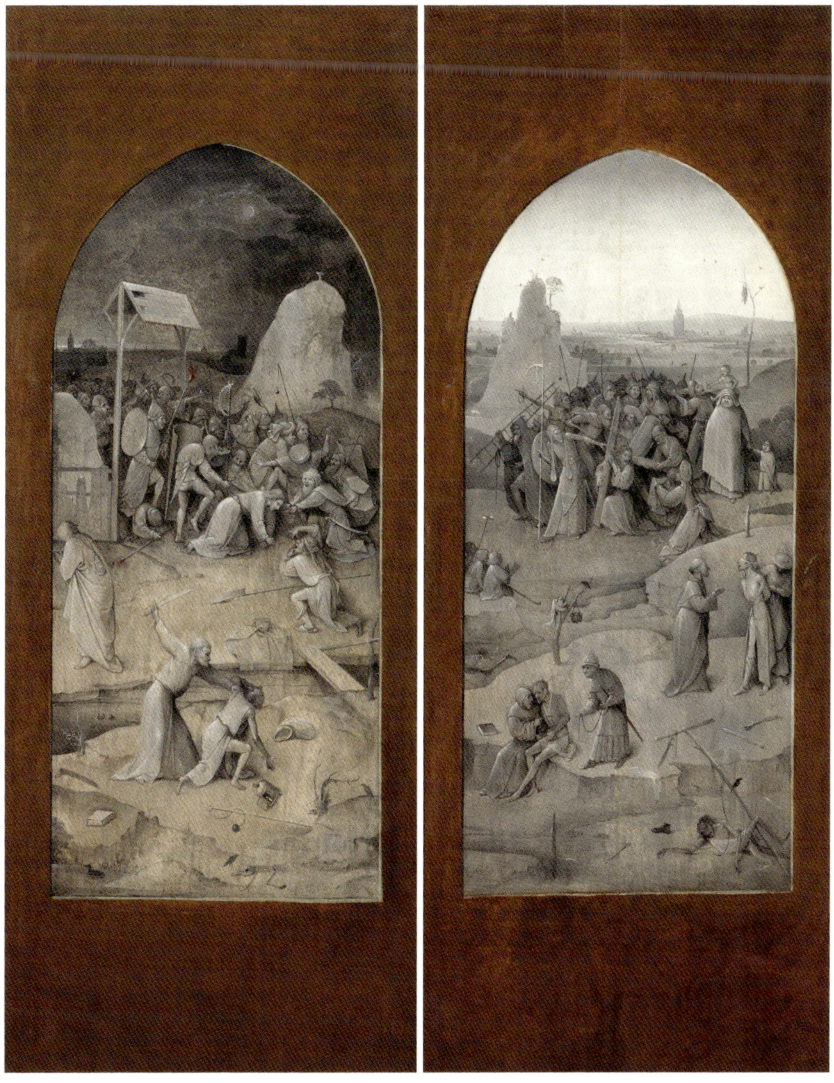

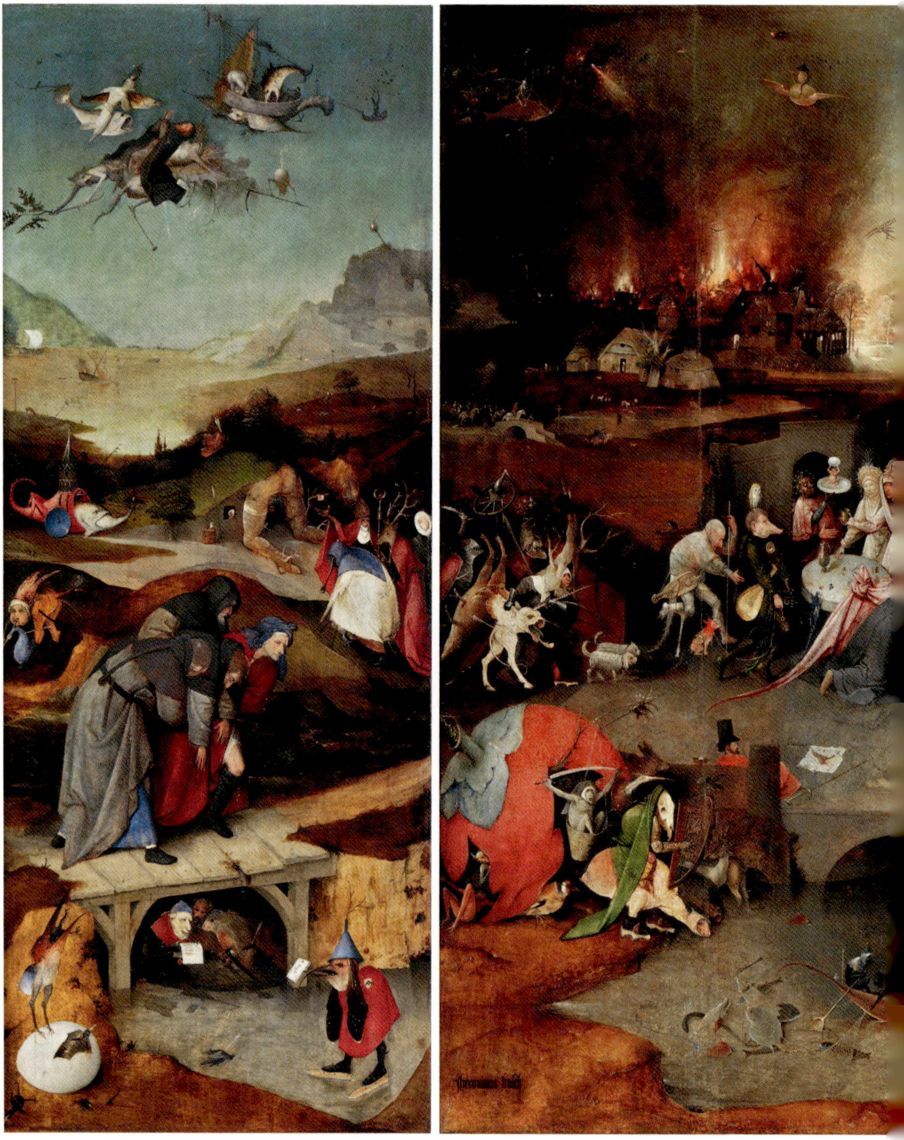

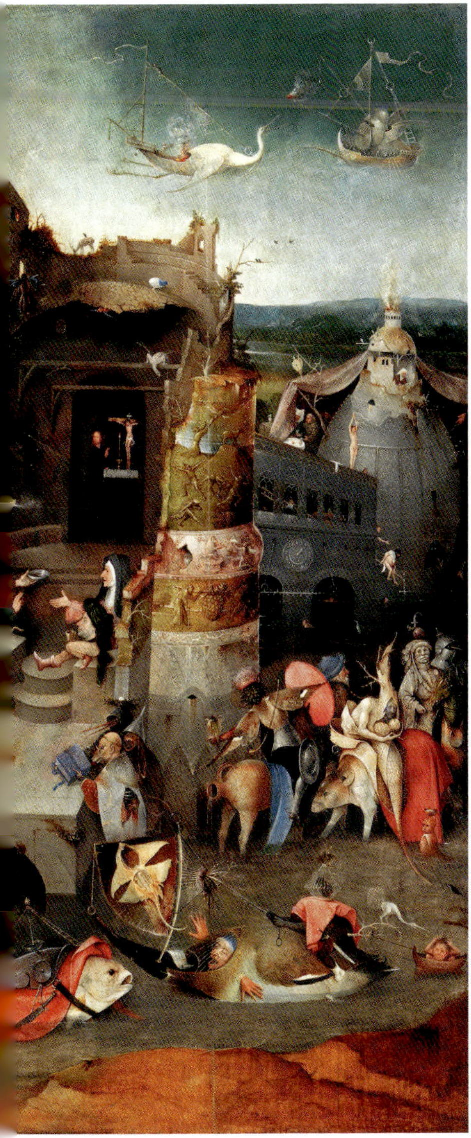

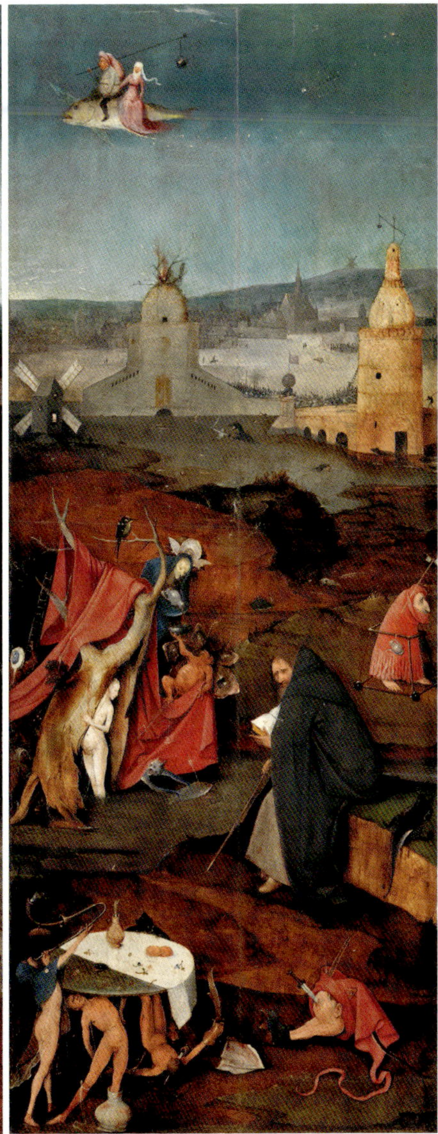

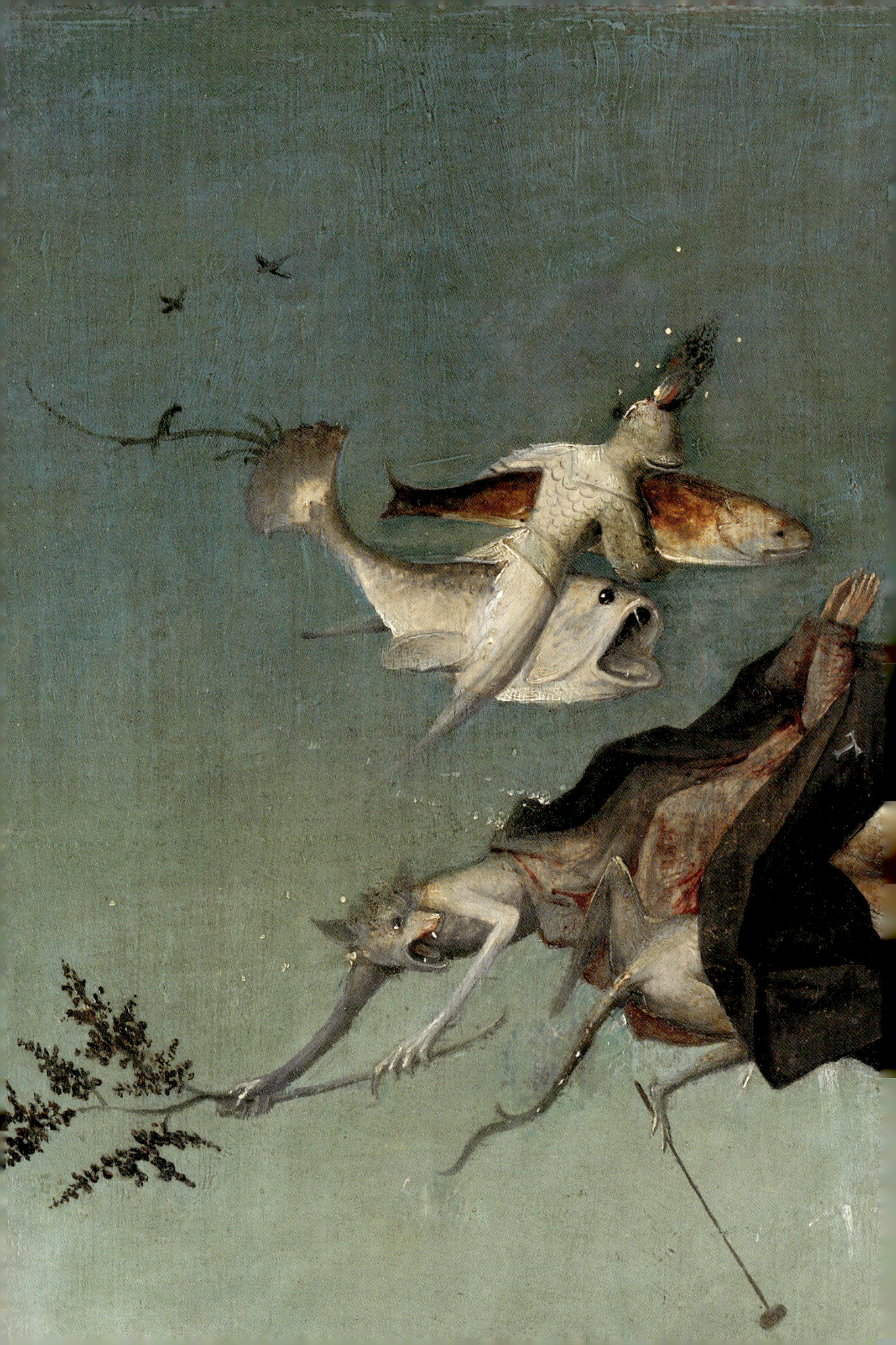

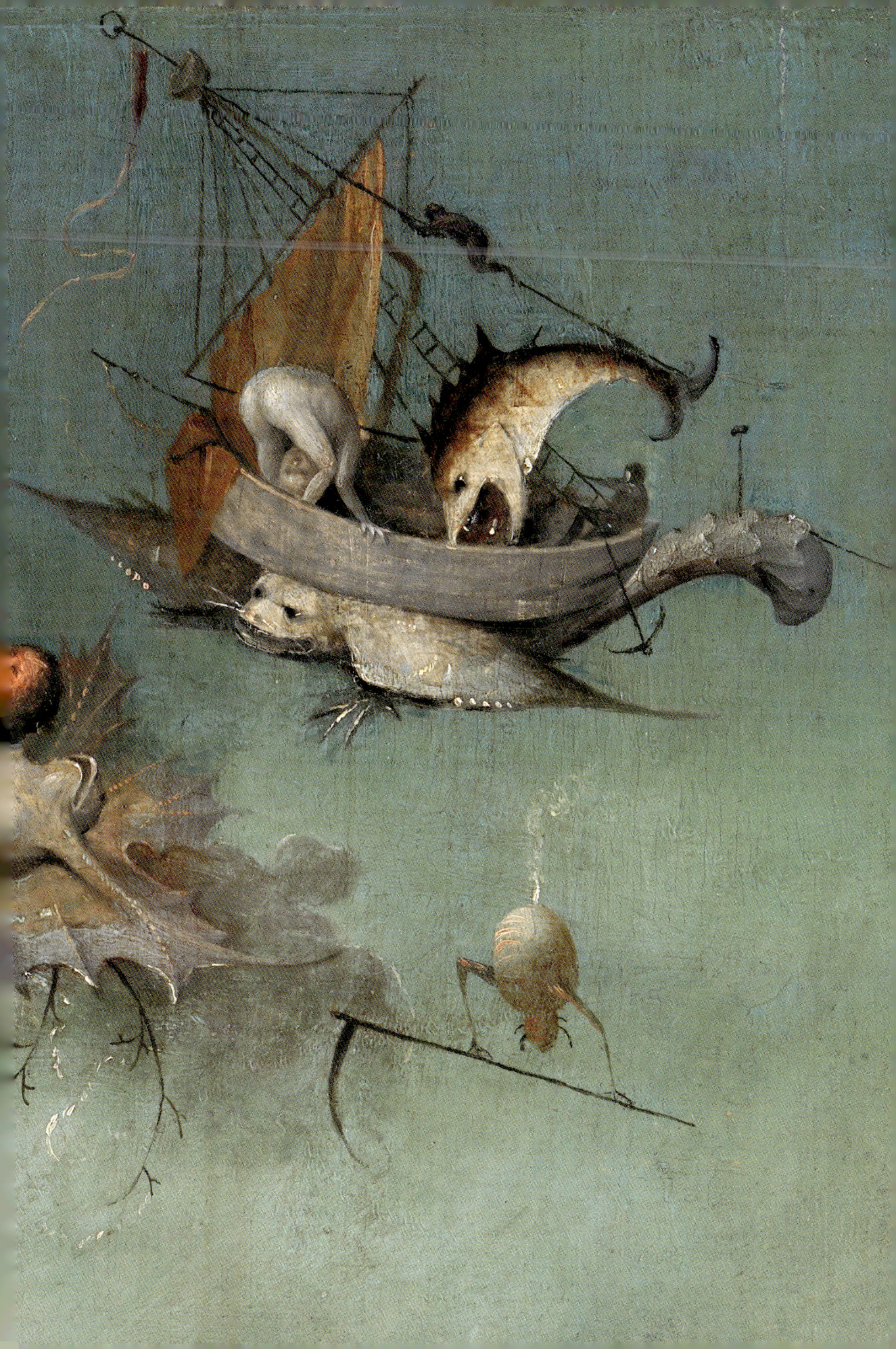

Pages 120/121, 123, 124/125
Details from: **Temptation of St Anthony**, *c.* 1502
Left inner wing: **St Anthony Accused by Devils**

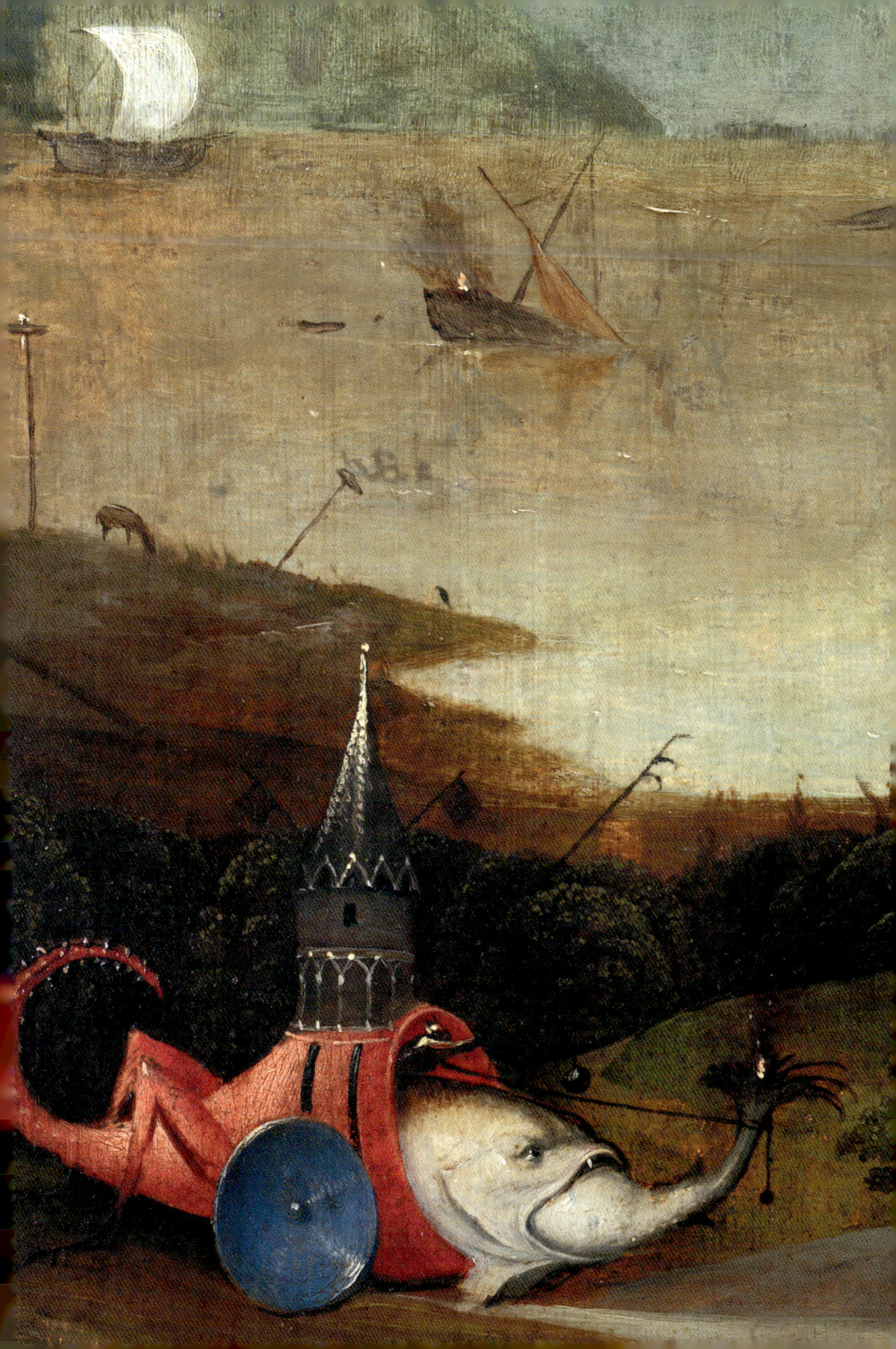

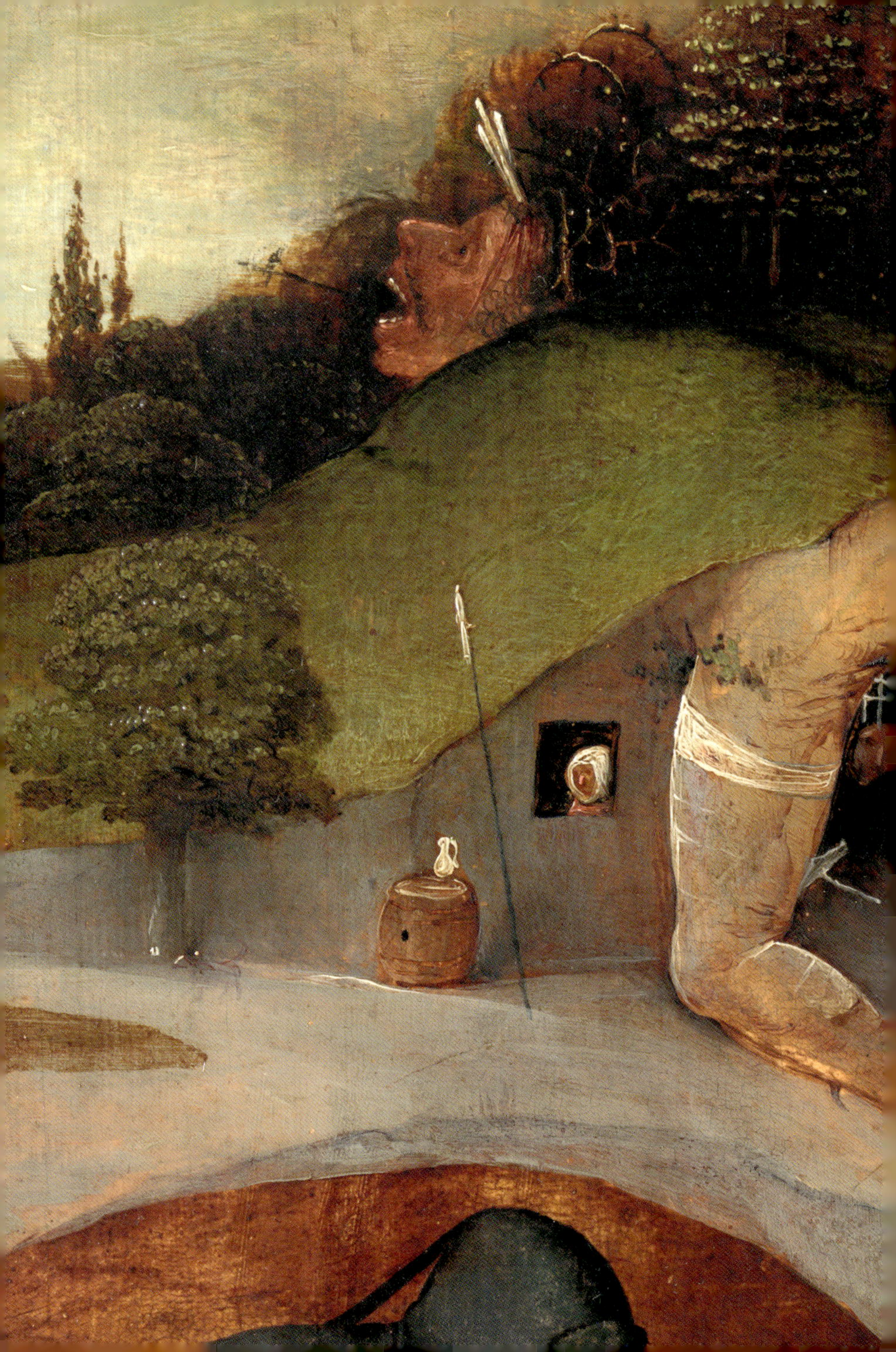

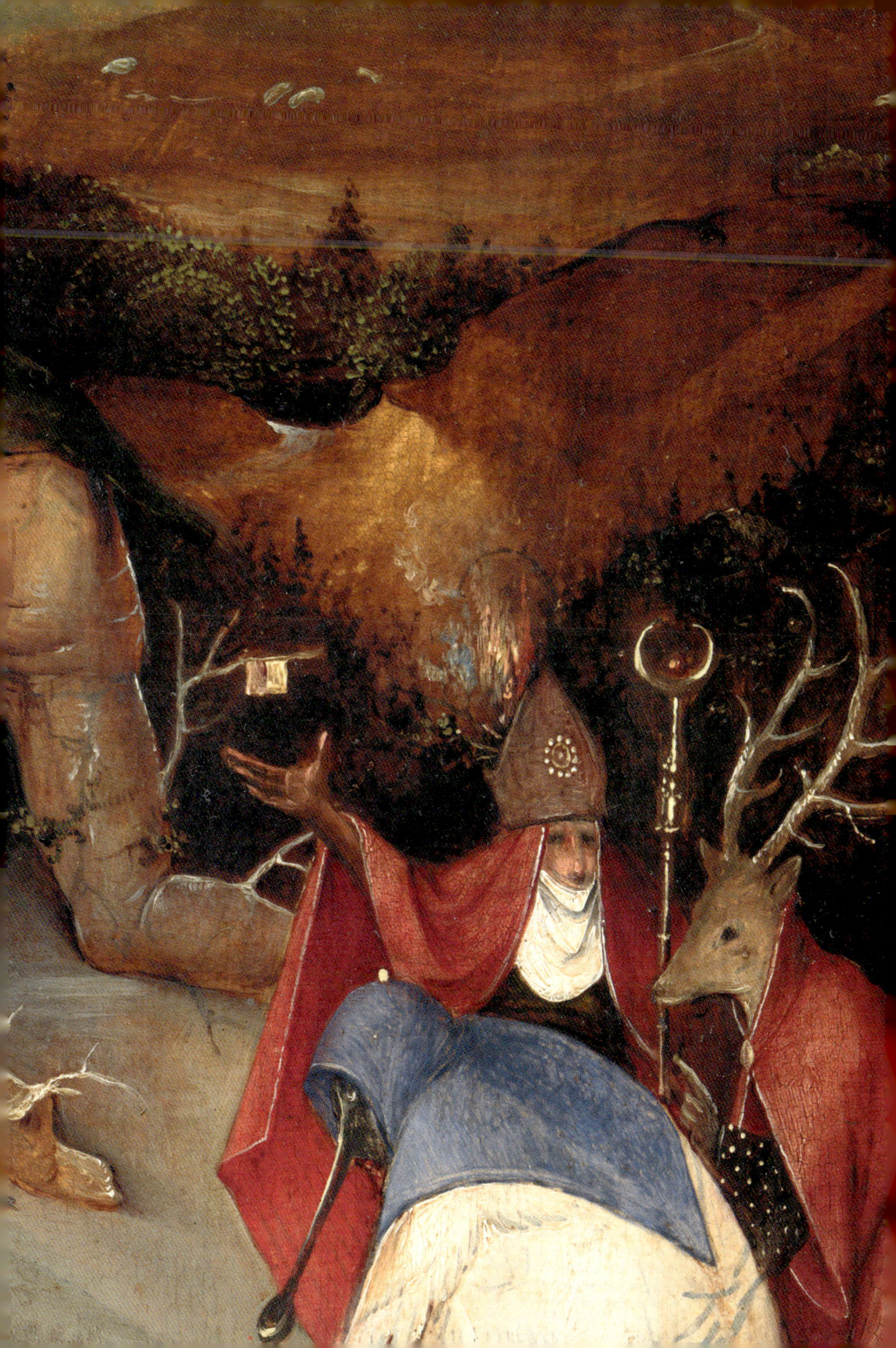

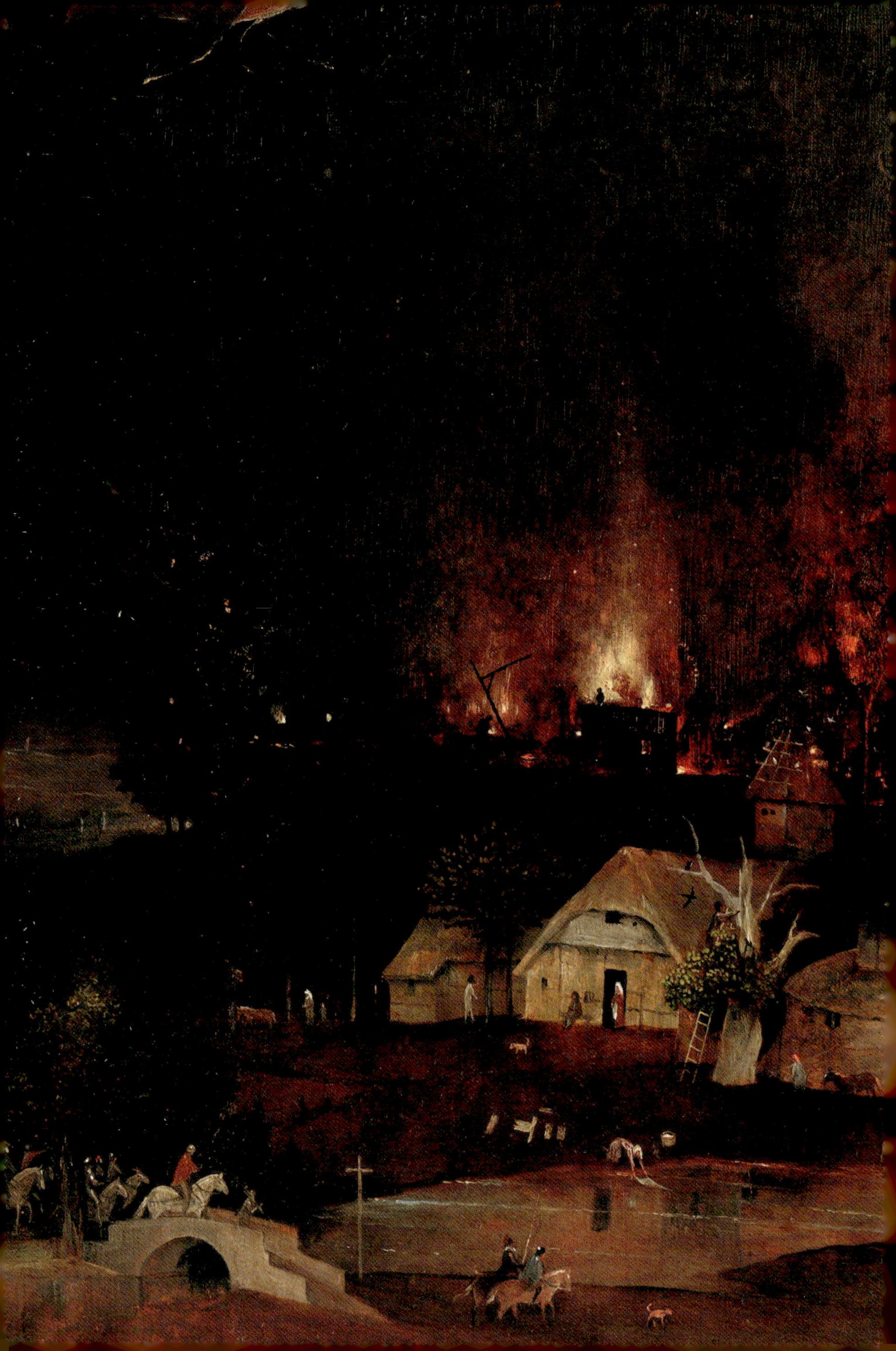

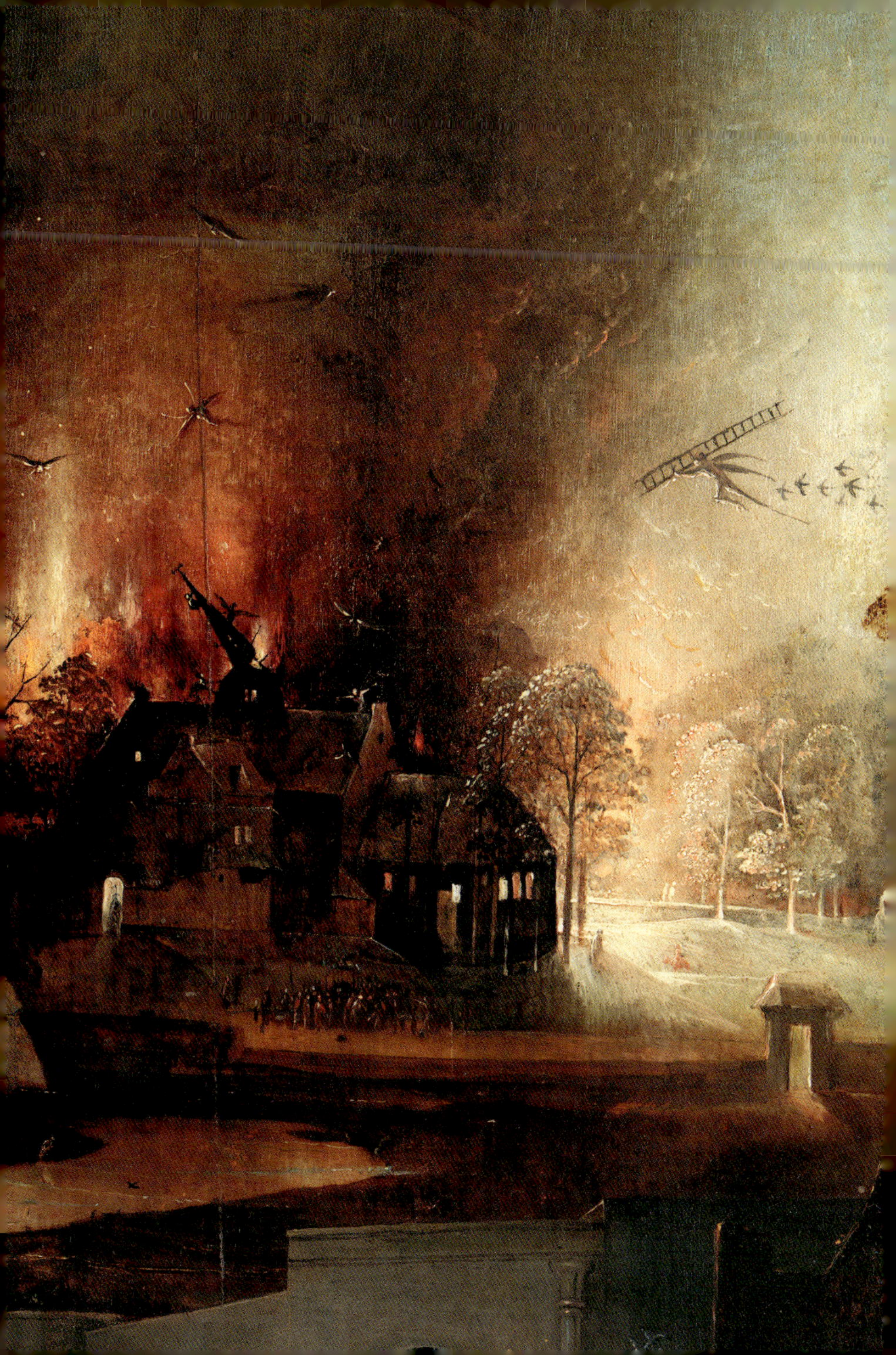

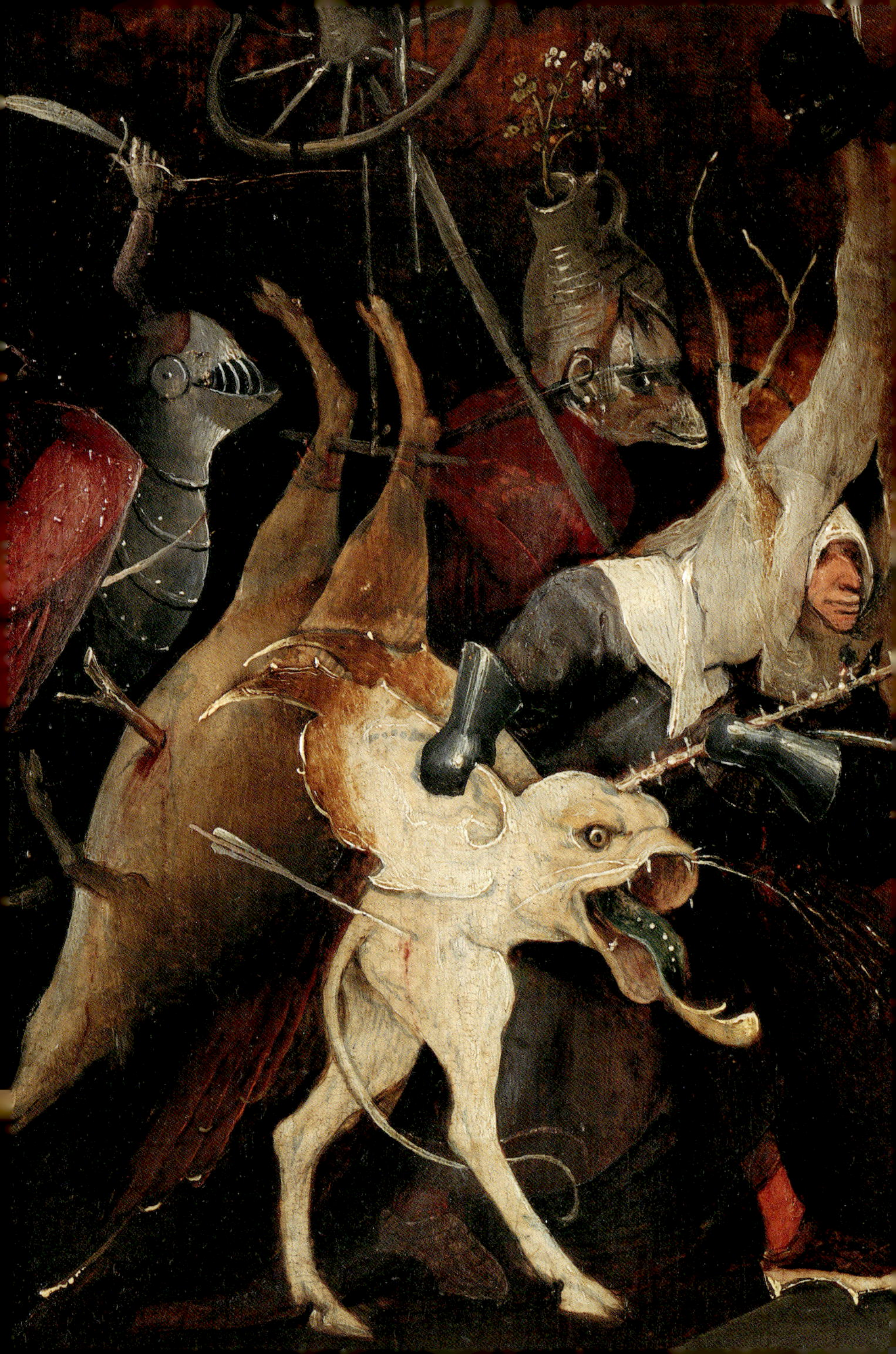

Pages 126/127, 128
Details from: **Temptation of St Anthony**, *c.* 1502
Central panel: **The Temptation of St Anthony** (see ill. pp. 118/119)

Pages 131, 132/133
Details from: **Temptation of St Anthony**, *c.* 1502
Central panel: **The Temptation of St Anthony** (see ill. pp. 118/119)

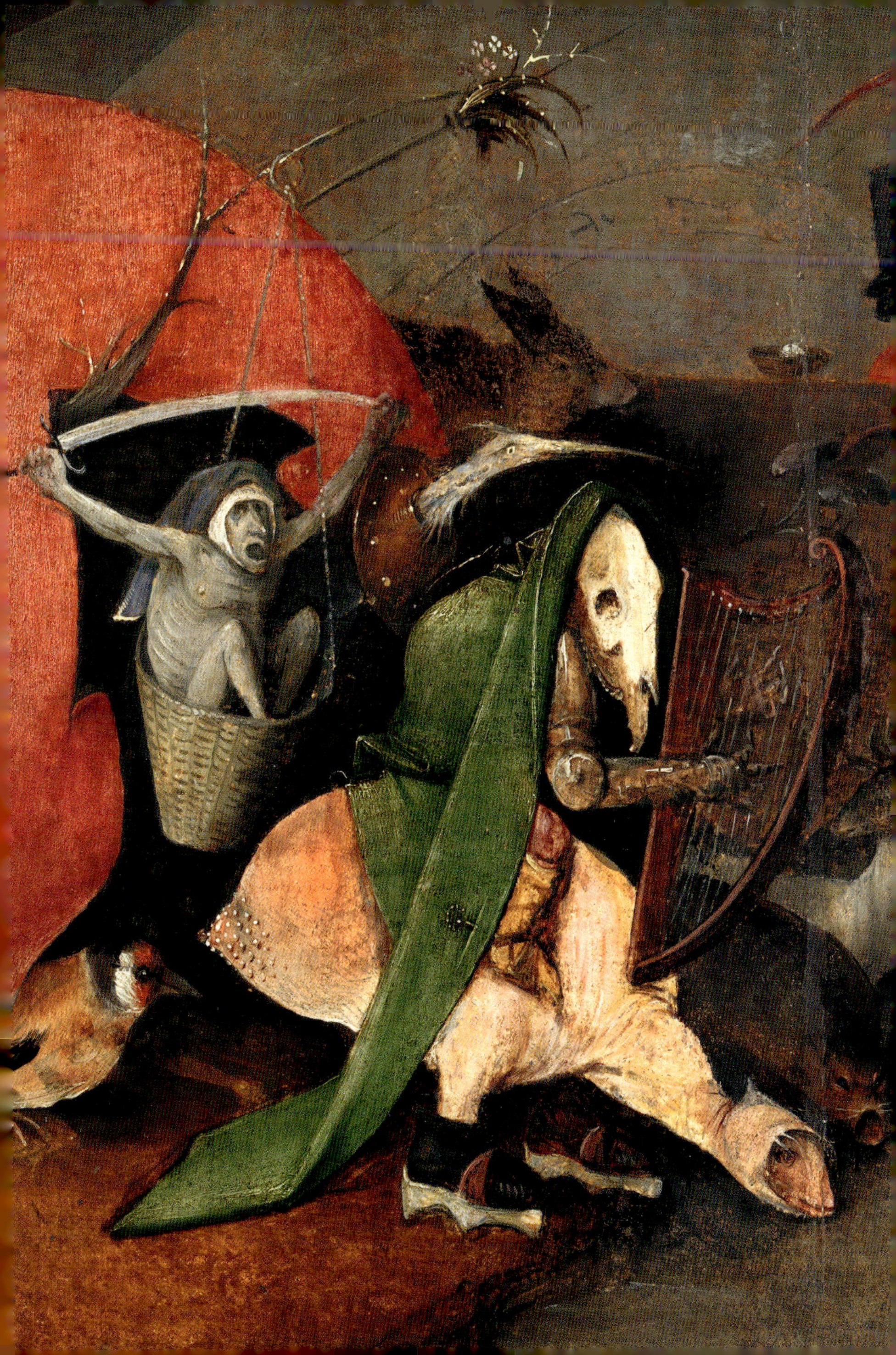

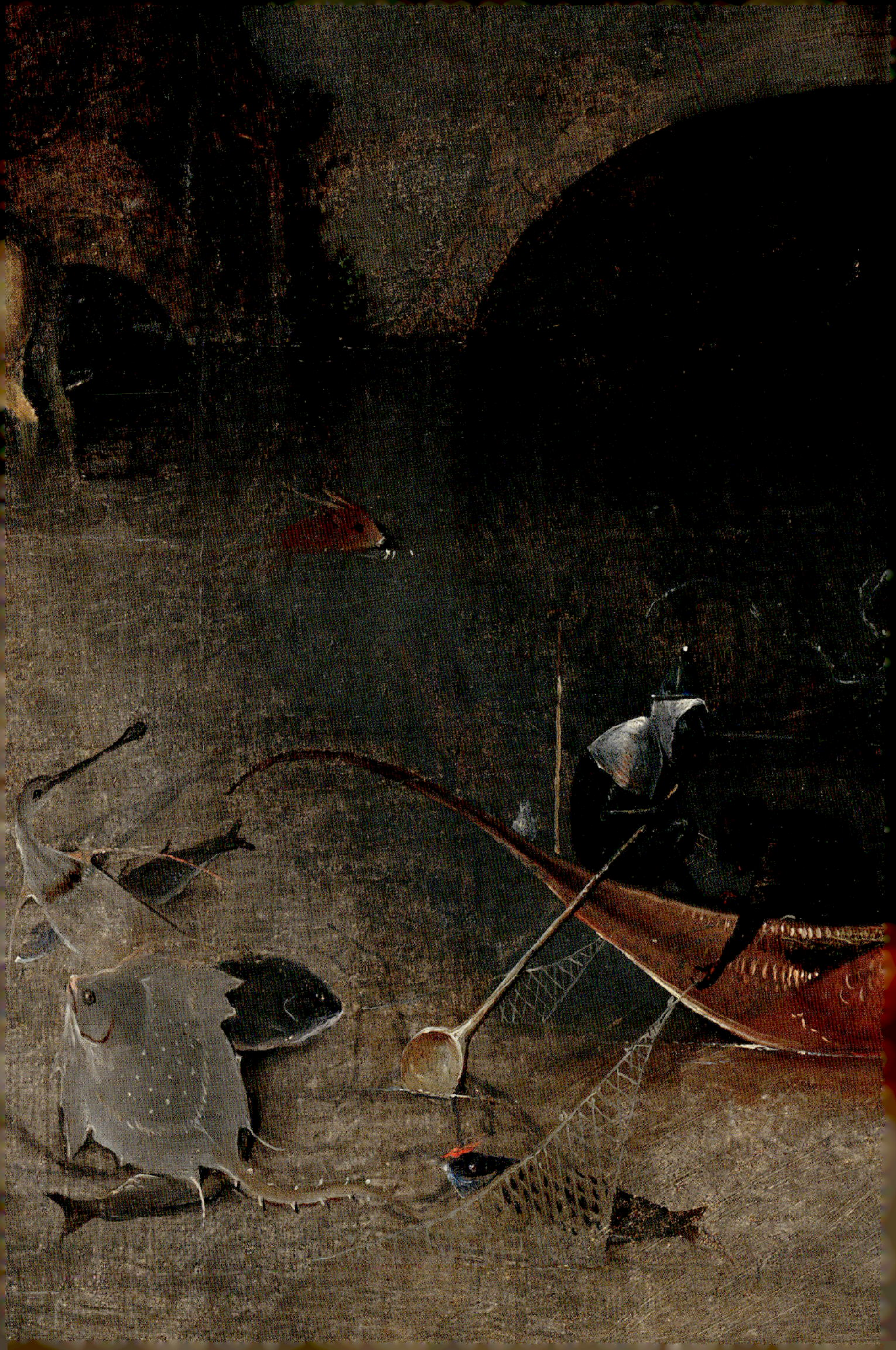

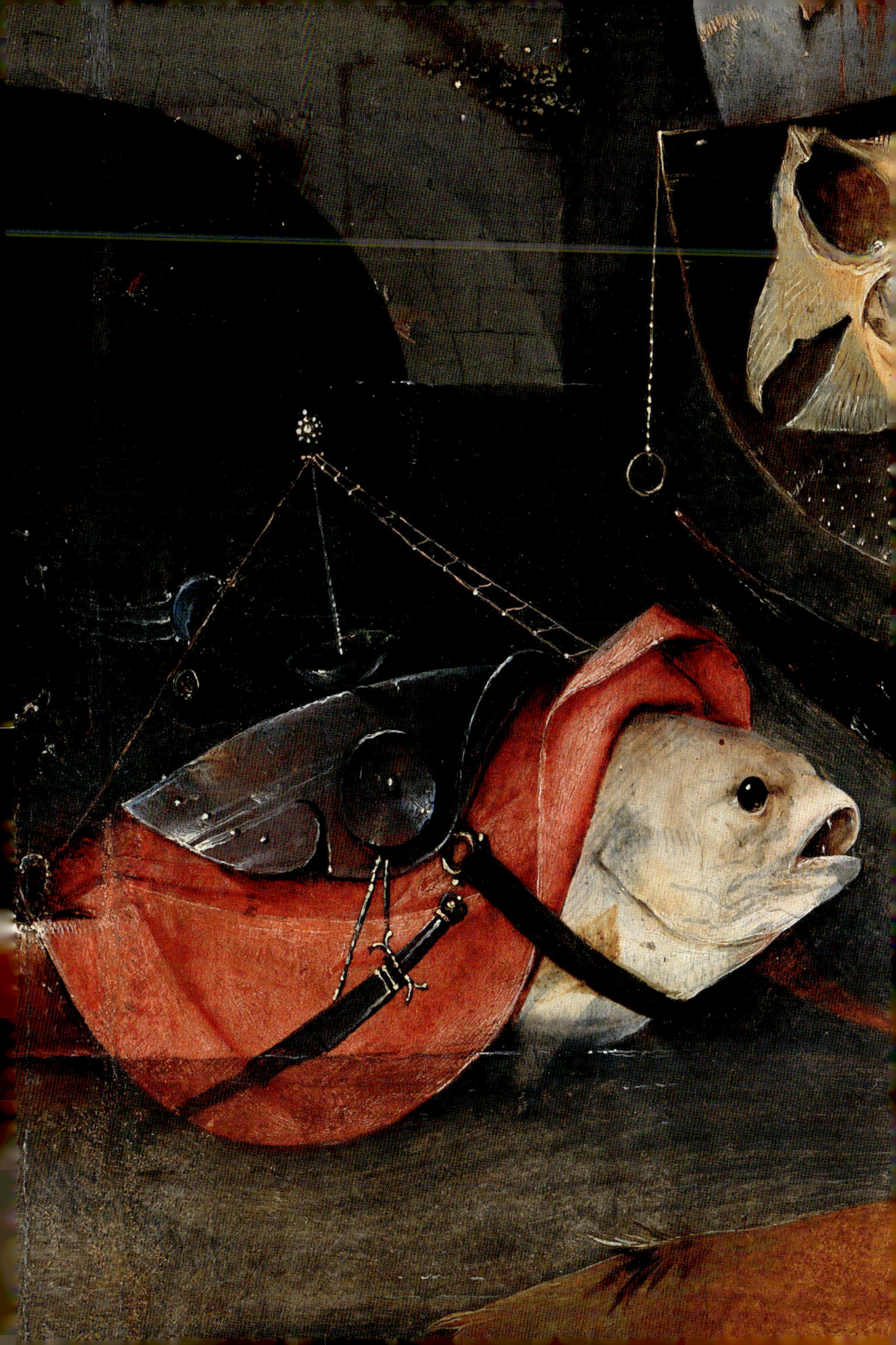

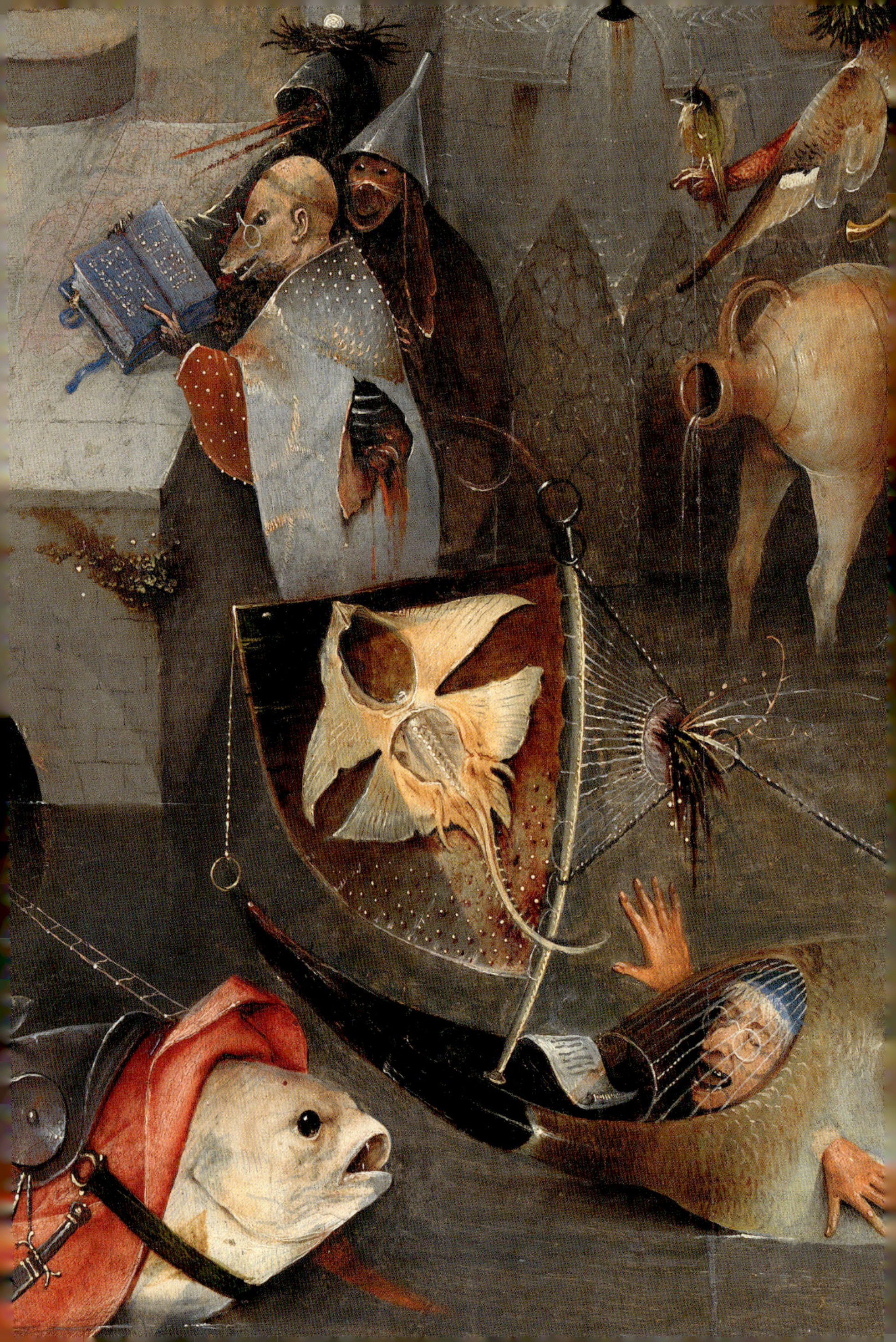

Detail from: **Temptation of St Anthony**, *c.* 1502
Central panel: **The Temptation of St Anthony**
(see ill. pp. 118/119)

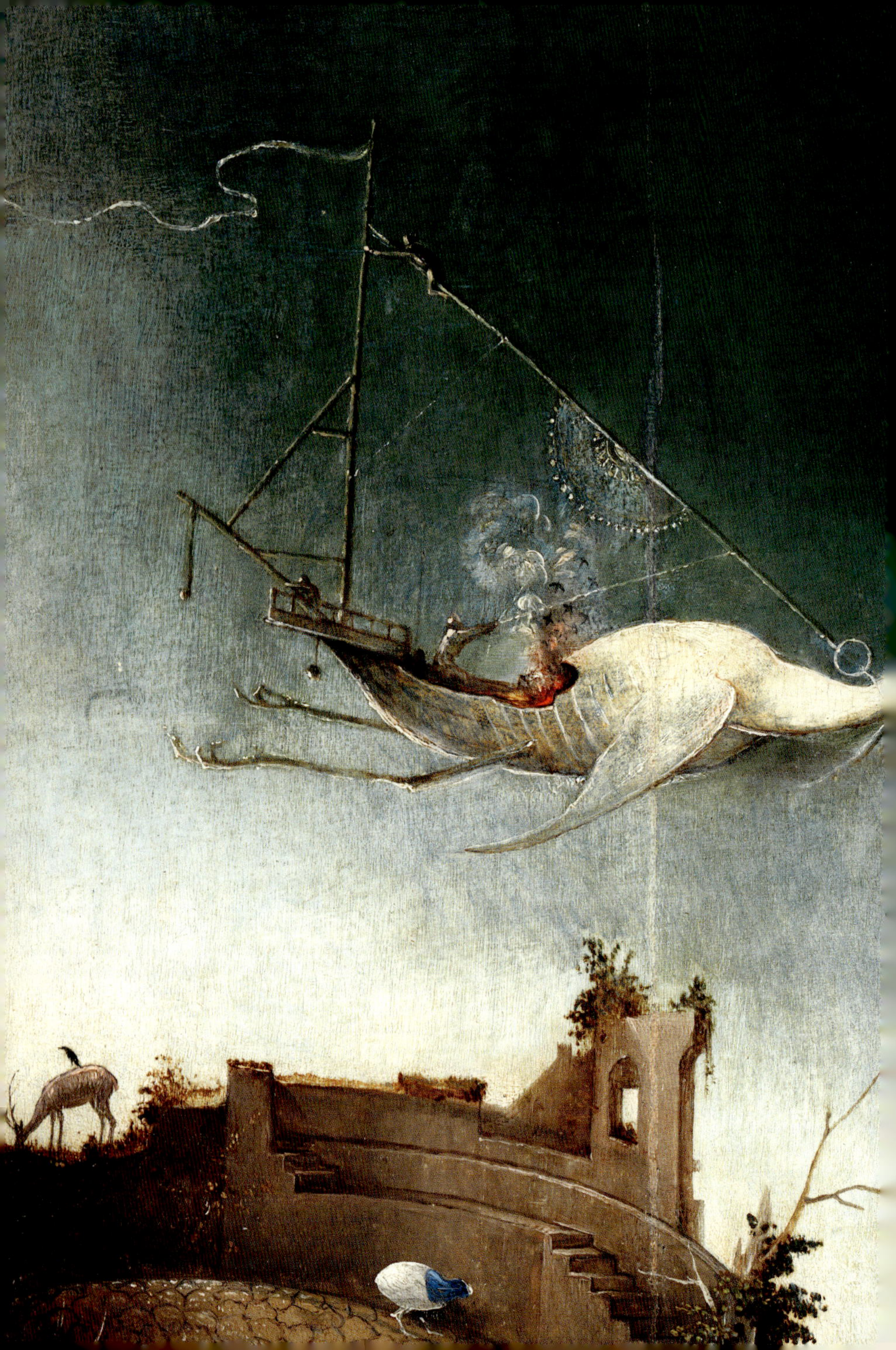

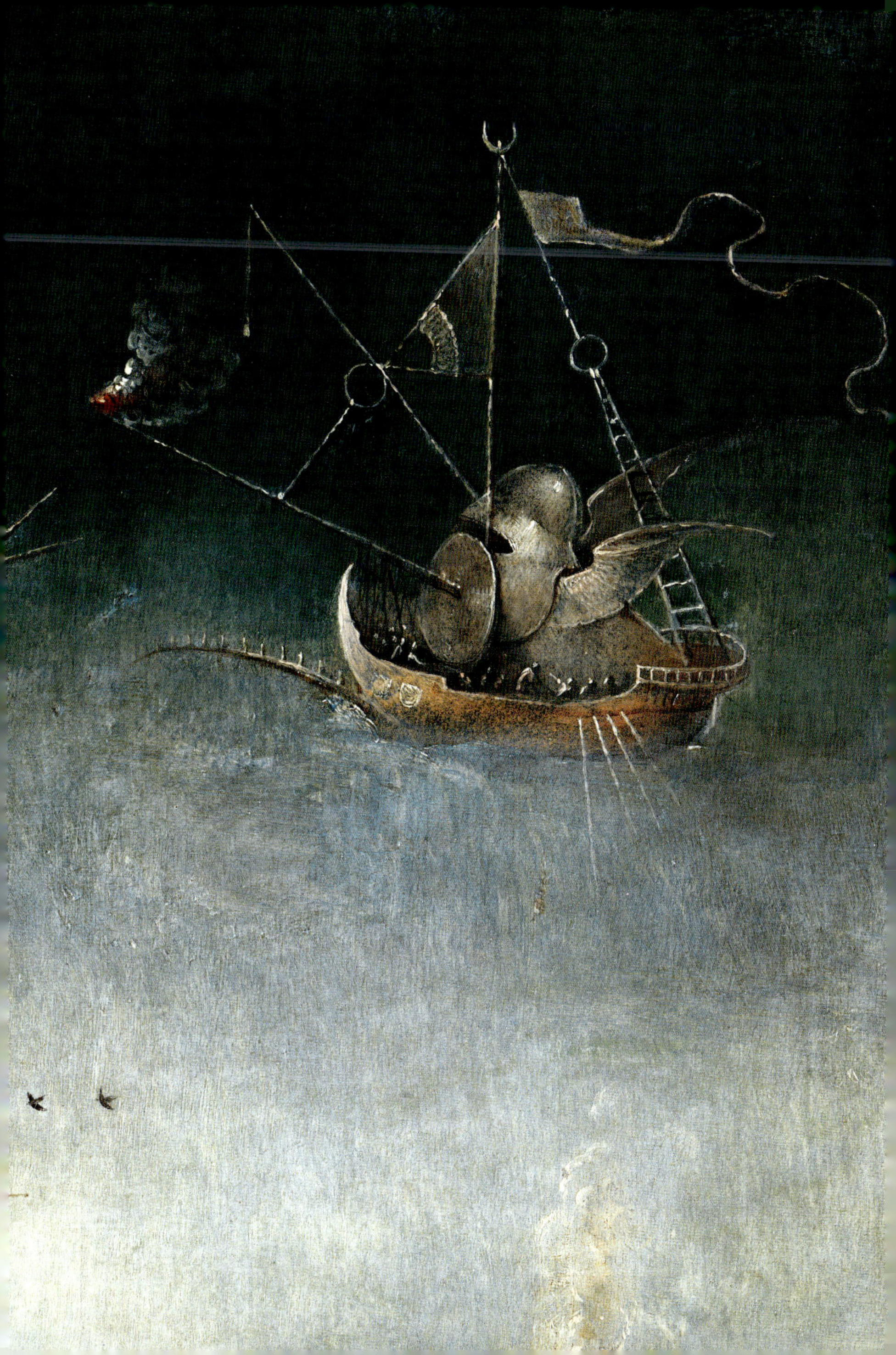

Pages 136/137, 139
Detail from: **Temptation of St Anthony**, *c.* 1502
Central panel: **The Temptation of St Anthony**
Right inner wing: **St Anthony in Meditation** (see ill. pp. 118/119)

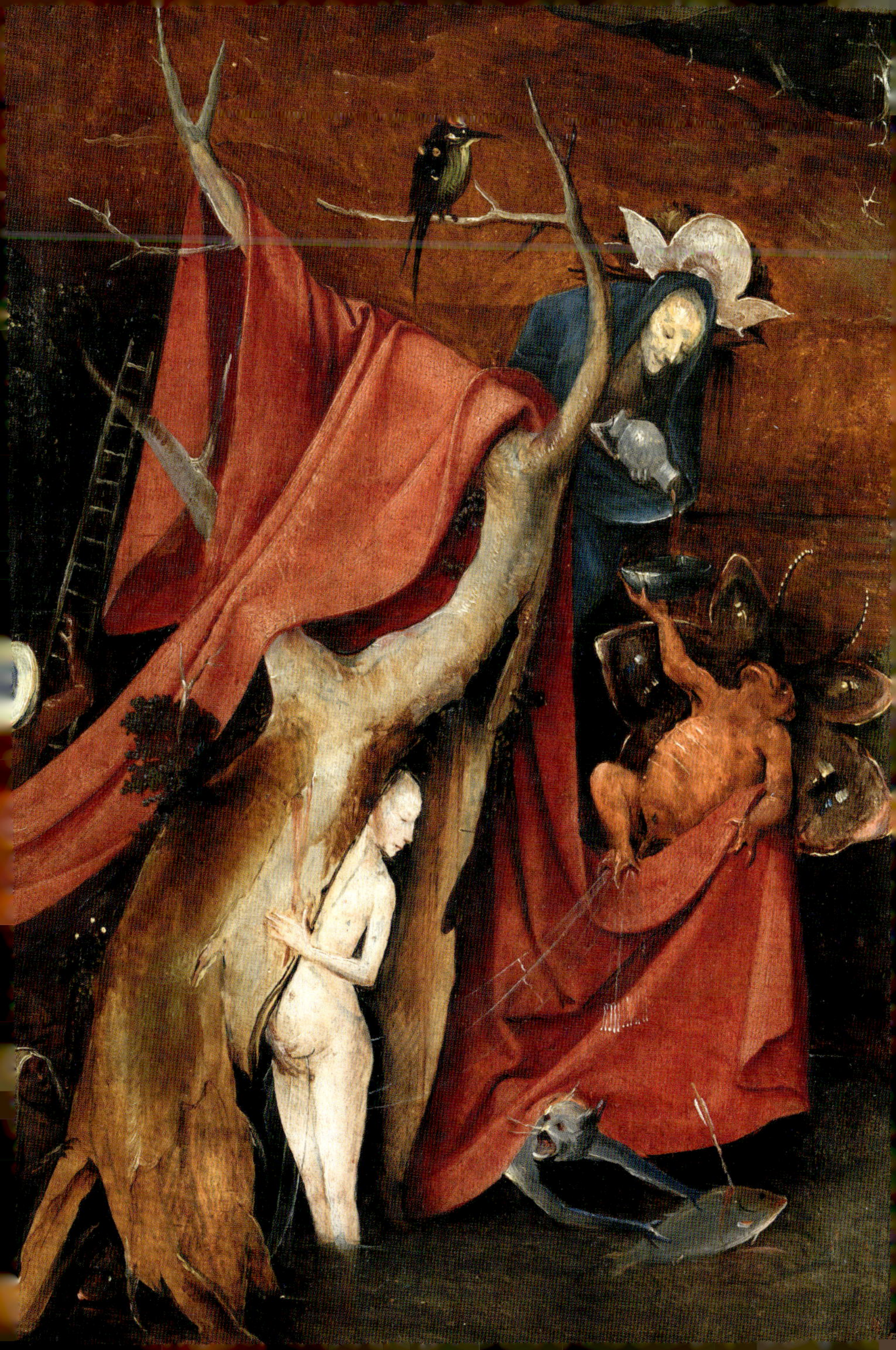

IV.

Nuptial art: *The Garden of Earthly Delights*

c. 1503

"Bosch is one of the very few painters who – he was indeed more than a painter! – who acquired a magic vision. He saw through the phenomenal world, rendered it transparent, and thus revealed its pristine aspect."

HENRY MILLER, 1957

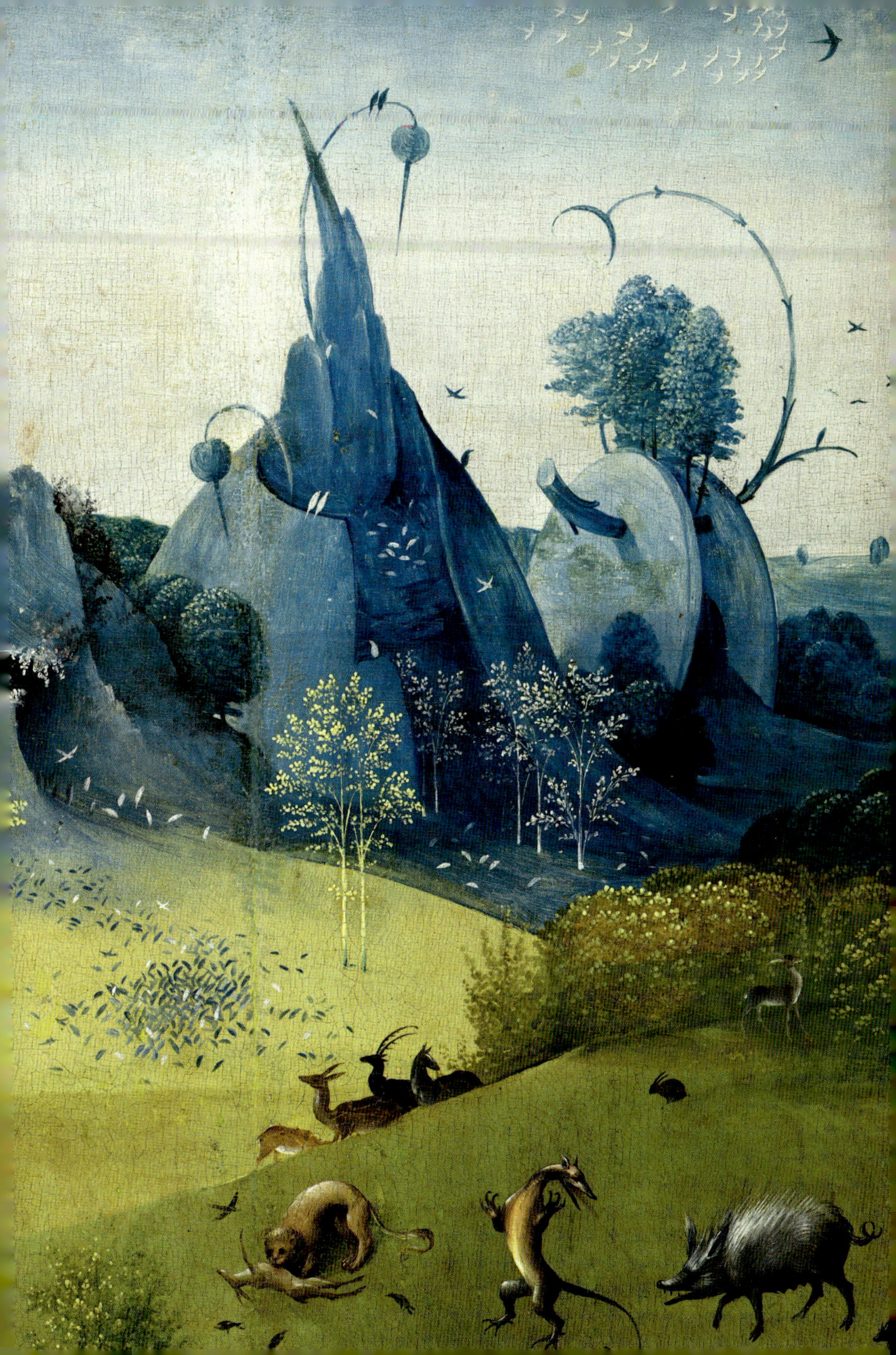

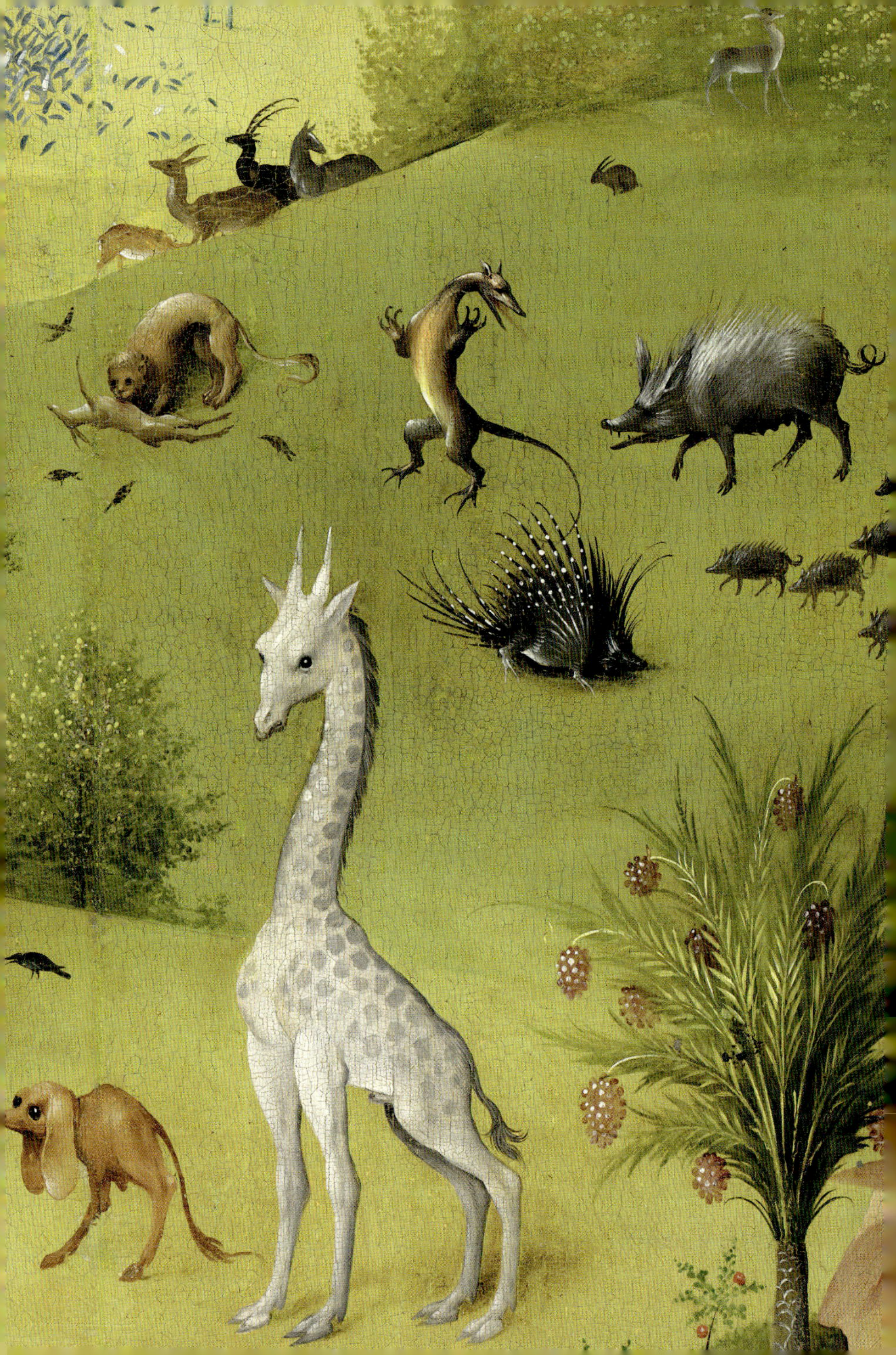

The Garden of Earthly Delights (Cat. 11), Bosch's most famous work, was in all probability painted in 1503, on the occasion of the marriage of Henry III of Nassau-Breda (p. 144); and it was intended to serve as a sort of "nuptial mirror" (*speculum nuptiorum*, Vandenbroeck 1990, p. 166, note 795), in other words as a guide to how to make a success of a marital alliance, and as an overview of its benefits and hazards. The painting is documented in 1517 as already installed in the Brussels palace of the Nassau family. The triptych, whose thematic material is based without doubt on the Bible and biblical exegesis, presents a succession of four directly related views. The *Creation of the World up to the Third Day* plays out across the two exterior shutters in the closed position. *Paradise and the Creation of Eve* are seen in the left inner wing. *Humankind before the Flood* is in the central panel. And *Hell* is in the right inner wing. According to Baldass in his early and highly perceptive analysis of the triptych, the *Garden of Earthly Delights* shows both "chronological and causally dependent events in the history of the world and humankind" and "simultaneously imagined possibilities of the state of the soul" thereby representing a "didactic, moralising *vanitas* world picture" (Baldass 1959, p. 234 f.). The function and intention of Bosch's triptych must be understood in a broader context, however, to include the dual aims of instructing and entertaining the viewer, encapsulated in the notion of *docere et delectare* (to instruct and to delight). This regularly invoked formula provided an important basis, and indeed legitimation, for secular poetry and the visual arts in the late Middle Ages and early Renaissance (cf. Raupp 1986, pp. 126–133; Fischer 2009, pp. 245–273). The phrase ultimately goes back to Horace, who observed in his *Ars poetica* V, 333–334: "*Aut prodesse volunt aut delectare poetae / aut simul et iucunda et idonea dicere vitae*" ("Poets aim either to benefit, or to amuse, or to utter words at once both pleasing and helpful to life ").

The earliest mention of the "pleasing" effect of the *Garden of Earthly Delights* is found in the journal kept by Antonio de Beatis, an Italian canon who accompanied Cardinal Louis d'Aragon (1475–1519) on a trip through Germany and the Low Countries, France and Italy. In July 1517 – barely a year after Bosch's death – their travels took them to the palace of Henry III of Nassau in Brussels. De Beatis writes of the *Garden of Earthly Delights*: "There are also some other panels with fanciful themes, on which seas, skies, woods, landscapes and many other things are reproduced, including people coming out of a sea-shell, others being excreted by cranes, women and men and white and black in various acts and states, birds and animals of all sorts and of great naturalness, the whole thing pleasing and fantastical in such a way that it is almost impossible to describe it properly to someone who has never

Pages 141, 142
Details from: **The Garden of Earthly Delights**, *c.* 1503
Left inner wing: **Paradise and the Creation of Eve** (see ill. p. 188)

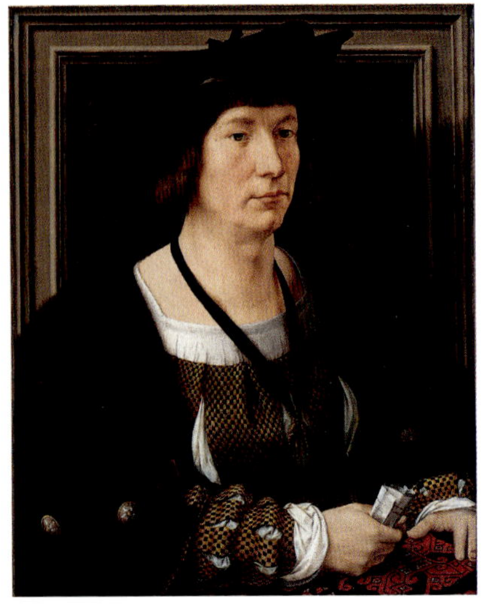

seen it." De Beatis emphasises the triptych's artistic and entertainment value in so far as he uses words such as *bizzerie* (fanciful themes), *piacevole* (pleasing) and *fantastiche* (fantastical). He also stresses the variety of motifs and rich diversity of figural scenes. In acknowledging, finally, how difficult it was to convey an accurate impression of the triptych, de Beatis also underlines the astonishing qualities of the work's depiction and the impossibility of doing it justice in words.

De Beatis's account also provides further information about the palace context within which the *Garden of Earthly Delights* appeared. The chamber in which the work hung was also decorated with other "most beautiful pictures", among them the well-proportioned nude figures of Hercules and Deianira,"and the story of Paris with the three goddesses, most perfectly worked" ("*In quello sono bellissime picture, et tra le altre uno Hercule con Dehyanira nudi di bona statura, et la historia di Paris con le tre dee perfectissimamente lavorate*"; de Beatis 1905, p. 116, line 30 f.). The *Hercules and Deianira* mentioned by de Beatis was probably one of the first mythological paintings by Jan Gossaert (known as Jan Mabuse, 1478–1532), produced in the years following his trip to Italy (1508/09) as part of Henry III's retinue. This is, however, unlikely to be the panel dating from 1517 and now in Birmingham (p. 146), in view of the latter's small size. The *Judgement of Paris* also mentioned by de Beatis was probably painted by Lucas Cranach, who explored the subject as a woodcut in 1508 and in several paintings from *c.* 1512/14 (for example, p. 147). Common to all three works is a moralising erotic content and an interest in the representation of the naked human body. Their subject is the relationship between the sexes and the sometimes fatal consequences for a man having a relationship with a woman. The moral of all three paintings is that beauty and feminine charms dazzle men's senses and unleash their desires. Hercules dies as a result of his own jealous bride's revenge, while Paris provokes the Trojan War by awarding the golden apple to Aphrodite and then by receiving Helen in return. Adam is expelled from Paradise because he follows Eve's suggestion rather than God's commandment. While the

Jan Gossaert, **Henry III of Nassau-Breda**, *c.* 1516/17
Oil on panel, 57.2 x 45.8 cm / 22½ x 18 in. Fort Worth, Kimbell Art Museum

Garden of Earthly Delights is alone in signalling the hazards of earthly love, all three paintings invoke the subject of the power of women and can thus serve to warn male viewers not to surrender to carnal desires. At the same time they hold up before our eyes the ideal beauty of the female body and are themselves a visual feast. That the interior furnishings of the Nassau palace, including the paintings on its walls, were intended to serve the pleasure and entertainment of guests can also be deduced from the diary entry of another foreign visitor: when Dürer visited the palace in 1520, he wrote enthusiastically about secret doors, a meteorite in the courtyard and a huge bed "which 50 people could lie in".

The description provided by de Beatis in his journal was followed just under a century later by the moralising exegesis of the *Garden of Earthly Delights* offered by José de Sigüenza, author of the first very detailed analysis of the triptych. Writing around 1605, Sigüenza interpreted the human figures, animals and plants in terms of the deadly sins and the transience and ephemerality of all earthly things, and thus along the same lines as many art historians of the 20th century. To appreciate the difference between the texts by de Beatis and Sigüenza from the point of view of art historiography, it is important to bear in mind the different periods in which each was written and the different intellectual backgrounds of their authors. De Beatis, who stresses the visually eye-catching and astonishing aspects of the picture, was a secular cleric and secretary whose duties were probably administrative. He saw the triptych only briefly and wrote down his impressions of it from memory later the same day. Sigüenza, on the other hand, who emphasises the moral and contemplative function and intention of the triptych, was a monk and chaplain who had the opportunity to study the work again and again. The polarity between the responses of de Beatis and Sigüenza to the *Garden of Earthly Delights* can thus be explained by the different circumstances of their respective encounters with the picture and their different perspectives as viewers. Both praise the artist; but, whereas Sigüenza sees Bosch as a good Christian painter, for de Beatis Bosch's triptych satisfies more general aesthetic interests and needs.

The exterior view, executed in grisaille and spanning both shutters (pp. 186/187, Cat. 11.1), shows Creation at the end of the third day in accordance with its description in Genesis 1:1–13. At God's command, the light has been divided from the darkness, the waters under the firmament from the waters above, and the land from the seas. God then created the vegetation: "plants yielding seed of every kind, and trees of every kind bearing fruit with the seed in it" (Gen 1:11). The world sphere, occupying almost the whole of the picture space, is not portrayed as a sequence of events, but in the form it had attained by the end of the third day. Dark clouds are gathering in the transparent vault of the sky. The lower part of the sphere is filled almost to the half-way point with water, on top of which floats the terrestrial disc, ringed by a narrow band of water. The land is flat in some places, hilly in others, and is dotted with escarpments, solitary trees and trees in groups. Strange, hollow, fruit-like

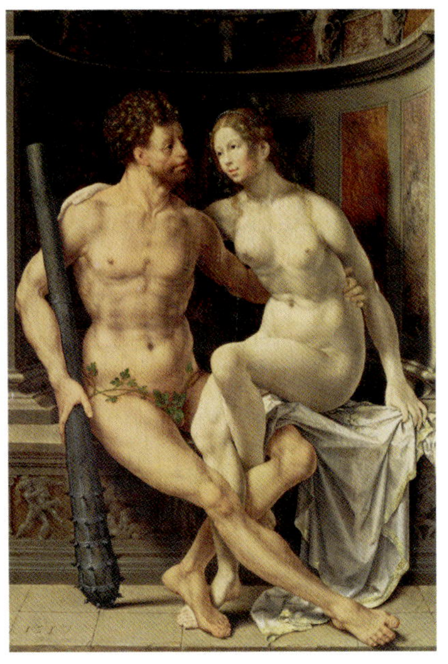

forms, pierced or bursting open and bristling with thorns, many of them curved, can be seen in the left foreground. The shape that Bosch has here given to the Earth's surface is unique in pictorial tradition and has been interpreted by Bax and Vandenbroeck, in line with contemporary late-medieval literature, as a symbol of fertility and sexuality. Bosch portrays the world sphere as a combination of the two pictorial types that were familiar in his day: the transparent globe and the terrestrial disc. The black background lightens in the top left spandrel; and here God is seated in the clouds, wearing a tiara and holding an open book (p. 182). His right hand with its pointing index finger adopts the gesture conventionally understood to indicate speaking. The inscription running across the top of both outer wings is taken from Psalm 33:9. It proclaims: "*Ipse dicit et facta sunt, Ipse mandavit et creata sunt*" ("For he spoke, and it was done; he commanded, and it stood fast"). The representation of God resembles that in Hartmann Schedel's *Chronicle of the World* (p. 183).

The paradise wedding

The left inner wing of the *Garden of Earthly Delights* (p. 188, Cat. 11.2) depicts the sixth day of Creation (Genesis 1: 20–31). Visually dominating the lower half of the panel in terms of colour and composition is the central figure of God, here in the person of Christ, standing between Adam and Eve and turned towards the viewer. Christ holds Eve, who kneels to the right (Christ's own left), by her right wrist and presents her to Adam, who sits upright on the grassy slope to the left (Christ's own right).

Adam's seated position and Eve's kneeling pose recall the traditional iconography of God calling forth Eve, as frequently found in representations of the Creation. But it is clear that Eve has long since emerged out of the side of her future husband and that

Jan Gossaert, **Hercules and Deianira**, 1517
Oil on panel, 36.8 x 26.6 cm / 14½ x 10½ in. Birmingham, University of Birmingham, The Barber Institute of Fine Arts

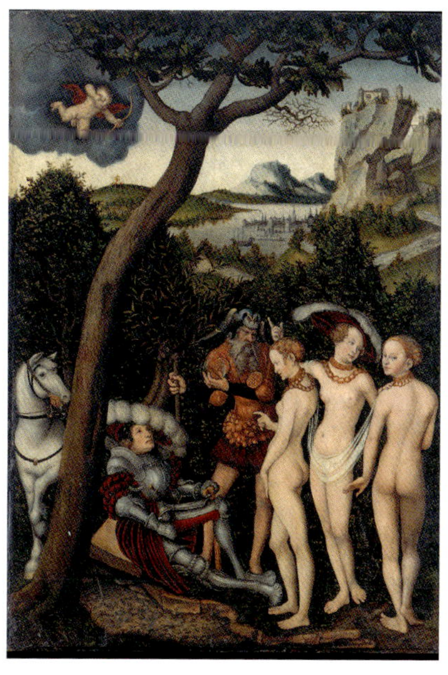

Adam has already sat up after awaking. As a moment in the biblical story occurring between the Creation of Eve (cf. Cat. 13.3, 20.2) and the more rarely portrayed joining of Adam and Eve in wedlock in the Garden of Eden (p. 163), the giving of Eve to Adam is a prototype of the sacrament of marriage (Erffa 1989, p. 158). With the gesture of Christ's raised right hand, the ideal relationship between man and woman receives divine ratification, and God's blessing upon their marriage is pronounced: "Be fruitful and multiply; fill the earth and subdue it; have dominion over the fish of the sea, over the birds of the air, and over every living thing that moves on the earth." (Gen 1:28)

Adam has woken up and is turning from inner contemplation of God to outer admiration of Eve in her pale and slender gracefulness: Eve is "already the image of temptation", Adam's gaze the "first step towards sin" (Tolnay 1965, pp. 31–32). According to St Augustine and medieval theologians, the Fall as a turning-away from God began when Adam, having continued to partake of the highest things in an ecstatic vision while asleep during the creation of Eve, cut himself off from them when, upon waking, he directed his gaze at the newly created woman and thus turned towards the world of the senses (Schade 1977, p. 475 ff.). In as far as Adam looks at Eve, he no longer submits to the will of God, but allows his own will to preside, leading him to sin. In Bosch's picture, however, the first man has not yet fallen from grace.

At the very bottom of the panel, directly underneath the first man and woman, the ground is teeming with more than a dozen birds, mythical beasts and imaginary creatures. They are frolicking in and around a dark waterhole, whose centre lies below Eve. We can recognise a genuine rebus in Bosch's representation of the *monnikvis* (monkfish) as a monk with a fish-tail reading a book. Looking at the way in which the animals are arranged in two rows across a broad strip of land underneath Adam and Eve, we may probably assume

Lucas Cranach the Elder, **The Judgement of Paris**, *c.* 1528
Oil on panel, 101.9 x 71.1 cm / 40⅛ x 28 in. New York, The Metropolitan Museum of Art, Rogers Fund 1928, inv. 28 221

that they are intended to illustrate the hierarchy of God's Creation, here still intact. Man literally appears one level higher than the birds and beasts and is also master of his own animal instincts. As attributes of the feminine, and particularly of fertility, the waterhole and the hares in front of the small burrow are specifically assigned to Eve (p. 149).

Rising behind Adam on the left edge of the panel is what we would now designate a Canary Islands dragon tree, *Draecena draco*, here imbued with a highly positive symbolism. Its brownish-red resin served as a plant remedy and a dye, among other uses. Winding its way up the trunk of the tree, most strikingly, is a vine with flat, circular leaves that resemble Communion wafers. Bosch normally uses small, amorphous dabs to depict foliage, and leaves in the shape of discs like this appear in none of his other works. Through its symbolic reference to the wine and the host of the Eucharist, the dragon tree can be identified as the third of the special trees in the Garden of Eden: the Tree of self-sacrificing Love ("*die boem der minne*", "*lignum amoris*"). Although rarely mentioned in the literature, this Tree of Love is specifically discussed by Dirc van Delf: love may here be understood as the love of God, since the combination of the tree and the vine clearly refers to the body and blood of Christ and hence also to his Sacrifice. The fact that the tree stands behind Adam underlines his particular role as the beloved likeness of God.

Appearing in miraculous fashion in the upper half of the panel, on the central vertical axis above Christ, is the fountain of paradise, here represented as a fountain of life and constructed from a wonderfully fanciful mix of architectural forms (p. 150). This motif is normally illustrated as a Romanesque or Gothic work of architecture and shows the source of the rivers of Paradise and the loveliness of the Garden of Eden. Bosch, by contrast, presents it as an essentially organic structure of the same pale red colour as Christ's robes. Five white discs recall both the five wounds of Christ and the Host as the body of Christ. In Christian exegesis the water streaming out of the fountain was often interpreted as analogous with the Blood of Christ. The shape of the fountain thus contains allusions to the Passion, the Son of God becoming man, the sacrament of the Eucharist and the divine sacrifice as part of the work of Salvation. Bosch's fountain of life thus also comes close to the pictorial tradition of allegories of Salvation, in which Christ is depicted in the fountain of life, in the wine-press, or in the mill where the host wafers were made (Marrow 1979, pp. 58–62). At the same time its organic, vegetal forms make it into an *opus naturae* (Vandenbroeck 1989, pp. 55–61), a work of nature. (This conclusion seems logical, since it was generally thought that man only acquired the ability to design and build things for himself *after* the Fall.) The precious stones at the foot of the fountain testify to its

Detail from: **The Garden of Earthly Delights**, *c.* 1503
Left inner wing: **Paradise and the Creation of Eve** (see ill. p. 188)

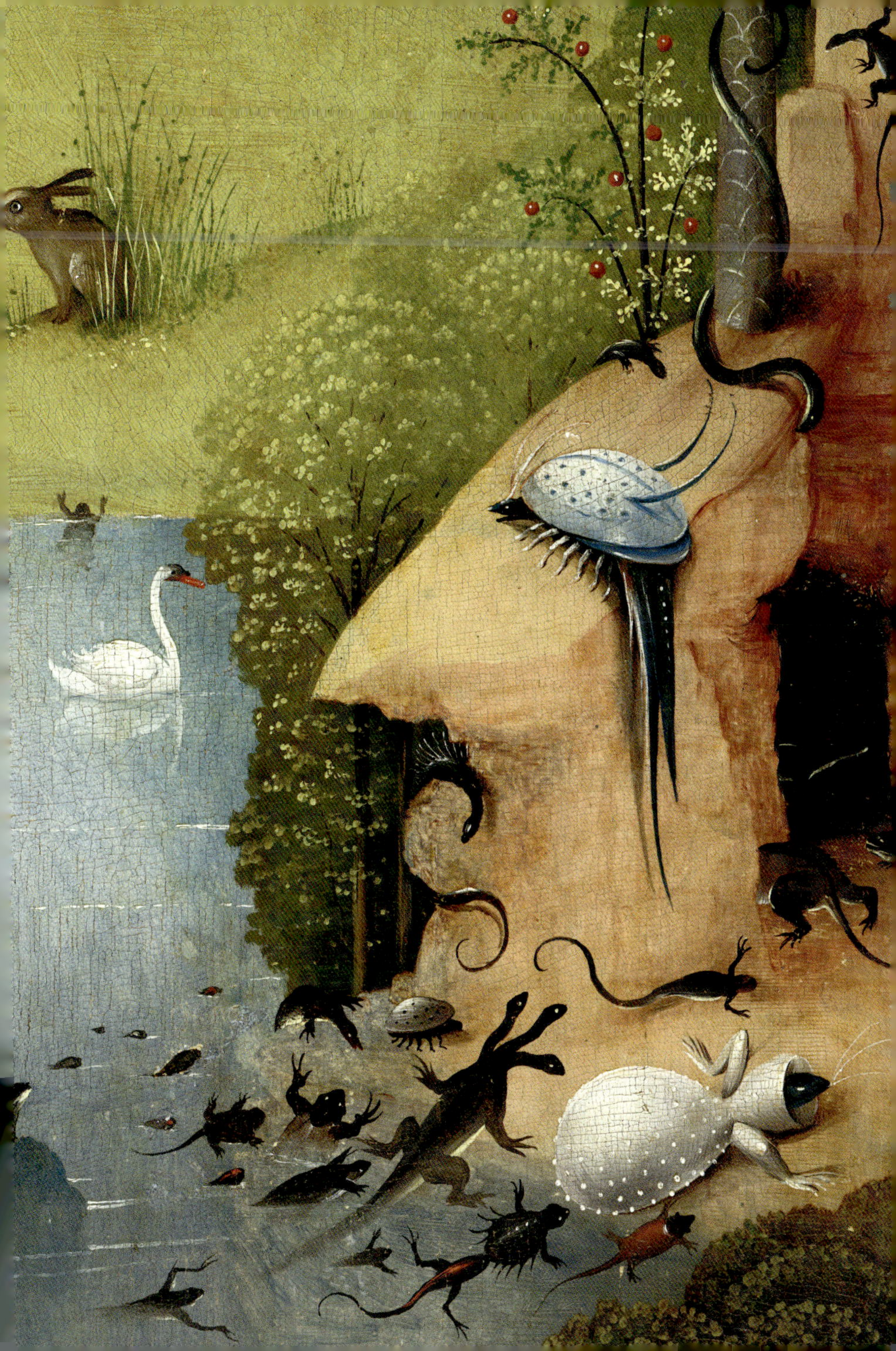

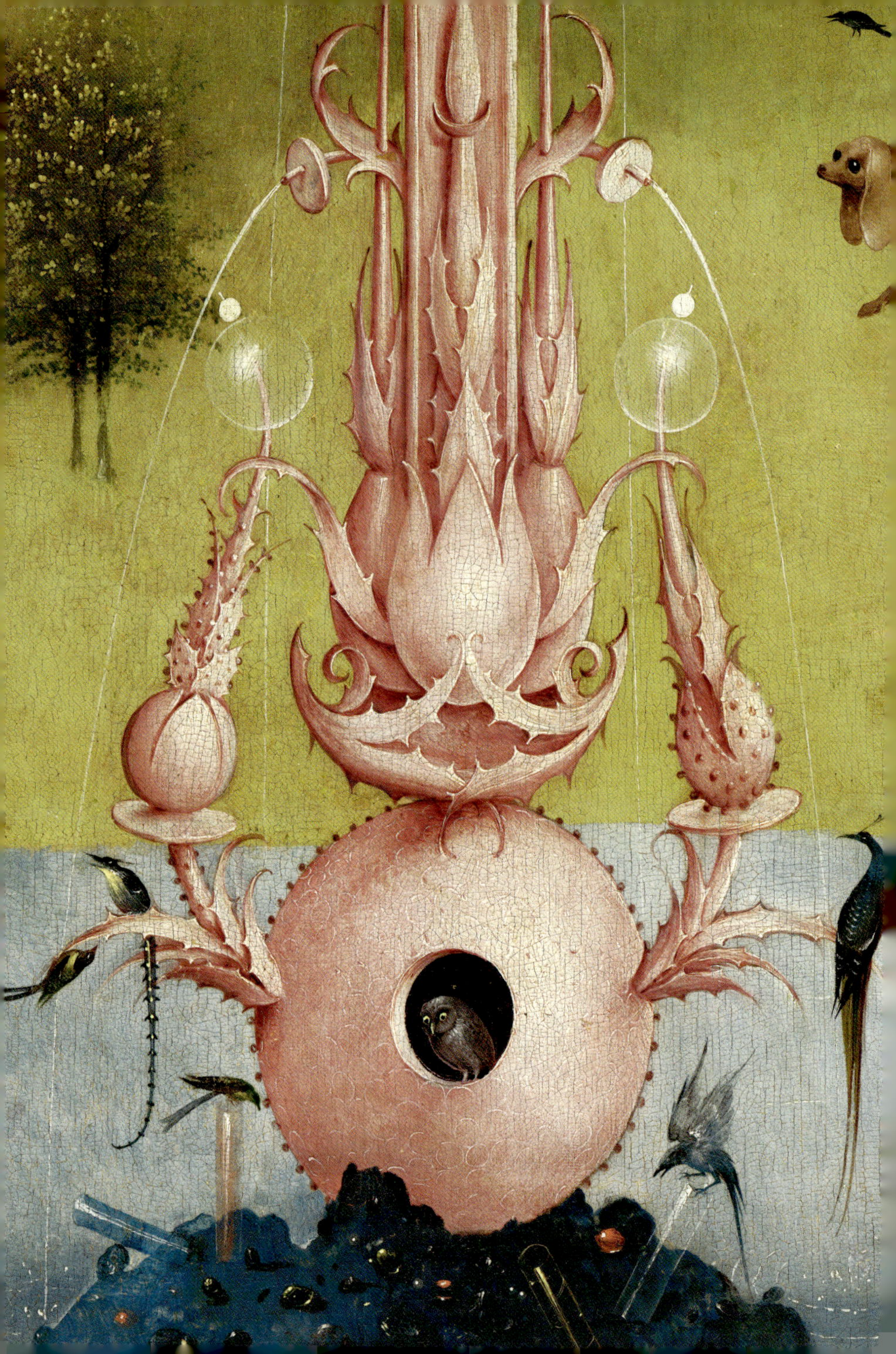

goodness and purity. They were a usual feature of literary and artistic representations of Paradise fountains in the late Middle Ages and early Renaissance. Like a picture that can present two faces, Bosch's fountain of life is thus both Christ and created nature, namely the mortal nature in which the Son of God took on human form in order to live among men until his death on the Cross.

The base of the fountain is shaped like a convex disc with a hole in the middle. Standing inside this hole is an owl. As in the drawing *The Wood Has Ears, the Field Eyes* (Cat. D3) the owl is thus located in the very centre of the panel. With its abundance of negative connotations – spiritual blindness, malevolence, sin, temptation and seduction – the owl may be interpreted in this context to mean that a potential for Evil is inherent to created and independently self-multiplying nature, an Evil to which the Son of God surrenders Himself and which is vanquished through Him. The owl embodies in very general terms the "satanic adversary of the work of redemption" (Bambeck 1987, p. 53); and it is employed by Bosch as the equivalent of the Tree of Knowledge with the serpent and the apple.

The goodness of the water springing from the fountain of life is illustrated by the hoofed animals drinking on the left edge of the panel. Particularly striking is the unicorn, which embodies virginity, chastity and purity and whose long horn (thought to be able to render poison harmless) touches the water. The unicorn is accompanied by two horses, a cow, stags and deer. The presence of these last alludes to the tormented souls seeking refuge with God, as David prays in Psalm 42:1–2:"As the deer pants for the water brooks, so pants my soul for You, O God. My soul thirsts for God, for the living God. When shall I come and appear before God?"

On the opposite, right side of the panel is a second tree, a date palm. This, like the dragon tree, bears clusters of grape-like fruit. Its identification with the Tree of Life is supported by the fact that a number of sources describe such a tree as bearing dates or, even more frequently, grapes or grape-like fruits (p. 153) and as standing at the highest point next to the fountain of paradise. This, it was believed, was the tree from which Christ's Cross would be made. The preacher Jan Brugman sought to engage his listeners with the following imagery:"Let us climb this palm tree of the Holy Cross with the bride [= the soul] and pluck its fruits" (Brugman, *Verspreide Sermoenen*, 13th sermon, lines 129–130:"*Laet ons opclymmen mitter bruut op desen palmbome des heilighen cruces ende plucken sine vruchten*").

The area below the date palm carries exclusively negative connotations. The serpent slithering down the trunk may be seen not only as a symbol of the Fall but also as the vanquished Satan. The barren rock is partly hollow and, within its green surroundings, signals

Detail from: **The Garden of Earthly Delights**, *c.* 1503
Left inner wing: **Paradise and the Creation of Eve** (see ill. p. 188)

life that has died as a consequence of sinful behaviour. Its strange shape alludes to Adam's tomb, which was said to lie on the Mount of Calvary (Golgotha, the "place of the skull"). The hill was occasionally represented quite literally in the shape of a skull, and Bosch has even given his rock a "face" seen in profile, inasmuch as he has shaped the projection on the left like a pointed nose and followed it underneath by fleshy lips, as outlined by the curving body of a second snake. Above it, a pale blue and black beetle-like animal forms the lid and eyelashes of a closed eye (p. 149). This head created out of a striking natural feature would be recognised centuries later by the Surrealist Salvador Dalí (1904–1989; *The Great Masturbator*, 1929, Museo Nacional Centro de Arte Reina Sofía). But artists in the late 15th and early 16th centuries were already looking for representational objects in the amorphous shapes of mountains and clouds, veined marble and peeling plaster. This process demonstrates that imagination went (and indeed still goes) hand in hand with the associative workings of the human brain.

The negative significance of the rocky outcrop is underscored through the presence of some amphibians that have left the health-giving waters in order to crawl along and into the rock. Also notable is the peacock perched on the extreme right edge of the fountain, a bird that was considered the antagonist of the serpent. The date palm on the barren rock thus symbolises humankind's deliverance by the new Adam, Christ, from the Fall of the first Adam, and its consequences. The branch growing on the left of the palm and bearing a number of fruits can be seen as a further sign of this new life. Neither the many hideous beasts nor the animals shown hunting and eating contradict the notion of this scene as a depiction of Paradise. Firstly, because the Garden of Eden was imagined as lying somewhere between Palestine and India and as being correspondingly full of exotic and monstrous creatures. Secondly, because, according to Thomas Aquinas (*c.* 1225–1274) the animals were not changed by the Fall.

The paradise in which Christ is present, and which has been regained as a paradise of souls, is a metaphor of the soul that is close to God. This spiritual state is also reflected in the harmoniously ordered layout of Bosch's picture. In compositional terms, Christ, Adam and Eve are arranged in a clear hierarchy: to the left (on Christ's own right) Adam is seated on a hillock, as if on a natural throne, as lord of the animals his feet on his Creator's robe. To the right (on Christ's left, heraldically the lesser side) we find Eve. A similar division of the composition into a male side on the left and a female side on the right, each furnished with typical attributes, can be found in Jan van Eyck's *Arnolfini Portrait* (London, National Gallery), a painting in which the wife is assigned to the domestic sphere and the husband to the outside world. On the left inner wing of the *Garden of Earthly Delights* this male/female principle extends to the organisation of many of the landscape details. Thus the characteristics and qualities represented on the left (that is to say, on Christ's own right)

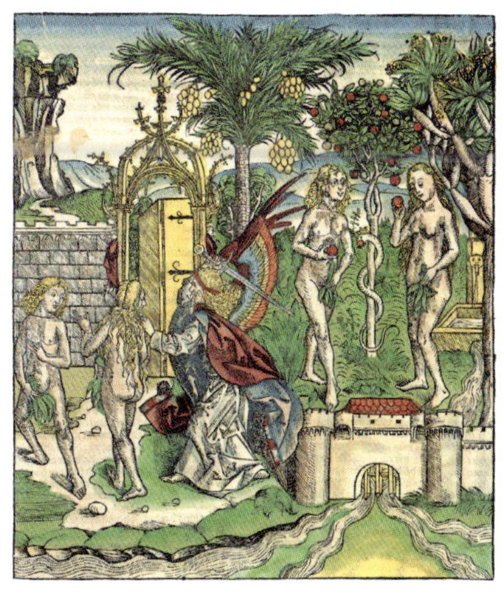

are primarily positive, while on the right (Christ's own left) we can recognise symbols of sin (Dittrich 2005, p. 506). The elephant, for example, stands for strength, intelligence, frugality, chastity and moderation. Horned animals, and ducks and birds with long beaks, also symbolise the male principle. The swan on Eve's side of the panel stands for renunciation and purity, but also for arrogance on account of its long neck. Giraffes make only rare appearances in art in the 15th century, and any symbolism they may contain remains elusive. It is interesting, however, to note the lowered head, the graceful descent of the slender neck, whose outline bends when it arrives at the giraffe's back and then runs out along the sloping spine, and lastly the rear legs, which extend backwards (p. 142). These characteristics correspond to the inclined head, kneeling pose and rounded and delicate anatomical forms characterising the representation of Eve. Gloomy hollows and the dark pond also belong to Eve's side. The landscape is generally more amorphous in its forms on the right and more geometric on the left, corresponding to matter (perceived as female) and form (understood as male). According to Aristotle (384–322 BC), whose ideas were reiterated by Bartholomeus Anglicus (*c.* 1190–1272) in his widely read *Liber de proprietatibus rerum* (On the Properties of Things, 1235), the various works of nature were born out of the interaction of these two principles. In the event of an insufficient will to form, the same two principles could give birth to the evil and the ugly. Throughout the Paradise landscape on this left inner wing, man and beast are separated and the animals grouped into categories: birds, land animals, aquatic animals. This grouping continues right into the background, with each category appearing in its appropriate habitat. The background terminates in four rock formations which assume rounded geometric forms and resemble those seen on the exterior shutters (p. 141).

The symmetry and order of the composition is also established through Bosch's use of colour. The pale flesh of Adam and Eve corresponds with the whitish grey of the elephant and giraffe stationed on either side of the fountain higher up the panel. Order, clarity and

Hartmann Schedel, **The Fall and the Expulsion from Paradise**, 1493
from: *Chronicle of the World*, fol. 7r (detail), Nuremberg 1493
Woodcut, 42 x 29 cm / 16½ x 11⅜ in. Weimar, Herzogin Anna Amalia Bibliothek

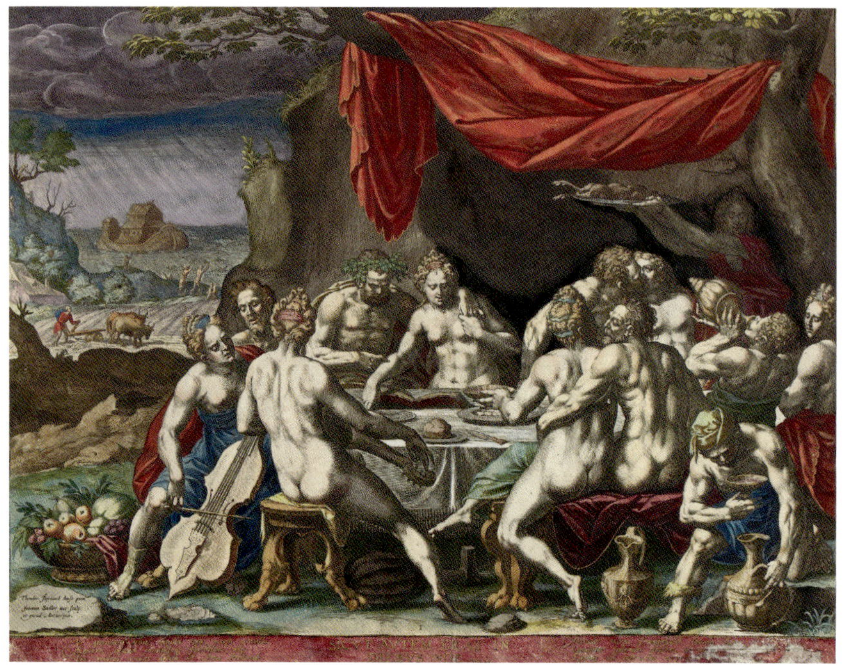

Jan Sadeler the Elder after Dirck Barendsz, **Sicut autem erat in diebus Noë**, *c.* 1581–1585
Copper engraving, 35.7 x 45.7 cm / 14 x 18 in. Amsterdam, Rijksmuseum

hierarchy signal that God's laws are in force. Christ is the representative and guarantor of divine order, of which He is Himself a part by dint of assuming physical form. As Word becomes Flesh, Christ is origin and goal. Everything around him is orientated towards Him; the entire picture, and indeed the entire triptych, unfolds outwards from His figure.

What we see in the left inner wing is not primarily the Creation or the Garden of Eden in the Old Testament sense, but the celestial paradise to which souls return as promised in the New Testament. The loss of the material security of the Garden of Eden can be overcome through the mystical union between souls and God in this heavenly sphere. Entrance to Paradise – be it for Adam and Eve or for any other Christian – is made possible through the love of humankind and the grace of God. The paradise wedding as a God-given union of love between man and woman legitimises marriage as a holy sacrament, one performed under the protection of Christ both at the spiritual and the practical level. Any possible future suffering is to be overcome through patience and love.

In terms of their narrative technique, the exterior shutters and the left inner wing may be seen as a shift from *narratio*, the re-telling of the events of the Old Testament, to *argumentatio*, a presentation of logical factual connections, which are taken up in the central panel in multiple ways. Bosch's other representations of Paradise (Cat. 13.3, 20.2) are far more conventional in that they adhere to the artistic tradition of portraying the six days of Creation as a chronological sequence, and serve simply as the prologue to the main scene in the central panel (Cat. 13.4, 20.3), which is largely self-contained.

Humankind in a false paradise

As de Beatis remarked so long ago, it is almost impossible to describe the full wealth of motifs in the central panel of the *Garden of Earthly Delights*. The composition is clearly divided into foreground, middle distance and background. Many elements repeat themselves: naked men and women (including some who are black-skinned), birds, land animals, aquatic animals, and hollow forms of a vegetal or artificial nature. Thematically, the central panel is based on the notion of *Humankind before the Flood* (Cat. 11.3), which in Bosch's day was considered a historical period, as described in Genesis 6:1–5: "Now it came to pass, when men began to multiply on the face of the earth, and daughters were born to them, that the sons of God saw the daughters of men, that they were beautiful; and they took wives for themselves of all whom they chose. And the Lord said, 'My Spirit shall not strive with man forever, for he is indeed flesh; yet his days shall be one hundred and twenty years.' There were giants on the earth in those days, and also afterward, when the sons of God came in to the daughters of men and they bore children to them. Those were the mighty men who were of old, men of renown. Then the Lord saw that the wickedness of man was great in the earth, and that every intent of the thoughts of his heart was only evil continually." This passage is taken up in the New Testament in Matt. 24:37–39 (and similarly in Luke 17:26–27 and 2 Peter 3:5–7): "But as the days of Noah were, so also will the coming of the Son of Man be. For as in the days before the flood, they were eating and drinking, marrying and giving in marriage, until the day that Noah entered the ark, and did not know until the flood came and took them all away, so also will the coming of the Son of Man be."

Although it is hard to trace a pictorial tradition for the subject of *Humankind before the Flood* within printmaking and painting of the 15th to 17th centuries, several examples can be found of the themes of *The Flood* and *Sicut erat in diebus Noë*. Based on the Old Testament, representations of the Flood typically show humankind's desperate attempts to escape the rising waters by taking to boats, clinging to pieces of flotsam and scaling trees and rocks, as seen in *The Flood* (Madrid, Museo Nacional del Prado) by Jan van Scorel (1495–1562) and to a certain extent on the right inner wing of the *Garden of Earthly Delights*. In the 17th and 18th centuries, both paintings hung in the Escorial, and specifically in the Galería de la Infanta, the picture gallery assigned to the ladies' apartments (Bassegoda 2002, p. 367). It is likely that the two shutters that have come down to us as fragments (Cat. 19) were once part of a triptych showing the Flood on its lost central panel. The second theme, *Sicut erat in diebus Noë*, meaning "Thus it was in the days of Noah" and based on Matthew 24, can be seen in an engraving (p. 154) after Dirck Barendsz (1534–1592), which shows a company of naked men and women indulging in food, drink and love. In line with this *Sicut erat in diebus Noë* theme, Bosch's central panel shows the likewise sinfully indulgent activities of men and women unaware of the impending Deluge, but in an incomparably more poetic fashion than in the work by Barendsz.

The history of humankind before the Flood, condensed into just a few obscure verses in the Book of Genesis, was substantially embellished in the writings of medieval authors, for example, in the *Historia Scholastica* (*c.* 1170) by Petrus Comestor (*c.* 1100–1178), the *Spiegel Historiael* (*c.* 1260) by Jacob van Maerlant (*c.* 1225–*c.* 1299), or the *Tafel van den Kersten Ghelove* (*c.* 1400) by Dirc van Delf. These texts all agree that the first age of man, which lasted from Adam to the Flood and Noah, was ruled by lust. The good descendants of Adam and his third son, Seth, succumbed to the wicked daughters descended from Cain, whereupon all humankind fell into sinful ways, and above all to lust. From this union, the race of giants was born – an idea that may have inspired Bosch's tree giant on the right inner wing (p. 213, Cat. 11.4). Several figures in the central panel are portrayed as black-skinned, a characteristic often associated with the fratricidal Cain and his descendants and intended as a mark of infamy (p. 195).

The three figures in the cave in the lower right corner of the central panel form a pictorial counterpart for the situation on the left inner wing and constitute a key scene in their own right as well (p. 207). Their identification with Adam, Eve and Noah (Bax 1956; see Fischer 2002b, pp. 28–29), the protagonists of the beginning and end of the first age, is based, in part, upon their facial expressions and gestures. Adam points ostentatiously at Eve, as if to blame her for the state in which humanity finds itself. In doing so he looks straight out of the picture, thereby reinforcing the fact that he is speaking directly to the viewer. Eve, meanwhile, dressed like Adam in an animal pelt, holds a fruit. Adam and Eve were regularly portrayed in medieval Christian art dressed in animal skins or cloaked in their own long hair in front of a hut or cave, as a sign of their expulsion from Paradise and their primitive status. Noah, the primogenitor of post-Deluge humanity, looks out over Adam's shoulder and wears leaves on his head, identifying him as the first wine-grower.

Detail from: **The Garden of Earthly Delights**, *c.* 1503
Central panel: **Humankind before the Flood** (see ill. pp. 190/191)

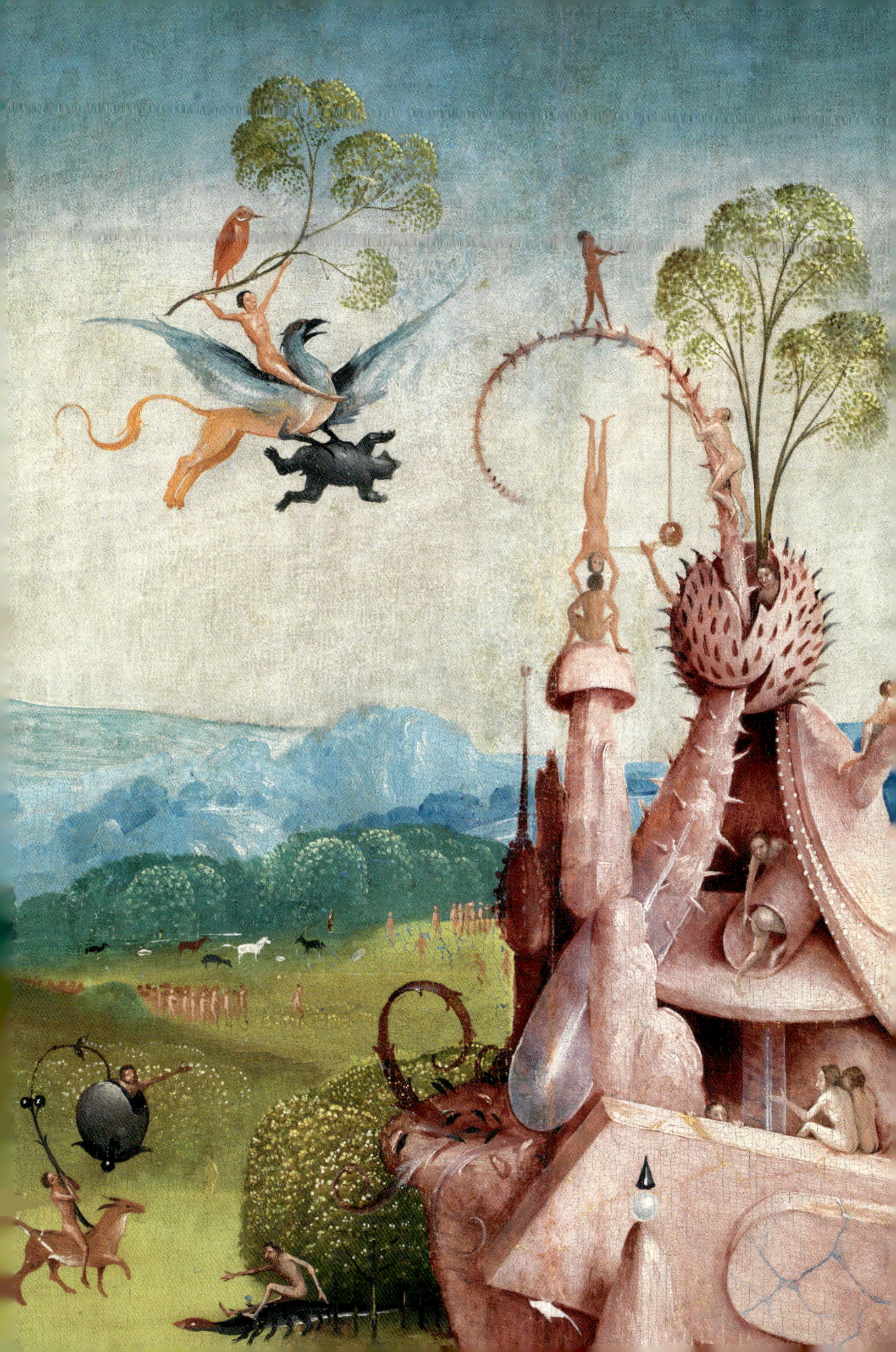

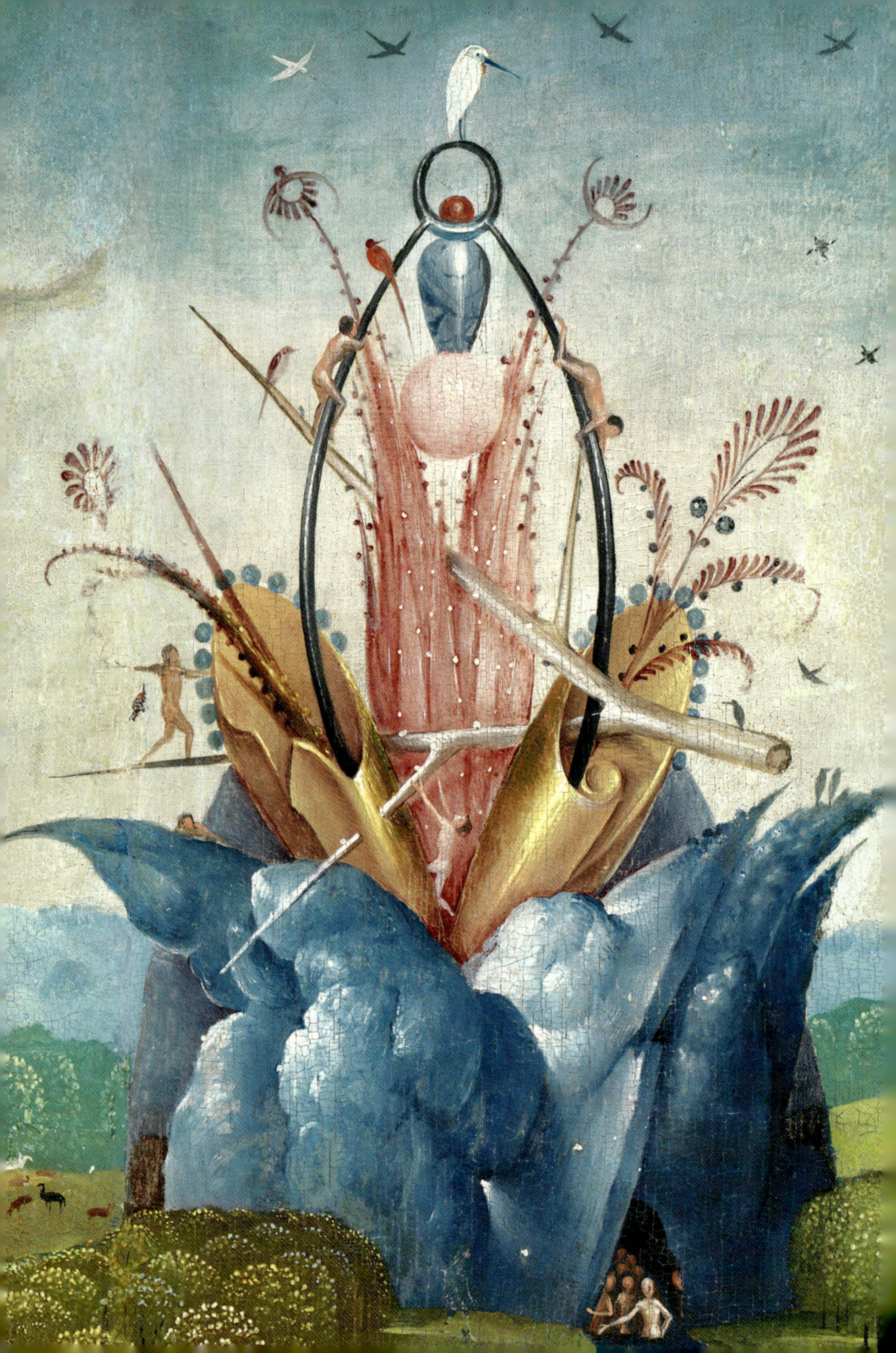

The men and women on the hill to the left of Adam and Eve can be seen as their descendants, since they no longer live in holes in the earth but in tent-like shelters – an indication of their gradually evolving civilisation. The juxtaposition of man and woman, fruit and cavity, repeats itself in several figural groups across the central panel. An eschatological dimension is implicit in the *Garden of Earthly Delights*, both in its allusions to the Flood and to sinful humankind after the Fall, and in the background of the central panel, where four hybrid architectural structures rise unsteadily towards the sky and look to be on the brink of collapse (pp. 157, 158, 165, 166).

In his interpretation of the Old Testament material and his visualisation of the landscape of paradise, Bosch invoked many of the characteristics of the *locus amoenus*. This fictive "pleasant place" had its roots in the literature of Antiquity; and during the Middle Ages it served to inform representations of secular paradisaical gardens, thereby serving as a pendant to the *hortus conclusus* ("enclosed garden") of sacred art (cf. Cat. 6.3). Features common to both include an enclosed green meadow with fragrant flowers and trees offering shade, songbirds and other creatures, and a fountain or stream. In secular compositions of this kind women and men are typically seen in conversation, playing games or making amorous advances to each other, while music is being played and food and drink lie close at hand. Examples can be seen in the *Large Garden of Love with Chess-players* (p. 160) by Master ES (*c.* 1420–*c.* 1468) and in the *Small Garden of Love* (*c.* 1440–1450) by the Master of the Gardens of Love (*fl. c.* 1430–1450). But whereas these two engravings represent sensual love primarily in the ideal, sublimated form of the courtly love of the German *Minne* tradition, Bosch amplifies this sensuality to the point of irony.

Bosch used the elements of the "pleasant place" in the Lust (*luxuria*) segment of *The Seven Deadly Sins and the Four Last Things* (pp. 308/309, Cat. 15), where they are joined by a jester, and on the right inner wing of the *Temptation of St Anthony* (pp. 118/119, Cat. 10.5), where they again symbolise lust and take on demonic shapes. There, a naked woman standing up to her knees in water looks out from the hollow and split trunk of a tree, over which a red *Minne* cloth is draped like a canopy, while a devil proffers a fish pierced with an arrow. The demon ostentatiously displaying his belly and being served a drink by an old woman is also part of this scene (p. 139). The red canopy and the split tree-trunk reappear under a new guise in the right foreground of the *Garden of Earthly Delights*: among a series of shelters recalling the tents of courtly *Minne* scenes they have transformed into the red, cylindrical object in which three persons are standing. In a process typical of his compositional style, Bosch has fused analogous forms – here a tent and a tree-trunk – into a

Detail from: **The Garden of Earthly Delights**, *c.* 1503
Central panel: **Humankind before the Flood** (see ill. pp. 190/191)

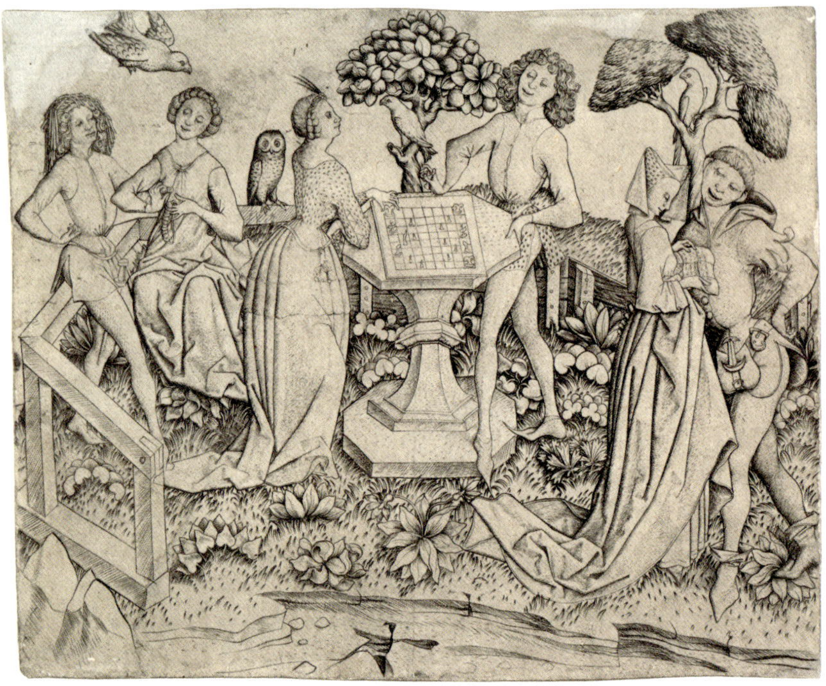

Master ES, **Large Garden of Love with Chess-players**, *c.* 1460–1467
Copper engraving, 16.4 x 20.8 cm / 6½ x 8⅛ in. Berlin, Staatliche Museen, Kupferstichkabinett

new, invented object (p. 204). This tree-tent has occasionally been mistaken for a branch of coral (Fraenger 1969). The many couples and groups of figures who can be seen standing, sitting or reclining in close physical proximity, whether touching, eating fruit or squeezing into vessels, all point to the sexual significance of the scene.

In the left foreground, a couple is sitting in a sort of bubble, the man with his hand on the woman's abdomen and she with her hand on his thigh (pp. 196/197). Bosch was evidently not content to restrict himself solely to allusions to heterosexual love: in front of the tree-tent, he presents a drastic contrast of innocence and coarseness in the motif of two kneeling men. The first is leaning forward and thereby thrusting upwards the two flowers protruding from his anus, while the second man gazes at them, one hand extended and the other holding another flower. Bax identifies the scene as an allusion to the *peccatum contra naturam*, the sin against nature, as homosexual acts were then known. Various sorts of fruit can be seen not just in the foreground but also throughout the middle distance, including cherries, blackberries, strawberries (pp. 176/177) and the fruits of the strawberry tree. In Spain around 1600 these last earned Bosch's painting the title of the "Strawberry Tree" since the attractive fruits of this plant were considered symbols both of visual temptation and of transience. Vandenbroeck has made a thorough study of the meaning of the fruits in the *Garden of Earthly Delights*. The cherry is associated with fertility, marriage, love and eroticism. Two cherries on a stalk were considered a phallic symbol. The blackberry refers to love and a lover's grief. All of these fruits can also signify parts of the female anatomy and the pleasures of love or the sexual act. Flowers, and in particular the rose, carry a similar symbolism. Songbirds (p. 195) and fish are likewise phallic symbols.

This orgiastic feast of sensuality, staged with the help of imagery drawn from the natural world, is new in its concrete interpretation, but not as a theme *per se*. A comparable, literary example in terms of allegorical complexity is the late medieval *Roman de la Rose*, a French copy of which was made for the Nassau palace library under Engelbert II. The *Roman de la Rose* was begun around 1235 by the French nobleman Guillaume de Lorris (*c.* 1205–after 1240) but left unfinished at his death. It was completed some 45 years later by the Paris scholar Jean de Meung (*c.* 1240–not later than 1305). This second part, written in a very different style, proved controversial; and at the start of the 15th century it was labelled misogynistic by other writers, including Christine de Pizan (1365–after 1430). In the first part of the *Roman de la Rose* we follow the narrator – who relates the story in the first person as if it were a dream – into a walled garden, where he proceeds to meet a series of allegorical characters, all of them personifications of the Virtues or properties of love. Cupid's darts arouse the dreamer from his passivity: he falls in love with the Rose of the title, but is able to reach her only briefly before she is abducted, whereupon he seems to fall into despair. It is at this point that Jean de Meung takes up the story. He abandons the refined, idealising style of Guillaume de Lorris and turns the garden of courtly love into a garden of earthly love. Here a battle breaks out, at the end of which the rose is vanquished and brutally broken. The second part as a whole has the form of a cynical, satirical, didactic offering in which heavenly and earthly love are irreconcilably opposed as Good and Evil. The woman, symbolised by the Rose, no longer offers the chivalric Lover a means of moral purification, but signifies only temptation and danger. Bosch's *Garden of Earthly Delights* undoubtedly comes closer to the latter train of thought; but, in the figure Adam, it also treats the theme of male responsibility.

While many of the pictorial motifs in the middle distance and background may not belong to the iconography of the Garden of Love, they can certainly be assigned to the thematic complex of sin and earthly love. In the centre of the panel, a cavalcade of vices (p. 199) has formed a ring around a circular pond in which white and black women are bathing. The acrobatic riders galloping endlessly around this pool are "fools of Venus", blinded and whipped up by their desire for love. Their assortment of mounts – the boar, unicorn, donkey, bear, billy goat, bull, dromedary (or camel), lion and panther – can be variously assigned to the vices of lust (*luxuria*), gluttony (*gula*), avarice (*avaritia*), wrath (*ira*) and pride (*superbia*), although the precise meaning is unclear since some vices can be represented by more than one beast. The middle of the central panel, with the men riding around the pool, ultimately symbolises nothing less than the power and dominion of women, which in Bosch's equation is the inevitable correlative of male sinfulness and folly. Losing control of his reason, man becomes "savage". According to Vandenbroeck, the motifs of riding in a circle and of riding wildly on animals can be traced back to popular fertility rites and fertility practices, to village squares with maypoles, to dances of invocation and binding, and dances of choosing and wooing a partner. Some rural Marian processions took up elements of pre-Christian water and tree cults, ritually walking or crawling around a tree or a pond not in worship of nature but because it had become associated with the presence, or an apparition, of the Virgin. The men riding around the women in the pond in Bosch's panel can be interpreted as a parody, in the sense of false reverence. Other motifs in the central panel, such as the savages, Africans, merknights and mermaids, likewise allude to carnal love and temptation, to uncivilised and wild behaviour. An investigation into Bosch's iconography reveals, in short, that the mêlée in the central panel illustrates the diametric opposite of courtly decorum and courtly behaviour – we are looking at an exotic and untamed counter-world. Male viewers of the *Garden of Earthly Delights* would certainly not have wished to let women rule at court; nor would they wish to surrender to their own baser instincts. Instead, self-mastery and composure were the order of the day.

The viewer can easily get lost in the myriad details of the panorama spilling across the central panel. Let us therefore take a closer look at their shape and significance, both as a whole and in detail, and at their contradictory relationship to the left inner wing. The owl perched inside the base of the fountain of life at the centre of the *Paradise* panel, for example, reappears twice in the central panel, at roughly the same height but on the left and right edges of the scene, accompanied by its blind "worshippers". The unicorn drinking from the stream flowing out of the fountain of life in the *Paradise* panel becomes, in the central panel, a rearing mount near the pool of women, its significance thereby switching from chastity to lust; something similar can be observed in Bosch's *St Jerome* (p. 304/305, Cat. 12.2). Following the principles of the world turned upside down, the central panel inverts the details of the *Paradise* panel into their opposites (Moxey 1994). This finds figural expression in the man upside down in the water in the left foreground, of whom we see only the legs and lower abdomen (pp. 196/197). The natural ratios of size between human, animal, plant and object are also abolished, so that the birds and fruits in the picture are often as large as or larger than the people around them. We have already encountered this

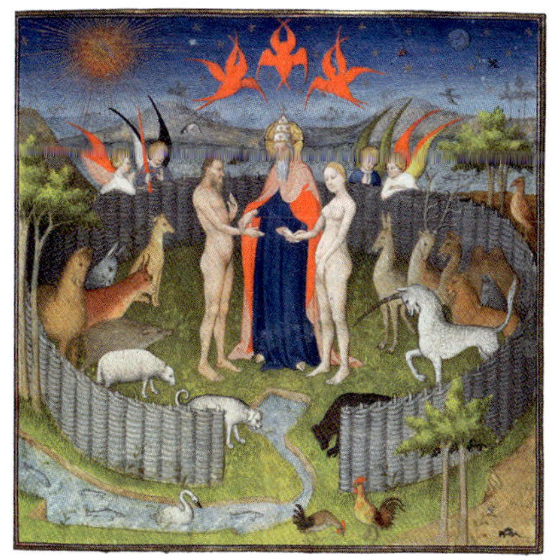

compositional principle, where size equals importance, in *St Christopher* (p. 78, Cat. 7). The hierarchy of things has been levelled. The animals depicted as near and subordinate to Adam and Eve in the *Paradise* panel are represented in the central panel on the same level as, and in direct physical contact with, their countless descendants. Men and women are no longer carefully segregated. Natural habitats are also confused, with birds in the water and fish on land or in the air. In contrast to the stillness and calm of the *Paradise* panel, everything is in motion. Even stationary pictorial elements are on the point of tipping over and are essentially fragile and unstable. This can be observed in particular in the right background, where tectonic elements are stacked on top of each other. Sin undoes the natural order given by God. The chaotic and the arbitrary become the new ordering principles.

Bosch employs parody as a tool in his creative process, in so far as he takes figures from the *Paradise* panel, with its more refined stylistic *niveau*, and inverts them to generate a host of figures of a baser kind. A good example is the group of Adam, Christ and Eve: in composition, gesture and facial expression these reflect the principles of hierarchy. Corresponding figures occur in two groups on the central panel. The first of these can be found in the lower right corner, right next to the man kneeling down with the flowers in his anus: here a woman is seated in the same position as Adam in the left inner wing. She sits there passively with her legs outstretched, one hand resting on the ground and the other on her thigh, with her face covered by the transparent, inverted cup of a flower, while all around the world sinks into sin and folly. A second woman in an identical sitting position, but in exact mirror-image, can be found further along the same axis in the right *Hell* panel. In each case a man to the left of the woman thrusts his posterior into the air, a gesture that unmistakably signals impurity. The woman in the *Hell* panel is associated with lust through the devil putting his arms around her, and with unchastity through the toad on her breast and the devil's backside. This last has a mirrored surface in which the reflection of the woman's face can be seen – a reference to the deadly sin of *superbia* (van-

Boucicaut Master, **God Presents Eve to Adam**, *c.* 1415
from: *Des proprietez de choses*, fol. 16r. Parchment, 40.5 x 28.5 cm / 16 x 11¼ in.
Cambridge, Fitzwilliam Museum, Ms. 251

ity, pride). This was considered the very first of all the deadly sins, the one to which Eve succumbed even in Paradise. Thus the woman in Hell, looking at herself, is the negative counterpart not just of Adam but also of Eve as she is portrayed before the Fall in the left inner wing. The seated woman in the central panel would thus represent the intermediary stage in the soul's descent into sin.

The object of parody is present within the parody itself. The unbroken line of the horizon between the left and central panels, in conjunction with the similarity between their landscape types, even suggests continuity. The background of the central panel is dominated by five partly red, partly blue structures. The one in the centre is entirely surrounded by water, from which rivers branch off to flow underneath the other four structures. These evidently illustrate the sources of the four rivers of Paradise (pp. 176/177, 181). The elements common to both panels – naked men and women, animals, plants and the landscape – are nonetheless combined in wholly different ways. The vertical axis between the two panels marks the point at which each becomes the inverted mirror of the other: whereas the left inner wing is Christocentric, the central panel is anthropocentric. The first presents the figure of Christ for the viewer's worship, while the second shows at its centre women being worshipped by the men circling around them. In the same way, the marriage of two faithful partners with the aim of producing offspring in the left panel is contrasted with uninhibited sexuality in the central panel. There is thus nothing to support the claim, regularly put forward ever since Fraenger, that Bosch's contemporaries would have understood the central panel, with its grotesque body language and unreal living conditions, as an ideal, positive or exemplary place. This does not mean, however, that they would not have found the painting "interesting" from an artistic point of view.

Humankind in an infernal brothel

The right inner wing presents a view of Hell that has a confusing, genre-like realism. The composition does not exhibit even the modicum of mirrored symmetry found in the central panel and can only be described as chaotic. Stabilising points of reference are offered at first sight by the giant figure in the centre, and upon closer examination by a number of other pictorial motifs developed from the left and central panels. Hell itself is not a diffuse darkness from which devils emerge in shadowy outline in order to inflict the most gruesome torments upon the damned, grouped according to the nature of their sins. Instead, it spreads out in the form of an infernal landscape with parched earth in the foreground, followed in the middle distance by a body of water that has burst its banks.

Detail from: **The Garden of Earthly Delights**, *c.* 1503
Central panel: **Humankind before the Flood** (see ill. pp. 190/191)

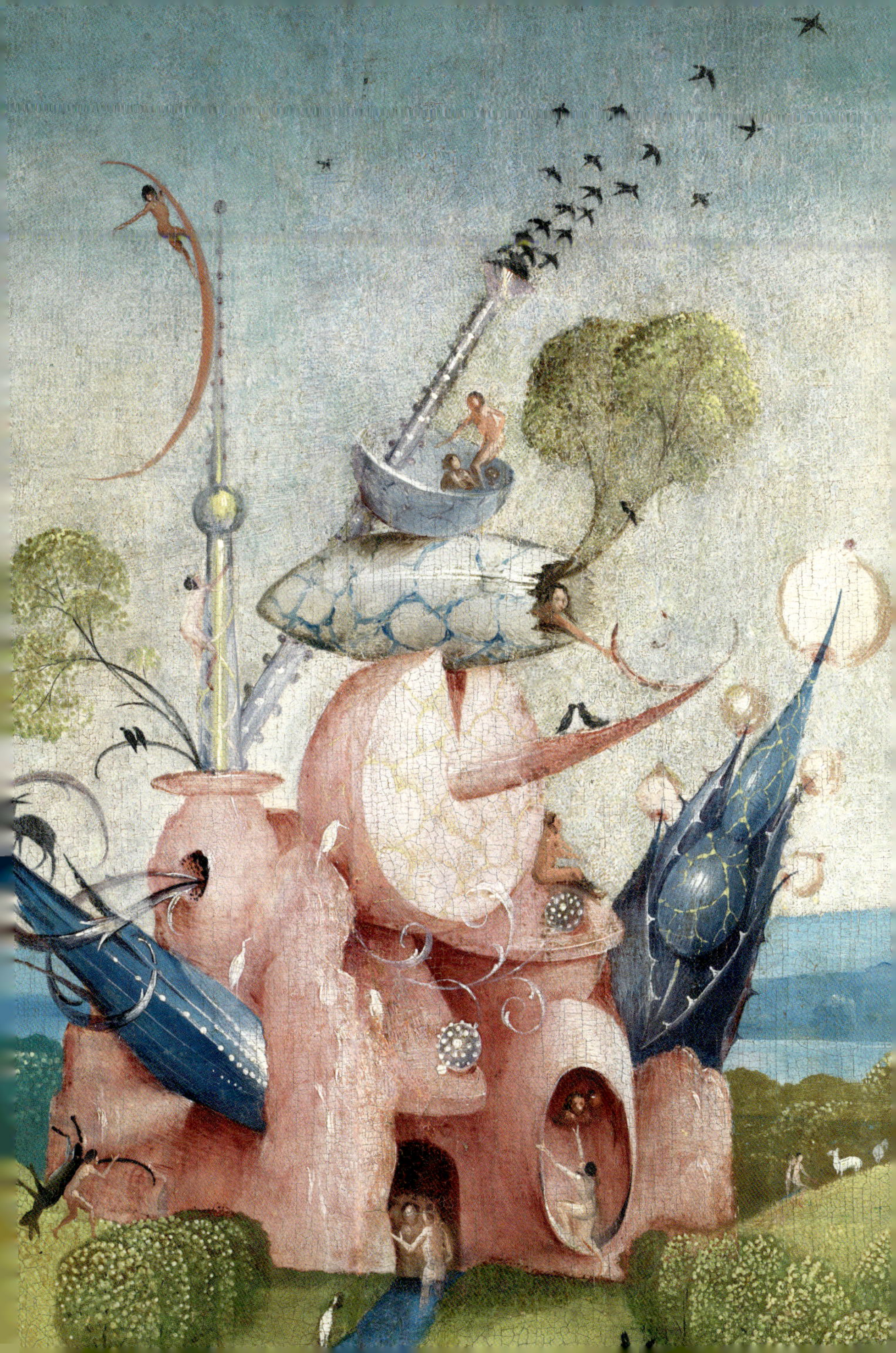

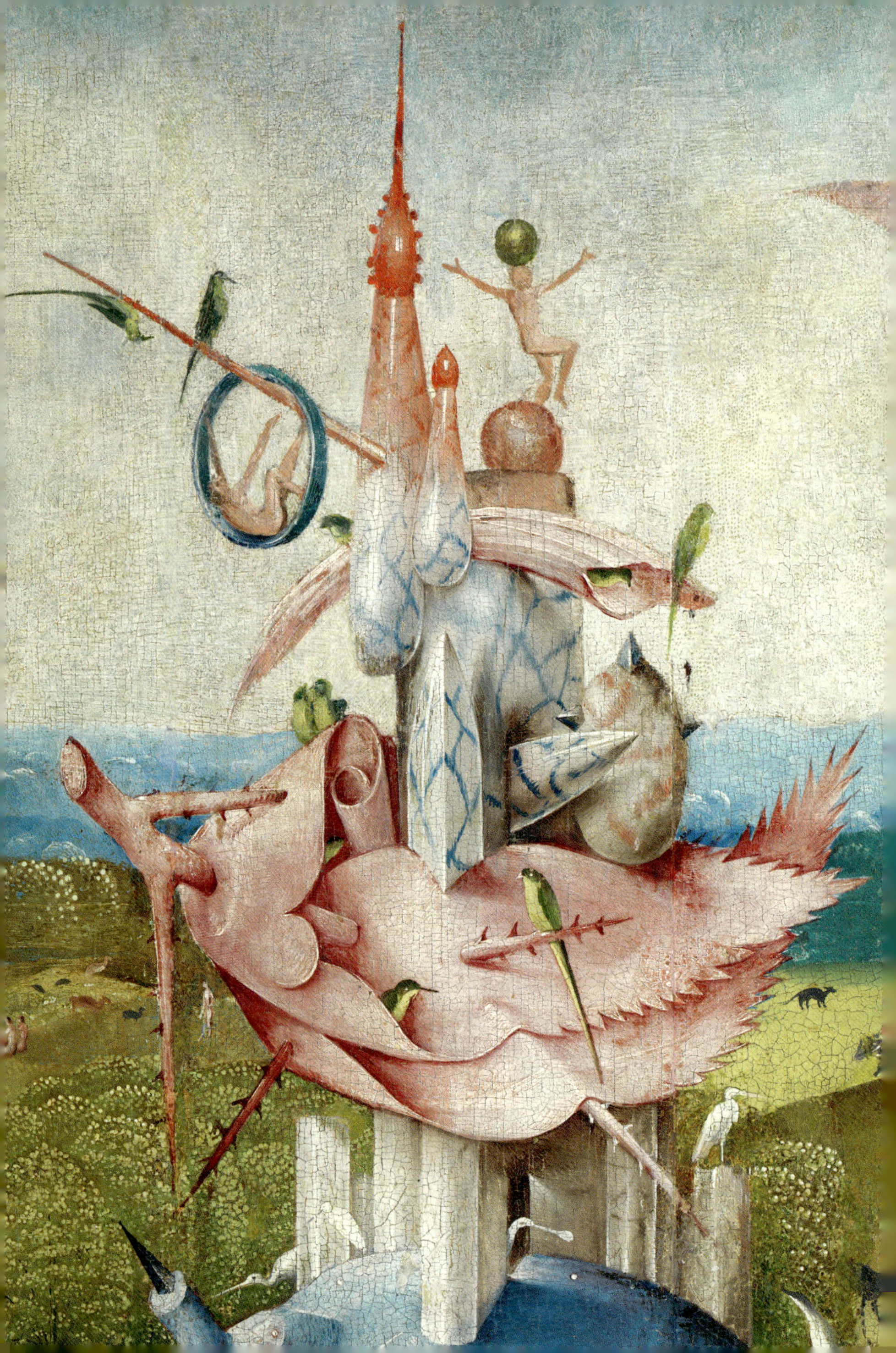

Beyond, this expanse of water is crossed by a bridge, while a city seen in silhouette burns on the horizon (pp. 208/209). The background calls to mind a foundering world at war and is a reminder of the devastating fire of 1463 that Bosch experienced at first hand. With its contemporary architecture, clothing and objects, this vision of Hell is clearly situated in the present or near future.

The so-called tree-man (p. 213, cf. Cat. D4, p. 212) in the centre is a huge, pale, anthropomorphic figure presenting his rear end to the viewer and looking back over his shoulder. He embodies, above all, the vices of *luxuria* (unchastity) and *gula* (gluttony). A large disc sits on his head like a grotesque hat, with three pairs of sinners and devils on its brim circling round a set of red bagpipes (pp. 210/211). They are watched by a fourth devil, while a fifth uses his whole body to play the smoking instrument. The tree-man's arms and legs have fused together and are depicted as leafless, hollow trees, each with one branch. His body is egg-shaped and houses a tavern, identified by a flag with the emblem of bagpipes on it. Inside, a woman is filling jugs from a barrel, and three men are sitting on a toad at a table (p. 213). Fire seems to be leaping towards them. Two branches grow up through the interior, one hung with a helmet and the other with a crossbow. At the front edge of the tree-man's cavernous body a man is leaning his head thoughtfully on one hand. The top of a ladder is propped against the edge beside him and two sinful souls are being sent up it by a demon below them that is part bird, part knight and part butterfly. Here and in most of the other scenes in the panel the damned are trapped in a situation from which there is no escape and in which they repeat their activities on earth; only rarely, however, do they suffer direct physical torture. The tree-man's feet take the form of ash-grey boats, each with a devil as helmsman or ferryman. Countless tiny heads can be made out in the rectangular openings in the floor of each boat. Each also has a tall mast; on the one that is fully visible a poor soul is clinging to the rigging beneath a burning crow's-nest.

The whole of the right inner wing is dominated by the topos of the "evil inn" (Dutch *quade herberge*; Bax 1956, pp. 91–92). Taken from contemporary literature, the term was applied to brothels and shady taverns in which it was asserted, secular music, gambling, alcohol and prostitution led to the sins of lust, quarrelsomeness, anger, vanity, greed, alcoholism and an addiction to gambling. Bosch indicates these connections not with a pointing finger but with a creative freedom of combination and bitter irony, as demonstrated by the motif of the couples walking hand in hand in apparent intimacy around the tree-man's hat: the set of bagpipes they are circling is itself the definitive symbol of secular music and at the same time a symbol of sex and unbridled licentiousness.

Detail from: **The Garden of Earthly Delights**, *c.* 1503
Central panel: **Humankind before the Flood** (see ill. pp. 190/191)

In line with the notion that one sin leads to another, the deadly sins often appeared together or in sequence. In his widely read treatise *De Imitatione Christi* (*c.* 1418; *On the Imitation of Christ*), Thomas à Kempis (*c.* 1380–1471) counsels the reader:"control the untamed appetite for food and drink, and you will more easily control all bodily desires." The body was viewed as a vessel intended as a container for the Holy Spirit. Its purity, however, was destroyed by sin and in particular by lust. A body contaminated by sin excluded a person from receiving the Eucharist. The impurity of the tree-man is clearly indicated by the scatological motif whereby he "bares his backside", allowing us to look right into his belly with its tavern scene. The body has quite literally become a dwelling-place of sin. The giant is, in every respect, the opposite of man in terms of their likeness to God. The giant musical instruments in the foreground – in particular the lute, harp, hurdy-gurdy, bass shawm and drum – are symbols of secular music like the bagpipes and in principle carry the same symbolism. Here, however, they also serve the devils as instruments of torture (p. 217).

While the topos of the "evil inn" is represented in concentrated form in the tree-man, it is elaborated in greater detail in the scenes in the lower left section of the panel (p. 218). The naked woman with the dice on her head is identified as a prostitute by the candle and jug in her hand; and she clearly also belongs to the milieu of the shady tavern, as a comparison with another picture makes clear (p. 219). Bosch has turned the hare beside her (a symbol of Eve and fertility) into a hunter who has bagged a couple of the damned. In line with the principle of the world turned upside down, fertility, as a natural state, has mastered its vehicle, man (cf. p. 169). In the left foreground a devil holds a trictrac board – similar to a backgammon board – menacingly in the air. Playing-cards lie scattered on the ground in the bottom left corner, and slightly above and to the right of them a man is leaning with his back against an overturned table, his right hand pierced by a dagger. A devil is standing over him and thrusting a sword into his body. The devil wears a shield slung over his shoulder; it bears the image of a skewered and severed hand balancing a dice on two fingers. This corresponds to the system of corporal punishment practised by the courts in the late Middle Ages and Early Modern era, whereby the punishment was inflicted upon the part of the body that had committed the sin. In this infernal trial the hand is the *corpus delicti*, the evidence linking its owner to the crime of gambling. Higher up the panel, next to the bagpipes and on the same vertical axis as the musical instruments, is a huge pair of ears. Shot through with an arrow and apparently severed by the knife lying between them (pp. 210/211), these ears could be interpreted in an analogous fashion, namely to signify that listening to secular music leads to sin. Corporal punishment found its origin and legitimation in the Bible. As part of His teachings to the disciples, Christ said with reference to adultery:"If your right eye causes you to sin, pluck it out and cast it

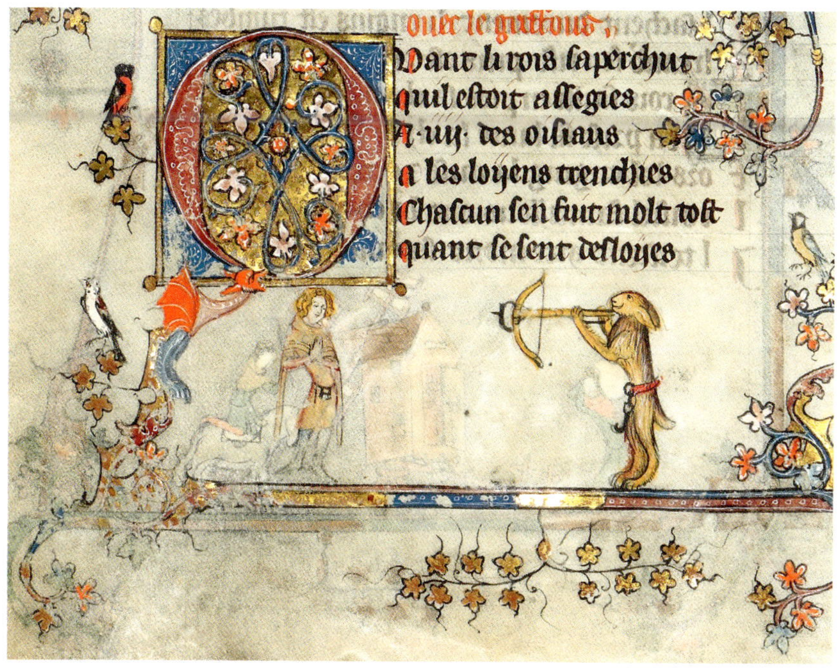

French artist, **The Hare as Hunter**, 1338–1344
from: *Romance of Alexander the Great*, fol. 81v (detail). Parchment. Oxford, Bodleian Library, Ms. Bodley 264

from you [...] And if your right hand causes you to sin, cut it off and cast it from you; for it is more profitable for you that one of your members perish, than for your whole body to be cast into hell" (Matt. 5:27–30). At the same time, Christ's gesture of blessing shown in the left inner wing is parodied by the severed hand on the devil's shield, where the fingers point to the dice – a gesture that can also be understood as breaking the commandment not to take God's name in vain.

Bosch was addressing themes that had a contemporary relevance. Towards the end of the 15th century, restrictions on prostitution were being tightened, while at the same time marriage was becoming increasingly institutionalised. Gambling, which was often accompanied by drinking, was considered to lead to over-excitement, arguments and outbursts of temper and was thus frequently banned. The combination of elements in the centre and in particular the lower part of the *Hell* panel, and their comparison with the ideal of marriage in the *Paradise* panel, may be compared to a didactic, aphoristic poem on "marriage proverbs" (*Dit zijn proverben van huwene*) from around 1450:"From bad people one can learn / unchastity, dicing, drinking and swearing, / unseasonable drinking and eating, / and also to forget days of fasting, / and thus all the commandments, / that one should observe before God" ("*An quade menschen mach men leeren,/Oncuusheit, dobbelen, drijncken en sweeren, / Tontide drijncken ende eten,/Ende oec die vastendaghe vergheten,/ Ende oec alle die ghebode,/Die men hauden zoude van gode*"; Braekman 1969, pp. 92–93).

By around 1500 the motif and theme of the "evil inn", encountered repeatedly in the late Middle Ages, had condensed into a symbol of all that was bad for the civic elite and the aristocracy. In an autobiographically slanted text of 1516, Erasmus of Rotterdam expressly mentions that his tutor did not engage in dicing, whoring or drinking. The reputation of young noblemen grew to include not just the desire to show off, a tendency for extravagance and a passion for hunting, but also gambling and drinking sprees. It is probably for this reason that a treatise on virtue composed by François Demoulins in 1509 warned the young François d'Angoulême, later King François I of France (1494–1547), against the demons of cards and dice. Bosch's works may similarly have served the young prince Henry III of Nassau-Breda and the Habsburg Philip the Handsome as visual reminders of the "discourteousness" of certain forms of behaviour. The "evil inn" motif is also found in Bosch's *Adoration of the Magi* (Cat. 6.3), *Temptation of St Anthony* (Cat. 10.3) and *Last Judgement* (Cat. 13.4), in the Wrath segment of *The Seven Deadly Sins and the Four Last Things* (Cat. 15) and in *The Pedlar* (Cat. 17.1).

Among the individual scenes and figures in the *Hell* panel of the *Garden of Earthly Delights* the eye is also struck by the devil seated on the "throne" at the lower right (p. 221). The blue bird-headed monster sits as if enthroned on a raised commode or high chair and is swallowing a sinner, from whose rectum birds, smoke and fire are escaping. The large cauldron on the devil's head illustrates his vast appetite. This monstrous defecator of sinners exhibits parallels with a passage in the *Vision of Tundale*, in which a giant winged beast punishes those convicted of the sin of lust by devouring and then excreting them:"Soon, they came upon a hideous creature that filled Tundale with terror. It seemed more evil and dangerous than anything he had ever seen before, with two enormous black wings and with claws of iron and steel protruding from its feet. Its neck was long and slender but held a huge head in which burned two red eyes, set wide apart, and its mouth was wide and spat fire in a seemingly inextinguishable stream. Its nose was tipped with iron! The beast sat in the middle of a frozen lake swallowing terrified souls which burned inside its body until they were nearly wasted away, but then they were expelled from this

Detail from: **The Garden of Earthly Delights**, *c.* 1503
Central panel: **Humankind before the Flood** (see ill. pp. 190/191)

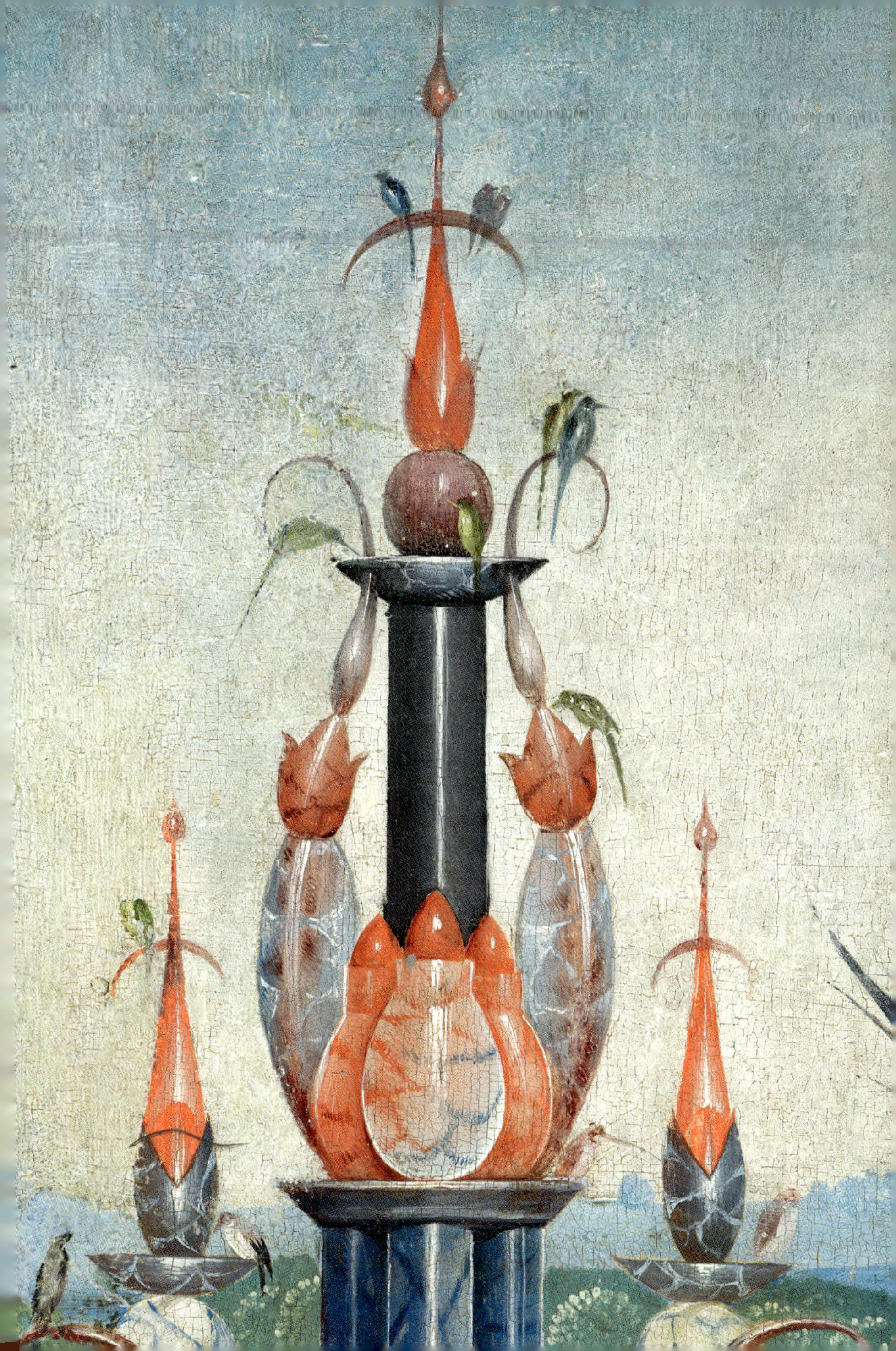

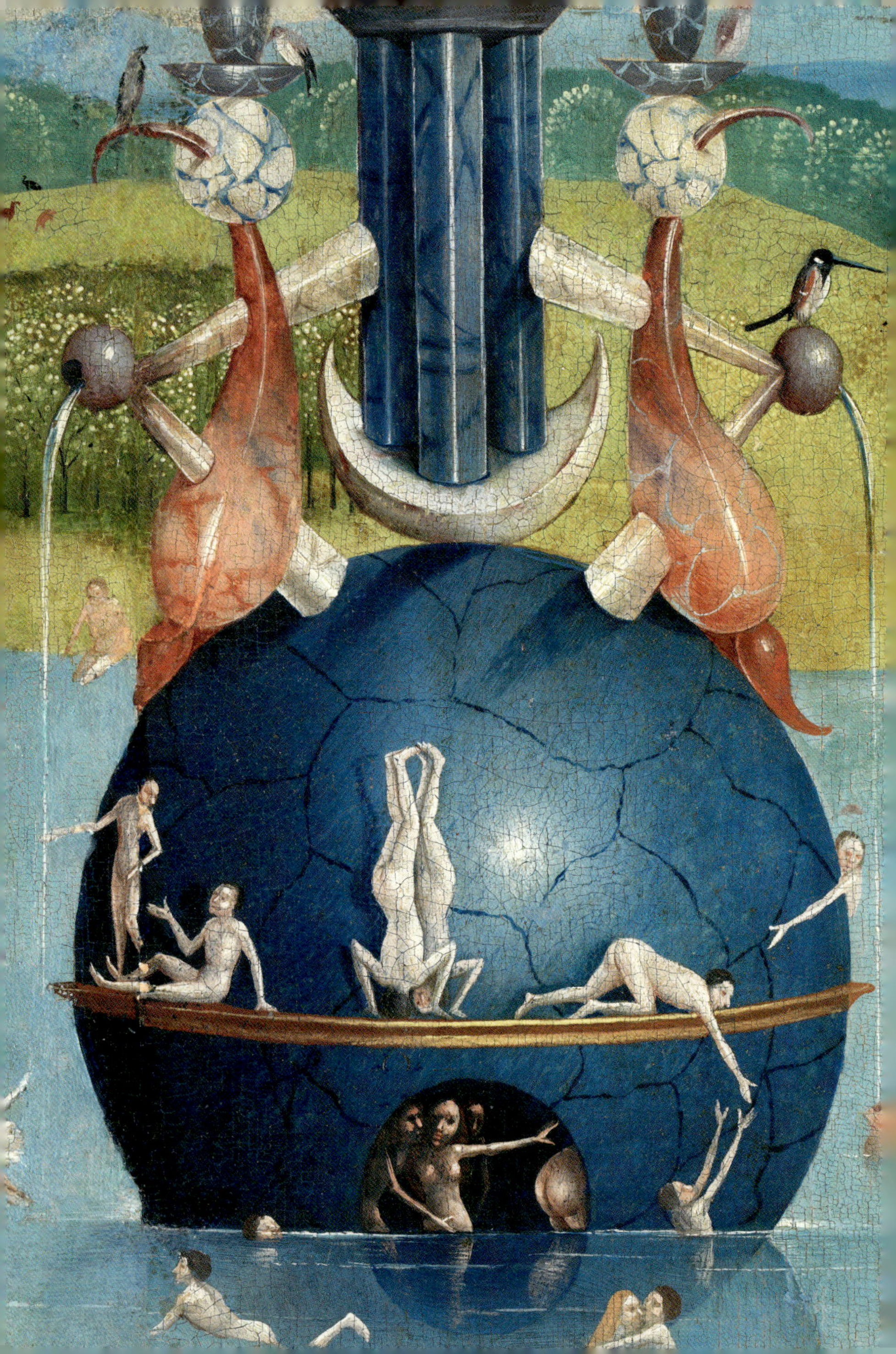

horror in the creature's excrement and left until they had recovered and become whole once again. [...] But they were not delivered from this pain, the cycle was renewed and they had to endure it again and again." This punishment was specifically ordained for "monks, clerics, priests and canons and other men and women of Holy Church who have indulged their carnal desires [...] ignoring the strictures of their order and leading their lives as they wish" (Passus VIII; cited here from Scott-Robinson 2008).

The *Vision of Tundale* (*Visio Tnugdali* in the original Latin) was written down in around 1149 by the Irish monk Marcus at the Scots Monastery in Regensburg. It tells the story of Tundale, a notoriously unscrupulous man who falls unconscious one day during dinner and is shown a vision of the afterlife. An angel guides him through numerous scenes of Hell and finally shows him a glimpse of Heaven. Beholding the dreadful punishments suffered by sinners (p. 220), Tundale repents of his previous conduct and, restored to consciousness, embraces a virtuous life. The *Visio Tnugdali* was widely known north of the Alps and remained extremely popular right up to the Early Modern era. It forms part of the same genre of vision literature as the *Divine Comedy* (written 1307–1320) by Dante Alighieri (1265–1321). Various vernacular translations were in circulation, with an edition appearing in 1482 in Antwerp and another in 1484 in 's-Hertogenbosch, printed by Gerardus Leempt. The subject of Hell evidently held a great fascination. Literary journeys into the afterlife, liturgical drama and pictorial representations of Hell *à la* Bosch also provided aesthetic vehicles through which a lay public could explore the afterlife and look ahead at what lay in store. Through these media, terrors and evil forces could take on a sensual reality, could be made visible and tangible, and could thus be exorcised. Texts of this sort opened up a world far removed from both the saintly and the mundane; but it was one in which surprise and even humour were to be found. This is witnessed not just by the devils taking a role in religious plays, with their tricks with fire, sly ruses and meaningless pseudo-Latin, but also by the devils in the *Garden of Earthly Delights*.

Causally, formally and in terms of content, the central panel and right *Hell* wing are far more closely inter-linked than they appear at first sight and demonstrate that here, too, the thematic and chronological cohesion of the triptych's interior extends to the smallest details. Both panels are eschatological in orientation and show a sort of implicit Last Judgement. The element of water is present in all three parts of the triptych, but to the right we can see that the relationship between land and water shifts in favour of the latter. Hell is indeed half covered by water and ice, a relatively large ratio that has no comparison in other Hell paintings of the 15th and 16th centuries. Like the Flood, the water is here

Detail from: **The Garden of Earthly Delights**, *c.* 1503
Central panel: **Humankind before the Flood** (see ill. pp. 190/191)

an instrument of divine punishment for sinners and is therefore assigned to Hell. Given that the Deluge of the Old Testament is equated in the Gospels with the Last Judgement to come, the flood in Bosch's *Hell* panel can be understood as itself heralding the Last Judgement and as one of its instruments of punishment. Against the thematic backdrop of the first, sinful age of man after the Fall and before the Flood, the tree-man – a giant descendant of the daughters of Cain – with boats for feet represents a kind of fraudulent or false Ark. Instead of providing sinners with shelter, it induces them to sin repeatedly. It thus also assumes the role of the tree to which drowning men and women cling for safety, another topos of Deluge representations.

The secular musical instruments are also directly connected with the theme of humankind before the Flood. During that first age, according to Hartmann Schedel in his 1493 *Chronicle of the World*, the "desires of the eyes" were aroused by the mining and working of precious metals, the "desires of the ears" by the art of song and the invention of musical instruments such as the organ and the harp, and the desires of the flesh by clothing. The first forms of civilisation and culture, that is to say, developed before the Flood.

In formal terms, all four segments of the triptych are linked by the motif of the circle: the spherical body of the Earth on the exterior shutters; the convex disc with the owl in the centre and the birds around it in the left inner wing; the round pond with female bathers and men riding around it in the central panel; and the circular brim of the tree-man's hat in the right inner wing, upon which three couples are walking around the bagpipes in the middle. Depending on context, the circle can symbolise the perfection of the cosmos, or it may betoken the sinner whose physical desires drive him to wander endlessly and meaninglessly in a circle, without ever reaching a destination.

The invention that Bosch brought to every last inch of his paintings is directly related to the process by which he and his workshop elaborated the details of the composition. While the main motifs and the basic structure of each panel were laid down at an early stage, many of the detail motifs in the central and *Hell* panels were only developed after the *Paradise* wing had taken shape, namely as contradictions, inversions and parodies of the motifs invented for this last. Bosch, that is to say, did not follow a preconceived, harmoniously planned overall design. Rather, he used the process of *amplificatio* to elaborate upon a theme in detail in a way that was as skilful and at times as labyrinthine as possible (Fischer 2009, pp. 175–178).

Instruction and entertainment for the nobility

Several documentary sources (see entry on Cat. 11), starting with the journal entry by de Beatis of 1517, make it likely that the *Garden of Earthly Delights* was commissioned by a member of the important Netherlandish branch of the noble house of Nassau-Breda. The

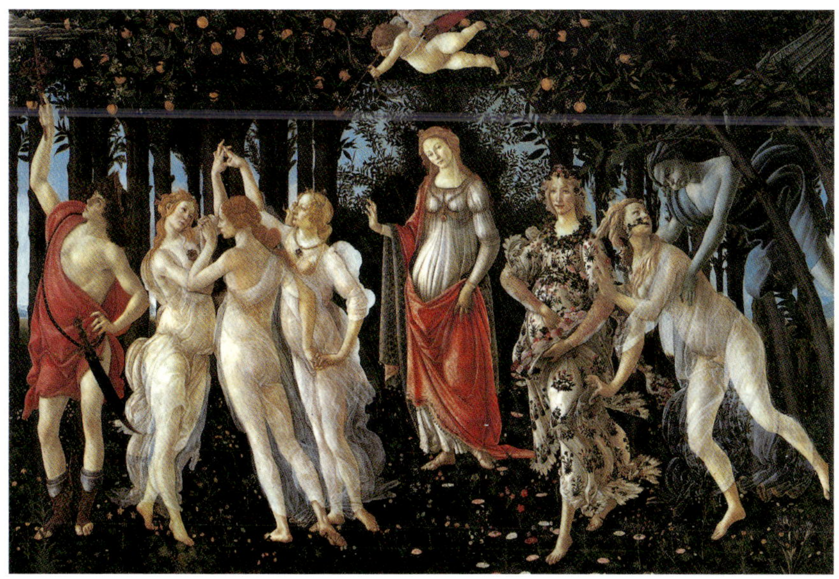

Sandro Botticelli, **Primavera (Allegory of Spring)**, *c.* 1482
Tempera on poplar, 203 x 314 cm / 79⅞ x 123⅝ in. Florence, Galleria degli Uffizi

Pages 176/177
Detail from: **The Garden of Earthly Delights**, *c.* 1503
Central panel: **Humankind before the Flood** (see ill. pp. 190/191)

two lords of Breda in the years immediately around 1500 were Engelbert II (1451–1504) and his successor Henry III of Nassau. Since Engelbert's marriage to Cimburga of Baden in 1468 had produced no children, in 1499 he summoned his 16-year-old nephew Henry to the Low Countries from the Nassau ancestral estates. Henry continued his education in the Nassau palaces in Brussels and Mechelen and at the court of Philip the Handsome in Ghent. Between 1501 and 1506 Henry's links with the Ghent court were so close that he was invited to accompany Philip on his visit of 1501 to 1503 to Spain, France and Germany and that of 1506, again to Spain. During the first of these extended trips Engelbert arranged for his elected successor to marry Louise-Françoise de Savoie (before 1486–1511). The couple were betrothed in November 1502 and married in August 1503. At the beginning of December, a month after the company had returned to the Low Countries, Engelbert II organised ten days of festivities at the Nassau palace in Brussels, thereby evidently also celebrating the marriage. These were attended, and greatly enjoyed, by the bride and her ladies-in-waiting (Gachard 1876, pp. 338–339). On 6 January 1504 the estates and

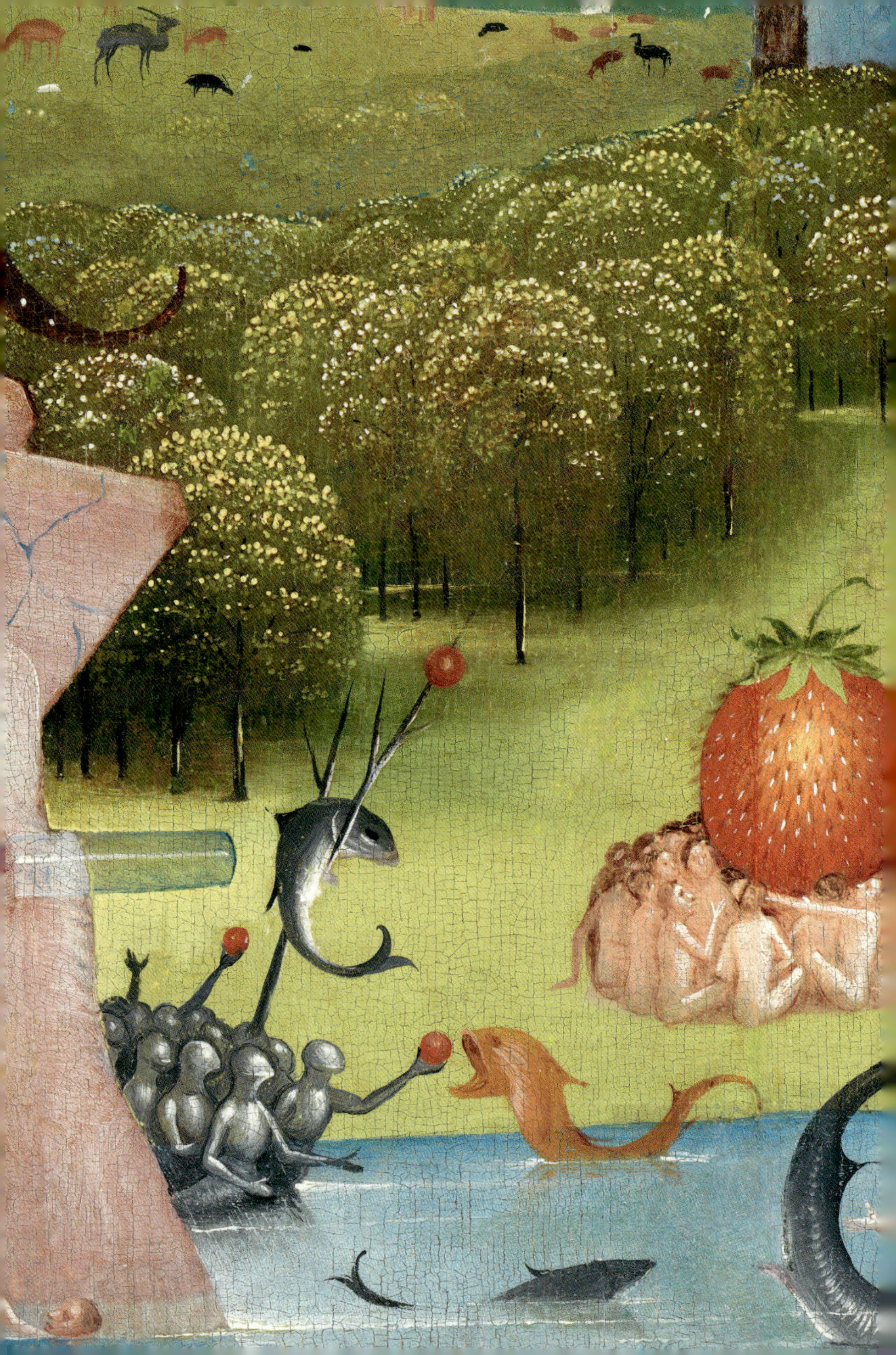

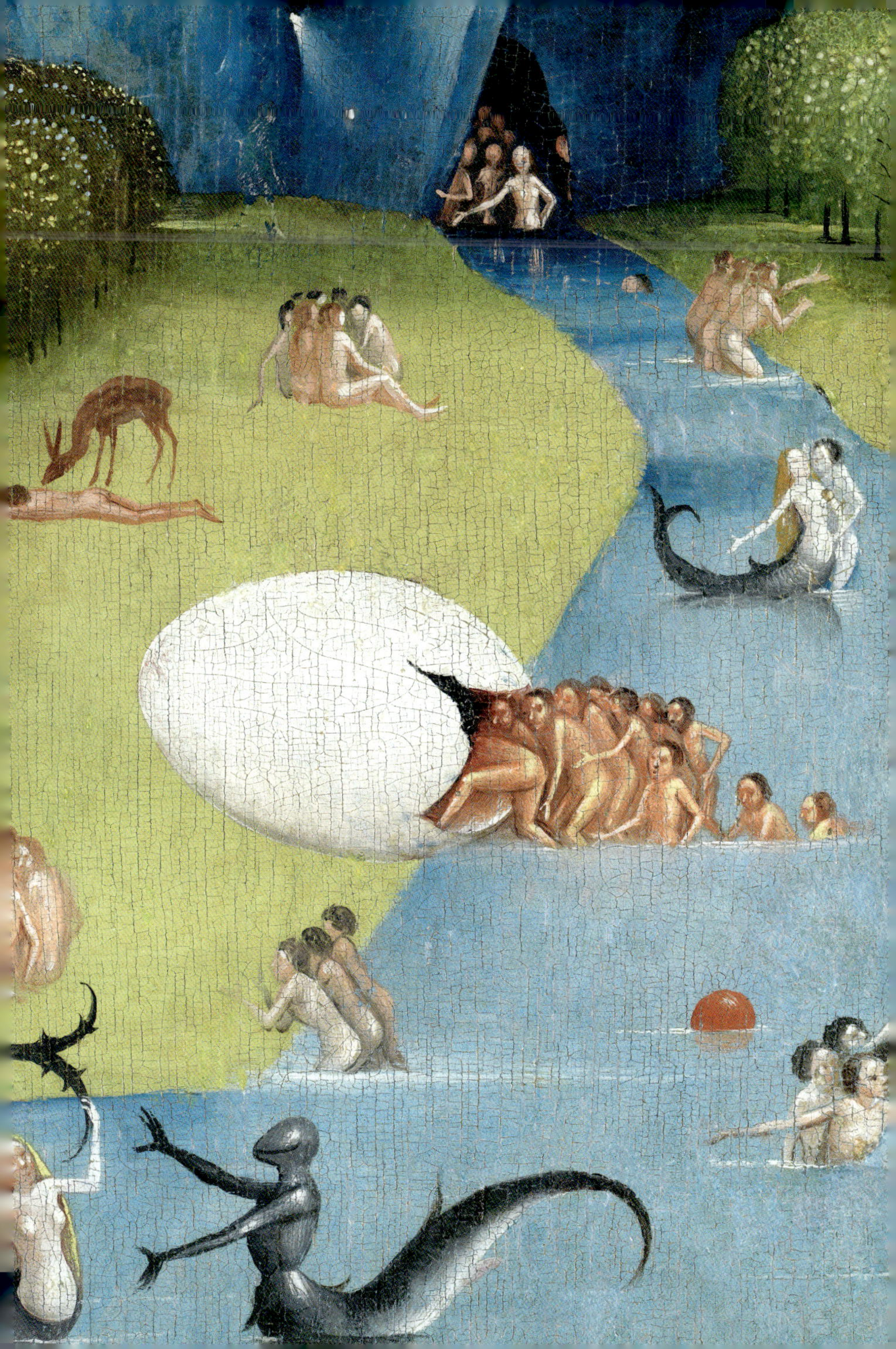

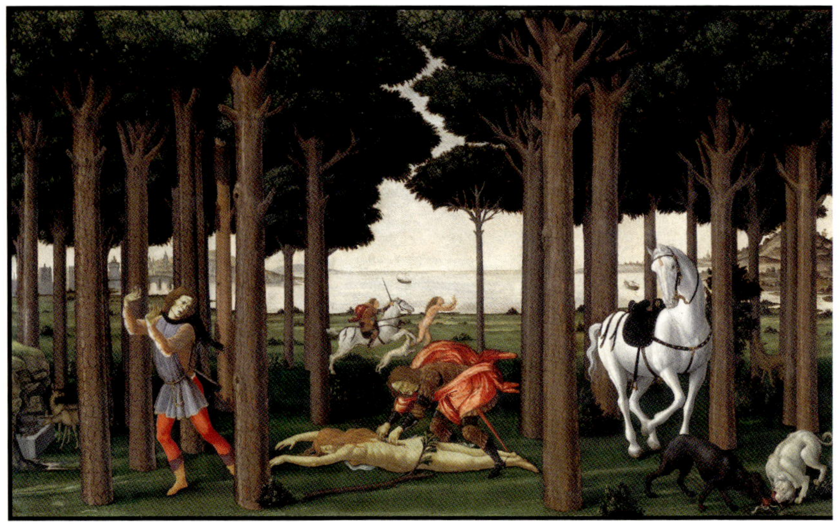

Sandro Botticelli, **Episode from the Life of Nastagio degli Onesti**, 1483
Tempera on panel, 82–84 x 138–142 cm / 32¼–33 x 54⅜–55⅞ in. Madrid, Museo Nacional del Prado

chancellor of Brabant organised a ceremony to mark the arrival of Philip the Handsome. Whether Bosch had already completed the *Garden of Earthly Delights* by August 1503 and whether the wedding guests were therefore able to see the work, commissioned only the previous year to mark Henry's engagement, we do not know.

Engelbert II died on 31 May 1504. He had served the Habsburgs Maximilian and Philip in a military capacity and had held other important political offices in the Low Countries. From his Brussels palace, of which only the chapel survives today, he had acted as governor of the Netherlands during Philip's absence. Henry inherited the Nassau properties in the Low Countries from his uncle and also followed, both militarily and politically, in his footsteps. On 31 July 1504 the 21-year-old took up residence in the Nassau palace in Breda, traditionally the family's main seat, at the same time commissioning extensions to the palace in Brussels. Breda only truly became Henry's main residence from 1515, when he celebrated his second marriage there and proceeded to organise a major programme of new building.

Whether the childless Engelbert II – who suffered from the very painful and protracted venereal disease of syphilis and very probably died of it in 1504 – intended that the *Garden of Earthly Delights* serve as a warning for Henry is a question that must remain unanswered. As was the custom among the aristocracy in the late Middle Ages, the education of the young Henry lay in the hands of one secular and one clerical tutor. Clues as to the nature of this education can be found in the libraries of Burgundian and Netherlandish princes and nobles and in the books that have come down us from the Nassau collection (see Fischer 2009, p. 354). These last include, in particular, historiographical works, compilations of exempla, theological and didactic works on morality, encyclopaedia and other religious literature, but also works treading the same ground as the *Garden of Earthly Delights*, such as the *Roman de la Rose*, chronicles of the world, works of biblical exegesis and *City of God* by St Augustine (354–430). The teachers of princes considered a cultivated mind and virtuous conduct more important than military values. Bosch's *Garden of Earthly Delights*, *Last Judgement* (Cat. 13) and *Temptation of St Anthony* (Cat. 10) are works that were suitable for the moral instruction of Henry III and Philip the Handsome: they had a spiritual dimension, but they sought to satisfy the artistic expectations of a courtly audience.

Both Engelbert and Henry were evidently lovers of art who preferred, where possible, to employ artists from the region. They maintained very close links with the cities of Brabant, including 's-Hertogenbosch. It is possible that they made contact with Hieronymus Bosch through the Brotherhood of Our Blessed Lady, as is suggested by a number of considerations. In 1504/05, for example, through his steward Bernt von Lutzenborch, Henry III made a present of a horse to the Brotherhood, perhaps to mark his own visit to 's-Hertogenbosch on 10 December 1504. As titular bailiff of Brabant from 1504 onwards, Henry was Philip's representative as Duke of Brabant. The actual function of bailiff was performed by Hendrik Masscherel, whose coat of arms was made for the chapel of the Brotherhood by Bosch's workshop; the journeymen were paid for the job in 1503/04. Henry, like his first wife, was an external member of the Brotherhood. In the period 1469–1502 the external members included fifteen Habsburg courtiers holding offices such as councillor, steward, doctor and chaplain. Between 1479 and 1514 they also included nine representatives of both the house of Nassau, closely allied to the Habsburgs, and of the Nassau court. From 1507, moreover, the members of the Brotherhood included "*Franssu de Savoy, vrou van Nassau, tot Breda*", that is to say Henry's wife, Louise-Françoise de Savoie. Henry himself is mentioned in Brotherhood records in 1517/18, but he must have been a member before this date.

For a work of art produced in conjunction with a marriage, such as the *Garden of Earthly Delights*, it was not unusual for serious and entertaining elements to appear in such close proximity. This combination was in accordance with the duty of secular art to instruct and delight, *docere et delectare*, functions that could only be fulfilled by means of an elaborate pictorial programme. By way of comparison, we may cite two work complexes by Sandro Botticelli (1445–1510), both connected with a marriage and both intended to decorate the bedrooms or antechambers of bridal couples. The first complex comprises

Botticelli's *Primavera* (p. 175) and *Minerva and the Centaur* (Florence, Galleria degli Uffizi) and the second his four-part *Nastagio degli Onesti* cycle, illustrating a tale from Boccaccio's *Decamerone* about a knight from Ravenna (p. 178). These paintings deliver very serious, didactic messages that are no less drastic than Bosch's representations of Hell, and that take as their chief theme the ambivalence and fragility of earthly love even as they celebrate the marriage of two young members of the aristocracy. Such unions were not private matters but highly political affairs; and for the bridal couple they marked a major new chapter not just in their personal lives. The biblical themes of the *Garden of Earthly Delights* and the mythological themes of Botticelli's paintings can be explained in terms of the different thinking on marriage north and south of the Alps. Bosch's triptych reflects the primarily religious and moral perspective from which marriage was viewed in northern Europe, as reflected in the writings of scholars such as Albrecht von Eyb (1420–1476), whose book *Ob einem manne sey zu nehmen ein eeliches weib oder niet* discussed "Whether a Man should take a Wedded Wife or Not". This book on marriage was particularly widely read and was published in numerous editions between 1472 and 1540, including a Dutch translation. In Italy, on the other hand, marriage was situated to a large extent in a socio-political context, with emphasis falling upon its significance for the State. *The Garden of Earthly Delights* was naturally unable to set forth the differentiated arguments of a written treatise on marriage.

The dual function of art to instruct and to delight was invoked in the context of a wedding in 1394, when Willem van Hildegaertsberge had delivered a poem at the governor's palace in The Hague as part of the festivities accompanying the marriage of Albert of Bavaria (1336–1404) and Margaret of Cleves (*c.* 1375–1411) (Oostrom 1987, no. LVI, pp. 46–53; Fischer 2009, pp. 270–271). Hildegaertsberge concentrates first of all upon instruction and opens his recitation with an appeal to the assembled company to remain peaceable and to enjoy the wedding festivities in harmony and concord, always mindful of the God-given union between man and woman in the shape of Adam and Eve, who were able to live in the Garden of Eden as long as they remained without sin. He then expounds the benefits of marriage as guarantor of the continued existence of humankind, firstly because its lawful consummation prevents humankind from dying out, and secondly because upholding the marital bond in loving partnership protects husband and wife from divine retribution. At this point the image of humankind before the Flood may well have occurred to his audience. This moralising line of argument stresses that disciplined conduct is the foundation of a good and likewise enjoyable life. The poem finally requests that listeners be not offended by the lesson it has delivered, since good teachings, when they are followed, often lead to

Detail from: **The Garden of Earthly Delights**, *c.* 1503
Central panel: **Humankind before the Flood** (see ill. pp. 190/191)

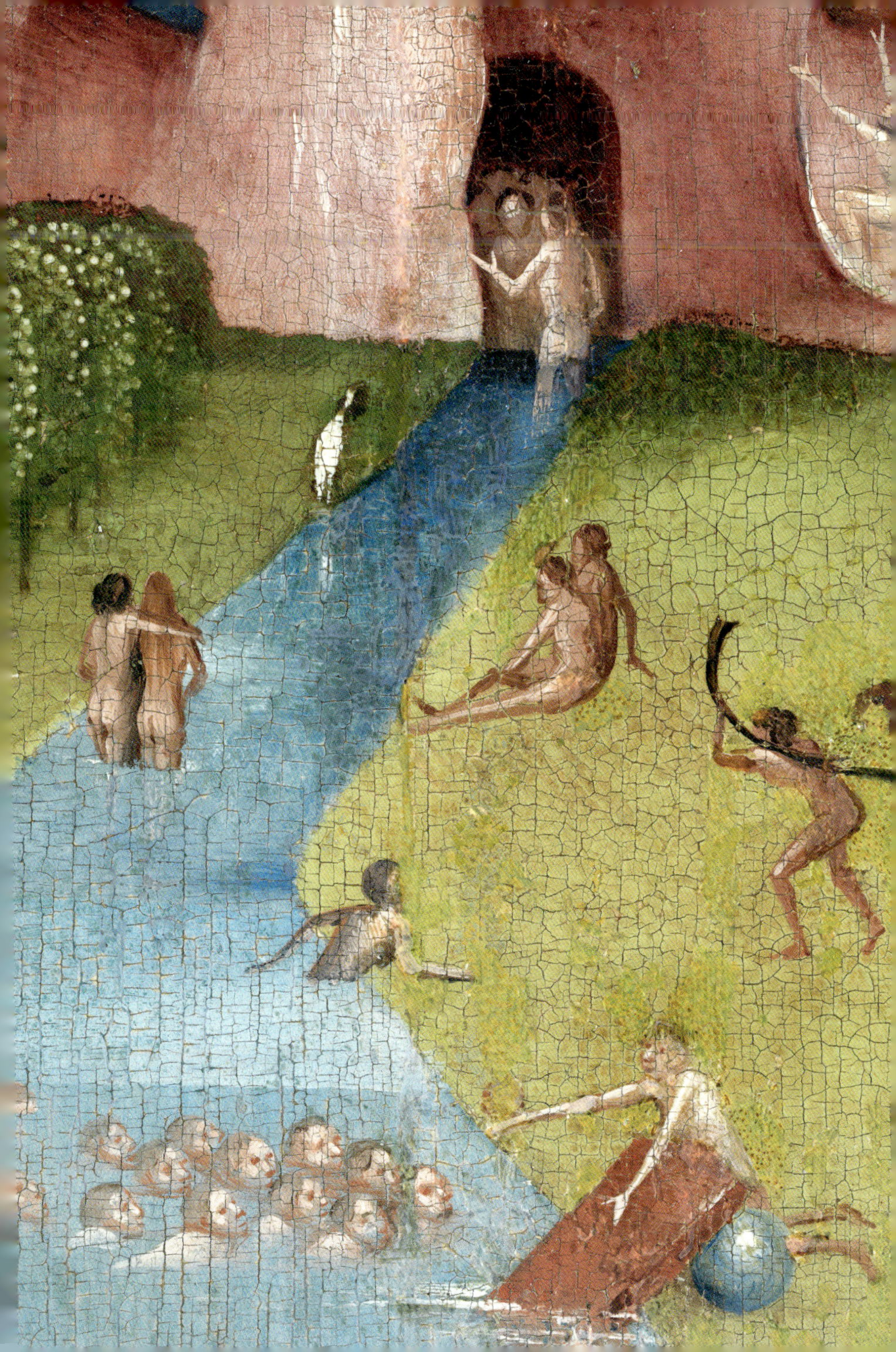

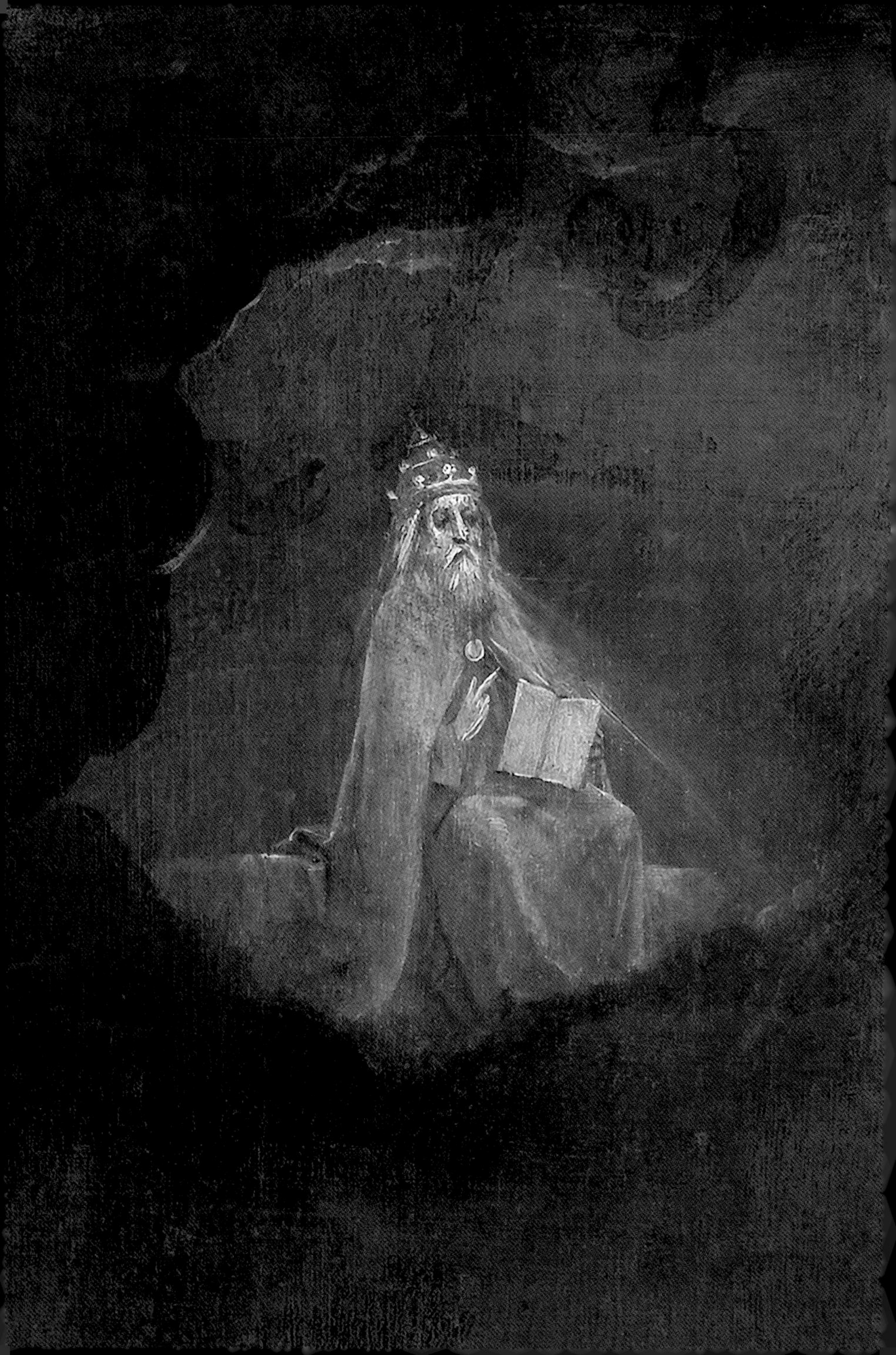

wisdom. Hildegaertsberge concludes with a few words on the role of the poet, which consists of maintaining the balance between entertainment and instruction. The moral should not be presented in too aggressive or forceful a manner, but nor should a poem be pure entertainment with no (moral) benefit. Bosch certainly seems to have designed the central panel of the *Garden of Earthly Delights* primarily in terms of visual appeal, with its colourful and strange panorama intended to intrigue and delight a courtly public.

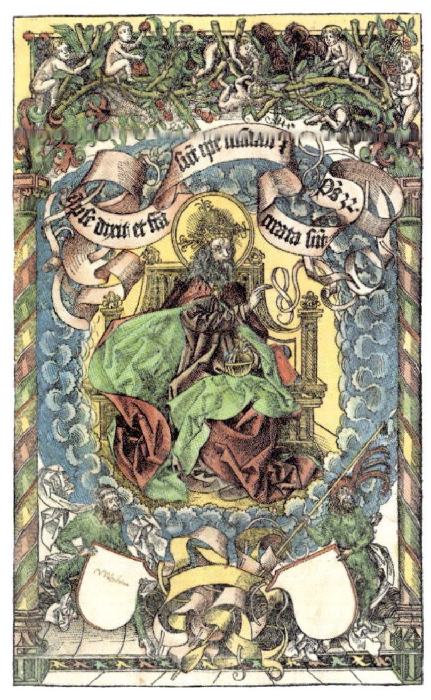

It could, in any case, surely have rivalled the colourful and exotic banquet staged for the wedding of Charles the Bold and Margaret of York (d. 1503) in 1468 in Bruges, devised by the Bruges *rederijker* Anthonis de Roovere. He recorded that the meal had included two dozen different dishes of game and three dozen desserts in the shape of trees made out of sugared fruits, these last served, as a final flourish, by a pair of dwarfs (Pleij 2000, p. 141). There were dashes of coarse humour, too, such as confectionery dogs that deposited fragrant piles of nutmeg. Such utopian elements were part of a fantasy of material abundance that would guarantee not just the satisfaction of desire but also security, peace and happiness: in other words, physical as well as mental welfare. There was no expectation that these wishful fancies would be realised; they were simply enjoyed for their own aesthetic and imaginative nature. The strange and the wondrous became a means through which the wedding guests could experience another, different world, one that transported them beyond the mundane bounds of daily life. There was a fascination at court for the shape and gleam of gems and precious metals, the colours of Gobelin tapestries and magnificent clothes,

Page 182
Detail from: **Creation of the World up to the Third Day**, *c.* 1503
Outer wings of: **The Garden of Earthly Delights** (see ill. p. 186/187)

Hartmann Schedel, **God the Father as Creator of the World**, 1493
from: *Chronicle of the World*, fol. IV, Nuremberg 1493
Woodcut, 42 x 58 cm / 16½ x 22⅞ in. Weimar, Herzogin Anna Amalia Bibliothek

and natural curiosities such as "unicorn" horns, whale teeth, coconuts and shells. These were all considered objects that showed nature as an artist at work and, *vice versa*, art as the imitator of nature.

The aesthetic interplay between nature and art is seen in the *Garden of Earthly Delights* in the fountain of life with the precious stones at its base in the left inner wing, and in the five massive fountain structures in the background of the central panel. Exotic and untamed nature was likewise associated at court with dark-skinned figures and "wild men". These allowed courtly society to linger on the fringes of a foreign, uncivilised world before slipping back into familiar roles and ceremonies. The *Garden of Earthly Delights* lastly also allows Paradise to be perceived to a certain extent via the senses through the magnificence of its palette, which is astonishingly fresh and bright. Bosch, indeed, succeeds in achieving a harmonious colour composition with red and blue, colours normally understood as extreme opposites.

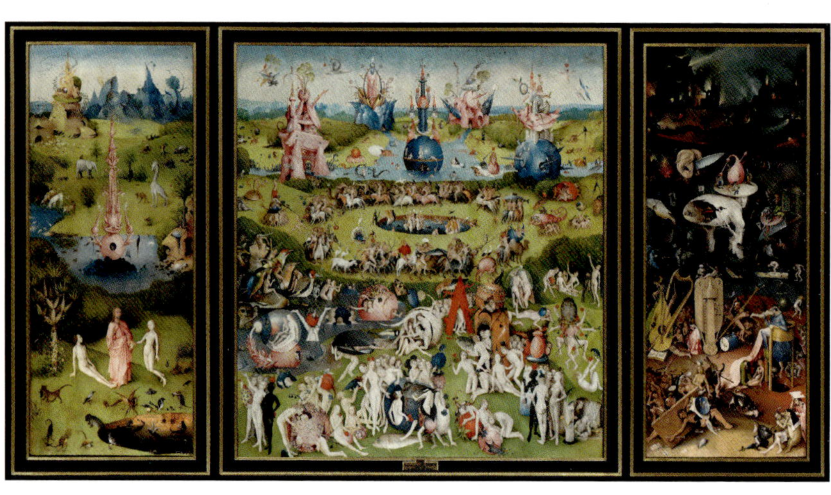

Pages 184-191
The Garden of Earthly Delights (exterior: Creation of the World), *c.* 1503
Oil on panel (oak), 220 x 195 cm / 86⅝ x 76¾ in. (central panel 190 x 176.7 cm / 74¾ x 69½ in. without frame), 220 x 97 cm / 86⅝ x 38¼ in. (wings)
Madrid, Museo Nacional del Prado

Outer wings: **Creation of the World up to the Third Day** *(Page 185, Detail; 186/187)*
Left inner wing: **Paradise and the Creation of Eve** *(Page 188)*
Central panel: **Humankind before the Flood** *(Page 190/191)*
Right inner wing: **Hell** *(Page 189)*

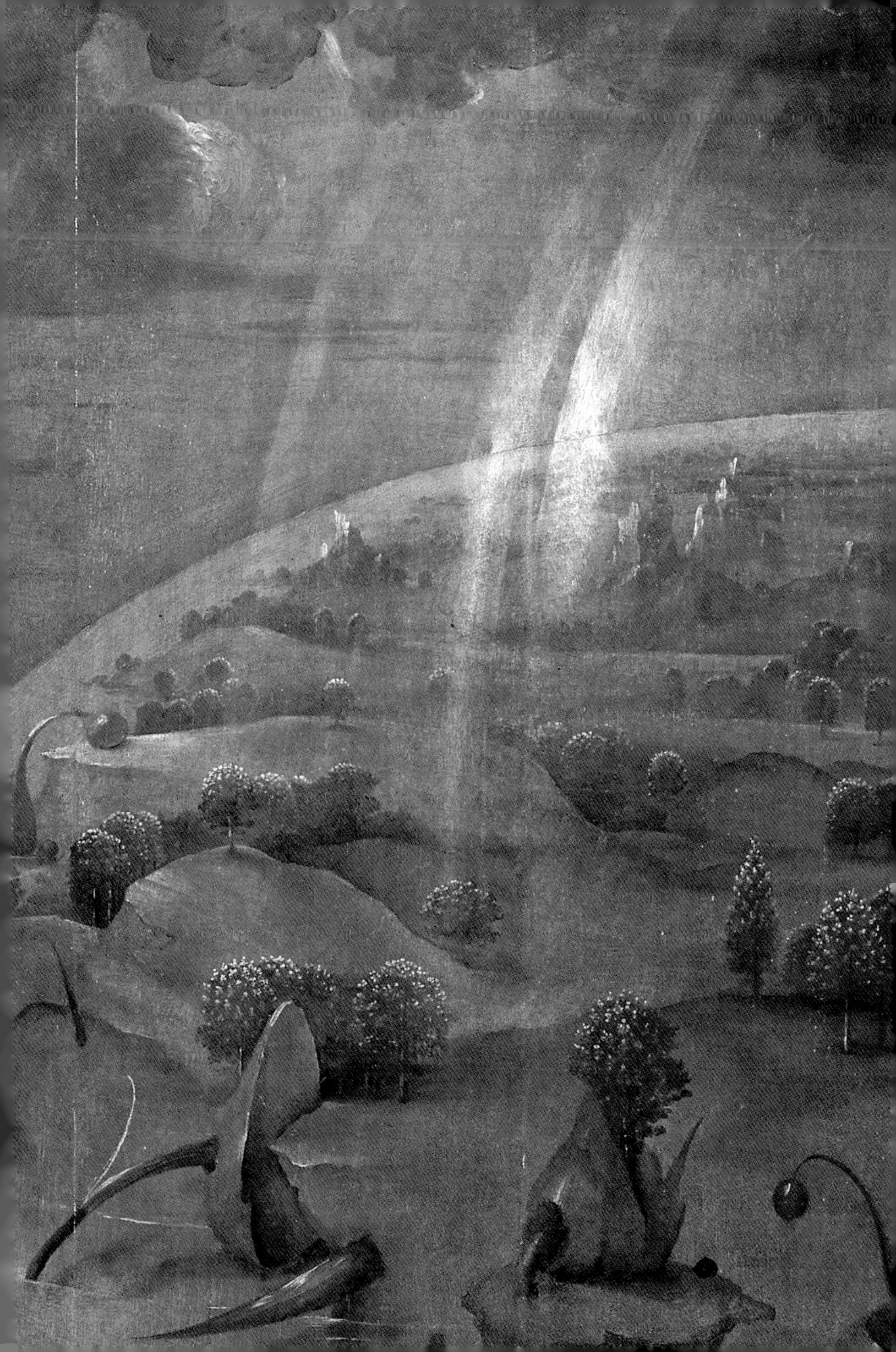

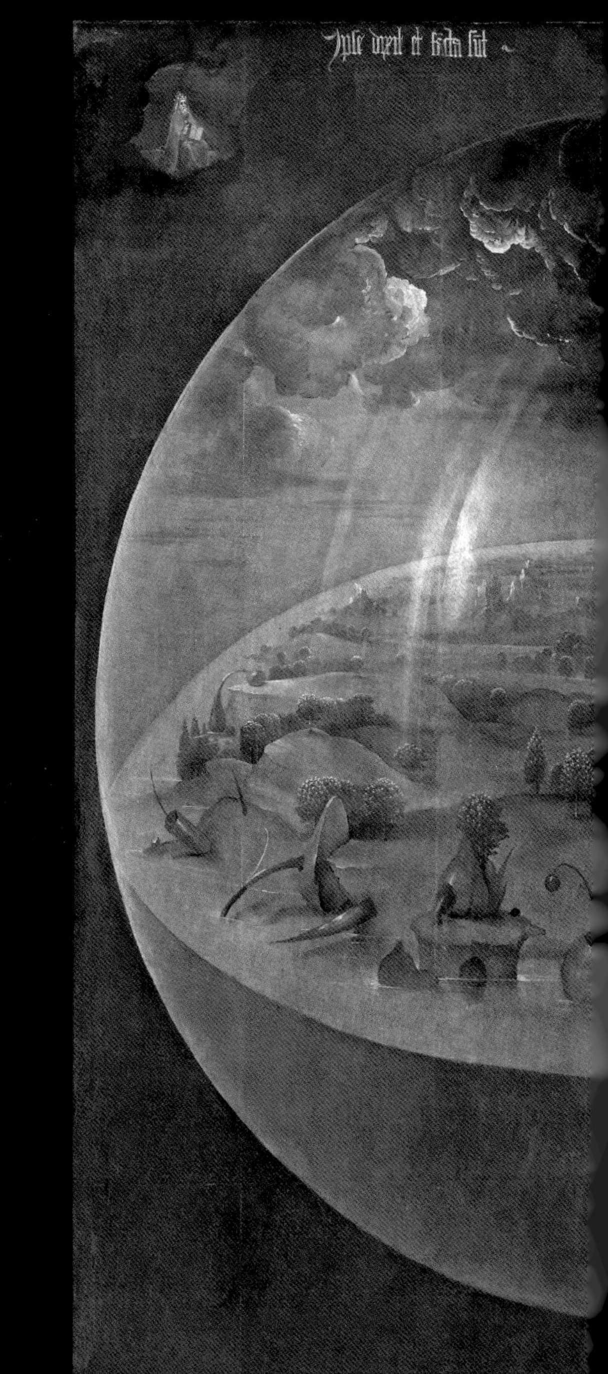
Ipse dixit et facta sunt

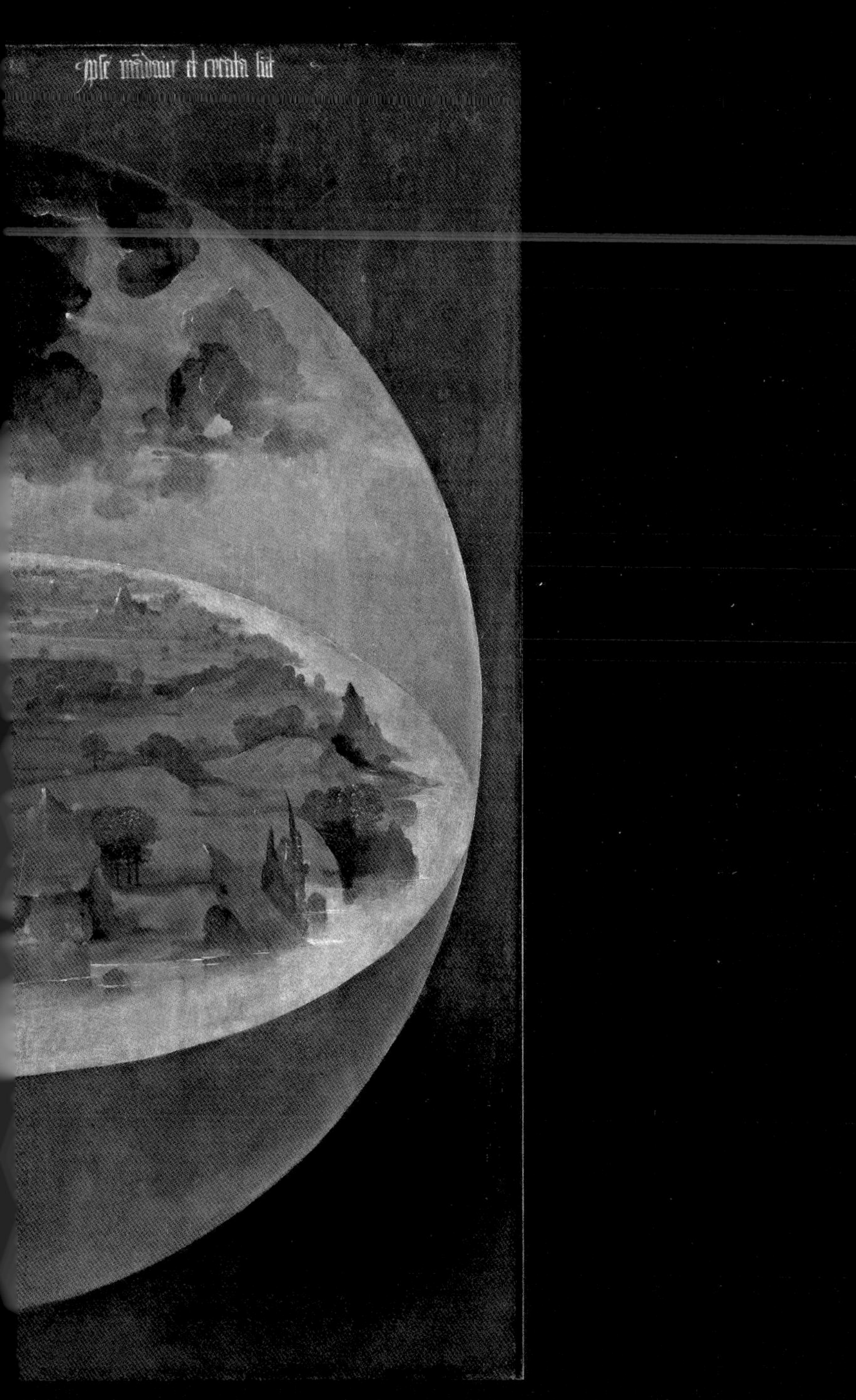
Ipse mãdavit et creata sũt

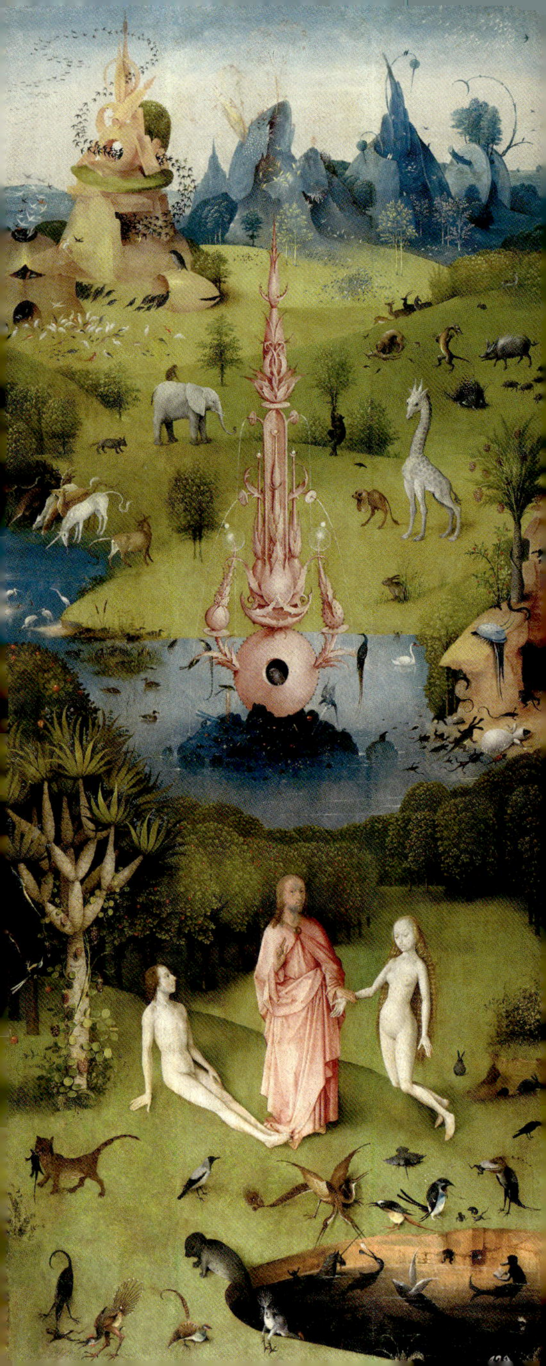

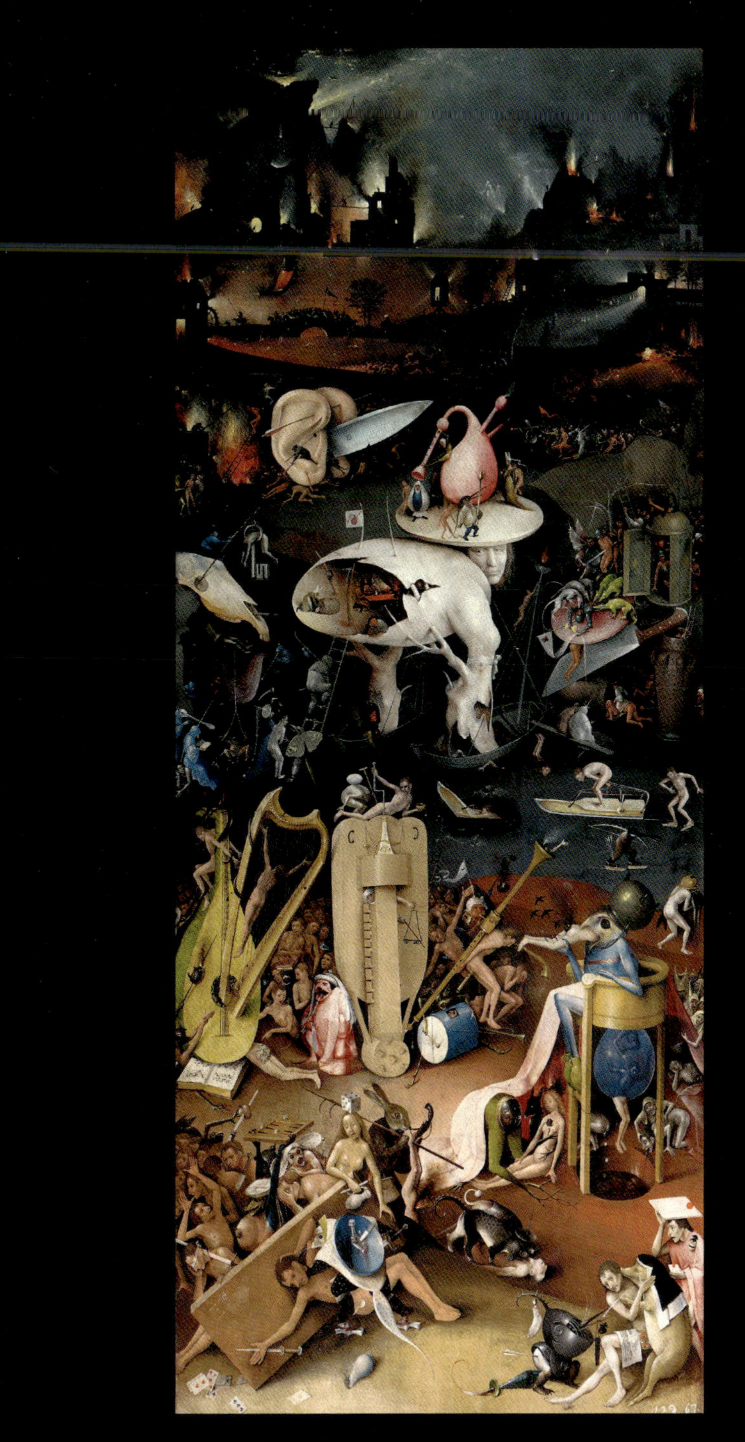

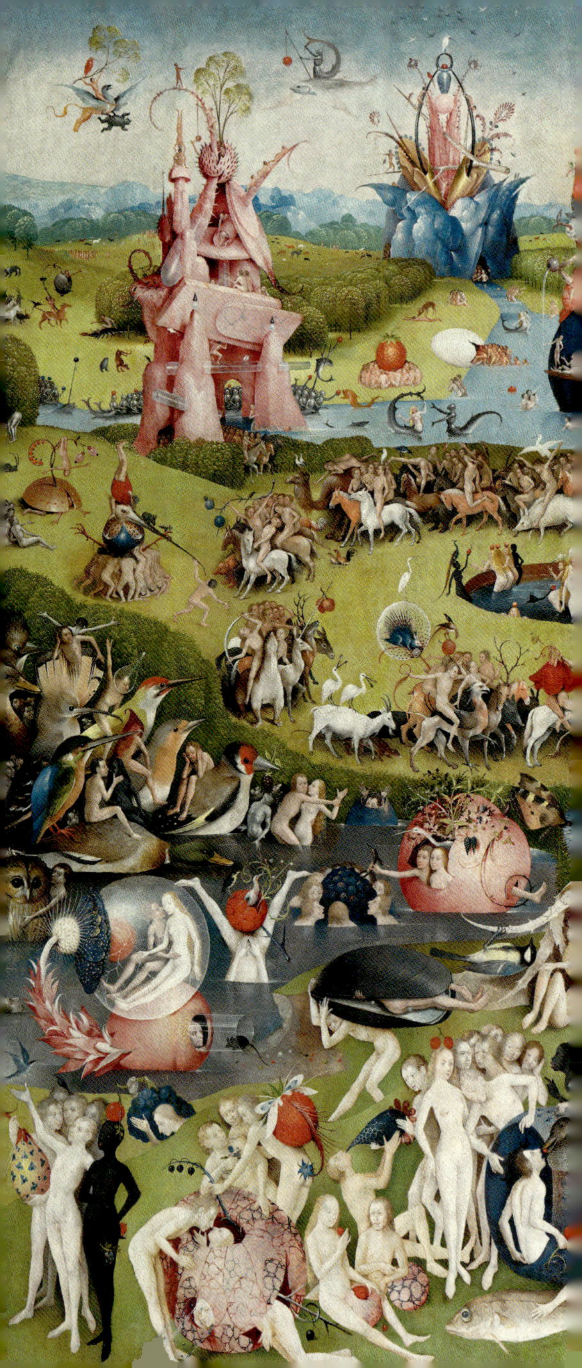

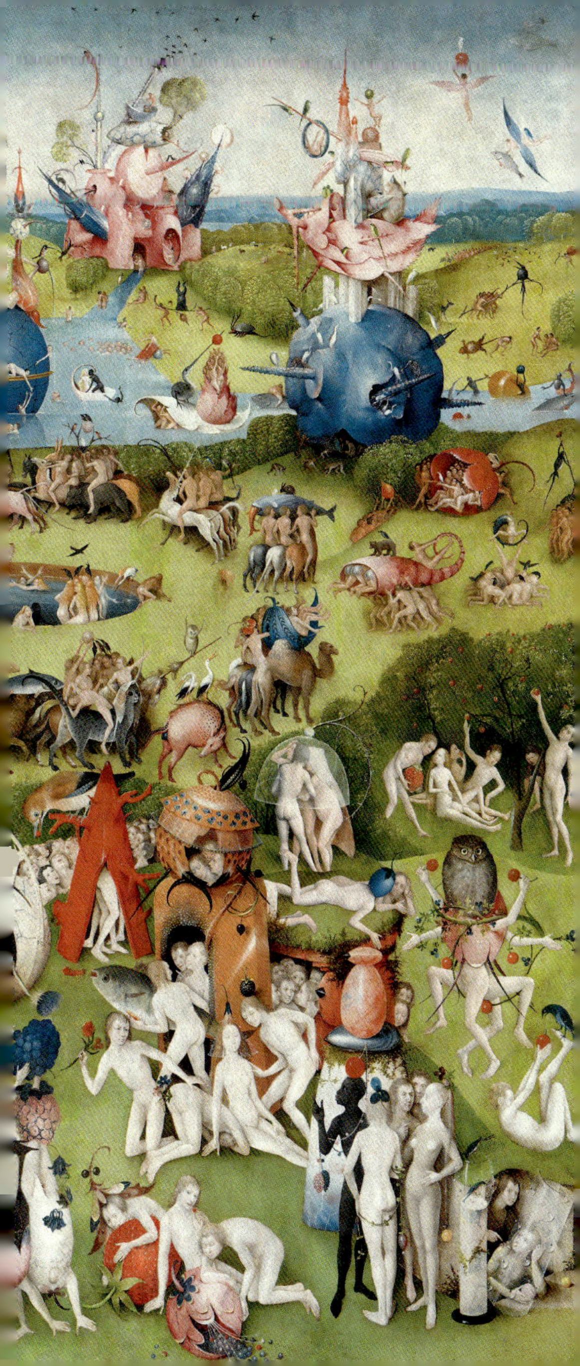

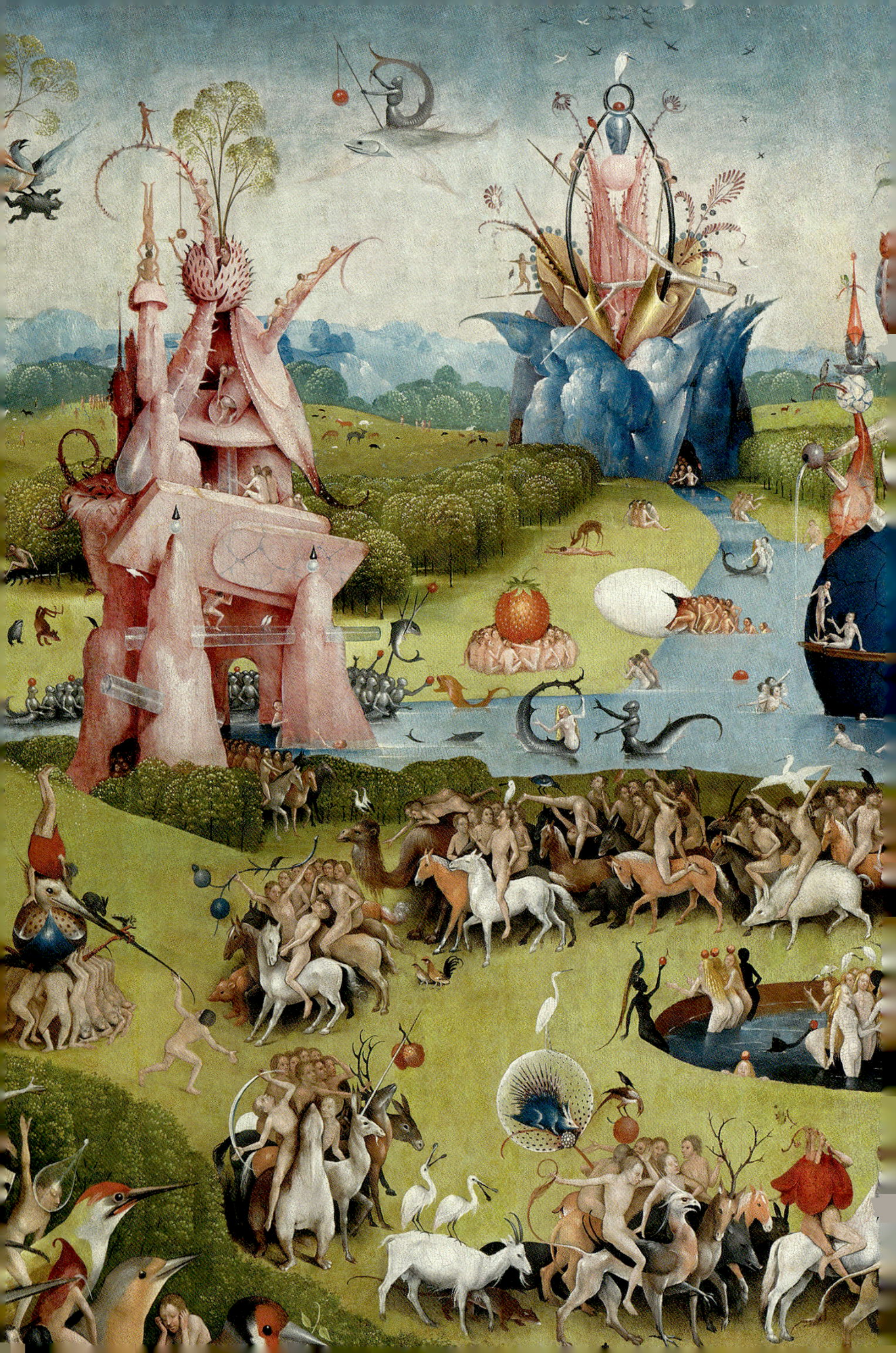

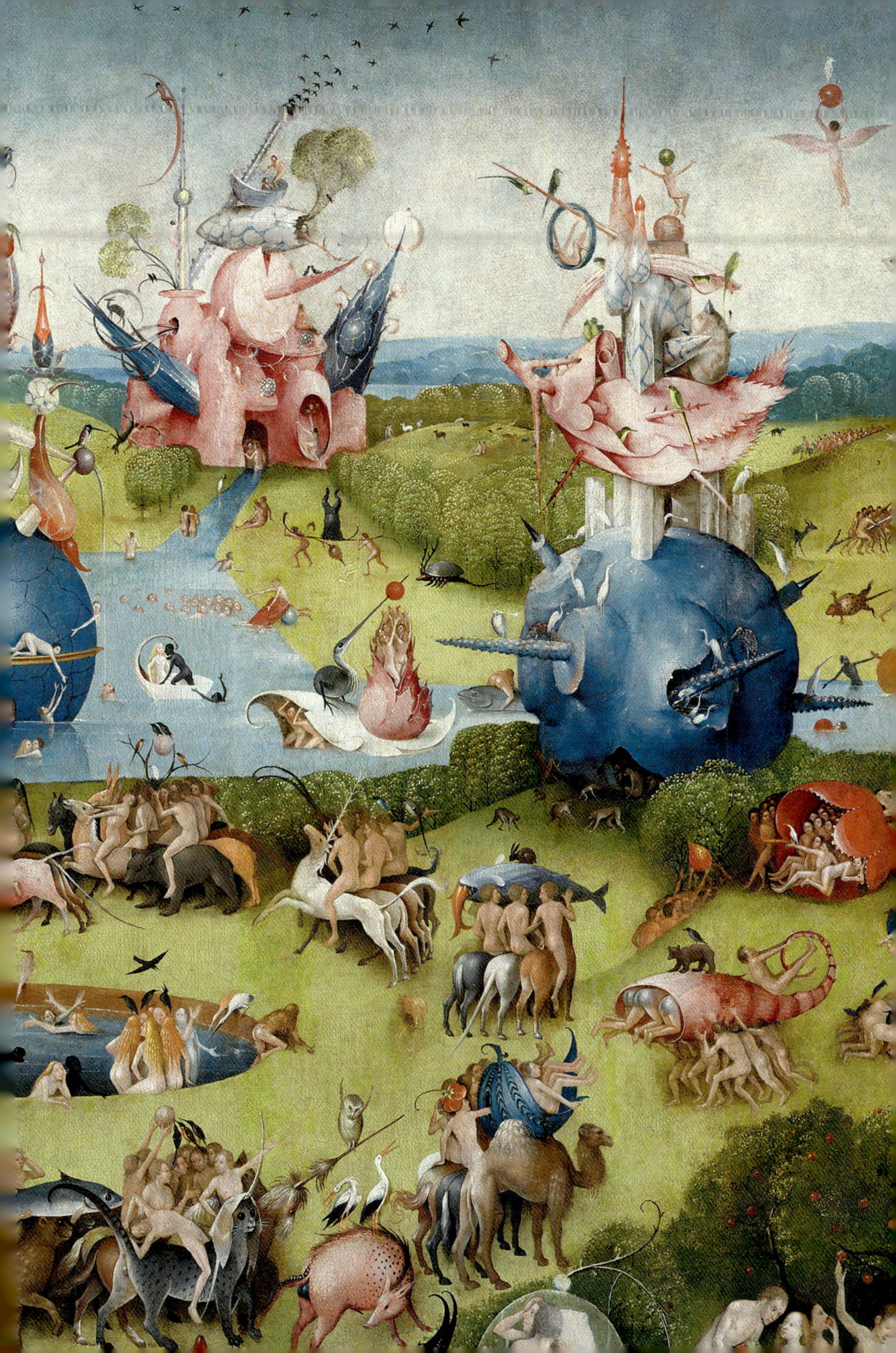

Pages 192/193, 195, 196/197
Detail from: **The Garden of Earthly Delights**, *c.* 1503
Central panel: **Humankind before the Flood** (see ill. pp. 190/191)

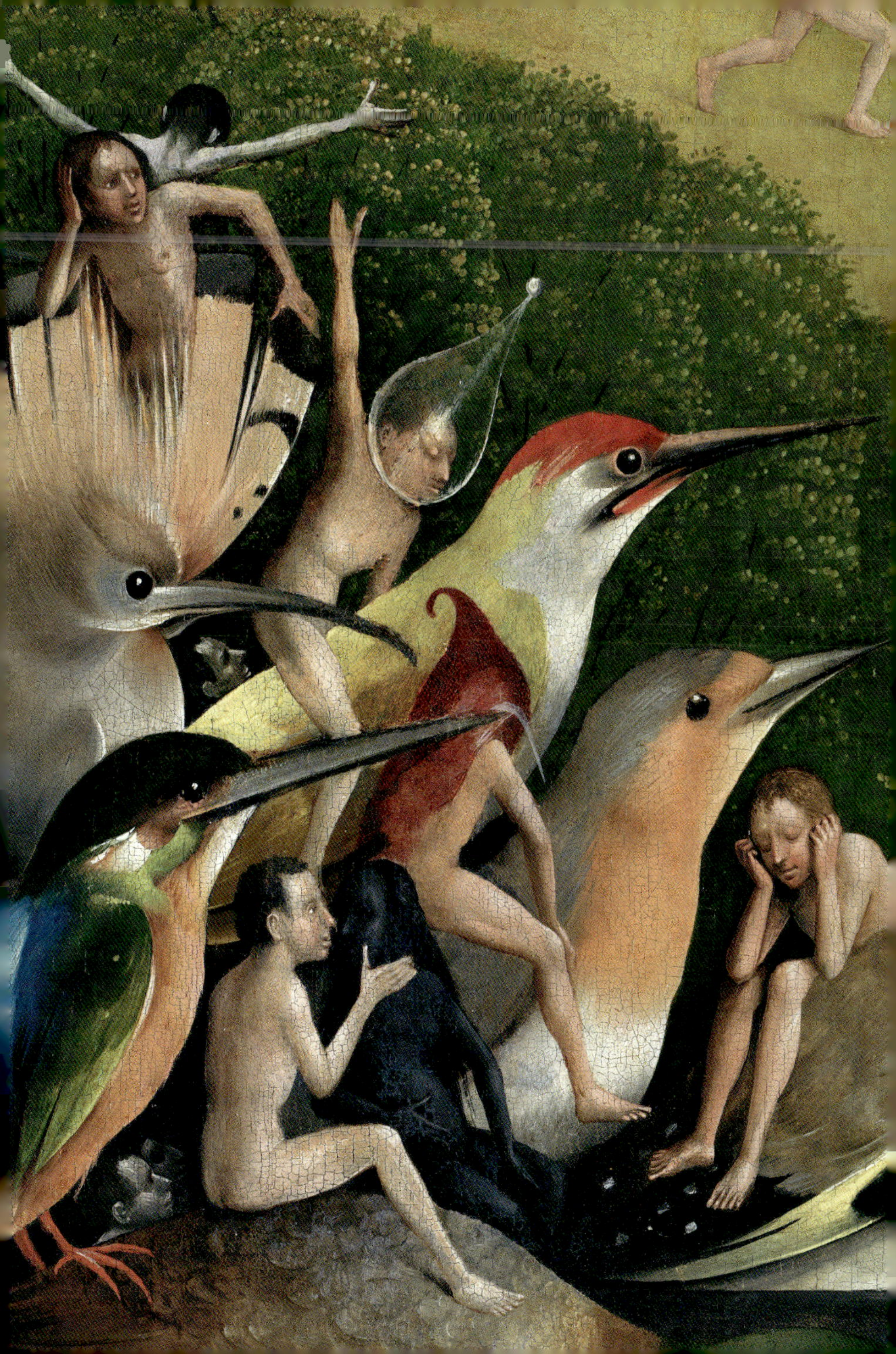

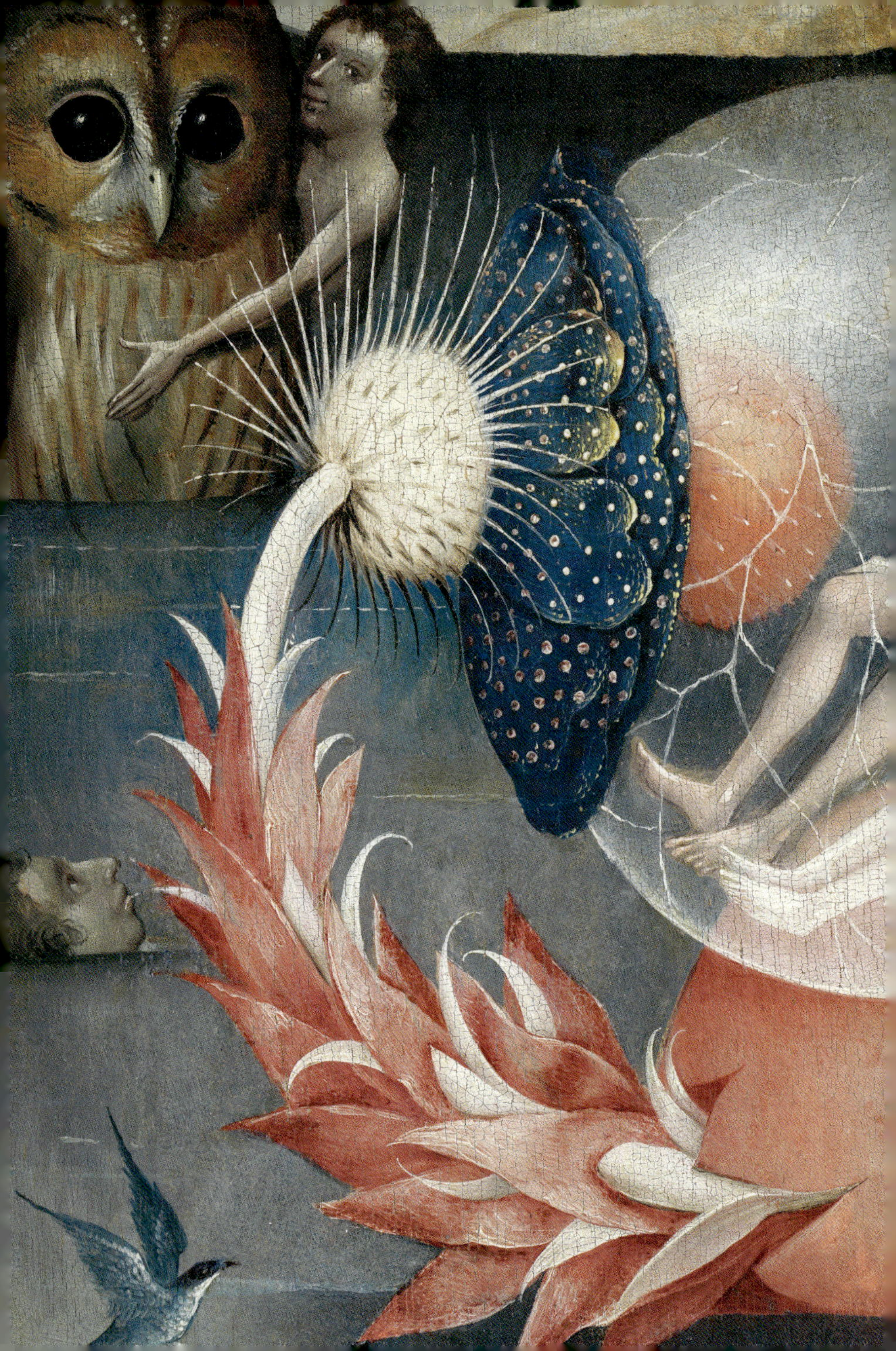

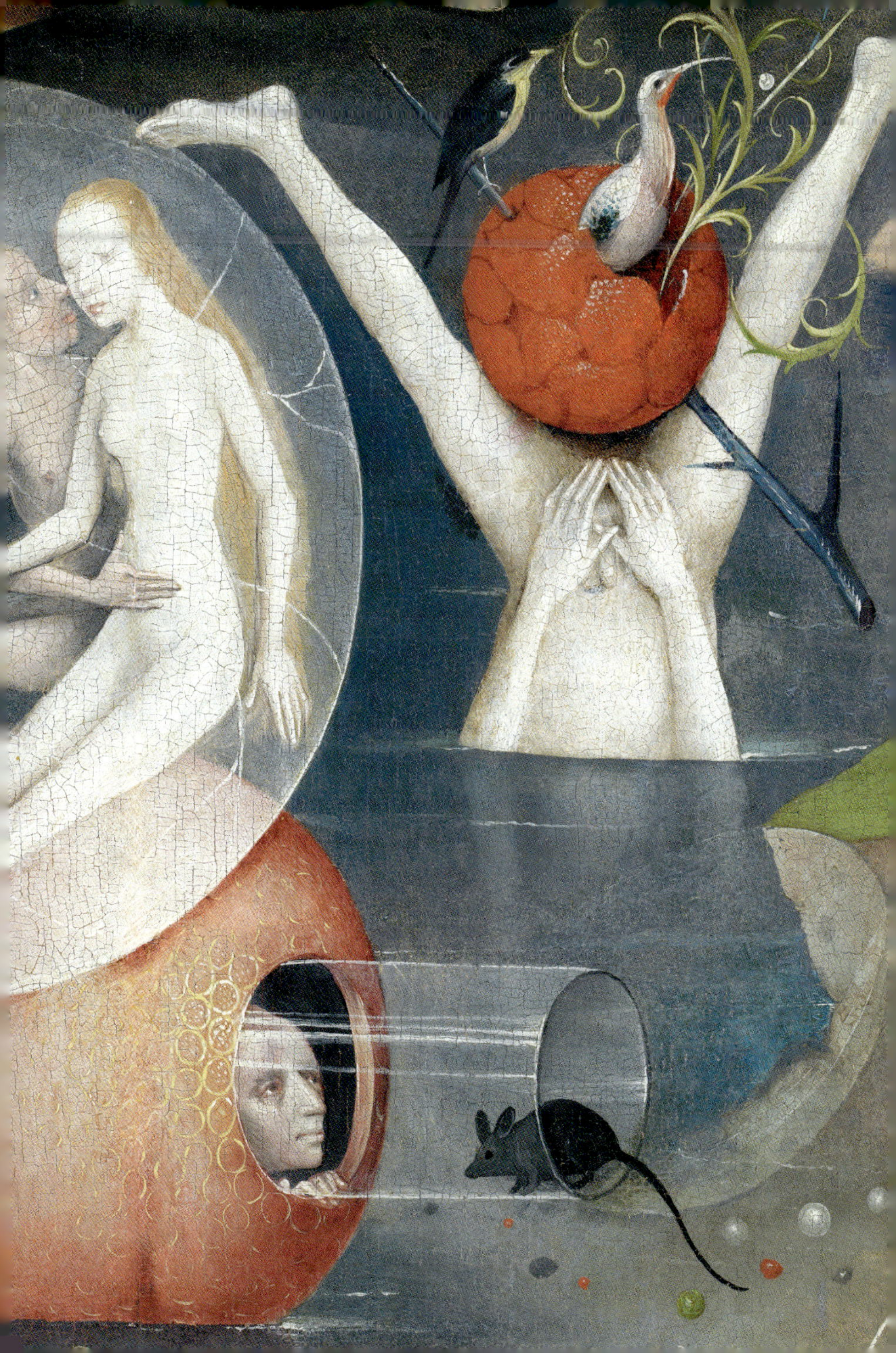

Pages 199, 200/201
Detail from: **The Garden of Earthly Delights**, *c.* 1503
Central panel: **Humankind before the Flood** (see ill. pp. 190/191)

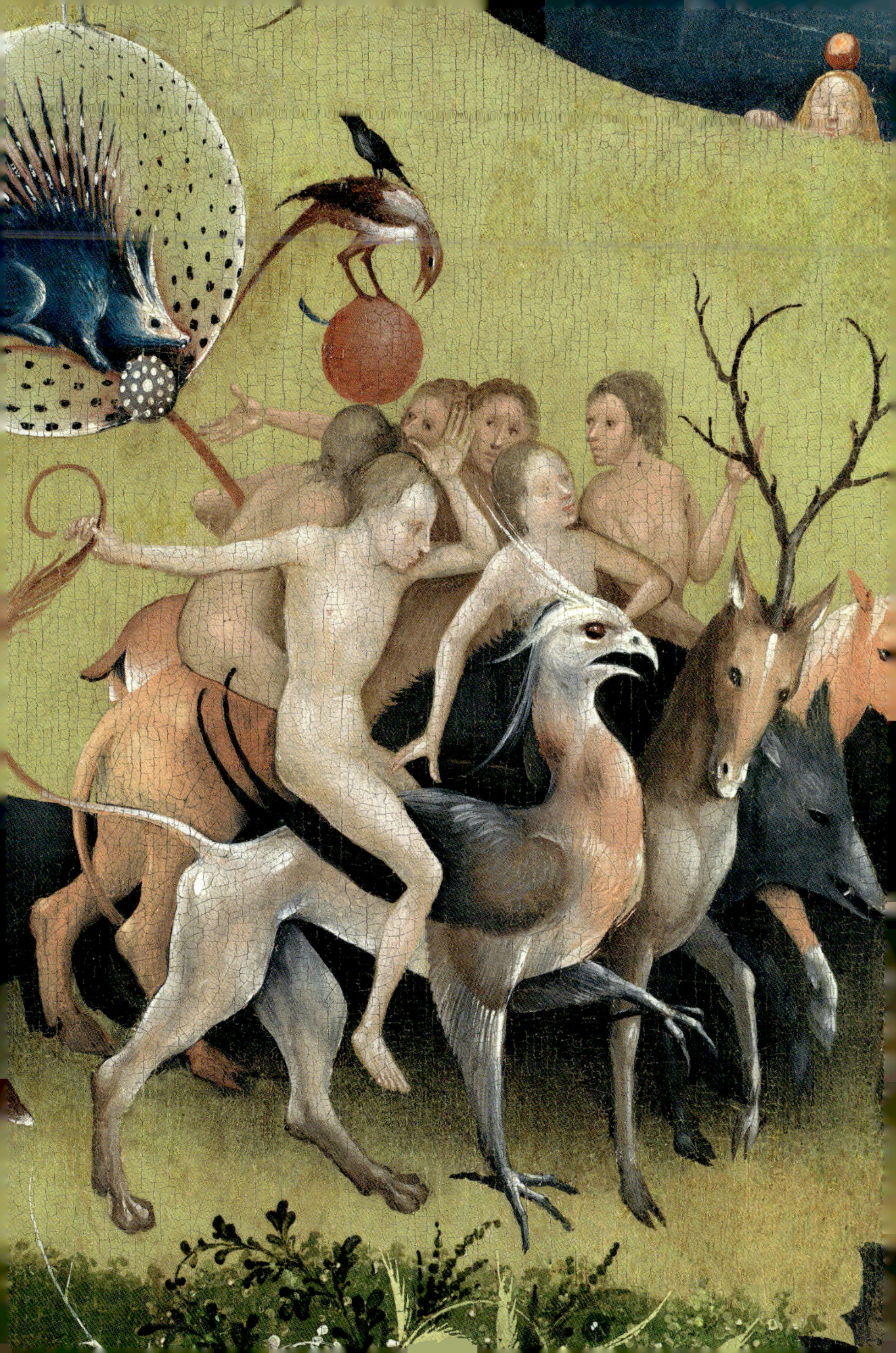

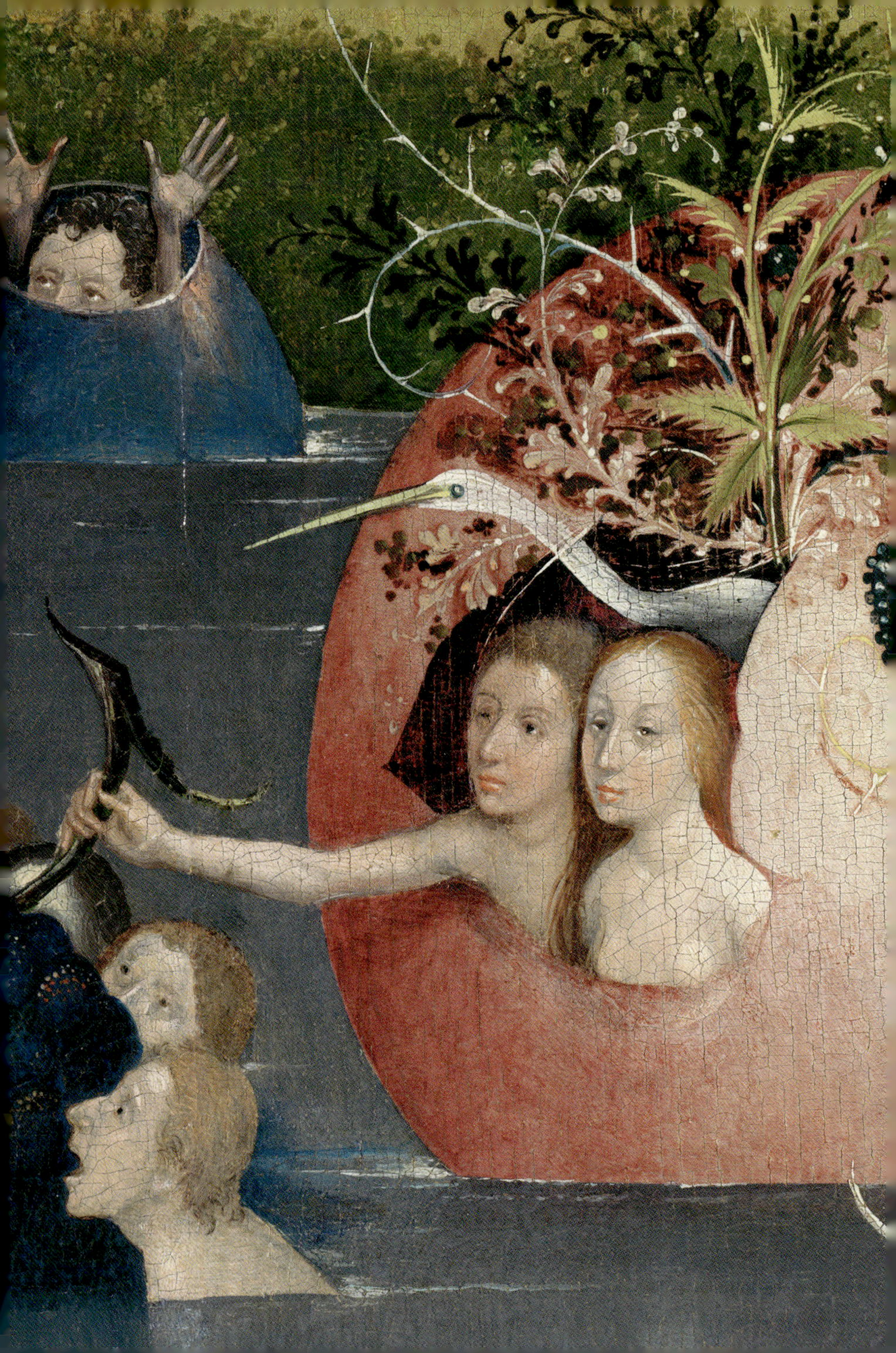

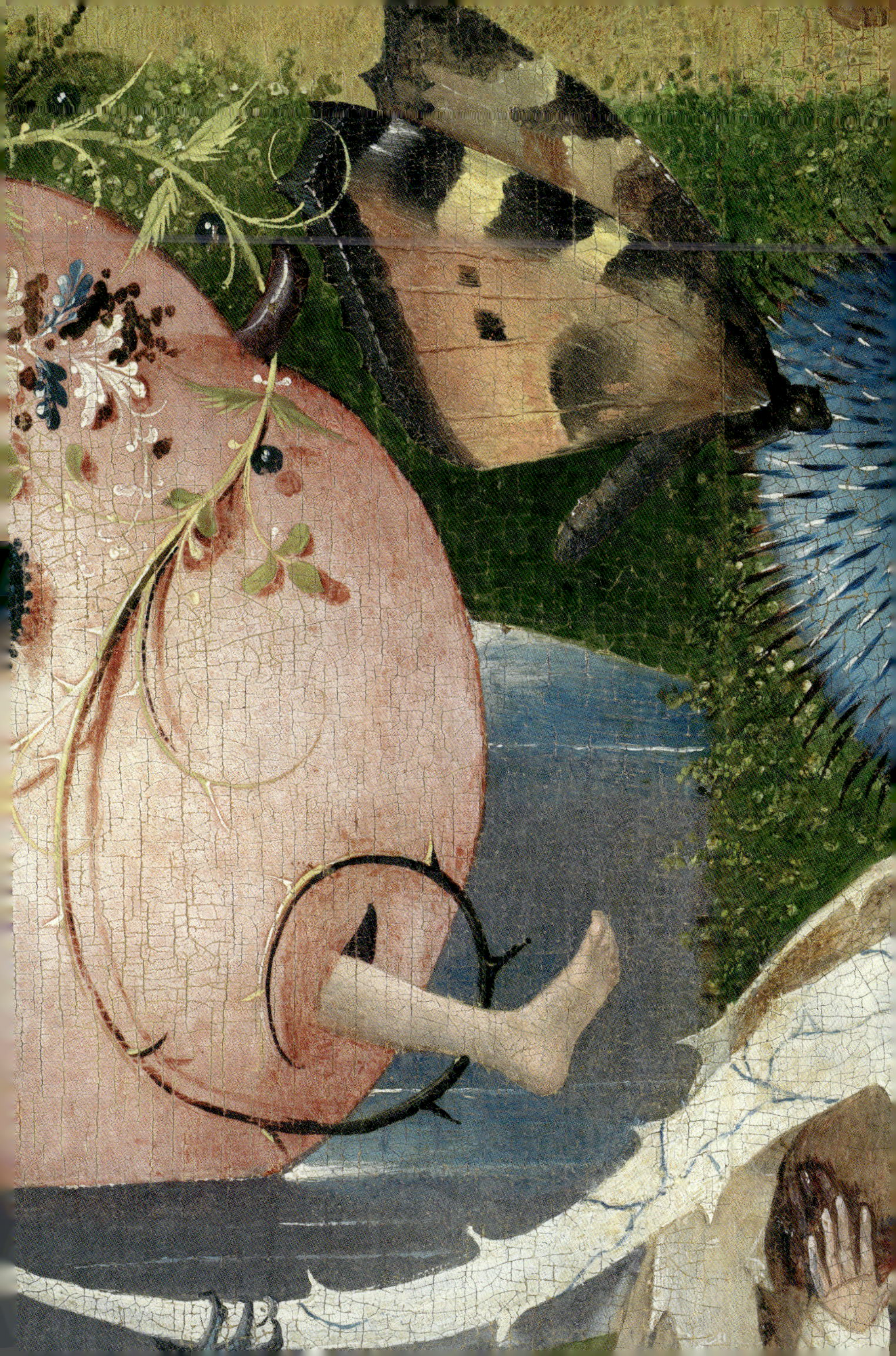

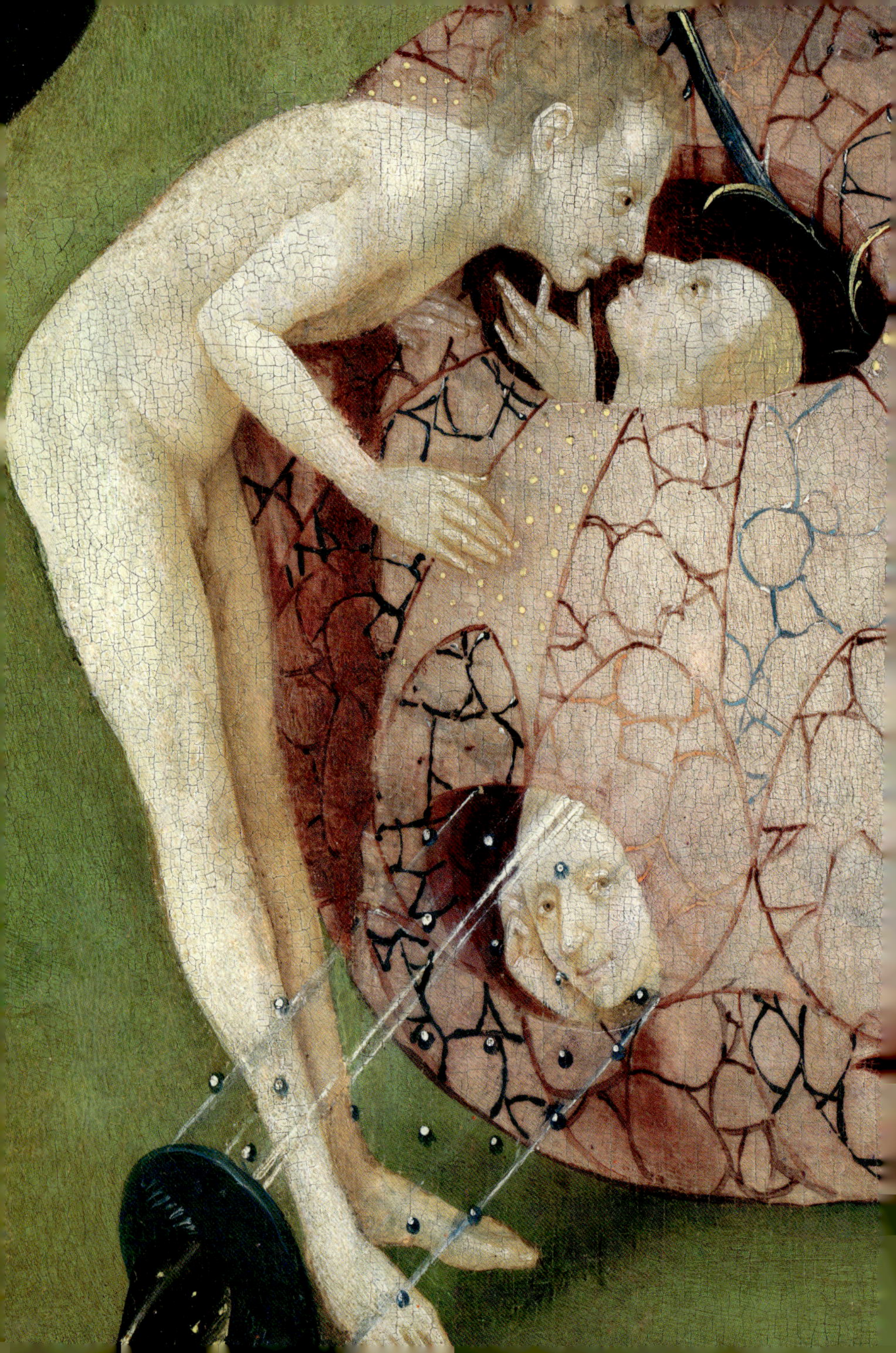

Detail from: **The Garden of Earthly Delights**, *c.* 1503
Central panel: **Humankind before the Flood** (see ill. pp. 190/191)

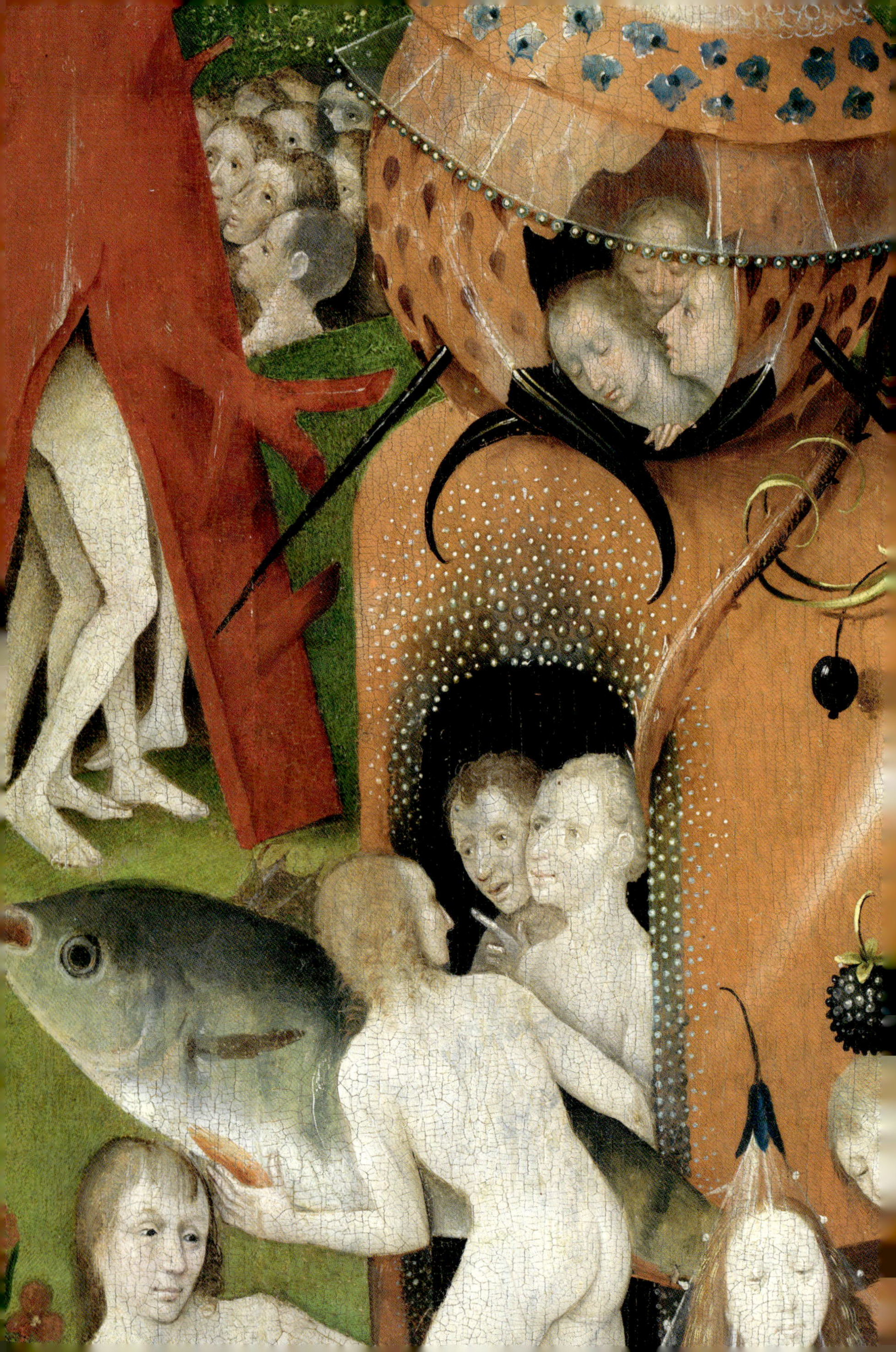

Detail from: **The Garden of Earthly Delights**, *c.* 1503
Central panel: **Humankind before the Flood** (see ill. pp. 190/191)

Details from: **The Garden of Earthly Delights**, *c.* 1503

Page 207
Central panel: **Humankind before the Flood** (see ill. p. 190/191)

Pages 208/209, 210/211
Right inner wing: **Hell** (see ill. pp. 189)

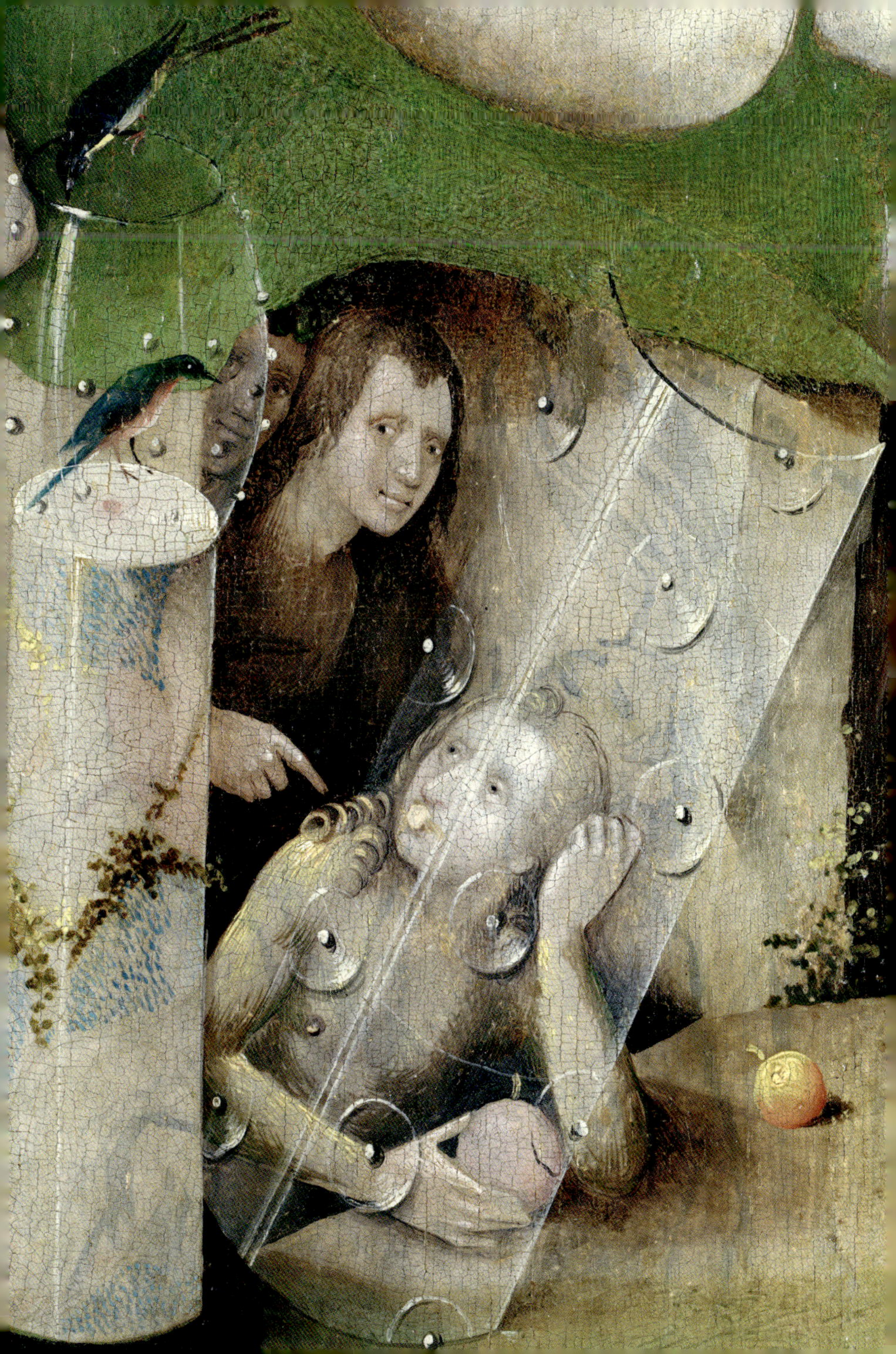

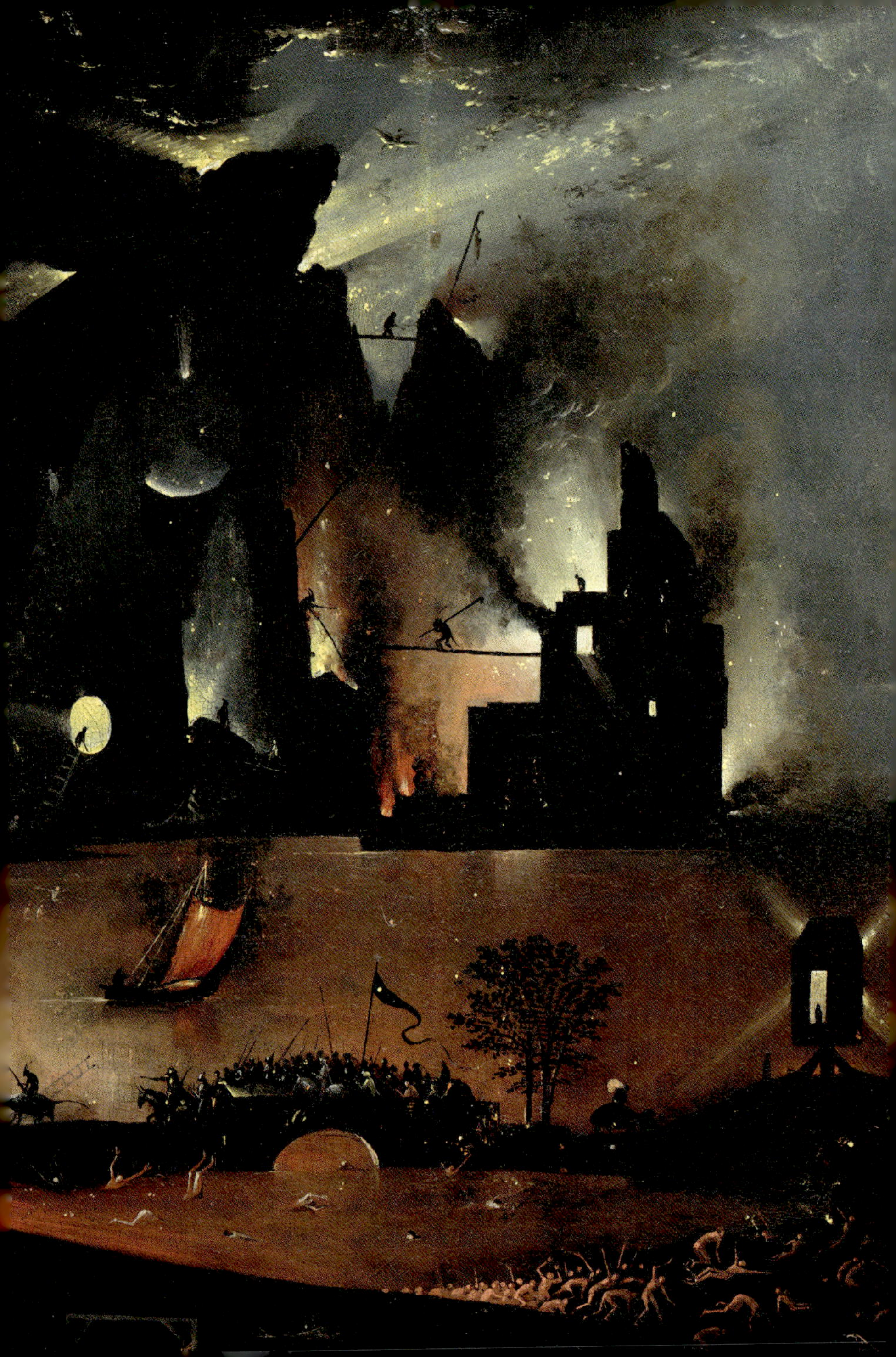

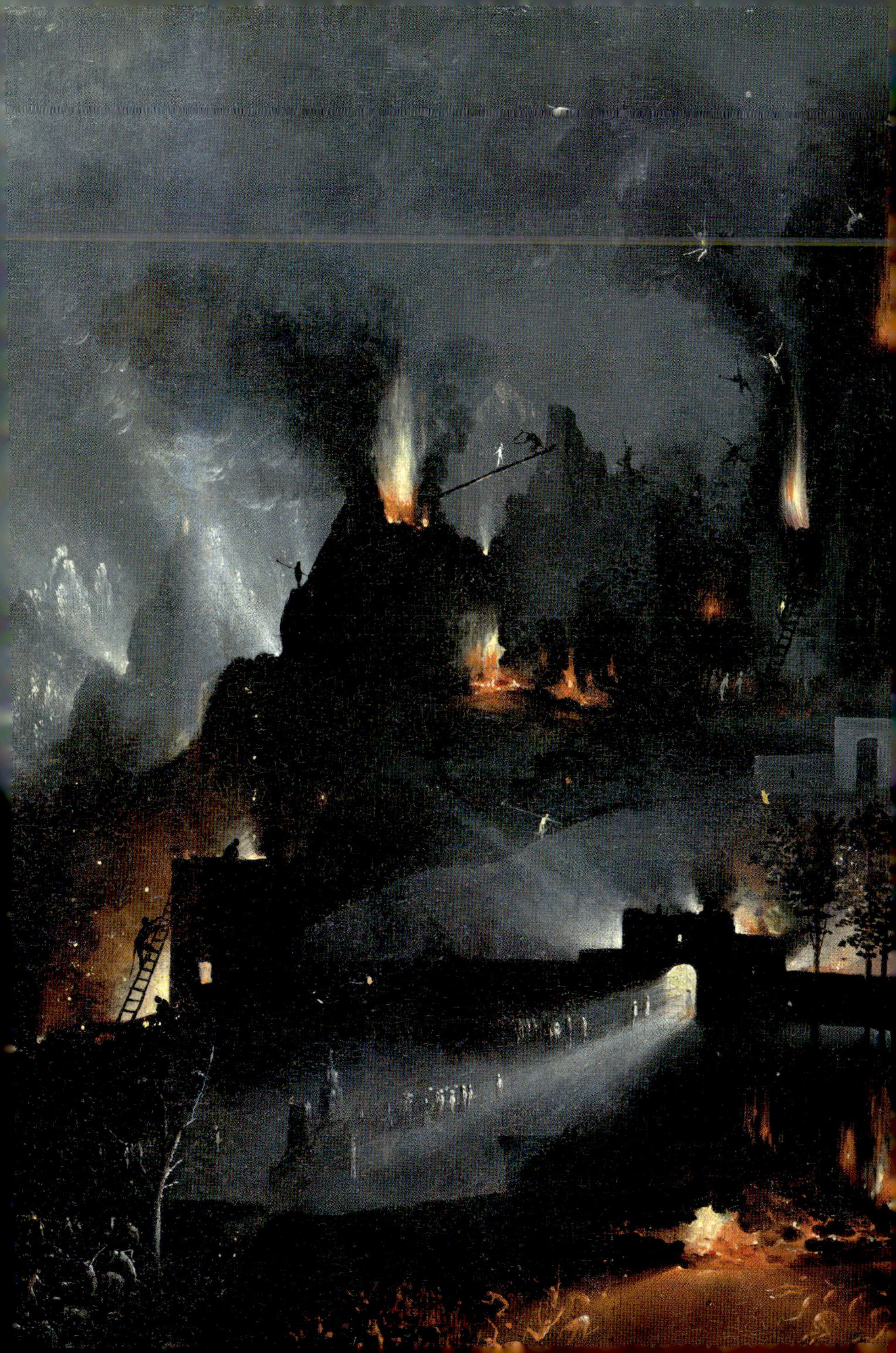

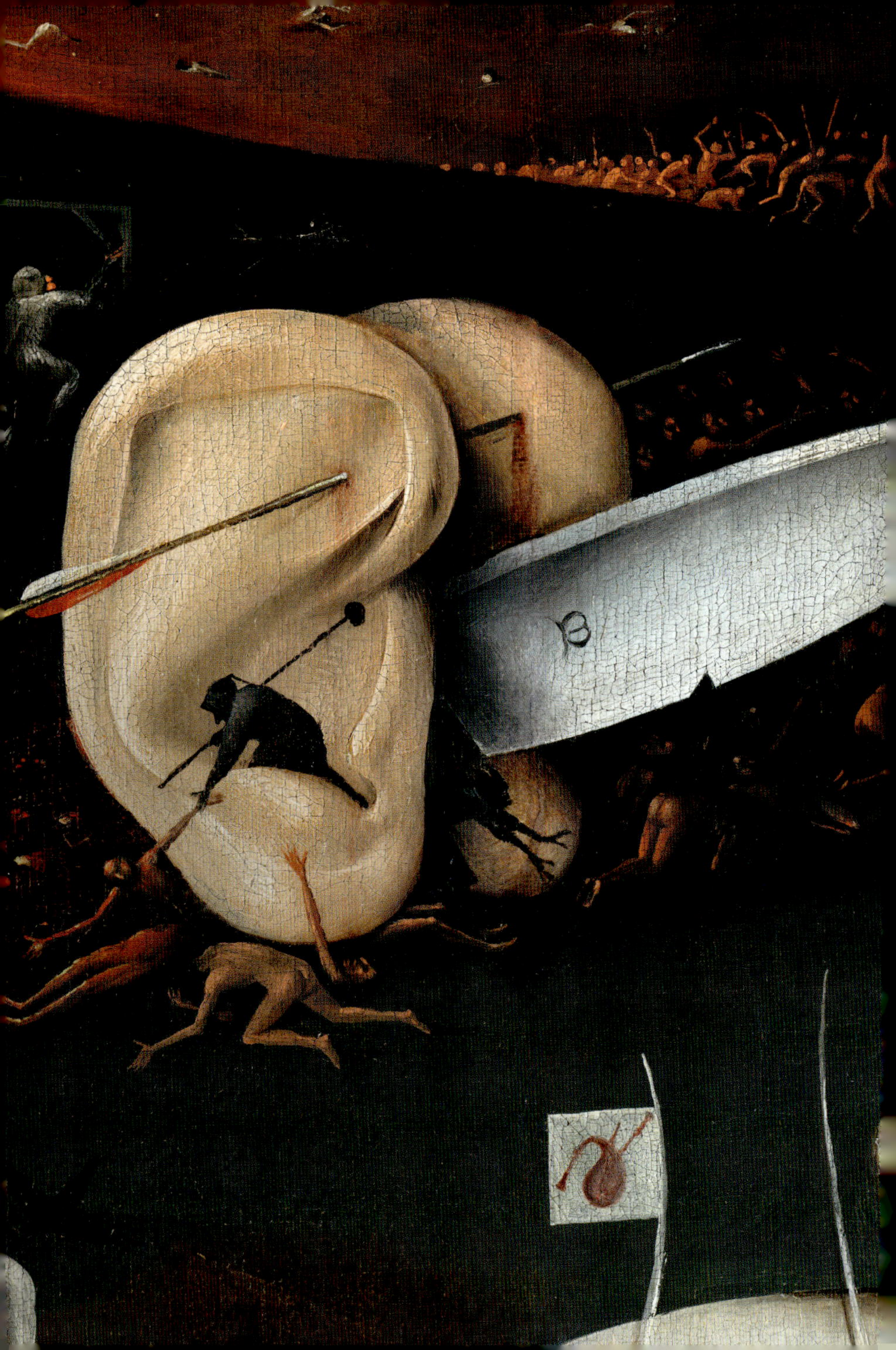

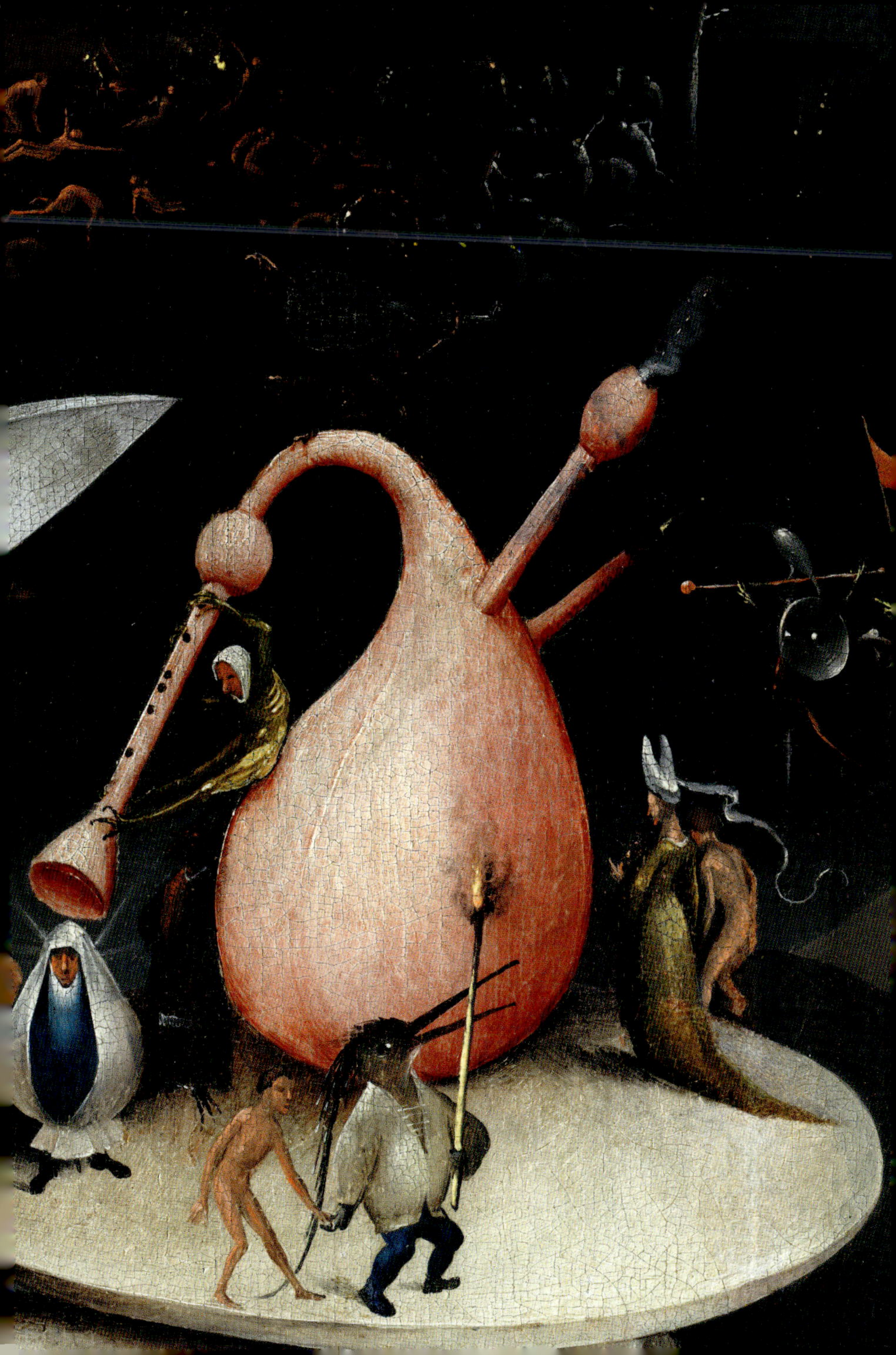

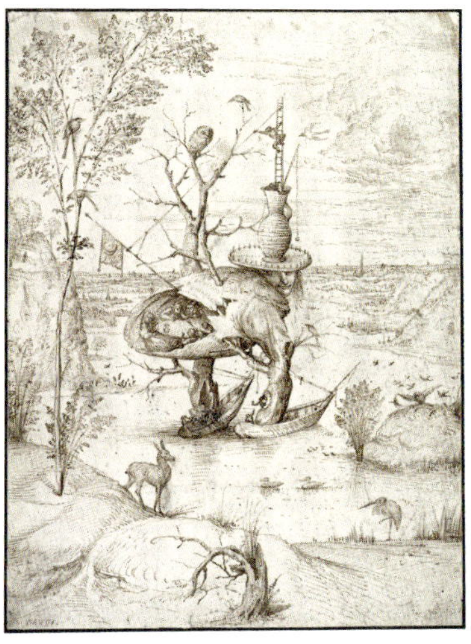

The Tree-Man, *c.* 1503–1506
Pen and brown ink on paper, 277 x 211 mm / approx. 10⅞ x 8¼ in. Vienna, Albertina
At the end of the 16th century, the name BRUEGEL was added in pen and ink by an unknown hand.

Page 213
Detail from: **The Garden of Earthly Delights**, *c.* 1503
Right inner wing: **Hell** (see ill. p. 189)

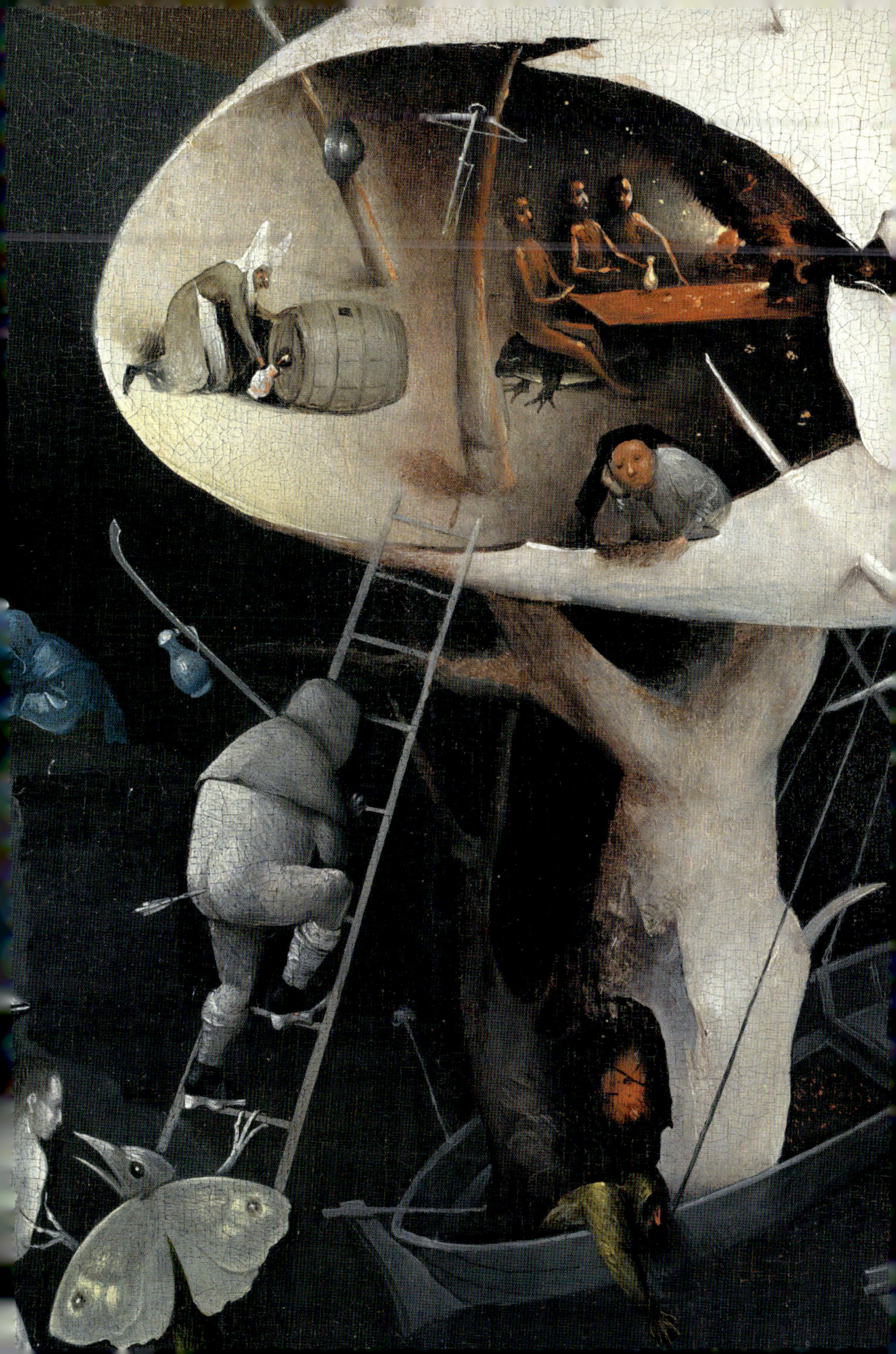

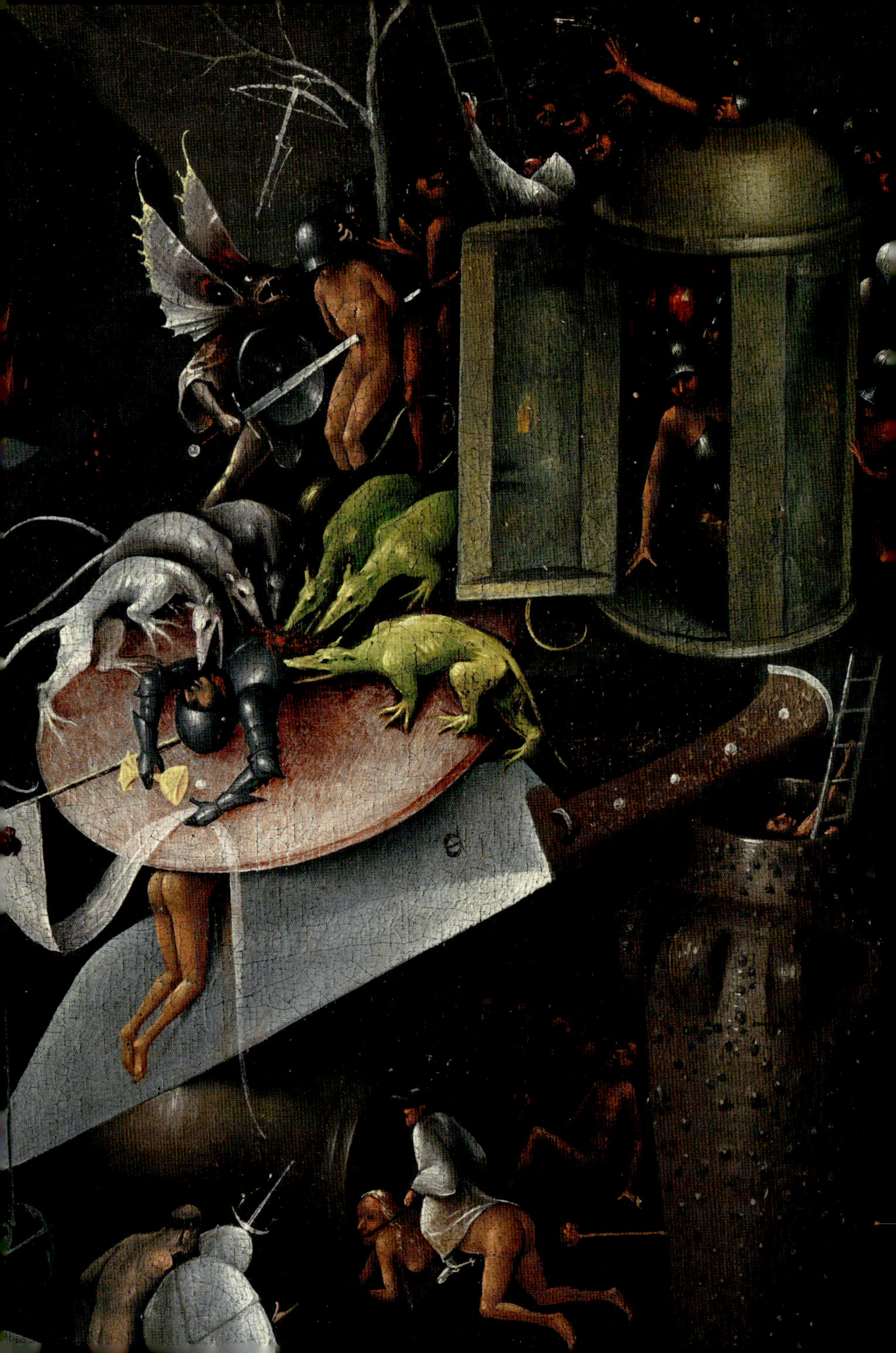

Detail from: **The Garden of Earthly Delights**, *c.* 1503
Right inner wing: **Hell** (see ill. p. 189)

Detail from: **The Garden of Earthly Delights**, *c.* 1503
Right inner wing: **Hell** (see ill. p. 189)

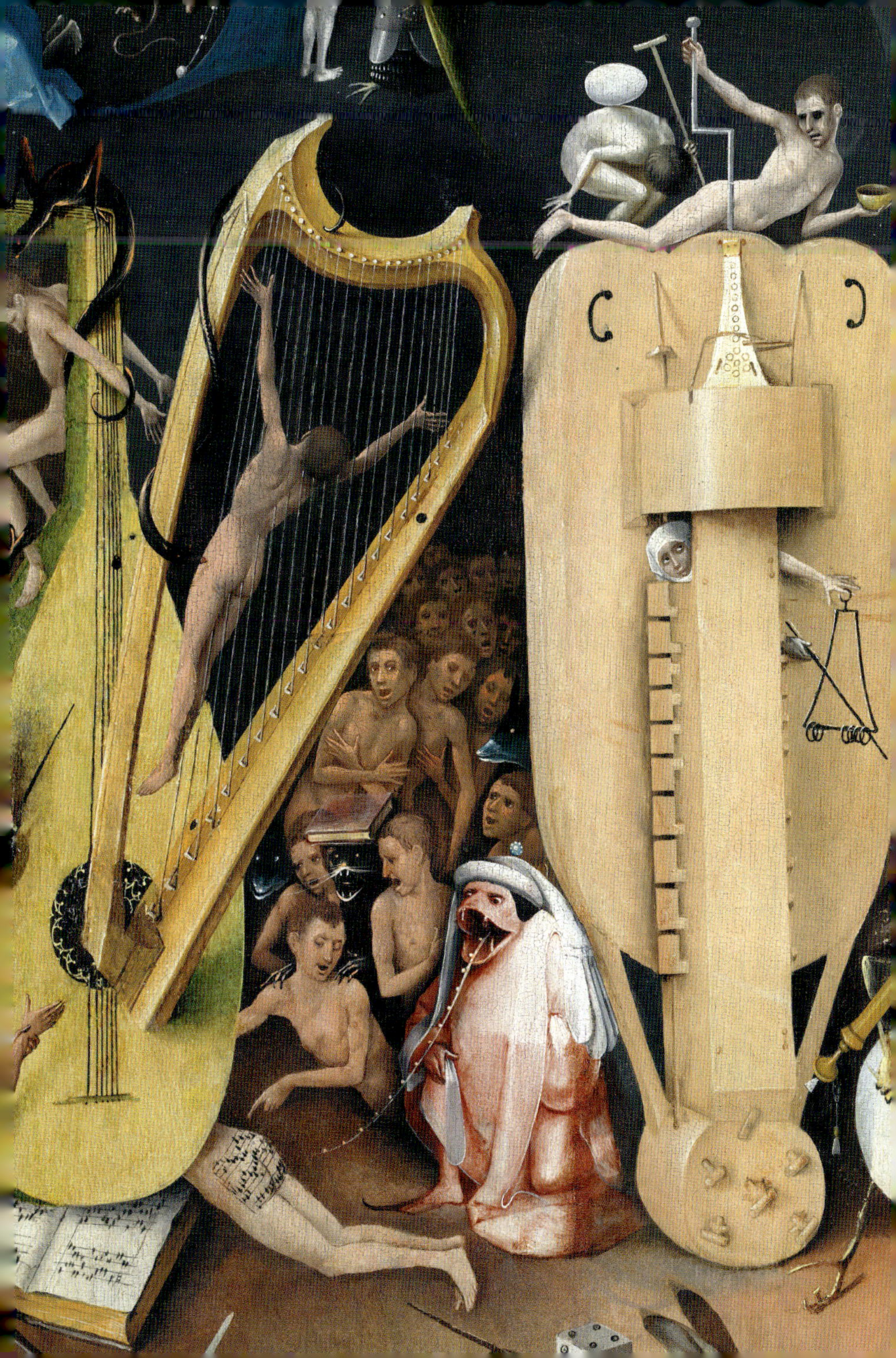

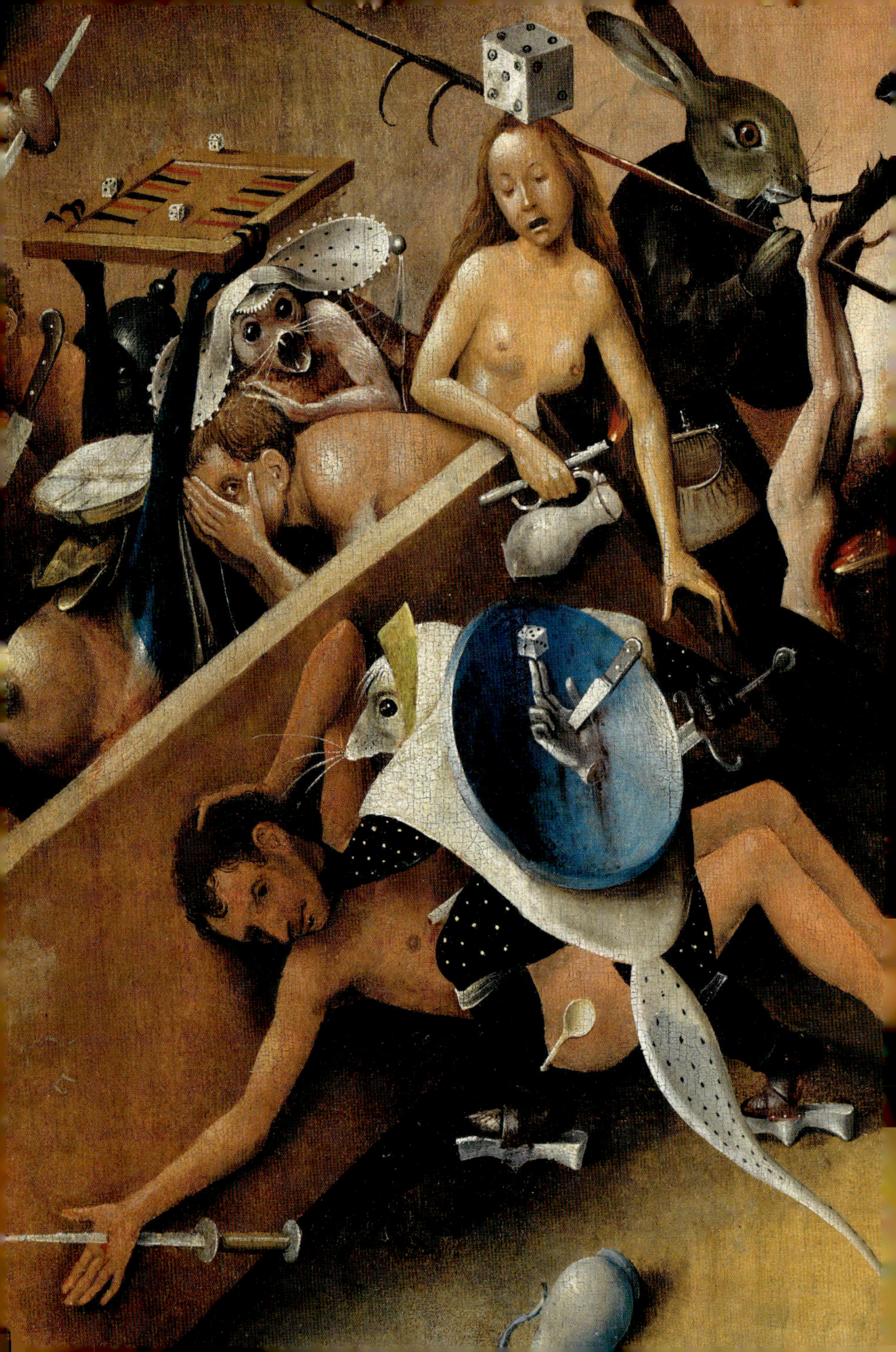

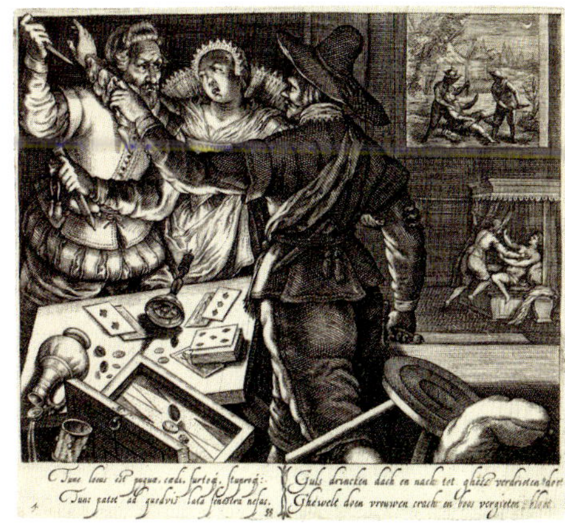

Jacob Matham, **The Consequences of Alcoholism**, *c.* 1600–1620
Copper engraving, 17.8 x 19.8 cm / 7 x 7¾ in. London, The British Museum

Page 218
Detail from: **The Garden of Earthly Delights**, *c.* 1503
Right inner wing: **Hell** (see ill. p. 189)

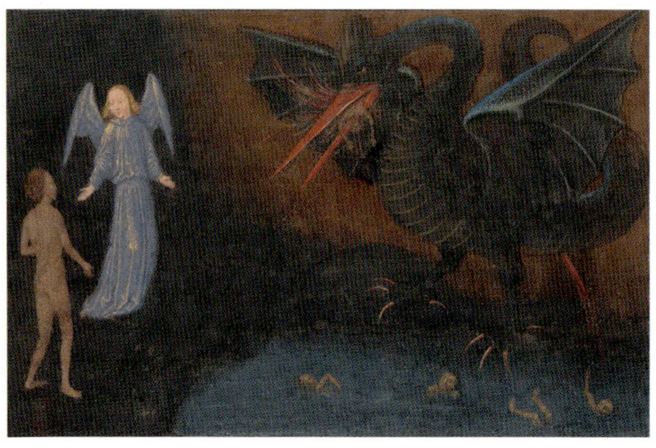

Simon Marmion, **The Torment of Unchaste Priests and Nuns**, *c.* 1474
from: *The Vision of Tundale for Margaret of York*, fol. 24v (detail)
Tempera colours, gold leaf, gold paint, and ink on parchment, 36.3 x 26.2 cm / 14¼ x 10⅜ in.
Los Angeles, The J. Paul Getty Museum, Ms. 30

Page 221
Detail from: **The Garden of Earthly Delights**, *c.* 1503
Right inner wing: **Hell** (see ill. p. 189)

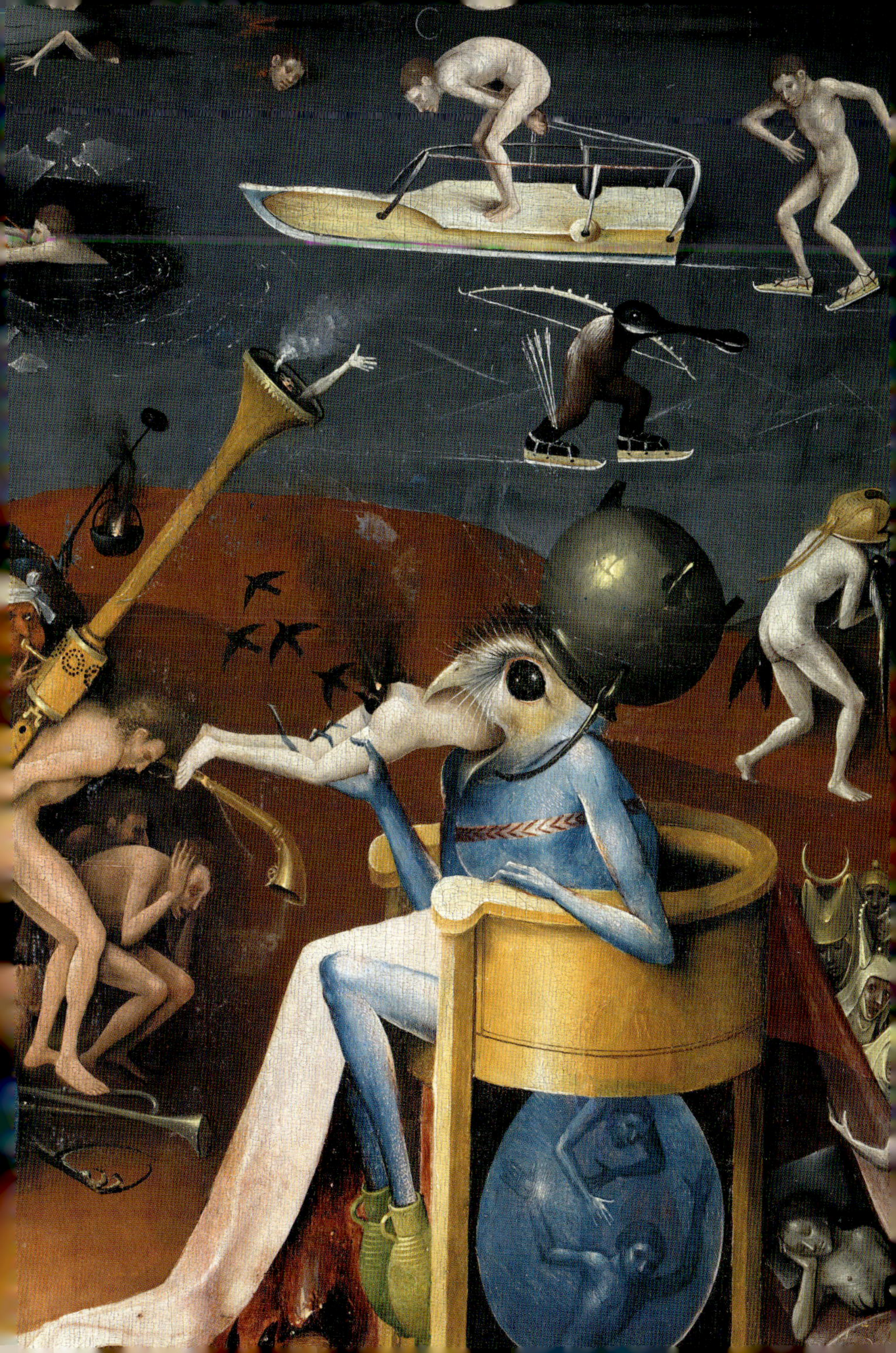

V.

Art for the king: *The Last Judgement*

c. 1506

"I cannot help feeling that the real secret of his magnificent nightmares and daydreams has still to be disclosed. We have bored a few holes through the door of the locked room; but somehow we do not seem to have discovered the key."

ERWIN PANOFSKY, 1953

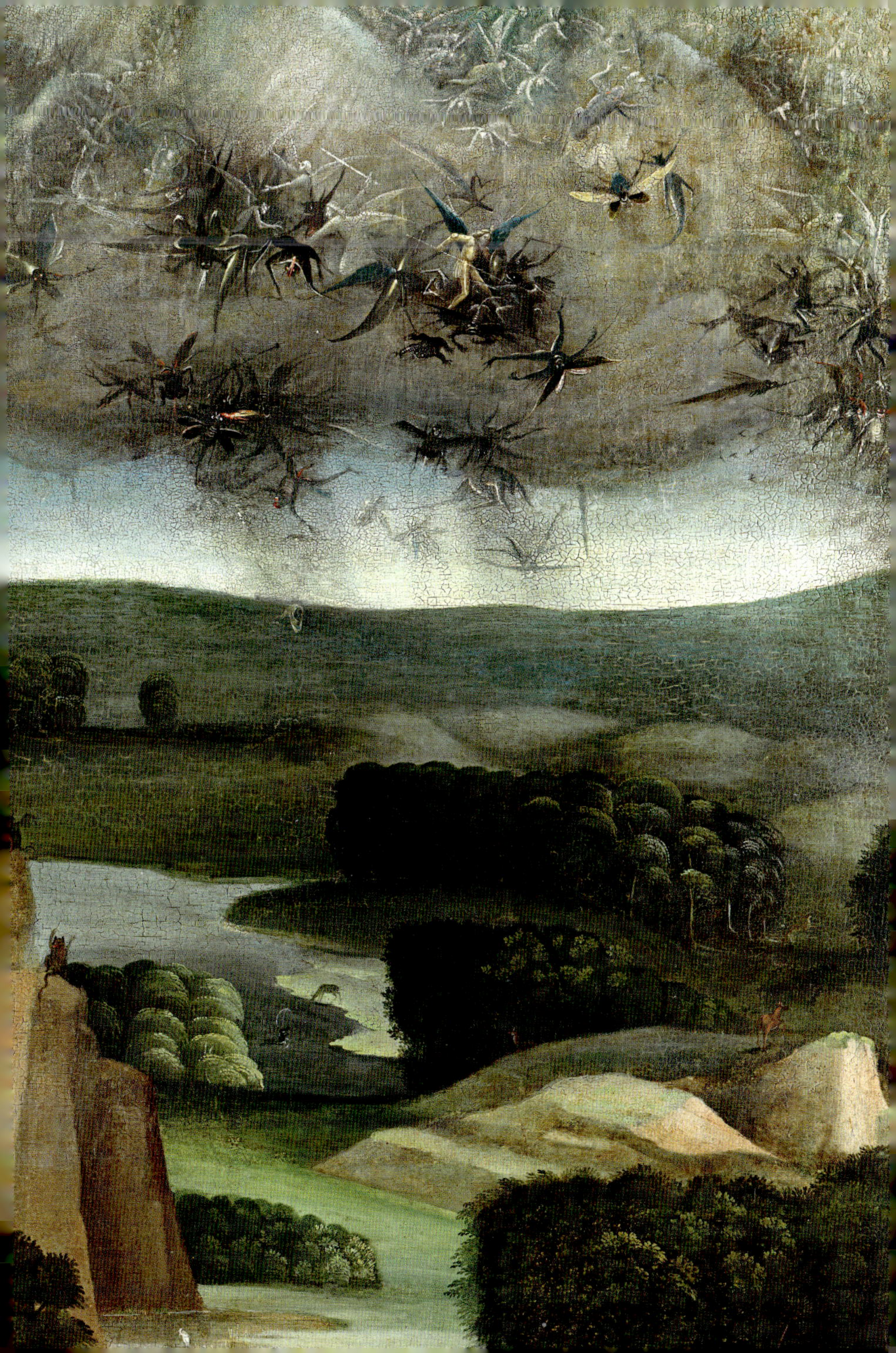

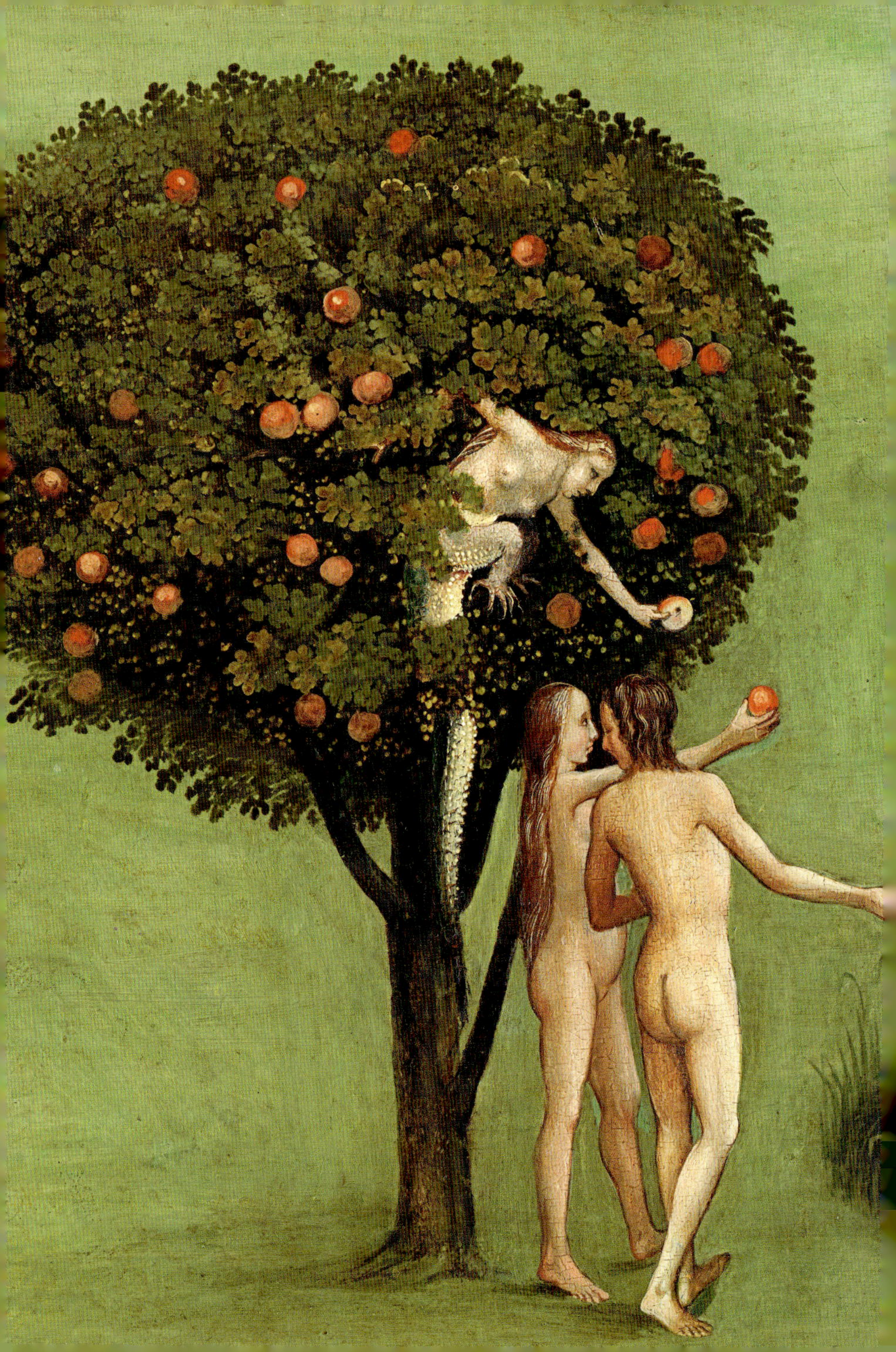

In the short period between 1497 and 1503, bracketed by two complex works, the *Adoration of the Magi* and the *Garden of Earthly Delights*, Bosch established an artistic reputation that drew him to the attention not just of the patriciate beyond the regional bounds of Brabant but also of the senior aristocracy. The popularity of Bosch's paintings at the princely and royal courts of Europe dates, at the latest, from the *Garden of Earthly Delights*, which opened the door to commissions from other noble patrons. The artist's international breakthrough came with the return from Spain of the Philip the Handsome's Habsburg court, in 1503. The inventory of the estate of Queen Isabella of Castile (1451–1504), drawn up in June 1505, six months after her death, shows that at least one painting bearing the signature of Hieronymus Bosch, namely a *Penitent Magdalene*, had already reached the Spanish court by the end of 1504 ("*una Magdalena penitente*": Sánchez Cantón 1950, pp. 182–184; Pita Andrade 2006, pp. 14 and 41). This panel probably reached Spain through dynastic links, possibly via Diego de Guevara (before 1442–1520; p. 227), the father of Felipe. An external member of the Brotherhood of Our Blessed Lady and himself the owner of paintings by Bosch, Diego de Guevara was major-domo to Joanna of Castile and Philip and later treasurer to Margaret of Austria. An alternative route may have been via Philip himself, who could, for example, have taken the *Penitent Magdalene* with him as a gift on his trip to Spain in 1502. Given Philip's elevated standing – as Governor of the Netherlands, son of the King of the Romans and later Holy Roman Emperor Maximilian, and from 1505 King of Spain – the commissions that he and members of his court awarded to Bosch served to heighten the artist's own reputation and status, as well as provide his painting with a stage. Other nobles now wanted to own the same pictures, or at least to get hold of copies. As a result, demand for Bosch's art at the courts of Europe's princes and kings grew steadily over the following years and decades.

In September 1504 Philip the Handsome commissioned a triptych for his own collection. The accompanying document refers to "Jheronimus van Aken, called Bosch, painter, living in 's-Hertogenbosch" ("*Jeronimus van Aeken dit Bosch paintre demeurant au Bois le Duc*"). This is one of the archival sources indicating that Jheronimus van Aken and Hieronymus Bosch (written Jheronimus Bosch) are one and the same person. The name Bosch as an abbreviation of 's-Hertogenbosch had already appeared on the *Adoration of the Magi* (Cat. 6.3) around 1496/97 and probably even earlier on *St John on Patmos* (Cat. 3.2). This means that these works must have been addressed to viewers from outside his home town. This same document records Bosch being paid a cash advance by Philip

Pages 223, 224
Details from: **The Last Judgement**, *c.* 1506
Left inner wing: **Fall of the Rebel Angels, The Fall and The Expulsion from Paradise**
(see ill. pp. 254/255)

the Handsome's administration for "a large panel painting nine feet high and eleven feet long, which is to show the Last Judgement, that is Heaven and Hell" ("*ung grant tableau de paincture de neuf pietz de hault et onze pietz de long, ou doit estre le Jugement de dieu assavoir paradis et infer*"). The subject to be portrayed and the dimensions of the finished painting were, then, stipulated – as was indeed the norm – along with the award of the commission, which also made provision for a down-payment of 36 *livres*. As a unit of currency, the *livre* (pound) roughly corresponded to the Rhenish guilder. Assuming that the deposit represented about a fifth of the total price, the job as a whole would have been worth at least 180 guilders (Fischer 2009, p. 20).

The commission for the *Last Judgement* had its roots in the general political situation and Philip's personal circumstances. Philip was based in 's-Hertogenbosch from September 1504 at the latest, and right through to May 1505, accompanied for some of this time by Henry III of Nassau-Breda. Within this period he left the city only briefly: in January and in late March/early April 1505, also returning for a final visit in August 1505. His stay was on account of the preparations for war against the Duchy of Guelders, which had revolted against Habsburg rule under its leader Duke Charles of Egmond (1467–1538). In September 1504 Philip assembled all his troops outside 's-Hertogenbosch and met his ally, the Duke of Cleves, for talks inside the city. That same month, as part of the terms of the Treaty of Blois signed on 22 September, it was agreed that France would not join the conflict.

After the death of Charles the Bold in 1477 parts of the Netherlands had seen the outbreak of civil war between pro- and anti-Burgundian factions as the Habsburgs fought to secure their succession to the lands of the collapsed Burgundian Empire. In the Low Countries the rule of Maximilian I was perceived as foreign tyranny; but through Philip the Handsome, to whom the Netherlandish estates were well disposed, continuity and normality were to be restored. In contrast to his father, Philip was seen by the Netherlandish estates as the country's natural prince ("*prince naturel*"). The son of Maximilian and Mary of Burgundy, Philip had been born in Bruges and raised in Malines by Margaret of York, the widow of Charles the Bold. He was educated by Netherlandish nobles and Humanists, who also exercised a fair degree of power in the years before the regency was gradually transferred to Philip from 1494. The members of Philip's royal household came from the Netherlandish nobility; and, in his pursuit of a conciliatory policy, Philip initially had the Netherlandish estates on his side. The Duchy of Guelders, however, declared itself independent, something that Philip for a long time did not challenge. Only at Maximilian's insistence did he eventually regain control of Guelders for the Habsburgs and the Empire.

Specific details of Philip's cultural policies and his activities as an art patron have only recently been brought to light (Onghena 1959, Rivière 1985, Zalama Rodríguez/Vandenbroeck 2006). Some three dozen portraits (including donor portraits), several altarpieces and other large paintings, tapestries, miniatures, stained glass, and a number of works mentioned in documents nevertheless testify to the fact that Philip both consciously and actively strove to furnish himself with the trappings of sovereignty during his youthful and relatively short-lived reign. He therefore turned in part to artists whose names he already knew, for example, employing the two sons of Lieven van Lathem (documented 1454–d. 1493), the important Flemish illuminator who had worked for the Burgundian dukes Philip the Good and Charles the Bold. Jacob van Lathem (documented 1493–1522) was a painter and in particular a portraitist, although it has not yet been possible to attribute any specific panels to his hand, while his brother Lieven (documented 1496–1506) was a goldsmith and seal carver. Bosch's *Last Judgement* (pp. 254/255, Cat. 13) was one of the most important paintings, if not *the* most important painting in Philip the Handsome's collection. Bosch is also the most famous painter to be employed by him.

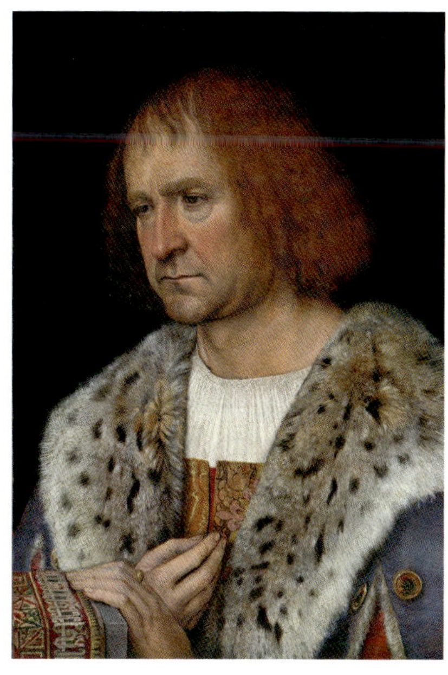

It is now widely accepted that the painting commissioned from Bosch in the abovementioned document of September 1504 is the *Last Judgement* now in Vienna. This identification is supported by the saints depicted on the exterior shutters, the dimensions of the triptych, the overpainted donor figure and the fact that the triptych was probably in the possession of the Habsburgs by 1508. The discrepancy in size between the Vienna triptych – whose dimensions are not much more than half those laid down in the contract (see entry on Cat. 13) – must be accepted in this case as a departure from, or modification of, the terms of the commission, be it through a mutual verbal agreement or as a result of Bosch's own decision. It is conceivable that money played a role: if Bosch made a start on the triptych only in 1505, for example, the year after receiving the initial deposit, sub-

Michiel Sittow, **Diego de Guevara**, *c.* 1516/17
Oil on panel, 33.6 x 23.7 cm / 13¼ x 9⅜ in. Washington D.C., National Gallery of Art, Andrew W. Mellon Collection

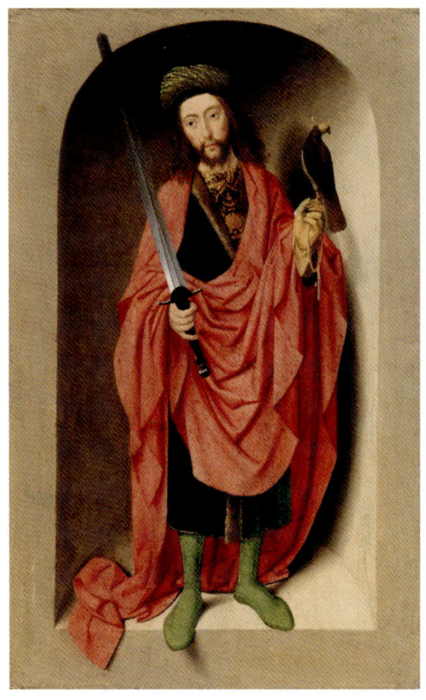

sequent payments may have been halted by Philip's ascent to the throne of Castile, Leon and Granada, his trip to Spain at the start of 1506 and his death in September of that year.

St James and *St Bavo*

In the closed position, the triptych's exterior shutters show *St James* (p. 253, Cat. 13.1) on the left. St James, in Spanish Santiago (d. *c.* 44), son of Zebedee, is known as James the Great to distinguish him from his fellow apostle James, son of Alphaeus, who is known as James the Less. According to legend, he travelled to Spain to preach the Gospel, but abandoned his mission when it appeared to be in vain. After his martyrdom in the Holy Land, however, his companions laid his corpse in a rudderless boat. Pushed out to sea, this eventually made landfall in Galicia in the northwest of the Iberian Peninsula. The saint's bones were buried but his grave was subsequently forgotten, only being rediscovered thanks to a miraculous star. A church was built on the spot and, by the Late Middle Ages, this church of Santiago de Compostela had become the most important site of Christian pilgrimage alongside Rome and Jerusalem, and the destination of pilgrimage routes from all over western Europe. St James became the patron saint of Spain, being invoked in particular during the long struggle with the Moors.

Bosch has painted the barefoot James, stooped under the burden of life's journey, in three-quarter view, comparable with his *St Christopher* (Cat. 7) and *The Pedlar* (Cat. 17.1 and 20.1). The compositional layout is also similar: scattered around the bent but unbending main figure are allegorical pictorial motifs on a small to miniature scale. James is dressed in a long robe. He carries his staff, gripped in both hands, across his right shoulder,

Master of the Brunswick Diptych, **St Bavo,** *c.* 1490
Detail of the exterior of the Brunswick Diptych. Oil on panel, 35 x 23 cm / 13¾ x 9 in.
Braunschweig, Herzog Anton Ulrich-Museum, Kunstmuseum des Landes Niedersachsen

with a long section of cloth looped over it and hanging down to the ground. Also across his shoulders is his pilgrim's hat, with a scallop shell fastened to its upturned front brim. Hanging from his belt are a bread bag, a dagger in a tattered sheath and a book pouch.

A number of scenes unfold in the arid surrounding countryside, possibly showing the events and episodes of a pilgrimage, but also representing stations along the road of life in allegorical terms. On the right, a brigand is stabbing a traveller, who is lying on the ground with all the items he was carrying scattered around him. By this means Bosch illustrates the danger that, in a pilgrimage through this world, a person through no fault of his or her own, might lose everything – worldly possessions, health, even life. Above this scene, deeper within the landscape, stands a cross of atonement, of the sort often erected out of remorse at the scene of a crime. In contrast, the snake slithering along the ground at James's feet is a symbol of Evil. Below it the edge of a small pool can be seen, with clumps of reeds, scallop shells, a creeping lizard and, further left, a strange frog with horns. The left side of the picture contains four scenes. A hooded crow is perched on a dead tree behind the saint's back and, as a bird of prophecy, warns against illness and an unshriven death (cf. Dittrich 2005, p. 320). Above it are three exempla that allude directly to the pilgrimage of life: a blind man, his face hidden deep beneath his pilgrim's hat, is holding fast to the person in front of him, a man with a maimed leg. Although their physical handicaps have made them beggars, the two men have nonetheless embarked on a pilgrimage. It is certain, however, that they will only be able to reach their goal with the help of St James, who is credited in his legend with healing a lame man. Above them a traveller is taking a rest beneath a tree with a flourishing canopy of leaves, expressing the faith in God that supplies the good pilgrim with shade and fruits, in a free interpretation of the Song of Solomon 2:3 ("Like an apple tree among the trees of the woods, so is my beloved among the sons. I sat down in his shade with great delight, and his fruit was sweet to my taste."). At the very top of the panel, on the other hand, someone has ended their life's pilgrimage by hanging themselves. This image of *desperatio*, despair, goes back to the representation of Judas and can also be found among the Passion scenes on the exterior shutters of Bosch's *Adoration of the Magi* (Cat. 6.1), where a figure accompanied by a second person likewise points to a hanged man in a tree. Bax has interpreted the scene as an episode from the life of St James: in some versions of his legend, the saint is credited by name with bringing back to life a man who had been wrongly hanged after his father made a pilgrimage to Santiago (Bax 1983, pp. 1296–297).

The exterior of the right wing shows St Bavo (p. 253, Cat. 13.2). According to legend, Bavo was a nobleman who renounced the life of the world and gave away all his possessions to the needy. He adopts the characteristic pose of a patron saint (cf. p. 228), upright and facing the viewer, albeit with his eyes slightly lowered and his head turned towards the right. He wears a tunic with sleeves and cuffs, and on top of this a knee-length cloak with one end draped over his right shoulder. His legs and feet are stockinged, and gold spurs identify him as a knight and noble. His right hand is reaching into a purse beneath his cloak, where he also carries his sword – symbols of his generosity and his aristocratic rank. On his left hand Bavo carries a falcon, his most important attribute, and on his head he wears a simple biretta.

Behind the saint on the left a beggar has laid out a severed foot on a piece of white cloth or paper, as proof of his disability. We cannot tell whether it is his own foot – cut off in corporal punishment – or one he has scavenged from a place of execution (cf. Bax 1983, pp. 305–307). This pictorial motif also appears in the central panel of Bosch's *Temptation of St Anthony* triptych (pp. 118/119, Cat. 10.4), where a beggar has likewise placed an amputated leg in front of him – doubtless pretending to have some dreadful disease or to have been unjustly punished, so as to appeal to people's charity. The beggar behind St Bavo has a circular sore or plaster on the wrist of his bent right hand and holds a round bowl in his left. Hanging from the bowl is a lead weight on a string, an official token issued by the authorities that identified the bearer as a "real" beggar and genuinely deserving of alms. Kneeling on the right side of the panel is an old woman with a protruding lower jaw, wearing a headscarf and a cloak. An infant balancing a bowl and spoon on its head is seated astride her right shoulder. Gruel is starting to spill out of the bowl: this can be interpreted as a token of the hunger tormenting the child or even as wasteful squandering. In front of this group another child or possibly a dwarf, with a small head and clothes that are too large, extends one arm beseechingly to Bavo, as do the old woman and the infant. The great difference in age between the woman and the children raises questions about the relationship between them. Sources report that beggars picked up children at random or used them to arouse compassion and so to bring in more alms. In both its actions and the pejorative characterisation of its outer appearance, this group embodies the negative image of importunate and false beggars, often described in late medieval Netherlandish literature (Steemers 1979, p. 119; Marijnissen 1987, p. 1221). The scene takes places beneath the flattened and unadorned arch of a roofed or tunnelled passage, through whose far archway we glimpse a view of the moderately busy street of a town with gabled houses typical of the late Middle Ages.

The figure of St Bavo on the outer right wing bears the features of Philip the Handsome (see entry on Cat. 13; cf. pp. 235, 252). St Bavo thus represents the Netherlandish branch of the house of Habsburg, and specifically Philip. St Bavo (Sint Baaf) was the

Detail from: **The Last Judgement**, *c.* 1506
Central panel: **The Last Judgement** (see ill. pp. 254/255)

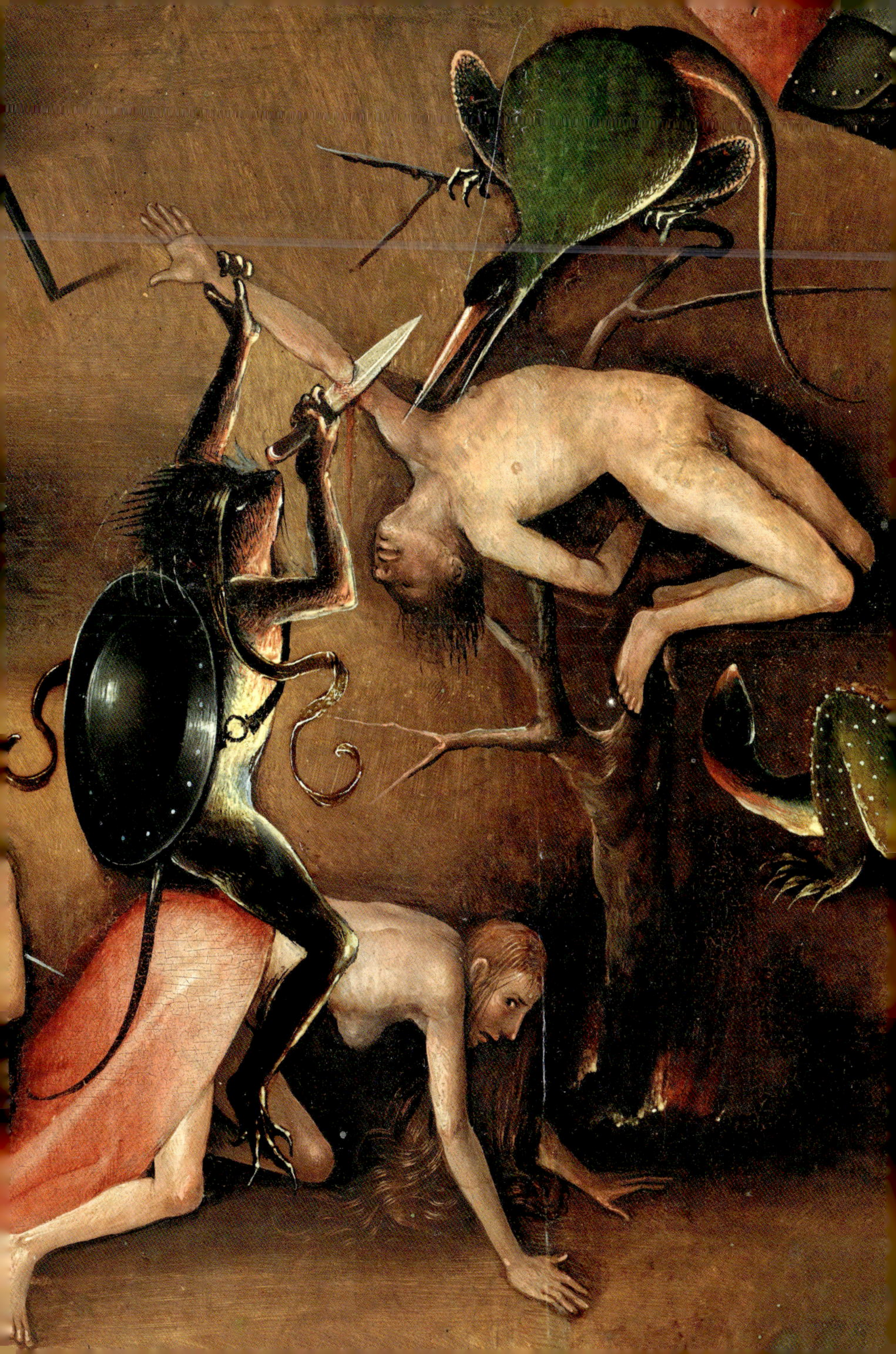

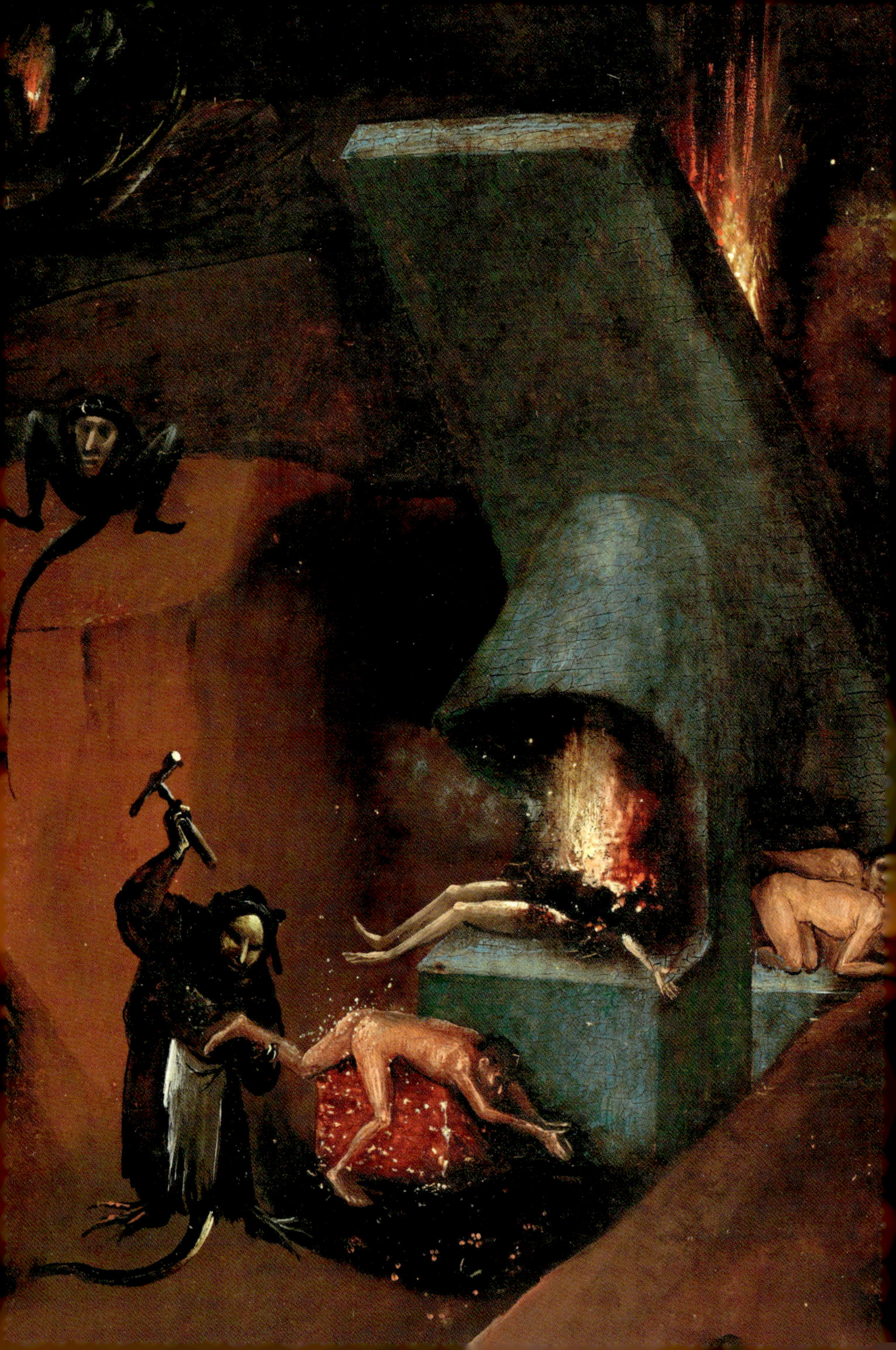

patron saint of the cities and bishoprics of Ghent and Haarlem and was also venerated in other towns and villages in the historical Netherlands, above all in West Flanders, including Bruges, which housed one of his relics and had one of its districts named after him. According to an inscription, St Bavo's heart is supposed to have found its final resting place in the Church of Our Lady in Philip the Handsome's native city. As the patron saint of Spain, St James – the second saint on the exterior shutters – represents the dynastic alliance of the house of Habsburg with the Spanish monarchy. This alliance was doubly forged: firstly, through the marriage of Philip the Handsome to Joanna of Castile (1479–1555; p. 235), later known as Joanna the Mad, in 1496; and secondly, through that of his sister Margaret of Austria (1480–1530) to Joanna's brother John of Aragon and Castile (1478–1497) one year later.

The paintings on the exterior shutters are both executed in grisaille. The gradations and contrasts of light and shade are elaborated in much greater detail than in Bosch's polychrome panels and those using a limited palette, so informing the figures with a correspondingly greater sculptural presence. This is especially evident when we compare them with grisailles by other artists. Such comparison also makes clear that the plasticity of Bosch's figures is enhanced by their monumentality. It is certainly true that monochrome painting is obliged to exploit chiaroscuro contrasts in order to be clear and effective. Bosch's two saints have a very finely chiselled appearance, almost as if they were carved out of marble or ivory. The underdrawing is visible as a dark blue in numerous parts of the panel. Whether it is more detailed than in Bosch's polychrome paintings is a question that can only be answered through technical investigation. The greys are cool in the shadow, but elsewhere warm, and are overlaid with white in the manner of a veil. Both panels terminate at the bottom in illusionistic Gothic tracery from which hangs a shield on a leather strap. Whether these shields are simply decorative or once showed, or were intended to show, coats of arms, has yet to be clarified.

Both the manner and the monumentality of this presentation serves to highlight – much more clearly than in Bosch's other such paintings – the function of St Bavo and St James as patron saints. Both were to be venerated and prayed to. As a devout nobleman who displayed charity towards those truly in need, St Bavo provided a model for Philip the Handsome. He embodied the ideal of the generous and just ruler; certainly Philip wanted to be seen as representing this ideal himself. St James, with his ability to work miracles, also embodied charitable action; even more importantly, however, he was a protector of pilgrims and a model to be imitated on the pilgrimage of life. We can thus

Detail from: **The Last Judgement**, *c.* 1506
Central panel: **The Last Judgement** (see ill. pp. 254/255)

imagine both saints as personal patrons of Philip, as a Christian and as a prince. In this sense St James and St Bavo are also connected with the interior of the triptych: good deeds and the avoidance of sin were essential criteria when it came to the Last Judgement, when every Christian would have to answer to God.

The genesis of Evil

With the triptych's shutters open, the left wing (pp. 254/255, Cat. 13.3) shows the birth of Evil and the loss of Paradise. At the top we see the Fall of the Rebel Angels, which is here, as so often, equated with the separation of light from darkness. Angels surround the mandorla containing the figure of God the Father, a dazzling vision reminiscent of sunlight bursting through storm clouds. The Archangel Michael, clad in golden armour, leads the host of white angels – indicated with just a few strokes of the brush – armed with swords and crosses. They are battling the rebel angels, who have assumed the shape of blackish insects and are plummeting earthwards, some of them headfirst and backwards (p. 223). The rebel angels here present the reversed and inverted image of their celestial counterparts and explain how Evil came into the world: like their bodies, their "character traits" are the opposite of those of the heavenly angels. Squatting on the precipitous rocky cliffs below are strange dark beasts with their front paws raised, as if lamenting or greeting the falling angels.

The chronology then jumps from the very top of the panel to the very bottom, as if to the picture's opposite extreme, in order to show the Creation of Eve from Adam's rib. Adam is sleeping, but the fact that he is propped on one elbow may be understood to signify that his mind is still active. He is in a state of inner contemplation, contemplation of the divine. The dog curled up nearby symbolises this striving through meditation towards divine knowledge. On Adam's other side God in the shape of Christ holds Eve by her left forearm and makes the sign of blessing over her. Eve here is the exact mirror-image of her figure in the *Garden of Earthly Delights* (Cat. 11.3). The figure of Christ has clearly been overpainted at a later date: although his red robes may be original, his moustache certainly is not. The two ducks in the marshy pool on the right are symbols of love and fidelity. Above the group of three figures a cockerel is keeping its distance from the fox slinking among the shadows of the trees, the former a symbol of faith and vigilance, the latter a symbol of Evil. A second cockerel is perched in a tree.

Present since the fall of the Rebel Angels, Evil is already lurking in Paradise. It finally strikes on the right side of the panel, where we see the Tree of Knowledge with its yellowish-red fruits (p. 224). Eve is looking appraisingly at the apple she is holding at arm's length, while Adam stands gesticulating beside her. The Devil, represented as a serpent with a face and golden hair resembling Eve, lurks outside her field of vision above her

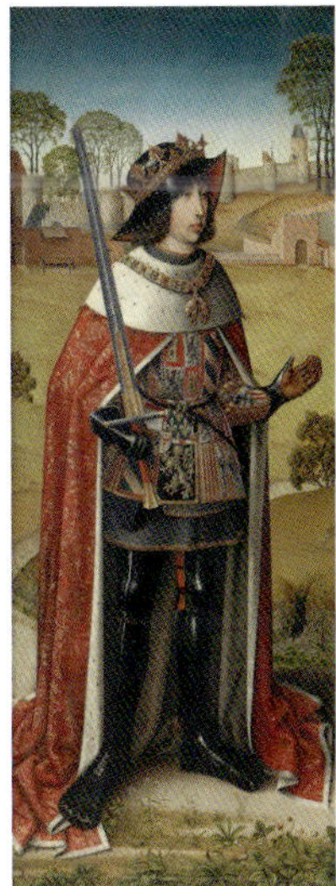
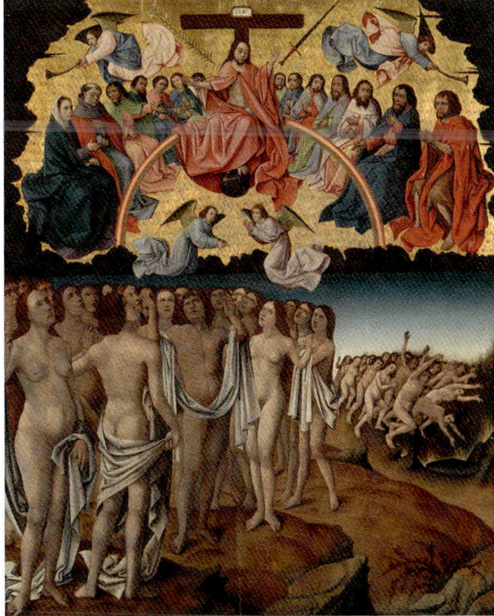
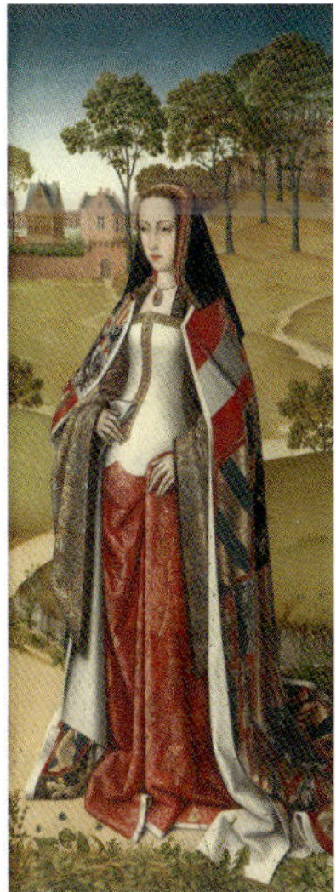

Master of the Joseph Legend, **Last Judgement with Philip and Joanna as Donors (for Zierikzee Town Hall)**, *c.* 1505/06
Oil on panel, 126 x 105 cm / 49⅝ x 41⅜ in. (central panel), 125 x 48 cm / 49¼ x 18⅞ in. (each wing)
Brussels, Royal Museums of Arts of Belgium

Pages 236/237
Detail from: **The Last Judgement**, *c.* 1506
Central panel: **The Last Judgement** (see ill. pp. 254/255)

head and offers a second apple. The Temptation of Eve by Satan is portrayed as trickery and cajolement. The porcupine on the right symbolises greed and the owl on the leafless branch the seductive power of Evil. The bird on the ground below has yet to be identified but is perhaps an ostrich or a crane. The Creation of Eve and the Fall are followed, halfway up the right side of the panel, by the Expulsion from Paradise. The Archangel Michael, here in red, is driving Adam and Eve out of the Garden of Eden through a dark wood. His figure is located on the vertical line connecting God the Father at the top with Christ below, while Eve makes all three of her appearances at equally spaced intervals along a diagonal.

The direction in which the "first parents" are fleeing on this left inner wing is distinct from the movement of the redeemed souls in the central panel, who are being accompanied by angels to Heaven in the top left corner. The right edge of the inner wing and the left edge of the central panel here form the boundary between the newly fallen Adam

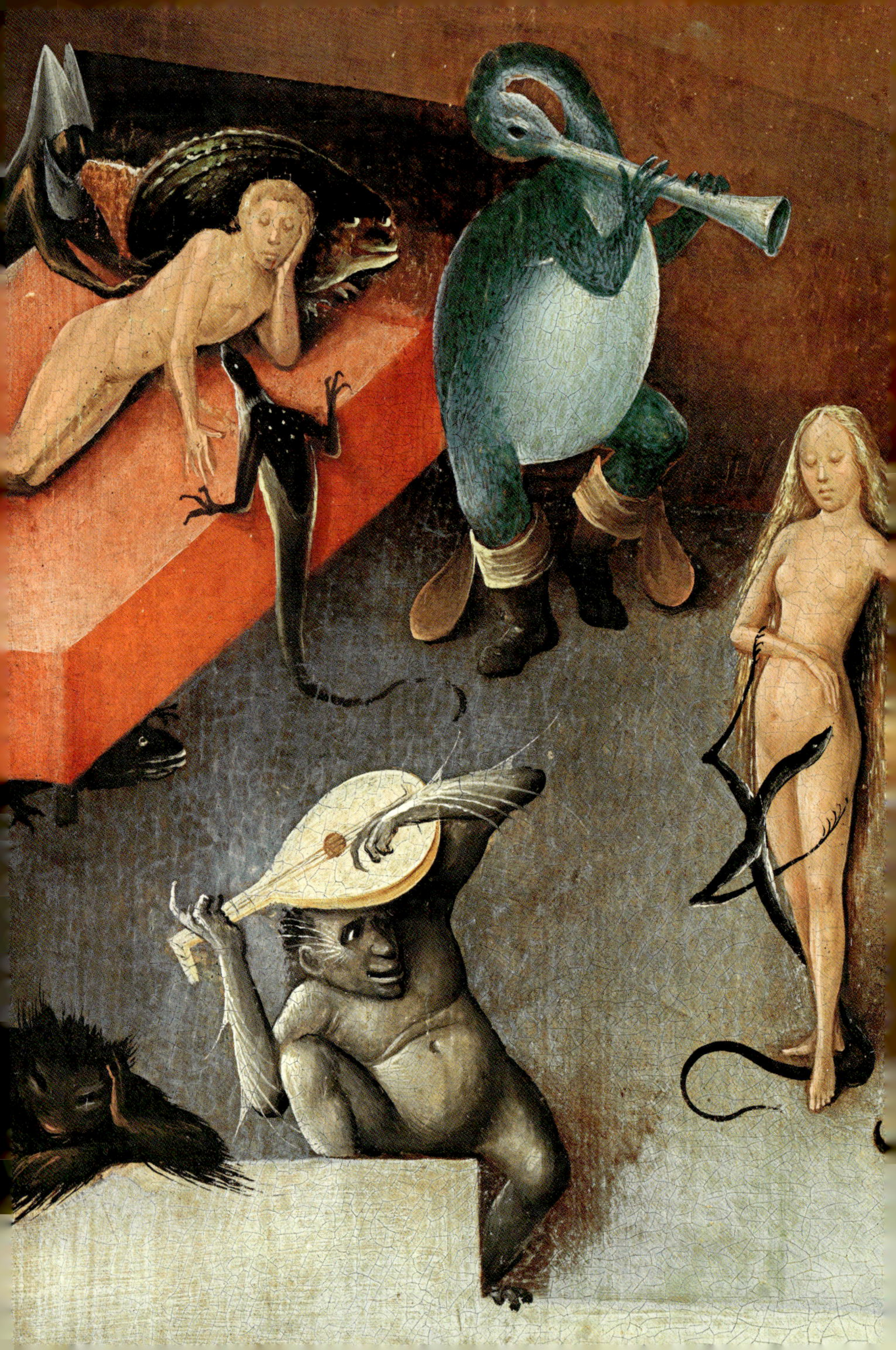

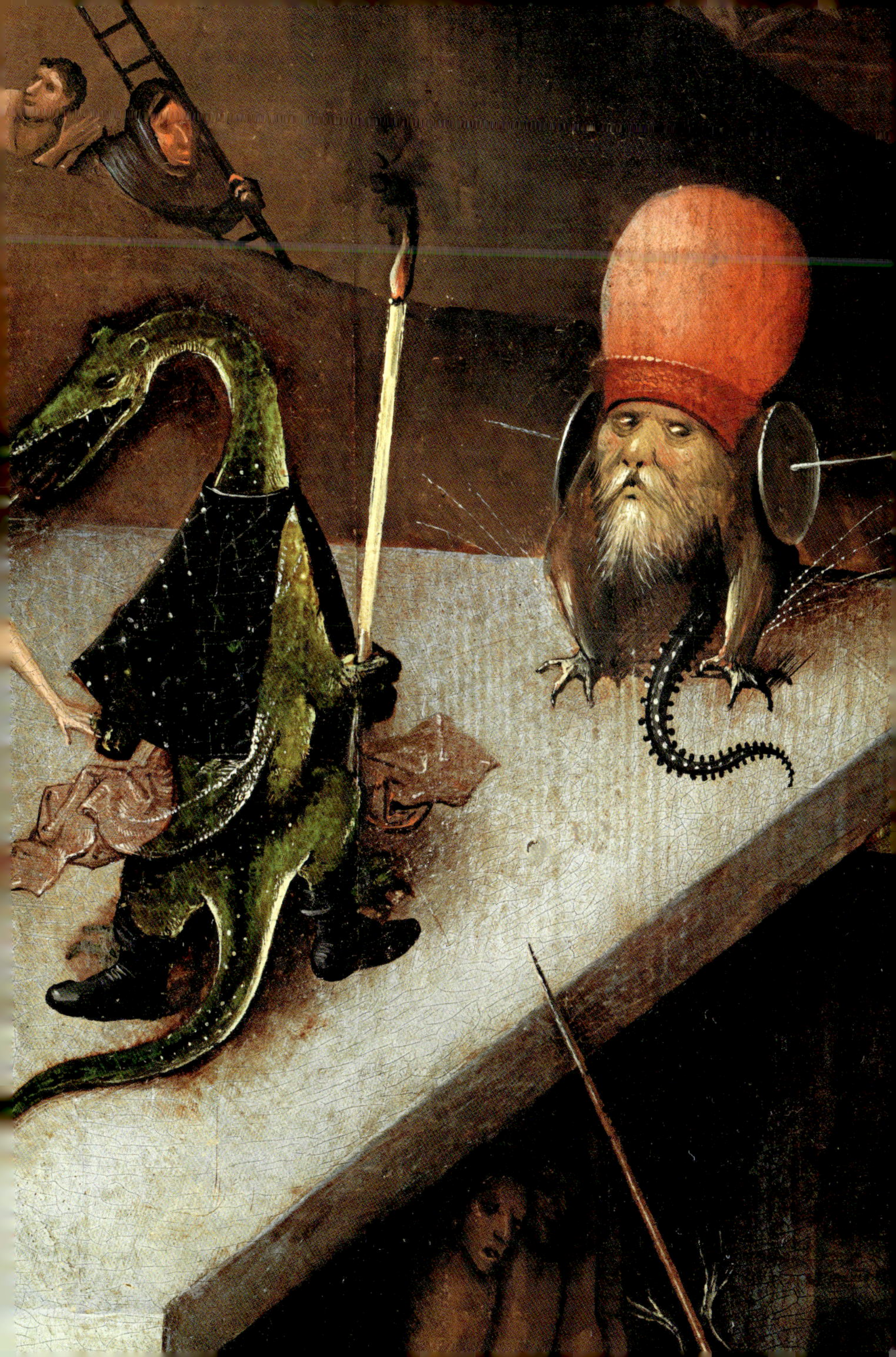

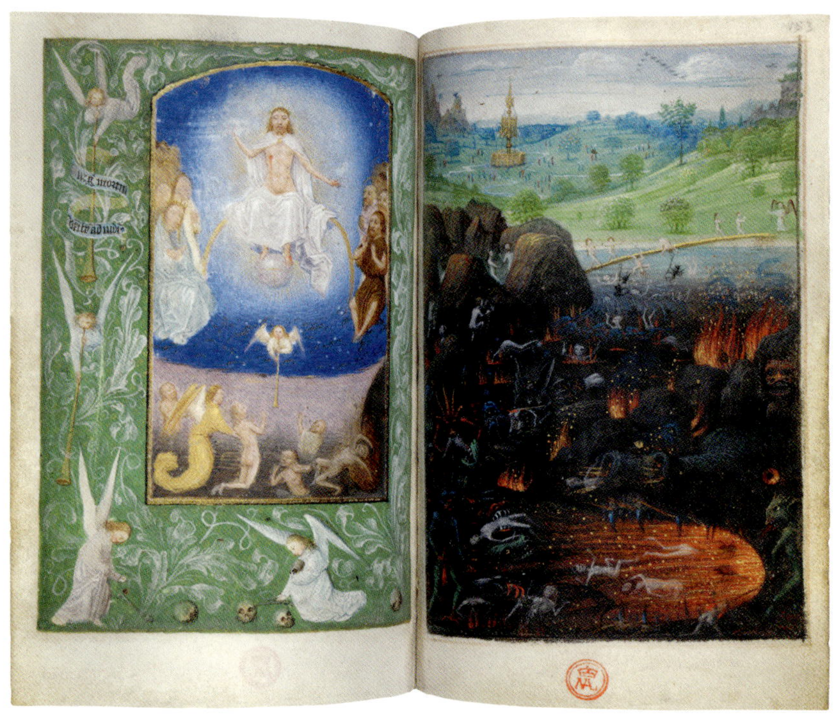

Simon Marmion, **The Last Judgement**, 1475–1481
from: *Book of Hours*, fol. 152v–153r
Parchment, 11 x 7.7 cm / 4⅜ x 3 in. London, Victoria and Albert Museum, Ms. Salting 1221

and Eve, who will later be redeemed, and those redeemed on the Day of Judgement. The left inner wing thus shows that God mercilessly punishes any offence against his divine order, whether perpetrated by angels or humankind. At the same time, the Fall of the Rebel Angels and the Fall of Man demonstrate the existence of Evil. In this respect the left inner wing forms the prologue to the two other interior panels.

The Last Judgement

The central panel (pp. 254/255, Cat. 13.4) shows the *Last Judgement* as it is described in Matthew: "When the Son of Man comes in His glory, and all the holy angels with Him, then He will sit on the throne of His glory. All the nations will be gathered before Him, and He will separate them one from another, as a shepherd divides his sheep from the goats. And He will set the sheep on His right hand, but the goats on the left." (Matt. 25: 31–33) Bosch represents the kingdom of Heaven largely in line with convention. Christ is enthroned on a rainbow. His right hand is raised, indicating the side of the elect. His left hand is lowered and signifies: "Depart from Me, you cursed, into the everlasting fire prepared for the devil and his angels." (Matt. 25:41). Standing out from the saints gathered on either side are the figures of the Virgin and St John the Baptist, who act as intercessors for the souls. Between them angels are holding a scroll of the same colour as the sky, possibly showing the instruments of the Passion. The Apostles are seated in council in two groups of six: in the left group Peter and Paul can be recognised from their traditional physiognomies. Two pairs of celestial blue angels are sounding golden trumpets to the left and right. In the top left (that is to say, on Christ's own right) a gap of golden light opens in the deep blue firmament to receive the elect. On the opposite side, only the blackest darkness yawns. Below this celestial zone a vast inferno fills the background. Fires flicker between pools, hills and buildings in a nocturnal landscape, as the damned, individually and in groups, are herded and tormented by devils, as foretold in Revelation: "But the cowardly, unbelieving, abominable, murderers, sexually immoral, sorcerers, idolaters and all liars shall have their part in the lake which burns with fire and brimstone, which is the second death." (Rev. 21:8). Halfway up the left edge of the panel an angel with fair hair and white robes is leading a redeemed soul to safety. Right at the top more angels are escorting some half a dozen redeemed souls to Heaven.

Bosch's patently asymmetric representation of the elect and the damned, and of Heaven and Hell, was unusual in panel painting. It was conventional to keep the numbers of the two groups more or less equal, as in the *Last Judgement* (p. 248) by Stephan Lochner (*c.* 1400/10–1451) and the *Last Judgement* triptych (1505/06) by an unknown master in Brussels, which was originally painted for the courtroom in Zierikzee Town Hall in Zeeland, and shows Philip the Handsome and Joanna as donors (p. 235). This even distribution evidently had something to do with the judicial context for which such pictures served a purpose: most *Last Judgement* paintings adorned tribunes and courtrooms, where they looked down upon the workings of the judiciary.

In manuscript illumination, on the other hand, both in books of hours and in vision literature (p. 238), we find examples of a different type of *Last Judgement* composition. Here Paradise is relegated to the background and thus appears smaller and more distant. The vision of a very narrow bridge of trial or judgement, which spans an abyss or a lake and across which the elect must first walk while carefully keeping their balance in order to reach Paradise, is described in a number of texts (Dinzelbacher 1973, 2002). Late medieval texts also describe the number of the damned as exceeding that of the redeemed by a thousandfold. The individual is thus urged to lead a godly life in order to earn a place amongst the elect. The basis for this belief in a limited admission to the kingdom of God is found in the Parable of the Wedding Feast related in St Matthew's Gospel: "Then the king said to the servants, 'Bind him hand and foot, take him away, and cast him into outer darkness; there will be weeping and gnashing of teeth.' For many are called, but few are chosen." (Matt. 22:13–14) This pictorial concept, with its patent surplus of damned souls, has nothing to do with pessimism or fatalism, in other words, but is a visual means of dramatising the Last Judgement for the individual worshipping in front of the triptych. Even such a large triptych could thus be personal in character, even if it could not be displayed in the donor's private chambers. The lower left corner of the central panel of Bosch's *Last Judgement* originally featured a lone donor portrait, probably that of Philip the Handsome (see entry on Cat. 13). The famous polyptych by Rogier van der Weyden, now in the Musée de l'Hôtel-Dieu in Beaune, is an example of a *Last Judgement* similarly oriented towards the salvation of its donor's soul, in this case Rolin and his wife.

Hell is divided into a number of distinct areas. An allusion to the resurrection of the dead, climbing out of their graves, can be seen in the left foreground, and possibly also in the background to the left of centre. This episode in the Last Judgement is not always represented. Foreground and middle distance are separated by the bridge to the hereafter leading across a swollen river. Although the bridge effectively divides the scene into areas behind and ahead of it, and to its left and right, the world already appears transformed into Hell everywhere we look. The fate of the lonely soul who is being led across this bridge on a mount, in the company of other souls and a jostling crowd of devils, is probably sealed in the truest sense of the word: a messenger devil carrying a bill of indictment hastens ahead of the column to announce its arrival to the gatekeeper, who stands in the mouth of a huge green jug serving as the base of an instrument of torture.

Certain deadly sins, grouped in variations, are also illustrated, although not all seven are shown (cf. Bax 1983). They can be identified with the help of the tondo of Hell in Bosch's *Seven Deadly Sins with the Four Last Things* (pp. 308/309, Cat. 15), in which the deadly sins and their attributes are depicted individually in scenes identified by a Latin caption. To the right of centre, beyond the bridge, we see Sloth (*acedia*) portrayed in an "evil inn" setting, as a man slumped over a barrel, propped on one arm and clasping a set of bagpipes. A woman wearing a horned hat (a double hennin) is looking out of the tavern door. Her hat identifies her as a procuress, and she therefore stands for Lust (*luxuria*). (This Burgundian item of headwear, including its conical variant with just a single point, had already fallen out of fashion around 1480.) Further right two souls are

Detail from: **The Last Judgement**, *c.* 1506
Central panel: **The Last Judgement** (see ill. pp. 254/255)

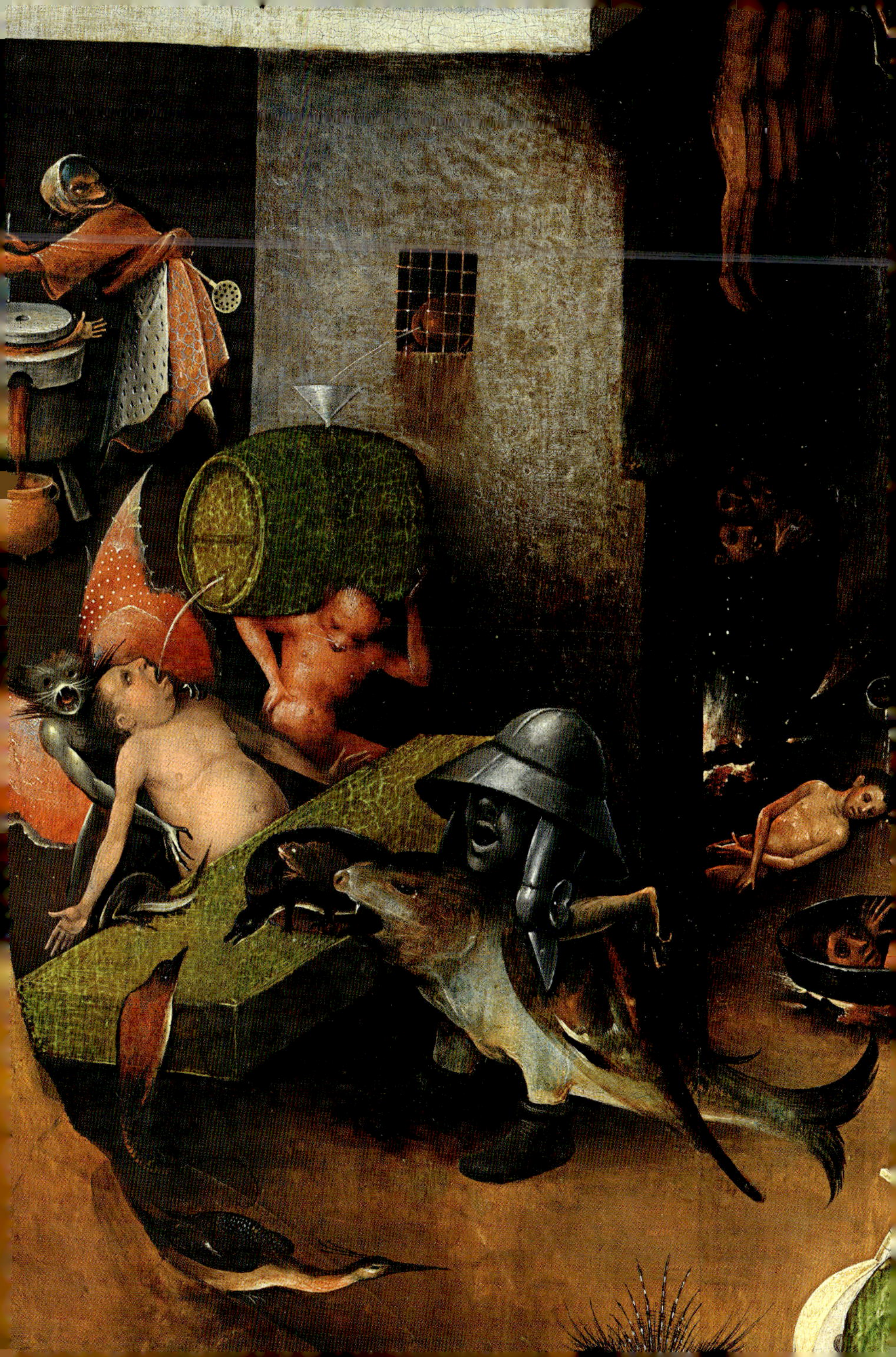

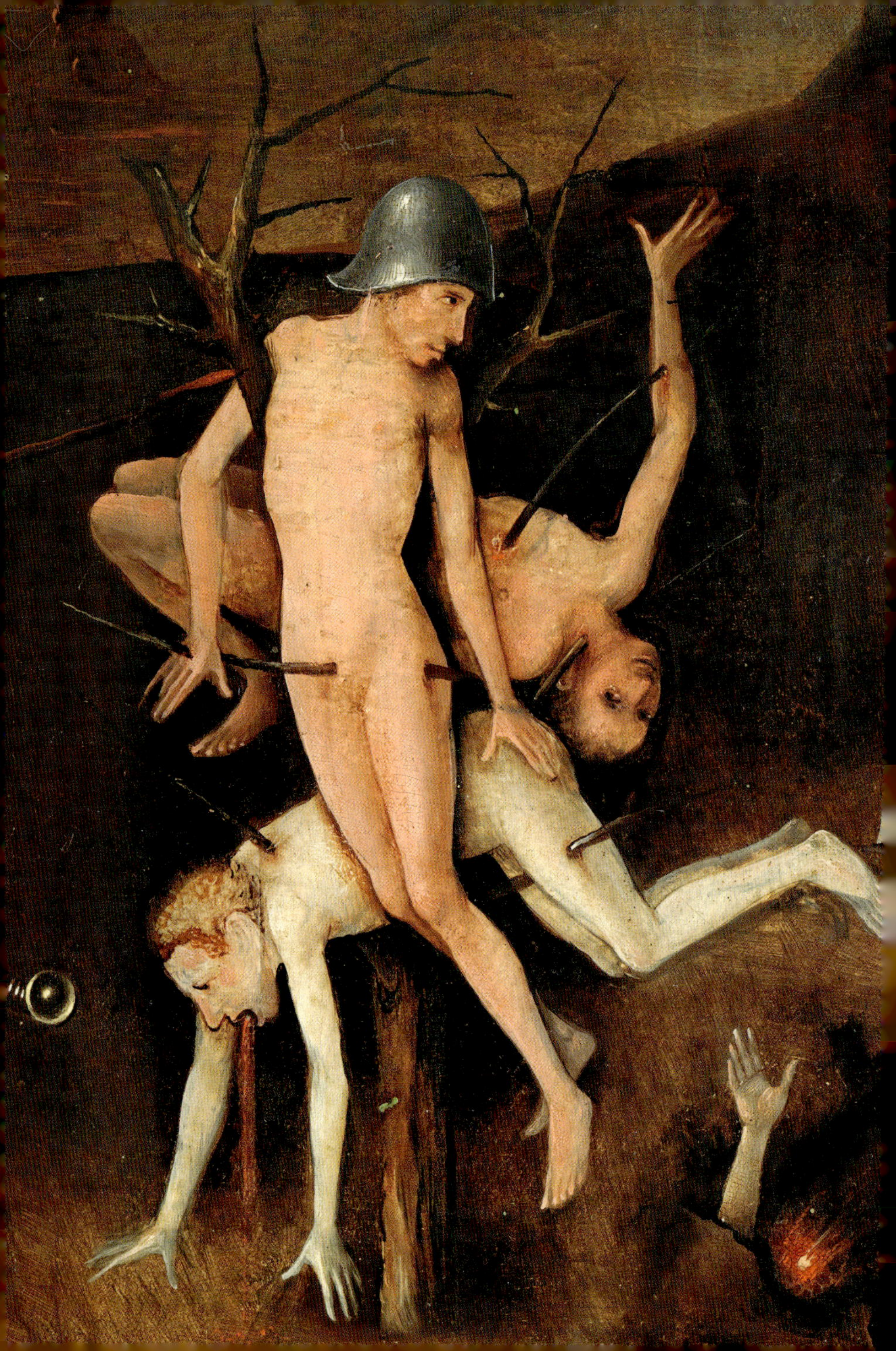

being shod with horseshoes by blacksmith devils (cf. Cat. 15), while others are roasting on the fire (p. 232). The scenes in the left foreground and on the left edge of the picture refer to the deadly sin of Wrath (*ira*), whose typical symbol is a raised naked blade (cf. Cat. 15). A strikingly large number of weapons and even war machines can be seen in the panel (pp. 246/247). Wrath was considered the cause of war, murder and arson, and it thus precisely summed up the triptych's historical context. Lust (cf. Cat. 15) makes further appearances in the immediate foreground and on the roof-like platform on the left, where a man is lying on a red bed. A woman in a horned hat leans over the edge of the bed behind him. Standing in front of the bed on the right is a naked woman with a serpent entwining itself around her body, her hand held in that of a dragon devil carrying a slender taper. Other devils are making music nearby (pp. 236/237). Bax has identified a model for the blue musical devil, whose snout forms a wind instrument, in 14th-century Netherlandish manuscript illumination (Bax 1979, p. 350). It is therefore probably an example of a monster drollery, as handed down in pattern books. The couple are an allusion to Adam and Eve, since they appear at the same height as their counterparts being driven out of the Garden of Eden in the left panel. Lust was considered one of the very first sins of all.

In front of the walls in the lower left corner the sin of Gluttony (*gula*) is being punished. The damned themselves are being turned into meals in the frying pan or on the spit, or are being forced to eat and drink. This latter fate is being suffered by a fat man at a table (cf. Cat. 15), who is drinking directly from a stream of liquid issuing from a barrel (p. 241). The liquid is in fact urine that has been passed by a devil. Here the central panel links to the scene of the Fall at the same height in the left panel: Gluttony was considered a driving force behind the eating of the apple from the Tree of Knowledge.

The gateway to Hell

In the foreground of the right inner wing (pp. 254/255) a host of devils are tormenting a handful of souls, including a woman who is being made to sing along with them from a large book. Further to the right a bulbous-nosed and bespectacled devil is reading out the charges against a man who has been blindfolded. It is almost as if the devils were requesting admission to their own Hell. The juxtaposition of a man and woman facing each other directly in front of the gateway to Hell calls to mind Adam and Eve, who were the original cause of human suffering. The boundary with Hell is established by a wall pierced by an arched gateway decorated with toads. Standing like a guard in front of the entrance is a black figure in Oriental dress with a green turban. Fire blazes in his stomach and on

Detail from: **The Last Judgement**, *c.* 1506
Central panel: **The Last Judgement** (see ill. pp. 254/255)

his head. Damned men are being lowered from the top of the gate, probably intended to serve as target practice for archers, just like the damned souls in the left foreground and on the green fish.

On the far side of the walls and gateway countless numbers of damned souls have been corralled into a red tent. To the right of the tent and in the background a total of four giants can be seen. Traditionally, only the Prince of Darkness and chief of all the devils, Satan or Lucifer, was represented as a giant. From the late Middle Ages, however, departures from this representational convention became increasingly common as the notion of the arbitrary face of Evil gained hold, granting artists greater scope to indulge their imagination. On the right a monochrome green giant throws back his long-haired head in order to spit out a vertical jet of fire (p. 251). This reveals the leg of one of the damned in front of his mouth. Behind him, a giantess clasps her bloated belly, which is sprinkled all over with white and red dots. She has whiskers on her face and a number of pustules on her nose. These last might be an allusion to a serious infectious disease, such as syphilis (Bax 1983, pp. 244–254), or may represent some kind of adornment – or is the giantess in fact adorning herself with the consequences of her sexual promiscuity? Her conical hennin undoubtedly signifies her vanity and lust. Behind her a giant devil squats beneath a blue sheet, an arrow protruding wince-inducingly from its anus. The emphasis upon eating, excreting and the digestive organs is typical of Hell, and in particular of Satan: these activities underline the impurity and vileness of sin. The fourth giant devil crouches on the left. He is wearing a brownish grey habit with white hair visible beneath his hood. This giant eats sinners, and large numbers of them appear to be in or beneath his stomach. On his back an insect devil is rolling a spherical red object that resembles the fruit of the strawberry tree: here, as in the *Garden of Earthly Delights*, this stands for the passing pleasures of the senses and their futility. Behind the giant, as in the central panel, an infernal landscape with pools, rocks and buildings appears in nocturnal silhouette, interspersed with columns of fire.

Bosch's careful planning of his triptych can also be seen in his use of colour. In the interior view brown and black in the central and right panels form an antithesis to the green on the left and establish a forceful contrast between the living and the dead. The powerful palette employed for Heaven and its occupants in the central panel is set against a brown background in Hell on the right. Red, blue and green are evenly distributed in particular across the lower half of the central panel. Blue is employed just once on the right inner wing, whereas green is prominent and establishes a link with the Garden of Eden on the left. This rhythmic orchestration of colour contributes to the compositional balance of the interior view and produces a relatively harmonious overall impression, notwithstanding the chaotic distribution of the figures.

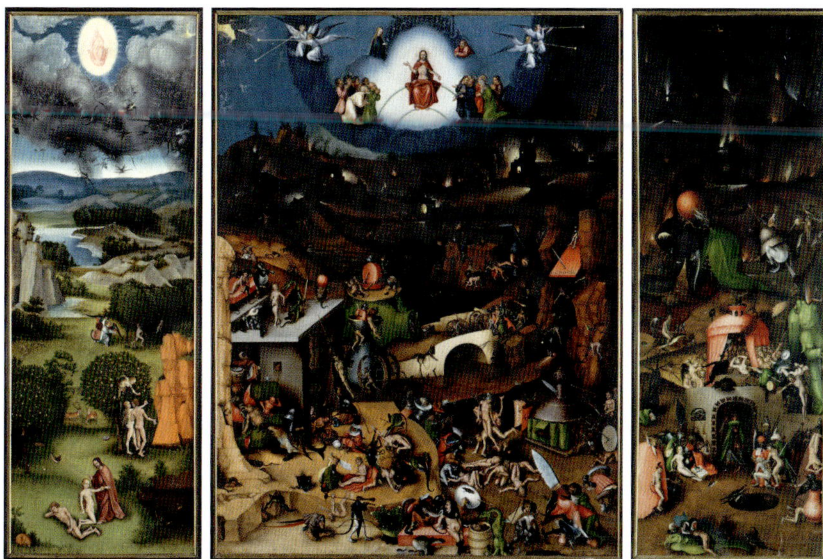

Lucas Cranach the Elder after Hieronymus Bosch, **The Last Judgement**, 1508 (*c.* 1520–1524?)
Oil and tempera on panel (lime), 163 x 125 cm / 64⅛ x 49¼ in. (central panel),
163 x 58 cm / 64⅛ x 22⅞ in. (each wing)
Berlin, Gemäldegalerie (For the original by Bosch, see ill. pp. 254/255)

Pages 246/247
Detail from: **The Last Judgement**, *c.* 1506
Central panel: **The Last Judgement** (see ill. pp. 254/255)

The late Middle Ages employed an especially complex system of colour symbolism. The symbolic value of individual colours varied depending on context, to the point that colours could signify partially contradictory meanings. Alongside black, grey, brown and white, Bosch uses the three powerful colours of green, blue and red for his devils. In this context green stands for inconstancy and unreliability, blue for trickery and illusion, and red for everything deviating from the Christian norm (Pleij 2004, pp. 77–88). These colours allude to some of the fundamental characteristics of devils as they were perceived in Bosch's day: they were thought to be constantly changing shape and assuming ever new guises, deceiving and confusing man about his true values and goals and upsetting his inner peace and equilibrium, until the sinner removed himself from the community or was expelled from it.

The interior wings of Bosch's *Last Judgement*, and in particular the upper halves of each panel, were extensively overpainted at a later date. Some clues to their original

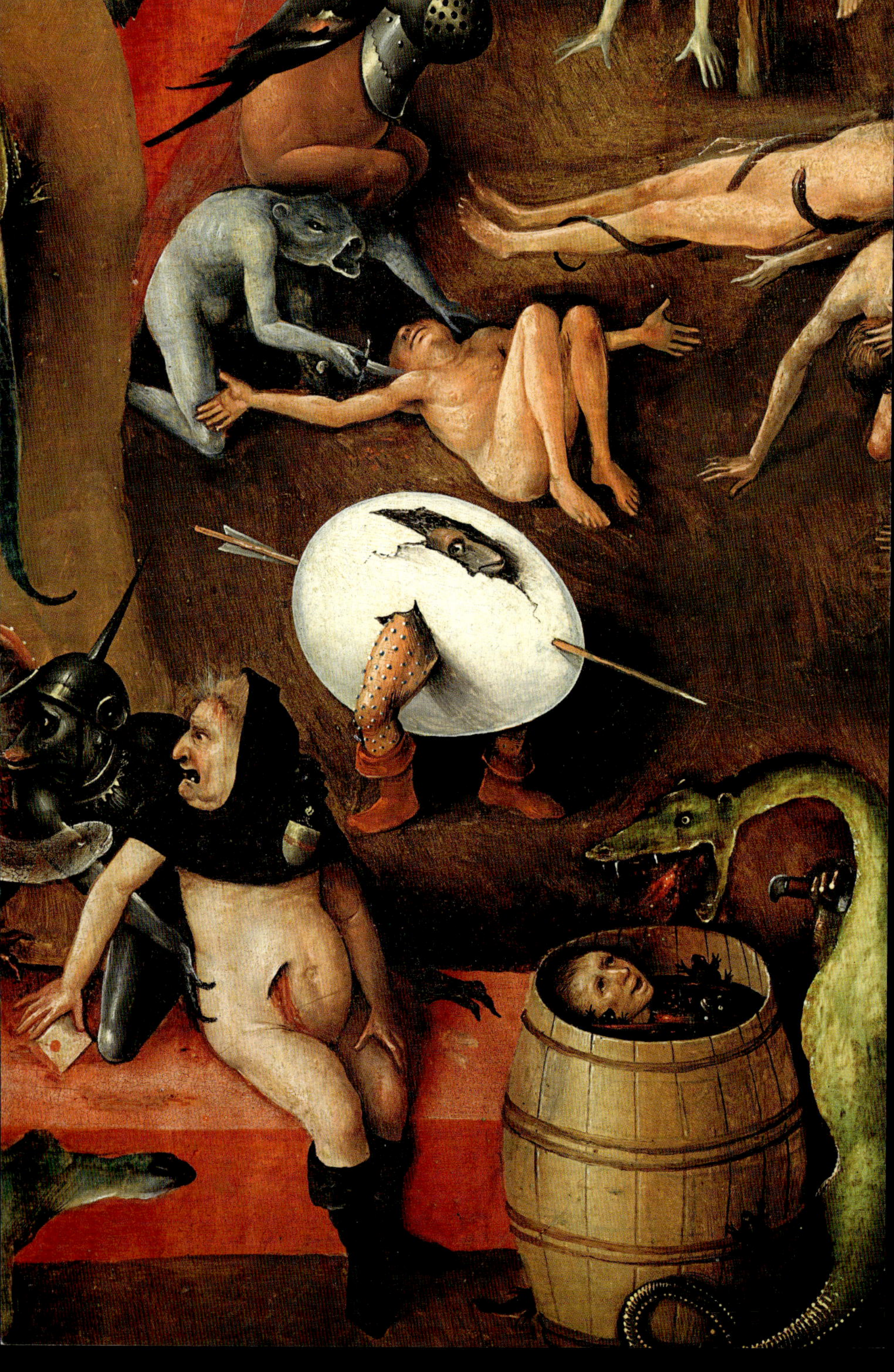

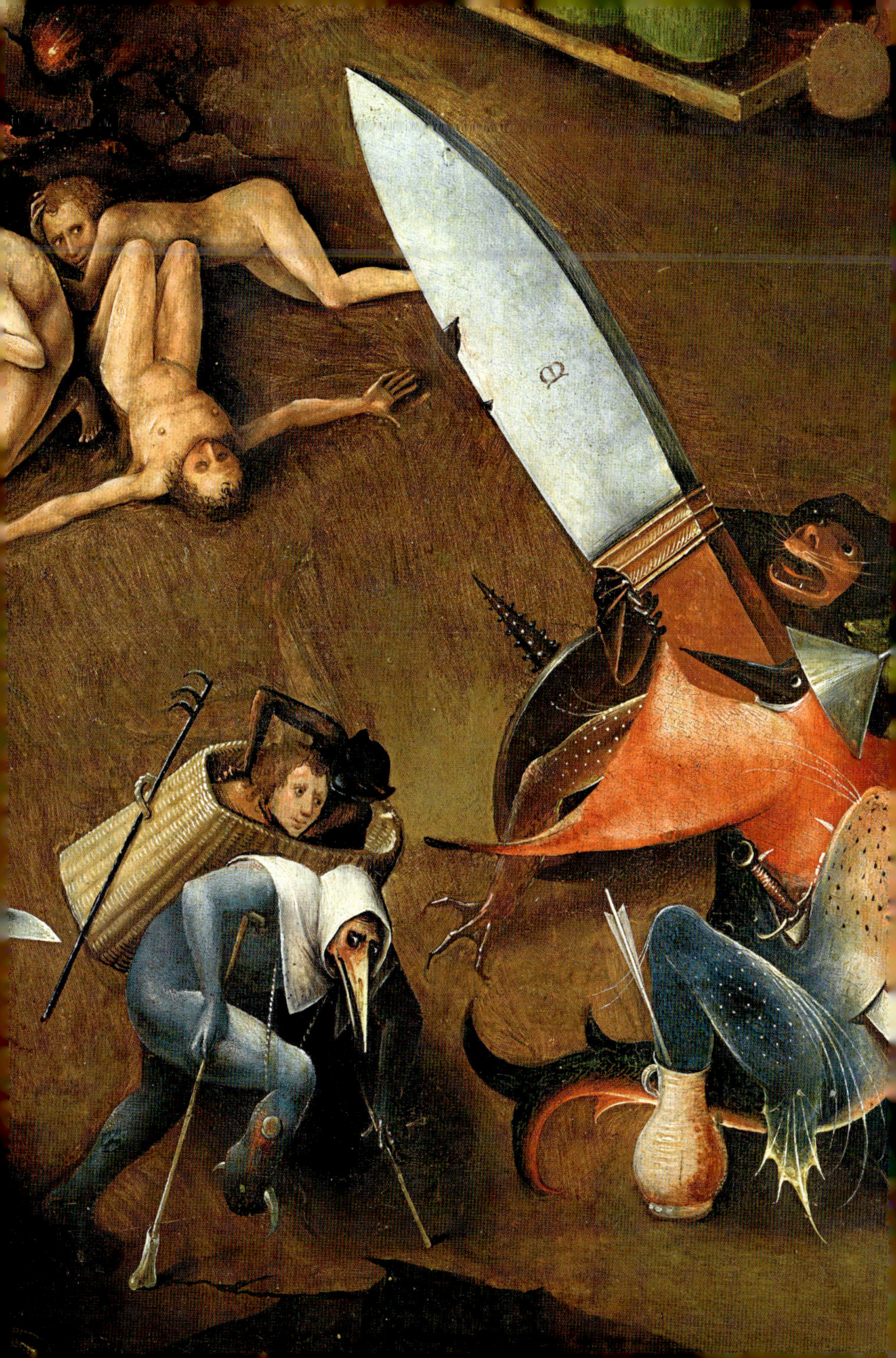

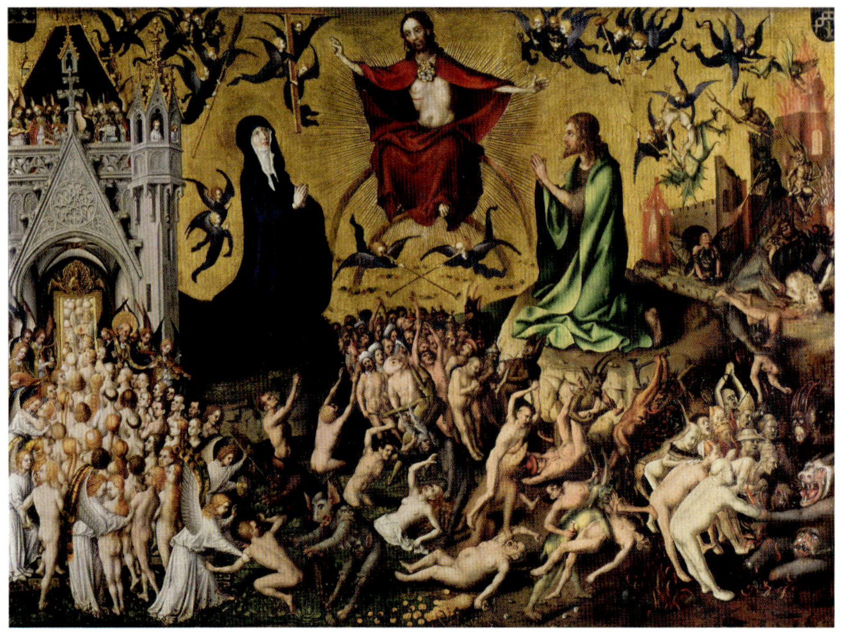

Stephan Lochner, **The Last Judgement**, *c.* 1435
Oil on panel (oak), 124.5 x 172 cm / 49 x 67¾ in.
Cologne, Wallraf-Richartz-Museum & Fondation Corboud

appearance may be gleaned, however, from a comparison with the *Last Judgement* by Lucas Cranach (p. 245), a copy of Bosch's work. This reveals that the background as far as the horizon, and especially the sky around God the Father, appears too green. In the left inner wing of the two *Haywain* triptychs (pp. 320/321, Cat. 20.2, p. 294), the sky is, as usual, blue.

Bosch represents the hereafter not as a glorious heavenly city but as a divine celestial light, in which even the corporeal state of the resurrected and redeemed souls is as if dematerialised and spiritualised, enabling them to see God mystically. The light does not merely symbolise God, but "manifests the very nature of God" (Benz 1969, pp. 326–328). This light cannot be represented *per se* since it exists outside the picture and the material realm. Bosch therefore merely hints at its presence. The only artist to have portrayed the hereafter in this fashion in a panel painting before Bosch was Dirk Bouts (1410/20–1475) in his *Earthly Paradise* (p. 261). In the *Last Judgement* panels (pp. 248, 281) by Stephan Lochner and Hans Memling (1433/40–1494), by contrast, the entrance to Heaven passes through the magnificent gateway to the celestial city, beyond which Heaven appears as a foil of gold leaf.

By contrast with the redeemed, the damned are conceived into intensely corporeal fashion that they are treated in pictorial representations like "meat" or "flesh" (Dutch, *vlees*). As if they were animals, they are caught like fish, hunted like game and slaughtered like cattle. In some cases they are cured, hung up to mature, roasted or boiled and so prepared as dishes for the Great Devourer: Satan, Lucifer or one of his representatives. To this end the devils employ utensils such as the long, three-pronged meat-hook called a *crauwel*, to catch, carry and cook their victims.

While the heavenly sphere is projected into the realm of the immaterial and unportrayable, Hell by comparison assumes great substance. It permits sins and punishments to be abundantly represented for the purposes of instruction. The viewer can wander through the pictorial landscapes of the *Last Judgement* in a sort of optical journey of the soul. As well as truths relating to humankind, the triptych offers variety and innovation both in its overall concept and in individual figures. We have already seen a very impressive instance of this in the *Garden of Earthly Delights* (Cat. 11), which the viewer can explore visually from left to right, starting in Paradise with the Creation of Eve, then traversing the central panel with humankind before the Flood, and continuing on to Hell. The *Last Judgement* is infused with a religious soberness and severity, however, whereas the *Garden of Earthly Delights* is indisputably more festive and fantastical, and at the same time funnier and more cheerful.

Philip the Handsome did not commission the *Last Judgement* for a courtroom, but for personal reasons connected with the forthcoming, probably decisive battle against the Duchy of Guelders. The work was intended to show Philip's consciousness of his duties as a Christian and as a prince. His plea for divine assistance for the Habsburg side was delivered by the intercessory portrait of him originally incorporated in the painting. The judgement upon this war, as upon all who would meet their death in it, was to lie in God's hand. Philip had long put off going to war, albeit probably less on his own account than to preserve the political peace between himself and the estates in the Low Countries, and was by no means confident about the outcome. In this respect he found himself in a difficult situation.

The *Last Judgement* is another example of the way in which Bosch's work was born out of the interplay of his personality, his environment and his patron. Only the senior aristocracy could commission works of this size. In Bosch, Philip engaged the services of a painter whose works fell in line with the tradition of Southern Netherlandish book and panel painting in the 15th century and at the same time imbued this tradition with fresh ideas. Bosch is also to a certain extent representative of the Brabant region, the new centre of power and commerce in the Low Countries following the shift away from West Flanders and the cities of Ghent and Bruges – a shift that had far-reaching consequences both for art and for the art market. Brussels the capital, Malines the princely residence and Antwerp the trade centre were now joined by 's-Hertogenbosch as a strategic military outpost.

The fact that admiration for Bosch was not limited to the sphere of Habsburg influence in the Netherlands and Spain, is demonstrated by the above-mentioned copy of the *Last Judgement* painted by Lucas Cranach the Elder (p. 245). In 1508 Cranach was sent to Malines as the envoy of Frederick the Wise (1463–1525), Elector of Saxony, in order to attend the festivities accompanying the homage and oath ceremony for the eldest son of Philip and Joanna, the young Archduke Charles, later Charles V (1500–1558). Cranach arrived at some point after the end of June and remained until 17 November, based in Malines and probably also in Brussels. It may have been during this period that he made his copy of Bosch's triptych. Although the copy is very accurate when it comes to the colour and shape of the figures, Cranach was unable to identify all the details; in the left inner wing, for example, he replaced the crane or ostrich with deer.

Detail from: **The Last Judgement**, *c.* 1506
Central panel: **The Last Judgement** (see ill. pp. 254/255)

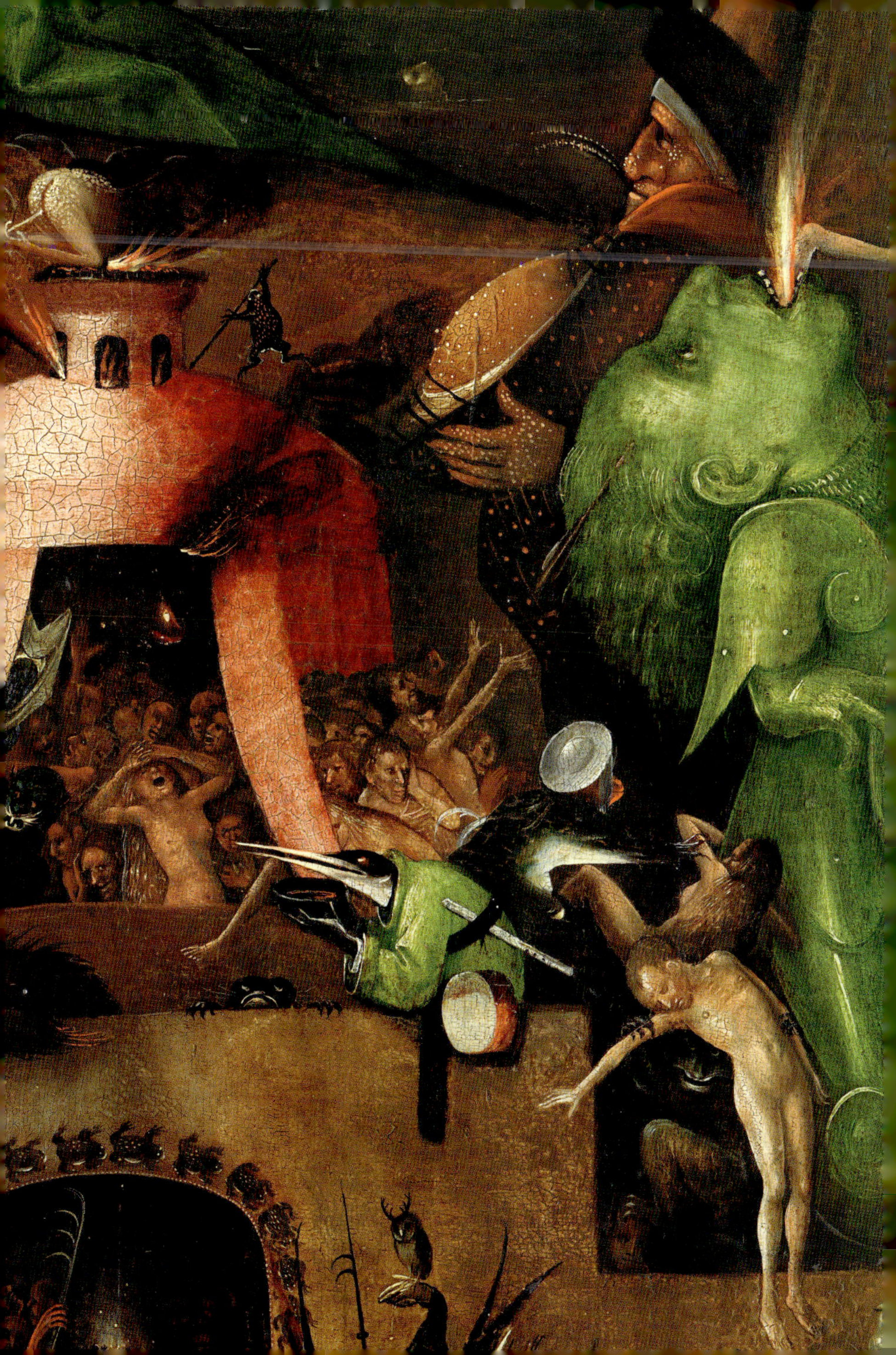

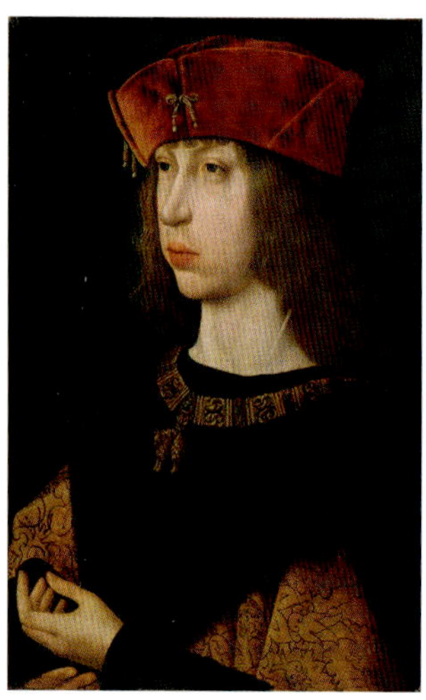

Master of the Magdalene Legend, **Philip I of Habsburg, called the Handsome**, *c.* 1501
Oil on panel, 41.8 x 26.9 cm / 16½ x 10½ in. Paris, Musée du Louvre, inv. 2085

Page 253

St James, *c.* 1506
Left outer wing of: **The Last Judgement**
Oil and tempera on panel (oak), 167 x 60 cm / 65¾ x 23⅝ in.
Vienna, Akademie der bildenden Künste, Gemäldegalerie

St Bavo, *c.* 1506
Right outer wing of: **The Last Judgement**
Oil and tempera on panel (oak), 167 x 60 cm / 65¾ x 23⅝ in.
Vienna, Akademie der bildenden Künste, Gemäldegalerie

Pages 254/255

The Last Judgement, *c.* 1506
Oil and tempera on panel (oak), 163 x 127.5 cm / 64¼ x 50¼ in. (central panel), 167 x 60 cm / 65¾ x 23⅝ in. (wings)
Vienna, Akademie der bildenden Künste, Gemäldegalerie
Left inner wing: **Fall of the Rebel Angels, The Fall and The Expulsion from Paradise**
Central panel: **The Last Judgement**
Right inner wing: **Hell**

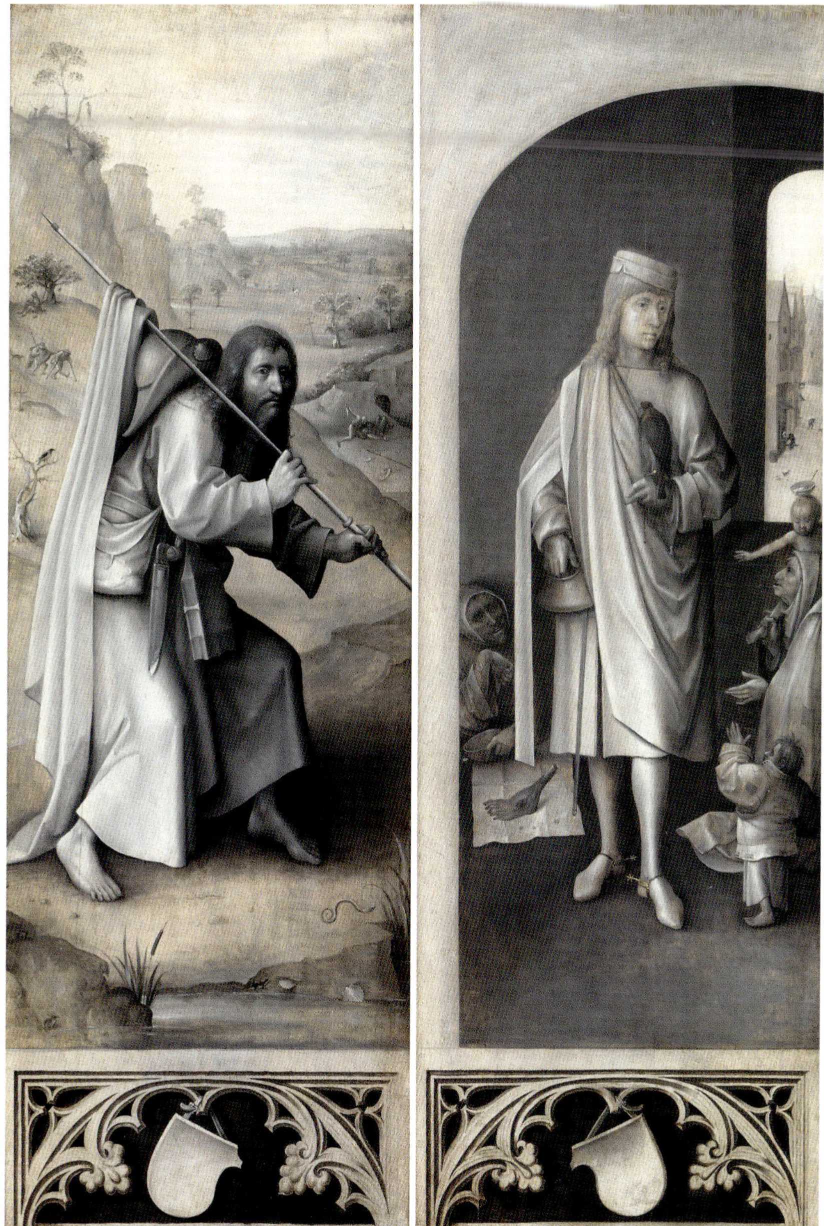

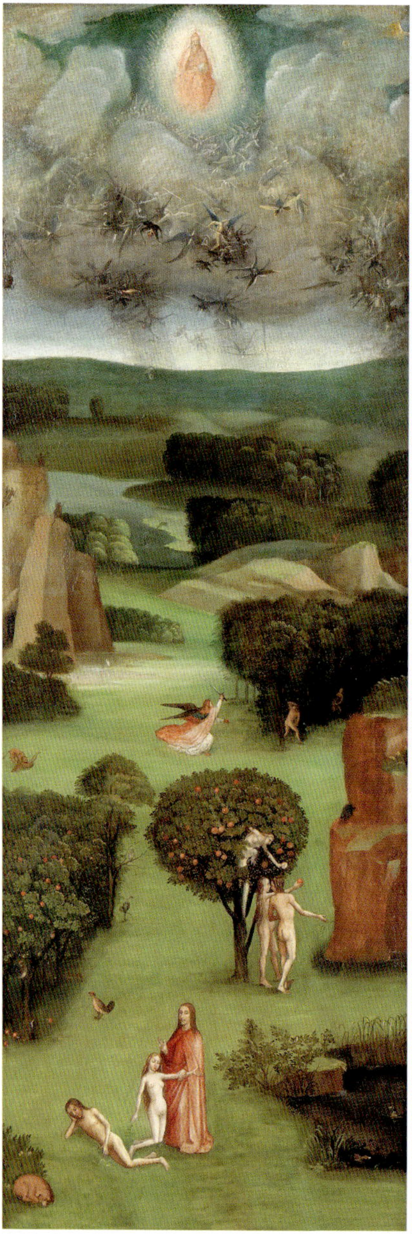

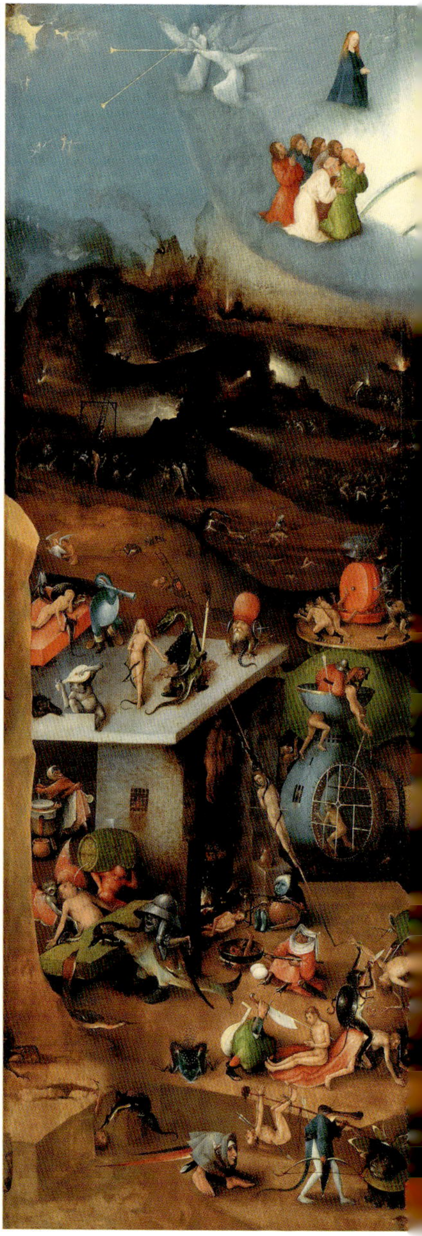

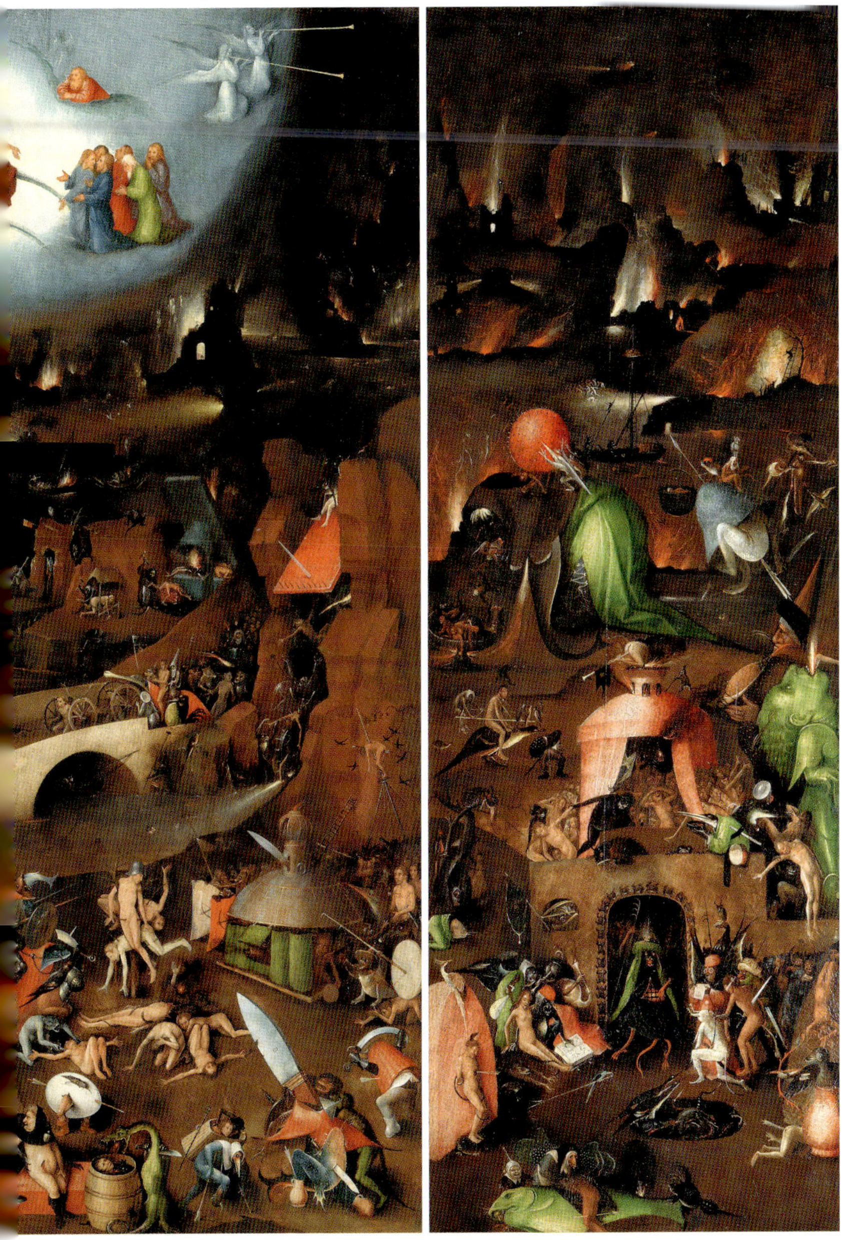

VI.

Exemplum docet: Late works

1504–1516

*"Of what did Bosch dream? Of Christ's Passion,
Of the wickedness and stupidity of the soldiers,
Of the vanity and transience of this earthly life,
Of Hell with its instruments of torture,
Of the temptation against which the holy men
are capable of putting up little resistance."*

MAX JAKOB FRIEDLÄNDER, 1941

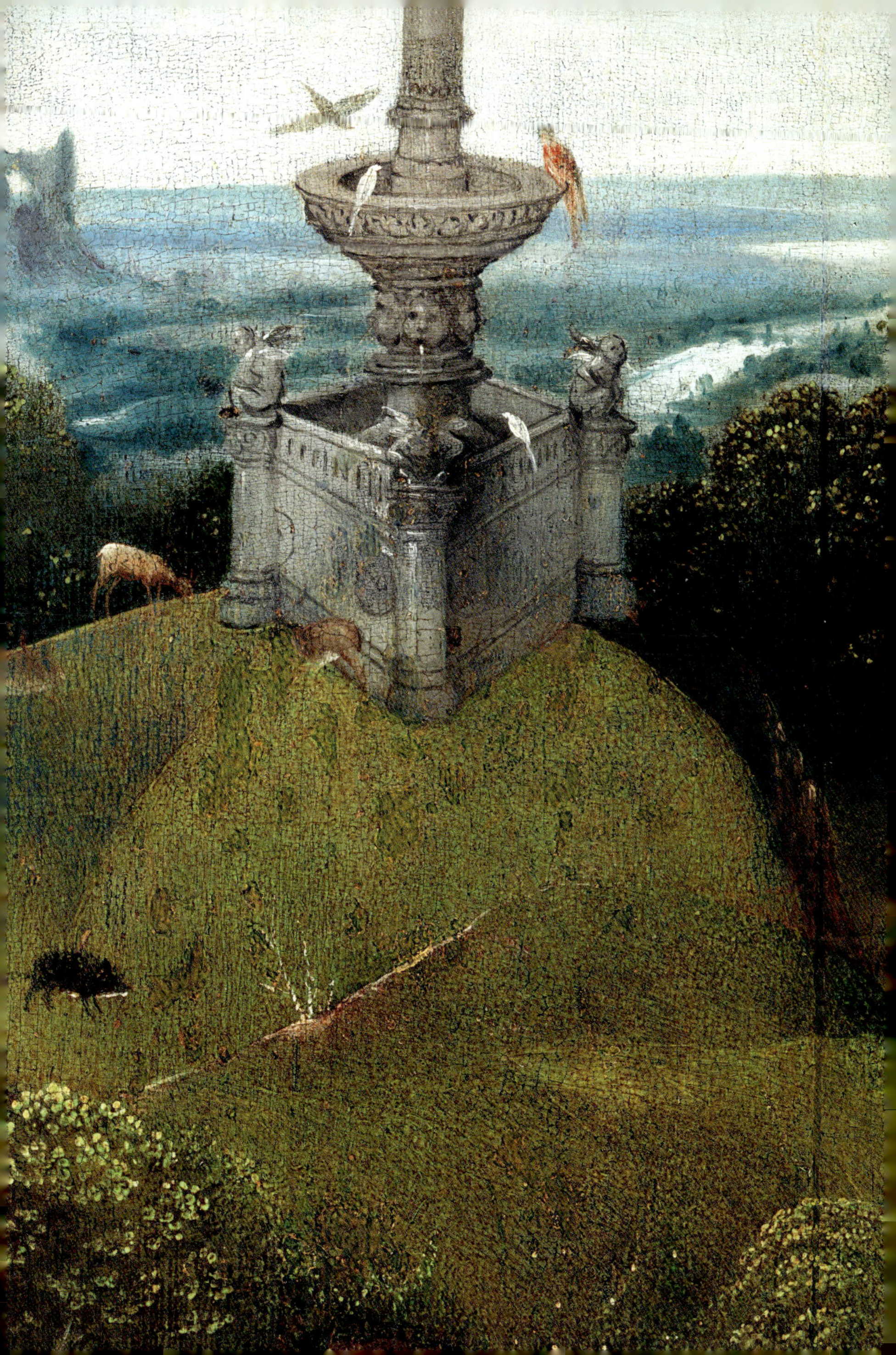

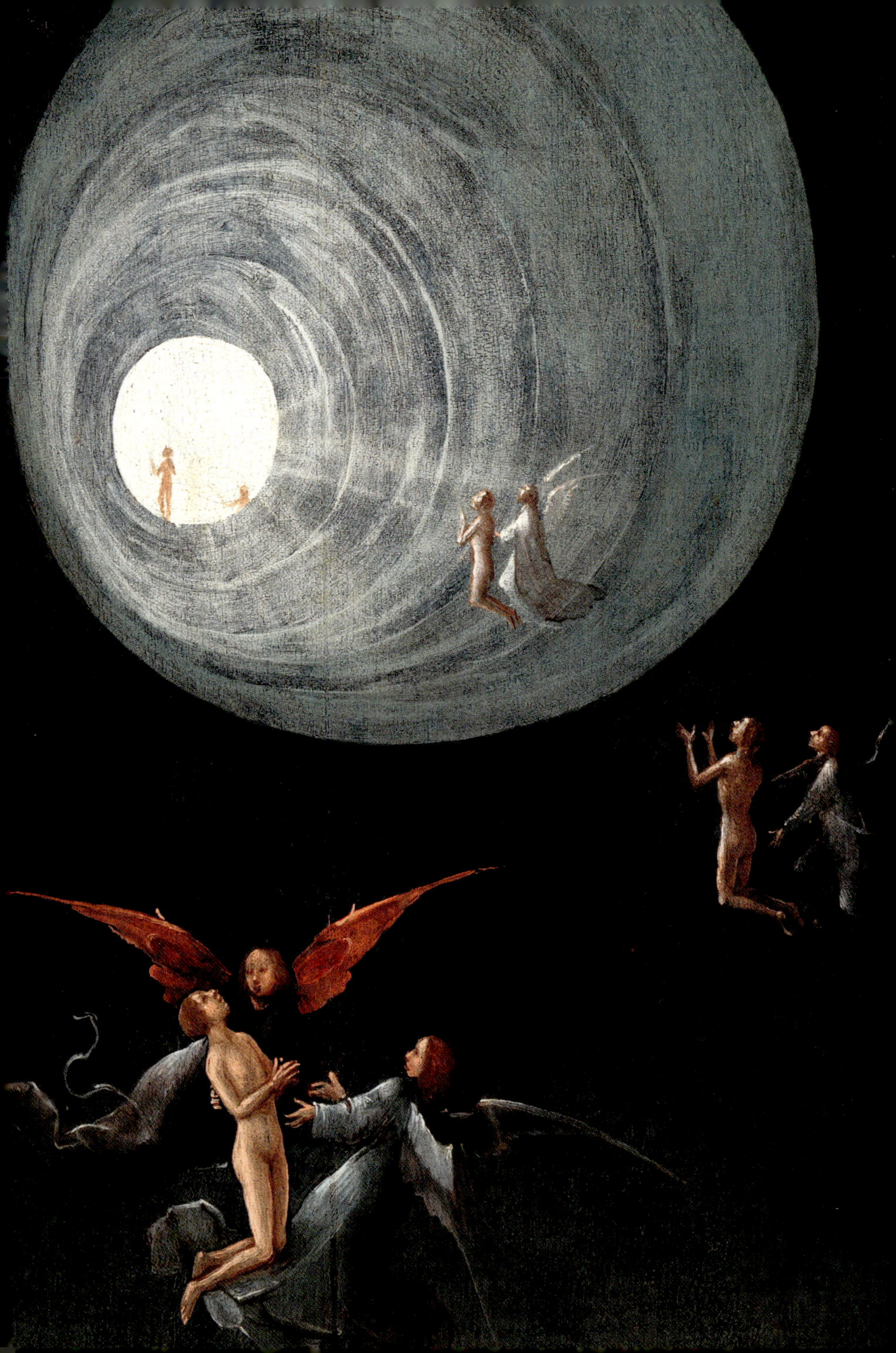

The quality of Bosch's art – as also of his patrons – reached a new height with his three large triptychs: the *Temptation of St Anthony* (Cat. 10), the *Garden of Earthly Delights* (Cat. 11) and the *Last Judgement* (Cat. 13). Yet it is these very paintings that were subsequently to contribute to the demotion of his work to the much narrower category of the grotesque. This trend had already begun in the 16th century, as revealed, for example, by the previously cited comments of de Beatis, and it was deplored by both Guevara and Sigüenza. Even if drolleries provided Bosch with a chance to make his art more varied, more lavish and more freely inventive, he chose this medium not on a mere personal whim, but in direct response to the subject-matter of the commission in hand and to his knowledge of the tastes of his patrons, in particular those from the courtly sphere, who were familiar with drolleries from books of hours. Not until the middle decades of the 16th century would there be a market for the smaller-format diableries produced in such numbers by Bosch's followers.

The reasons for Bosch's success lay, instead, in a whole range of innovations that he introduced into painting. His *Adoration of the Magi* (Cat. 6), which does not fall within the sphere of drolleries, provided an influential model for many workshops and early followers. Among the paintings that issued from Bosch's own workshop during the final decade of his career, some (Cat. 12, Cat. 14, Cat. 21, Cat. 22) continue in the vein established in particular by the *Temptation of St Anthony* (Cat. 10), while in others Bosch explored new directions (Cat. 15–20). One factor was of great significance for Bosch during these last years of his life: in a paradigm shift to which many of his fellow artists likewise had to adjust, the interests of potential customers were turning increasingly towards the Renaissance and the Humanism flourishing in Italy. Yet this also presented Bosch with an opportunity, as it opened up a new market for his paintings.

An illuminating insight into the reception of Bosch's art in Italy during the last decade of his life is offered by the three works in Venice (Cat. 12, Cat. 14 and Cat. 16). We shall discuss them here as a group, since they have all come down to us from the same collection, even though the two triptychs were conceived for a religious context and not for ostentatious display in a private art collection. This nevertheless became their destiny, as is shown by a note made by the patrician Marcantonio Michiel (1484–1552) in 1521, and by a 1528 inventory of the paintings belonging to Marino Grimani (1488/89–1546). The latter was the nephew and heir of Cardinal Domenico Grimani (1461–1523), from whose collection the three Bosch paintings can confidently be said to derive. The Grimanis were

Pages 257, 258
Detail from: **Paradise and Hell**, *c.* 1505–1515
Interior of the inner left wing: **Earthly Paradise**
Interior of the outer left wing: **Heavenly Paradise**
(see ill. pp. 312/313)

sone of the most important noble families in Venice. Domenico supported the idea of reform within the Catholic Church, maintained contacts with Jewish intellectuals, was open to developments in the North, and supported Pope Hadrian VI (1459–1523), who came from the Low Countries (Limentani Virdis 2010).

The person who imported or brokered the sale of Bosch's paintings may have been Daniel van Bomberghen (also called Daniel Bomberg, *c.* 1485–1553), originally from Antwerp and active in Venice from 1516 onwards as a publisher of Hebraica and a dealer in luxury goods, who also had links with Cardinal Grimani (Aikema 2001a, Limentani Virdis 2010). Another possible candidate, unconsidered until now, is the 's-Hertogenbosch merchant Lodewijk Beys, who was related to Bosch through his nephew, Jan Goessens, and who owned a house on the market square very close to that owned by Bosch. Beys's home was so grand and well-appointed that Maria Bianca Sforza (1472–1510), wife of Emperor Maximilian I, lodged there during an imperial visit of 1502. In 1500, 1504 and 1513 Beys made lucrative pilgrimages to Jerusalem and Mount Sinai, whence he brought back relics of St Catherine (van Dijck 2001a, p. 54 f.). Such pilgrimages to the Holy Land, which were undertaken by nobles and patricians and proved very costly, departed from Venice in spring and autumn. Beys, who is known to have combined his pilgrimages with business transactions, might have negotiated or organised a delivery of Bosch's works while waiting to set sail.

In 1521, when Michiel made his notes on the art works he saw at the (now publicly accessible) Palazzo Grimani near the church of Santa Maria Formosa, the building housed a collection of manuscripts and paintings from the Low Countries. The manuscripts included the *Breviarium Grimani*, acquired in 1520; and among the paintings were works by Hans Memling, Joachim Patinir (*c.* 1485–1524) and Herri met de Bles (*c.* 1500/10–1555/60). After Domenico Grimani's death most of the works in the collection were put into storage in crates. These were reopened only in 1615, after which date the *Triptych of the Crucified Female Martyr* (Cat. 14) hung elsewhere in Venice: in a room at the Doge's Palace.

Hermit Saints Triptych

The *Hermit Saints Triptych (with Sts Jerome, Anthony and Giles*; pp. 304/305, Cat. 12) was produced around 1504, and so probably even before the *Last Judgement*. Who commissioned it, and for what purpose, are unknown. The originally arched top of the triptych was cut down at some point and the backs planed off and reinforced with struts, with the consequent loss of any information that might have been gleaned from painted coats of arms or even portraits of donors. The pictorial concept governing the interior, with each panel devoted to one saint, suggests that we may be looking at three patron saints, here venerated in a triptych perhaps intended to stand on an altar. The central panel – and the main one by dint of both its central position and its surface area (which is twice that of the wings) – shows the emaciated *St Jerome* (Cat. 12.2) in a sweeping hilly landscape, kneeling in front of a crucifix in a ruin serving as a chapel. His long red cloak covers all but his bare feet, hands and chest. In his right hand, which is raised in front of his chest, St Jerome holds a rock with which to chastise himself. His left hand reaches out towards a polychrome crucifix propped on a small altar in a miniature apse. Its low wall supports three monochrome reliefs (p. 277). This main scene is based on a passage in one of St Jerome's letters to Eustochium (*Ad Eustochium de custodia virginitatis* 22,7):"Now, although in my fear of hell I had consigned myself to this prison, where I had no companions but scorpions and wild beasts, I often found myself amid bevies of girls. My face was pale and my frame chilled with fasting; yet my mind was burning with desire, and the fires of lust kept bubbling up before me when my flesh was as good as dead." An early edition of the letter was printed in Hasselt in 1490. In the three mural reliefs, which serve as pictures-within-a-picture, Bosch illustrates Jerome's inner conflict, in which the saint must choose between chastity (*continentia*) and lust (*luxuria*), between humility (*humilitas*) and pride (*superbia*). These virtues and vices are exemplified by the two reliefs mounted on either side of the choir apse. The relief on the right, nearer the viewer, shows the positive exemplum of the Old Testament figure of Judith, who cut off the head of Holofernes, commander of the Babylonian army besieging the Jewish city of Bethulia, after first using her charms to make him drunk (Deuteronomy, Book of Judith 13:1–17; p. 262). The man who paid for his carnal instincts with his head thus becomes a negative exemplum. Judith, by contrast, symbolises the victory of intelligence, courage and chastity over blinding lust. Although Jerome, in his letter to Eustochium, does not use the example of Judith to illustrate his own inner battle, he does

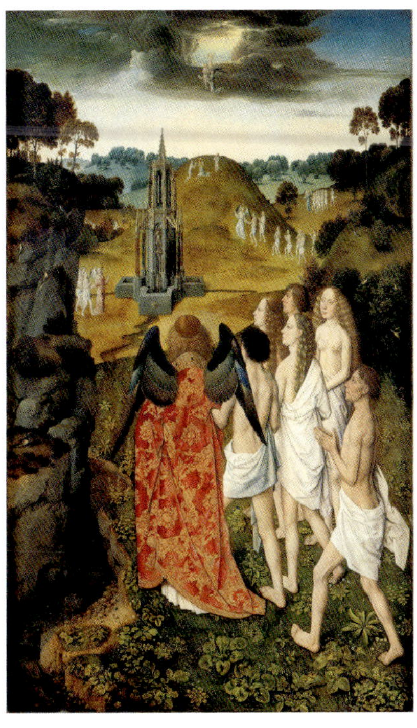

Dirk Bouts, **Earthly Paradise**, *c.* 1470
Oil on panel, 115 x 69.5 cm / 45¼ x 27⅜ in. Lille, Palais des Beaux-Arts

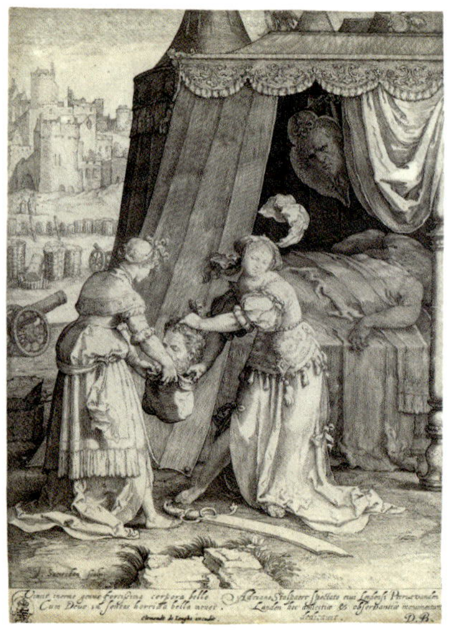

cite the stories of Samson and Delilah and of David and Bathsheba, which likewise revolve around the theme of lust.

A separate negative counterpart to Judith can be recognised in the relief further back on the left, beside the crucifix. Here, an acrobat or dancer is attempting to climb up on to the back of a unicorn. According to legend, this fabulous beast was wild and extremely strong and could only be tamed by a virgin, making it a symbol of chastity, in particular of the Virgin Mary. The figure corresponds to the beribboned Morris dancers (cf. Israhel van Meckenem, p. 104) worshipping the Golden Calf in the painted relief in the central panel of the *Temptation of St Anthony* (p. 105, Cat. 10.4). The third relief is situated below the first two and shows a man with his head and torso inside a beehive, leaving only his naked buttocks exposed to view. The same visual device is found on an incense burner, several centuries older and converted into a reliquary (Fischer 2009, p. 162), in Venice: a classic instance of the wide temporal and geographical dissemination of such motifs. After its use in Bosch's workshop, it was taken up in a drawing by an assistant or a follower (p. 460/461, Cat. D9r); and it was later employed by Pieter Bruegel (p. 275). A withered stick is poking out of the anus of the naked man in the basket; and, perched at the far end of this, with a number of other birds flying around it, is an owl, which probably stands here, as elsewhere, for spiritual blindness. The bare backside – a motif common in Bosch and widespread from the 14th to the 16th century – is a metaphor that illustrates very directly the uncleanness resulting from the sins of a life reduced to the merely physical. Another bird is sitting on a branch above Jerome's head, and is thus located on a notional line that runs from the naked man in the basket through the relief with unicorn and acrobat. As a symbolic animal representing the free soul or the state of grace, the unicorn is evidently an antitype to the naked man trapped in sin.

Jan Pietersz Saenredam after Lucas van Leyden, **Judith and Holofernes**, *c.* 1600
Copper engraving, 28.7 x 20.9 cm / 11¼ x 8 ¼ in. (trimmed)
Dresden, Staatliche Kunstsammlungen, Kupferstich-Kabinett

Evidence of the collapse of a pre-Christian heathen culture can be found in the wild landscape around Jerome (p. 278). The saint is kneeling in a ruin that resembles a chapel with the apse of a choir. Fragments of ornamental stone-paved flooring still survive. On the left is the stump of a column, painted with a picture showing a man kneeling in prayer to the cosmos and surrounded by stars. The cracks in the pillar, the frog at its base and the withered branches beside it bestow a sinister air. On the far side of the paving is a sculpture that seems to be toppling over. The historical Jerome did in fact distance himself from ancient astrology, heathen scholarship and the belief in pagan idols. On the right a flight of steps leads up towards Jerome from the darkness of a subterranean vault: a fitting metaphor for both the descent and the ascent of the soul (p. 285). In the middle distance, to the left, behind a lion (Jerome's traditional companion) we can see various birds and a group of wild animals. Bosch achieves a forceful representation of St Jerome even without portraying his emotions, physical suffering and self-chastisement (cf. Cranach, p. 269). Leaving aside the barren surroundings and the wild beasts, the real threat here comes from the sin of unbelief, doubt and unchastity.

Not unlike the Ghent *St Jerome* (Cat. 2), where the details of the surrounding landscape point to what is occurring in the saint's inner life, the Venice painting externalises Jerome's spiritual battle through the device of the picture-within-a-picture. The contrast between the painted reliefs, and the gestures made by Jerome illustrate the inner battle of the soul. The reliefs here provide the arguments. The saint's right hand points to the relief with the exemplum of unchastity, while his left hand motions towards the exemplum of Judith, so that his arms cross. Commanding the greatest presence of all, however, is the crucifix, sculpturally modelled and painted in naturalistic colour; and it is towards this that Jerome is ultimately reaching. The top of a dead tree behind it has burst back into full leaf. The saint thus chooses faith and redemption. Bosch had already employed a comparable pictorial structure, including pictures-within-a-picture, in the central panel of his *Temptation of St Anthony* triptych (pp. 118/119, Cat. 10.4).

The interior of the left and right wings offers little space in which to portray the lives of the saints in great detail. The left inner panel shows *St Anthony* (Cat. 12.1) drawing water from a well, his eyes downcast, as if in meditation. Opposite him a devil is pouring out liquid as if wishing to ape the saint. Other devils also parody St Anthony, for example the two holding an open book in front of them (pp. 272/273). Three of the demons in the foreground have stylised peacock's eyes, as seen also on the clothing of the *Crucified Female Martyr* (Cat. 14). A number of key motifs, including the burning monastery and the naked woman standing beneath the tree draped with a red cloth (p. 271), as a symbol of Anthony's temptation by lust, are taken from Bosch's *Temptation of St Anthony* triptych (Cat. 10.4 and Cat. 10.5).

The right inner panel shows *St Giles*. The cult of St Giles (*c.* 640–*c.* 720), also known as St Aegidius, was widespread in the late Middle Ages, owing to the fact that he was counted as one of the Fourteen Holy Helpers. Giles originally came from Athens and lived for a number of years as a hermit in a cave at the mouth of the Rhône. According to legend, he nourished himself with the milk of a doe. When Wamba, king of the Visigoths, arrived one day with a hunting party Giles placed himself in front of the doe to protect her and was shot by an arrow. In his humility he prayed to God that his wound should not be healed. By way of atonement, the king founded the Benedictine abbey of Saint-Gilles in the south of France. Bosch portrays Giles as a hermit praying before a simple altar in a gloomy cave, with his traditional attributes: a book, a Benedictine habit and a doe. In a departure from pictorial tradition, the saint in Bosch's picture wears a priest's tonsure, and the arrow protrudes not from his arm but from the area around his heart. Lying in front of the saint, in addition to the book, is a letter or document, perhaps the abbey's foundation charter or the letter delivered by an angel and confirming, in another episode of the saint's legend, that the sins of Charlemagne (747/48–814) had been forgiven. A face can be seen peering into the cave through a hole in the rear wall: perhaps that of a member of the hunting party.

The steeply sloping landscape is home to a few plants and animals. Bosch's palette, which fluctuates between moss green and reddish brown, has suffered over time along with the rest of the triptych, whose condition is only mediocre. Numerous small animals are arranged around St Giles in his cave (Dittrich 2005, p. 506), of which those above him can probably be interpreted in a positive light: the porcupine on the left as a symbol of strong faith, the grey heron at the centre as an emblem of love and fidelity to Christ, the chamois on the rocky outcrop as divine wisdom, and the great titmouse on the right at the entrance to the cave as a symbol of the soul. In the foreground, below the saint, the raven perched on a carcass symbolises Evil. Lying nearby, at the lower left, is a boar's head and, at the lower right, the skull of a horse, both symbols of pride (*superbia*). The lizard crawling along a withered tree root stands for sin in general. Through the emphasis upon his self-sacrifice and his life as a hermit, St Giles appears as a model of prayer and penitence. The figure of St Giles praying in his cave may well have formed the starting-point for the paintings of St Paul and St Mary Magdalene on the exterior shutters of the *Adoration of the Magi* (Cat. 24.1/2), a product of the Bosch workshop.

It has yet to be established whether the *Hermit Saints Triptych* was already installed in the setting for which it was originally intended when it was sold, or if it never served the purpose for which it was conceived, or if it was in fact destined for export from the start.

Detail from: **Paradise and Hell**, *c.* 1505–1515
Interior of the inner right wing: **Fall of the Damned** (see ill. pp. 312/313)

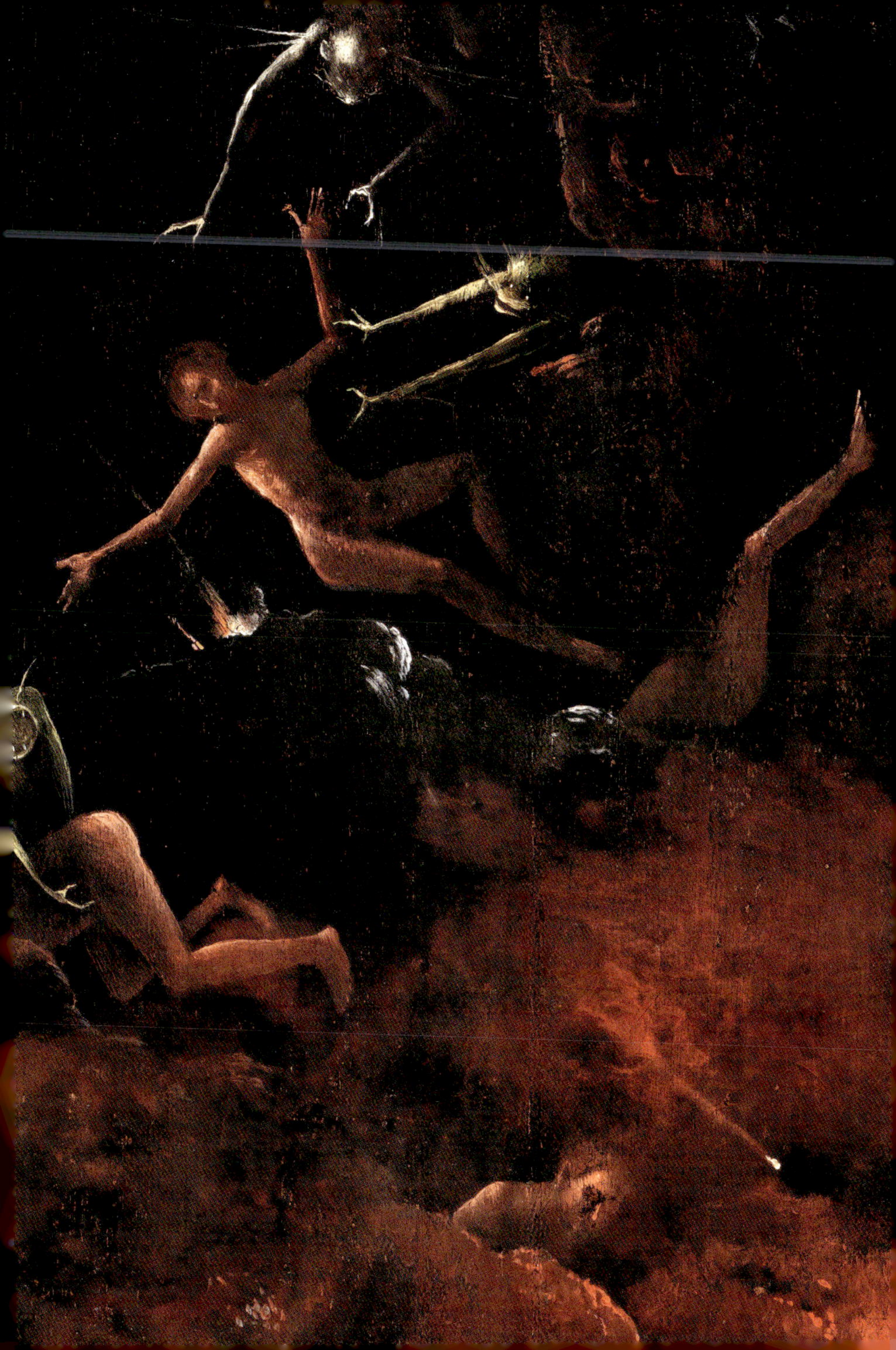

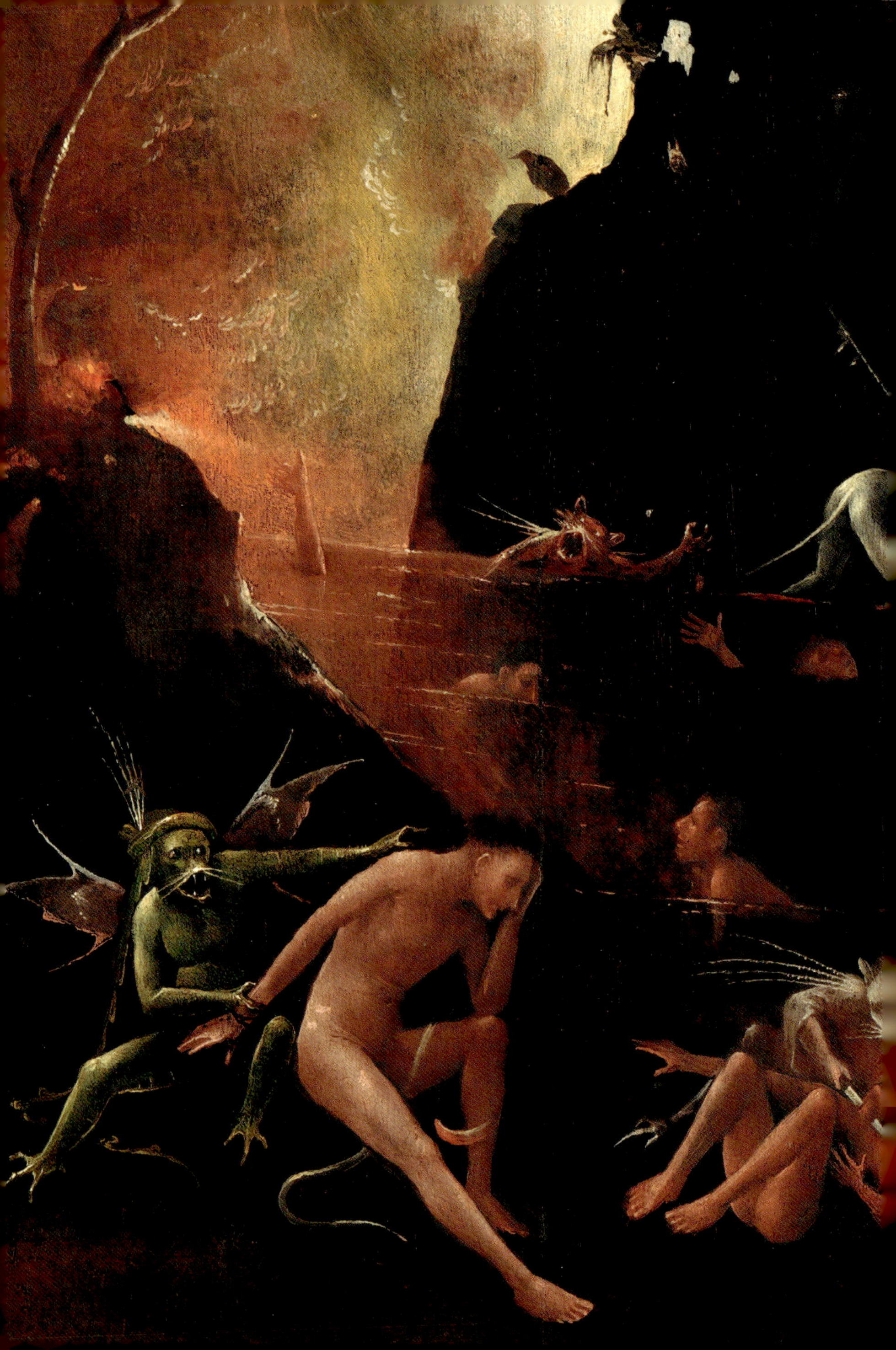

Be that as it may, its three saints are well suited to the Venice region. St Jerome, an ascetic and a translator of the Bible, had been a popular figure in Italian art centuries before he appeared in painting north of the Alps around 1500. St Giles and St Anthony were likewise widely venerated in Italy. St Anthony, in view of his association with demonic creatures and infernal landscapes, also fulfilled Italian expectations of the work of 16th- and 17th-century Flemish and Dutch painters, who were lauded as specialists in this genre in art literature from south of the Alps (Aikema 2001a/b/c).

A virgin on the Cross

As revealed by the presence of two donor figures beneath the visible paint layer, the *Triptych of the Crucified Female Martyr (St Wilgefortis;* pp. 310/311, Cat. 14) originally functioned as a memorial or altarpiece commissioned as part of the endowment of a requiem mass intended to help secure for these same donors a place in the hereafter. The donors are in each case identified, by their style of dress, as members of the educated civic elite, in common with the donors of other Bosch paintings (e. g. Cat. 6 and Cat. 21). The triptych is dated to the years between 1505 and 1515, a period that includes both its original production and its subsequent over-painting. How much time elapsed in between is unclear. It is equally unclear whether the work was rejected by the clients – on account, for example, of alleged artistic deficiencies – or whether it for a time served its intended purpose before being removed from its ecclesiastical context and sold. The identity of the female saint in the central panel was long a matter of conjecture. A definitive pronouncement on this matter is effectively impossible, since a distinction has to be made between the original painting and its modified version. The work was produced as a triptych of St Wilgefortis, a legendary female saint venerated in the Low Countries as Sint-Ontcommer. Over the course of the 14th and 15th centuries her cult spread in various forms from Brabant and the Middle Rhine to Germany, where she was known as Kümmernis (Schweizer-Vüllers 1997; King 2003). According to the legend that accompanied her from the 15th century onwards, Wilgefortis was the daughter of a heathen king and, as a young woman, converted to Christianity, taking a vow of virginity. When her father found her a husband she prayed to God to make her unattractive in order to escape the unwanted marriage, with the result that she grew a beard. Her suitor was indeed repulsed, but her father had her killed in the same fashion as her heavenly bridegroom: by crucifixion. She hung on the cross for three days, praying, converting others and giving comfort. After angels had finally carried her up to Heaven a violent storm broke out and her father's palace went up in flames (Bax 1961, pp. 31–32).

Detail from: **Paradise and Hell**, *c.* 1505–1515
Interior of the outer right wing: **The Damned in Hell** (see ill. pp. 312/313)

As befitting a princess, the saint is clothed in a full-length red over-dress with deep slits, wide sleeves and a belt, and an anthracite-coloured under-dress embroidered in silvery gold. On her head, which is inclined slightly backwards and to one side, she wears a gold crown. Her dark under-dress is trimmed with dots, delicate branches and stylised peacock-feather eyes, symbols of the Resurrection. Wilgefortis has been bound with ropes to a T-shaped cross. Her long, chestnut-golden hair falls loose far down her back: a sign of her true virginity. A shadow running from her chin to her temples no more than hints at a beard, perhaps because the paint surface has eroded over the centuries. It is possible that the beard was still visible in the 18th century, since Zanetti (see entry on Cat. 14) could not decide if the crucified martyr was male or female. But in a number of other paintings of St Wilgefortis her beard is only lightly indicated.

For a deeper understanding of Bosch's *Triptych of the Crucified Female Martyr* it is important to bear in mind that it is based on the standard layout for a multi-figural Crucifixion scenes: in its portrayal, for example, of the bystanders' emotions, or its organisation of the figures to left and right of the cross into a good and a bad side. St Wilgefortis's imitation of Christ (*Imitatio Christi*) thus reveals itself both in the overall composition and in the details. She appears in the centre: not hanging in agony from the Cross, but halfway between life and death. She embodies Salvation, resurrection and triumph over death. On the right of the cross the two men nearest the foreground are dressed in magnificent fantastical costumes. They might represent the royal fathers of the bridal couple, or the princess's father and a counsellor, accompanied by further courtiers in the group behind. One of them is pointing to a scene decorating his belt, which shows the confrontation between a bear and an ape, the latter armed with the lance-like trunk or bough of a tree. This detail has been interpreted as an allusion to the unequal battle between the bride and groom (Bax 1961, p. 22). To the left of the cross the bridegroom has fainted (p. 300): his position and pose correspond to those of the swooning Virgin in many Crucifixion scenes, but also to those of the dead Christ in the Deposition carved by van Wesel (p. 24) as part of his altarpiece for the Brotherhood of Our Blessed Lady in 's-Hertogenbosch. It is interesting to note the formal similarity between the clothing of bride and bridegroom, in particular as regards the colour and embroidered decoration of their undergarments; while the ornamental details – respectively, peacock feathers and an owl – set positive against negative. The folds of the bridegroom's red cloak have in fact fallen open to reveal an owl, a symbol of folly and blindness, on his thigh. The shovel lying prominently in front of him, and the uneven surface of the ground, call to mind Psalm 7:15:"He made a pit and dug it out, and has fallen into the ditch which he made." It might also stand for the bridegroom's failed plans, or serve as a warning of God's impending judgement, as formulated in Luke 3:17:"His winnowing fan [occasionally translated as "winnowing shovel"] is in His hand, and He will thoroughly clean out His threshing floor, and gather the wheat into His barn; but the chaff He will burn with unquenchable fire." A priest and other courtiers or servants have rushed to the prince's aid. Further men are standing in front of and inside a hollow tree, its lower branches leafless, constituting a further symbol of sin on this side of the cross. (A similar *St Wilgefortis* composition with the king and bridegroom on either side of the cross and the palace in the background is found in a wall painting, today largely destroyed, in Rostock).

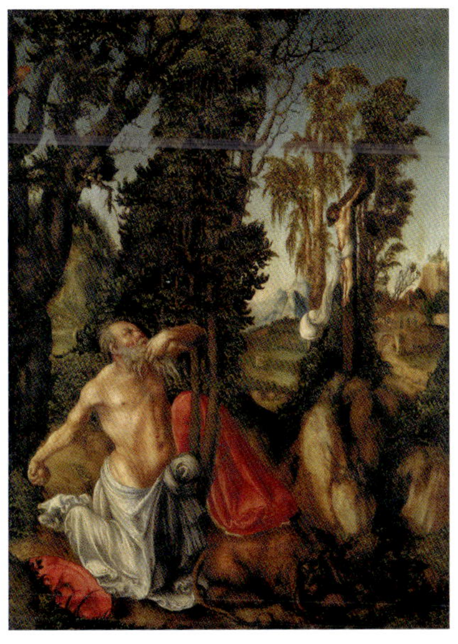

The figures within the Bosch triptych achieve their animated effect not so much through their facial expressions as through their body language. Such a rich and varied concentration of poses, looks and, above all, gestures is to be found nowhere else in Bosch's work. A clear distinction is made here between the figural groups on either side of the cross. Among the crowded figures on the left some are covering their faces or clutching their heads as if blinded by the sun, while others are turning away from Wilgefortis on the cross or do not register her presence. Since they are not receptive to the teachings of Christianity and are afraid of the divine omnipotence and retribution issuing from the crucified saint, they represent the negative side. By contrast, the figures on the right should be interpreted positively, as the enlightened and converted. The fact that they also include the father of the bride is only at first sight surprising: according to some versions of the legend of St Wilgefortis, he converted to Christianity after his daughter's death. The figures on this "good" side appear calmer and look towards the crucified female martyr. She in turn seems to be turned towards them, her body slightly angled in their direction.

The triptych's left and right inner wings show events that followed the female martyr's death on the cross. On the left a fire rages in the palace, represented as a collection of gabled houses around a courtyard with a tower. Goods are being taken to safety across a bridge (p. 297). Opposite, on the right, we see the damage caused by a storm. A huge fish

Lucas Cranach the Elder, **The Penitence of St Jerome**, 1502
Oil on panel (limewood), 55.5 x 41.5 cm / 21⅞ x 16⅜ in. Vienna, Kunsthistorisches Museum, Gemäldegalerie

lying on the shore is being promptly dragged away, three boats have capsized and just one armoured vessel remains unscathed in the harbour.

The fire motif on the left inner wing was subsequently modified when the figure of the donor was over-painted with a representation of St Anthony, although in this case no devils were added at the top (cf. Cat. 10.4, Cat. 12.1, Cat. 22). The tower visible behind the hermit saint exactly follows the outline of the donor's back and head. St Anthony is immersed in studying a book and is surrounded by a number of small demons. On the right inner wing, which in contrast to *St Anthony* takes up the landscape of the central panel, the donor figure has been over-painted with those of a priest and an executioner. Behind them, between two hills, some robbers are attacking a traveller, while a bear trots along the same path in the opposite direction. The over-painting of one of the donors with the popular motif of the *Temptation of St Anthony*, in conjunction with the variety characterising the figures on the central panel, may well have appealed to Italian art-lovers.

Paradise and Hell

From Marcantonio Michiel's note we may conclude that the two wing fragments, *Paradise and Hell* (pp. 312/313, Cat. 16), dating from *c.* 1505–1515, were also housed in Cardinal Grimani's palace in Venice. Michiel mentions two paintings "by the hand of Bosch", which he erroneously describes (perhaps because he gave them only a fleeting glance) as works on canvas: one "a canvas of Hell and a great variety of monsters" and the second "the canvas of dreams". In comparison with Bosch's large triptychs it is hard to recognise "the great variety of monsters" ("*la gran diversità de monstri*") that Michiel saw in the first picture (Cat. 16.3, *Fall of the Damned*); and it is likely that he is referring, rather, to the wealth of different poses assumed by the figures, among whom it is at first difficult to distinguish between damned and devils. Michiel's phrase may also be understood as a formulaic tribute drawn from a still somewhat limited range of categories of praise. In the case of the second picture (Cat. 16.4, *The Damned in Hell*), the damned man in the foreground, his head resting in melancholic fashion on one hand, explains Michiel's interpretation of the motif as the "canvas of dreams"(p. 266). This mounting of *Paradise and Hell* as two separate pictures clearly shows that Bosch's original work, if indeed it ever included a central *Last Judgement* panel or shrine, had long been dismantled into its individual parts. Michiel makes no mention of the two *Paradise* panels, perhaps because he saw nothing spectacular in them.

Pages 271, 272/273
Hermit Saints Triptych (with Sts Jerome, Anthony and Giles), *c.* 1504
Left inner wing: **St Anthony** (see ill. pp. 304/305)

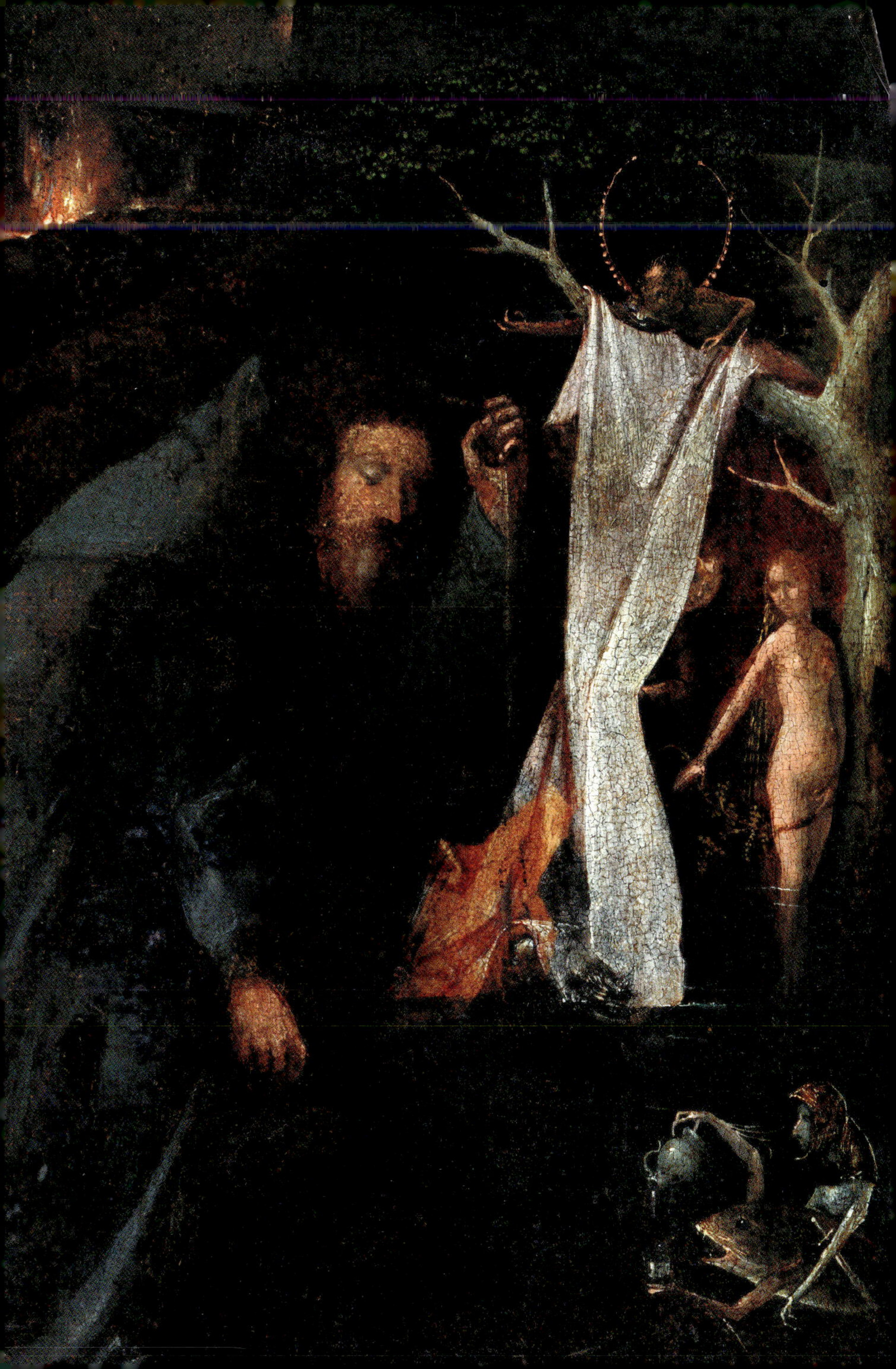

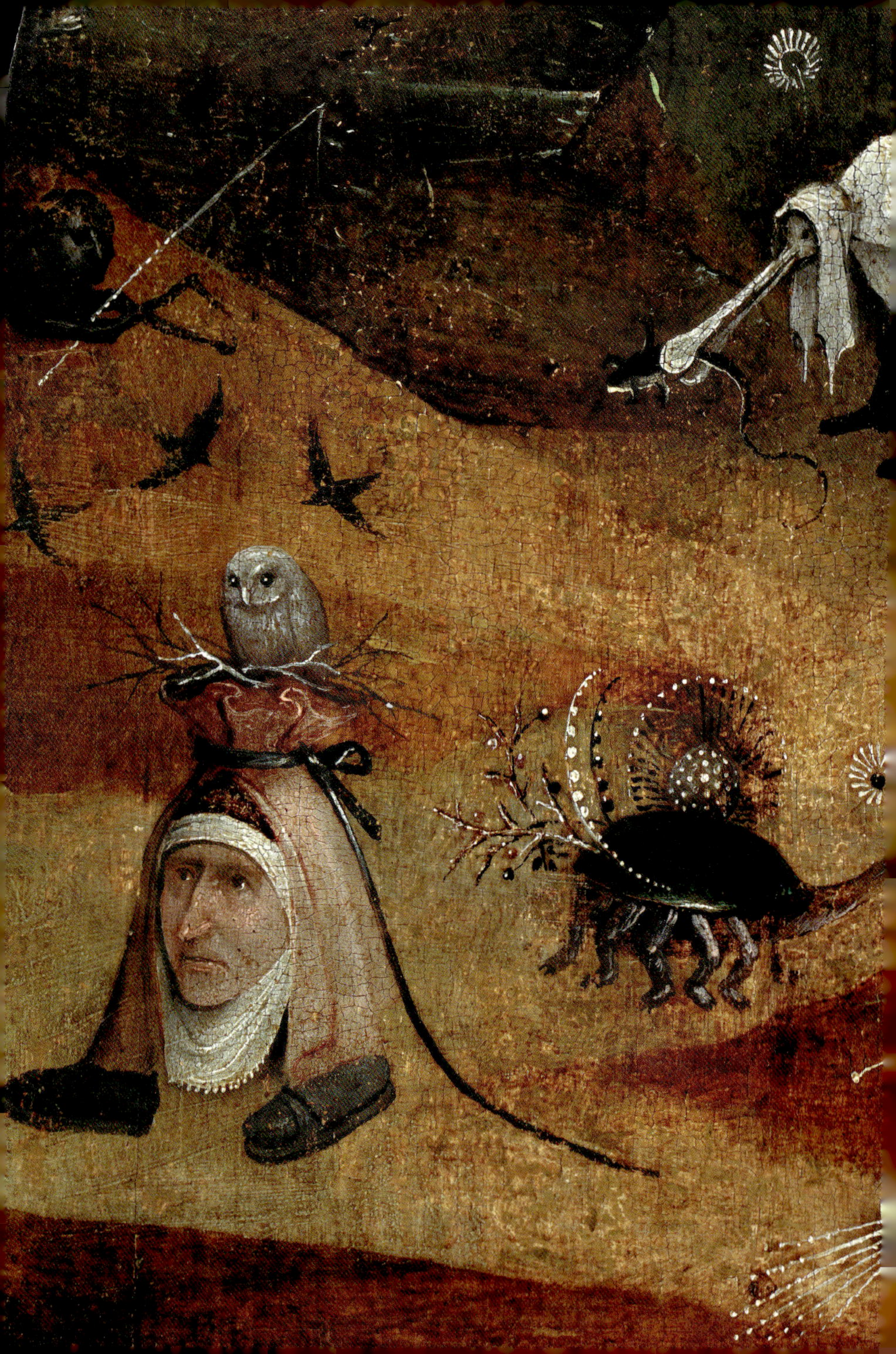

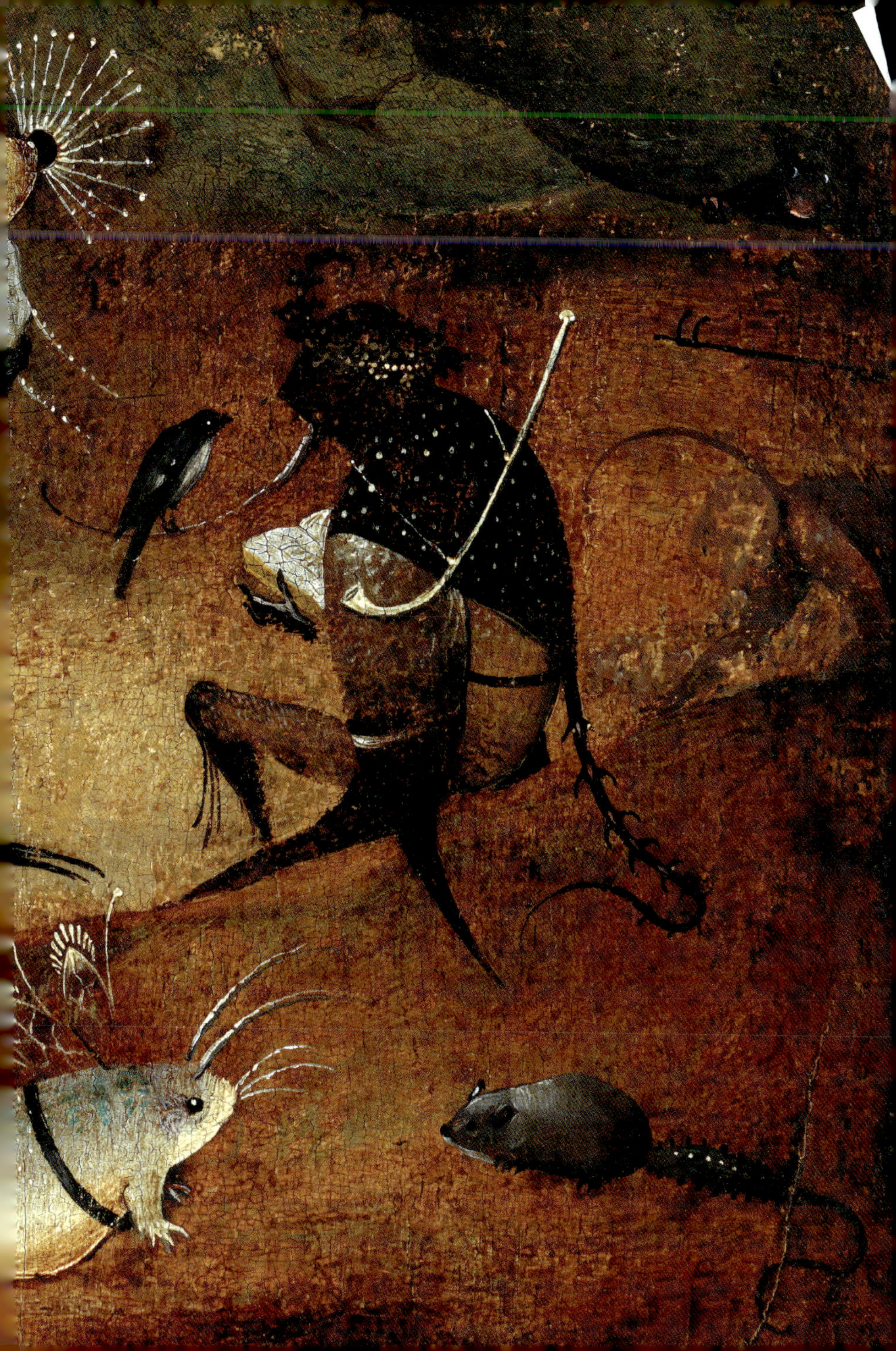

The original function of these four panel paintings is completely unknown. It almost seems as if they were destined for export right from the start, in order to appeal to potential clients on the far side of the Alps (see Aikema 2001). Whatever the case, Bosch has here created impressive effects with minimal means, in particular in the *Fall of the Damned* and *The Damned in Hell.* With the reduction in their pictorial elements and their palette, and with their figures floating, often like cut-outs, in diffuse and boundless spaces that flicker and glisten, these paintings are perhaps even more oppressive and fascinating than the other visions of Hell in Bosch's oeuvre, even though the works concerned are larger (Cat. 11.4, Cat. 13.4/5). Any initial disappointment that we, as modern viewers, may feel at the poor condition in which these panels survive is thus rapidly compensated by a sense of enrichment.

The two left inner panels depict the *Earthly Paradise* followed by the *Heavenly Paradise*. The *Earthly Paradise* shows the first stage in the journey to Heaven undertaken by the souls of the Elect, or more accurately the Redeemed. Angels are reintroducing them to the lost Garden of Eden. The fountain architecture, based on simple geometric forms and bodies, alludes to the style of Antiquity, although the plump masks spouting water from the central column and the naked winged cherubs crouched on the corners are wholly uncharacteristic of Bosch's usual rendering of either paradise fountains or angels. In the outermost left panel, where the souls continue their journey up to Heaven, a surprising pictorial invention awaits: the souls, each accompanied by an angel, ascend towards a celestial sphere conceived as a sort of tunnel, where they disappear into the gleaming light of Heaven. The conception of this divine realm as a dazzling radiance calls to mind the final canto of Dante's *Divine Comedy* (*Paradiso* XXXIII). A heavenly Paradise comparable in motif, if not in expression, can be seen in paintings produced shortly before Bosch's panel by Dirk Bouts (p. 261) and Simon Marmion (p. 238) – even though neither of these artists includes the tunnel reminiscent of descriptions of near-death experiences. Hans Memling's *Last Judgement* (p. 281) also includes the motif of the Fall of the Damned and the symmetrical overall layout of Paradise on the left and Hell on the right. Nowhere has Bosch employed his painting technique with such economy and to such great effect as in the *Fall of the Damned* and *The Damned in Hell.* Over a barely detectable under-drawing he has applied a layer of black paint, into which he has then placed bright reddish, yellowish and greenish accents, executed *alla prima*, that is to say, rapidly painting wet in wet.

It is unsurprising that the works that reached Venice at an early date should testify to a change in Bosch's approach to painting, since the artist was in this way responding to a general trend. From around the turn of the 16th century the upper aristocracy in the Low Countries also increasingly surrounded itself with Humanist scholars and poets, and from 1509 made a point of patronising the visual arts of the Italian Renaissance (Coburg 2010).

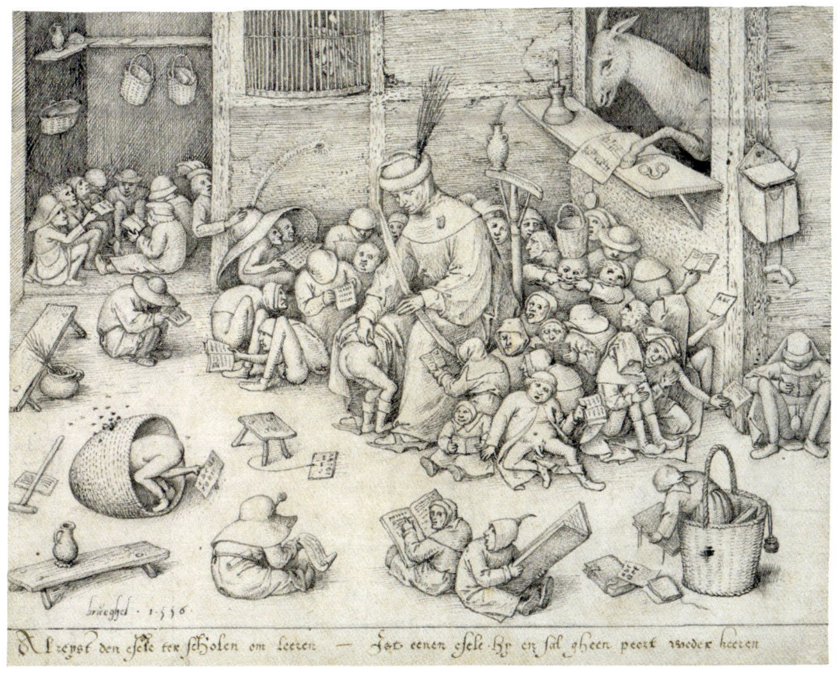

Pieter Bruegel the Elder, **The Ass at School**, 1556
Pen and black ink on paper, 23.2 x 30.7 cm / 9⅛ x 12 in.
Berlin, Staatliche Museen zu Berlin, Kupferstichkabinett, KdZ 11 641

This opening to the Italian Renaissance occurring in genuinely Netherlandish art – a development inherited from the era of the Dukes of Burgundy – first really got underway when Margaret of Austria was appointed regent of the Netherlands on 18 March 1507 by her father, the later Emperor Maximilian I, following the death of her brother Philip the Handsome (d. 25.9.1506). In 1508/09 Jan Gossaert travelled to Rome in the company of Henry III of Nassau-Breda and Philip of Burgundy (1464–1524) – by 1517 the latter's art collection would include Bosch's *Extracting the Stone of Folly* (Cat. 18) – in order to make a number of studies and sketches, some after statues from Antiquity. In 1510 Margaret appointed the Venetian painter, engraver and draughtsman Jacopo de' Barbari (1440/60–1516) as her court painter in Malines. Henry III and Margaret of Austria – successors to the patron to whom Bosch owed his most important commissions, Philip the Handsome – thus now became major patrons of Renaissance art. Even if this did not signify an overnight stylistic revolution within the arts in the Low Countries, it nevertheless marked the start of a long-term change, at least in some areas, that saw local pictorial traditions facing competition from new forms of representation. Bosch evidently reacted to this development with clearer compositional structures, less grotesque depictions of devils and an increase in genre-like elements. The character of many of the works from the last ten years of his career can be summed up in the traditional notion of teaching by example: *exemplum docet.*

The almost square panel of *The Seven Deadly Sins and the Four Last Things* (pp. 308/309, Cat. 15) was produced around 1505–1510. Its original destination and patron are unknown. The Spanish words *tabla* and *mesa,* used by Bosch connoisseur Felipe de Guevara when describing the work in his *Comentarios de la pintura* of *c.* 1560, in conjunction with the layout of the painting, have encouraged commentators to assume that the panel served as a table top. The picture combines a main frontal view with the need for the eye to travel in a circle around the panel and thereby change its viewpoint in order to study the representations of the seven deadly sins. It does not follow from this, however, that the painting was intended to be displayed horizontally, in the manner of a table top.

Deadly Sins and Last Things

The Seven Deadly Sins and the Four Last Things is executed in the same serious stylistic vein as the *Last Judgement* (Cat. 13.3–V), but it is structured in a much clearer fashion. It adopts a traditional circular format, with contents additionally labelled and explained by Latin inscriptions. The primary purpose of these inscriptions was to enable the viewer to identify all seven of the deadly sins, each in turn and then as a whole. This suggests that the panel was employed for the religious instruction of clerics, such as future priests, or of lay congregations, for whom didactic panels employing diagrammatic layouts were used in church. Only a few such panels have come down to us, however, or are known today (Boockmann 1994; Slenczka 1998). The intention was that they be regularly studied and their contents learned by heart. *The Seven Deadly Sins* thus also provided a visual checklist for any viewer examining his or her conscience prior to confession – among them Philip II, who kept the work in his apartments in the monastery palace of San Lorenzo de El Escorial. Written in Latin across the top of the panel, in the manner of an inscription, are two verses from the Old Testament Book of Deuteronomy:"*Gens absque consilio est et sine prudentia/Utinam saperent et intelligerent ac novissima providerent*" ("For they are a nation void of counsel, nor is there any understanding in them. Oh, that they were wise, that they understood this, that they would consider their latter end!" Deut. 32:28–29). These

Detail from: **Hermit Saints Triptych (with Sts Jerome, Anthony and Giles)**, *c.* 1504
Central panel: **St Jerome** (see ill. pp. 304/305)

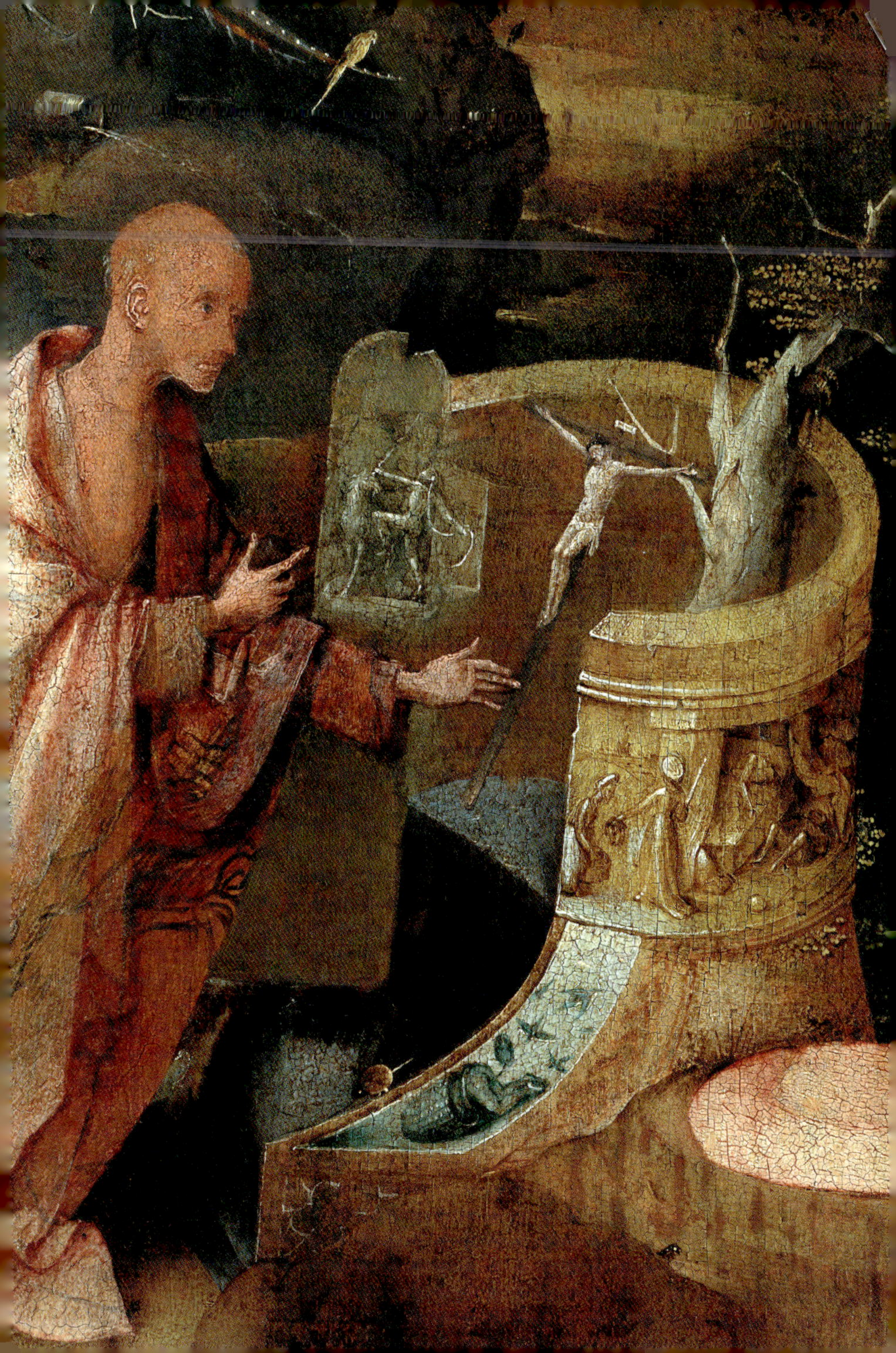

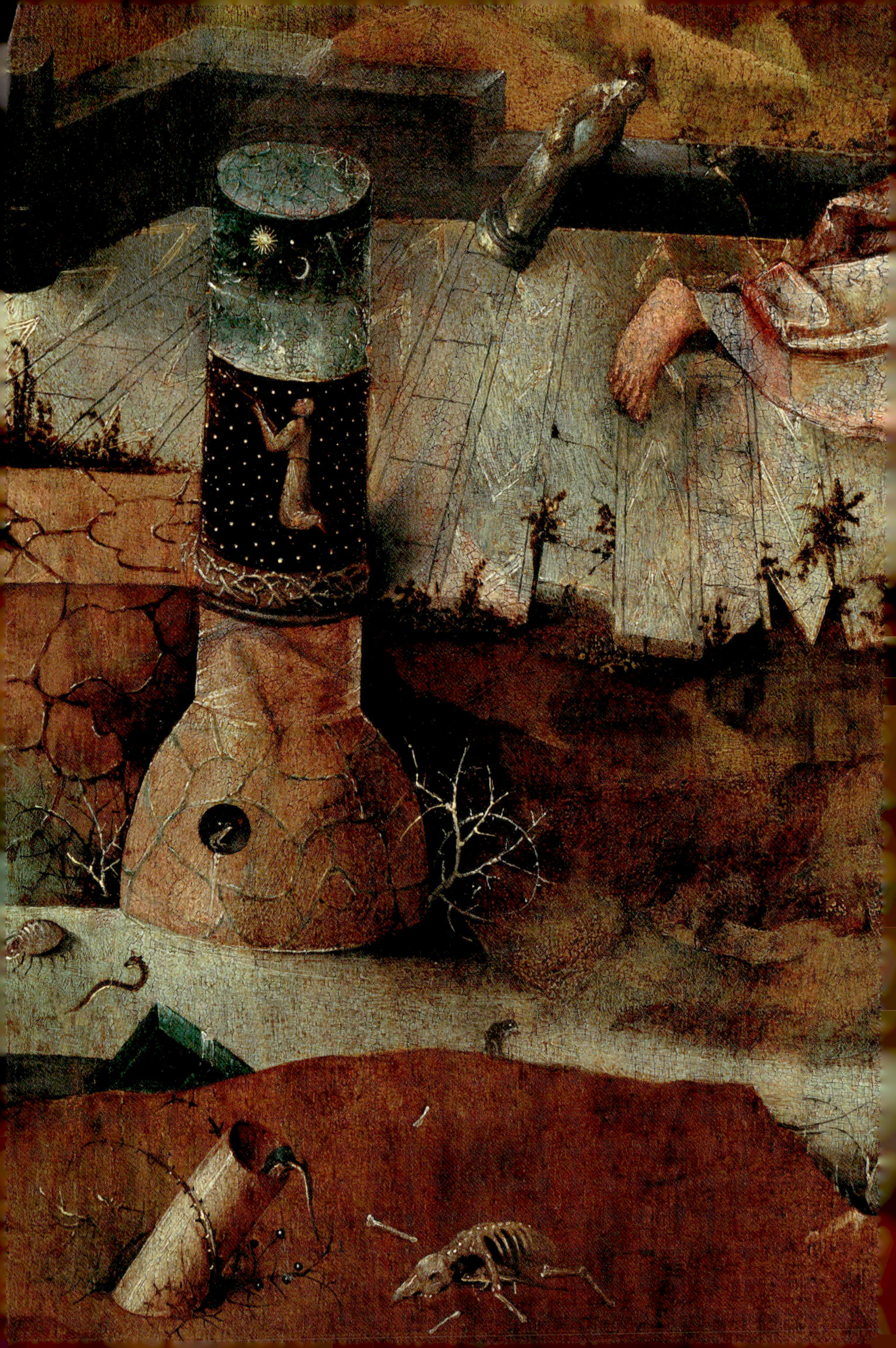

sentences refer to the large tondo underneath, occupying the centre of the panel, which represents the ignorance of the great majority of the faithful. Bosch peoples his exempla of the seven deadly sins with figures representing most levels of society: nobles, lawyers and officials, various members of the middle classes, the common people and peasants. Given the panel's religious function, and in contrast to what we find in *The Haywain* (Cat. 20.3), only the clergy are not directly associated with a sin. Among the representations of the seven deadly sins our eye is drawn first to Wrath (*ira*), which is aligned with the main view: under the influence of drink, two peasants in front of a tavern have got into a fight, perhaps over a woman, and are going at each other with daggers and a stool. This sort of brawl fully matched the contemporary cliché of the oafish and choleric peasant. Reading clockwise, we find that Wrath is followed by Pride (*superbia*), embodied in a middle-class woman adjusting her elaborate head-dress (it is in fact no longer of the latest fashion) in a mirror held up by a devil wearing a lace-trimmed cap. Next, Lust (*luxuria*) presents an lmost classic depiction of a courtly rendezvous in a garden. One couple withdraws into the privacy of a tent while a second is entertained by a jester. Sloth (*accidia*; properly *acedia*) is represented by a middle-class man who has grown sluggish in both body and soul, and who refuses to be roused by the rosary proffered by his devout wife. In Gluttony (*gula*) the male members of a shabby household are eating and drinking in a disgusting manner. The representation of Greed (*avaritia*) shows a judge, seated in the centre holding his staff of office, being bribed by two men while his two companions are otherwise occupied. In Envy (*invidia*) a man with pointed features and an overbite clutches a gnawed bone while looking askance at a proud nobleman with a falcon. Beside him a young couple are forging tender bonds despite the bars between them, the man offering the object of his suit a pink flower.

At the centre of this radial arrangement of the seven deadly sins is the stylised solar Eye of God. Its golden rays issue from Christ, who appears in its pupil as the Man of Sorrows. The words "*Cave, Cave Dominus videt*" ("Beware, beware, the Lord sees!") can be read in the iris: a reference to the omniscience of God. The Man of Sorrows also refers to the Son of God and the Saviour's death on the Cross, and to the possibility of Redemption that this death offers to penitent sinners.

The representation of the Four Last Things begins with Death in the top left corner, portrayed in the *ars moriendi* tradition of the exemplary good end (p. 291, cf. also Cat. 17.5). It continues with the Last Judgement at the upper right, likewise employing a conventional compositional formula. With its Christ enthroned and its celestial royal city, it comes closer to Hans Memling's *Last Judgement* (p. 281) than to Bosch's Vienna triptych

Detail from: **Hermit Saints Triptych (with Sts Jerome, Anthony and Giles)**, *c.* 1504
Central panel: **St Jerome** (see ill. pp. 304/305)

(Cat. 13.4). These two tondi are followed at the bottom of the panel by Hell (left) and Heaven (right), appearing as "simultaneous" stadia, so to speak. A banderole between them carries another verse from the Book of Deuteronomy: –"*Abscondam faciem meam ab eis et considerabo novissima eorum*" ("And he said, 'I will hide my face from them, I will see what their end will be'"; Deut. 32:20). The verse underlines the eschatological orientation of the work and issues a warning to those who have turned away from God: the seeming absence of God is the calm before the storm of judgement. For those who do not seek God, their fate is sealed, while the refusal to recognise God leads to punishment and damnation. The Hell tondo contains further exempla of sin and the specific torments that each sin incurs, here again captioned with Latin inscriptions. Behaviour in the present world is thus linked with its consequences in the beyond. The representation of Heaven as a magnificent city gate is similar to what we find in the work of Memling (p. 281): St Peter admits the Elect under the supervision of the enthroned world judge, while angels play music and female saints and the Elders watch the scene from a sort of tribune.

The background areas of the panel are a dark, disquieting blackish green dotted with small, irregular dabs of paler colour. These, however, do not resolve themselves into the figures of monsters, as seen in the background of the early *Eye of God with Scenes from the Passion* (Cat. 3.2.2), on the exterior surface of the right wing that Bosch contributed to the altarpiece for the Brotherhood of Our Blessed Lady. Here, as there, the black surface represents the chasm of darkness in contrast to the solar eye.

With its evocation of a menacingly watchful God and the infernal punishments awaiting sinners, *The Seven Deadly Sins and the Four Last Things* seems typically "medieval". Bosch's painting is, nevertheless, intellectually more complex than other didactic panels of its day, and also aesthetically more sophisticated. Bosch was abreast of the latest trends in his use of exempla. These, even if tracing their roots back to the preaching techniques employed by Franciscans and Dominicans in the late Middle Ages, marked the beginnings of genre painting in the Early Modern era (Bruyn 1987). In his *Comentarios de la Pintura*, Felipe de Guevara waxed positively lyrical over the realism of Bosch's portrayal of Envy (see entry on Cat. 15). A sensitive artistic handling of the subject was of secondary importance in the case of these exempla, however. What mattered was to frighten and admonish the viewer with a negative image, here seasoned with a liberal dash of satire, as in the images signifying Wrath, Pride and Lust.

A rediscovered triptych

Within the surviving body of Bosch's paintings the triptych is the dominant pictorial format. Of the twenty undisputed autograph works that have come down to us, nine are triptychs and at least four others are fragments of triptychs. In the older German

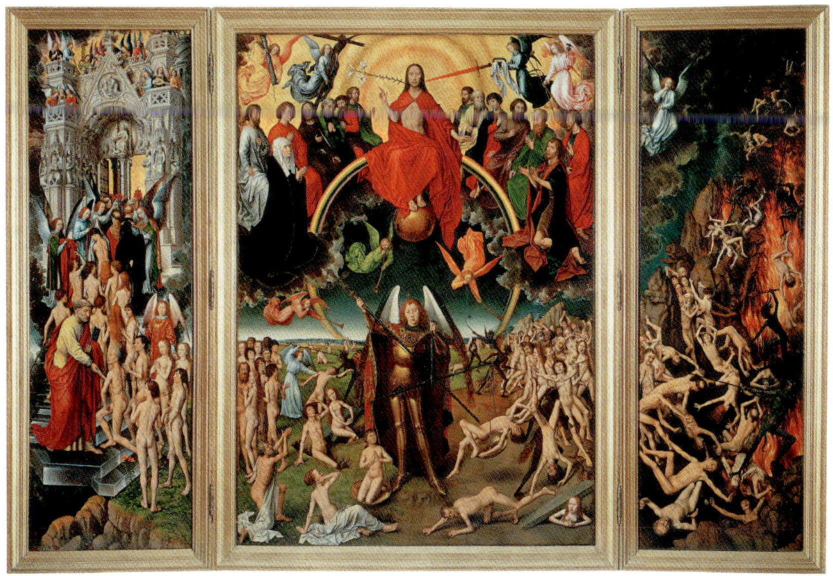

Hans Memling, **Last Judgement**, 1467–1471
Oil on panel, 221 x 161 cm / 87 x 63⅜ in. (central panel), 242 x 90 cm / 92¼ x 35½ in. (each wing)
Gdańsk, Muzeum Narodowe

literature and occasionally even today, triptychs are sometimes described as *Altäre* (altars). This designation, employed in approval of the work in question, is in fact misleading. An altar dedicated to a saint serves as a repository of relics and is the place where Mass is celebrated; from a liturgical standpoint it is therefore more important than its altarpiece, which in most cases may be viewed as an illustrative accessory and ornament. Nor is it true that every triptych is an altarpiece, or that the triptych is a sacred format *per se*. It was this assumption that led Fraenger to misinterpret the *Garden of Earthly Delights* (Cat. 11) as an apotheosis of sensuality. Nor, however, do Bosch's triptychs provide any evidence of a general secularisation of this format, for the themes he treats are always religious. Alongside the *Garden of Earthly Delights* and the *Last Judgement* (Cat. 11 and Cat. 13), Bosch's known innovative triptychs include one that survives only in four shutter fragments (pp. 306/307, Cat. 17), which together allow us confidently to reconstruct the original exterior and interior surfaces of the wings: *The Pedlar* (Cat. 17.1), *The Ship of Fools* (Cat. 17.2), *Allegory of Intemperance* (Cat. 17.3) and *Death and the Miser* (Cat. 17.5). The central panel, which has not survived, probably showed the *Wedding at Cana* (see Cat. 17.4a and Cat. 17.4b). The representation of *The Pedlar* (p. 303, Cat. 17.1) on the exterior shutters suggests a number of parallels with the parable of the Prodigal Son (Luke 15:11–32): both characters fall into bad ways, squander their money in disreputable establishments and end up impoverished and disgraced. Even so, the pedlar is a distinct pictorial type (cf. p. 302). Whereas the Prodigal Son, full of remorse, returns to his real father and is joyfully welcomed back into the family, the pedlar can only hope to be welcomed back by his heavenly father. While Bosch alludes to this possibility in his painting, whether it will actually come to pass is by no means certain. What Bosch shows in concrete terms is the protagonist in the centre of the picture walking along a path: behind him to the left is a brothel in a dilapidated house, in front of him on the right a gate with a cow on the other side. The gate stands for the narrow opening through which one may gain entry to the heavenly Paradise. Here we once again encounter one of the fundamental constants in Bosch's oeuvre: the idea that life is a pilgrimage towards God. The left and right sides of the picture are not only opposite each other. When read from left to right they show a chronological progression from life in this world to death and the hereafter. The profligacy and lust featured on the left were traits especially associated with youth. The older and wiser pedlar, representing the viewer, takes the role of the penitent individual facing the end of his life.

A similar principle underlies the conception of the interior surfaces of the shutters. In the triptych as reconstructed here these two inner wings present extremes of sinful behaviour which stand in rhetorical opposition to the central panel, showing the state of wedlock blessed by God. In *The Ship of Fools* (pp. 289, 306, Cat. 17.2), which originally formed the upper section of the left inner wing, a Franciscan friar and a nun of the Order of the Poor Clares, the latter playing a lute, are seated in the middle of the boat nearest the viewer. The combination is particularly piquant since the tonsured friar, as a priest, is strictly speaking in charge of the nun's spiritual welfare and should be guiding her along the right, that is to say, religious, path. Both appear to be singing, and a loaf of bread hangs down from above, within reach of their mouths. A pewter beaker and a plate of cherries, symbols of carnal lust (Vandenbroeck 1989, p. 162 f.), stand between them on a plank that projects out over the side of the boat like a springboard. A similarly exuberant trio of men, the one furthest to the right holding a spoon-shaped paddle or rudder, are clustered behind this couple, dressed in red and russet in keeping with their heated state. Further left, a man dressed in red and another woman with her head covered are engaged in a light-hearted fight over two jugs, the one held by the woman seemingly empty, the one in the water full. To the right of the main group, perched on a branch that projects from the stern of the boat like a mast or bowsprit, is a personification of Folly, a jester sipping reflectively from a bowl. To his left another man, dressed in red and holding a knife in one hand, is scaling the main mast in order to cut down a trussed and plucked chicken: a symbol of Gluttony. A pennant similar to that of the Ottoman Empire, with a yellow crescent on a red background, flutters above the chicken and below the top of the mast, which ends in the leafy crown of a tree or a maypole, with an owl peering out of its depths. Two naked men swim in the dark water in front of the boat, one trying to climb on board, the other holding his full bowl above the water line. Further objects complementing the figural composition are a barrel in the boat, a fish dangling from the right branch and a jug hanging upside down at the end of a long branch rising diagonally upwards on the left: a symbol of Lust. Gluttony, Lust, Folly and sheer obliviousness to the world are evidently the vices illustrated here.

The lower section of the left inner wing, with its *Allegory of Intemperance* (Cat. 17.3), contains two further scenes. In the upper left corner the representation of Gluttony and Folly continues with the four almost naked figures in the water, clinging with obvious intent to a barrel that is evidently very full. Sitting astride the floating barrel is a stout buisine player, carrying over his right shoulder a maypole with a ball hanging from it, and wearing on his head a hood and an inverted funnel. He represents Prodigality. Nearer the foreground another figure swims about aimlessly; in place of a hat he wears a poultry pie served on a plate or circular tray and with the head of a small spoonbill sticking out of it. The foreground scene at the bottom of the panel treats the theme of Lust in a manner similar to that of the exemplum in *The Seven Deadly Sins and the Four Last Things* (Cat. 15). On the bank near the water a man and woman, whose style of dress suggests that they belong to the middle classes, have withdrawn into a furnished, pale red tent for a tête-à-tête. On the ground in front of the tent entrance are wooden clogs, a hat in the Burgundian style on top of a belt, and a section of trumpet. Further items of clothing, probably belonging to the swimmers, are draped over the withered half of an otherwise leafy tree and scattered on the ground nearby. Here, too, a jug is hooked upside down over a branch. The association of drinking, eating, music-making and lust is one we have already encountered in the *Garden of Earthly Delights* (Cat. 11). Here, as there, flourishing nature becomes a symbol of the uncurbed human instincts that seek only sensual pleasure.

The unbridled indulgence of the senses invoked on the left inner wing finds its pendant in *Death and the Miser* on the right (pp. 290, 307, Cat. 17.5). The New Testament parable of the Rich Man and Lazarus the beggar (Luke 16:19–31) offers only an indirect biblical source for Bosch's painting, whose iconography is more closely related to late Medieval prints of the *ars moriendi*, the art of dying (p. 291). Such works advised those who wished to get to Heaven of the right way to prepare for death (cf. Death in *The Seven Deadly Sins and the Four Last Things* Cat. 15). Bosch shows an old miser, in his bedchamber and on the point of death, being exposed to temptation one decisive last time by a monster devil who offers him a bag of money. The drama of the scene is heightened by the arrival of Death, who is already standing in the open doorway. An angel kneels beseechingly behind the dying man and directs him towards his only Salvation: a crucifix that stands in front of a window, through which light is streaming. The miser is shown a second time, in the foreground of a parallel scene, leaning on his stick and holding his rosary, but at the same time filling a money bag being held open by a devil crouching inside a chest. As a contrast to this, Bosch includes, in the lower right corner, a group of weapons and pieces of armour arranged like a still life. These are the symbols of the Christian soldier, the means with which the faithful can arm themselves against Evil. The conflict of Good and Evil, eternal life and eternal damnation, are clearly represented in the picture, both sides present in equal measure.

The triptych's central panel, showing *The Wedding at Cana* (Cat. 17.4), has only come down to us in the form of several copies. The copy now thought to be the most faithful to the original is the pen drawing in the Louvre (p. 287, Cat. 17.4a). The best painting is thought to be that now in Rotterdam (pp. 306/307, Cat. 17.4b), although it is incomplete at the top, unlike another version, now in the Huis Bergh (p. 286). The episode in which Jesus turned water into wine during a wedding feast at Cana in Galilee is told in John 2:1–11. Jesus, his mother and the disciples were invited to a wedding. When the wine ran out Mary spoke to Jesus, who instructed the servants to fill six jars with water. The water in the jars then turned into the best wine. The bride, dressed in white, correspondingly appears in a central position between John and Mary. The guests are seated around the L-shaped table, with Christ on the right making the sign of blessing. The banqueting hall is filled with numerous subsidiary scenes, most of which are hard to interpret, as in the case of the short figure with the goblet before the table. Beyond the figure of the bride we see into a vaulted chamber with a baldachin at its far end, beneath which stands a magnificent dresser (in Dutch, *tritsoor*). Its shelves are lined with expensive metal containers, perhaps used to serve the best wine. A strangely comical scene is being acted out on top of the capitals of the pillars: a young Cupid with a pot over his head, indicating his blindness, is attempting to loose one of his darts at a similarly small and naked figure who takes refuge in a hole. One of several unusual things about this scene is the fact that, up until around 1500, Cupid was traditionally shown in long robes and in most cases as a young man. It was not until shortly after 1500 that Lucas Cranach, for example, started to paint him in the shape of a putto. Bosch has here pictured a naked boy, but without basing him on the putti of the Renaissance (cf. the angel in Hans Memling, p. 281). The two musicians playing on a balcony on the left are another symbol of secular pleasure.

The assumption that *The Wedding at Cana* originally stood at the centre of a triptych with *The Ship of Fools, Allegory of Intemperance* and *Death and the Miser* as its wings is sup-

Hermit Saints Triptych (with Sts Jerome, Anthony and Giles), *c.* 1504
Central panel: **St Jerome** (see ill. pp. 304/305)

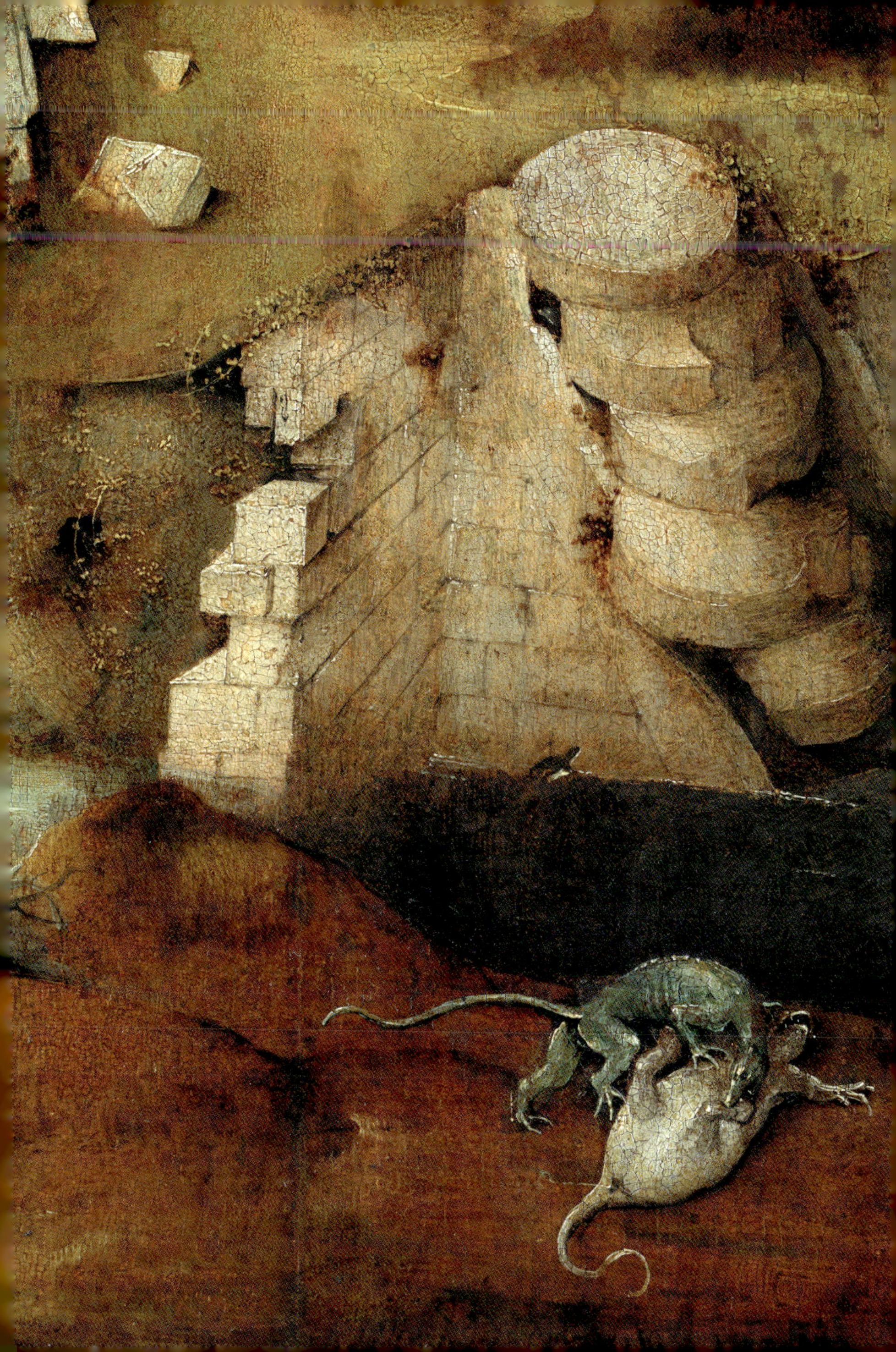

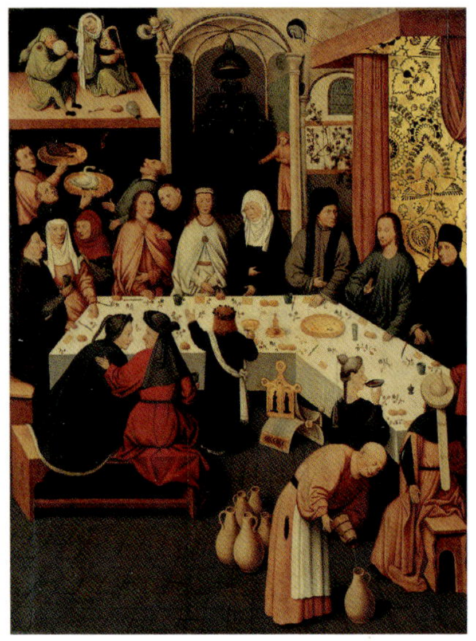

ported by the matching dimensions of the panels, their play on contrasts – a typical structural device employed in sermons on the Wedding at Cana – and their compositional links (see entry on Cat. 17). These include recurring pictorial motifs such as the draperies falling in folds in the foreground of all three interior panels, the laid tables in the centre and on the left (which, in addition, together form a symmetrical U-shape), and the canopy over Christ and the miser. The explanation for these apparent coincidences lies in the fact that, as we have seen in the case of the *Garden of Earthly Delights*, the subsidiary motifs are derived from the main scene in an almost parodic process. Hence the wings, which represent allegories of the deadly sins in a low-brow style, make reference – in their function as secondary or peripheral components of the overall work – to the central panel as the main picture, whose own biblical theme is treated in an appropriately high-brow style. The extremes found on the triptych's interior surfaces also appear in *The Pedlar* on the exterior shutters (p. 303). As noted above, the left exterior shutter shows the life of excess, and above all lechery, associated with youth, while the right shutter represents old age and the question of what our status will be in the hereafter. The pedlar is "on the outside" in the truest sense: he is outside the Christian fellowship of the central panel and not yet close to Salvation, or at least not as close as are the guests at the Wedding at Cana. He is, nevertheless, a repentant sinner.

This leads us to the matter of Bosch's patron, whose name is unknown, and the possible function of this triptych. The donor appears in the under-drawing of the central panel (p. 287, Cat 17.4a), where his style of dress shows him to be a canon (a member of the secular clergy). As the setting for the miracle in which Jesus turned water into wine, a transformation interpreted as a symbol of the Eucharist, the Wedding at Cana was popularly invoked as proof that marriage was indeed a holy state and a sacrament. Marriage was also

Anonymous artist after Hieronymus Bosch (?), **The Wedding at Cana**, *c.* 1515–1540
Central panel of "The Cana Triptych". Oil on panel, 93.5 x 72 cm / 36¾ x 28⅜ in.
's-Heerenberg, Foundation Huis Bergh, Collection Dr J. H. van Heek

presented in sermons, for example, as having a moral utility. If the donor of the triptych chose its theme in his own interests, as one that would intercede with Heaven on his behalf and ensure his Salvation, and if his choice thereby fell specifically on a theme relating to wedlock, we might well speculate that the canon, whether or not a priest himself, was also a married man who, as a penitent sinner (like the pedlar), sought to justify this status or underline its sanctity. It is true that representations of the Wedding at Cana may also be found in monastery refectories. In works intended for such a destination, however, the thematic emphasis would have to fall either upon the communal repast or upon the mystic marriage between God and the soul, for example by showing the Virgin and Christ seated side by side or by giving more prominence to the disciples.

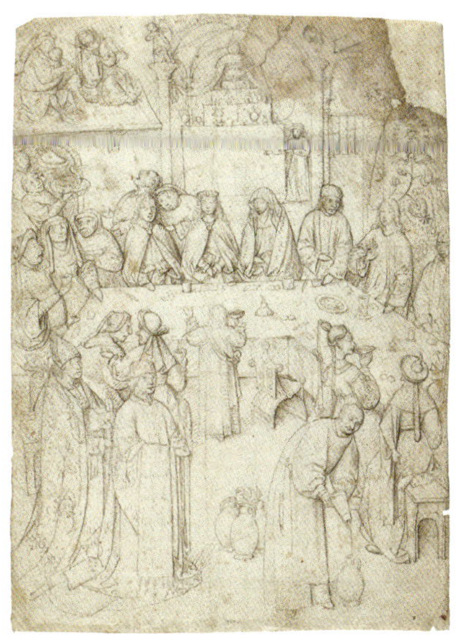

Bosch has repeatedly been described as a preacher of morality and a pessimist. The function of Bosch's pictures did not escape even his very early interpreters: Guevara, for example, described a number of Bosch's paintings as *moralidades*. Within Bosch's pronounced moralism two strands converge: contemporary religious concepts of the hereafter, and the desire to live a good life while still on Earth. But his moralism neither points a finger nor is it purely subjective. Its concrete form of expression can only properly be understood with reference to Bosch's specific patrons and his membership of the 's-Hertogenbosch Brotherhood of Our Blessed Lady as an institution of the bourgeois elite (and of the aristocracy). The values and standards espoused by the brotherhood were those characteristic of bourgeois morality (Vandenbroeck 1987a). The elite middle classes were particularly anxious to distinguish themselves by their morals, and to this end they modelled their behaviour in many respects upon that seen to prevail at aristocratic courts. While shared moral values provide a group or a class with ideological reassurance and encourage

Anonymous artist after Hieronymus Bosch (?), **The Wedding at Cana**, *c.* 1505–1515
Central panel of "The Cana Triptych", copy
Pen drawing on paper, 28.1 x 20.8 cm / 11 x 8¼ in. Paris, Louvre, Rothschild Collection

a sense of community, they also entail the exclusion of other social classes and groups, in so far as they stigmatise and denigrate certain forms of behaviour (Vandenbroeck 1987a, pp. 247–280).

Moral teachings undoubtedly also served as maxims intended to make life in this world easier, if not exactly pleasant. Appropriate and useful rules of conduct would enable the individual to lead an ethical, honourable life that was pleasing to God. The importance of moderation and of finding the right middle ground between discipline and pleasure is also documented by the rules governing the ceremonial communal meal taken by the Brotherhood of Our Blessed Lady (see p. 63), which sworn members were required to host at regular intervals. On Sunday 10 March 1510 it was Bosch's third turn to entertain the Brotherhood and he again invited its members to his own home. It was recorded "that the sworn brothers went two by two, pair by pair from the church to the house of brother Hieronymus van Aken, painter" ("*dat die gezworen bruderen twee ende twee, paer ende paer gegaen zyn vuyt der kercke inden huise ons medebruders Jheronimi van Aken scilder*"; van Dijck 2001a, p. 182). The gathering was occasioned by the death of fellow sworn member Jan Back. Although the banquet consisted of several courses, and the list of dishes included a dozen different kinds of fish, as well as nuts and fruit, the fact that no meat was served is again a sign of religiously motivated moderation during Lent (Unverfehrt 2003, pp. 62–63; source edited in van Dijck 1973, p. 451).

Extracting the Stone of Folly

Within Bosch's surviving oeuvre there is just one painting with a secular theme and function. It is also, and perhaps for this very reason, the smallest. *Extracting the Stone of Folly* (p. 315, Cat. 18) can be dated only very approximately to the years around 1505–1515. Series of illustrations treating secular themes – establishing, for example, a link between foolishness and love – had appeared in the form of prints in the 15th century. Only in the 16th century, however, was this thematic complex seen to be worthy of a panel painting (p. 314; cf. also Cat. 28). It is possible that Philip of Burgundy was the first owner or purchaser of this particular work (it seems unlikely that such a small picture would have been a commissioned piece). In 1517 the original, or a copy of it, is documented as hanging in the dining hall of his palace in Wijk bij Duurstede, southeast of Utrecht. Philip of Burgundy, an illegitimate son of Duke Philip III, known as Philip the Good (1396–1467), enjoyed close links with the Habsburg court in the Netherlands (Cools 2000, Sterk 1980). In 1497 he was appointed chamberlain to Philip the Handsome, who in 1498 made him an admiral. In

Detail from: **The Wedding at Cana with Exempla ("The Cana Triptych")**, *c.* 1500–1510
Left inner wing, above: **The Ship of Fools** (see ill. pp. 306/307)

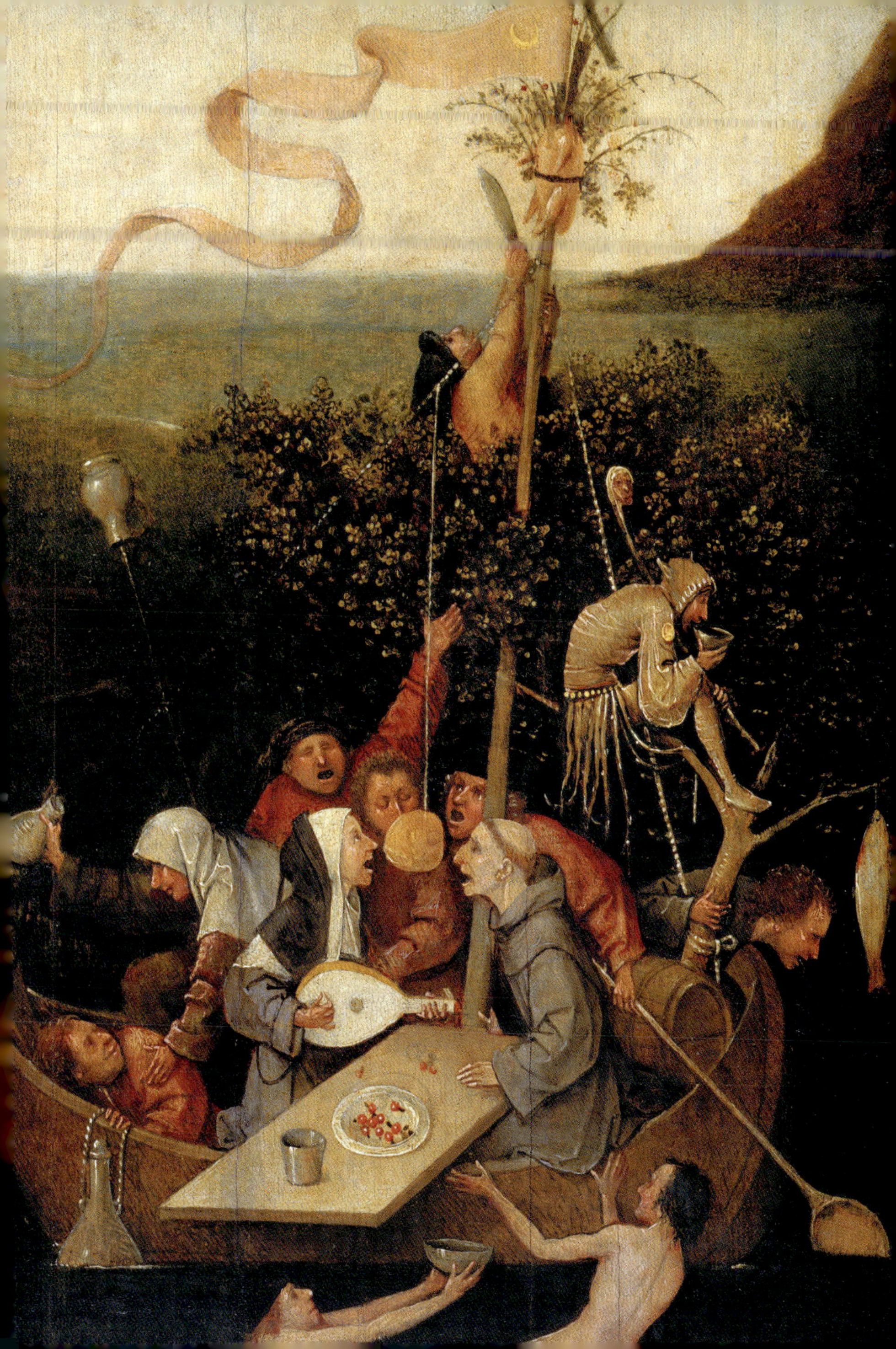

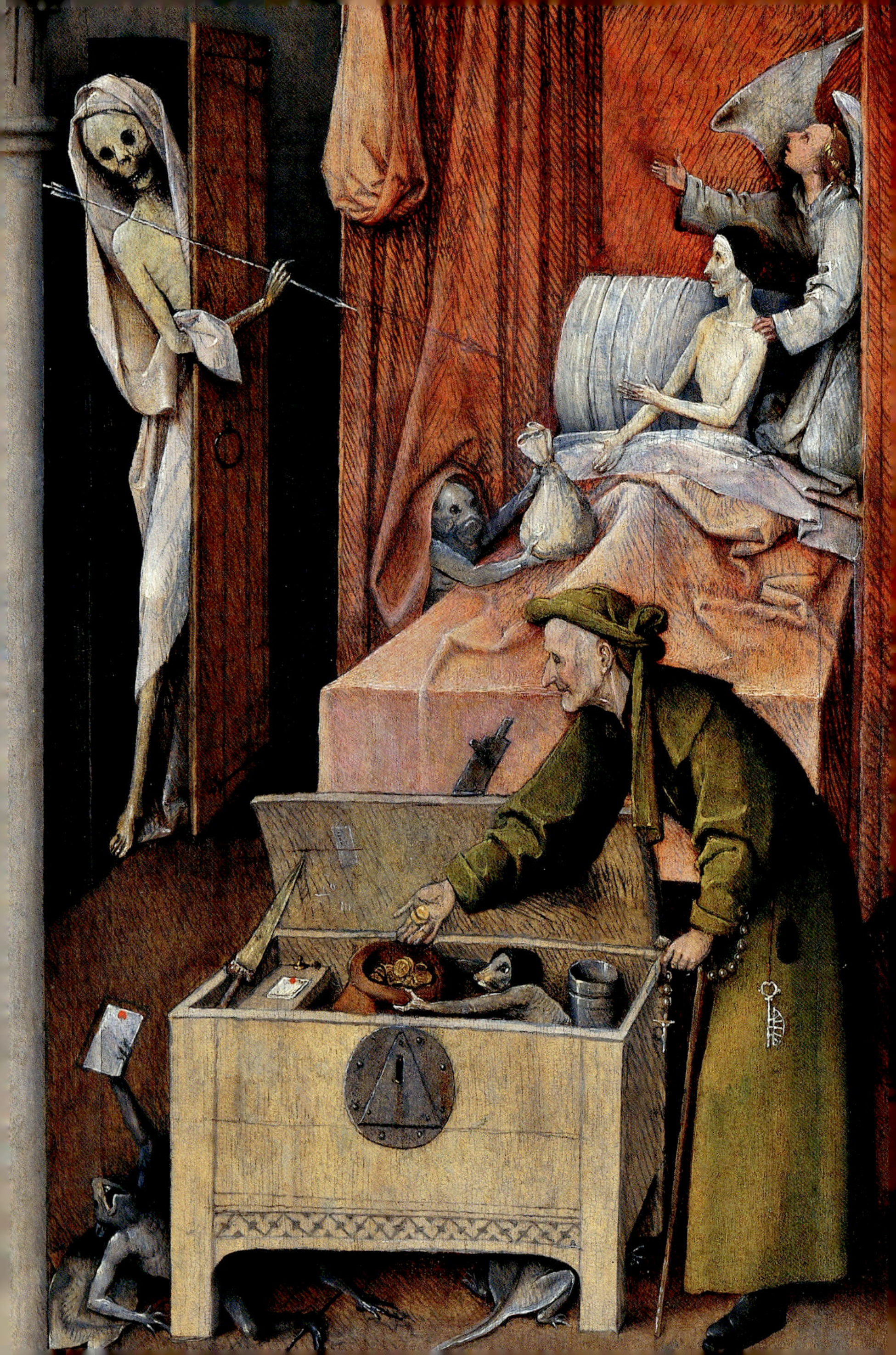

1501 he became a member of the Order of the Golden Fleece, and between 1504 and 1511 he took an active military part in the wars with the Duchy of Guelders. In 1508, as we have already seen, he visited Italy with Henry III of Nassau-Breda. Through the latter's good offices he was installed as Bishop of Utrecht in 1517. Philip of Burgundy is thought to have been a weak bishop and a weak politician. But, as patron of the arts and *bon viveur*, he was a typical Renaissance prince.

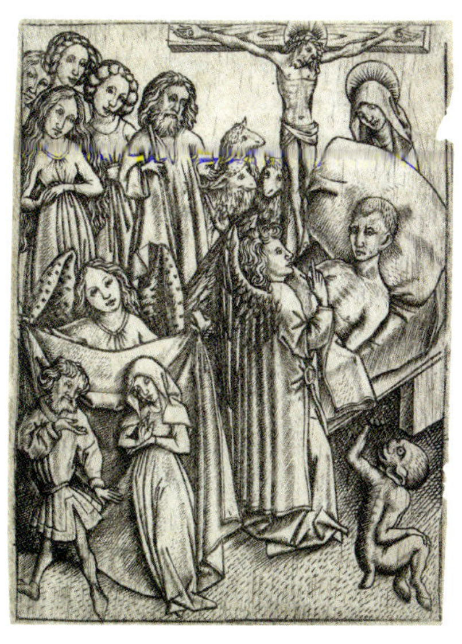

Both in its subject matter and in its function of delivering a lesson in an entertaining manner, *Extracting the Stone of Folly* resembles the simple, popular farces performed in the Low Countries from the 14th to the 17th centuries. This comic genre of theatre (in Dutch, *Klucht*) often centred upon the theme of the deceived husband and his cunning wife, in which the gender roles were communicated in humorous incidental ways. Bosch's portrait-format painting, whose iconography is studied in detail in Koldeweij 1991, shows a circular scene with four figures in a landscape, set against a dark background carrying an inscription in ornamental gold lettering. The protagonist is the man seated on a sturdy chair to the left of centre, into whose mouth Bosch has mockingly placed the rhyming couplet:"*meester snijt die keye ras /Myne name Is lubbert das*" ("Master, cut the stone out / My name is Lubbert Das"). The top line plainly commands the "master" to remove the stone and thus describes the main event in the picture: the man is undergoing an operation on his head to remove his folly. The line along the bottom of the panel reveals the protagonist's character since it contains a verbal pun: in addition to the obvious alternative translation,"My name is Lubbertus", it can also be read as:"My name is castrated fellow". When run together, Lubbert Das sounds like "Lubbertus", the Latinised name of a popular figure of satire in the 16th century. Both

Master ES, **Consolation through turning away from earthly things**, *c.* 1450–1460
From the series: *Ars moriendi*, Copper engraving, 8.9 x 6.7 cm / 3½ x 2⅝ in.
Oxford, Ashmolean Museum, Department of Prints and Drawings

Page 290
The Wedding at Cana with Exempla ("The Cana Triptych"), *c.* 1500–1510
Right inner wing: **Death and the Miser** (see ill. pp. 306/307)

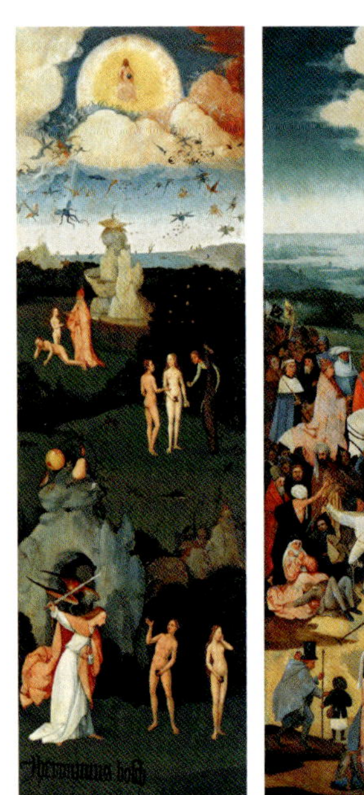
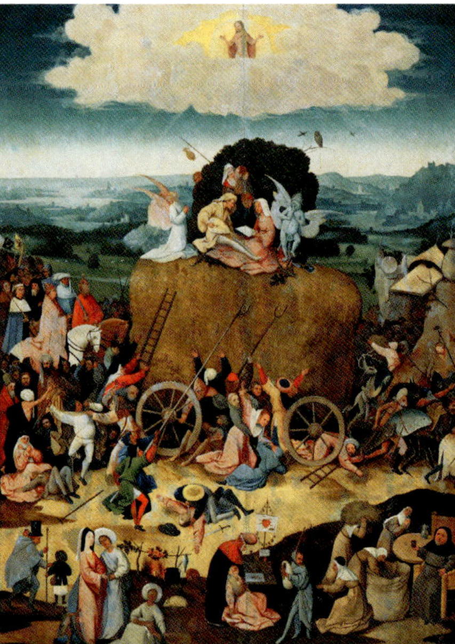
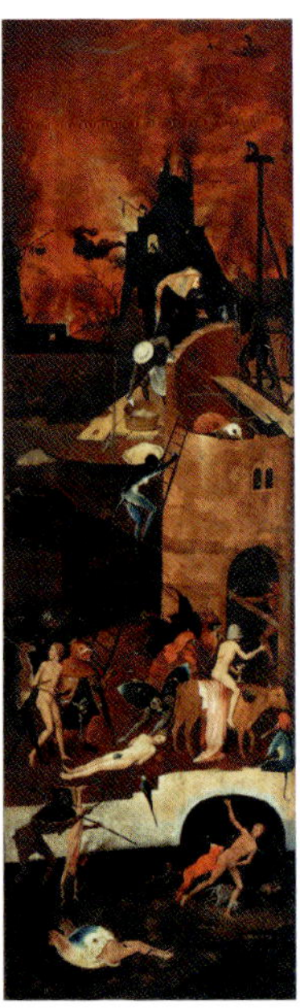

Anonymous artist after Hieronymus Bosch, **The Haywain**, copy, *c.* 1550
Oil on panel (oak), 140 x 100 cm / 55⅛ x 39⅜ in. (central panel), 140 x 50 cm / 55⅛ x 19⅝ in. (each wing)
Madrid, Monasterio de San Lorenzo de El Escorial (For the original by Bosch, see ill. pp. 320/321)

Generally speaking, all of these works are less complex and clearer in their composition than the *Garden of Earthly Delights* (Cat. 11) and the *Last Judgement* (Cat. 13).

What is interesting about the present, fragmentary work is that the grisaille technique employed for the exterior shutters has also been used for the interior panels. There were essentially two reasons why this technique was employed in painting, one religious and the other artistic. The latter was rooted in the rivalry between painting and sculpture: with its imitation of stone, grisaille painting represented an attempt to surpass even sculpture by illusionistic means. From a religious point of view, grisaille signified a renunciation of the splendour, immediacy and illusionism of colour. This is in line with the words of St Augustine:"And, indeed, the knowledge of created things contemplated by themselves is, so to speak, more colourless than when they are seen in the wisdom of God, as in the art by which they were made." (Augustine, *City of God*, Book XI, Ch. 7). The absence of colour may therefore be understood as a lack of intensity and completeness. The presence of God or a saint was made manifest in polychrome representation, and hence the interior of an altarpiece, its feast-day side, was usually executed in colour, in contrast to the exterior, everyday side, which was frequently painted in grisaille. At the same time, however, a monochrome palette can also express ascetic poverty, humility, seriousness and grief – an interpretation that seems appropriate in the present case.

All the world follows the haywain

The Haywain triptych (pp. 320/321, Cat. 20), produced around 1510–1515, was originally a highly colourful work, as we can deduce from a copy (p. 294). As if it were a résumé of Bosch's oeuvre to date, it unites the clarity and simplicity of the artist's early panels of saints and Passion scenes with the multi-figural density and complexity of the primarily eschatological triptychs of his middle phase and the genre-like allegories of his late paintings. The exterior shutters (p. 319, Cat. 20.1) present a variation on the pictorial motif of *The Pedlar* (cf. p. 303, Cat. 17.1). Here, too, the itinerant hawker is an ambivalent symbol of life as a pilgrimage towards God. Stooped under the burden of life, poor and emaciated, the pedlar turns his head to contemplate the scenes taking place around him and thereby also draws the viewer's attention to them. Beside the narrow trail along which he makes his way a russet dog with a spiked collar (cf. Cat. 5, Cat. 17.1) closes in from behind. The dog is an incarnation of the Devil, as comparisons with literary and pictorial sources have demonstrated (de Bruyn 2001a, pp. 258–268). In the lower left corner two hooded crows are perched on the skeletal remains of a dead horse: like the gallows standing on the hill in the background, they allude to the danger of meeting a bad end though sin. Behind the pedlar, further back along his route, as if this were an event from his own past, we see three robbers fleecing a traveller. This reference to the loss of material possessions not only evokes a very real threat facing travellers in Bosch's day. It can also be understood, in the figurative sense, as an admonition that those who pass through life without paying due attention must reckon with such a loss. Opposite, on the right, we come upon a further exemplum: peasants or shepherds, oblivious to the world around them, neglecting their flocks as they dance and make music, unaware of the sinfulness of their actions. The pedlar is, however, offered an alternative path that, if followed, will lead him away from vice. Amid all the bleakness, a narrow bridge at his feet, although no more than a wobbly plank with a makeshift handrail resting in the fork of an upright prop, offers him safe passage over a dark stream. This is, indeed, nothing less than a symbol of the path to Salvation and everlasting life. It combines the notion of the bridge to the hereafter (Dinzelbacher 1973; cf. Cat. 10.3, Cat. 11.4, Cat. 13.3, Cat. 20.4) with the image of the narrow gate (cf. Cat. 17.1; Matt. 7:13–14:"Enter by the narrow gate; for wide is the gate and broad is the way that leads to destruction, and there are many who go in by it. Because narrow is the gate and difficult is the way which leads to life, and there are few who find it.").

The interior of the *Haywain* triptych embeds the symbolism of hay within an allegory flanked on the left by major events from the story of Creation and on the right by a representation of Hell. The interior view as a whole thus unfolds in a chronological sequence from left to right. The left inner panel shows, at its top, the enthroned figure of God the Father, who is thus situated above and at the beginning of everything. Positioned directly behind is a depiction of the Fall of the Rebel Angels, which was often equated with the divine act of separating light from darkness. In a background scene, played out in front of a rock-like paradise fountain, we see the creation of Eve from Adam's rib, which is followed, at the centre right, by the Fall and finally, in the foreground, by the Expulsion of Adam and Eve from the Garden of Eden by the Archangel Michael. The birth of Evil and the uprooting of humanity having thus been introduced and explained, the haywain in the central panel takes up the established left-to-right momentum, continuing it in a linear fashion running parallel to the picture plane. The haywain motif which Bosch here unfolds in such an inventive and detailed manner goes back, as Sigüenza immediately recognised, to the Old Testament, and specifically to Isaiah 40:6–8:"The voice said, 'Cry out!' And he said, 'What shall I cry?' 'All flesh is grass, and all its loveliness is like the flower of the field. The grass withers, the flower fades, because the breath of the Lord blows upon it; surely the people are grass. The grass withers, the flower fades, but the word of our God stands forever.'" It also refers to Psalm 103:15–19:"As for man, his days are like grass; as a flower of the field, so he flourishes. For the wind passes over it, and it is gone, and its place remembers it no more. But the mercy of the Lord is from everlasting to everlasting on those who fear Him, and His righteousness to children's children, to such as keep His covenant, and to those who remember His commandments to do them. The Lord has established His throne in heaven, and His kingdom rules over all." In practice, the passage from the Bible was interpreted and reformulated in the vernacular literature in numerous ways, and occasionally condensed as a figure of speech into the exclamation "*tis al Hoy*" –"'tis all hay!". The hay motif, with its connotations of flesh, transience and vanity, was so widespread in the late Middle Ages that it may be considered a definitive literary topos. As far as we know, however, Bosch was the first to translate this topos into an image.

In the central panel the heaped up hay becomes a screen upon which humanity projects its wishes, weaknesses and desires. The many figures and scenes within this central panel correspondingly illustrate behaviours related to temptation, blindness, greed, deception and transience (de Bruyn 2001a). With its yellow colour resembling gold, the haywain, or rather the hay that it contains and transports, is perceived by people of all

Detail from: **Triptych of the Crucified Female Martyr (Sint-Ontcommer)**, *c.* 1505–1515
Left inner wing (see ill. pp. 310/311)

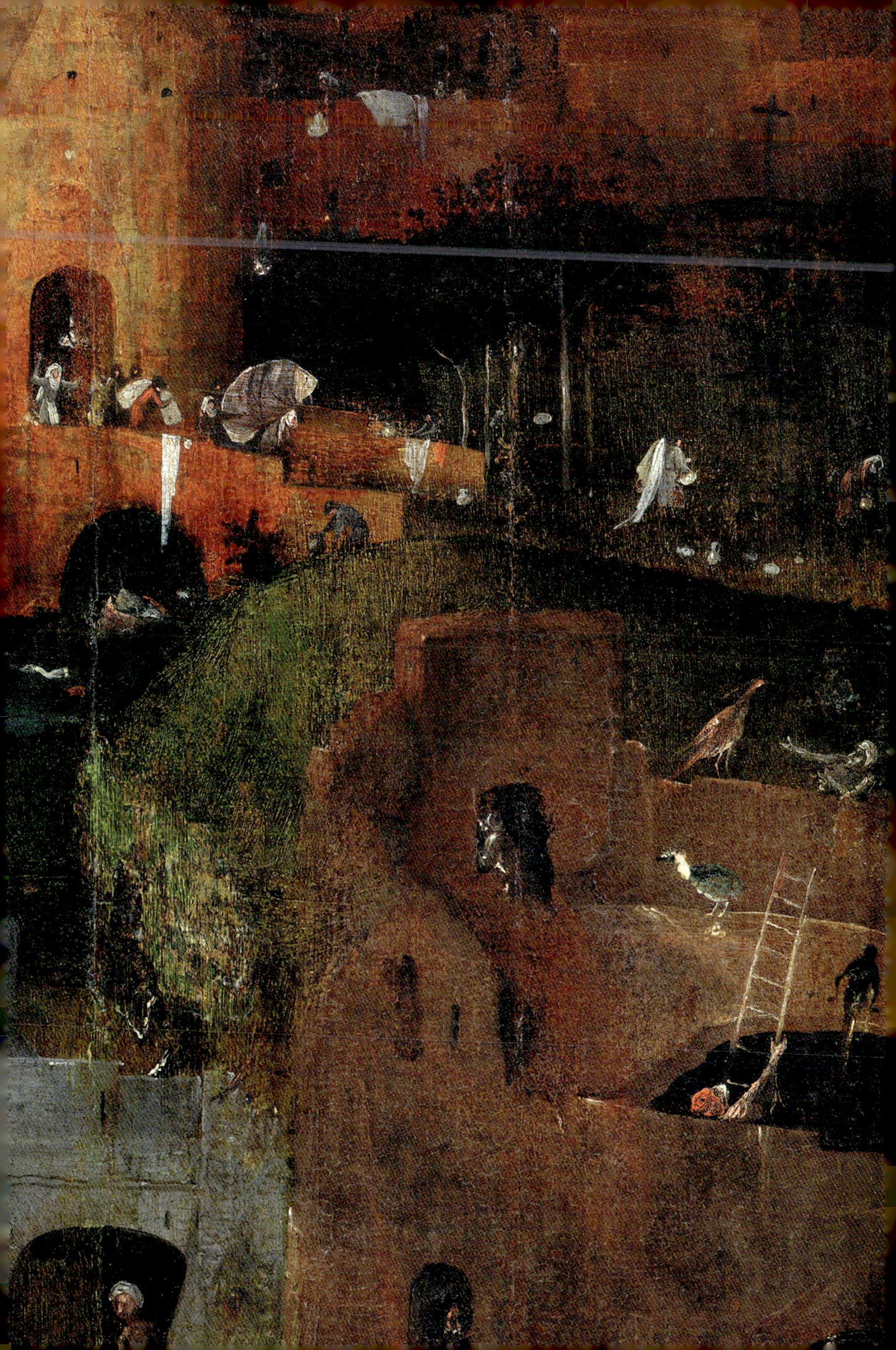

classes as having an enduring and absolute value. Through the sheer volume of hay, however, Bosch makes its worthlessness all the more apparent.

Representatives of very different strata of society are caught up in the "Adoration of the Hay" in Bosch's painting. At the very pinnacle are the emperor and the pope, who appear on horseback directly behind the haywain, accompanied by a king and a prince. Although the remaining social hierarchy is not illustrated in strictly descending order in the procession behind them, the picture nevertheless contains clearly recognisable members of other classes, such as the men and women in religious garb in the lower right corner. These are evidently Franciscans – an Order supposedly pledged to a vow of poverty. While their confessor relaxes in a chair, some of the nuns are busy gathering up hay while another flirts with a bagpiper. Members of the clergy and devout individuals are not, however, portrayed by Bosch solely in a critical manner: among the central group at the foot of the haywain, for example, a monk behaves in exemplary fashion in so far as he is attempting to break up a fight, while in the foreground just below him an isolated pilgrim apparently being attacked by another person manages to remain impassive. Typical secular figures, impossible to assign to a specific profession or social group, alternate with individuals in oriental dress – Christians are obviously not the only ones struck by blindness. The man in the beaver hat in the lower left corner is quite literally blind: he is being guided by a boy with the help of his staff. To the right some "gypsies" are trying to sell a (stolen) baby to an apparently childless middle-class woman. Trading in children was one of the slanderous rumours surrounding the Roma, who were at that time still only recent immigrants. Between this scene and the monk-and-nuns group, a quack doctor has set up his booth: already he is relieving a patient of her money rather than her toothache.

The young people at the far left of the composition, and especially those seen on top of the haystack (pp. 322/323), reveal themselves to be utterly oblivious to the world. Of the latter group, one couple are making the most of the visual protection afforded by a bush to surrender to their sensual desires, accompanied by secular music from the figures seated on the hay. They embody the flowers of the field in the quotation from Isaiah: their youthful beauty and young love are only short-lived and will fade like flowers. This love scene on top of the haystack is the crucial component of the central panel of the triptych, as is also testified by its exposed position between an angel on the left and a devil playing a fanfare on his nose on the right. Christ, as the Man of Sorrows, looks down from a cloud above and raises His hands in order to display the stigmata – a reminder of the inevitable Last Judgement. Christ's gesture is, however, observed only by the angel. As so often, Bosch here employs mirror symmetry on either side of a vertical axis in order to allow the viewer – who is him- or herself a potentially redeemed or damned soul – to compare the two sides and make a choice. Here, the axis descends from Christ, as the tip of a pyramid,

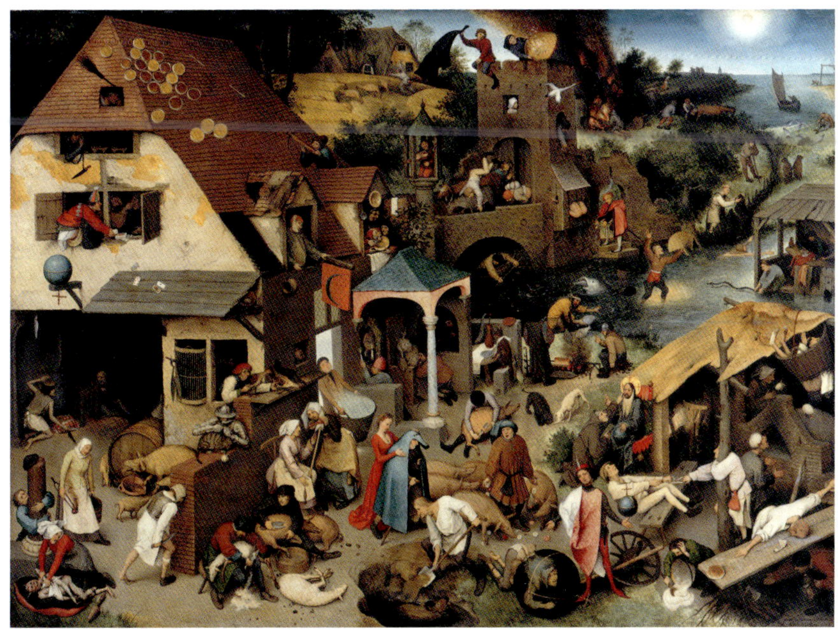

Pieter Bruegel Elder, **Netherlandish Proverbs**, 1559
Oil on panel (oak), 117.2 x 163.8 cm / 46⅛ x 64½ in. Berlin, Staatliche Museen, Gemäldegalerie

down through the group "rolling in the hay". On the right the devil visually "mirrors" the angel through the shape of his wings and in his unusual pale blue colouring. (Blue – in this respect like air or smoke – stood for deceit, futility and transience; and in Bosch's day people spoke of looking at the world through "blue-tinted", rather than "rosy-pink", spectacles.) Again we find the ubiquitous owl, in this case perched on a branch on the right, surrounded by other birds, and matched on the left by a jug hanging from a stick. The owl is even wearing a leash, identifying it as a lure (the lure of sin) to ensnare sinners. José de Sigüenza readily recognised the scene on top of the haystack as the most important within the entire composition. He described it most fittingly as follows:"One of these pictures has as its basic or principal subject a loaded Haywain, and atop it sit the sins of the flesh, fame and those who signify glory and power, embodied in several naked women [*sic*] playing instruments and singing, with glory in the figure of a demon who proclaims his greatness and power with his wings and trumpet." (Sigüenza 1605, p. 839; cited here from Snyder 1973, p. 38). On the right inner wing the very front of the haywain procession crosses a bridge (leading to the hereafter) and arrives at its final destination: Hell,

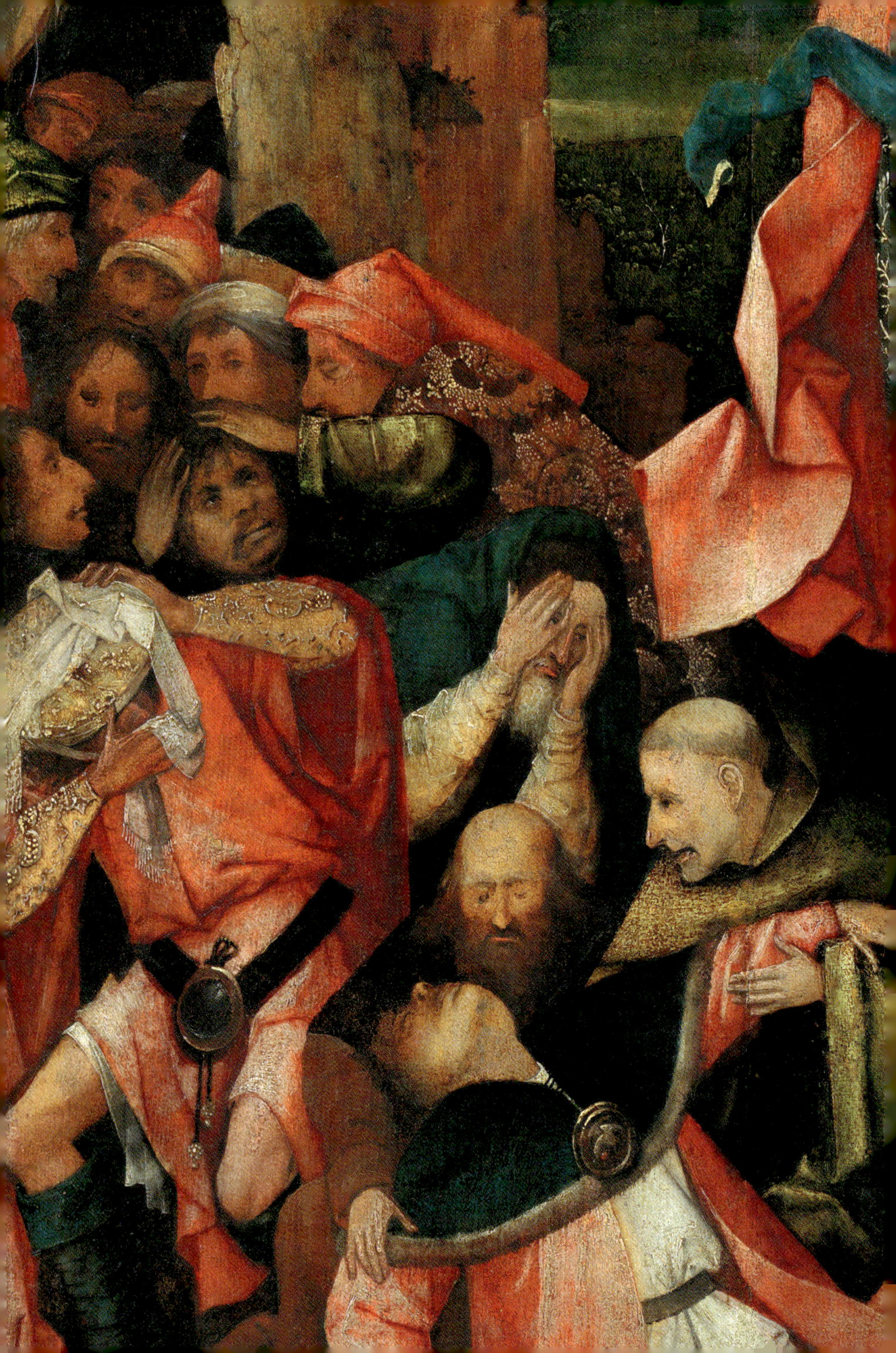

bathed in fiery reds and browns. With the help of scaffolding and tackle blocks, devils are skilfully constructing a masonry tower, which – in parallel with the tower of hay – grows with each new sin committed by humankind (p. 328). In the foreground hybrid devils are leading and dragging the Damned into Hell. A hunter devil herds his quarry in front of him (pp. 330/331). The message of the interior of the *Haywain* triptych is clear: those who surrender themselves blindly to worldly values will ensure their own passage to Hell. The only certain remedy is to reflect upon Christian values in order, with God's aid, to follow the path to Salvation. Bosch has taken the eschatological undercurrent of the biblical passages cited above and stated it with complete clarity. The pedlar on the exterior, however, breaks out of the trapped and hopeless situation of those in the interior. He epitomises the sinner who endeavours to improve his life by leaving the road of sin and following the path of redemption.

For those seeking somewhat lighter entertainment, however, *The Haywain* triptych – in particular the central panel – also has much to offer in as far as it is an astonishingly original pictorial invention that overflows with anecdotal scenes, each in itself a worthy subject for a painting. The sheer number and variety of figures ensure that the narrative unfolds by means of the rhetorical figure of *accumulatio*, that is to say, the accumulation of analogous scenes and figures relating to the symbol of "hay". Bosch herein demonstrates both his artistic and his intellectual mastery. This process was later also used by Pieter Bruegel the Elder (*Netherlandish Proverbs*, p. 299; *Children's Games*, *c.* 1560, Vienna, Kunsthistorisches Museum, Gemäldegalerie).

During the last years of his career Bosch was not so wholly occupied with panel painting that he could not fulfil other requests and obligations as an artist. In 1508/09, for example, Wouter van der Rullen invited Bosch and Jan Heyns, a fellow member of the Brotherhood of Our Blessed Lady, to his home to discuss whether and how to provide a polychrome decoration for Adriaen van Wesel's altarpiece; while in 1511/12 Bosch produced a design for a cross on a chasuble and in 1512/13 a design for a candelabrum. These were not minor activities but services readily rendered by a member of the Brotherhood, and they were of the kind that Bosch regularly undertook. They even speak in his favour, since the work of designing, advising and organising commanded greater respect than the related manual labour.

Hieronymus Bosch continued to enjoy success and prosperity. The invoice for the Brotherhood banquet he hosted in 1510 mentions his *maeghden*, maids (whom Bosch evidently employed at that time as part of his domestic staff, in keeping with his social

Detail from: **Triptych of the Crucified Female Martyr (Sint-Ontcommer)**, *c.* 1505–1515
Central panel (see ill. pp. 310/311)

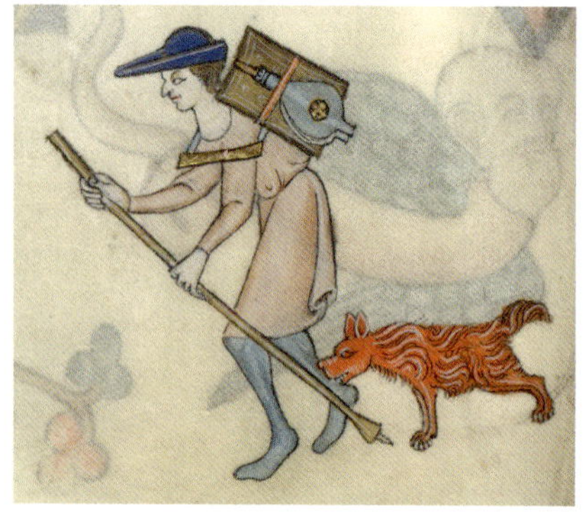

standing). A sum of 68 guilders that he received in 1515 may derive from sales of wood or payment for artistic commissions. But the very next year Hieronymus Bosch died. After a ceremonial Requiem Mass attended by his friends and fellow Brotherhood members, he was buried on 9 August (see document in the chapter "Documentary sources"). Bosch had fallen victim to the severe epidemic of pleurisy that swept through 's-Hertogenbosch around 1516, and which also claimed the lives of his nephew, Anthonis, of the architect Jan Heyms, and of countless others. For the local population, already decimated by the war of independence waged by the Duchy of Guelders against the Habsburgs, it was yet another blow.

That same year the Duke of Brabant, the later Emperor Charles V, awarded Bosch's widow, Aleid van der Mervenne, a life annuity of ten pounds (van Dijck 2001a, p. 185), which can only really be explained as remuneration for art works received. Bosch had profited all his life from his marriage to Aleid; now she was able to benefit financially from her artist husband after his death. It is also likely that she inherited his estate, including the material in his workshop.

English artist, **A Pedlar**, *c.* 1325–1335
Parchment, 35.5 x 24.5 cm / 14 x 9⅝ in. From: *Luttrell Psalter*, fol. 70v (detail)
London, British Library, Add. Ms. 42130

Pages 304/305
Hermit Saints Triptych (with Sts Jerome, Anthony and Giles), *c.* 1504
Oil on panel (oak), 85 x 60 cm / 33½ x 23⅝ in. (central panel), 85 x 29 cm / 33½ x 11⅜ in. (wings; panels cut down, original height *c.* 110 cm / 43¼ in. with an arched or curved top)
Venice, Museo Palazzo Grimani
Left inner wing: **St Anthony**
Central panel: **St Jerome**
Right inner wing: **St Giles**

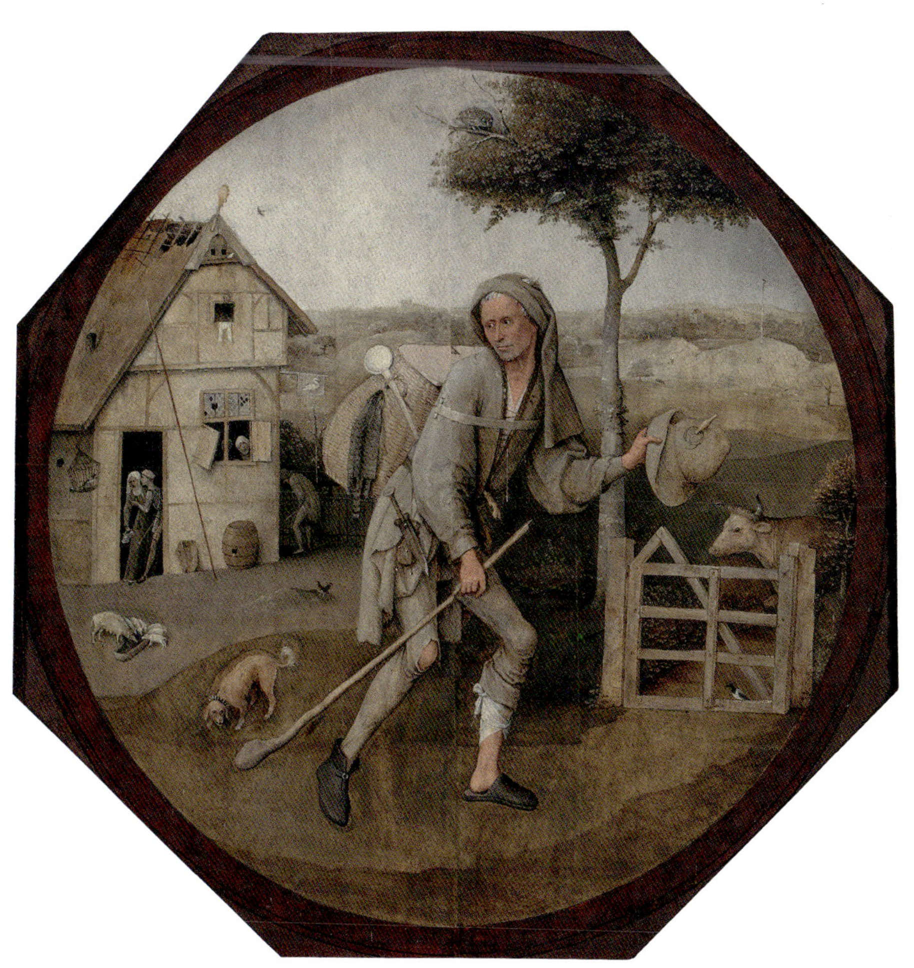

The Pedlar, *c.* 1500–1510, Outer wings of: **"The Cana Triptych"**
Oil on panel (oak), 71 x 70.6 cm / 28 x 27¾ in. (originally *c.* 94 x 72 cm / 37 x 28⅜ in.)
Rotterdam, Museum Boijmans Van Beuningen

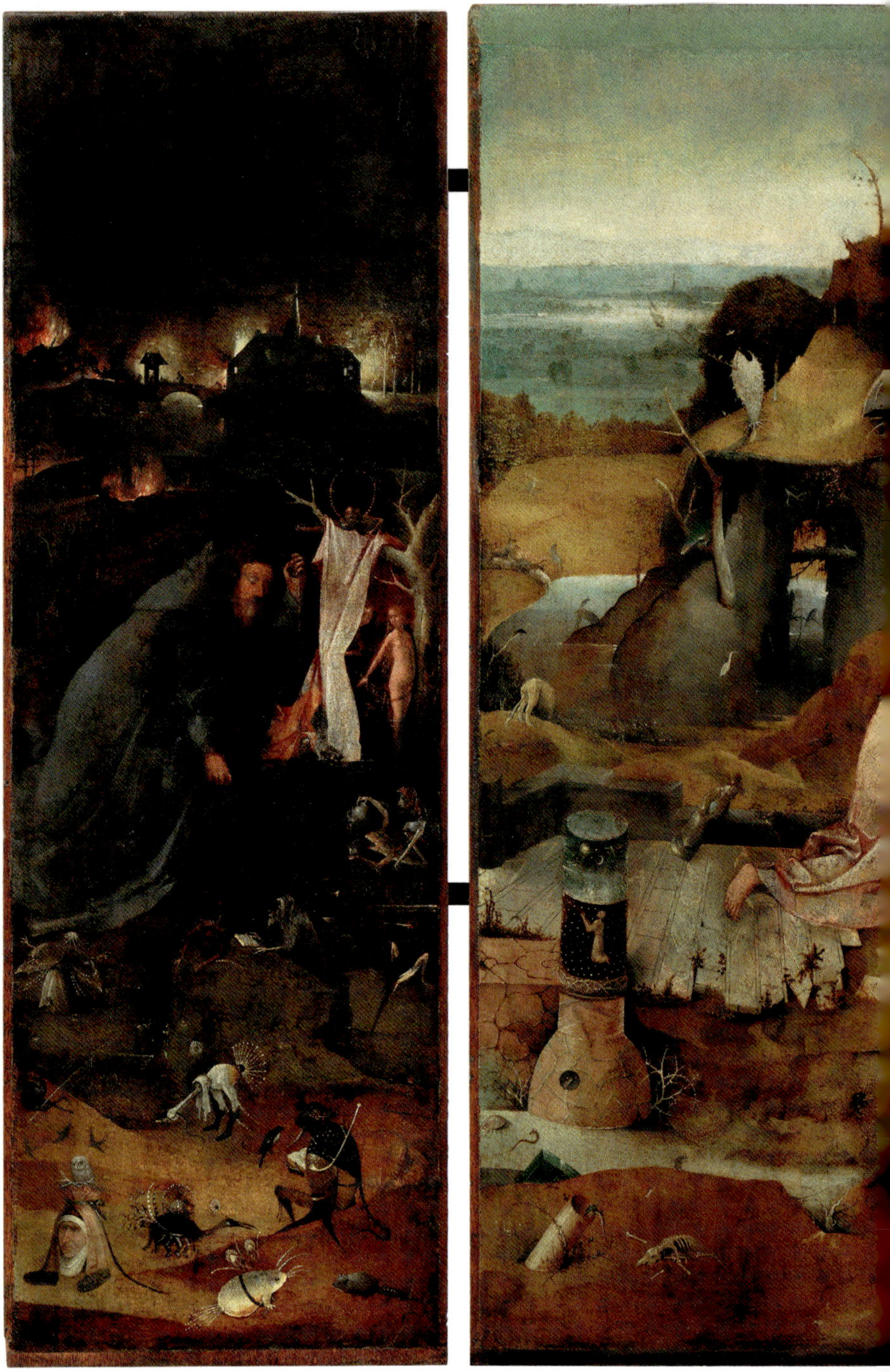

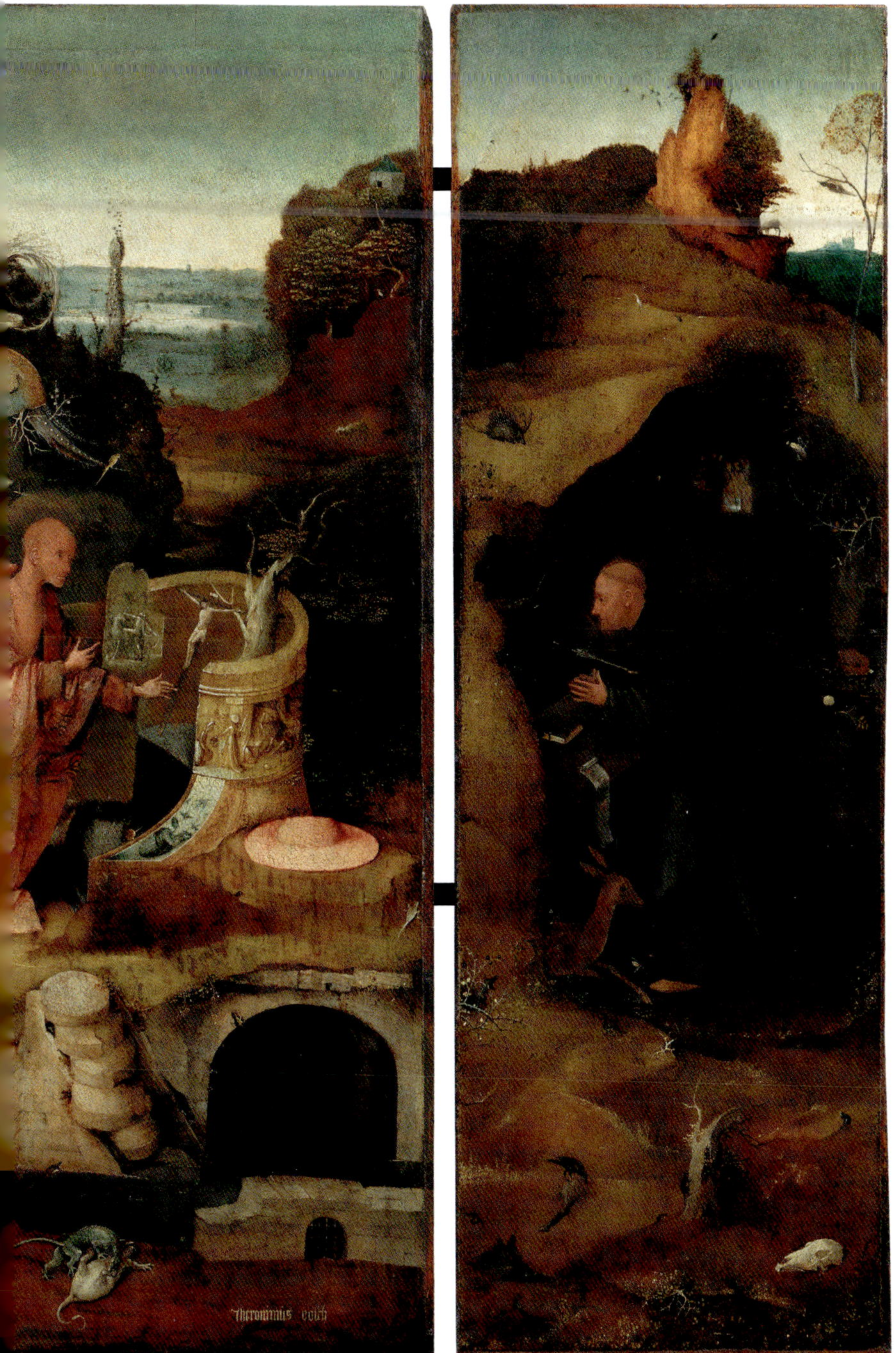

jheronimus bosch

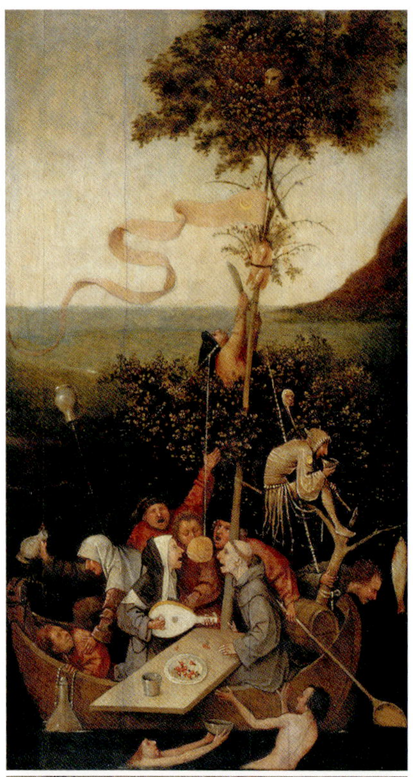

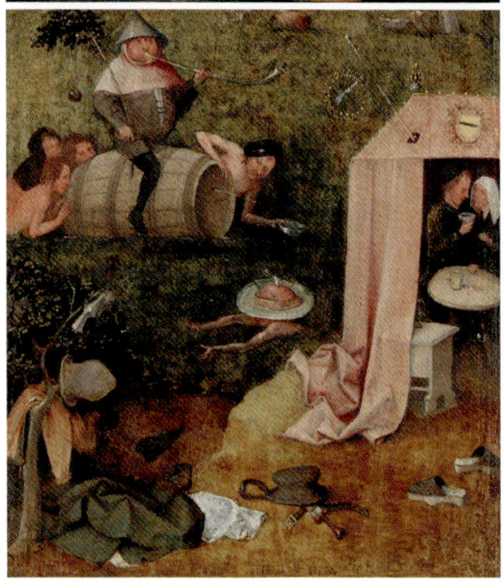

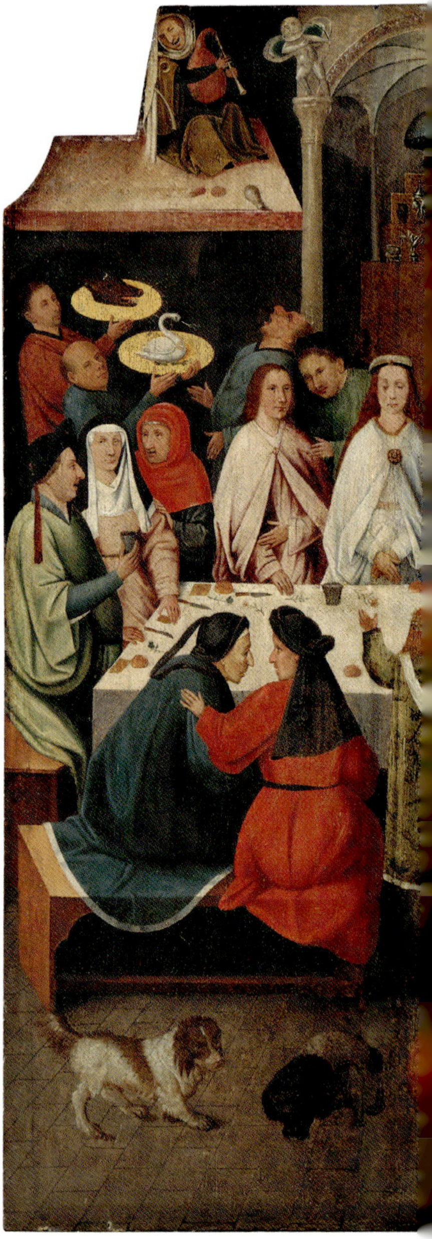

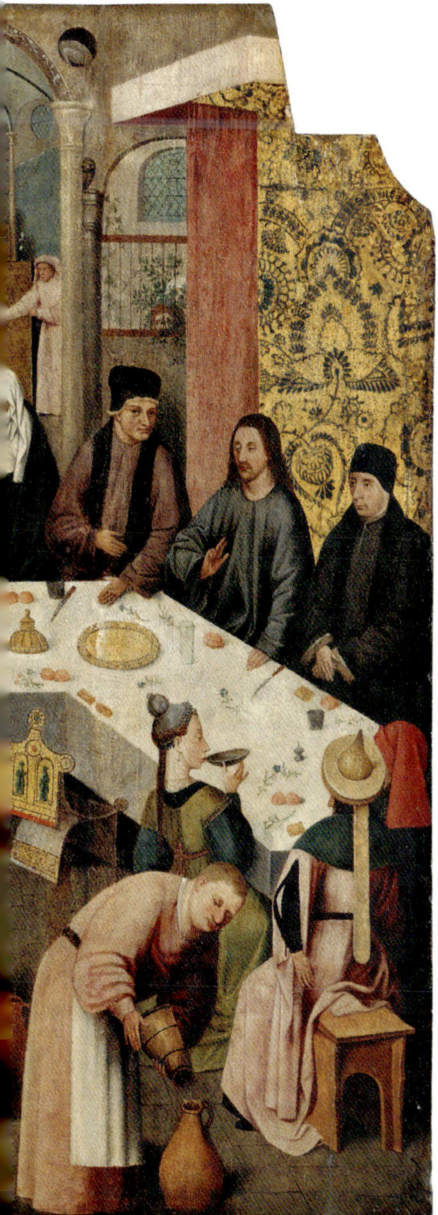

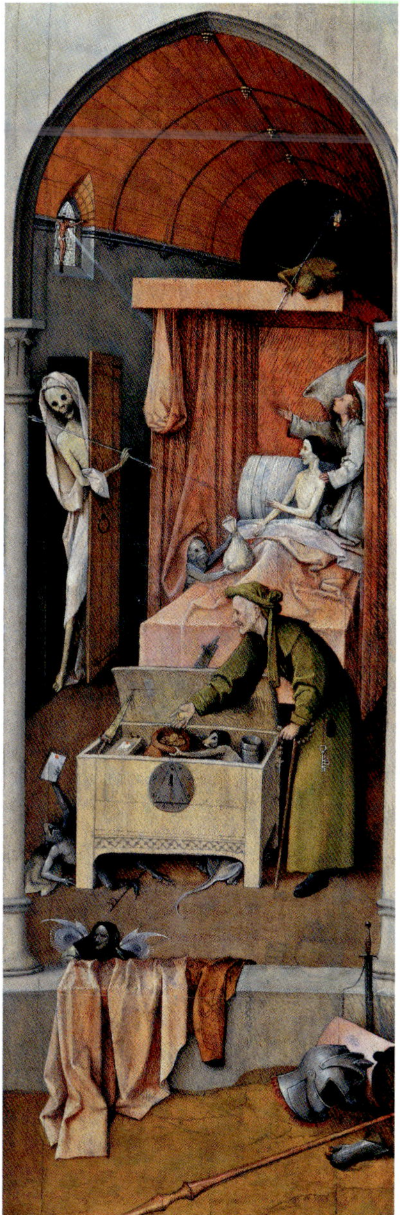

The Seven Deadly Sins and the Four Last Things, *c.* 1505–1510
Oil on panel (black poplar), 120 x 150 cm / 47¼ x 59 in.
Madrid, Museo Nacional del Prado

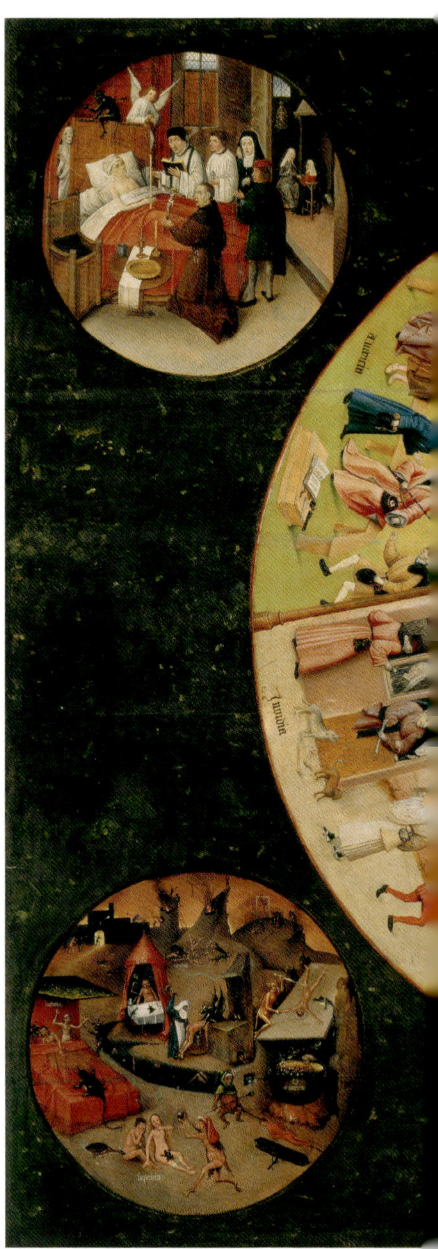

Pages 306/307
The Wedding at Cana with Exempla ("The Cana Triptych"), *c.* 1500–1510
Oil on panel (oak), *c.* 94 x 72 cm / 37 x 28⅜ in. (central panel),
94 x 32.6 cm / 37 x 12¾ in. (wings)
Triptych, reconstruction

Left inner wing, above:
The Ship of Fools, *c.* 1500–1510
Oil on panel (oak), 57.9 x 32.6 cm / 22¾ x 12¾ in.
(originally *c.* 94 x 32.6 cm / 37 x 12¾ in.)
Paris, Musée du Louvre

Left inner wing, below:
Allegory of Intemperance, *c.* 1500–1510
Oil on panel (oak), 35.9 x 31.4 cm / 14⅛ x 12⅜ in.
(originally *c.* 94 x 32.6 cm / 37 x 12¾ in.)
New Haven, Yale University Art Gallery, inv. no. 1959.15.22; Gift of Hannah D. and Louis M. Rabinowitz

Central panel, copy:
Anonymous artist after Hieronymus Bosch (?)
The Wedding at Cana, after 1555–1561
Oil on panel (oak), 93 x 72 cm / 36⅝ x 28⅜ in.
Rotterdam, Museum Boijmans Van Beuningen

Right inner wing:
Death and the Miser, *c.* 1500–1510
Oil on panel (oak), 92.6 x 30.8 cm / 36⅜ x 12⅛ in.
Washington DC, National Gallery of Art, Samuel H. Kress Collection

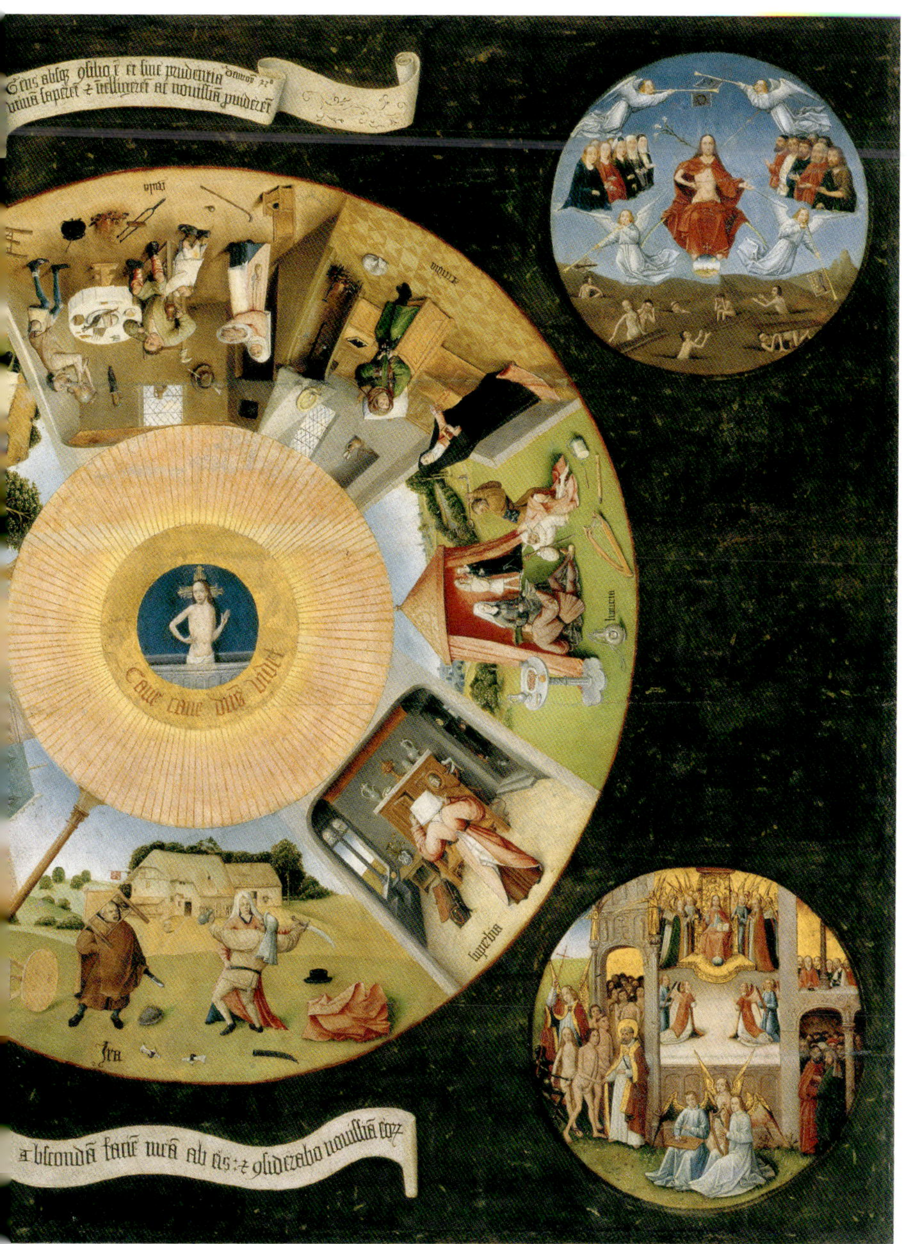

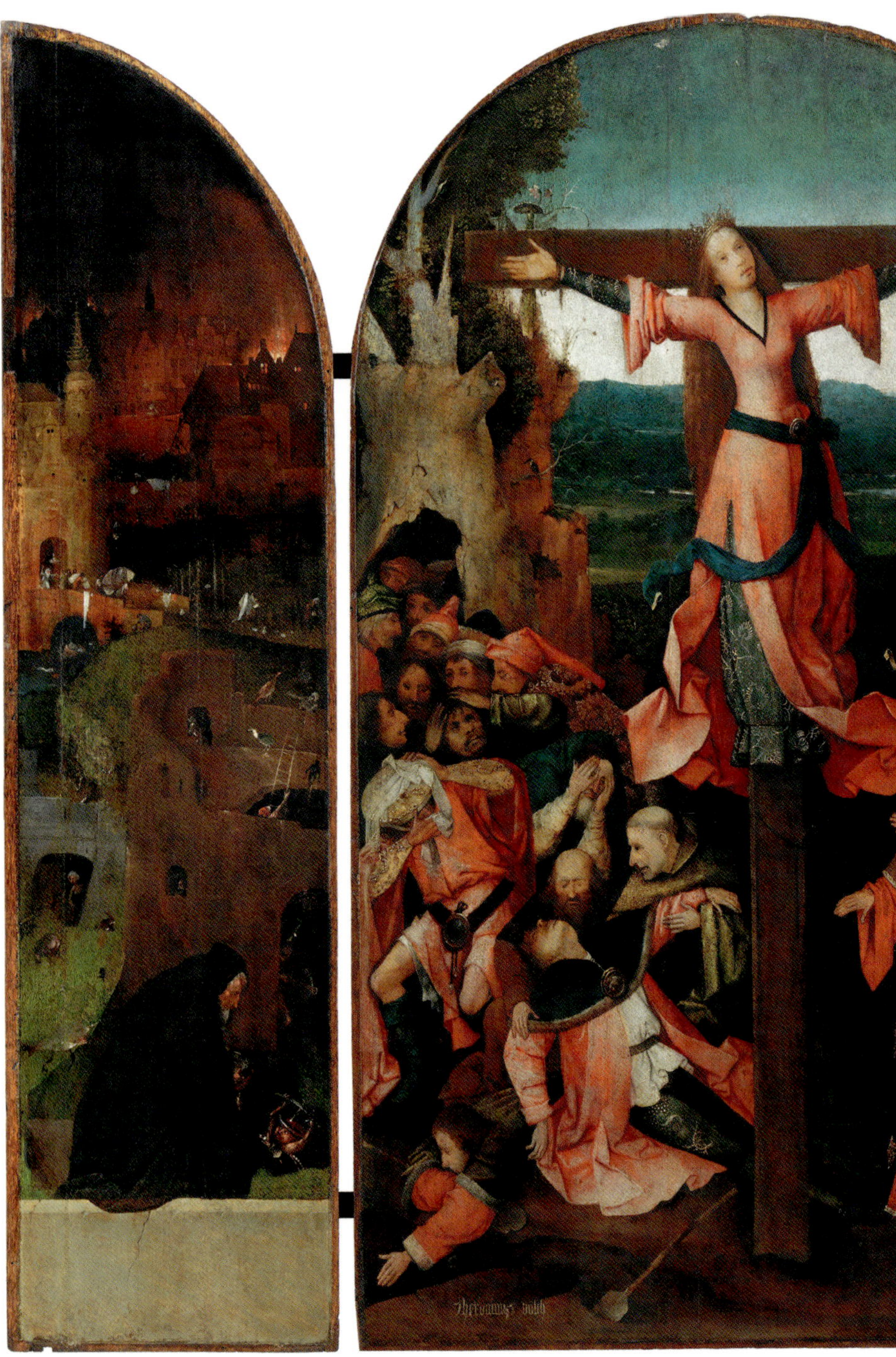

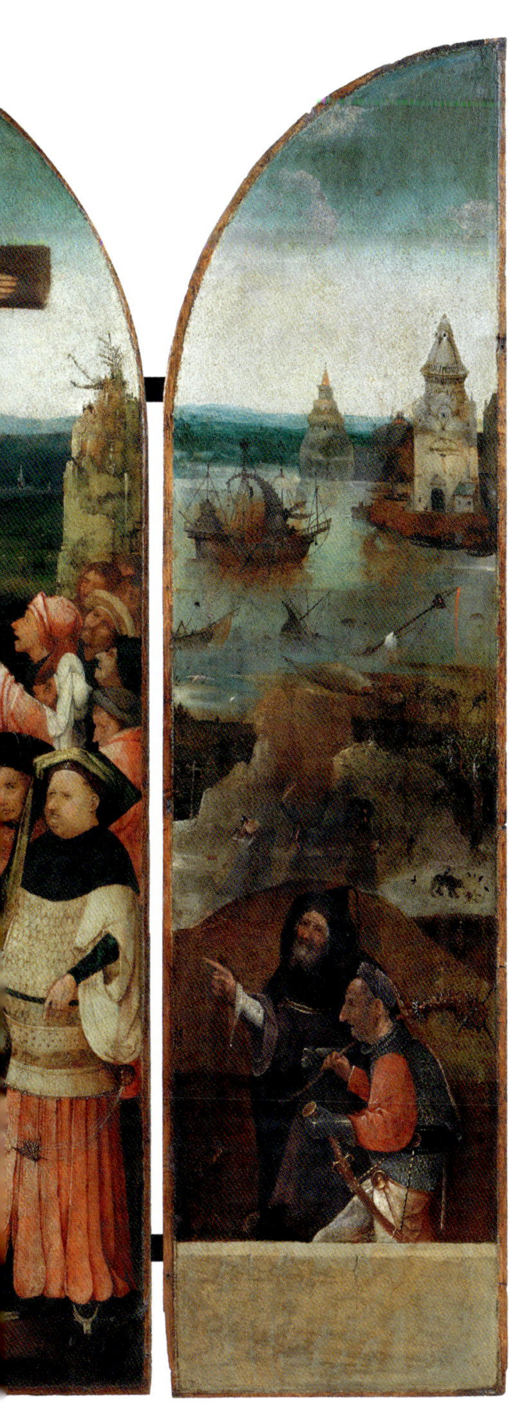

Triptych of the Crucified Female Martyr (Sint-Ontcommer), *c.* 1505–1515
Oil on panel (oak), 105 x 63 cm / 41⅜ x 24¾ in. (central panel), 105 x 28 cm / 41⅜ x 11 in. (wings)
Venice, Museo Palazzo Grimani

Pages 312/313
Paradise and Hell, *c.* 1505–1515
Oil on panel (oak), 86.5 x 39.5 cm / 3⅜ x 1½ in. (each wing panel)
Venice, Museo Palazzo Grimani
Left and right pairs of wings
Interior of the outer left wing:
Heavenly Paradise
Interior of the inner left wing:
Earthly Paradise
Interior of the inner right wing:
Fall of the Damned
Interior of the outer right wing:
The Damned in Hell

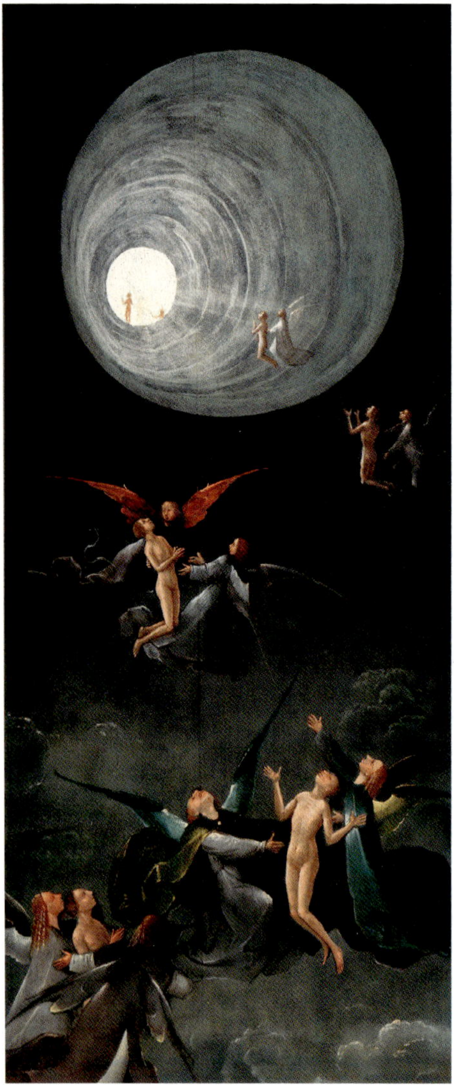

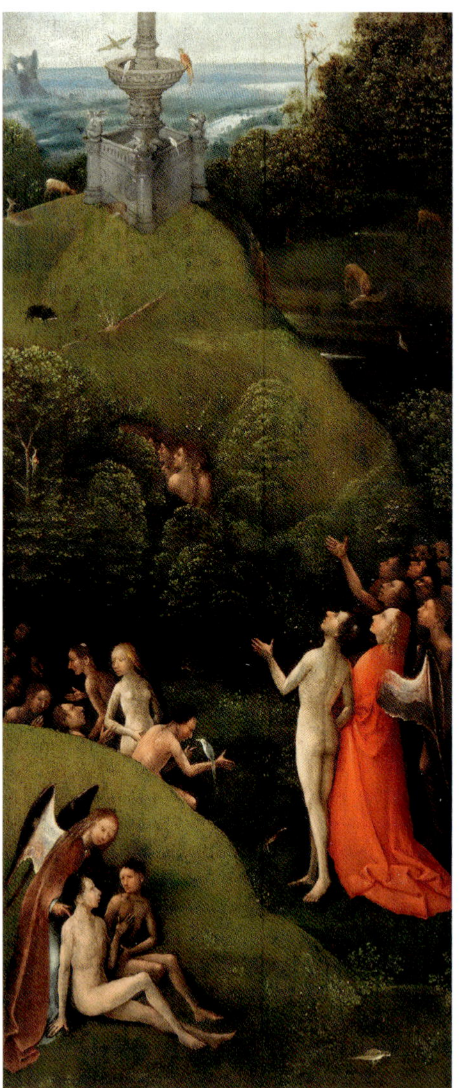

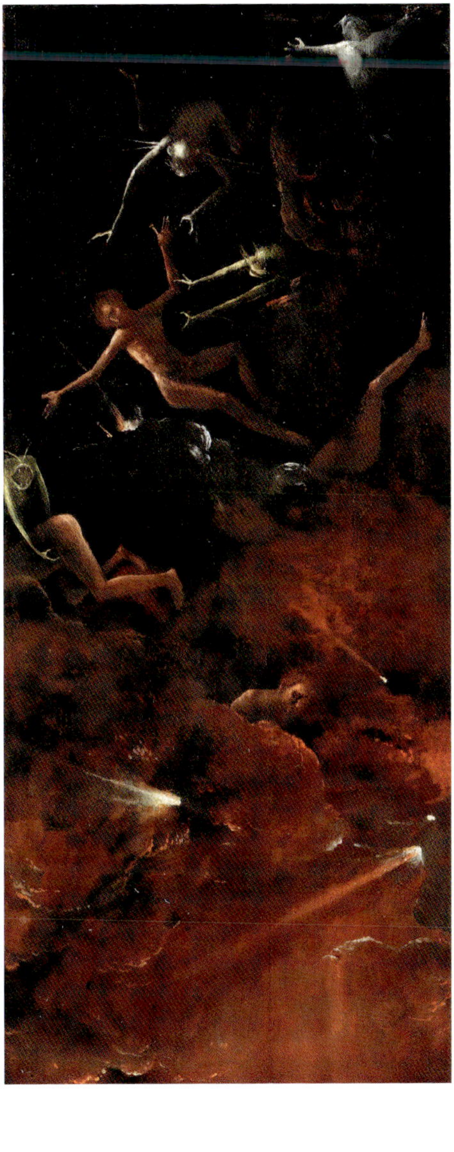

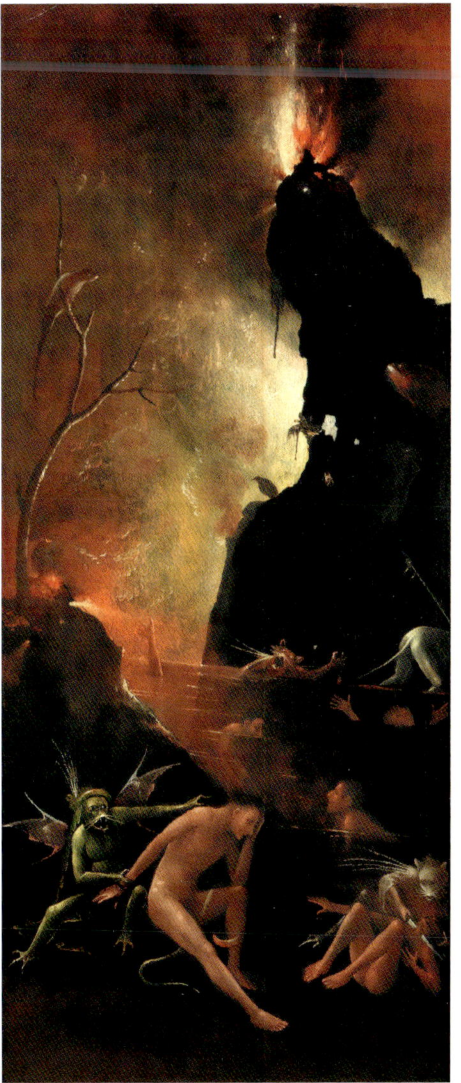

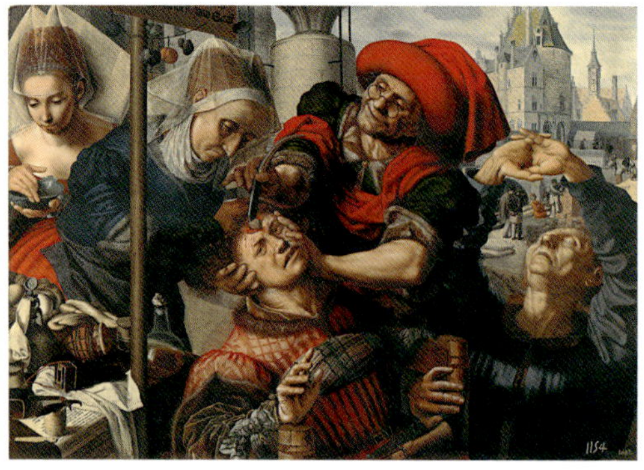

Jan Sanders van Hemessen, **Extracting the Stone of Folly**, *c.* 1550–1555
Oil on panel, 100 x 141 cm / 39⅜ x 55½ in. Madrid, Museo Nacional del Prado

Page 315
Extracting the Stone of Folly, *c.* 1505–1515
Oil on panel (oak), 47.5 x 34.5 cm / 18¾ x 13½ in. Madrid, Museo Nacional del Prado

Pages 316/317
Fragments of a representation of The Flood (exterior: The Temptation and Deliverance of Job), *c.* 1510–1515
Oil on panel (oak), 69 x 36 cm and 69 x 38 cm / 27⅛ x 14⅛ in. and 27⅛ x 15 in.
Rotterdam, Museum Boijmans Van Beuningen
Outer wings: **Four tondi showing the Temptation and Deliverance of Job**
Left inner wing: **The World Before the Flood**
Right inner wing: **The Animals Leaving Noah's Ark**

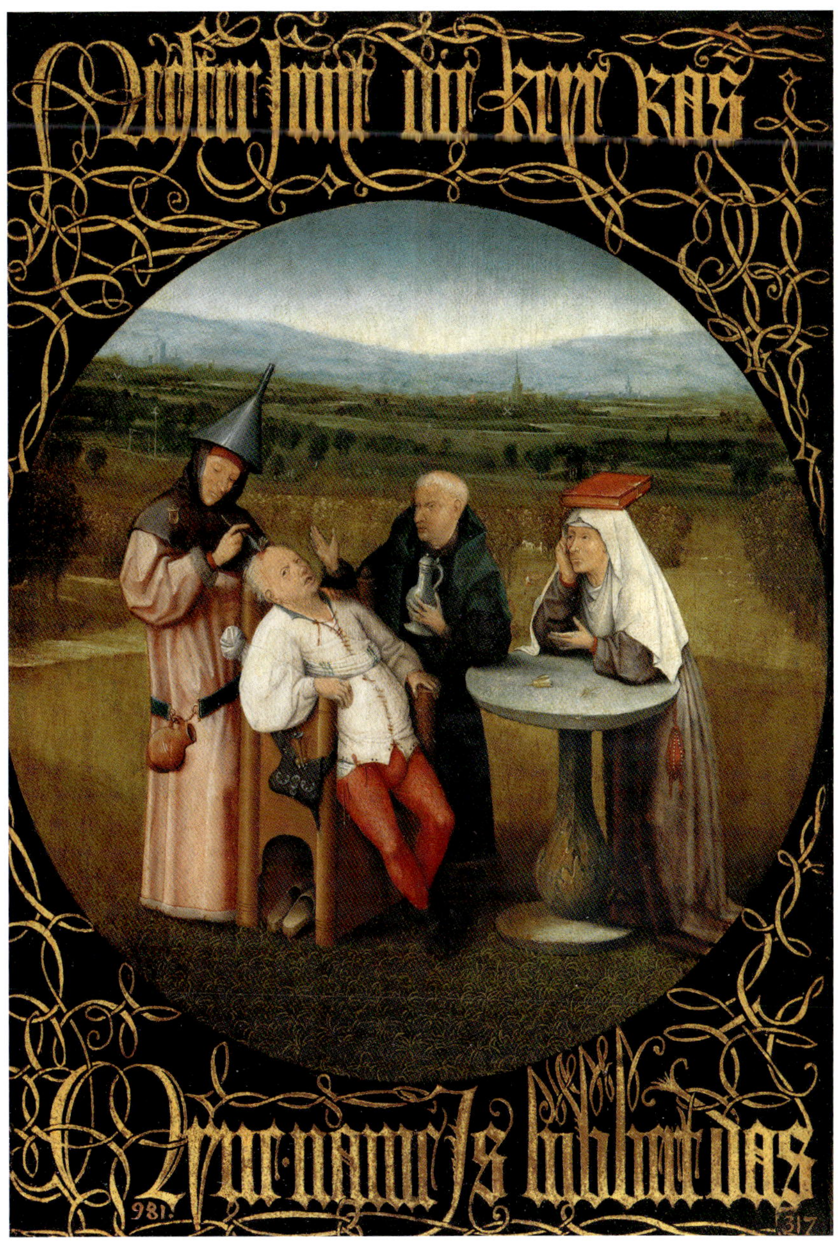

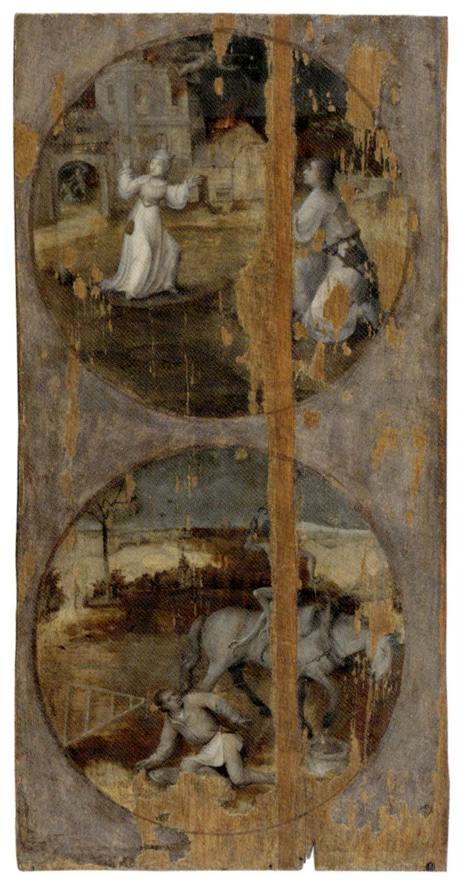

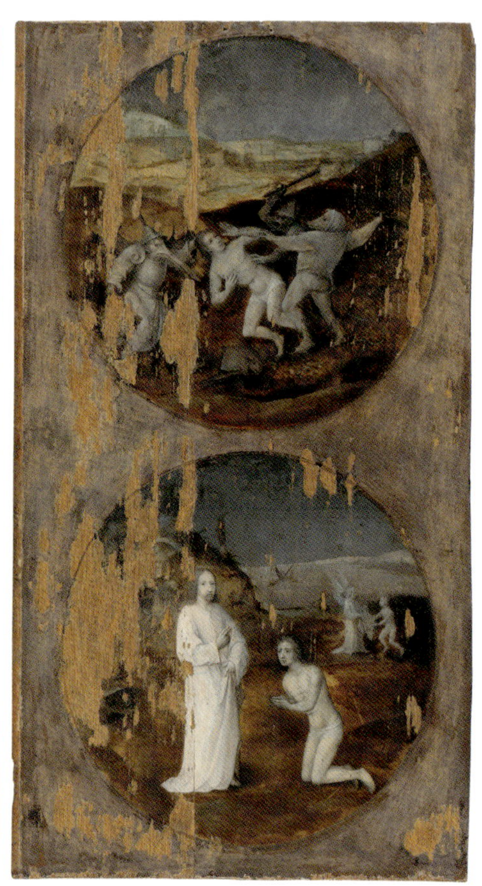

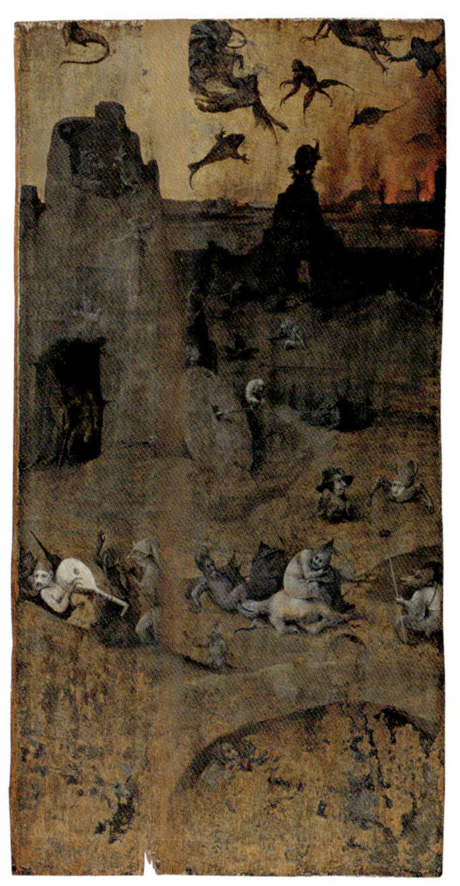

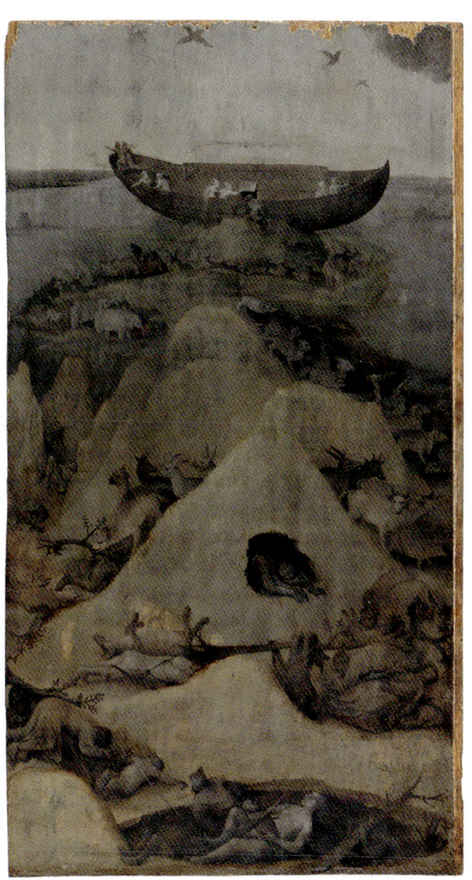

The Pedlar, *c.* 1510–1515
Outer wings of: **The Haywain**
Oil on panel (oak), 147 x 56 cm / 57⅞ x 22 in. (each wing)
Madrid, Museo Nacional del Prado

Pages 320/321
The Haywain, *c.* 1510–1515
Oil on panel (oak), 133 x 100 cm / 52⅜ x 39⅜ in. (central panel), 147 x 56 cm / 57⅞ x 22 in. (wings)
Madrid, Museo Nacional del Prado
Left inner wing: **The Genesis of Evil and the Loss of Paradise**
Central panel: **The Haywain**
Right inner wing: **Hell**

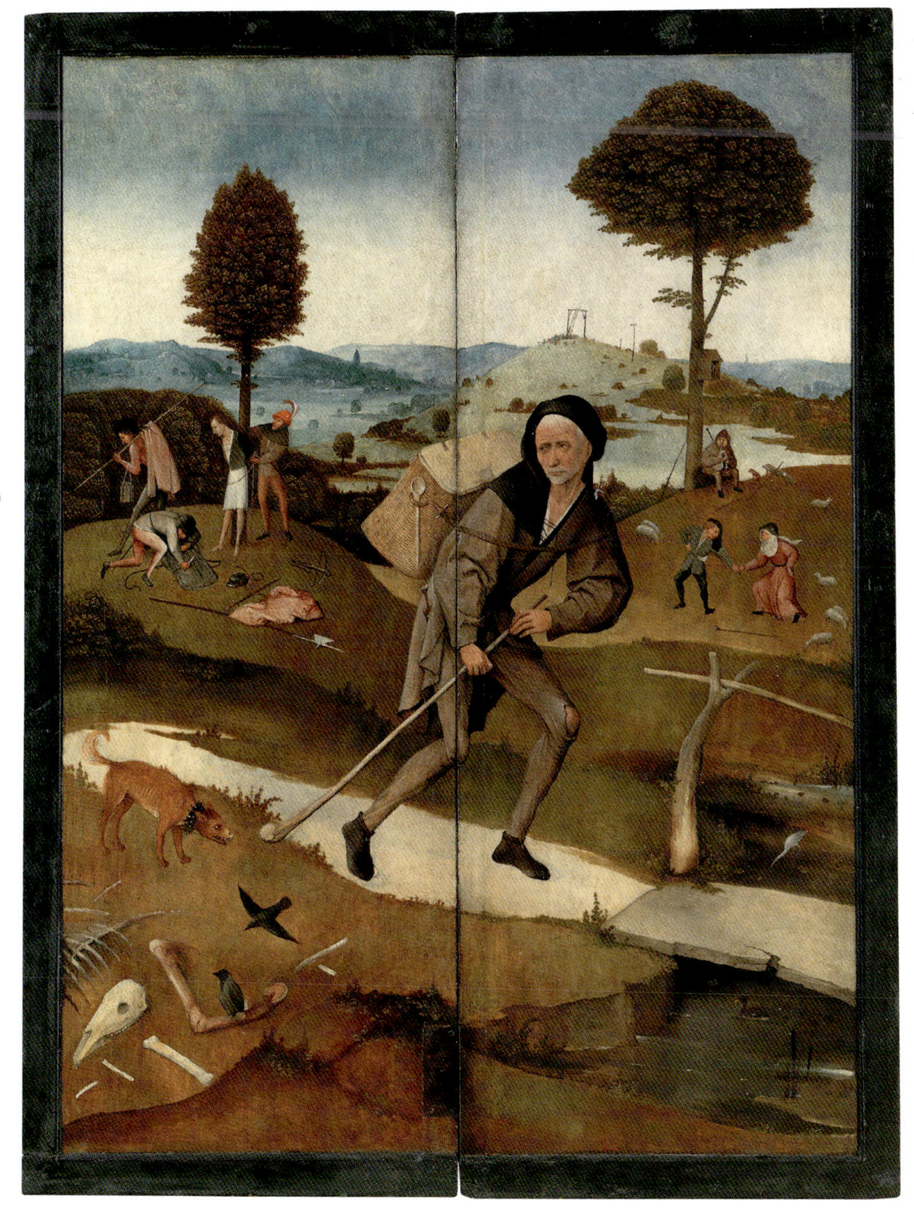

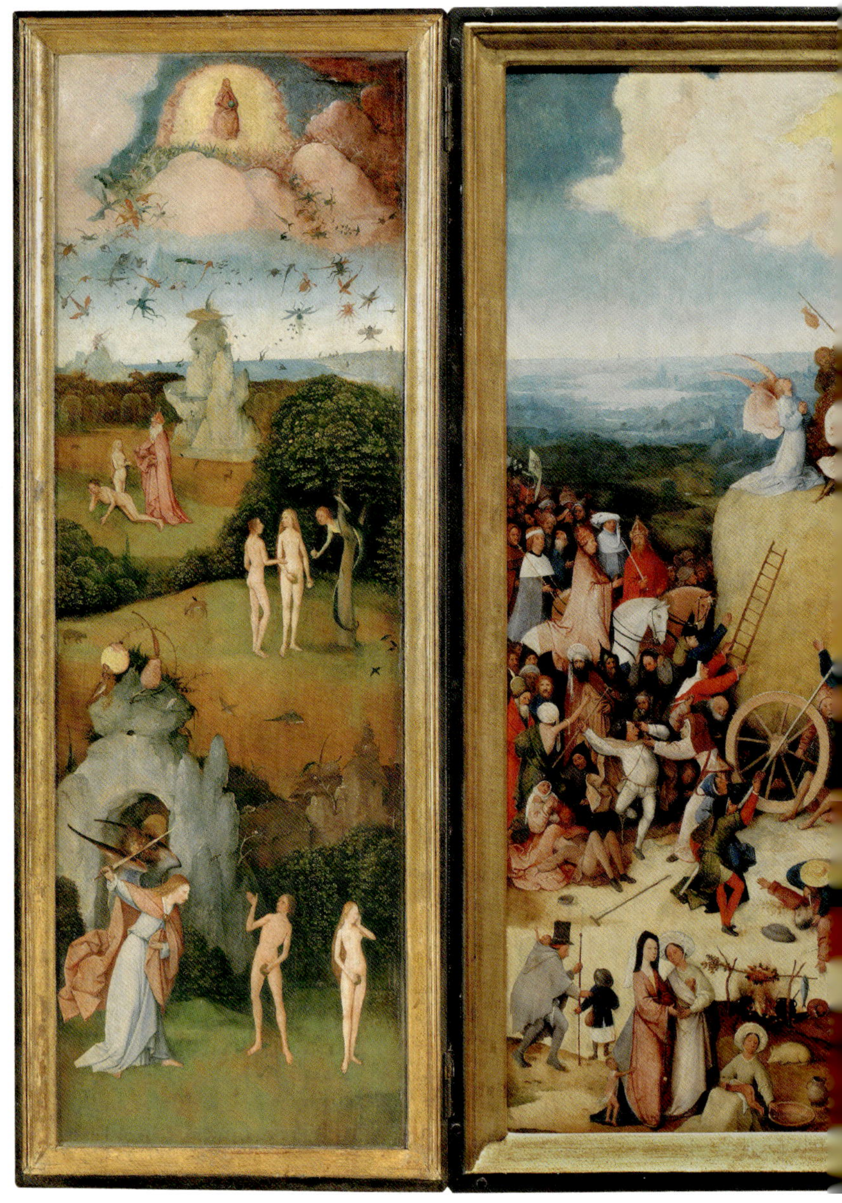

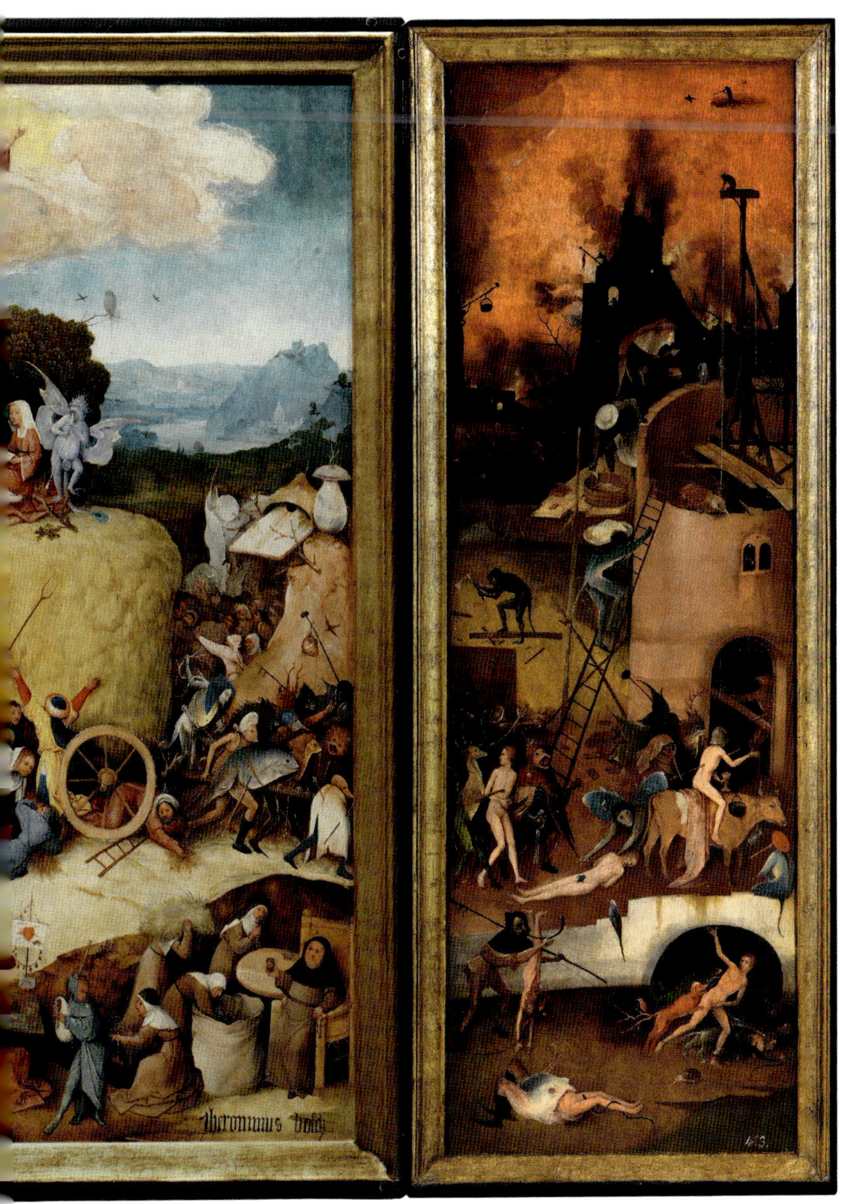
Jheronimus bosch

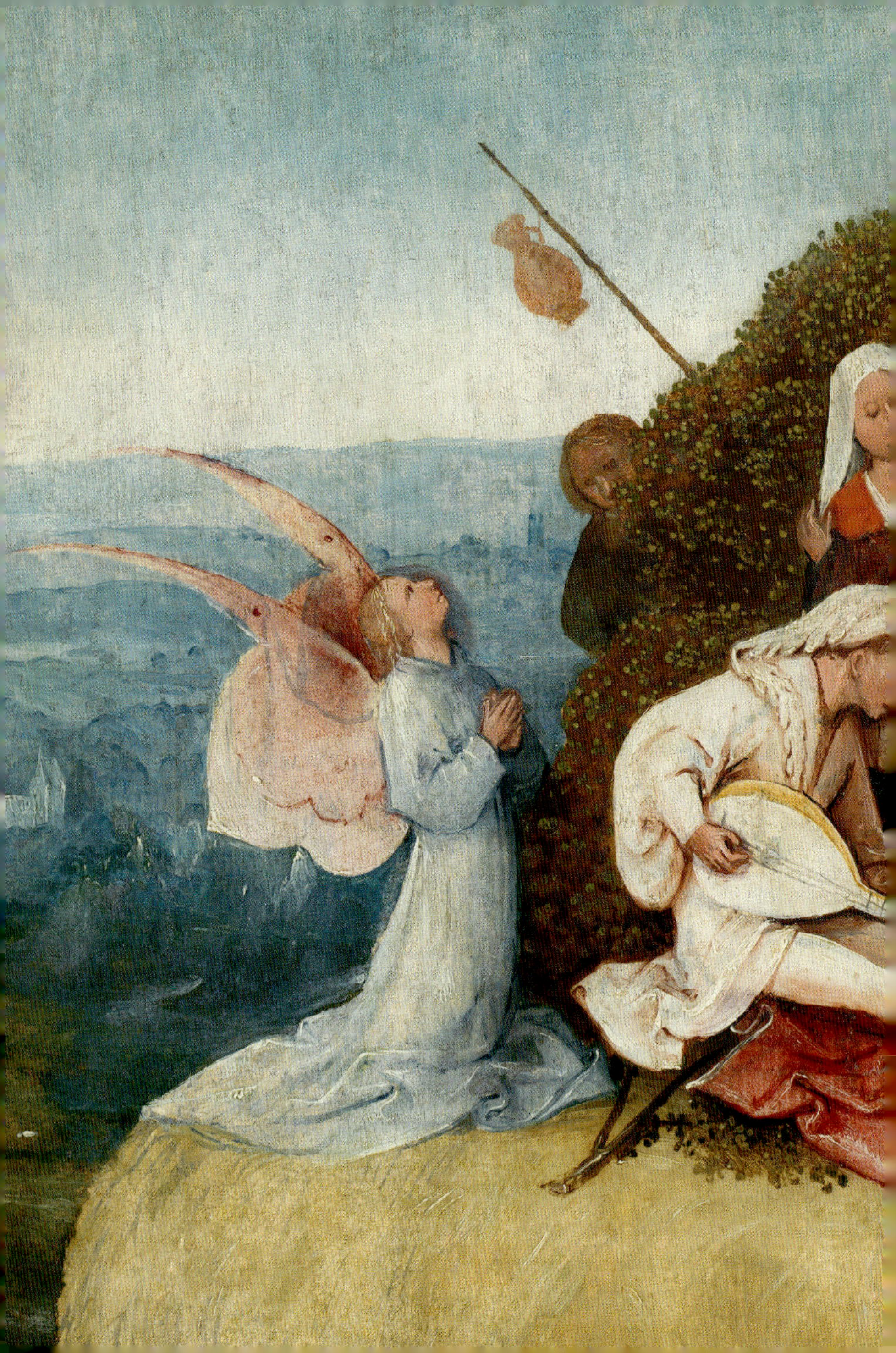

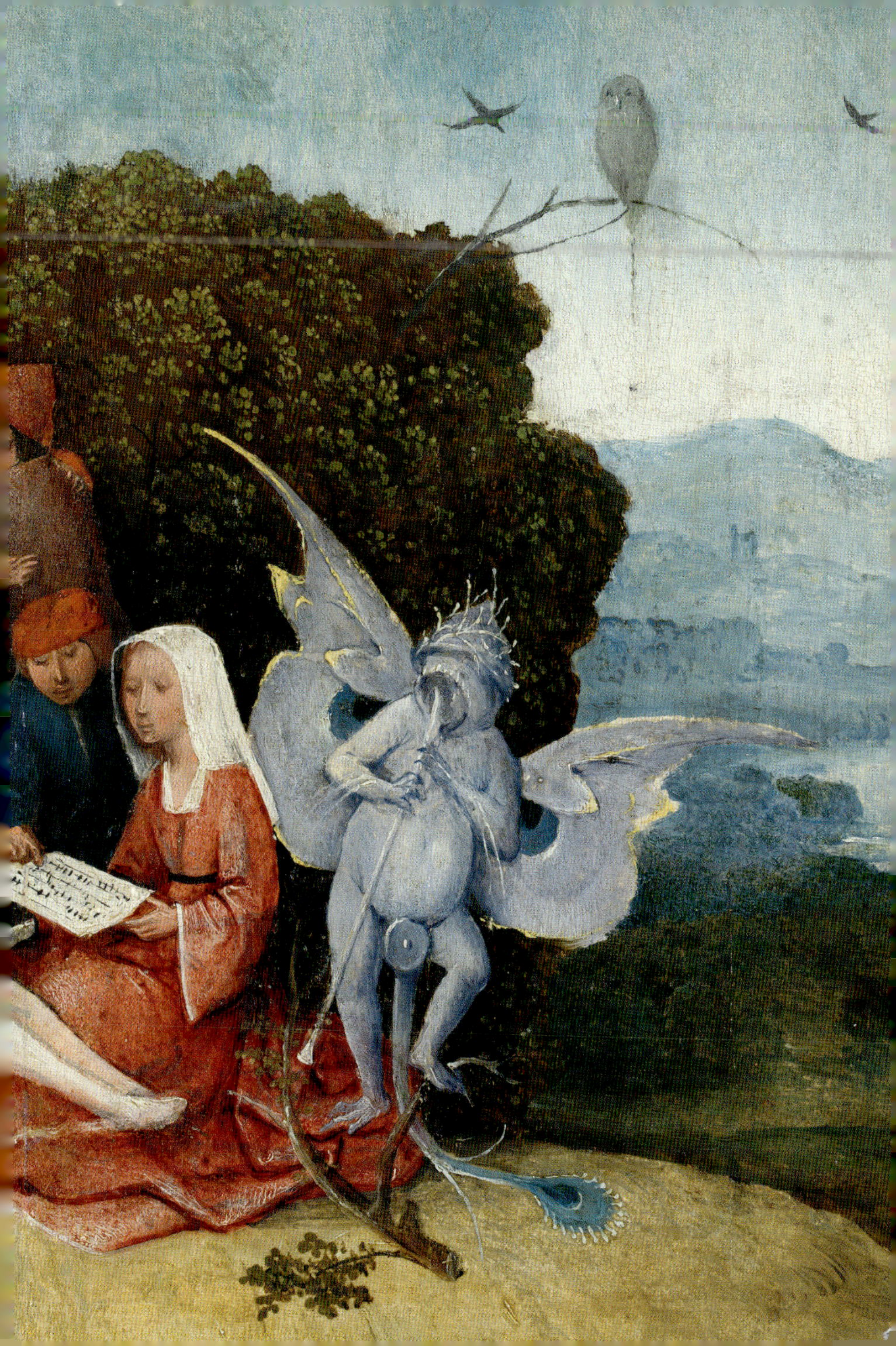

Pages 322/323, 325
Details from: **The Haywain**, *c.* 1510–1515
Central panel: **The Haywain** (see ill. pp. 320/321)

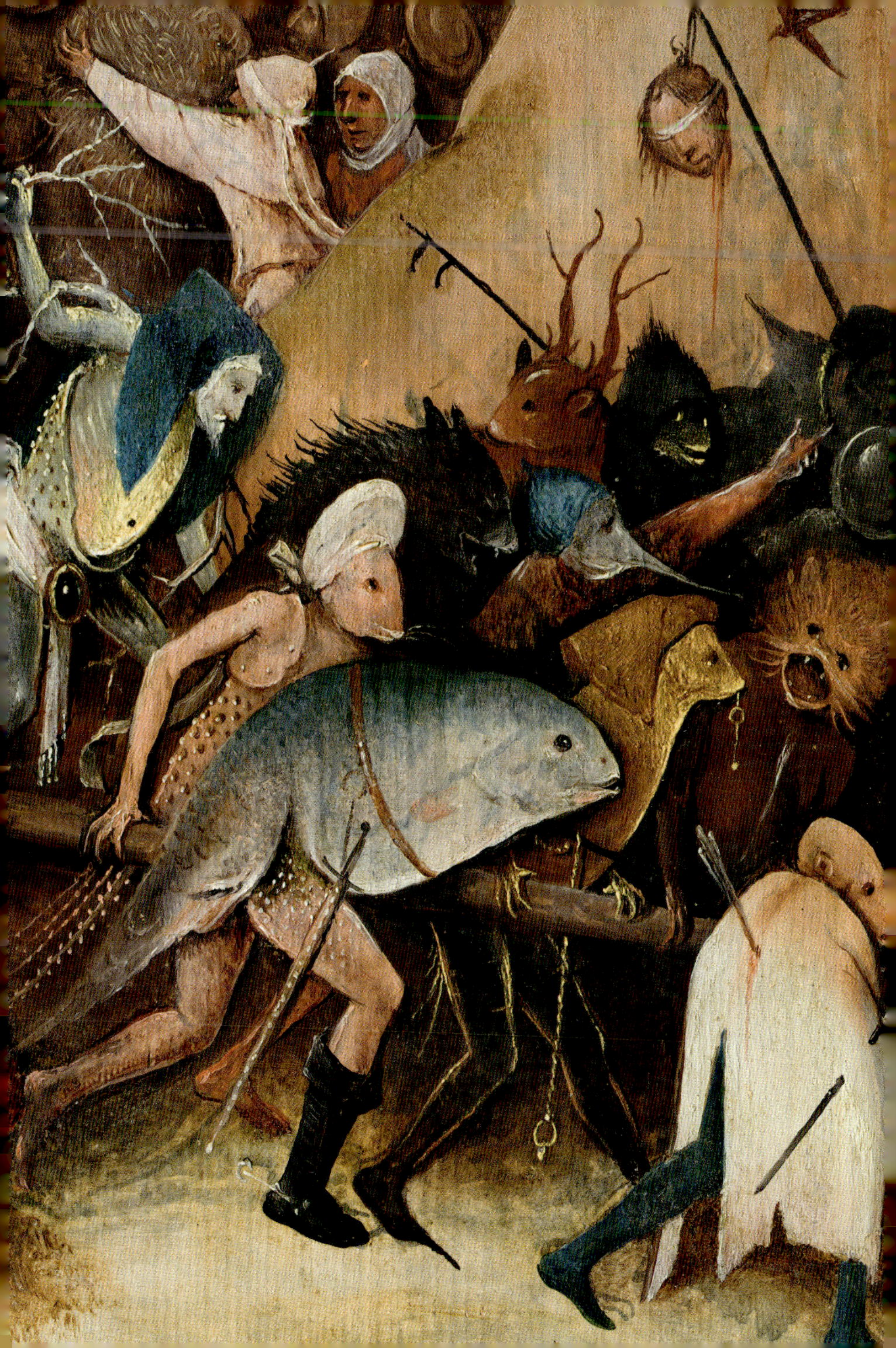

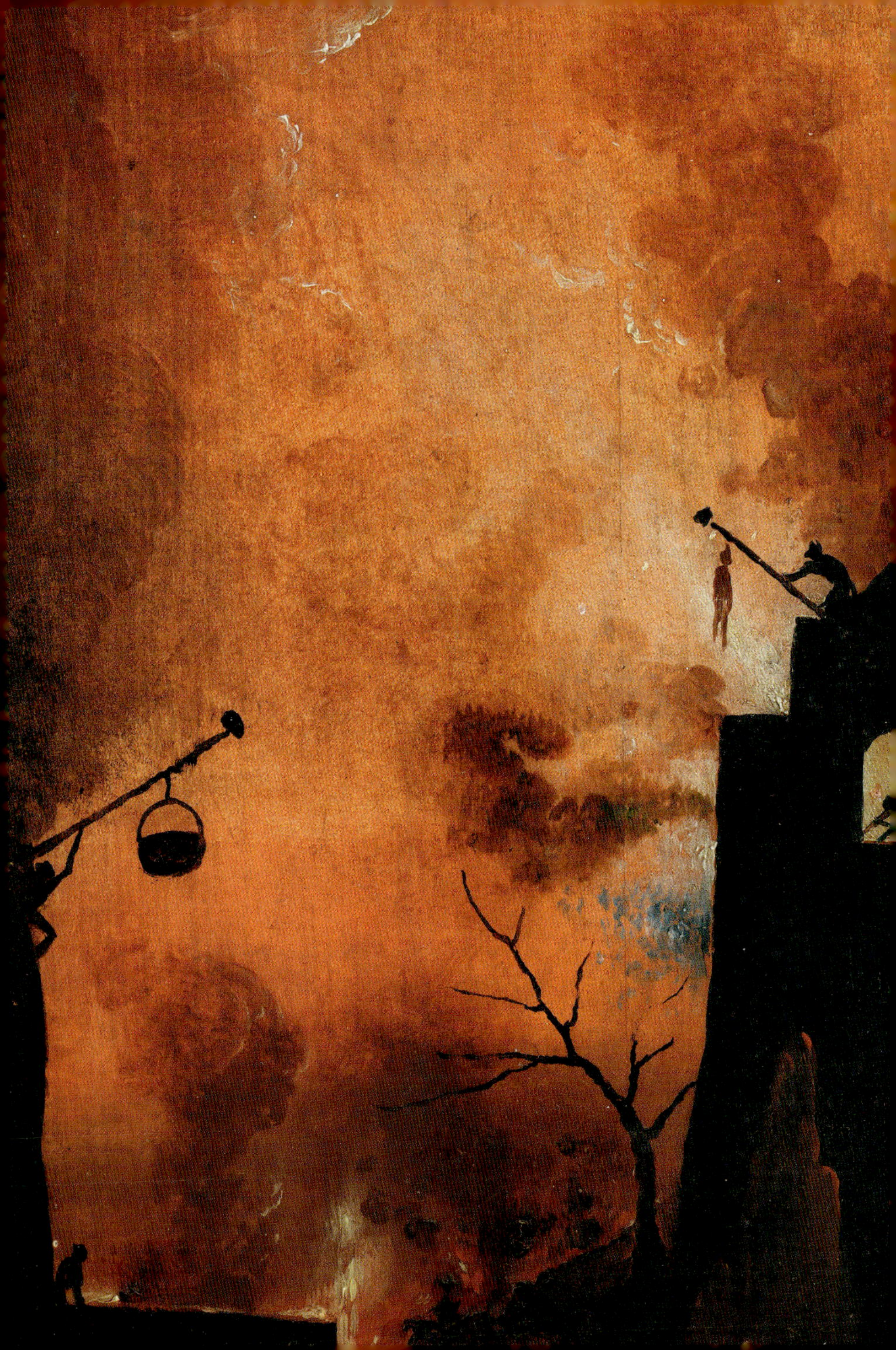

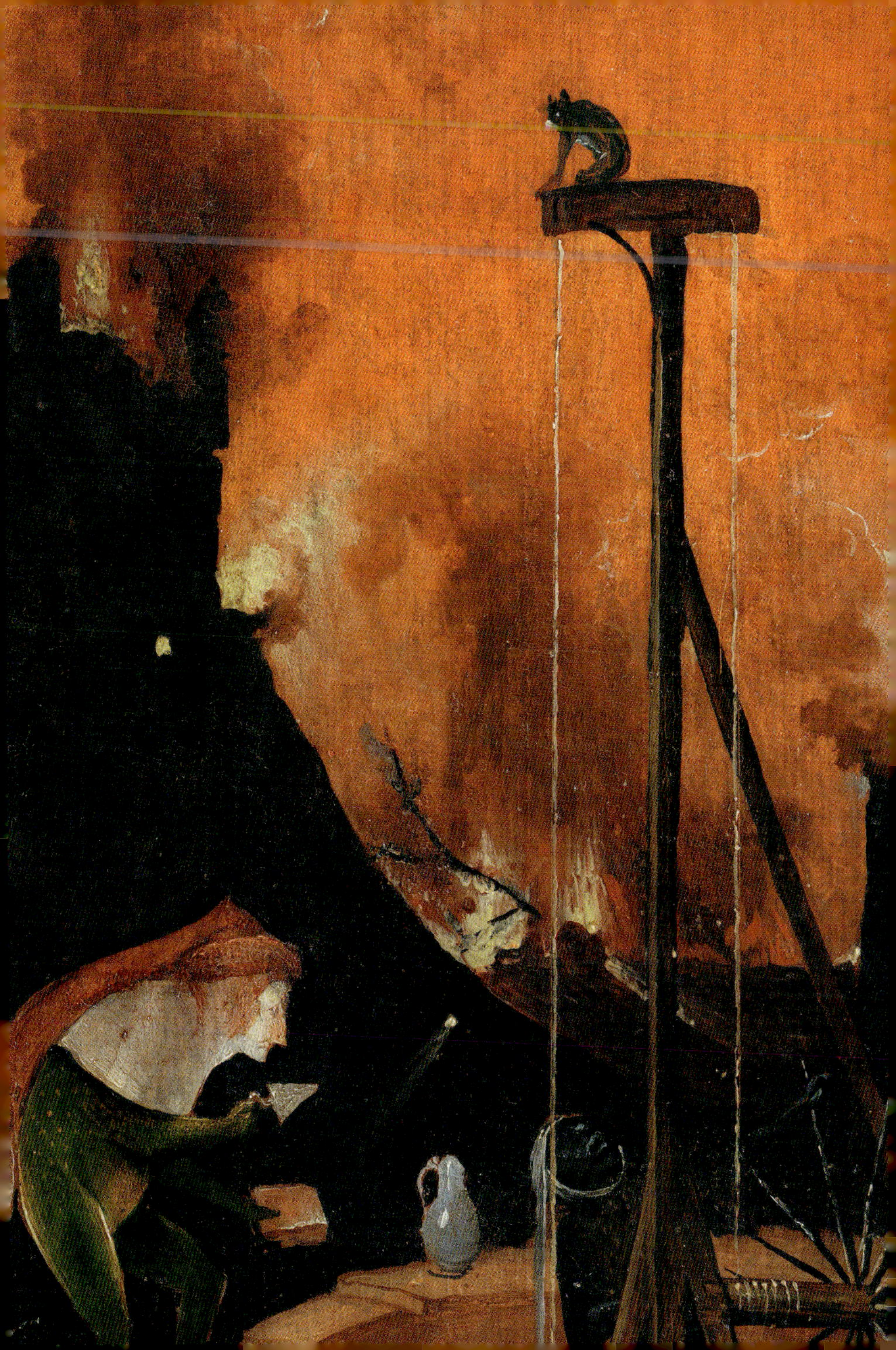

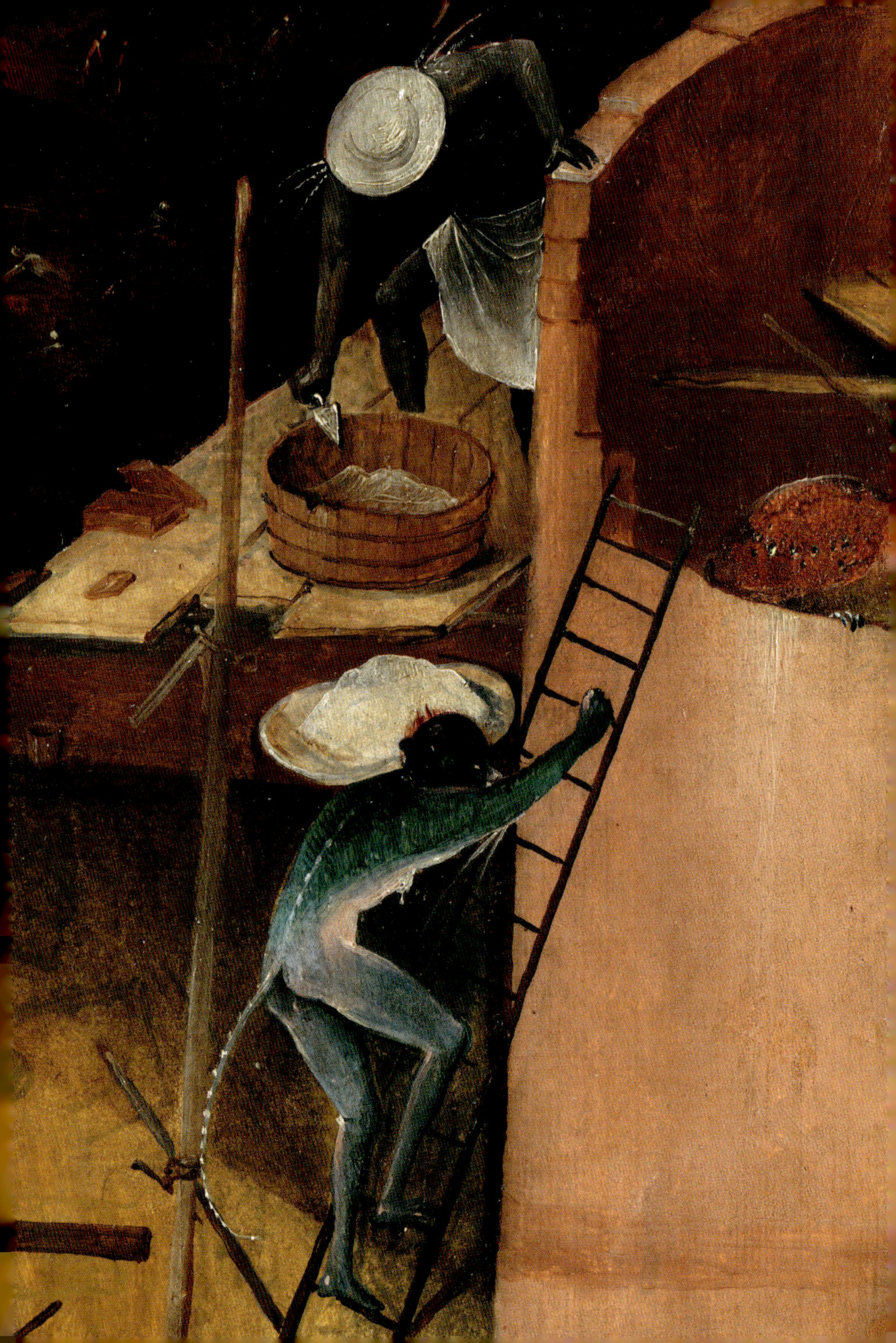

Pages 326/327, 328, 330/331
Details from: **The Haywain**, *c.* 1510–1515
Right inner wing: **Hell** (see ill. pp. 320/321)

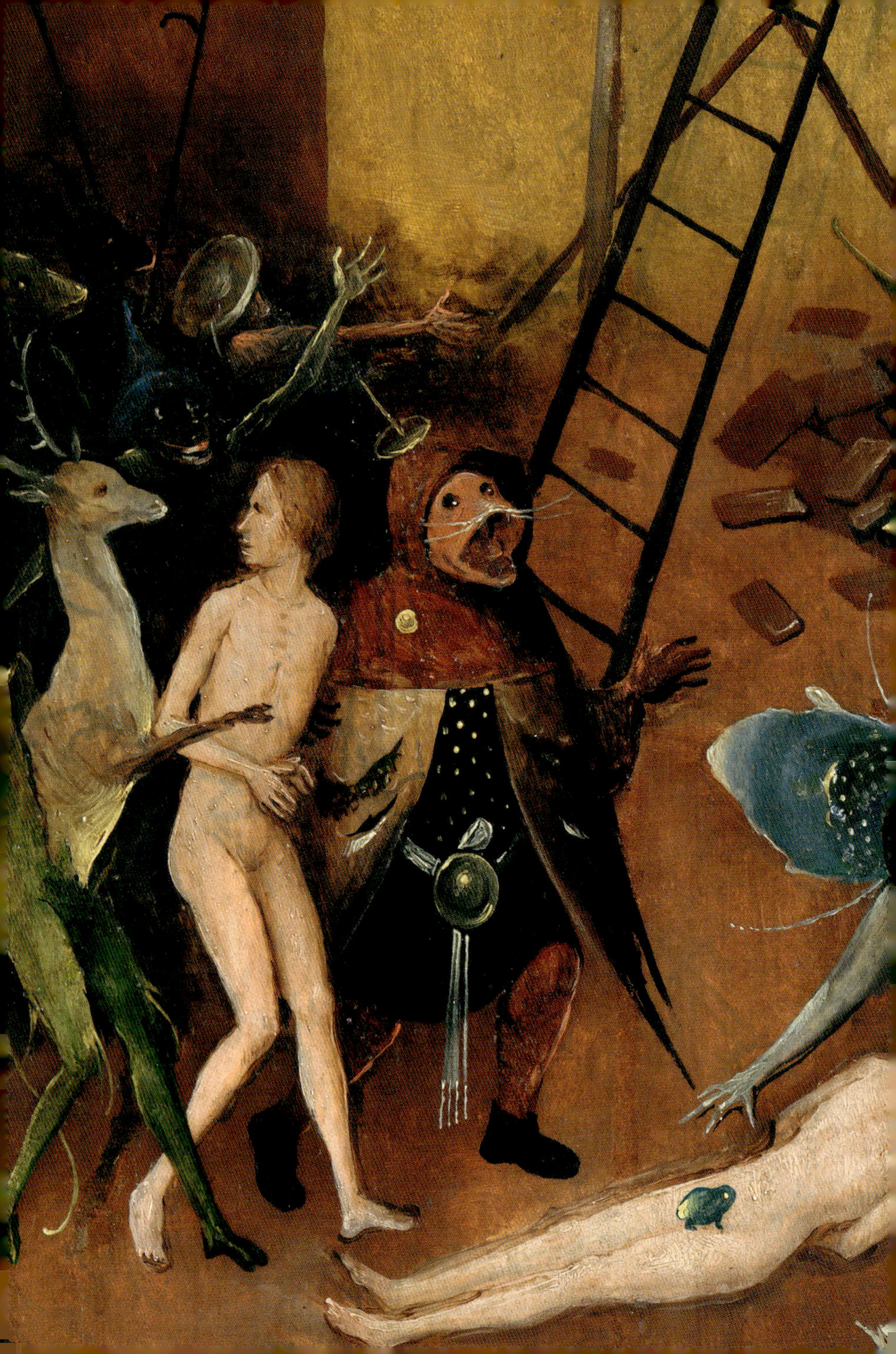

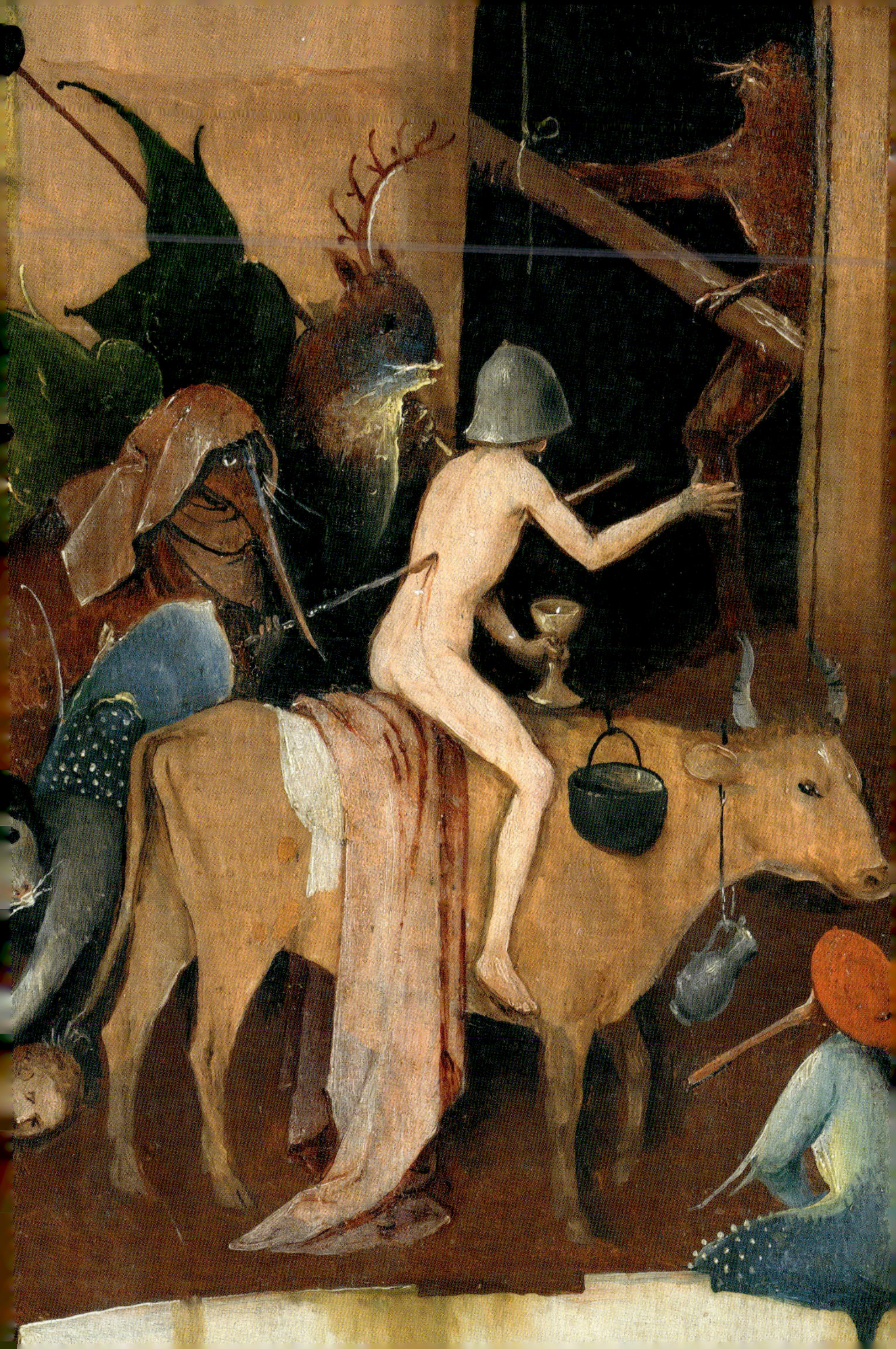

Epilogue: An enigmatic bequest

"In the portrayal of strange apparitions and hideous and terrifying dream worlds, the Fleming Hieronymus Bosch was unique and truly divine."

GIOVANNI PAOLO LOMAZZO, 1584

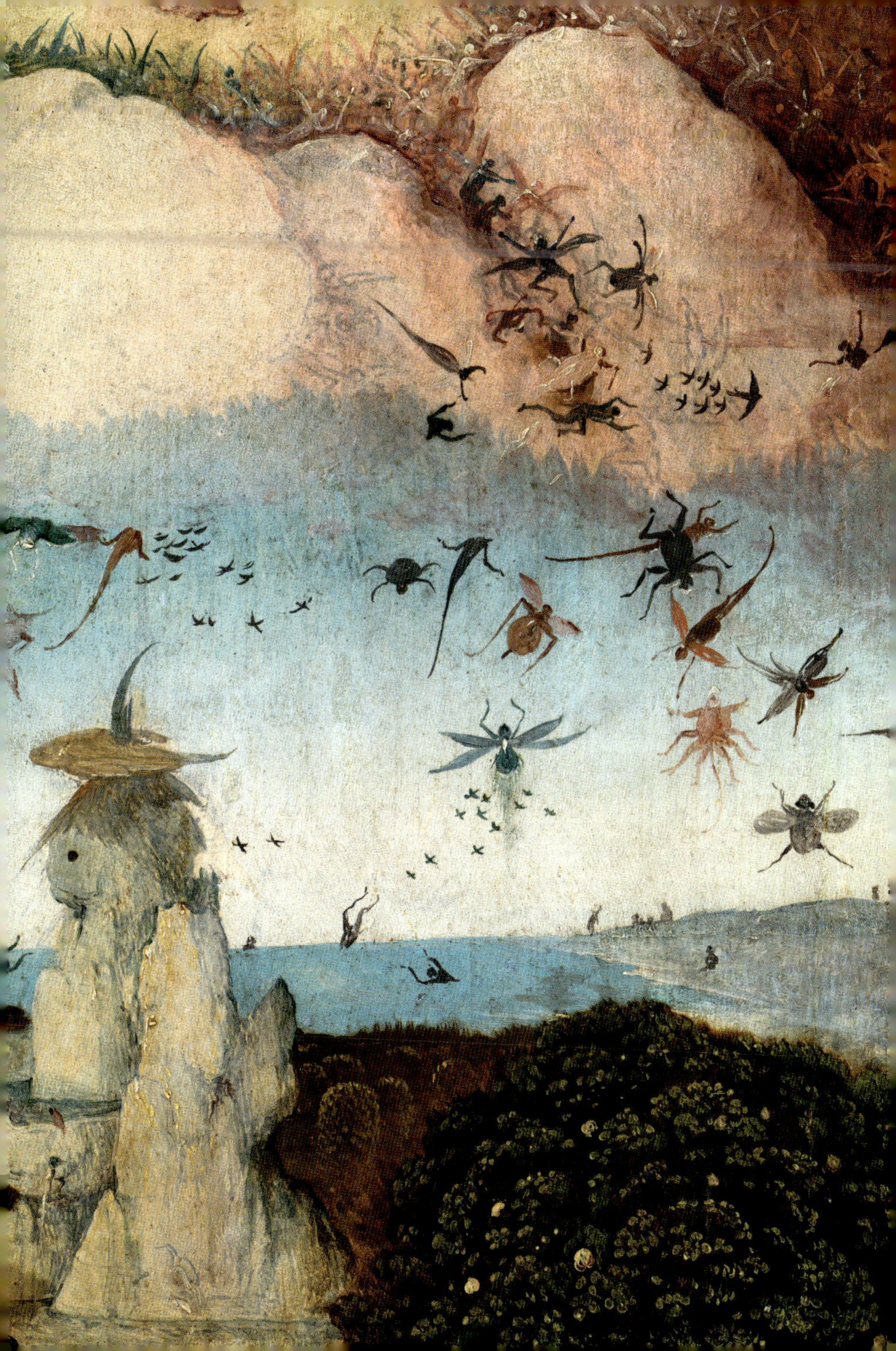

In the last few years of his life it would seem that Hieronymus Bosch increasingly left the execution of his commissions to his workshop. He probably employed assistants on a more or less permanent basis from 1499 at the latest, and certainly from around 1503–1505 (see document of 1503/04; cf. Cat. 12, 14, 17, 21, 22). Exactly how many individuals were involved and the nature and extent of their contribution to his paintings are questions that remain to be answered. One commission definitely carried out by the Bosch workshop is the *Triptych with Sts Job, Anthony and Jerome* (Cat. 22), which cites four existing works by Bosch and was produced around 1505. It seems logical to assume that other members of the van Aken "painter dynasty" were also active in the workshop. An especially likely candidate is Anthonis Goessens van Aken (*c.* 1478–1516), a nephew of Bosch (on his biography: van Dijck 2001a, p. 35; Vink 2001a, p. 96). Trained by his father, Goessen, he was probably competent enough to work for his uncle Hieronymus. In 1513/14 Anthonis made the effigy of Christ on a donkey that was pulled through the town during the Palm Sunday procession. He also executed a commission for the Brotherhood in 1514/15, and in 1515 painted a number of heraldic shields on behalf of the municipal authorities for the "Joyous Entrance" (*Joyeuse Entrée* or *Blijde Inkomst*) of Charles V on his first visit to 's-Hertogenbosch as Emperor, in July 1515.

The role of the workshop in the dissemination of Bosch's art is likewise largely unclear. There seems to have been a smooth transition from paintings issued by the workshop to paintings by followers of Bosch, i. e. to artists who operated within the same pictorial genre, copied Bosch's works and directly quoted or modified his motifs (Unverfehrt 1980, Gibson 1992, Mechelen 2003, Aikema 2001a). A work of particular interest for our understanding of Bosch's reception is the triptych of *The Last Judgement* (Cat. 26), which dates from *c.* 1515. In the closed position, the triptych shows *The Flagellation* (Cat. 26.1) on its exterior. It was not conceived as a dazzling piece of "artifice" intended purely for display purposes, but for traditional use with an everyday and a feast-day aspect. In the open position, it presents the Last Judgement with the Earthly Paradise on the left panel and Hell on the central and right panels, with Christ as Judge of the World enthroned above the whole. The work draws clearly – albeit without exact citations – upon pictorial motifs from Bosch's three great triptychs: the *Garden of Earthly Delights* (Cat. 11), the *Last Judgement* (Cat. 12) and *The Haywain* (Cat. 20). It is none the less clearly identified as Bosch's invention by the signature "jheronimus bosch" in the lower right corner of the central panel. While this does not prove that it was actually produced in Bosch's workshop, the painter demonstrates such a thorough knowledge of the master's oeuvre that he must either have worked for a while in the workshop or based his painting upon material taken from it. Whatever the case, he reinterprets his source in an independent fashion and with great technical sophistication. The number of works attributed to Hieronymus Bosch in inventories and records is astonishingly high (Tolnay 1965, Cinotti/Schlégl 1966, Vandenbroeck 2003, pp. 308–340). Even today the number of listed copies and imitations exceed the number of surviving Bosch originals by a factor of somewhere between 15:1 and 20:1 (cf. Unverfehrt 1980), allowing us to assume that not too many works remain unknown. How cautiously we must proceed in the case of archival references to works by Bosch, however, is demonstrated by the case of a painting presented, in 1516, to Margaret of Austria by a lady-in-waiting of Eleanor of Castile (1498–1558). In an inventory drawn up that same year, this gift is described as a medium-sized single panel of St Anthony ("*Ung moyen tableau de Sainct Anthoine*"; van Dijck 2001a, p. 92). In 1524 another inventory describes the same painting in more detail: St Anthony, surrounded by strange figures, is holding a crook with one arm and a book and a pair of spectacles in his hand (Eichberger 2002, p. 269, van Dijck 2001a, p. 93). This last attribute, in particular, carries only negative connotations when deployed by Bosch, for whom it symbolises external, sensory sight (see the devil in Cat. 3.2.1 and Cat. 10.4); the attribution of the panel in question to the painter from 's-Hertogenbosch thus seems implausible. Another inventory, from 1542, lists no fewer than five tapestries in the possession of King François I of France (1494–1547), all of them allegedly designed by Hieronymus Bosch (van Dijck 2001a, pp. 95–96, Kurz 1967, 's-Hertogenbosch 1967, pp. 28–37, Koldeweij/Vermet/Vandenbroeck 2001): a Temptation of St Anthony, a Haywain (p. 336), the *Garden of Earthly Delights*, a St Martin and a war elephant. The first four can today be admired in Madrid, while the fifth has come down to us as both a print and a painting. Only the tapestry of the *Garden of Earthly Delights* is a copy after Bosch; the others simply imitate his style. Bosch's originality and evident popularity led to the emergence, over the course of the first half of the 16th century, of a number of followers, in particular in Antwerp and Brussels. These artists met the demands of the art market with many dozens of paintings and prints, often signed with Bosch's name, and thereby helped shape our image of the master right down to the present day. The most important of these followers included Joachim Patinir, Herri met de Bles and Pieter Bruegel the Elder in Antwerp and the Verbeeck brothers in Mechelen. Other masters who borrowed heavily from Bosch's themes and motifs were Jan Mandijn (*c.* 1500–1559), Pieter Huys (*c.* 1520–1581/84) and probably also Marcellus Coffermans (1520–1578). Others, again, made overt copies of Bosch's works, as in the case of Michiel Coxie (1499–1592), who worked for the Habsburgs.

The research carried out into Bosch's life and works to date has succeeded in shedding much light on the following: Bosch as a member of the van Aken family of painters, his financial circumstances and his social sphere (van Dijck 1973 and 2001b, Blondé/Vlieghe 1989, Gerlach 1988, Vink 2001a/b, Huys Janssen 2007), his iconography (Bax, Gibson, Marijnissen, Vandenbroeck, de Bruyn and many other individual studies; see the bibliographical listings in the catalogue of works), stylistic analyses aimed at establishing the

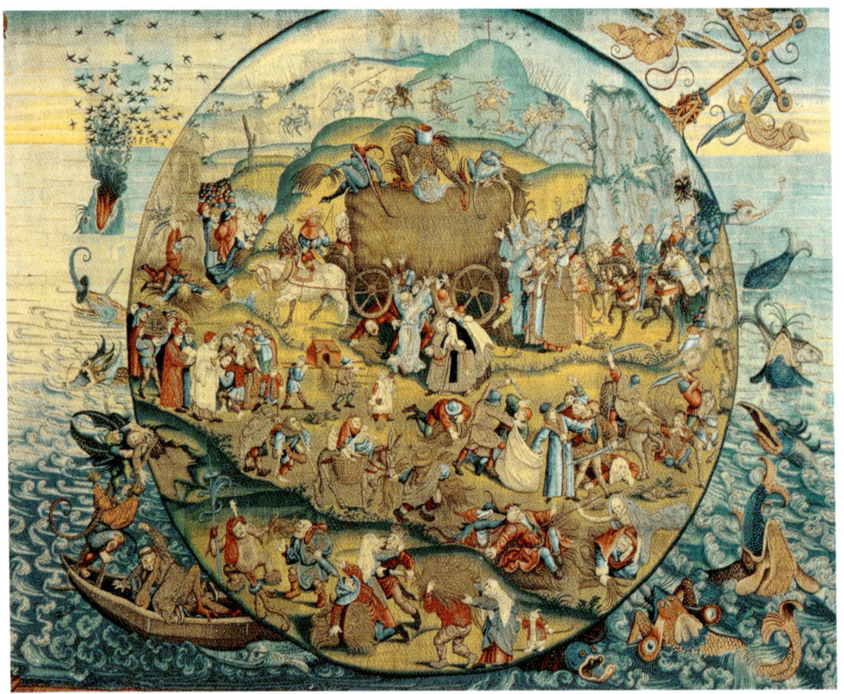

Brussels Workshop, **Haywain in the Terrestrial Globe**, *c.* 1550–1570 (design before 1542)
Tapestry, 298 x 373 cm / 117⅜ x 146⅞ in. Madrid, Patrimonio Nacional, Palacio Real

Page 333
Detail from: **The Haywain**, *c.* 1510–1515
Left inner wing: **The Genesis of Evil and the Loss of Paradise** (see ill. pp. 320/321)

authenticity of works attributed to Bosch (Filedt Kok 1972/73, Unverfehrt 1980, Koreny 2002/03 and 2012) and technical investigations in the context of restoration campaigns (van Schoute et al.). Extensive scientific analyses of the work lie at the core of the Bosch Research and Conservation Project, launched in 2010 as part of *Jheronimus Bosch 500*, a ten-year international programme marking the 500th anniversary of Bosch's death in 1516. The aim of this project is to yield new insights in response to questions of attribution and the artist's working process.

With regard to areas of research still remaining to be explored, it is only possible to offer a subjective opinion here. There is still much to be learned about the members of the Bosch workshop and their contribution to individual works, as also the matter of whether and to what extent they perpetuated the master's ideas and pictorial motifs during their time in his workshop and thereafter. The paintings firmly attributed to the workshop and its members (Cat. 21–28) constitute an important point of reference in this respect, including, above all, an explanation of the diverse types of underdrawing. In considering the questions of style that inevitably play a role here, it will be necessary to apply a complex concept of style itself, which takes account of the division of labour within the workshop and the dependence of the painter and his art works upon the demands and expectations of the patron and the subject matter, function and stylistic genre. Colour symbolism and combination in Bosch's works have so far received almost no attention.

Thanks to the discoveries made by scholars over the last few decades, however, it is already possible to situate Bosch clearly within the context of the society, culture and prevailing ideas of his day and to identify some of the factors that contributed towards the "Bosch phenomenon". These shaping factors include: the regional character of art in 15th-century 's-Hertogenbosch, away from the major centres of art; the town's pronounced religious climate, due to the local presence of monastic orders and religious communities; the ideas of Christian reform and Humanism; the increasingly varied and complex expectations placed upon art; and the growing competition among artists, to which Bosch, as the third eldest son, evidently responded with ambition and self-confidence. For him, the Brotherhood of Our Blessed Lady and its social network also provided the link to his princely patrons. The Spaniard Diego de Guevara, from 1496 an external member of the Brotherhood of Our Blessed Lady, also acted as an important intermediary.

From a broader art-historical perspective, Bosch may be assigned to the wide-ranging and multi-faceted tradition of the moral satire, the absurd and the grotesque, as represented by drolleries in the 15th and 16th century visual arts. This same tradition was familiar to Bosch's followers and is also present in literature before and after Bosch, in such well-known comic and didactic works as *Der Ring* by Heinrich Wittenwiler (active around 1400), the satires and sermons centred upon German proverbs by Thomas Murner (1475–1537), *Baldo* by Teofilo Folengo (1491–1544) and *Gargantua* and *Pantagruel* by François Rabelais (*c.* 1494–1553). Where beauty, harmony and illusionism were the highest ideals, namely in the Netherlandish painting of the 15th century and the art of the Renaissance, it was equally possible to invoke their polar opposites: an anti-classical aesthetic, and an anti-classical concept of art that deliberately offended against the principles of harmony – in line with the Christian notion that outer beauty was the beauty of a transitory world, whereas true harmony was present in the soul of a heart purified by truth. Hieronymus Bosch took the grotesque as an artistic and indeed aesthetic principle and sought to renew pictorial art on a Christian basis, rather than on that of Antiquity. Even if he was neither a non-conformist nor an avant-gardist, he still went against the current of his day – to produce an oeuvre of timeless magnetism.

Catalogue of paintings

"For God often gives the ability to learn and the wit to make something good to [an artist] who has no equal in his day, and whose like has not been seen for many a year previously, nor shall soon come again."

ALBRECHT DÜRER, 1528

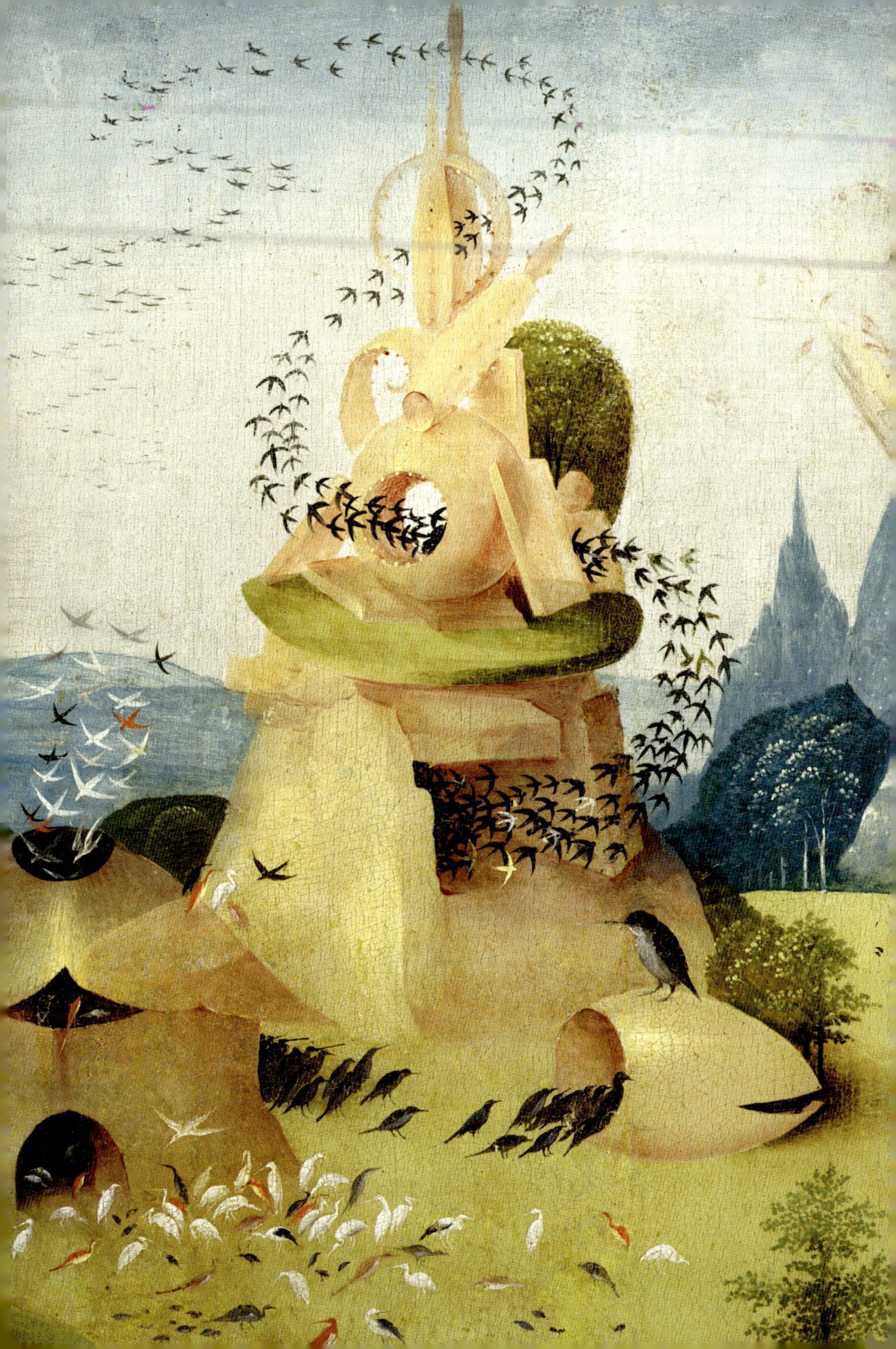

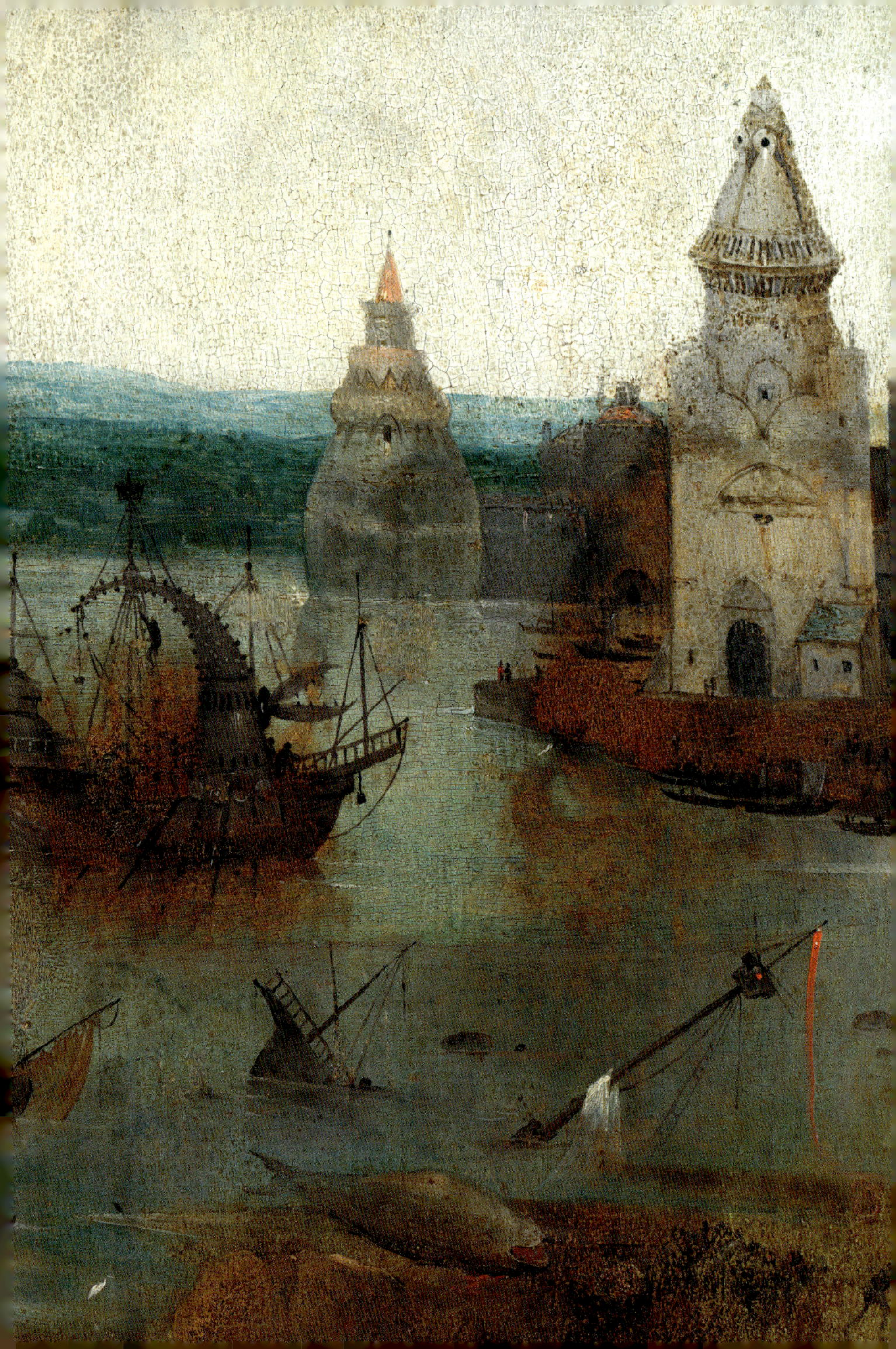

Notes on the catalogue

The individual works making up Bosch's œuvre have received far from equal attention. This may be on account of their respective size, the condition in which they have come down us, or the familiarity or strangeness of their iconography. Bosch's triptychs present a particular challenge for the viewer: the artist interpreted this format with such freedom, and infused it with such complexity, that these works may be regarded not so much as large paintings than as pictorial cycles.

Alongside iconographic studies and the examination of Bosch's œuvre within the context of the history of ideas, Bosch scholarship has focused intensively on the personal style and developmental phases of his art. In the course of several decades findings based on connoisseurship have been complemented by ever more objective methods of assessment (dendrochronology, archival research), enabling Bosch's works to be dated more accurately and many previous attributions to be dismissed, leaving almost no works whose origin is still disputed. Bosch's œuvre as recognised today comprises just twenty paintings and eight drawings. Half a dozen panel paintings and as many drawings are attributed to members of his workshop. Occasional attempts are nevertheless made to reduce Bosch's œuvre yet further and even to distinguish between the work of Bosch and the work of a particularly gifted apprentice (Koreny 2002/03, 2012). Not included in this catalogue are the numerous works documented only in inventories of the 16th and 17th centuries, since their attribution to Bosch is in many cases highly dubious.

In his annotated bibliography Gibson (1983) systematically assembles all the publications on Bosch and provides a brief summary of their contents. The standard work by Marijnissen, which has appeared in several languages and editions (first English edition 1987), continues to provide a well-organised insight into Bosch's paintings and the prevailing state of research. In our catalogue, attribution and chronology are essentially based on the work of Unverfehrt (1980) and the publications accompanying the 2001

Page 339
The Garden of Earthly Delights, *c.* 1503
Left inner wing: **Paradise and the Creation of Eve** (see ill. pp. 188)

Page 340
Detail from: **Triptych of the Crucified Female Martyr (Sint-Ontcommer)**, *c.* 1505–1515
Right inner wing (see ill. pp. 310/311)

Rotterdam exhibition (Koldeweij/Vermet/Vandenbroeck 2001; Koldeweij/Vermet/Kooij 2001, pp. 96–131), as well as on the individual studies listed under the corresponding catalogue number. Between now and 2016 we can expect further new insights to emerge from the work of the Bosch Research and Conservation Project, under whose aegis comprehensive documentation of the technical analyses of Bosch's paintings is also being compiled (Spronk 2011). Cinotti (1966), Vandenbroeck (2003) and the various publications by van Schoute all shed useful light on the question of attribution and on Bosch's followers, including lists of works.

With regard to chronology, dendrochronological analyses – i.e. the calculation of the felling date of the wood used for a particular panel as deduced from its tree rings – make it possible to establish the earliest point in time from which a panel could have been available as a painting support. Other factors playing a role in the chronological ordering of Bosch's œuvre include the identity of the patron, the function and complexity of the work, the pictorial motifs cited within it, and the technique and style of the underdrawing and painting. Datings based on the general criteria of a stylistic development have not, in my view, proved sufficiently objective.

Bosch's chief patrons are to be found among the ruling nobility of the Low Countries and among the civic secular and secular-clerical elite. His greatest collector, without a doubt, was Philip II of Spain (1527–1598): inventories show that Philip owned 26 paintings now viewed as either by Bosch or attributed to him (Silva Maroto 2001; Vandenbroeck 2001a).

Bosch also left his traces in the literature of the 16th and 17th centuries. Salazar (1955), Heidenreich (1970), Cinotti (1966), Marijnissen (1987) and the source texts themselves (see Appendix) shed light on the history of Bosch's literary reception and interpretation.

The number of surviving works by Bosch's followers exceeds the master's own production more than tenfold. Unverfehrt's study of the reception of Bosch's art in the early 16th century, written at the start of the 1970s and published in 1980, lists well over 250 works by followers of Bosch – from workshop products and copies to paraphrases and paintings in the *diableries* style established by the master. The number of known copies of Bosch's best-known works is impressive in itself: a good thirty of the *Temptation of St Anthony* (Cat. 10) and about a dozen of the *Garden of Earthly Delights* (Cat. 11). An ambitious copy of the latter also exists as part of a series of four tapestries after Bosch originals or replicas (Kurz 1967; 's-Hertogenbosch 1967, pp. 28–37; see pp. 336). In contrast, only two copies or paraphrases are known to exist of the Vienna *Last Judgement* (Cat. 13) (one of them, however, attributed to no less an artist than Lucas Cranach the Elder), a further two copies or paraphrases of the Frankfurt *Ecce Homo* (Cat. 4) and three of the Vienna *Small Christ Carrying the Cross* (Cat. 9).

The catalogue is divided into two parts. It starts with the paintings considered by the author to be original works by Bosch; it then covers the paintings by Bosch's workshop and followers, where attribution occasionally remains a contentious issue. Two copies of the *Wedding at Cana* are also included, since they allow us to reconstruct the lost original by Bosch. The works within each part of the catalogue are presented, as far as possible, in chronological order. Unless otherwise stated, the dimensions given do not include the frame.

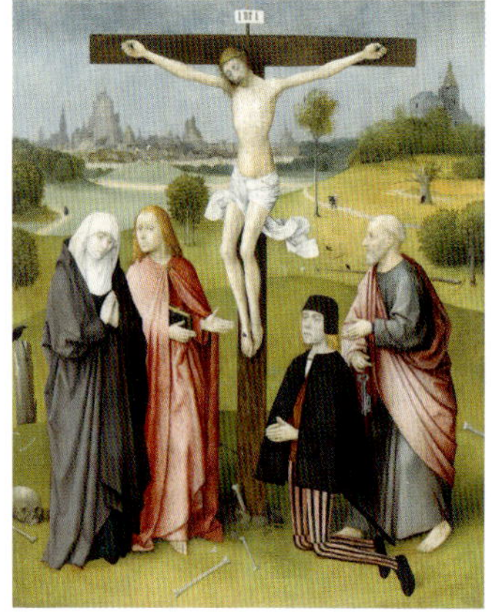
1

Catalogue of paintings – autograph works

1

Crucifixion with Saints and Donor, *c.* 1485–1490
Oil on panel (oak), 74.7 x 61 cm / 29½ x 24 in.
Brussels, Musées royaux des Beaux-Arts de Belgique/Koninklijke Musea voor Schone Kunsten van België, inv. no. 6639

The painting shows the Crucifixion with the Virgin and St John the Evangelist as intercessors on the left and a kneeling donor with St Peter on the right, in front of a spacious landscape with a contemporary 15th-century city silhouetted on the skyline. Where the panel originally stood, what function it served and within what context, are all unknown. It has not yet been possible to identify the donor. Since St Peter is standing directly beside him as his patron saint, it is likely that the donor's own forename is Petrus, Pe(e)ter, Pieter or Piet. In the absence of documentary evidence, provenance or a coat of arms, however, this does not really bring us any closer to an answer. The donor's manner of dress provides a clue to his social status and the period in which the panel was painted. His short cape, vertically striped hose, hat and sword allow us to conclude that he was a relatively young man from courtly civic circles, vested with judicial policing powers, who came from a social class either directly below or among the lowest echelons of the aristocracy or patriciate. Such clothing ceased to be worn in the 16th century, except by landsknecht mercenaries. Art historians are almost unanimous in viewing the *Crucifixion* as an early work. The argument for an early dating (*c.* 1477–1483 or later) is supported by the results of dendrochronological analysis, the donor's style of dress and the artistic pretensions of the panel as a whole. The background landscape is conceived in a similar fashion to the right-

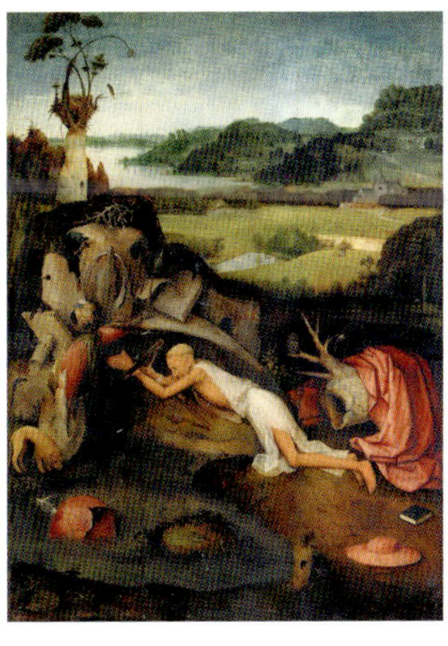

2

hand inner wing of the Boston *Ecce Homo* (Cat. 21), making 1499 the *terminus ante quem*. In its theme and function, the *Crucifixion* shows that Bosch also produced thoroughly "normal" pictures in line with the requirements of his day. The surprising conventionality of the composition may, however, be seen as a factor not only of the panel's presumed early dating, but also of the donor's social status and the conceptually conservative nature of the ubiquitous Crucifixion theme, which left little room for innovation. A greater degree of artistic originality is found only in the landscape, a prominent factor within the composition with details that are not as idyllic as in most 15th-century Netherlandish painting. The middle ground, in particular, contains a hint of the more typical Bosch: strolling couples and tokens of death such as bones, skulls and ravens are dotted about in a seemingly random fashion between the distant city and the mound of Calvary. The figure of the donor was at one stage overpainted with an image of St Mary Magdalene, subsequently removed during restoration in 1966/67, which may explain the poor quality of the portrait of the donor's face. A "painting on panel with the Crucifixion of Christ, done by Hieronymus Bosch with a wooden frame", documented in 1664 in 's-Hertogenbosch, may have been the panel discussed here. Whatever the case, in the 19th and 20th centuries the work was in a number of private collections in Brussels, before entering the Musées royaux. See also pp. *21*, 26/27.

LITERATURE: Marijnissen 1987, pp. 346–351; Koldeweij 2001, p. 81; van Schoute/Verougstraete/Garrido 2001, p. 116; Stroo 2001, pp. 71–83; Fischer 2009, pp. 81–84.

2

St Jerome in the Wilderness (St Jerome in Penitence), *c.* 1485–1490
Oil on panel (oak), 80.1 x 60.6 cm / 31½ x 23⅞ in.
Ghent, Museum voor Schone Kunsten, inv. no. 1908 H

St Jerome lies semi-naked on the ground in a sort of hollow with a hill behind him, surrounded by stone slabs, plants and animals. Beyond, there extends a sweeping central European landscape. Born Eusebius Sophronius Hieronymus (347–419/20) in Stridon, St Jerome was one of the four Latin Doctors of the Church in Late Antiquity. His authority rested upon his translation of the Bible into Latin (the Vulgate), and he was considered by Humanists to be the prototype of the learned scholar. In the visual arts he is often portrayed in his study, as in the paintings by Domenico Ghirlandaio (1449–1494) and Antonello da Messina (*c.* 1430–1479) and the engraving by Albrecht Dürer (1471–1528), or during the ascetic period of his life, as in the unfinished painting by Leonardo da Vinci (1452–1519) of St Jerome chastising himself. One of the few depictions of the saint from the Low Countries in the 15th century is the painting by Rogier van der Weyden (1399/1400–1464).

Bosch steers Netherlandish art in a new direction here, too, with this variation on the theme of St Jerome. In her in-depth study, Ruppel (1988) shows how Bosch has based his iconography on the Bible and mystic religious texts, and how – even in a relatively small work such as *St Jerome* – he has embedded the devotional aspect of the panel firmly in the details of his composition.

The parameters for the panel's dating (1476–1482 or later) are established by dendrochronology and by the re-use of the pictorial motif of St Jerome in a sort of hollow in the *c.* 1505 triptych of *Sts Job, Anthony and Jerome* (Cat. 22). Measured against the evolution of Bosch's œuvre as a whole, *St Jerome in the Wilderness* – although already displaying an innovative streak – is both smaller and less complex than Bosch's other paintings and is thus probably an early work. This conclusion is supported by its stylistic handling in general and by the treatment of the landscape in particular. The unpainted margin is missing from the top and bottom, but the picture itself has survived intact and has only suffered small areas of wear, which have been lightly retouched. The work was owned by a family in northern France before being purchased by the Ghent museum in 1908.

See also pp. *29*, 31–33.

LITERATURE: Tolnay 1965, p. 34; Graziani 1983; Marijnissen 1987, pp. 388–393; Ruppel 1988; Wiebel 1988; van Schoute/Verboomen 2000, pp. 107, 211; Koldeweij/Vermet/Vandenbroeck 2001, pp. 22, 168, 173; van Schoute/Verougstraete/Garrido 2001, p. 117; Klein 2001, p. 124.

3

Two small shutters of a carved altarpiece for the Brotherhood of Our Blessed Lady, after 1488

Bosch painted the two small panels showing *St John the Baptist* (Cat. 3.1) and *St John on Patmos* (Cat. 3.2) on behalf of the 's-Hertogenbosch Brotherhood of Our Blessed Lady or one of its members. They served as shutters that, when closed, concealed the upper scenes of the wooden altarpiece carved by Adriaen van Wesel (*c.* 1417–between 1490 and 1499) for the Brotherhood's chapel in the church of Sint-Jan (pp. 24, *24*, *38*, 40; Halsema-Kubes 1980; Koldeweij 2001). The church was dedicated to St John the Baptist and St John the Evangelist, the latter being traditionally equated with the author of *Revelation* and serving as the Brotherhood's chief patron saint alongside the Virgin.

The commission was not awarded by the Brotherhood as a whole, or at least not in the first instance, since the painting of *St John the Baptist* originally included a donor figure, subsequently painted out by Bosch himself. This man appeared not among the brethren or as their representative, but as an individual. It was common for Brotherhood members to make personal donations to the furnishing and use of their chapel: in 1503/04, for example, the knight Jan Back (d. 10

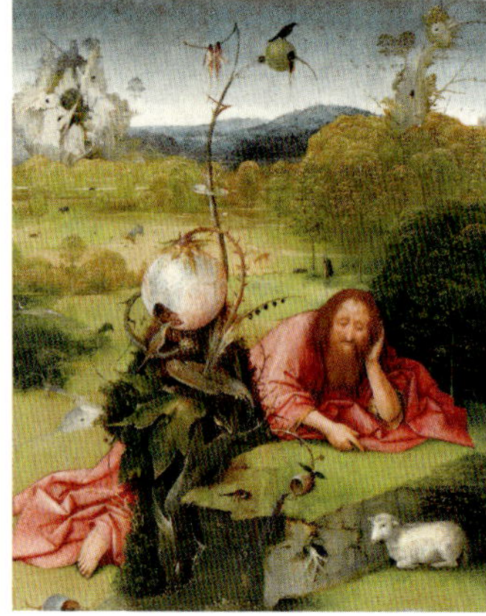
3.1

February 1509) commissioned Bosch's journeymen to produce his escutcheon for just such a purpose. In 1509/10 his widow Adriana van Wylic endowed the same chapel with a Requiem Mass, something that is mentioned in the *Regulations* printed in 1518, which otherwise names only the Brotherhood's collective contributions (*Regulations*, fol. 5r).

Dendrochronological analysis has established 1489 as the earliest possible year in which the two panels could have been painted and thereby provides an important basis for their dating. At this same point in time – during the accounting year 1488/89 – the Brotherhood purchased two wood panels from a carpenter with its own funds. It is likely that Bosch painted the two *St John* pictures on these panels at some point thereafter (Vink 2001a, p. 101; Wattel 2001, p. 13). Since this was the first commission that the Brotherhood awarded to Bosch after he had been sworn in as a member, it may be assumed that the artist executed them promptly out of a sense of obligation and gratitude.

Elevated to a bishopric in 1559, 's-Hertogenbosch fell to the Protestants in 1629, after which van Wesel's altarpiece lost its function. By no later than the 19th century it had been dismantled and its components scattered. Parts are today housed in Berlin and Amsterdam. Only the carved reliefs at the top of the altarpiece, taking the form of shallow cabinets with Bosch's *St John* panels as their doors, still remain in the possession of the Brotherhood of Our Blessed Lady and are preserved in its headquarters in 's-Hertogenbosch.

See also pp. 38, 39.

LITERATURE: Halsema-Kubes 1980, 1992; Koldeweij 2001, pp. 70–78; Hoffman 2008.

3.1

St John the Baptist (in Meditation), after 1488

Oil on panel (oak), 49 x 40.5 cm / 19¼ x 16 in. (trimmed along the lower edge,

originally *c.* 63 x 43 cm / 24¾ x 17 in.)
Madrid, Fundación Lázaro Galdiano,
inv. no. 8155
Left wing, interior

St John the Baptist is propped up on one elbow in a semi-recumbent position on the ground. A thistle-like plant with a fruit resembling a pomegranate rises in front of him in the central foreground, inpinging on the viewer's attention. The plant, which has been the object of several studies (Clark 1994, Graziani 1983), is an imaginary creation that borrows from actual flora. The focus of interest now is not so much on identifying the plant as on determining its meaning and purpose within the composition as a whole – apart from its role in disguising and concealing the donor, whose figure originally appeared at this spot. On the basis of studies of the symbolism and rhetorical function of individual elements in other Bosch paintings, we may assume that this dominant pictorial motif, which embraces one large and three small fruits, as well as three birds pecking at the plant and one lying dead in front of it, has an explicative purpose and illustrates three different states of the human soul between salvation and damnation. The plant's main fruit, round and whitish in colour and with one of the birds pecking a hole in its lower left side, reappears in a very similar form on the left inner wing of the *Haywain* triptych (Cat. 20.2).

X-rays of the painting (Fúster Sabater 1996, van Schoute/Verboomen 2000) clearly reveal – in a paint layer underneath the thistle-like plant – the figure of a man dressed in the manner of the educated, probably secular-clerical upper middle class, the stratum of society that was found within the Brotherhood and which we can recognize in the persons of Peeter Scheyve (see Cat. 6) and Peter van Os (see Cat. 21). It is unclear whether and to what extent the overpainting of this single donor figure delayed the panel's completion. At some point in or after the 17th century the

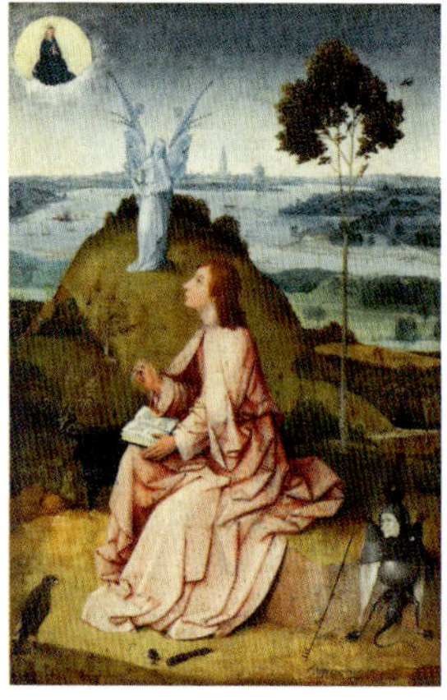
3.2.1

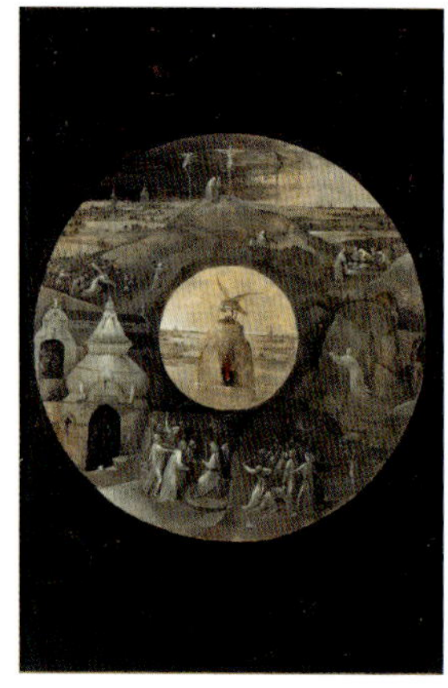
3.2.2

front and rear surfaces of the panel were separated. A strip was also sawn off along the lower edge, reducing the height by about a quarter. The picture is recorded as having been in the collection of José Lázaro Galdiano in 1920. Following his death in 1947, the panel went on display in 1951 in the newly founded Museo Lázaro Galdiano in Madrid, where it remains. See also pp. 37, 40, 41.

LITERATURE: Graziani 1983; Marijnissen 1987, pp. 394–401; Clark 1994; Fúster Sabater 1996; van Schoute/Verboomen 2000, pp. 108–109, 181, no. 18; Klein 2001, p. 124; van Schoute/Verougstraete/Garrido 2001, p. 117; Fischer 2009, pp. 275–278, 334–337.

3.2

St John on Patmos (exterior: The Eye of God with Scenes from the Passion), after 1488

Oil on panel (oak), 63 x 43.3 cm / 24¾ x 17 in.
(exterior tondo: ∅ 39 cm / 15⅜ in.)
Berlin, Staatliche Museen, Gemäldegalerie, inv. no. 1647A
Right-hand wing
3.2.1 Interior: St John the Evangelist on Patmos
3.2.2 Exterior: The Eye of God with Scenes from the Passion

The picture on the interior surface of the right wing shows St John witnessing the Revelation. The anecdotal motif of the devil, who is contemplating stealing the saint's inkwell as a way of sabotaging the divine plan for salvation, is inspired by a legend about the saint that was very popular in the Low Countries and northern France (Gelder 1972).

The exterior shows a stylised, all-seeing eye of God, executed in grisaille. At the centre, as it were in the pupil of the eye, a pelican is feeding its young. The surrounding iris shows scenes from the Passion. Beyond its circumference, the white of the eyeball gives way to unrelieved darkness.

St John on Patmos bears what is probably the

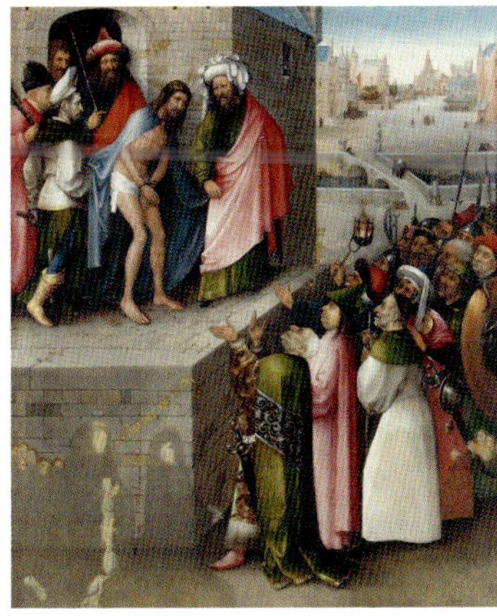
4

earliest surviving example of Bosch's signature on a work: it is signed "jheronimus bosch" in the bottom right corner. The panel was purchased by the Berlin Museums in 1907 from a London private collection.

See also pp. *42*, 43, 44, *45*, 46–48.

LITERATURE: Bax 1953; Gelder 1972; Marijnissen 1987, pp. 284–291; Bock 1996, p. 21; Asmus/Grosshans 1998, pp. 156–159; Jacobs 2000; van Schoute/Verboomen 2000, pp. 110–113, 176; Klein 2001, p. 125; Fischer 2009, pp. 90, 235–236, 339–341.

4

Ecce Homo with Donors, *c.* 1490–1495
Oil on panel (oak), 71.1 x 60.5 cm /
28 x 23¾ in.
Frankfurt am Main, Städel Museum,
inv. no. 1577

This particular *Ecce Homo* is among the few works in which Bosch employs inscriptions (for the others, see Cat. 11.1, 15 and 18). In contrast to the *Ecce Homo* by Bosch's workshop (Cat. 21.3), the situation is here clarified and reinforced by means of Latin phrases in gold lettering. "*Ecce Homo*" ("Behold the man!") is addressed to the public both inside and outside the picture and is answered blindly by the rabble on the right side with "*Crucifige eum*" ("Crucify him!"). Conversely, the donors at lower left (and right) pray fervently for deliverance with "*Salva nos xp*[=Christ]*e redemptor*" ("Save us, Christ the Redeemer"). The picture thereby articulates its primary eschatological purpose of securing for the donors a place in the hereafter. In 1983, following the removal of earlier overpainting, the donors were again made visible, as pale shadows. The head of the donor family, a patrician, is seen kneeling towards the front on the left side, a relatively large figure. The similar-sized figure behind him is probably his eldest son, a Dominican monk, and behind him in turn are six more sons extending to the far left. His wife and six daughters are represented as very small

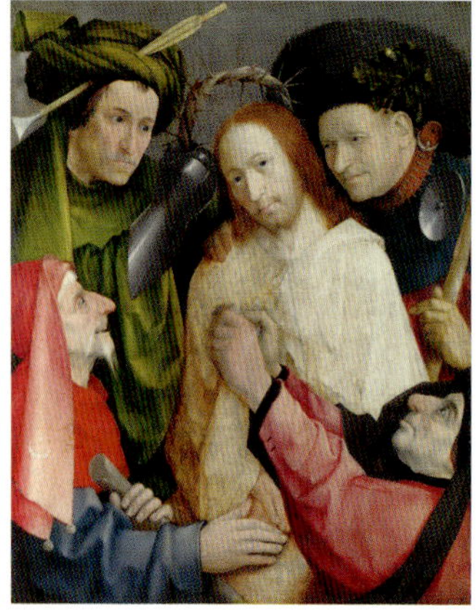

5

figures on the right side. In three other paintings (Cat. 3.1, Cat. 13.1, Cat. 14), the donors were overpainted during Bosch's own lifetime either by the master himself or his workshop; in the case of the present *Ecce Homo*, however, they were only painted out at a later date, once the picture had lost its original function, probably in the early 16th century. Dendrochronological analysis indicates that the picture must have been produced after 1470. And comparison with the Boston *Ecce Homo* (Cat. 21) suggests that it was painted before 1499. It is generally dated to the early 1490s on the grounds of its stylistic development and artistic accomplishment.

The underdrawing, executed with a brush, contains a number of pentimenti, above all in the background. They include a double semi-circle, not found in the final painting, which may have been intended to represent an arched gateway, as frequently found in the background of 15th-century *Ecce Homo* scenes. In the process of painting, Bosch appears to have opted for an unimpeded view across the townscape, such as he favours in other works. An illuminating example of how Bosch's approach to landscape differed from that of other early painters can be been in the small pictorial motif of a couple who have their backs turned to the viewer and are looking into the depths of the picture.

There are at least two copies or paraphrases of the picture without the donors, of which the one in the Rijksmuseum in Amsterdam dates from *c.* 1530–1550 and is documented from the middle of the 16th century onwards as being in the possession of the Brigittine convent in Koudewater, near 's-Hertogenbosch. The original was therefore probably destined for 's-Hertogenbosch or somewhere in the neighbourhood, although its provenance can only be traced back to the start of the 20th century, when it arrived in Berlin from a Belgian private collection; in 1917 it was purchased by the Städelscher Museums-Verein.

See also pp. *49*, 56, 58.

LITERATURE: Unverfehrt 1980, pp. 90, 262–263, no. 50; Sander 1993, pp. 28–45; Marijnissen 1987, pp. 368–377; van Schoute/ Verboomen 2000, pp. 202–203; Klein 2001, p. 123; Fischer 2009, pp. 89, 278–280.

5

Christ Mocked (The Crowning with Thorns), *c.* 1495

Oil on panel (oak), 73.5 x 59.1 cm / 28⅞ x 23¼ in.

London, National Gallery, inv. no. NG 4744

The symmetrically constructed painting shows Christ at its centre, tightly surrounded by four guards, one in each corner. The nature of the system according to which these four figures have been characterised is unclear (Marijnissen 1987). The suggestion that they represent the four temperaments (Dixon 2003) is unconvincing. It is true that the figure at lower right could be viewed as a sanguine type on account of his bulbous nose, the grim-faced figure at lower left as a choleric, the man at upper left with the pursed lips as a phlegmatic, and his counterpart with the furrowed brow at upper right as a melancholic. Other than these specific details, however, the remaining characteristics and attributes of the four men do not correspond to the usual pictorial conventions (cf. Lütke Notarp 1998). Nor does the answer appear to lie with physiognomy. In this system, large, bulging eyes, such as those exhibited by the man at upper left, are associated both with jealousy and with shameless, disobedient and indolent behaviour (Braekman 1970, p. 124). This last trait is associated with the phlegmatic type in the theory of the four temperaments. According to physiognomy, however, indolence (along with foolishness) was also signalled by large lips, such as those displayed by the man at lower right, who would therefore likewise be characterised as a phlegmatic (Braekman 1970, p. 129). When applied to the men tormenting Christ in Bosch's painting, in

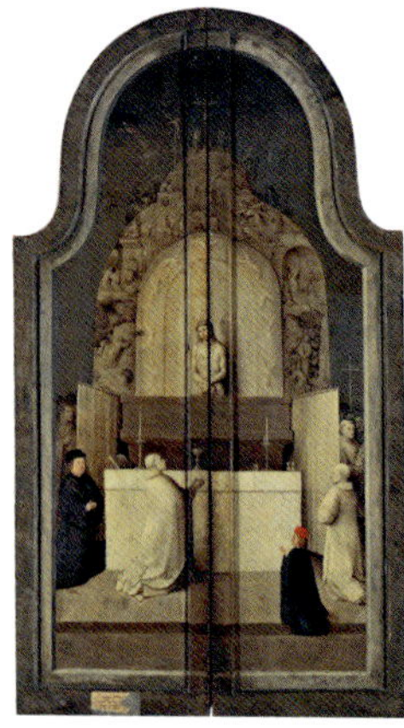

6.1

other words, the theories of physiognomy and the temperaments lead to contradictory conclusions. The four figures could also be interpreted as a Muslim, a Jew, a heathen and a personification of eternal death (anticlockwise from bottom left; Marijnissen 1987).

The dating is based on the painting's more ambitious character yet still relatively small format, and on the size and monumentality of the figures. The attribution to Bosch has occasionally been rejected in the past, either on the grounds that the panel does not appear sufficiently grotesque or because the position of Christ's arm seems clumsy. This detail nevertheless follows the literary sources (Psalm 22:14 and 17), and the arms of Christ's four tormentors are all anatomically correct. The Christ here mirrors the corresponding figure in the Crowning with Thorns scene found at upper left in the Passion scenes in the *Mass of St Gregory* (Cat. 6.1). The top paint layer has worn away in places, as is particularly evident in Christ's pale cloak. Here, the bluish underdrawing shimmers through, revealing a number of pentimenti vis-à-vis the final painting. The staff held by the man at lower left, for example, was originally longer, while the man at top right had both his right and his left hands on Christ's shoulders. The underdrawing also contains a preliminary design for a St Christopher and the Christ Child seen in frontal view (Campbell 1999). The painting was in a private collection in Britain up to the beginning of the 20th century, and was then in Rome, before being purchased by the National Gallery in 1934.

See also pp. *59*, 60, 61.

LITERATURE: Schmidt 1960; Ringbom 1965; Wuyts 1968; Braekman 1970; Marrow 1977, 1979; Unverfehrt 1980, p. 145; Marijnissen 1987, pp. 352–359; Lütke Notarp 1998; Campbell 1999; Bray 2000, pp. 114–115; van Schoute/ Verboomen 2000, pp. 64–66, 176, 199–202; Klein 2001, p. 124; Dixon 2003, p. 130; Fischer 2009, pp. 337–339; Spronk 2011.

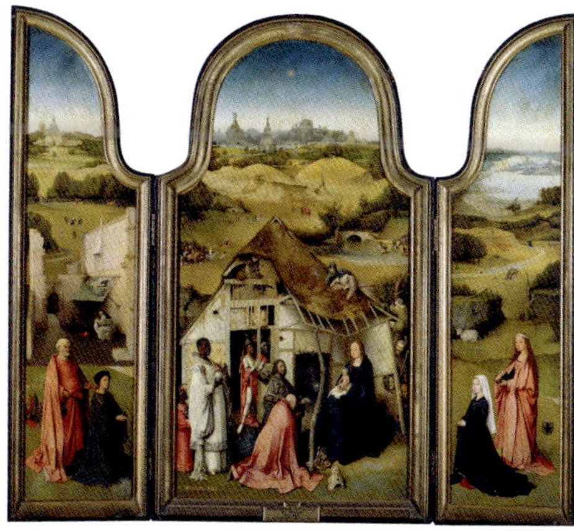

6.2–6.4

6

Adoration of the Magi with Donors (exterior: Mass of St Gregory with Donors), *c.* 1496/97

Oil on panel (oak), 146.7 x 84 cm / 57¾ x 33 in. (central panel), 146.7 x 42.3 cm / 57¾ x 16½ in. (wings, including frame)

Madrid, Museo Nacional del Prado, inv. no. 2048

6.1 Outer wings: Mass of St Gregory with Scenes from the Passion and Donor's Family

6.2 Left inner wing: St Peter with Male Donor

6.3 Central panel: Adoration of the Magi

6.4 Right inner wing: St Agnes with Female Donor

The triptych, which shows the *Adoration of the Magi* set in a sweeping landscape on the inside, and the *Mass of St Gregory* with scenes from the Passion on the outside, was painted for a married couple in Antwerp, who appear on the interior of the wings with their coat of arms and their patron saints, Peter and Agnes. The donor Peeter Scheyve (d. 1506, also Scheyfve) was a tax collector for the city of Antwerp from 1495 and a lay judge from 1505. His wife Agnes de Gramme, whom he married in 1495, died just a few years later in 1500 (Vandenbroeck 2003, p. 314) and possibly even as early as 1497 (Huys Janssen 2005, p. 132). The triptych must therefore have been produced between 1495 – the probable year it was commissioned, to mark Peeter Scheyve's marriage and new office – and 1499. This latter date is corroborated by the re-use of the figure of St Peter on the left inner wing of the Boston *Ecce Homo* of 1499 (Cat. 21.2). The oak panels were made in Brussels (van Schoute/Verougstraete/Garrido 2001, p. 117). The donors were in the past erroneously identified with the von Bronc(k)horst-Bosch-huysen nobility. This conclusion was reached not by identifying the coats of arms but solely on the basis of an inventory of the family's estate drawn up in 1567, which includes a *Three Kings* triptych and attributes it to Hieronymus Bosch. It is interesting to note that the trail of that similar-sounding triptych – now lost – also leads back to Bosch's native city and to well-known members of the upper nobility. Its donor, Wilhelmina Bronchorst, had previously been married to an illegitimate son of Henry III of Nassau (1483–1538), owner of the *Garden of Earthly Delights* (Cat. 11), and thus had links with the latter's court (Renson). Her family was resident in the neighbouring duchy of Guelders, but also had roots in North Brabant. In 1501 a certain Herbrech, daughter of Theodoricus, Sir van Bronckhorst en Batenburg, and widow of Sir Johannes Dicbier, Sir van Mierlo, was granted a burial place in the Dominican monastery of 's-Hertogenbosch (Meijer 1897, p. 232).

As many as 22 copies of the *Adoration of the Magi* may still exist, of which six are reproduced in Unverfehrt and the remainder listed with their sources (Unverfehrt 1980, pp. 259–262; Garrido/van Schoute 2001, figs. pp. 118–119). To these copies we may add a few variants of Bosch's composition, and of the central panel in particular, a trend that started with the Boston *Ecce Homo* and extends to Jan Bruegel the Elder (1568–1625). The *Adoration of the Magi* is thus one of the most frequently copied, imitated and re-used works in Bosch's œuvre. The triptych is also mentioned in 1574 in the list of pictures earmarked by Philip II as suitable furnishing for the Escorial, at that time still under construction: "Another panel with two wings: the Birth of Our Lord Christ is painted on the central panel, by the hand of Hieronymus Bosch, it is five feet high and three wide, without the wings." These dimensions may be converted to approximately 139 x 84 cm / 54¾ x 33 in. (1 Castilian foot = 27.86 cm or 11 in.) and probably include the original curved frame which is still in place. In 1839 the triptych was transferred from the Escorial to the Prado, where it remains. In terms of its technical quality, the well-preserved *Adoration of the Magi* ranks among

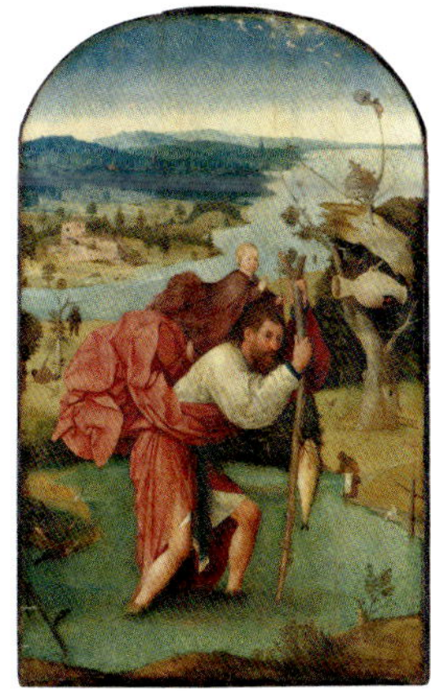
7

Bosch's finest works. Its exquisite painting technique and complex layout suggest that the triptych was intended to impress the Antwerp public and bring its artist to the attention of a wider clientele. The work is painstakingly executed right down to the details. This is true not only of the landscape but also of the Magi's clothing and gifts, for example, which are decorated with typological scenes. See also pp. 62, 63, *65*, *66/67*, 71.

LITERATURE: Brand Philip 1953; Tolnay 1965, pp. 12–13; Unverfehrt 1980, pp. 259–262; Garrido/van Schoute 1985; Raupp 1986, pp. 200–201; Marijnissen 1987, pp. 234–259; Venice 1992, pp. 57–58; Jacobs 2000; Garrido/van Schoute 2001, pp. 96–119; Renson 2001; van Schoute/Verougstraete/Garrido 2001, p. 117; Schlie 2002, pp. 153–155; Anfam 2003; Vandenbroeck 2003; Huys Janssen 2005; Büchse 2006; Falkenburg 2007b; Higgs Strickland 2007; Duquenne 2009; Fischer 2009, pp. 179, 279–284.

7

St Christopher, *c.* 1495–1500
Oil on panel (oak), 113 x 71.5 cm / 44½ x 28⅛ in. (cut down at the top; originally *c.* 120 cm / 47¼ in. high)
Rotterdam, Museum Boijmans Van Beuningen, inv. no. St. 26

St Christopher is shown, in wholly traditional fashion, carrying the Christ Child across a stretch of water in the centre of the panel. Motifs found in the surrounding landscape, on the other hand, are unconventional, and represent the dangers along life's path. De Bruyn has published several detailed studies of the iconography, showing that the landscape motifs either symbolise or exemplify specific sins and dangers. Bosch's re-interpretation of St Christopher as a model of Christian behaviour rather than as a patron saint, and the innovation this represents vis-à-vis the representational tradition of the 15th and early 16th century, is discussed by Fischer (2009).

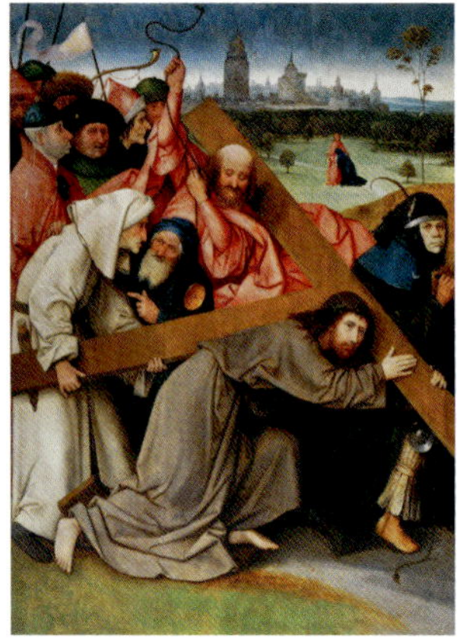

8

The wealth and variety of diableries directly sourced from *St Christopher* by Bosch's successors is documented by Unverfehrt. It is thus remarkable that, in contrast to many other Bosch works, no copies of the composition as a whole have come down to us. It is likewise remarkable that there is only one painting directly connected to Bosch's *St Christopher* and which may perhaps be situated within the circle of the master's immediate successors, in contact with the Bosch workshop (Unverfehrt 1980, no. 16). Other such works take their inspiration from Bosch's early successors in Antwerp: Alart Du Hamel (*c.* 1450–*c.* 1506), Joachim Patinir (1475/80–1524) and Jan Wellens de Cock (*c.* 1475/80–1527/28).

The paint surface is in reasonably good condition. A concentric arrangement of wispy clouds, which are possibly grouped around the sun, can be detected just below the panel's trimmed upper edge. The small and badly worn signature "jheronimus bosch" appears in the bottom left corner. Dendrochronological evidence indicates that the work must have been executed after 1490, and probably towards the end of the decade given its innovative and forward-looking pictorial concept and its abundant use of grotesque elements. *St Christopher* paintings by Bosch are mentioned in Habsburg inventories from the early 17th century onwards (Lammertse 1994, p. 87; Vandenbroeck 2001a, pp. 58–59); but none of these can be linked with the present panel. The original was formerly in an Italian private collection and entered the Museum Boijmans Van Beuningen as a loan in 1935 and as a gift in 1941.

See also pp. *78, 80*, 89, 90.

Literature: Schönbach 1874; Stahl 1920; Unverfehrt 1980; Marijnissen 1987, pp. 402–409; Lammertse 1994, pp. 84–89; de Bruyn 2000, 2001b; Klein 2001, p. 125; van Schoute/Verougstraete/Garrido 2001, p. 118; de Bruyn 2005; Fischer 2009, pp. 106–117.

8

Large Christ Carrying the Cross, *c.* 1500
Oil on panel (oak), 150 x 103 cm / 59 x 40½ in.
Madrid, Palacio Real (Monasterio de San Lorenzo de El Escorial), inv. no. 10 014 379.

The scale of the figures in *Christ Carrying the Cross* – along with Cat. 15, the biggest individual panel within Bosch's œuvre – is unusually large for the artist. The Virgin and St John are seen through a gap that has opened up as if by chance in the crowd accompanying Christ along the road to Calvary. In contrast with the hectic activity of the soldiers, their pose – St John supporting the Virgin – reveals their intrinsic and absolute participation in the events of the Passion. The picture also shows an early instance of inversion, in so far as the most important secondary figures, St John and the Virgin, are positioned in the background, even if the main figure of Christ remains in the foreground. A visual axis into the middle ground is thus created at right angles to the movement of the procession across the foreground.

Dendrochronological evidence indicates that the painting was produced at the earliest between 1492 and 1498, while its size and monumentality date it to probably soon after this period. It is unclear whether the work was conceived as a single panel or as part of an altarpiece. The scene, in particular on account of the figure of Christ, corresponds in its formal design to the Christ carrying the Cross in the *Mass of St Gregory* (Cat. 6.1). The composition and a number of the figures are also clearly related to the *Small Christ Carrying the Cross* (Cat. 9).

Among the first batch of pictures that Philip II ordered to be delivered, as part of the furnishings for his still unfinished Escorial in 1574, was "a panel on which is painted Christ Our Lord carrying the Cross, with Simon of Cyrene dressed in white, and other figures, by the hand of Hieronymus Bosch, which is 6

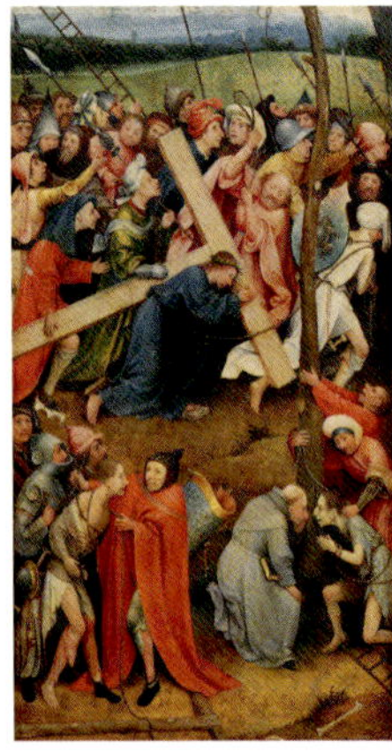
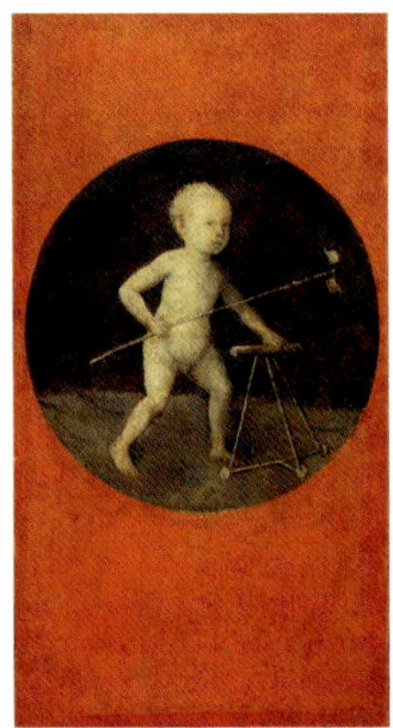

9.1–9.2

feet high and 4¾ wide." The description and the dimensions – which, when converted, correspond to approximately 167 x 132 cm / 65¾ x 52 in., including the frame – more or less match Bosch's *Large Christ Carrying the Cross*. The picture is mentioned by Sigüenza, in whose eyes it showed the misguided understanding of the Pharisees and scribes who, in their envy and rage, would not rest until they had put Christ on the Cross.

See also pp. 77, 82, 83.

LITERATURE: Sigüenza 1605, p. 838 [trans. in Snyder 1973, pp. 34–41; here p. 36]; Gibson 1972/73; Marrow 1979; Marijnissen 1987, pp. 280–283; Klein 2001, p. 126; van Schoute/Verougstraete/Garrido 2001, p. 116; Vandenbroeck 2001a, p. 50; van Dijck 2001a, pp. 104–106.

9

Small Christ Carrying the Cross (exterior: Christ Child with Walking Frame and Whirligig), *c.* 1502–1510

Oil on panel (oak), 57.2 x 32 cm / 22½ x 12½ in. (cut down by a quadrant at the top and minimally along the bottom, originally *c.* 77–80 cm / 30–31½ in. high; exterior fondo: ∅ *c.* 30 cm / 11¾ in.)
Vienna, Kunsthistorisches Museum, inv. no. GG 6429
Left-hand wing
9.1 Interior: Small Christ Carrying the Cross
9.2 Exterior: Christ Child with Walking Frame and Whirligig

The interior surface of this left wing of a triptych shows Christ dragging his Cross. His suffering is heightened yet further by the nail-studded boards attached to his ankles. These small instruments of torture are frequently found in Netherlandish treatments of this subject (Marijnissen 1987). The crowd jostles behind Christ in a dense mass of bodies. A number of guards are clustered around the bad thief in the left foreground, while on the right the good thief is making his confession to a monk, dressed anachronistically in the robes of a Franciscan. The other figures are also wearing a fanciful mixture of contemporary and Oriental-style clothing. The procession has already arrived at the mound of Calvary: bones and a cross lie scattered on the ground.

The *Small Christ Carrying the Cross* originally formed the left inner wing of a triptych with an arched, semi-circular top and suitable for a modestly sized altar or perhaps a private chapel. Given the prevailing compositional tradition, it is likely that the triptych took the story of the Passion as its theme. Possible motifs for the central panel include a Nailing to the Cross, a Raising of the Cross or the actual Crucifixion, and for the right inner wing a Deposition or Ascension. An Entombment or Lamentation is unlikely on account of the wing's extremely tall and narrow format: the idea of Christ's body being sliced by the edge of the panel or presented in pronounced foreshortening is barely conceivable in Bosch's art.

As a stylistic feature, the crown of thorns is not loosely woven but is twisted tightly like a rope, as is always the case in Bosch. The figure beside Christ, or more accurately behind him, is cited – by Bosch or an assistant – from the *Large Christ Carrying the Cross* (Cat. 8). The man's pale red robes, full beard and bald pate identify him as St Peter. He is also either holding up a rope or pulling down on it. It is unclear whether he is lashing Christ with it, as soldiers can be seen doing in other treatments of the subject, or whether he is trying to ease Christ's burden. One Bosch follower has interpreted Bosch's original more specifically, lending this figure the martial appearance of a guard and sheathing his arms in armour (see Unverfehrt 1980, no. 125).

It is possible that the *Small Christ Carrying the Cross* was executed with the assistance of a workshop member who also painted the inner wings of an *Adoration of the Magi*, fragments of which are now in Philadelphia (Cat. 23; Unverfehrt 1980, pp. 256–257, no. 37). Whatever the case, a very similar figure wearing a

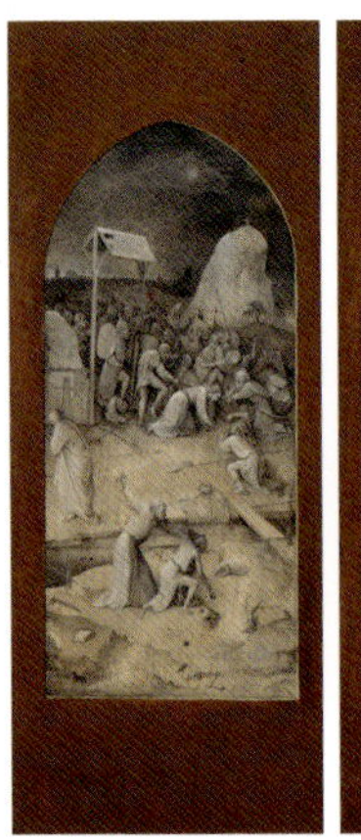
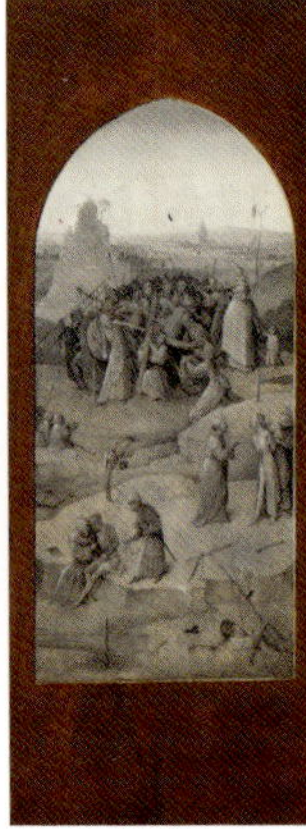

10.1–10.2

sort of turban and looking out of the picture at the viewer can be found at the extreme left of the composition both here and in the right wing fragment. The exterior of the wing shows a tondo of the *Christ Child* with a walking frame and a whirligig, executed in a palette of browns against a red background. We must imagine an Infant John the Baptist as his pendant on the opposite outer wing, engaged in a sort of joust or test of strength with the Infant Jesus (Willemsen 2001), as seen in an engraving by Israhel van Meckenem the Younger (*c.* 1440–1503). The whirligig – a children's toy also found in other pictures of this period – is formally analogous in its direction and angle of inclination, to the Cross carried by Christ on the interior. Other representations of the Infant Christ with a walking frame are known (Marijnissen 1987, ill. p. 272). The image makes no association between the Christ Child and foolishness, since the Child is not portrayed in a pejorative manner as elsewhere in the paintings of Bosch, where children appear as prototypes of unenlightened humanity. One example can be found on the exterior of the right wing of the *Temptation of St Anthony* (Cat. 10.2), where a small group of children, dressed in clothes that are far too big for them and with their hands and much of their faces concealed, are seated by the edge of the road. Holding their toys – one of them a whirligig – like good boys and girls, they watch with unconcern as the procession makes its way to Calvary. On the right outer wing of the *Last Judgement* (Cat. 13.2), a rough, almost malformed boy is entreating St Bavo's aid, while an infant balances a small bowl symbolically on its head: it has only its next meal on its mind. A revoltingly filthy child appears in the Gluttony scene on the panel illustrating the *Seven Deadly Sins* (Cat. 15). Bosch depicts only the children of donors and the Christ Child in a non-pejorative fashion.The present panel, which is painted on both sides, was executed after the *Large Christ Carrying the Cross*, as revealed by its adoption of figures from the

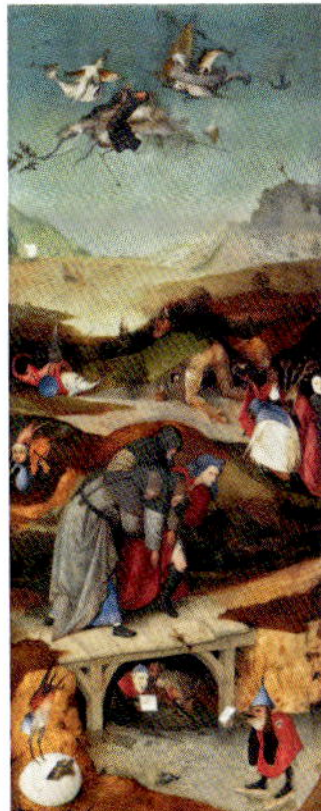
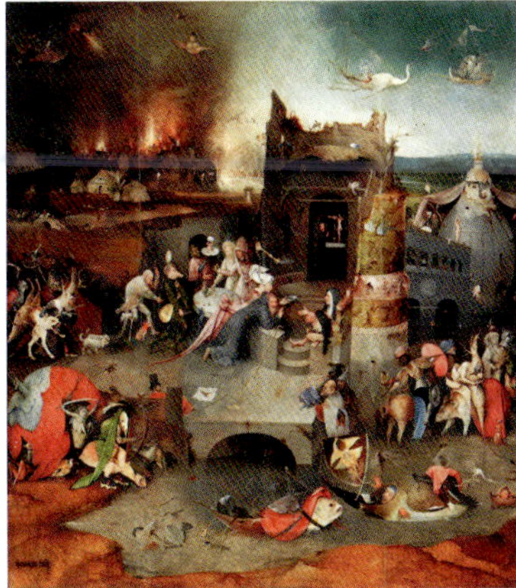
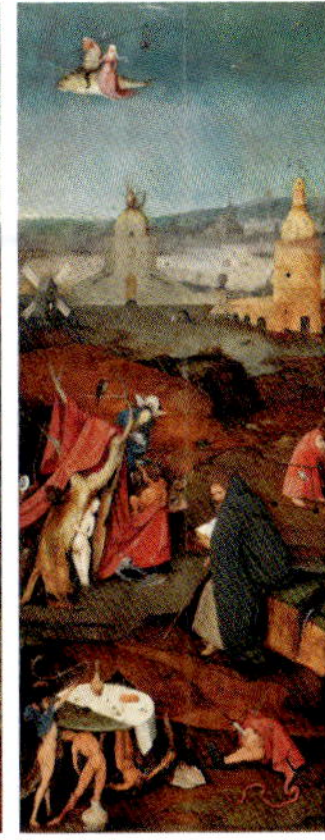

10.3–10.5

latter. It was purchased by the Kunsthistorisches Museum in Vienna in 1923 from an Amsterdam art-dealer.

See also pp. 82, 83, *84*, *91*.

LITERATURE: Ringbom 1965, pp. 168–169; Gibson 1972/73; Gibson 1975/76; Vos 1979, p. 26; Unverfehrt 1980; Marijnissen 1987, pp. 271–279; Jacobs 2000; van Schoute/Verboomen 2000; Willemsen 2001, pp. 193–195; Fischer 2009, p. 210.

10

The Temptation of St Anthony (exterior: The Arrest of Christ and Christ Carrying the Cross), *c.* 1502

Oil on panel (oak), 131.5 x 119 cm / 51¾ x 46¾ in. (central panel), 131.5 x 53 cm / 51¾ x 20¾ in. (wings)

Lisbon, Museu Nacional de Arte Antiga, inv. no. 1498 Pint

10.1 Left outer wing: The Arrest of Christ

10.2 Right outer wing: Christ Carrying the Cross

10.3 Left inner wing: St Anthony Accused by Devils

10.4 Central panel: The Temptation of St Anthony

10.5 Right inner wing: St Anthony in Meditation

This triptych is one of Bosch's most famous pictorial inventions and one of the most copied and imitated by artists in his wake (Unverfehrt 1980). Even if the identity of the patron and the original function for which the triptych was conceived remain unknown, we can conclude from the many replicas and re-interpretations it inspired, and from the inventories of pictures belonging to the upper aristocracy, that the work must have been prominently stationed in front of a correspondingly high-ranking audience at a relatively early date. The conception is targeted at courtly taste and its preference for *curiositas*, but without thereby losing its religious and moral function.

Queen Isabella I of Castile, known as Isabella the Catholic (1451–1504) and mother-in-law of Philip the Handsome (1478–1506), had two *St Anthony* pictures in her possession at the time of her death in late November 1504, as emerges from the inventory of her estate (van Dijck 2001a, pp. 59, 91–92). In view of the early date, we may confidently assume that these pictures were executed by Bosch or his assistants, and were not works by his imitators. Unless they were procured through the offices of Diego de Guevara (before 1442–1520), it is possible that Philip the Handsome brought the two works with him to Spain as gifts in 1502 or had them delivered not long afterwards.

A document from 1505 mentions a multi-figural triptych with the story of St Anthony (*c.* 251–356), also richly painted on its outer wings, with a value of 312 pounds (Fischer 2009, p. 99). Philip the Handsome purchased this *St Anthony* triptych towards the end of 1505, probably in December while staying in Bruges shortly before his departure for Spain, as a farewell present for his father, Maximilian I (1459–1519). The St Anthony theme was an apt choice in as far as Maximilian I had successfully overcome a difficult political situation at home and abroad and was at that time at the height of his power and fame. The triptych mentioned in the 1505 document could feasibly be identical to Cat. 10. But, although the description would fit, it is not detailed enough to be able to draw any firm conclusions.

On the evidence of dendrochronological analysis, the *Temptation of St Anthony* was painted at the earliest between 1495 and 1501. The time frame for its production is significantly narrowed by the fact that some of its pictorial motifs reappear in a similar or identical guise in the St Anthony scenes in the triptychs of the *Hermit Saints* (Cat. 12) and *Sts Job, Anthony and Jerome* (Cat. 22), dated respectively *c.* 1504 and *c.* 1505. The signature "jheronimus bosch" can be seen in the bottom left corner of the central panel.

The artistic significance of the St Anthony theme in Bosch's œuvre was evident even to Sigüenza in 1605: "Several times he painted the Temptation of St Anthony (this is the second category of paintings) as a subject through which he could reveal singular meanings" [Snyder 1973, pp. 36–37]. Sigüenza then documents the existence of at least five *St Anthony* pictures as he offers us a guide to where, within in the Escorial complex, pictures in the manner of Bosch were to be found: "This painting is seen often enough. In the Chapterhouse there is one, another is in the prior's cell, two are in the Gallery of the Infanta, and in my own cell there is a fine one in which I often read and lose myself." These pictures evidently fulfilled a religious function: for example, as a focus for meditation.

Despite the wealth and diversity of studies already published, art-historical research into the triptych is not yet exhausted. A good overview of the various viewpoints and areas of discussion can be found in Marijnissen (pp. 154–156), Gibson and Uhrig. Among the many interpretations advanced, the iconographic and iconological study by Dirk Bax stands out. Bax, who focuses on the pictorial details, bases his interpretation on contemporary literary sources of a religious and Humanist nature, although he does not take account of the Lives of St Anthony. Bosch's *Temptation of St Anthony* was considered so unconventional that art historians for a long time dismissed as pointless any systematic comparison of its contents with pictorial tradition and the legends of the saints (*Vitas patrum*). Yet it is precisely in this way that many of the work's details, and also its structure, can be explained (Fischer 2009).

The significance of the enigmatic inscription, variously interpreted, on the sealed letter held by the devil wearing ice-skates in the foreground of the left inner wing, has been deciphered by Massing in an illuminating essay. It can be conclusively read as *protio*, an abbreviation of *protestatio*, identifying it as a letter of protest, objection or accusation. The devils envy St Anthony, who is being borne up to heaven in ecstasy by angels, and want to prosecute him for sins committed in his youth, for which he has long atoned. The word, or more accurately the letter itself, serves to clarify the scene but is not mentioned in the saint's legend. It shows that Bosch has portrayed the episode along with its meaning: the brief inscription provides an additional tool with which to understand both this subsidiary scene and the overall representation in the left inner wing.

The triptych also offers evidence that monster drolleries were not *per se* the spontaneous and subjective inventions of the painter, but could also be sourced from traditional pattern-books. On the right inner wing, for example, the naked man blowing a buisine at lower left is a pictorial motif that can be found in much earlier manuscript illumination, namely in the marginalia of a 14th-century English psalter (Bax 1979, p. 350). Motifs of this kind are found in pictures in which secular music is represented as a cause of vice.

The scenes on the exterior of the triptych's wings have been largely ignored. Framed within a generous passe-partout that rises to a pointed arch, they are relatively small vis-à-vis the inner wings and, moreover, leave unused the pictorial space in the foreground and the sky. They show two Passion scenes: on the left the Arrest of Christ in the Garden of Gethsemane, and on the right Christ Carrying the Cross accompanied by numerous soldiers and spectators. Comparisons of the style and pictorial motifs of these outer wings with other works by Bosch and his followers would undoubtedly have much to tell us.

In more recent times the well-preserved triptych has undergone detailed scientific analysis and conservation (Lisbon 1972; van Schoute/Verboomen 2000; Mesquita e Carmo/Antunes de Sousa 2003). The detailed and relatively fine underdrawing (in places employing parallel hatching) and the lower paint layer both contain various minor and major pentimenti. These are most significant in the middle of the central panel, where Bosch originally inserted a tent with devils – a pictorial motif that goes back to the biography of St Anthony in the *Vitas patrum*.

The works of Hieronymus Bosch also reached the Iberian Peninsula via the Portuguese Humanist and collector Damião de Góis, also Goes (1502–1572), who purchased a number of Bosch's paintings in the Low Countries. De Góis was a diplomat and historiographer who, between 1523 and 1544, worked for the Portuguese trading post in Antwerp on behalf of King John III of Portugal (1502–1557). During these years he travelled widely throughout central and northern Europe, apparently more in pursuit of his Humanist studies than for diplomatic reasons. After his return to Portugal he presented a *St Anthony* painting and a *Temptation of Job* to the bishop and later cardinal Giovanni Ricci (1498–1574), from 1544 to 1550 papal nuncio in Portugal. De Góis also sold a *St Anthony* triptych to Philip II of Spain, probably a copy of the Lisbon work. Lastly, he bequeathed a *Crowning with Thorns* to the church in his native Alenquer, where he was also buried. In 1570 he was arrested and interrogated by the Inquisition for alleged Lutheranism. The statements de Góis provided about Bosch paintings in his current or former possession are preserved in the records of his trial (Feist Hirsch 1967, p. 48).

It is possible, therefore, that the triptych had already entered the Portuguese royal collection even before the second half of the 16th century. It is documented for the first time, however, only during the reign of King Ferdinand II (1815–1886), a German prince by birth, who sent it back to Germany for restoration. At the end of the 19th century the triptych hung in the Palácio das Necessidades in Lisbon, from where it passed into the National Museum in 1913.

See also pp. 96–139, *117*, *118/119*.

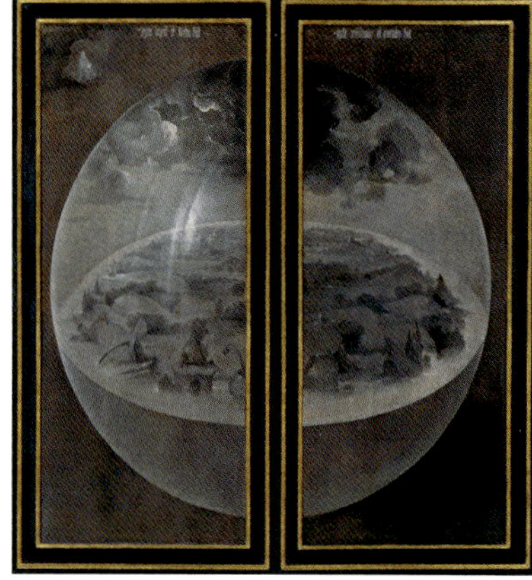

11.1

Literature: Sigüenza 1605, p. 838; Bax 1949/1979; Tolnay 1965, pp. 25–27; Lisbon 1972; Dinzelbacher 1973; Unverfehrt 1980; Gibson 1983, pp. 105–109; Marijnissen 1987, pp. 154–209; Venice 1992, pp. 54, 59–60; Lisbon 1994; Massing 1994; Uhrig 1998, pp. 98–103; Jacobs 2000; van Schoute/Verboomen 2000, pp. 178–180; Klein 2001, p. 126; Vellekoop 2001; Koreny 2002/03; Mesquita e Carmo/Antunes de Sousa 2003; Waadenoijen 2003; Silver 2006, pp. 218–234; Bango Torviso 2006b; Fischer 2009, pp. 304–323.

11

The Garden of Earthly Delights (exterior: Creation of the World), *c.* 1503
Oil on panel (oak), 220 x 195 cm / 86⅝ x 76¾in. (central panel 190 x 176.7 cm / 74¾ x 69½ in.
without frame), 220 x 97 cm / 86⅝ x 38¼ in. (wings)
Madrid, Museo Nacional del Prado, inv. no. 2823

11.1 Outer wings: Creation of the World up to the Third Day
11.2 Left inner wing: Paradise and the Creation of Eve
11.3 Central panel: Humankind before the Flood
11.4 Right inner wing: Hell

In the closed position, the grisaille shutters of Bosch's most famous triptych show the world on the third day of Creation, overseen by the figure of God enthroned. God has divided light from darkness and created the heavens, land and sea as well as the plants and trees. Inside the triptych, the story of Creation continues on the left wing, where it culminates in the introduction of Eve on the sixth day. Form and content then change, with the central panel showing *Humankind before the Flood* and the interior of the right wing a vision of *Hell.*

Bosch scholars have already shed substantial light on the triptych's iconography (above all

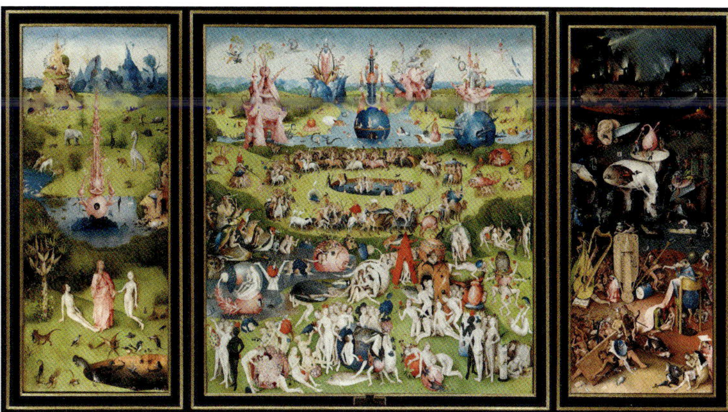

II.2–II.4

Bax 1956 and Vandenbroeck 1989 and 1990, but also *inter alia* Marijnissen 1972, 1977, 1987; Gibson 1973a; Yarza Luaces 1998; de Bruyn 2001c). More recently, the relationship between the triptych's main theme, its patron and its function has received increasing attention (Gibson 1973c; Wirth 1988 and 2000; Vandenbroeck 1989 and 1990; Moxey 1994; Belting 2002). The artistic character of the work, its pictorial invention and its compositional structure are areas only gradually being explored (Wirth 1988; Moxey 1994; Fischer 2002b and 2009).

After a number of earlier misinterpretations, art historians are in principle agreed that the innovative conception of this densely populated triptych, with its iconography centred upon Adam and Eve, was probably occasioned by the wedding of a prince. Henry III of Nassau seemed to be the primary candidate for the bridegroom until Vermet sowed doubts by speculating that the triptych was in fact painted *c.* 1480–1490, a dating that would make the *Garden of Earthly Delights* one of Bosch's earliest works. Vermet bases his argument on the results of dendrochronological analyses, according to which the panels could have been painted as early as 1460–1466. Such an early date can be reconciled neither with Bosch's artistic development nor with the biography of the prince at that earlier time, Engelbert II of Nassau (1451–1504), who was married in 1468. The argument that the gap between the felling of the original tree and the painting of the panels in *c.* 1503 is uncommonly long is unconvincing: in the case of the copy of the left wing of the *Garden of Earthly Delights* in the Escorial (inv. no. 2053), this time lapse is even greater than in the case of the original (Vermet 2001, p. 88; Garrido/van Schoute 2001, p. 192)! With this in mind, it is instead worth considering Pokorny's suggestion that the triptych might have been prompted by the marriage of Philip the Handsome in 1496. In that event, however, we would need to explain how the triptych entered the collection of Henry III, where it was documented by Antonio de Beatis in 1517. The stronger arguments support the assumption that the painting was produced *c.* 1503 to mark the marriage of Henry III of Nassau and Louise-Françoise, Duchess of Savoy.

The triptych's journey from the Brussels palace of Henry III of Nassau to the collection of Philip II of Spain can be clearly reconstructed (Steppe 1967; Gombrich 1969). After Henry III's death in 1538, the work passed to his son René of Châlon (1519–1544) and, after the latter's death, to his nephew, Dutch national hero William of Orange (1533–1584). In 1567/68 it was confiscated, along with other valuables found in the palace, by the Spanish under their governor, the 3rd Duke of Alba (1507–1582), who used every means – including torture – to get his hands on the triptych (Vandenbroeck 2001b). An inventory drawn up at that time lists "a large panel painting over the fireplace by Hieronymus Bosch" in the great hall of the palace. Alba sent the triptych back to Spain shortly afterwards. In 1591 it was bought for the Escorial by Philip II of Spain, who acquired it from the estate of Don Fernando de Toledo (1527/28–1591), Alba's illegitimate son. In 1939 the *Garden of Earthly Delights* was transferred from Philip II's collection in the Escorial to the Prado in Madrid.

The *Garden of Earthly Delights* was a highly popular pictorial invention. Unverfehrt's study of its reception shows that, after the *Temptation of St Anthony* (Cat. 10), the *Garden of Earthly Delights* is the most copied or imitated painting in Bosch's œuvre. Of the eleven surviving copies, largely dating from the years 1535–1550, the majority are single panels. One of the copies exists in the form of a tapestry, made in Brussels and in the possession of the Archbishop of Malines in the third quarter of the 16th century. As well as the original, another copy also reached Spain, probably via Diego de Guevara. The *Hell* panel became the object of numerous paraphrases and pastiches on the themes of the Last Judgement and the *Visio Tnugdali* (Vision of Tundale), the tale of a journey through Hell and Heaven by the knight Tundale dating from the 12th century and widely known around 1500 (Unverfehrt 1980, nos. 148–154, figs. 214–226).

The name *Garden of Earthly Delights* is a modern invention that, in the absence of a historical title, became established in the various European languages at the end of the 19th century. The earliest known title goes back to the period around 1593, when the work reached the Escorial with the last delivery of furnishings for the palace interior. The inventory lists "a panel painting in oil, with two wings, of the variety of the world, allegorised in farces by Hieronymus Bosch, which is called the Strawberry Tree [*del Madroño*], with gilt mouldings: it has a height, with the shutters closed, of two and a half *varas* [approx. 209 cm / 82¼ in.] and a width of two and a third [195 cm / 76¾ in.]. It was bought at the auction of Prior Don Fernando." José de Sigüenza, in his 1605 *History of the Order of St Jerome*, refers to the triptych by a similar title, describing it as "a painting of vainglory and the brief taste of strawberries or the strawberry tree".

While the Escorial inventory and Sigüenza derive their "Strawberry Tree" title for the triptych from the work's expressive content and from striking motifs within its composition, an archival trail leads to the potential biblical theme behind the conception of the *Garden of Earthly Delights* (Gombrich 1969, p. 166; Vandenbroeck 1990, pp. 73–74). In 1595 Archduke Ernst (*1553), residing in Brussels, acquired a *Sicut erat in diebus Noë* painting by Bosch through the offices of Jacques Grameye. The purchase was recorded by his secretary Blasius Hutter. Archduke Ernst died that same year. One of his four brothers and heirs was Emperor Rudolf II (1552–1612), into whose famed Prague collection of art and precious objects the work now probably passed. An inventory of this collection drawn up in 1621 lists, under entry 1287, "Licentious living before the Flood (copy)", and under entry 1288 "Two altarpiece wings, how the world was created" – a triptych, in other words, that has evidently been separated into its three component parts and which treats Old Testament subjects. In the inventory of 1635, only no. 1288 remains: "Historia with naked people, sicut erat in diebus Noe [Thus it was in the days of Noah]". It is possible, therefore, that a copy of the *Garden of Earthly Delights* was purchased in Brussels and subsequently came to Prague, where – as was standard practice at that time – the wings were detached. Even if the triptych in question was not the *Garden of Earthly Delights*, it testifies to the presence of the subject in Bosch's œuvre.

No Bosch painting has been subject to as many different interpretations as the *Garden of Earthly Delights* (overview: Marijnissen 1987, pp. 84–102; Gibson 1983, pp. 84–97; Fischer 2002b). Bosch scholarship in the second half of the 20th century was for a long time widely divided. A key factor in this situation was the iconological approach expounded by Erwin Panofsky, which art historians now applied to the art of Bosch. Panofsky himself chose not to offer an interpretation of the triptych, stating: "This, too high for my wit, I prefer to omit" (Panofsky 1953, p. 358). His 'modesty' was undoubtedly rooted in the fact that relatively little was known about Bosch's biography at that time and, moreover, that Bosch's œuvre did not fit into the conventional iconography of Renaissance Humanism.

Many other authors showed no such reserve, but drew liberally on the history of symbols and ideas in their interpretation of Bosch's paintings, linking them with alchemy, astrology, heresy and secret societies. Such speculations kept the art world on the edge of its seat from the late 1940s to the 1990s and left serious scholarship looking almost a little tame. Prominent in this approach was Wilhelm Fraenger, who made Bosch the painter in a heretical sect. Securely based criticism of Fraenger's untenable hypotheses was slow to emerge (Bax 1956; Hartlaub 1957; Vandenbroeck 1986b and 1990).

The various attempts that have been made to rename the triptych convey an idea of the different interpretations that have been placed upon it. Following Fraenger's bold baptism of the painting as the "Thousand-Year Empire" (*Tausendjähriges Reich*; 1947), Baldass proposed a more general "World Triptych" (*Welttriptychon*), Wertheim-Aymès (1957) an idealising "Garden of Heavenly Delights" (*Garten der himmlischen Freuden*), Reuterswärd (1970) the cautious formulation "The Large Triptych" (*Das grosse Triptychon*) and Chailley (1978), following Combe (1946), the speculative "Alchemical Garden" (*Le Jardin Alchimique*). Gombrich suggested *The Lesson of the Flood* or *Sicut erat in diebus Noë*, Bax "The Garden of Unchastity" (*Het tuin der onkuisheidsdrieluik*) and Vandenbroeck (1990) "The False Paradise of Love" (*Het valse liefdeparadijs*). Bosch does not, however, idealise or spiritualise sensual pleasure, but shows it as unchecked and uninhibited and hence in a manner that – here as in his œuvre as a whole – conveys his disapproval.

Bosch's largest extant work has been cleaned and restored on several occasions, most recently in 1998/99, when its bright, fresh, almost cool colours were once again brought to the fore. Despite its many small or tiny blemishes, the triptych remains in good condition. The greyish underdrawing is executed with sketch-like brevity and only becomes more detailed in the figural group with Christ. The underdrawing and the lower paint layer contain numerous pentimenti, of which the most clearly discernible are found on the *Hell* panel in the area of the devils and monsters, where Bosch evidently considered reiterating some of the pictorial motifs from the central panel: thus a large tower crowned by a sphere can be found in the lower paint layer at the right edge of the picture, and beneath it a transparent sphere containing a man. A sort of whale-fish with arms can also be found in the centre of the picture (Madrid 2000, p. 87).

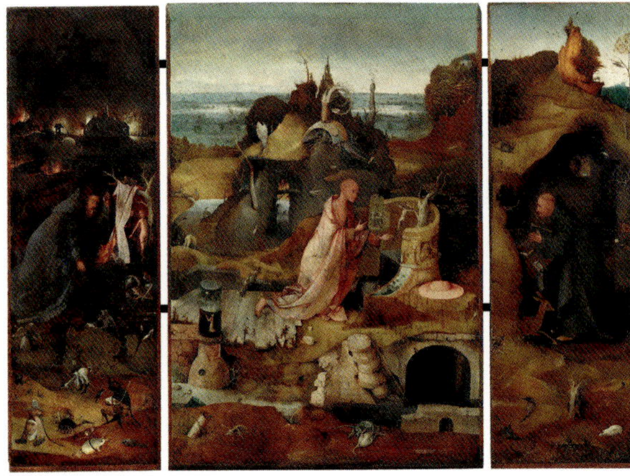

12.1–12.3

See also pp. 140–221, *186–191.*

LITERATURE: Beatis 1517–1518 [1905]; Sigüenza 1605; Justi 1889; Dollmayr 1898; Baldass 1943; Bax 1956; Dürer 1956–1969, vol. 1, p. 155, col. 70–81; Baldass 1959; Tolnay 1965, pp. 29–32; Spychalska-Boczkowska 1966; Gombrich 1967; Kurz 1967; Steppe 1967; Gombrich 1969; Calas 1969/70; Heidenreich 1970; Mateo Gómez 1972; Gibson 1973a; Hammerstein 1974; Glum 1976; Koch 1976; Boczkowska 1977; Unverfehrt 1980; Bax 1983, pp. 335–360, 378–388; Cook 1984; Marijnissen 1987, pp. 84–153; Mateo Gómez 1988; Wirth 1988; Vandenbroeck 1989 and 1990; Rooth 1992; Moxey 1994; Yarza Luaces 1998; Madrid 2000; van Schoute/Verboomen 2000; Wirth 2000; de Bruyn 2001c; Garrido/van Schoute 2001, pp. 29, 32, 158–193; Klein 2001, p. 123; van Schoute/Verougstraete/Garrido 2001, p. 117; Vandenbroeck 2001b; Vellekoop 2001; Belting 2002; Fischer 2002b; Fransen 2003; Unverfehrt 2003, pp. 19–26; Urbach/Garrido 2003; Silver 2006, pp. 21–80; Falkenburg 2007a; Gibson 2008; Fischer 2009, pp. 245–273; Mandabach 2010; Marías 2010; Pokorny 2010a; Falkenburg 2011.

12

Hermit Saints Triptych (with Sts Jerome, Anthony and Giles), *c.* 1504
Oil on panel (oak), 85 x 60 cm / 33½ x 23⅝ in. (central panel),
85 x 29 cm / 33½ x 11⅜ in. (wings; panels cut down, original height *c.* 110 cm / 43¼ in. with an arched or curved top)
Venice, Museo Palazzo Grimani
12.1 Left inner wing: St Anthony
12.2 Central panel: St Jerome
12.3 Right inner wing: St Giles

The triptych shows three saints as hermits: St Jerome in the central panel, St Anthony on the left inner wing and St Giles (*c.* 640 – *c.* 720) opposite him on the right inner wing. If it was originally produced for 's-Hertogenbosch, it might have been installed in the chapel of the Brethren of the Common Life or else on the St Jerome altar in Sint-Jan's church. The signature "jheronimus bosch" can be found in very small lettering in the lower right corner of the central panel.

The dating can be narrowed down considerably on the basis of dendrochronological analysis (1487–1493 or later) and compositional links with two other triptychs. Firstly, a number of pictorial motifs on the *St Anthony* wing (Cat. 12.1) can be traced back to the right inner wing and central panel of the *Temptation of St Anthony* triptych of *c.* 1502 (10.5 and 10.4). These include the group beside the water with the naked woman standing by the split tree and draped with a long red cloth; the devil with his pointed 'antlers'; and the blazing village with a church and a bridge beside a wood. Secondly, pictorial motifs from both the *Temptation of St Anthony* and the *Hermit Saints* triptychs resurface in the *Sts Job, Anthony and Jerome* triptych of *c.* 1505 (Cat. 22). It is possible that the left wing of the *Hermit Saints* triptych was largely executed by Bosch's workshop: although it takes up elements from the *Temptation of St Anthony*, the demons are scattered in an even, additive manner within the landscape around the saint, something unusual in the case of Bosch's works. The figure of the hermit, leaning on his staff as he draws water, is found in a stylistically similar painting in Kansas City (Unverfehrt 1980, no. 34b).

The triptych, whose palette is largely confined to greys, greens and browns, is in poor condition. The panels originally had an arched or curved top. The back has been planed and reinforced with a lattice of wooden struts to prevent the oak boards from warping. The exterior surfaces of the wings have thus lost the painting they probably carried. The badly worn and spotted paint surface strikes the eye as aqitated. There is evidence of just one pentimento. In the right section of St Jerome's red cloak, the relatively thick lines of the bluish underdrawing can be seen shimmering

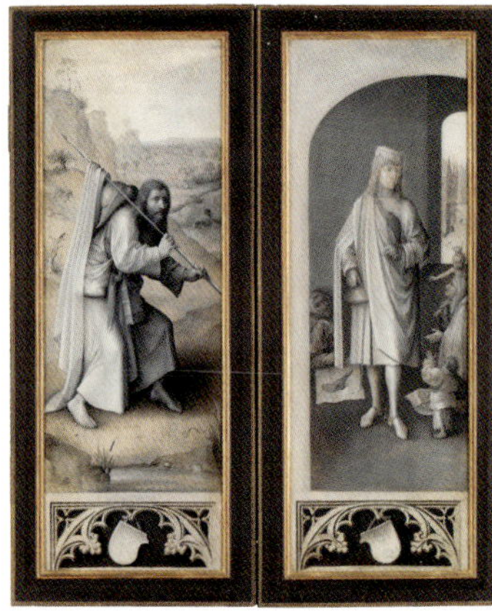

13.1–13.2

through. The painter subsequently shifted the main figure further upwards into the centre of the picture.

The work shares the provenance of the *Crucified Female Martyr* (Cat. 14) and the fragments of *Paradise and Hell* (Cat. 16). It had already reached Venice by 1521, when Marcantonio Michiel (1484–1552) saw it in the Venetian home of Cardinal Domenico Grimani (1461–1523), Patriarch of Aquileia, in the company of paintings that Michiel attributed firmly to Bosch, and a "Saint Jerome in the Wilderness" that he judged to be a work by Joachim Patinir (Venice, p. 18; Aikema 2001a). It is nonetheless possible that this last-named work was Bosch's *Hermit Saints* triptych, since the 's-Hertogenbosch artist was frequently confused with Patinir and Herri met de Bles (*c.* 1500/10–1555/60) – a mistake evidently also made by Karel van Mander in his Life of Bosch, for example (Fischer 2009, pp. 124–125). Michiel must in this case have missed Bosch's signature, however.

After Grimani's death, his collection passed as a gift to the Venetian Republic. In the case of the sculptures, a condition of the bequest was that they should go on public display in honour of their donor. Many paintings and a few sculptures were taken to a convent on Murano, while another eight crates of pictures were placed in storage in the cellars of the Doge's Palace. In 1528, after a complaint about the execution of the will, several works were returned to Grimani's heirs, among whom was Marino Grimani (1488/89–1546), who then had almost two dozen paintings sent to Rome. In 1592 his direct heir bequeathed the works definitively to the Venetian State. In 1615 it was decided to return works from the private chambers and storerooms in the Doge's Palace to public display.

A. M. Zanetti made a clear reference to the present painting in his 1773 publication *Descrizione di tutte le pubbliche pitture della città di Venezia*, in which he reported that a triptych of St Jerome and two other saints

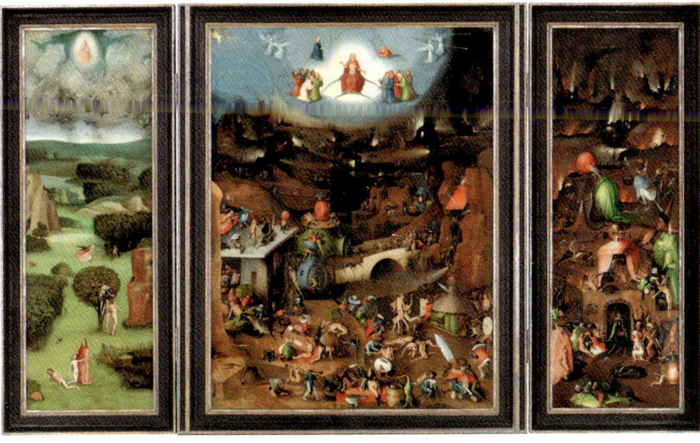

13.3–13.5

was housed in the Doge's Palace. In 1838 the work was removed to the Kunsthistorisches Museum in Vienna. It was returned only in 1919.

See also pp. 260–264, *304/305*.

Literature: Tolnay 1965, pp. 34–35; Unverfehrt 1980, p. 256; Marijnissen 1987, pp. 210–213; Wiebel 1988; Venice 1992; Peacock 1995; van Schoute/Verboomen 2000, pp. 104–106, 210–211; Aikema 2001a; Aikema 2001b; Aikema 2001c; Klein 2001, p. 125; Koldeweij 2001, pp. 18–19; Laemers 2001, p. 83; Fischer 2009, pp. 211–214; Venice 2010.

13
The Last Judgement
(exterior: St James and St Bavo), *c.* 1506
Oil and tempera on panel (oak),
163 x 127.5 cm / 64¼ x 50¼ in.
(central panel), 167 x 60 cm /
65¾ x 23⅝ in. (wings)
Vienna, Akademie der bildenden Künste, Gemäldegalerie, inv. nos. 579–581

13.1 Left outer wing: St James
13.2 Right outer wing: St Bavo
13.3 Left inner wing: Fall of the Rebel Angels, The Fall and The Expulsion from Paradise
13.4 Central panel: The Last Judgement
13.5 Right inner wing: Hell

It is fairly certain that the triptych of the *Last Judgement*, today in the Vienna Academy of Fine Arts, is the one named in a well-known document preserved in Lille. The document records that in September 1504 Hieronymus van Aken, called Bosch, painter, residing in 's-Hertogenbosch, was granted an advance of 36 *livres*, which was paid to him by the adviser and chief receiver, Simon Longin. The artist was to make a large panel painting nine feet high and eleven feet long, which was to show the Last Judgement with Paradise and Hell and was intended for Archduke Philip the Handsome's own use.

The huge dimensions stipulated in the document, which exceed those even of the *Garden of Earthly Delights* (Cat. 11), are clearly not the same, however, as those of the Vienna triptych, which – at roughly 5 ft 4 in. high by 8 ft 1 in. wide – measures not much more than half the size. Perhaps, when ordering the new triptych, Philip consciously wanted something even bigger than the *Garden of Earthly Delights* commissioned in 1503 (Belting 2002, p. 74). The war against the Guelders and Philip's departure for Spain probably hindered further payments, so that the work was carried out on a smaller scale than originally planned. The empty escutcheons on the outer wings and the overpainted donor figure in the lower left corner of the central panel also point to changes in the patron–artist relationship.

The commissioning of the triptych by Philip the Handsome is supported by several details. The figure of St Bavo on the right outer wing is clearly a portrait of Philip, whose features are documented in numerous contemporary works of art (Bax 1983, Onghena 1959). The typical Habsburg physiognomy is here combined with the soft, youthful characteristics that earned Philip his epithet of "the Handsome": long hair, large eyes, a slender nose, a full lower lip and a round chin. Saints in several paintings from around 1500 bear Philip's portrait: the figure of St George appearing in a 1496 painting of the Malines Guild of Archers is a case in point. A representation of Philip with a falcon and a cap-like hat – both common attributes of St Bavo – has likewise come down to us (*Master of the Legend of St Mary Magdalene*, *c.* 1490, Paris, Louvre [Depot]) and was also used for the young Duke Charles of Burgundy, the later Charles V (1500–1558), in a drawing by Hans Holbein the Elder (*c.* 1465–1524). Philip, who was born in Bruges and whose heart is buried there, and Charles, who grew up in Ghent, evidently identified with the charitable, noble local saint of West Flanders.

The combination of patron saints on the outer wings undoubtedly relates to Philip the Handsome. While St Bavo stands for the Netherlandish branch of the house of Habsburg, St James – Spain's national saint – represents the Spanish branch. The two countries had become dynastically linked through Philip's marriage to Joanna of Castile in 1496. In late 1504 the couple inherited the Spanish throne, but because of the war against the Guelders Philip was only able to make the pressing trip to Spain a year later.

This specific background explains why Joanna was not also included in the triptych as a female donor: the work was not a joint endowment by the royal couple, but arose in conjunction with Philip's preparations for war, which reached a climax in September 1504 – precisely when the commission was awarded. A similar situation can be seen, for example, in the Rolin Madonna painted by Jan van Eyck (*c.* 1390–1441) around 1435 for the Burgundian chancellor Nicolas Rolin (1376–1462), which shows neither Rolin's children nor his third wife, Guigone de Salins (1403–1470). In a *Last Judgement* triptych today housed in Brussels (inv. nos. 2405, 2406 and 4168), on the other hand, executed by an unknown master and dating to 1505/06, Philip is joined by the figure of Joanna, although not by the couple's five children (see p. *235*).

The interior surfaces of the wings, in particular, are in poor condition and have also been extensively overpainted. Their thick, cracked paint film with its fine craquelure is not a feature of the central panel or the outer wings. In the collections of the Early Modern era, triptychs were frequently dismantled, with wings and central panel subsequently following separate paths. This explains the differences in the condition in which they have come down us. Comprehensive analyses with the aid of modern diagnostic scanning techniques, including X-ray and infra-red reflectography, would be able to shed light on the extent to which the overpainting is genuine, and to show which changes were made by Bosch himself in the course of painting. A number of pentimenti are visible even to the naked eye on the middle

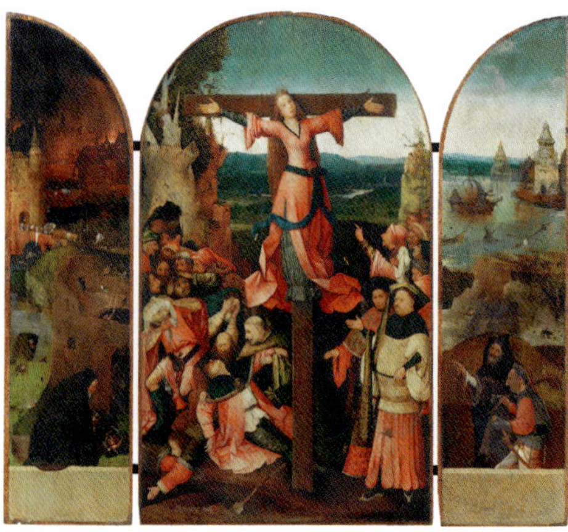

14

and lower left side of the central panel. A long, scrolling cartouche is likewise visible with the naked eye beneath the young nobleman in a cloak, while X-rays have revealed a secular donor figure – subsequently overpainted – in the underlying paint layer (van Schoute/Verboomen 2000, p. 181, no. 19).

In his painstaking investigation of the iconography of the *Last Judgement*, Bax showed that monster drolleries were recorded and handed down in pattern-books. He traced, for example, the musical monster on the left edge of the central panel, with its mouth and nose forming a wind instrument, back to 14th-century Netherlandish manuscript illumination (Bax 1979 [1949], p. 350).

It is probable that the triptych remained in the possession of the Austrian Habsburgs for a long time. It passed first to Margaret of Austria (1480–1530), who took over the running of affairs from her palace in Malines after the death of Philip the Handsome in 1506. In 1659 it appears in an inventory of the possessions of Archduke Leopold William of Austria (1614–1662), Governor of the Spanish Netherlands from 1647 to 1656, where it is described as "an altarpiece with two wings". The work was bequeathed to the Vienna Academy by Count Anton von Lamberg-Sprinzenstein (1740–1822) and passed into the Gemäldegalerie after his death.

See also pp. 222–225, *253*, *254/255*.

LITERATURE: Onghena 1959; Steemers 1978; Bax 1979 [1949]; Bax 1983; Marijnissen 1987, pp. 214–233; Trnek 1988; Michaelis 1989/90; Esser 1991; Venice 1992, pp. 56–57; Jacobs 2000; van Schoute/Verboomen 2000, pp. 178–180; Klein 2001, p. 124; van Schoute/Verougstraete/Garrido 2001, p. 119; Silver 2006, pp. 337–347; Fischer 2009, pp. 95–97; Pokorny 2010a.

14

Triptych of the Crucified Female Martyr (Sint-Ontcommer), *c.* 1505–1515

Oil on panel (oak), 105 x 63 cm / 41⅜ x 24¾

in. (central panel), 105 x 28 cm / 41⅜ x 11 in. (wings)
Venice, Museo Palazzo Grimani

The crucified virgin in the central panel of the triptych, whose attribute – a beard – was often only hinted at in pictures, was venerated in the Low Countries as Sint-Ontcommer and in Britain as St Uncumber or St Wilgefortis. Other names for this female martyr include Liberata and Kümmernis. One centre of her cult was Steenbergen, west of Breda. In 's-Hertogenbosch she had her own altar in Sint-Jan's church, where this triptych may originate. The inner wings originally portrayed events from the Life of St Wilgefortis, namely two catastrophes: on the left a palace fire, and on the right a storm striking unbelievers as a punishment, God having heard the prayers of the saint on the cross (Schnürer/Ritz 1934, pp. 14–16, plate IX, fig. 19; Bax 1961, p. 3). Both scenes can still be recognised in the background of the respective wings.

Either during or just after completing the triptych, Bosch and his workshop painted over the two donors on the interior wings (Cat. Venice 1992; Marijnissen 1987, pp. 262–263), replacing them with figural scenes, on the left specifically with a Temptation of St Anthony. The true subject of the work was consequently obscured and the triptych was then capable of being used for another purpose. Indeed, the idea of exporting the work to Italy was probably already in the artist's mind when he painted out the donors. The interpretation of the crucified virgin as St Julia, an identity still frequently ascribed to her in the literature even today, probably only established itself in the late 19th century.
The donors' style of dress does not characterise them perforce as Italians, as has been regularly claimed since Bax. Rather, it identifies them as belonging to the civic elite, whose members can also be found in other works by Bosch. It is noteworthy, however, that they are two middle-aged men. The kneeling pair are

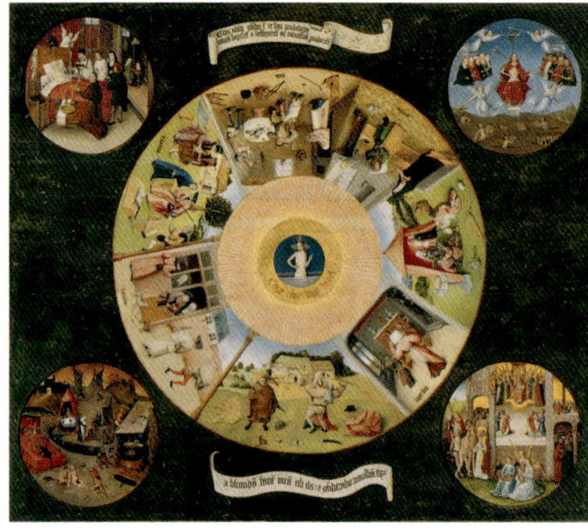

15

probably not related by family ties but appear as representatives of a corporation, perhaps of a religious fraternity such as the 's-Hertogenbosch Brotherhood of Our Blessed Lady. Dendrochronological evidence indicates that the *Triptych of the Crucified Female Martyr* was painted at the earliest shortly before 1500. Since the seated St Anthony in the left wing bears a strong mirror-image resemblance to the figure of St Anthony in Meditation on the right inner wing of the *Temptation of St Anthony* (Cat. 10.5), it may be assumed that Bosch and his workshop carried out the overpainting after completing the Lisbon triptych. If the tower behind St Anthony is based on corresponding motifs in *The Haywain* (Cat. 20) or the *Last Judgement* (Cat. 26), the two donor figures cannot have been overpainted until 1510–1515, probably by a member of the workshop.The triptych's paint surface is worn and exhibits blemishes in particular on the right inner wing. The underdrawing is barely visible and almost no pentimenti can be detected. The central panel bears the signature "jheronimus bosch" in the lower left corner. The panels, which are arched at the top, have not been trimmed, as revealed by their unpainted edges. The original frame is lost, however. The back has been planed down and reinforced with a lattice of wooden struts to prevent the wood from warping. Like the *Hermit Saints* triptych (Cat. 12) and the *Paradise and Hell* wings (Cat. 16), the work probably once formed part of the collection of the Venetian Cardinal Domenico Grimani. In view of the challenge presented by its iconography, it is entirely conceivable that the triptych of the *Crucified Female Martyr* is the work mentioned by Marcantonio Michiel in his report of 1521, but erroneously identified as a *St Catherine* by Joachim Patinir. Whatever the case, in his Venice city guide of 1664, *Le minere della pittura*, Marco Boschini noted that "a triptych with a crucified female saint by Girolamo [=Hieronymus] Basi" hung in the corridors of the Doge's Palace. In 1733 Zanetti wrote in his own book that the painting in question was a triptych by Bosch, but he was uncertain as to whether it depicted a male or a female saint (quotation in Limentani Virdis 2010, p. 240, note 5). In a painting by Gabriel Bella (1730–1799), executed *c.* 1780–1790, Bosch's triptych can be seen hanging in the *Sala dei Tre Capi*, next door to the Chamber of the Council of Ten in the Doge's Palace. In 1838 the triptych was removed to Vienna. It was returned only in 1919.

See also pp. 267–269, *310/311* and Cat. 12.

LITERATURE: Schnürer/Ritz 1934, pp. 14–16, plate IX, no. 19, pp. 22–23, 54–56; Gessler 1937; Bax 1961, pp. 3, 34–35; Marijnissen 1987, pp. 260–269; Venice 1992, p. 58; van Schoute/Verboomen 2000, pp. 116–119, 181, 213; Aikema 2001a, 2001b; Klein 2001, pp. 126; Fischer 2009, pp. 90–91; Limentani Virdis 2010; Venice 2010.

15

The Seven Deadly Sins and the Four Last Things, *c.* 1505–1510
Oil on panel (black poplar),
120 x 150 cm / 47¼ x 59 in.
Madrid, Museo Nacional del Prado,
inv. no. 2822

The Seven Deadly Sins and the Four Last Things falls clearly within the tradition of didactic, diagrammatic paintings for display inside churches. It has its starting point in medieval teachings in which each of the deadly sins and the four last things are clearly categorised, as in a treatise by Denis the Carthusian (1402/03–1471), for example. Bosch has none the less furnished each of the sins with a Latin inscription, in a circular layout that starts at the bottom with Wrath (*ira*) and continues anticlockwise with Pride (*superbia*), Lust (*luxuria*), Sloth (*accidia*, correctly speaking *acedia*), Gluttony (*gula*), Greed (*avaritia*) and Envy (*invidia*). These deadly sins form a ring around the central figure of Christ, who appears as a Man of Sorrows in the pupil of a stylised solar eye. Of the Four Last Things in the corners, Death is positioned at top left, in first place so to speak, followed by the Last Judgement at upper right and – to a certain extent, simultaneously – Hell at lower left and Heaven at upper right.

Bosch conveyed this clear-cut classification system in visual terms by deploying a pictorial topos found in painting in various contexts since antiquity: a centred partitioning system for square to rectangular surfaces, featuring a large circle divided into segments in the middle and further pictorial zones in the corners (p. 308). Instead of portraying the Deadly Sins as relatively abstract personifications, Bosch illustrates them in instantly recognisable and at times earthily humorous exempla in order to convey their meaning more effectively.

Bosch also incorporated three Latin inscriptions in the panel. These were not added as an afterthought but form the theological and thematic basis of the work, and they thus exerted a profound influence upon the creative process. Text and image overlap, complement and mutually reinforce each other. The signature "jheronimus bosch" is located at the bottom of the picture beneath the lower cartouche.

The Bosch connoisseur Felipe de Guevara (d. 1564?) was familiar with the painting even before it reached the royal collection in Madrid. It is possible that he or his father purchased it in the Low Countries. In his *Comentarios de la pintura* of *c.* 1560, he describes it admiringly as a "table owned by H. M. [His Majesty], in which the seven deadly sins, illustrated in figures and exempla, are painted in a circle, and while the whole painting is marvellous in itself, the picture of Envy in my opinion is so rare and inventive and expresses the effect of it in such a way that it could compete with Aristides, the inventor of those paintings that the Greeks called *Ethics*, which in our Castilian means paintings that show the properties and affects of the human soul". With these words, Guevara not only provides a defence and justification of Bosch's picture at the level of art theory, but goes even further: he places the artist on a par with the most famous and authoritative of the painters of Antiquity.

In the context of his discussion of the *Seven Deadly Sins*, Guevara also mentions one of Bosch's pupils; and this has led a number of art historians to wonder whether the panel is in fact the work of the student, not the master. Guevara does not attribute the painting to the pupil, however, but merely refers to him as a very careful imitator and as the only one of any worth who really came close to the spirit of Bosch. He does not cite the panel of the *Seven Deadly Sins* as an example of the pupil's work or style, but as an example of the kind of work by Bosch that was so successful in Flanders. On a number of occasions Guevara uses the phrase "*este género de pintura*", which may be translated not as "this method" or "this style of painting", but more accurately as "this kind of painting","this kind of picture", or better still as "this genre of painting" or "this pictorial genre". He was thus thinking of the artists of Greek Antiquity, such as the portraitist, satirist and genre painter Antiphilos of Naucratis (2nd half of the 4th century BC), a pupil of Ktesideno. According to Guevara, Antiphilos painted in a genre that in Antiquity was called *grillo* and of which Bosch was also a practitioner. Guevara is therefore referring to a lowlier genre of art known in the 16th and 17th centuries as *grillen* or *drollen* in the Low Countries and Germany and as *capricci* in Italy (Raupp 1986, pp. 304–312). These are collective names for highly inventive, fantastical and grotesquely comical representations. Today we call such works drolleries, genre pictures or more generally grotesques. As emerges from the quotation above, the only segment of Bosch's *Seven Deadly Sins* panel that Guevara compares with the style of Aristides of Thebes (1st half of the 4th century BC), an ancient

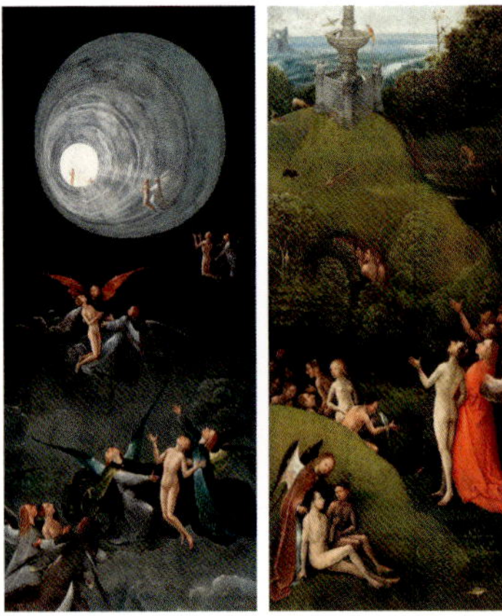

16.1–16.2

Greek painter famous in the Hellenistic and Roman era, is the exemplum of Envy (*invidia*). The annotator of the first edition of the *Comentarios de la pintura*, which was not published until 1788, likewise attributes the *Seven Deadly Sins* indisputably to Bosch in his footnote to this passage. This is supported by the panel's traditional attribution to Bosch in Spain and by the findings of technical analysis. Guevara furthermore judged Bosch's pupil to be "more careful and more patient" than his master, qualities that argue against his authorship of the panel in view of the clumsiness occasionally imputed to certain figures.

The work is regularly described as a tabletop, but there is no material evidence that it was conceived or used as such. It was produced after 1500, as revealed by the broad shape of the biretta in the depiction of Greed (*avaritia*), which only came into fashion at this point. The underdrawing is detailed and executed for the most part in fine strokes. Hatched shading running from upper left to lower right is a recurring feature. Numerous small pentimenti, most of them visible to the naked eye, can be found in the four corner tondi and in the exempla pictures in the segments of the central circle. The dog laid out in the underdrawing in the lower right corner of the Death tondo, with its representation of a dying man, was not developed any further, but was included instead in the exemplum of Sloth (*accidia*). The position of the cupboard in the representation of Pride (*superbia*) was altered in the course of painting, and in the Sloth section of the Hell tondo a damned soul on the chimneystack was never executed.

Unusually, the support is made of black poplar. Although poplar is still found in the Rhine region even today, it was used only occasionally by central European painters, for example by Hans Baldung Grien (1484/85–1545) for his *Aschaffenburg Virgin with a Dagger*, by the Westphalian painter Ludger tom Ring the Younger (1522–1584) and on several occasions by Lucas Cranach the Elder.

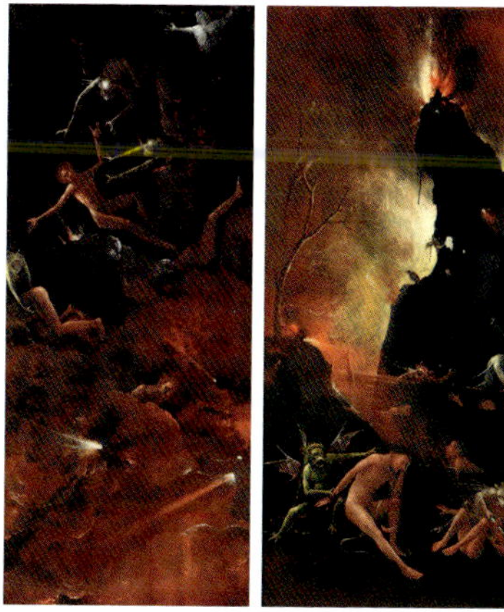

16.3–16.4

In southern Europe, on the other hand, and especially in Italy, poplar panels were in regular use.

The work is mentioned relatively frequently in sources in the 16th and 17th centuries. In 1574 it appears in the inventory of the first delivery of pictures ordered by Philip II for the adornment of the Escorial: "A panel painted with the Seven Deadly Sins, with a circle roundabout, and in the middle the figure of Christ our Lord; and in the four corners of the panel another four circles are painted: one with Death, another with the Judgement, another with Hell and in the other Paradise; by the hand of Hieronymus Bosch, it is four feet high and five wide". These dimensions, expressed in Castilian feet, convert to approximately 111 x 139 cm or 43⅞ x 54¾ in. – an indication that measurements were not taken quite as accurately as they are today.

Although José de Sigüenza is not entirely correct in his formal description of the work, he does correctly identify its iconography and he documents its location in Philip II's private rooms: "In the chamber of His Majesty, where he has a bookcase like those of the monks, there is another excellent piece. In the centre, in a circle of light and glory, he placed our Saviour; around Him are seven circles in which are seen the Seven Deadly Sins [...]" (Sigüenza 1605, pp. 838–839; cited here from Snyder 1973, p. 37). The painting forms part of the Patrimonio Nacional and has been in the Prado since 1939.

See also pp. 276, 279, 280, *308/309*.

LITERATURE: Schwartz 1959; Gibson 1973b; Raupp 1986, pp. 198–199; de Bruyn 1987; Marijnissen 1987, pp. 329–345; de Bruyn 1991; Schüssler 1993; Moser 1997; van Schoute/Verboomen 2000, pp. 122–131, 214–215; Garrido/van Schoute 2001, pp. 35, 76–95; van Schoute/Verougstraete/Garrido 2001, p. 117; Gielis 2003; Silver 2006, pp. 305–317; Pokorny 2010b; Gelfand 2010; Lentes 2011.

16
Paradise and Hell, *c.* 1505–1515
Oil on panel (oak), 86.5 x 39.5 cm /
3⅜ x 1½ in. (each wing panel)
Venice, Museo Palazzo Grimani, inv. no. 184
Left and right pairs of wings
16.1 Interior of the outer left wing:
Heavenly Paradise
16.2 Interior of the inner left wing:
Earthly Paradise
16.3 Interior of the inner right wing:
Fall of the Damned
16.4 Interior of the outer right wing:
The Damned in Hell

Assuming that the lost or merely planned central panel adhered to the traditional concept of the Last Judgement, it would probably have portrayed, in the upper zone, the enthroned figure of Christ in Judgement, accompanied by the Virgin and St John, the twelve apostles and the angels with trumpets (cf. Cat. 13.4), and in the lower zone the figures of the resurrected. The wings should correspondingly be read from the inside to the outside. The interior surfaces of the two left wings show, on the right, the Earthly Paradise and, on the left, the Heavenly Paradise. The right wings show first, on the left, the Fall of the Damned into Hell followed, on the right, by Hell with its torments.

In Venice in 1521 Marcantonio Michiel saw two works by Bosch in the house of Cardinal Domenico Grimani,"a canvas of Hell and a great variety of monsters, by the hand of Hieronymus Bosch. / The canvas of dreams, by the hand of the same". This last-mentioned picture might refer to the right panel of the right pair (16.4), since the melancholy pose of the man propping his head in his hand could suggest associations with reflection and dreaming. An inventory of Cardinal Grimani's estate includes "a Flemish panel painting of Hell in oil".

Dendrochronological evidence indicates that the wings must have been painted after

1484–1490. In the *Earthly Paradise* (16.2), i.e. the right panel of the left pair, the geometric, block-like shape of the fountain, in conjunction with its decoration and figures reminiscent of putti, argue in favour of a date after 1500, since they evoke the stylistic repertoire of the Renaissance rather than the Gothic era. Renaissance elements are found in Netherlandish art prior to 1510 only in very isolated cases in Bruges and in Antwerp, chiefly in the work of Gerard David (*c.* 1460–1523) as from 1495. Even in the earliest documentary sources, no central panel is mentioned.

The condition of the paintings is relatively poor. The exterior surfaces of the four panels are faintly marbled in a single colour, two in black and two in red (Marijnissen 1987). The paint surface of the *Earthly Paradise* contains a number of blemishes. The artist has made relatively frequent use of impasto white heightening which intensifies the chiaroscuro atmosphere. The underdrawing and any pentimenti are barely detectable.

The wings had found their way to Venice by 1521 at the latest, and then passed into the possession of the Venetian State at the end of the 16th century.

See also pp. 270, 274, *312/313*, Cat. 12 and Cat. 14.

LITERATURE: Marijnissen 1987, pp. 300–309; Venice 1992; Aikema 2001a, 2001c; Klein 2001, p. 124; Vandenbroeck 2003, p. 377, notes 880/881; Venice 2010.

17

The Wedding at Cana with Exempla (“The Cana Triptych”), *c.* 1500–1510
Oil on panel (oak), *c.* 94 x 72 cm / 37 x 28⅜ in. (central panel), 94 x 32.6 cm / 37 x 12¾ in. (wings)
Triptych, reconstruction

Following scientific analysis of the oak panels and likewise of the paint layers and underdrawing, Bosch scholars gradually recognised that the wing fragments of this reconstructed triptych originally belonged together. A striking feature of all the panels is their clearly visible parallel hatching, running from upper left to lower right as if executed by a left-handed artist. While both the exterior and interior views of the wings have now been reconstructed, debate continues to surround the subject of the original central panel. Koldeweij (2010, p. 20) has suggested the *Last Judgement*, but there is more reason to think that the central panel showed the *Wedding at Cana*.

The Wedding at Cana (Cat. 17.4) is unanimously accepted as a Bosch composition but has come down to us only in one drawn and four painted copies, of which the highest-quality painted copy is housed in the Museum Boijmans Van Beuningen in Rotterdam (Lammertse 1994, pp. 111–113; Unverfehrt 1980, nos. 19–20). In the Rotterdam painting (Cat. 17.4b), the two dogs at lower left are stylistically untypical of Bosch and were evidently added in order to fill a gap. In the drawing (Cat. 17.4a), probably the most accurate copy of the original, the same spot is filled by a male donor, a canon in typical white liturgical robes with a narrow collar and an almuce (a fur cape such as formed part of the vestments of a canon) draped over his forearm. The figures to the left and right of Christ, who are visible both in the Rotterdam painting (Cat. 17.4b) and the drawing (Cat. 17.4a), probably represent further donors. The aspirations of the donor or donors, relatively wealthy as a consequence of their elevated clerical status, go hand in hand with an innovative pictorial concept, namely the combination of a traditional theme with allegories of the vices.

The surviving painted copies of *The Wedding at Cana* each measure 93 x 72 cm (36⅝ x 28⅜ in.) and thus match the required height and width of the central panel being sought. The reliability of size as a gauge can be tested against other Bosch triptychs and their copies: owing to the use of a transfer cartoon, the dimensions of the copy are in most cases the same as the original.

A thematic constellation similar to that in this reconstructed triptych is to be found in sermons on the Wedding at Cana, as recorded in Middle High German manuscripts from around 1400 onwards and in particular in the third quarter of the 15th century, often in conjunction with the "Sermon on Matrimony" (Kruse 1995). This last sets out the good reasons for marriage and expounds its benefits. Thus the miracle that Christ performs at his mother's request during the wedding at Cana, when he turns water into wine, is considered to honour the state of wedlock. Furthermore, the sermon presents ethical arguments for marriage and illustrates its point with forceful comparisons. When selecting his bride, for example, the bridegroom should take care not to choose a woman who is beautiful on the outside but weak of character inside, while the father of the bride would do better to entrust his daughter "to a wise poor man than to a rich fool". The mutual care and concern of husband and wife shall protect them both from sins such as lust, arrogance and foolishness. Their union acts as a curb upon their behaviour, for both will have to practise restraint. As in Bosch, Temperance as the virtue of moderation and right measure is a fundamental theme of the sermon, while in the triptych the volume of wine being consumed serves as a traditional metaphor for moderate behaviour as opposed to its negative opposite, unrestrained over-indulgence.

As so often in Bosch's work, Biblical events and the acts of the saints are here, too, accompanied by allegorical exempla, a didactic rhetorical device disseminated by the Dominicans and the Franciscans and employed in sermons at the latest from the 13th century onwards. This combination of the sacred and the profane is thus most certainly not a sign of secularisation. Bosch's innovations also coincide with a period in which the triptych format was employed in a great many contexts and for a wide range of purposes. We can identify at least four types

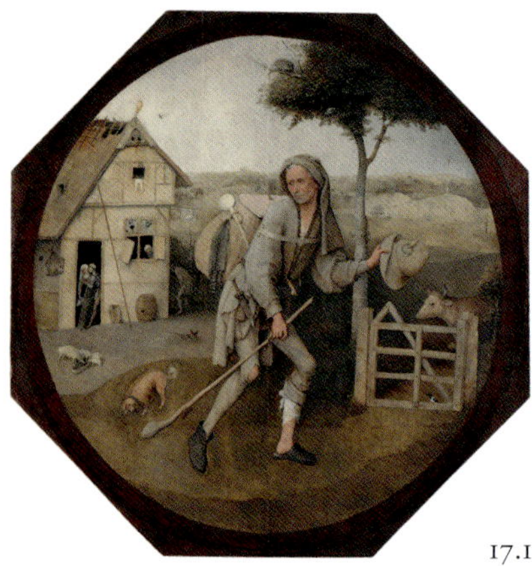

17.1

of triptych that were not in general used as altarpieces (see overview in Fischer 2009, p. 243): firstly, instructional pictures or pictorial sequences illustrating the portents of the Last Judgement or the Ten Commandments, as found relatively frequently inside churches in earlier times; secondly, small triptychs of a private devotional nature that were likewise relatively common but which seldom stood on altars; thirdly, the somewhat rarer type of triptych of a moralistic secular character; and fourthly, also fairly uncommon, heraldic or portrait triptychs. For all four groups, the three-panel format was advantageous both on pragmatic pictorial grounds and for reasons of conservation.

Dendrochronological evidence indicates that the wings cannot have been painted before 1488–1494. The naked cupids on the capitals on the central panel show an ironic and not an ideal representation of Renaissance putti and instead point to a dating after 1500.

See also pp. 282–284, *303*, *306/307*.

Literature: Kruse 1995; Jacobs 2000; van Schoute/Verboomen 2000; Klein 2001, p. 125; Hartau 2001a, 2003, 2005; Silver 2006, pp. 239–259; Fischer 2009, pp. 243–245; Pinson 2010.

17.1

The Pedlar, *c.* 1500–1510

Oil on panel (oak), 71 x 70.6 cm / 28 x 27¾ in. (originally *c.* 94 x 72 cm / 37 x 28⅜ in.)

Rotterdam, Museum Boijmans Van Beuningen, inv. no. 1079

Outer wings

The main figure shown is a pedlar and not, for example, the Prodigal Son, an interpretation often proposed. For all his similarity with the character in the biblical parable, this impoverished, itinerant hawker is present as a type in his own right in late medieval period, both in literature and in the visual arts (de Bruyn 2001a). The painting's message may be read to mean that humankind can reduce and over-

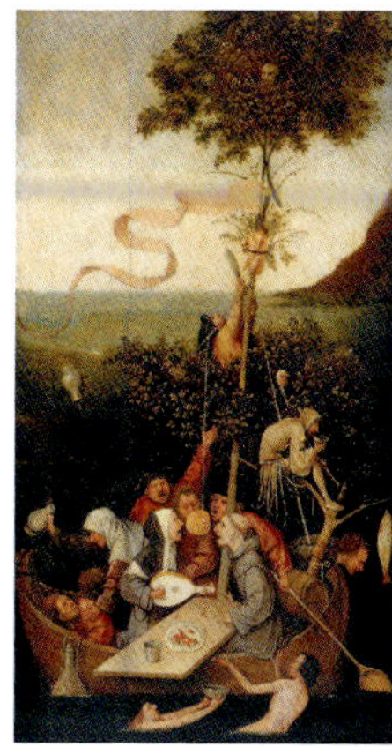

17.2

come the breadth and variety of sinful paths by turning to God. In *The Pedlar* the path thus leads from the yard in front of a brothel to the "narrow gate", beyond which are waiting an ox (a sacrificial beast and a symbol of Christ) and a magpie (which stands for the liberated soul) (de Bruyn 2001a, pp. 355–363). The pictorial motif of the pedlar is found again, in a slightly different form, in *The Haywain* (Cat. 20.1).

The panel, whose palette is dominated by greys and greens, has been cut down on all sides to form an octagon and the two halves of the original shutters joined almost seamlessly to form a single picture. The paint layers deviate only minimally from the composition laid out in detail in the underdrawing. Prior to 1904 the work was in a French private collection, before passing to Vienna and to Berlin. In 1931 it was purchased by the Museum Boijmans Van Beuningen.

Literature: Bax 1953; Brand Philip 1958; Tolnay 1965, pp. 41–42; Renger 1969; Vandenbroeck 1985; Bambeck 1987; Marijnissen 1987, pp. 410–419; Falkenburg 1988, pp. 88–90; Lammertse 1994, pp. 90–95; van Schoute/Verboomen 2000, p. 177; Buck 2001, p. 210; de Bruyn 2001a, 2001d; Lammertse/Roorda Boersma 2003; Unverfehrt 2003; Pinson 2005, pp. 52, 57–84; Sullivan 2008.

17.2

The Ship of Fools, *c.* 1500–1510

Oil on panel (oak), 57.9 x 32.6 cm / 22¾ x 12¾ in. (originally *c.* 94 x 32.6 cm / 37 x 12¾ in.)

Paris, Musée du Louvre, inv. no. RF 2218

Left inner wing, above

The main motif of this middle and upper fragment of the left inner wing can be clearly assigned to the iconographical tradition of the Ship of Fools. Harder to identify and interpret, however, are some of its individual pictorial motifs, in particular the figures with their heads draped: are they nuns, housewives

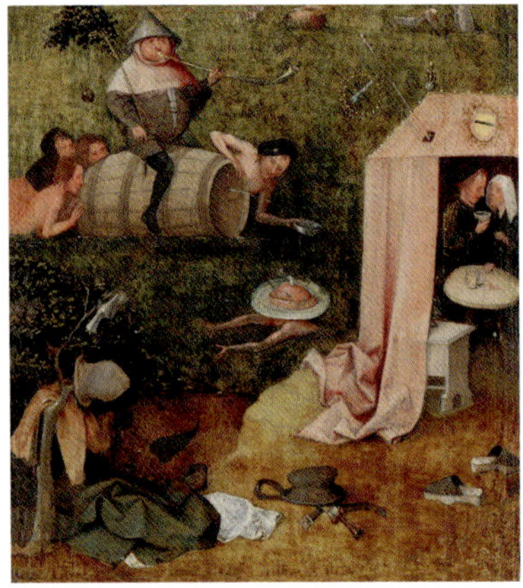

17.3

or even men in disguise? Material analyses prove that the *Ship of Fools* and its fellow fragment the *Allegory of Intemperance* (Cat. 17.3) were originally attached and together formed the left inner wing.

The lower section of the inner wing is already absent from a drawn copy on tinted paper in the Louvre (RF 3714r). In contrast to the foreground, where just a few details are modified, the background has been composed entirely freely. The sheet was in the past thought to be a master copy or even a design drawing (Unverfehrt 1980, pp. 44, 78); but the fact that it lacks the very part that was sawn off the bottom of the finished painting (Cat. 17.3) argues against this. A second drawing (RF 6947) in an identical style also exists, moreover, and this is clearly a copy of *Death and the Miser* (see Cat. 17.5).

The picture is badly worn in places and has been overpainted in the area of the crown of the tree. In 1914 it was in the collection of Camille Benoît, conservator of paintings at the Louvre, who bequeathed it to the museum in 1918.

LITERATURE: Boczkowska 1971; Unverfehrt 1980, pp. 44, 78; Pleij 1983; Morganstern 1984; Marijnissen 1987, pp. 310–319; van Schoute/Verboomen 2000, pp. 176, 187; Hartau 2001b; Landau 2010.

17.3

Allegory of Intemperance, *c.* 1500–1510
Oil on panel (oak), 35.9 x 31.4 cm / 14⅛ x 12⅜ in. (originally *c.* 94 x 32.6 cm / 37 x 12¾ in.)
New Haven, Yale University Art Gallery, inv. no. 1959.15.22
Gift of Hannah D. and Louis M. Rabinowitz
Left inner wing, below

Various material analyses have proved that this small oak panel, depicting allegories of the deadly sins of Gluttony (*gula*) and Lust (*luxuria*), forms the lower section of the inner left wing and was originally attached to the *Ship of Fools* (Cat. 17.2). Much of its paint

film has been lost, especially at the top, so that the pale colour of the wood shines through. The originally dark green paint layer still visible on the upper fragment has consequently here disappeared. The work came to light in 1928 at Christie's in London. After passing through various private hands it entered the Yale University Art Gallery in 1959.
LITERATURE: Marijnissen 1987, pp. 310–319.

17.4a
Anonymous artist after Hieronymus Bosch (?)
The Wedding at Cana, *c.* 1505–1515
Pen drawing on paper, 28.1 x 20.8 cm / 11 x 8¼ in.
Paris, Musée du Louvre, Rothschild Collection Central panel, copy (see p. 287)

This high-quality drawing was probably made from the lost original of Bosch's *Wedding at Cana*. It is executed in great detail and modelled with hatched shading whose lines are drawn primarily from lower left to upper right, instead of from upper left to lower right, as on the triptych's inner wings. The donor, who is accompanied by his patron saint, an otherwise unidentified bishop, fits perfectly into the composition and corresponds stylistically, including his costume, to the period around or shortly after 1500. The inclusion of the donor and his patron saint indicates that the drawing was made very early on, probably in and by the Bosch workshop, as an exact copy of what was evidently considered a model pictorial invention. This copy then served as the starting point for future pictures or as the direct basis of copies showing other or no donors, as in the case of the painting discussed here as Cat. 17.4b. See also the general introduction to Cat. 17.
LITERATURE: Unverfehrt 1980, no. 20; Kessler 2001.

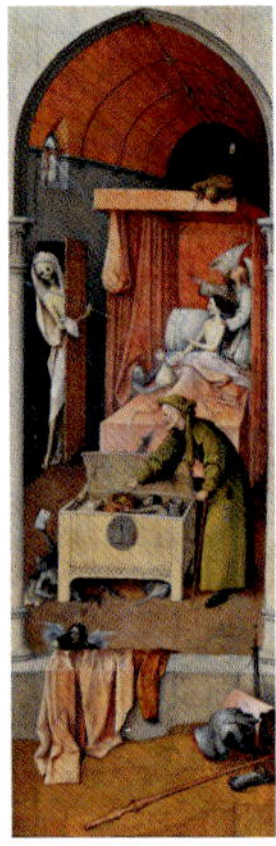
17.5

17.4b
Anonymous artist after
Hieronymus Bosch (?)
The Wedding at Cana, after 1555–1561
Oil on panel (oak), 93 x 72 cm /
36⅝ x 28⅜ in.
Rotterdam, Museum Boijmans Van
Beuningen, inv. no. St. 25
Central panel, copy (see pp. 306/307)

Dendrochronological dating confirms that the panel is a relatively late copy made in the second half of the 16th century. The group of donor and patron saint probably present in the original, but now redundant, has been replaced by two dogs that were most certainly not executed by Bosch – their naturalistic style rules this out – and probably not by his workshop either. The two rear-view figures seated at the table, who in the drawn copy remain largely obscured by the donor and his patron saint, have had the missing areas of their backs filled out in a sculptural style with loosely indicated draperies falling in generous folds. Such draperies are unusual for Bosch, as a comparison with other rear-view figures reveals. See also Cat. 17.4a and the general introduction to Cat. 17. LITERATURE: 's-Hertogenbosch 1967, pp. 93–97, no. 17; Unverfehrt 1980, no. 19; Dixon 1982; Marijnissen 1987, pp. 420–431; Lammertse 1994, pp. 108–113; van Schoute/Verougstraete/Garrido 2001, p. 118.

17.5
Death and the Miser, *c.* 1500–1510
Oil on panel (oak), 92.6 x 30.8 cm /
36⅜ x 12⅛ in.
Washington, National Gallery of Art, Samuel
H. Kress Collection, inv. no. 1952.5.33
Right inner wing

The iconography of this representation of a miser who has reached his final hour has been compared with pictures from the *ars moriendi* tradition and illustrations of "pointless

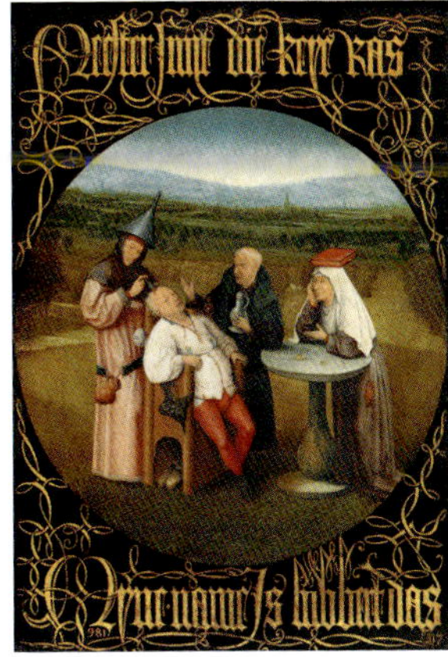

18

wealth" (Morganstern, Marijnissen, Vinken/Schlüter, Colenbrander). Areas of overlap can be found in the dying man's confrontation, for one last time, with the temptations that have ruled his life, here represented by devils, exempla and symbolic objects, and the promise of salvation extended by the Church, in the shape of clerics, angels, saints and Christ. A striking feature of the panel is the detailed underdrawing with its densely hatched shading (Antwerp 2002, p. 165, no. 2). This was probably visible right from the start since it appears in a very similar manner in a drawn copy in the Louvre (RF 6947). It is unclear when this drawing was made, but it was not a master copy or a design drawing (Unverfehrt 1980, Colenbrander 2003). While it is true that all its pictorial motifs – with the exception of the crucifix in the arched recess on the wall – appear in the painting, not all the motifs in the painting are found in the drawing. The drinking vessels standing on the wall at the lower right, for example, and the fish near the helmet, are not present in the painting's underdrawing (Metzger 2003). Moreover, the arrow held by Death in this underdrawing is shorter than the corresponding arrow in the drawn copy and the finished painting. The modification of certain pictorial motifs can be explained by the slightly wider format of the sheet vis-à-vis the panel. The panel came to light around 1826 in a British private collection; it was in Belgium in the 1930s and has been in Washington since 1951.

See also the general introduction to Cat. 17.

LITERATURE: Unverfehrt 1980, pp. 36, 44–45, 54, 78–79; Morganstern 1982; Hand 1986; Marijnissen 1987, pp. 320–327; McNamee 1998; van Schoute/Verboomen 2000, pp. 197–198, 215–216; Vinken/Schlüter 2000; Koreny 2002/03; Colenbrander 2003; Metzger 2003.

18

Extracting the Stone of Folly, *c.* 1505–1515
Oil on panel (oak), 47.5 x 34.5 cm / 18¾ x 13½ in.

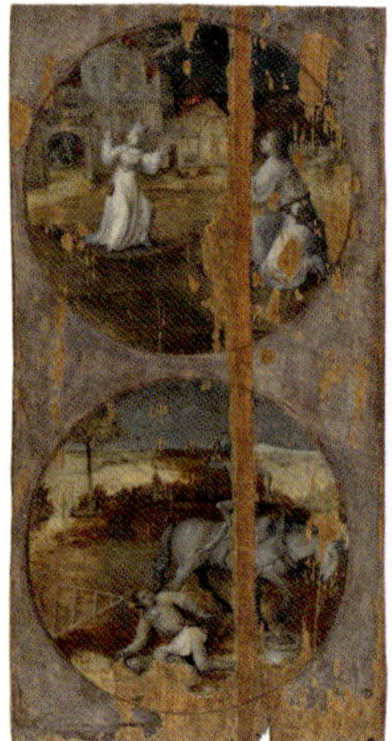 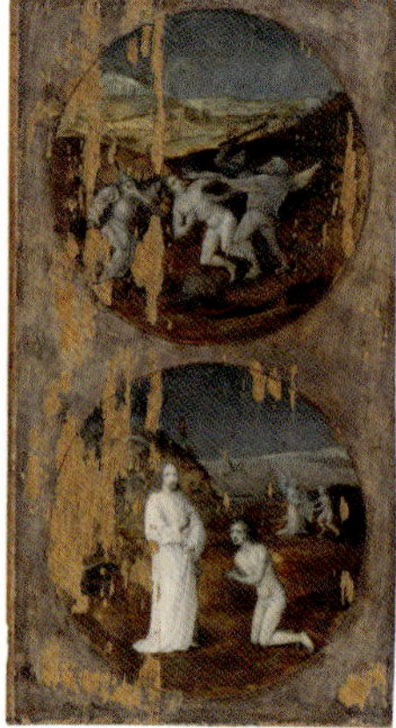

19.1

Madrid, Museo Nacional del Prado, inv. no. 2056

Extracting the Stone of Folly is the only painting in Bosch's œuvre with a purely secular theme and function; and for this very reason, we may suspect, it is also the smallest. The central theme of foolishness is the only aspect of the composition that can be traced back in very general terms to the Bible. The iconography has been studied in great detail by Koldeweij (1991), according to whom the seated man is vainly seeking to have his lack of intellectual vigour and virility cured by a quack doctor (far left), watched by his ostensibly pious wife (far right) and her illicit lover, the cleric (second from right). The composition exists in a number of variations, of which a group coming closest to the original (Unverfehrt 1980, nos. 50a/50b) largely adopts the seated central figure and modifies the appearance and pose of the other figures. Although *Extracting the Stone of Folly* is occasionally rejected as autograph, it falls entirely within the framework of Bosch's œuvre in terms of its painting technique. Its insignificant pentimenti are confined to corrections to the position of body parts or objects, although this would not be usual for a composition of such a lucid kind (cf. Cat. 7, 15, 17). The picture (or a copy of it) is mentioned in 1517 in an inventory of the Wijk bij Duurstede palace of Philip of Burgundy (1464–1524), where it is described as "a painting of Lubbertas having the stone cut out" ("*een taeffereel van Lubbertas die men die keye snijt*"). In 1524 it appears again, as "*een tafreel van Lubbert Tas die men die keye uyt snyt*".

In July 1527 Philip's collection was put up for auction. It is possible that the present work was acquired by Felipe de Guevara. A painting of *Extracting the Stone of Folly*, along with a further five works attributed to Bosch, was in the possession of his wife Beatriz de Haro in January 1570, when it passed to the Spanish King Philip II, entering the Escorial

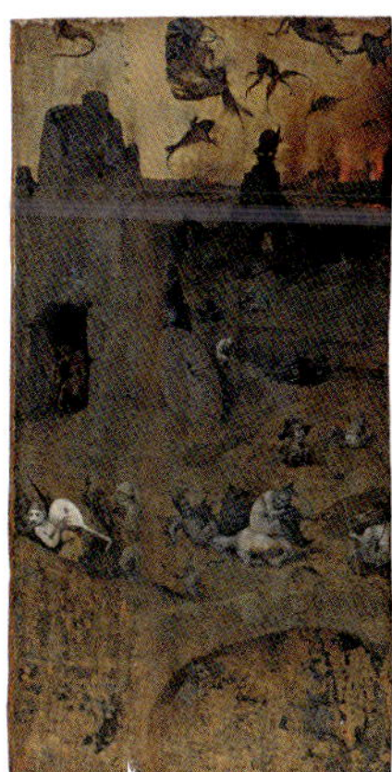
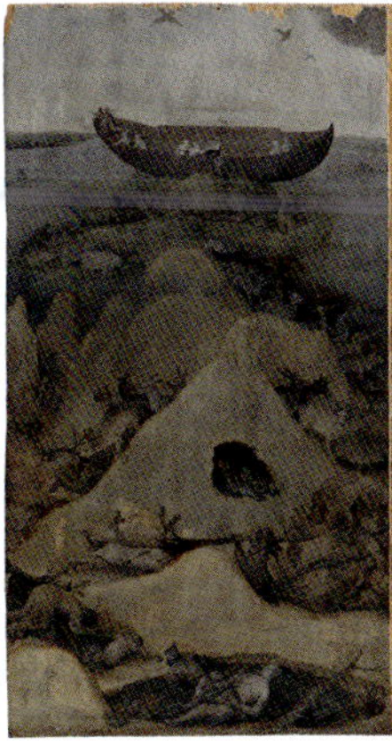

19.2–19.3

in 1574. While it is true that its description in the inventory as "*otro lienzo quadrado donde se cura de la locura*" ("another square canvas where lunacy is being cured") matches the content of the picture, it seems to deviate in two technical points: the picture is neither on canvas, nor is it square. But panel paintings were often described as canvases in inventories at that time, and "*quadrado*" can mean rectangular as well as square. What is certain is that in 1745 the original passed as a gift from the Duke of Arco's country estate near Madrid into the royal collection. Records indicate that it has been in the Prado since the middle of the 19th century.

See also pp. 288, 291, 292, *315*.

LITERATURE: Unverfehrt 1980, pp. 263–264, no. 55; Marijnissen 1987, pp. 440–445; Koldeweij 1991; Garrido/van Schoute 2001, pp. 50–57; van Schoute/Verougstraete/Garrido 2001, p. 117; Fischer 2009, p. 159.

19

Fragments of a representation of The Flood (exterior: The Temptation and Deliverance of Job), *c.* 1510–1515

Oil on panel (oak), 69 x 36 cm and 69 x 38 cm / 27⅛ x 14⅛ in. and 27⅛ x 15 in.

Rotterdam, Museum Boijmans Van Beuningen, inv. nos. St. 27, St. 28

19.1 Outer wings: Four tondi showing the Temptation and Deliverance of Job

19.2 Left inner wing: The World before the Flood

19.3 Right inner wing: The Animals leaving Noah's Ark

The interpretation of the iconography of these fragments remains a matter of dispute, particular in the case of the exterior wings. Although the Flood is clearly recognisable as the central theme of the interior, even here it remains to be clarified whether the left inner wing, which is populated by monsters as symbols of the wicked and the sinful, does indeed

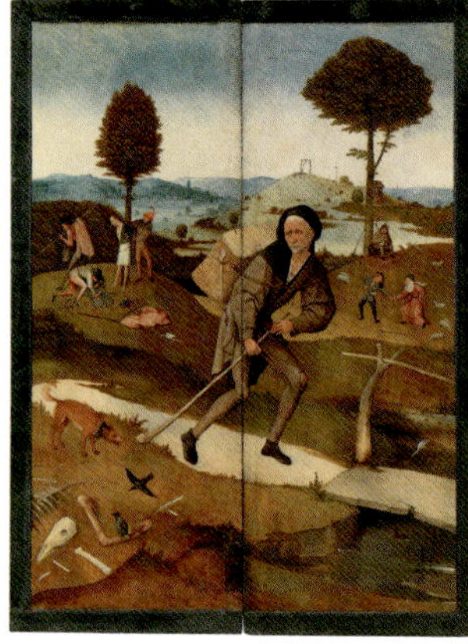

20.1

show the Earth before the Flood, or whether it represents the Fall of the Angels (Wuhrmann 1998). In the scene on the right inner wing, the animals are shown leaving Noah's Ark. Between the barren rocks, the receding waters reveal the monsters, animals and people drowned by the Flood. The interior of the triptych has evidently been laid out in chronological order; and in this respect it is comparable with eschatological works by Bosch, which show Paradise in the left wing and Hell in the right (Cat. 11, Cat. 13, Cat. 16, Cat. 20). In the present case, the central panel may have shown the Ark floating on the waters of the Flood or with the animals making their way on board. Wuhrmann argues instead for a representation of humankind before the Flood, comparable with the *Sicut erat in diebus Noë* theme in the *Garden of Earthly Delights* (Cat. 11).

Four tondi are visible on the exterior. In the first, to the upper left, devils are attacking a large farm and killing the people and cattle. A woman flees, while a man, evidently the owner of the estate, kneels in supplication. In the tondo beneath a farmer has been surprised by a devil while ploughing a field. From his perch on the back of the draught-horse, the devil is threatening to flog the man, who has fallen to the ground. In the tondo at upper right three demons with cudgels are attacking a man, naked to his undergarments. In the tondo at lower right Christ appears as Redeemer, his hand raised to bless the victim. In the middle distance an angel is clothing another – or the same – man, who seems to be the survivor of a shipwreck since a boat is sinking in the background.

The four tondi can be understood in general terms as allegories of temptation and deliverance (Lammertse 1994). Wuhrmann, with whom I concur, identifies the four tondi on the outer wings as representations of the Temptation and Deliverance of Job. Demons and devils here serve in place of soldiers and other tribulations. Job's sufferings intensify with each episode. The exterior and interior

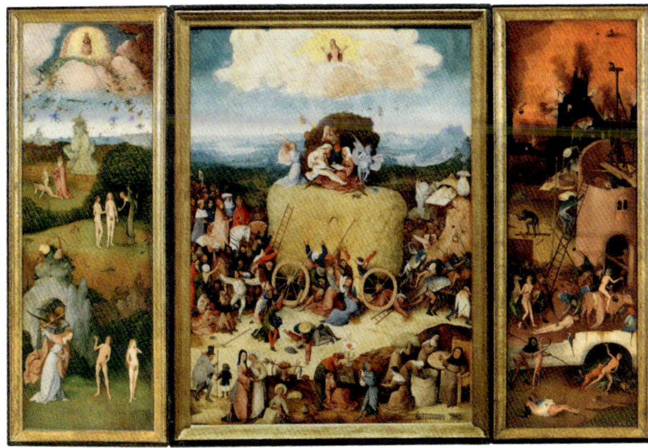

20.2–20.4

surfaces of the wings thus correspond to one another, in so far as they begin with scenes of worsening evil, but end with the deliverance of the steadfast believer through God's grace. Job and Noah are both examples of the salvation of the soul. Dendrochronological dating situates the period of production after 1508. Executed in grisaille inside and out, the wings are in poor condition, with the exception of the right inner panel. The wings are badly damaged in places, making it even harder to identify the iconography and the scenes portrayed. On both the inside and outside of the wings the underdrawing has been corrected and in some places deviates from the paint layer. In the tondo at lower left, for example, the devil and the horse have been shifted from the centre closer to the right edge. Another detail on the outer wings provides an important clue to the working process in Bosch's studio. The small monster reminiscent of a beetle or possibly a cat in the upper right tondo was transferred from a Bosch drawing which is today in Berlin (Cat. D8). This may have been done by a member of the workshop.

The two panels are documented in 1927 as being in the Madrid private collection of the Marquis de Chiloeches (the spelling Chiloedes is incorrect). In the 17th and 18th centuries the Chiloeches family was dynastically related to Guevara. In 1935 the wings passed, by way of the art trade, to the Museum Boijmans, first as a loan and then in 1941 as a gift. See also pp. 292–295, *316/317*. LITERATURE: Wittrock 1979; Bax 1983; Lammertse 1994, pp. 96–105; Marijnissen 1987, pp. 292–299; Wuhrmann 1998; Buck 2001, pp. 208, 210; Klein 2001, pp. 126–127; Silver 2006, pp. 322–329.

20

The Haywain (exterior: The Pedlar),
c. 1510–1515
Oil on panel (oak), 133 x 100 cm / 52⅜ x 39⅜ in. (central panel),
147 x 56 cm / 57⅞ x 22 in. (wings)

Madrid, Museo Nacional del Prado,
inv. no. 2052
20.1 Outer wings: The Pedlar
20.2 Left inner wing: The Genesis of Evil and the Loss of Paradise
20.3 Central panel: The Haywain
20.4 Right inner wing: Hell

When closed, the wings show a pedlar on the road, as in Cat. 17. The interior view opens on the left inner wing with events from the story of Creation up to the Expulsion from Paradise. On the central panel, moving in the same direction as Adam and Eve, is the haywain with its train of followers as an allegory of "the world, the flesh and the devil" (de Bruyn). The procession concludes on the right inner wing with the representation of Hell. In his thorough iconographic study, de Bruyn scrutinised all the details on the triptych's exterior and interior in the light of other pictorial representations, passages from the Bible and in particular Netherlandish texts of the Late Middle Ages and 16th century (de Bruyn 2001a). According to his findings, the figures and scenes on the central panel may be understood, within the overall symbolic meaning of hay, as variations on themes such as deception, greed and vanity.
In 1586 the eminent Spanish historiographer Ambrosio de Morales (1513–1591) appended a lengthy description and iconographical analysis of *The Haywain* to the publication of the writings of his uncle, the Spanish Hellenist Fernán Pérez de Oliva (*c.* 1494–1531). Born in Cordoba, Morales studied in Salamanca from 1524 up to the death of his uncle de Oliva in 1531. He then returned to Cordoba and in 1533 took his vows and joined the Order of St Jerome. He was subsequently ordained to the priesthood. In 1540 he began teaching at the University of Alcalá de Henares, east of Madrid, from 1550 onwards as professor of rhetoric. He died in Cordoba in 1591. His text on *The Haywain*, as Morales states in his preface, was written during his student days (i.e.

in the years up to 1531). It is much more likely, however, that it was composed in or around 1540, by which time the original *Haywain* (or a copy of it) had reached Madrid as part of the collection of Felipe de Guevara. Morales would have had ample time to study *The Haywain* at the latest from 1544/45, when he became tutor to the eldest son of Felipe de Guevara and Beatriz de Haro, Diego (1537/38–1566). In 1570 he also brokered the sale of works from Guevara's posthumous estate to Philip II. From 1572 to 1582 he served as historiographer to the Spanish monarchy, a role to which he was appointed by the king himself.

Morales compares *The Haywain* with the *Tabula Cebetis* (Tablet of Cebes), a fictitious, allegorical dialogue also known as the *Pinax* and at that time ascribed to Cebes of Thebes (*c.* 400 BC), and considers it an equally successful work. "With subtle detail and skilful execution [Bosch] shows us a panorama of our miserable lives and the great enchantment that we seem to find in its vanities. For those who have not seen the painting, I will describe it so that they may, in some manner, enjoy it if only by my words. It is a large piece with three parts, the largest in the middle, the smaller panels to the sides. In the first of the smaller, on the right side [from Christ's perspective within the picture;] where the sequence begins, the creation of the world is represented with the sin of Adam and the angel who casts him and his wife from the terrestrial paradise. It appears that the angel is leading them from that panel (which represents the beginning of man's life) directly into the larger central panel where the activities of men who have come into our world, tainted with the evil tendencies of original sin, are depicted.

In the upper part of the larger panel, in the centre, appears a very large wagon loaded with hay, resembling a tower, with a throng of people milling about it. This "wagon of hay", as it is called in Flemish, means the same thing as a "wagon of nothingness" [*carro de nonanda*] in Castilian. So, as a wagon of hay, it is in truth a wagon of nothingness, a name most appropriate for it. The wagon is pulled by several demons who guide the driver, carrying the yoke, towards the third panel, where the ultimate departure from this world and life is represented. Atop the great load of hay, or nothingness, or vanity, are several youths and maidens seated at leisure; some are plucking musical instruments, others dancing, and yet others eating, drinking and enjoying themselves in diverse ways. A devil making music with a hornpipe serves as their guide, while behind them kneels an angel, tearful and sad with his eyes and hands lifted towards heaven, bemoaning such great perdition as he prays to God in supplication and in tears.

Lower down, around the wagon, an infinite and diverse crowd of people follows on, who, filled with extraordinary desire and persistence, try to grab more hay and more vanity from the wagon. Some use hooks, others have shovels and other types of implements, and they wear themselves out grasping for the hay; others, with ladders, climb up in a frenzy to reach the top before more people arrive, and try to take more than they can carry. One of them falls because of his heavy load, another one snatches by shrewdness or by force the hay someone else has gathered, and yet another one kills somebody in order to steal his hay from him. And so they all continue, very satisfied, as if they were really acquiring some rich booty. They rush in order to be first to grab the hay, pushing others aside. Some of the brasher ones push forward, opening a path, while others collapse on the ground as the fury that has driven them on is spent, only to be trampled on by those who follow.

Behind the wagon, in the principal and honoured positions, ride the king and princes, and in a clever warning from the painter they appear immediately beside the wagon but because of their authority and importance do not reach out to grab any of the hay, the vanity, as all the others are doing. Instead, with a marked seriousness, the king gestures for his servants to move ahead and fetch quantities of hay for everyone.

Further down some people are returning with their bundles, contented but very tired and sweaty. Represented here are the different types and estates of man, many of whom are engaged in fierce quarrels, some killing as they grab a little more hay, vanity, nothingness from one another. Many run towards the wagon, tormented by the thought that it might get away or that the hay might run out. Parents take their children by the hand to show them the great riches, passing on their excitement so that even they approach the wagon and eagerly carry away their own bundles, not content with what their parents have fetched. Others pay large sums of money to buy the hay that others have brought back. There are so many details of this sort that it is impossible to describe them all, and there is really no reason for doing so. All of this ends abruptly as the demons guide the wagon into the final panel, where man's fate after this life is represented. Hell is symbolised by the variety of tortures that the miserable souls, whose lives were passed in the vanity of sin, must now suffer, being themselves just like the hay that dries out and dies away without the fruit of virtue." (Morales 1586; cited here from Snyder 1973, pp. 31–33).

Who commissioned *The Haywain*, and for what occasion, are questions that remain to be answered. The triptych is religious but not sacred, and can thus best be compared with the *Garden of Earthly Delights* (Cat. 11). Both works can be understood in relation to a courtly context. The Spanish upper nobility in the Low Countries evidently admired *The Haywain*, which is first documented in the 1530s. Around 1536, after his time at Charles V's court, Felipe de Guevara settled in Madrid with his wife Beatriz de Haro. He brought back with him a number of works by Bosch which he had most probably inherited from his father Diego, and which probably included the original *Haywain*. Whatever the case, in 1570 Philip II purchased from the collection of the deceased Guevara, or, rather, Guevara's widow, a "panel one yard and two-thirds high, with two wings, which when opened is three yards wide; and it is the Haywain by Hieronymus Bosch, by his own hand". These dimensions may be converted to approximately 139 x 250 cm / 54¾ x 98¾ in. (1 Castilian yard = 83.5 cm or 32 909 in.), giving a height that corresponds roughly to that of the central panel today, but a total width some 35 cm / 15 inches less than that of the Prado triptych in the open position. In 1539 Mencia de Mendoza (1508–1554), the third wife of Henry III of Nassau, who lived in the Low Countries from 1530 to 1533 and again from 1535 to 1539, instigated a hunt for a second *Haywain* ("*carro de Geronimo Bosque*") to replace one only recently purchased but already destroyed (de Bruyn 2001a, pp. 34–35; van Dijck 2001a, pp. 94–95). The search appears to have yielded nothing, as no *Haywain* can be identified in the inventories of Mencia's collection drawn up in 1548, 1554 and 1560, even though these list a number of other works attributed to Bosch.

The triptych is mentioned again and in more detail in the inventory of works sent to the Escorial in 1574 as part of the furnishings for the new palace:"A panel painting with two shutters, on which is painted with a brush a Cart of Hay from which every class is helping itself, which signifies the vanity that all chase after, and on top of the hay the figure of a guardian angel and the devil and other figures, and at the very top God the Father [*sic*], and on the panel on the right side [again from Christ's perspective within the picture;] the Creation of Adam and other figures from the same story; and on the left one [ditto] Hell and the punishment of the mortal sins; this is five feet high and four wide, without the shutters: it is by Hieronymus Bosch." With the exception of the erroneous identification of Christ as God the Father, the content of the central panel is here aptly summarised.

No mention is made of the paintings on the exterior shutters. The dimensions, which convert to approximately 139 x 111 cm / 54¾ x 43⅞ in., come close to those of the central panel.
The colours have suffered badly, especially on the left inner wing and in the background of the central panel, as shown by a comparison with the copy in the Escorial (see p. 294), which conveys an impression of the original palette. Where the paint has worn away, the underlying ground shimmers through more strongly, causing the paint surface to appear uneven. For this reason, the colour composition at first sight seems oddly undecided between monochrome and polychrome. Amongst Bosch's late works, it is true that he used grisaille on the inner wings of his *Flood* triptych (Cat. 19). On the present case, however, the tendency towards a brown tonality in the figures and landscape background is outweighed by Bosch's usual broad palette of colours.
The underdrawing largely corresponds with the visible picture. Numerous minor deviations can be seen on all the panels, but these chiefly relate to the size and details of individual figures and objects, and only rarely to their position. The only clear instance of hatching is found on the robe of the angel expelling Adam and Eve. The strokes descend from upper left to lower right as in Cat. 17, but in a manner that suggests no more than sketching. In 1939 the triptych was moved, along with other works by Bosch, from the Escorial to the Prado in Madrid.
See also pp. 295, 296, 298, 299, 301, *320/321*.
LITERATURE: Guevara 1560; Morales 1586; Sigüenza 1605; Salazar 1955; Brand Philip 1958; Tolnay 1965, pp. 401–405; Steppe 1967; Snyder 1973, pp. 31–41; Unverfehrt 1980, pp. 239–240; Raupp 1986, pp. 199–200; Marijnissen 1987, pp. 52–83; Vandenbroeck 1985; Jacobs 2000; de Bruyn 2001a, 2001d; Garrido/van Schoute 2001, pp. 38, 120–157; van Schoute/Verougstraete/Garrido 2001, p. 117; Klein 2001, p. 127; Koreny 2002/03; Silver 2006, pp. 260–273.

Catalogue of paintings – workshop and followers

Documentary sources and technical analyses of Bosch's works indicate that, by 1499 at the latest, he was employing at least one workshop assistant, in 1503/04 at least two journeymen and around 1505 likewise at least one assistant. In those days, as a rule apprentices remained with a master for three or four years, while journeymen might stay for as little as a few months and as much as several years. It has so far proved impossible to determine more closely the number and origin of the members of Bosch's workshop.

The attempt to attribute specific paintings and drawings to the anonymous artist characterised by Bosch collector Felipe de Guevara as a particularly talented Bosch pupil ("*discipulo*") has yielded very varied results (Unverfehrt 1980, p. 233 ff.; Vandenbroeck 1987a, p. 181 and 2003, pp. 196–199; Koreny 2002/03). Guevara explains that this painter, "who was his pupil [...], either out of reverence for his master or in order to increase the value of his own works, signed them with the name of Bosch rather than with his own." Guevara was in no doubt as to the artistic quality of the works by this unnamed pupil, however: "In spite of this fact his paintings are very praiseworthy, and whoever owns them ought to esteem them highly; for in his allegorical and moralising subjects he followed the spirit of his master, and in their execution he was even more meticulous and patient than Bosch and did not deviate from the lively and fresh qualities and colouring of his teacher." On the basis of the criteria cited in this passage, up to five paintings and approximately four drawings can be tentatively attributed to this "Pupil of Hieronymus Bosch".

The possibility that members of the van Aken "painter dynasty" were also active in the Bosch workshop cannot be ruled out. Bosch's brother Jan Anthonis van Aken (*c.* 1448–1498/99) died too early, however, for us to be able to link his name with works such as the Boston *Ecce Homo* (Cat. 21). Perhaps the most likely family member to have been employed in the Bosch workshop would have been Anthonis Goessens van Aken (*c.* 1478–1516), a nephew of Bosch (on his biography: van Dijck 2001a, p. 35; Vink 2001a, p. 96). He was probably trained by his father, Goessen, and was around 18 years old when the latter died. At this age he would not yet have been in a position to take over the orphaned van Aken workshop, which was run instead by his mother Katelijn (Katharina, d. 1523/26), as the master's widow. In 1499/1500 Katelijn carried out the polychrome decoration of a statue of St Barbara for the Grootziekengasthuis the 's-Hertogenbosch town hospital, or had the work done under her name (van Dijck 2001a, pp. 29–31). Whether Anthonis indeed worked for his mother or for his uncle Hieronymus, however, and where he lived and worked, are questions that remain to be answered. Whatever the case, he probably did not have his own workshop. Shortly after 1500 Anthonis married Gertrudis Pontheniers, whose parents lived on Verwerstraat on the south side of the market. Even though, on November 21, 1508, his mother Katelijn granted him usufruct of the van Aken house on the marketplace, in 1516 Anthonis was nevertheless living in Postelstraat in the west of the town, along with his brother Jan.

Documented works by Anthonis Goessens van Aken include a Tafel van de Heilige Geest, a Palm Sunday effigy of Christ on a donkey, which he produced in 1513/14 for the municipal alms-house, and a number of heraldic shields that he painted on behalf of the town's ruling body for the 'Joyous Entrance' (*Joyeuse Entrée* or *Blijde Inkomst*) of Charles V on his first visit to 's-Hertogenbosch as Emperor in July 1515. He also executed a commission for the Brotherhood of Our Blessed Lady in 1514/15. When Anthonis died in August 1516, the Brotherhood reduced the "death debt" (*doodschuld*) owed by his relatives on account

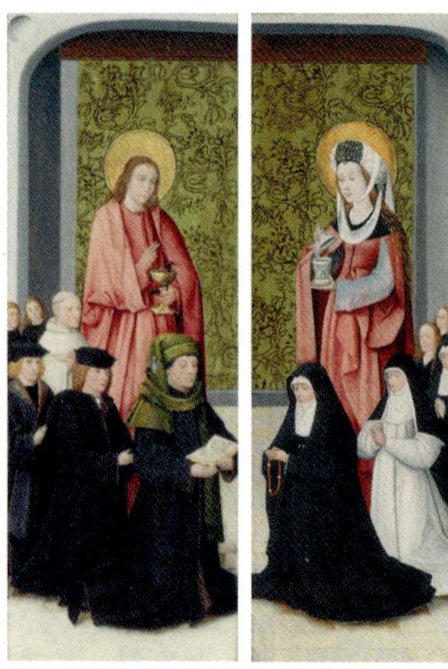

21.1

of paintings that he had made for them as an external member ("vanwege enkele schilderien die hy deser bruederscap voerttyden gemaect heft").

This second part of the Catalogue of Paintings starts with items produced by Bosch's workshop under the master's overall supervision but not executed by his hand (Cat. 21, Cat. 22). These are followed by works that demonstrate, through the similarities in their style and motifs, a clear connection with Bosch and which can probably be traced back to former members of his workshop (pupils, journeymen; Cat. 23–28). Last comes a painting by a follower of Hieronymus Bosch that is frequently still attributed to the master (Cat. 29).

Literature: Guevara 1560, p. 43 (cited here from Snyder 1973, p. 29); Cinotti 1966; Unverfehrt 1980; Schoute/Verougstraete/Garrido 2001; Vermet 2001, pp. 92–93; Koreny 2002/03; Elsig 2004.

21

Workshop of Hieronymus Bosch

Ecce Homo with Saints and Donors (exterior: Saints and Donors), 1499

Oil on panel (oak), 73.2 x 57.1 cm / 28¾ x 22½ in. (central panel), 79 x 36 cm / 31⅛ x 14¼ in. (wings), 16 x 57 cm / 6¼ x 22½ in. (predella)

Boston, Museum of Fine Arts, inv. nos. 53.2027 and 56 172 (predella)

William K. Richardson Fund, William Francis Warden Fund, and Juliana Cheney Edwards Collection

21.1 Outer wings: St John and St Mary Magdalene with members of the donors' family

21.2 Left inner wing: St Peter with male donor

21.3 Central panel: Ecce Homo

21.4 Right inner wing: St Catherine with female donor

21.5 Predella: Instruments of the Passion

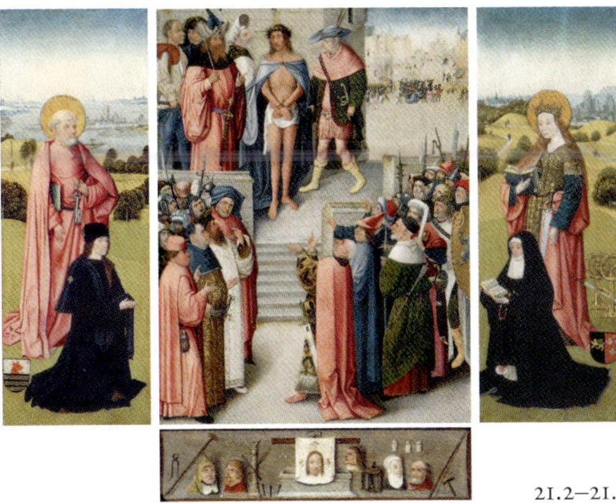

21.2–21.5

This triptych was commissioned by Peter van Os (*c.* 1467/69–1542), an accredited member of the Brotherhood of Our Blessed Lady since 1496/97, and his wife Hendrixke van Langhel (d. 1499/1500). It was painted on the occasion of their marriage and to mark Peter van Os's appointment as town clerk. The two donors, respectively accompanied by St Peter and St Catherine, face each other on the inner wings. On the outer wings, Vranck van Langhel, also known as Franco van Langel, (*c.* 1440–1497) is depicted with his sons and St John the Baptist on one side, and his wife Heilwig van der Rullen and her daughters with St Mary Magdalene on the other. Vranck van Langhel, who was already dead when the triptych was painted, had been Peter van Os's father-in-law, a fellow member of the Brotherhood and his predecessor as town clerk.

On the basis of the donors' biographies, the date of the original commission can be narrowed down to late 1498 and the completion of the painting to the year 1499. In September 1498 van Os became one of 's-Hertogenbosch's four town clerks. He married van Langhel's daughter somewhere between the middle and the end of 1498; at the start of 1499 they are already recorded as married. In conjunction with his marriage, in 1499 van Os was granted full citizenship. This improvement in his social status was also noted in the records of the Brotherhood of Our Blessed Lady for the accounting year 1498/99. Serious complications during her first pregnancy led Hendrixke to draw up her will at the end of December 1499; she died shortly after giving birth. The infant depicted on the right inner wing was added retrospectively on top of the final paint layer, which signifies that the donor portrait of Hendrixke was completed before the child's birth, in other words while she herself was still alive.

Bosch undoubtedly received the commission for this triptych on the basis of personal connections via the Brotherhood. Despite the importance of the client Bosch did not execute

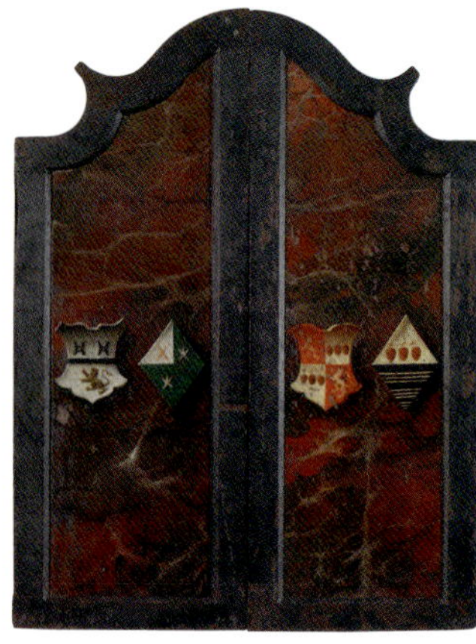

22.1

the painting himself but entrusted it to his workshop, on account of his own absence. It is possible that up to three painters were involved in the work (Elsig 2001). Alongside successful figures and the donor portraits, the treatment of the figures at the back on the central panel, next to Christ, is occasionally less confident.

This triptych is a compilation of four Bosch works. The central panel is modelled on the Frankfurt *Ecce Homo* (Cat. 4), from which the workshop copied a substantial proportion of the figures, architecture and townscape. The St Peter in the left inner wing has his roots in the St Peter in the left inner wing of the Madrid *Adoration of the Magi* (Cat. 6.2), although his head has here been enlarged so that his proportions seem more compressed in relation to the original. Visible in the background is a Christ carrying the Cross and surrounded by a throng of people, resembling the same scene on the exterior of *St John on Patmos* (Cat. 3.2.2). The background of the right inner wing looks back to the *Crucifixion* (Cat. 1).

We can assume that the triptych was originally installed inside a church or chapel in 's-Hertogenbosch, possibly Sint-Jan though more likely still the Dominican church in which Peter van Os and one of his sons are buried. In the late 19th century the work was in a private collection in London; its parts have been united at the Boston museum since 1956.

See also p. 79.

LITERATURE: 's-Hertogenbosch 1967, p. 113, no. 27; Unverfehrt 1980, pp. 137–139; Bichelaer 1998, suppl. 1, nos. 292 and 236; van Dijck 1998a; van Schoute/Verboomen 2000, pp. 202–203; Elsig 2001, p. 98; Klein 2001, pp. 124–125; Wattel 2001; Fischer 2009, pp. 71–73, 89.

22

Workshop of Hieronymus Bosch

('Pupil of Hieronymus Bosch'?)

Triptych with Sts Job, Anthony and Jerome (exterior: the four coats of arms of the donors), *c.* 1505

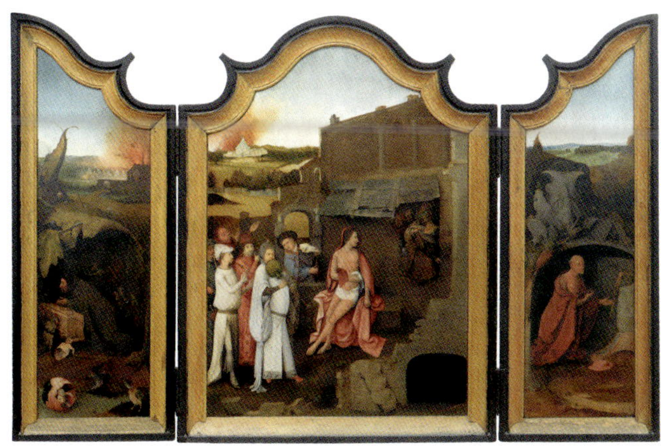

22.2–22.4

Oil on panel (oak), 98 x 72.1 / 38⅝ x 28⅜ in. (central panel), 97.8 x 30.2 cm / 38½ x 11⅞ in. (left wing), 98.1 x 30.5 cm / 38⅝ x 12 in. (right wing)
Bruges, Groeningemuseum, inv. no. 209
22.1 Outer wings: The four coats of arms of the donors
22.2 Left inner wing: St Anthony
22.3 Central panel: The Temptation of St Job
22.4 Right inner wing: St Jerome

The donors can be traced to 's-Hertogenbosch and once again to the Brotherhood of Our Blessed Lady. The exterior of the triptych bears the coats of arms of the de Haro and Pijnappel families. Johanna Pijnappel from 's-Hertogenbosch was first married to Jacob van Driele, also from 's-Hertogenbosch. He must have died in 1506 or earlier, since Johanna was able to remarry in Antwerp in 1507, having completed the standard twelve-month period of mourning. Her second husband was Diego de Haro, a Spanish merchant who from 1491 to 1513 ran an extremely successful import/export business in Antwerp, the most important centre of international shipping and trade in the Low Countries. Since the coat of arms of Johanna's first husband can still be detected beneath that of de Haro, it follows that the triptych was commissioned while Driele was still alive, in other words not later than 1506, and was completed at the latest in 1507, before Johanna's remarriage. It is worth mentioning that another de Haro – Jacob – is recorded in 1502/03 as being a member of the Brotherhood of Our Blessed Lady. His daughter Beatriz married Felipe de Guevara. The de Haros moved in Spanish court circles.
Over and above these biographical facts about the donors and the results yielded by dendrochronological analysis, which indicates that the oak panels were painted at the earliest around 1501–1507, the triptych's date can be narrowed down further by referance to its compositional models. The triptych is a compilation of four

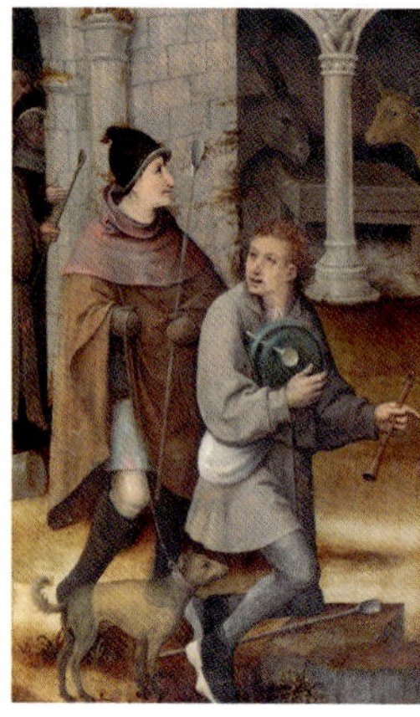
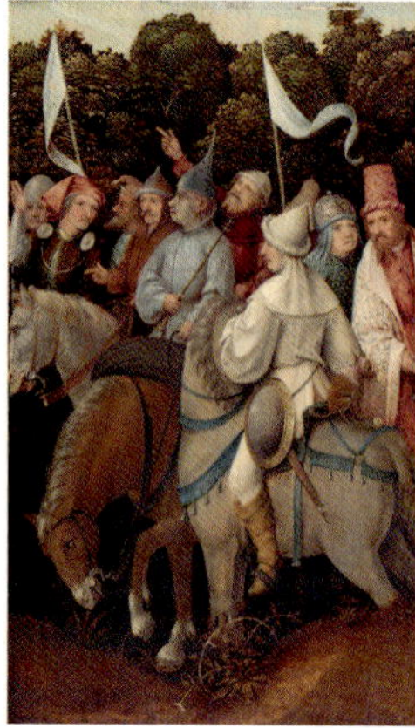

23.1–23.2

works by Bosch and for this reason must have been painted by an artist or artists thoroughly familiar with the master's œuvre. Since a Bosch follower can be ruled out in view of the early date, we can therefore assume that the triptych was produced within the immediate context of Bosch's workshop. In the *St Anthony* scene in the left inner wing, the background with the burning abbey, and in particular the two devils flying over the rooftop, cite the central panel of the Lisbon *Temptation of St Anthony* executed *c.* 1502 (Cat. 10). The figure of St Jerome and the curved section of low wall on the right inner wing, and the short flight of steps on the central panel, are taken from the central panel of the *Hermit Saints* triptych (Cat. 12.2), which was painted *c.* 1504 and whose left inner wing is likewise indebted to the *Temptation of St Anthony* triptych. On the right inner wing, the grotto with its bizarre rock formations overhead is adapted from the Ghent *St Jerome* (Cat. 2) and the architecture of the central panel from the *Adoration of the Magi* (Cat. 6).

The work was documented in 1858 in West Flanders, in the church of St James the Elder in Hoeke, and it entered the Bruges museum in 1931.

See also p. 334.

LITERATURE: 's-Hertogenbosch 1967, p. 58, no. 1; de Vos 1979, pp. 90–92; Unverfehrt 1980, pp. 116–121; van Schoute/Verboomen 2000, p. 214; van Dijck 2001a, pp. 64–67; Klein 2001, p. 126; van Schoute/Verougstraete/Garrido 2001, pp. 108–109, 116; Vandenbroeck 2003, pp. 175–176, 312–313.

23

Workshop of Hieronymus Bosch or former workshop member ("Pupil of Hieronymus Bosch"?)

Fragments of the inner wings of an Adoration of the Magi triptych: Adoration of the Shepherds and Retinue of the Magi, 1505–1515

Oil on panel, 37.5 x 22.5 cm / 14¾ x 8⅞ in. (left inner wing), 36.2 x 21.3 cm / 14¼ x 8⅜ in.

(right inner wing)
Philadelphia, Philadelphia Museum of Art, John G. Johnson Collection, inv. no. 1276 ("Two Shepherds") and inv. no. 1275 ("Retinue")
23.1 Left inner wing: Two Shepherds
23.2 Right inner wing: Retinue

These two wing fragments display similarities with paintings by Bosch and his workshop in some of their motifs and stylistic features. At the left edge of the right *Retinue* wing, for example, as in the interior of the *Small Christ Carrying the Cross* (Cat. 9.1), a man in a turban looks out of the picture at the viewer. In the case of the left, *Two Shepherds* wing, the architecture resembles that in the *Sts Job, Anthony and Jerome* triptych (Cat. 22). There are also parallels with the Anderlecht *Adoration of the Magi* (Cat. 24): there, as in the *Two Shepherds*, we find a shepherd's staff ending at the top in a sort of scoop, a distinctive design that also appears in Bosch's Madrid *Adoration of the Magi* (Cat. 6). Further similarities can be seen in the conception of the wall on the left, the terrain in the foreground and the ox and the ass facing each other across the wooden manger. By the same token, the numerous faces with heavy eyelids and bulbous noses seen in profile in the right, *Retinue* wing are also a characteristic of the Anderlecht *Adoration*. A general resemblance likewise exists in terms of palette, which is characterised by a rich variety of browns, dark greens and greys combined with striking reds and a blue that at times almost becomes turquoise. The *Retinue* is also notable for the banners carried by the riders and the decorative harnesses worn by their horses, with their strong colour contrasts – features otherwise absent from Bosch's works. The little brown dog crouching on the back of the horse in the foreground, dressed in a red hood without a peak in a style not unlike a fool's cap, is found in reverse in the painting *The Conjuror*, formerly attributed to Bosch, in Saint-Germain-en-Laye (Cat. 28).

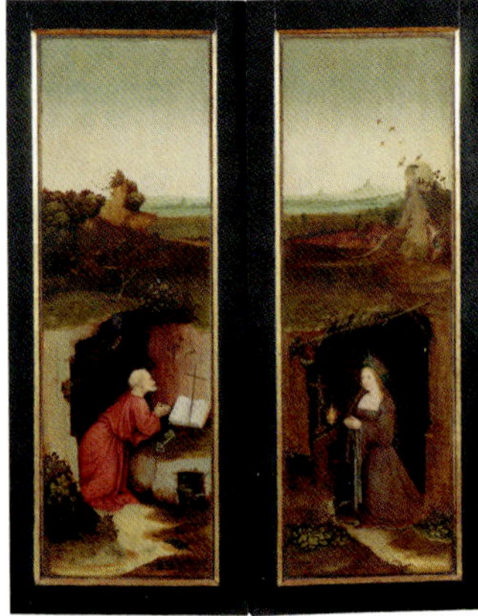

24.1–24.2

X-rays have revealed a use of lead white that comes very close to that found in autograph works by Bosch, as well as a number of pentimenti, in particular in the right inner wing. In the underlying paint layer, for example, the second figure from the right wears a metal disc with a spike on his head, and further differences in clothing are also found in the region of the horses' necks and riders' torsos at the left edge of the panel. These pentimenti suggest that at least the *Retinue* is not a copy of an existing Bosch painting, but an original composition by another painter, namely a member of Bosch's workshop.

Reconstructions of the triptych either assume that copies of the wings and perhaps even of the entire interior view are preserved in the *Adoration of the Magi* in the Noordbrabants Museum in 's-Hertogenbosch (inv. no. 15 257; formerly Vught, private collection), or posit the existence of a lost triptych by Bosch (see Unverfehrt). The two fragments, which have been trimmed on all sides, entered the collection of the Philadelphia Museum of Art in 1917.

LITERATURE: Unverfehrt 1980, pp. 102–111, nos. 12, 43; van Schoute/Verboomen 2000, pp. 193–196; van Schoute/Verougstraete/Garrido 2001, p. 118; Silver 2006, pp. 180–184.

24

Member of the workshop of Hieronymus Bosch ('Pupil of Hieronymus Bosch'?)

Adoration of the Magi (exterior: St Peter and St Mary Magdalene in the Wilderness), *c.* 1510–1520

Oil on panel, 78 x 62 cm / 30¾ x 24⅜ in. (central panel), 80.5 x 26.5 cm / 31¾ x 10½ in. (wings)

Anderlecht, Erasmushuis (on loan from the collegiate church of Sts Peter and Guido, Anderlecht)

24.1 Left outer wing: St Peter in the Wilderness

24.2 Right outer wing: St Mary Magdalene in the Wilderness

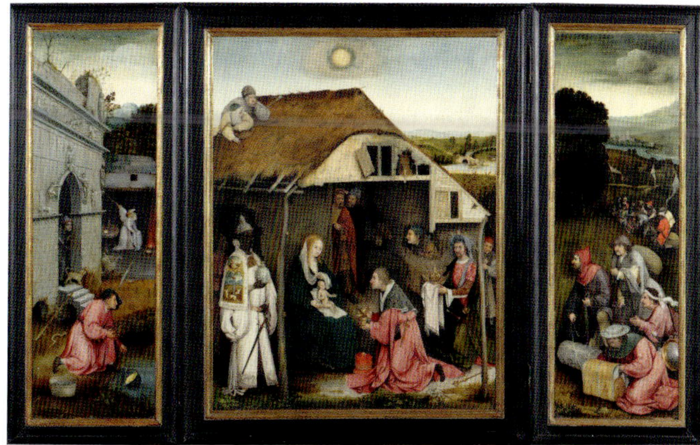

24.3–24.5

24.3 Left inner wing: Joseph, Angel and Shepherd
24.4 Central panel: Adoration of the Magi
24.5 Right inner wing: Retinue of the Magi

In 1549/50, when the *Adoration of the Magi* triptych was cleaned in Brussels, it was already the property of the collegiate church housing the tomb of St Guido, patron saint of Anderlecht. The same church was also dedicated to St Peter, increasing the likelihood that the triptych – with its exterior showing St Peter as a hermit – was created specifically for this church.

The composition and a large number of the figures are clearly derived from the Madrid *Adoration of the Magi* (Cat. 6). The stable and the Virgin are reversed and a number of figures relocated within the pictorial space.

The Anderlecht triptych displays stylistic similarities and areas of overlap with the *Fragments of an Adoration* in Philadelphia (Cat. 23, see above). Both works heavily exploit the Madrid *Adoration*, but with differing degrees of freedom. The black king at the left of the central panel here is related not only to his Madrid counterpart but also to *Sts Job, Anthony and Jerome* (Cat. 22): several details of his white robes are taken from this latter triptych, for example, such as the belt slung low beneath the rounded belly, the slit in the puffed sleeve falling down from his right elbow, and the way in which the tassels spill on to the ground. Even if the present triptych was not necessarily produced in the workshop under Bosch's supervision, the knowledge it displays of the Madrid *Adoration* and the Bruges *Sts Job, Anthony and Jerome* means that its maker was unquestionably someone very close to Bosch, i. e. a (former) assistant. Overall it makes freer use of Bosch's magnificent original than is the case in Cat. 20 and Cat. 22, something that supports a later dating. The classicising treatment of the façade on the left inner wing, with its ornamentation and ignudi, likewise argues for a later dating.

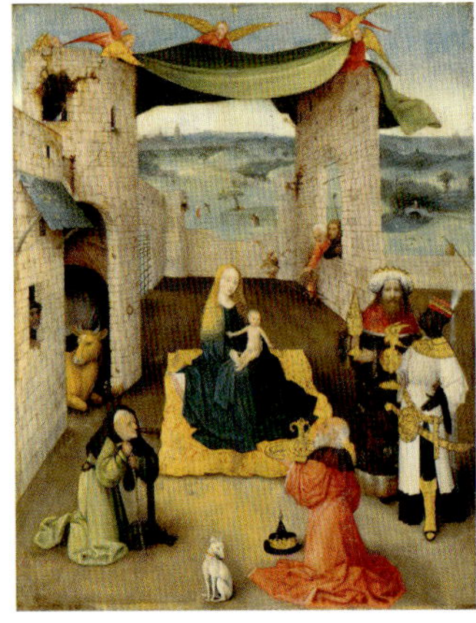

25

The Anderlecht *Adoration* also has numerous similarities and areas of overlap with the *Sts Job, Anthony and Jerome* triptych. In its left and right outer wings respectively, St Peter and St Mary Magdalene are shown kneeling in prayer in a cave-like grotto within a landscape setting close to that found in the inner wings of the *Job* triptych. The draperies of the kneeling king in the central panel likewise resemble those of St Anthony in the left inner wing of Cat. 22.

The thoroughly unusual portrayal of St Peter as a humble hermit rather than as the powerful representative of the papacy is also entirely in keeping with Bosch, who regularly depicted the saints as hermits (cf. Cat. 2, Cat. 3, Cat. 7, Cat. 10, Cat. 12 and Cat. 14) and from whom asceticism and moderation were leitmotifs. The partly bare, partly wooded hillside with the birds flying overhead behind St Peter strongly resembles the hill behind St Giles in the *Hermit Saints* triptych, just as the caves on both exterior shutters resemble that inhabited by St Giles (Cat. 12.3). A drawing for *St Peter* (Unverfehrt 1980, no. 37a) may be a preliminary sketch or a later copy. The underdrawing of the figures here is very much more precise than is usual for Bosch and comes closer to the style of Flemish painting of the 15th century (Venice 1992). The painting is also more delicate and characterised by more pronounced illusionistic and haptic properties.

The theme of the Penitent Magdalene in the Wilderness is linked with Bosch's name elsewhere, too. The mother-in-law of Philip the Handsome, Queen Isabella I of Castile, called Isabella the Catholic, had at least one *Penitent Magdalene* bearing Bosch's signature in her possession at the time of her death in late November 1504, as emerges from the inventory of her estate (van Dijck 2001a, p. 59 and pp. 91–92).

LITERATURE: 's-Hertogenbosch 1967, p. 86, no. 13; Unverfehrt 1980, pp. 102–111, 257–258; Venice 1992, pp. 55–56; van Schoute/Verboomen 2000, pp. 193–196; van Schoute/Verougstraete/Garrido 2001, pp. 111–112, 116.

25
Workshop or follower of Hieronymus Bosch
Adoration of the Magi, *c.* 1508–1515
Oil, tempera and gold on panel (oak),
71.1 x 56.5 cm / 28 x 22¼ in.
New York, Metropolitan Museum of Art, inv. no. 13.26, John Stewart Kennedy Fund, 1913

Attributed in some quarters to Bosch, this painting is in fact an extraordinary pastiche. The foreground scene of the Adoration of the Magi, observed by Joseph, three shepherds and four angels, is staged within a soaring architectural setting that obeys, in almost every respect, the centralised perspective embraced by the Renaissance. Even if this is not true of the brocade cloth on which the Virgin is seated on a cushion, with the Infant on her lap, or the figures themselves, it is none the less an astonishing discovery. Although principles of linear perspective had been employed in Netherlandish painting since around 1430/35, their application was sporadic and arbitrary. It was only with the absorption of Italian influences from 1508/09 (following Jan Gossaert's trip to Italy) that pictures gradually began to be constructed entirely on the basis of centralised perspective. In the case of Bosch and his workshop, only a few compositions demonstrate a use of perspective, in each case confined to a wall or a section of ground whose lines converge upon a single vanishing point (Cat. 4, Cat. 6.2, Cat. 17.5, Cat. 21 and Cat. 24). The present *Adoration* in other words, testifies to a knowledge of perspective that did not come from Bosch. The dog in the foreground reappears in almost identical form in *Antonio Siciliano and St Anthony*, the right wing of the diptych painted by Jan Gossaert in *c.* 1510–1515 (Galleria Doria Pamphilj, Rome).
The situation is different in the case of the landscape background, which strongly resembles a number of Bosch paintings, most notably the *Adoration of the Magi* (Cat. 6). Thus the dancing peasants can be compared with those on the left inner wing of the Mad-

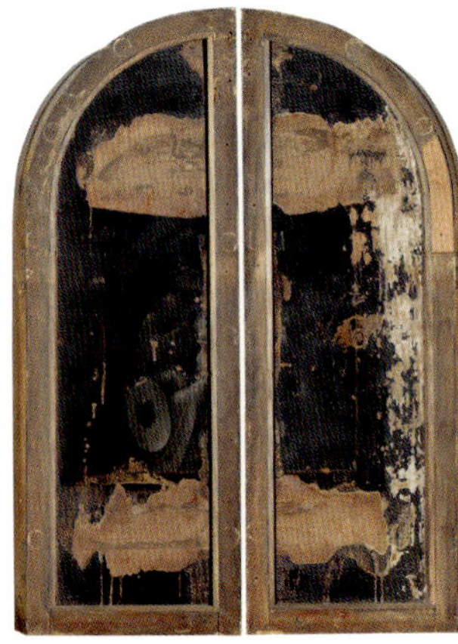

26.1

rid triptych, and the bridge and tree with a similar motif in the latter's central panel. The silhouette of the town, the birds beside the scattered bones on the right and the couple crossing the bridge followed by a white dog all resemble details in the background of the *Crucifixion* (Cat. 1). The crooked wayside cross on the right of the panel is similar to the one in *St John on Patmos* (Cat. 3.2), and the great white heron on a sandbank is also found in *St Christopher* (Cat. 7) and *St John the Baptist* (Cat. 3.1). These motifs are not literal quotations, yet are so characteristic of Bosch that one might wonder whether he painted them, and whether indeed he painted the whole background, though not the foreground. Are we looking at an early work by Bosch, or a panel in which more than one artist was involved – a landscape specialist and a figure painter, perhaps? This would be a division of labour that we encounter, for example, in the case of Joachim Patinir and Quentin Massys (*c.* 1466–1530).

Striking stylistic features of the gracefully built figures include their almond eyes, their narrow or absent eyebrows, their rosebud lips and their incisive linearity with its forceful outer contours – characteristics that, in the œvre of Bosch, are otherwise found only in *The Conjuror* (Cat. 28). Further features shared with this latter work include the emphatically empty and bare ground, the towering walls with their masonry construction, scattered tufts of vegetation and small windows in which birds are nesting. Lastly, a comparison may also be drawn between the two small, slender dogs.

The picture was in a Berlin collection prior to being purchased by the Metropolitan Museum of Art in New York shortly before the First World War.

LITERATURE: Unverfehrt 1980, pp. 123–125, no. 23; Ainsworth 1992, pp. 66–73; Ainsworth/Christiansen 1998, pp. 258–259, no. 66; Klein 2001, p. 123.

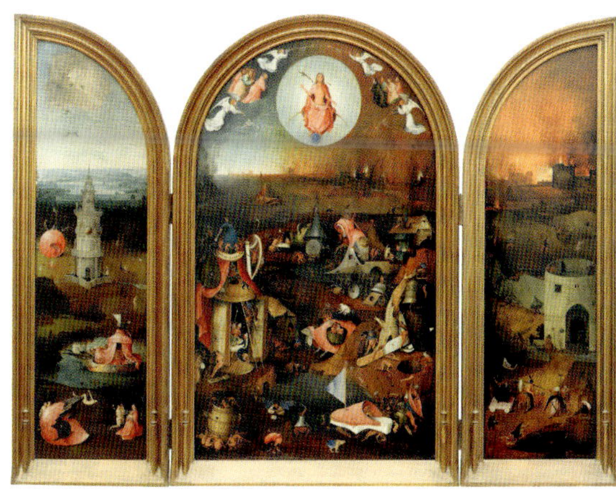

26.2–26.4

26
Workshop of Hieronymus Bosch or former workshop member ("Pupil of Hieronymus Bosch"?) **The Last Judgement (exterior: The Flagellation)**, *c.* 1515
Oil on panel (oak), 99.2 x 60.5 cm
39 x 23¾ in. (central panel),
99.5 x 28.7 cm / 39⅛ x 11¼ in. (wing)
Bruges, Groeningemuseum, inv. no. 208
26.1 The Flagellation
26.2–26.4 The Last Judgement

When open, the triptych shows the Last Judgement in the centre, flanked by the Earthly Paradise on the left and Hell on the right, its focal point a fiery inferno on the horizon. Structures and instruments of torture of all kinds are concentrated in the central panel in particular, all of them serving for the punishment of sinners. Christ as Judge of the World is enthroned overhead, accompanied by saints and angels. The triptych lacks rigour in its treatment of the Last Judgement theme: only angels – i. e. no souls of the saved – are seen rising heavenwards on the Paradise wing, for example, and the Resurrection of the flesh, i. e. the dead rising from their graves, is not shown. On the badly damaged and dark exterior with the Flagellation, a soldier – possibly kneeling – can be made out with difficulty in the lower left corner. He is wearing a helmet whose decoration resembles a Crown of Thorns and is dressed in a robe or coat, with a round shield slung over his back. He is raising his hands towards Christ whom we must imagine at the centre of the composition, where the edges of the two shutters meet. Behind the soldier, a bearded man in a gown stands facing us, probably with a book in his hand and his eyes lowered (a scholar?). On the far right, a man is shown in profile, looking left, with a long plume.

The present composition adopts and elaborates on at least three major triptychs by Bosch. The fruits, the sinners dancing around a bagpipe, the musical instruments, the harp

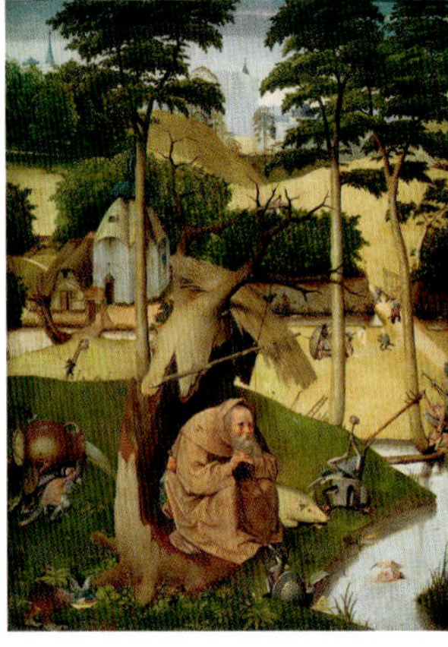

27

serving as a support for a crucifixion and the open lantern are all derived from the *Garden of Earthly Delights* (Cat. 11). The huge green jug, the millstone standing upright on its edge and pulled by sinners, the treadmills, the blue chimney and the anvil, the giant knife, the two men hanging upside down over a hearth with the devil beside them and the man on the spit, the red tent and the giant all originate from the Vienna *Last Judgement* (Cat. 13). The tower and the helmeted man with the golden goblet riding an ox or bull are taken from *The Haywain* (Cat. 20). The inferno on the horizon, and the murky pools with devils crawling out of them, are also typical of Bosch. All of these motifs resurface here not as quotations in the literal sense, but rather as free variations, albeit in a high concentration. Although this does not prove that the triptych was actually produced in Bosch's workshop, it can nevertheless be claimed that the painter was very familiar with the master's œuvre. We may therefore assume that he either worked in Bosch's workshop for a while or had access to material from it. Whatever the case, he reinterprets his source in an independent fashion and with great technical sophistication.

The work is signed "jheronimus bosch" at lower right on the central panel, which may be interpreted either as the signet of the Bosch workshop or as a deliberate forgery. The painting technique is more atmospheric and more delicate than that of Bosch, especially in the background of the central panel. Numerous pentimenti can be seen with the naked eye. The underdrawing in particular shimmers through the thin, ochre-brown paint layer – something that again situates the artist close to Bosch. This work, or rather its artist, probably played a certain role in the dissemination of Bosch's pictorial ideas and is therefore also of interest with regard to Bosch's reception. Hieronymus Cock (*c.* 1510–1570) used motifs from the Paradise wing in a copper engraving of 1560 and credited Bosch as their "inventor" in the accompanying inscription.

LITERATURE: de Vos 1979, pp. 87–89; Unverfehrt 1980; Klein 2001, p. 124; van Schoute/Verougstraete/Garrido 2001, p. 116; Vellekoop 2001; Silver 2006, pp. 352–359.

27
Member of the workshop or follower of Hieronymus Bosch ('Pupil of Hieronymus Bosch'?)
The Temptation of St Anthony, *c.* 1510–1515
Oil on panel (oak), 73 x 52.5 cm
28¾ x 20⅝ in.
Madrid, Museo Nacional del Prado,
inv. no. 2049

This painting, which is universally agreed not to be an original by Bosch, shows the seated St Anthony in three-quarter view, undisturbed in his meditation by the strange demons around him. In terms of style it exhibits a number of parallels with the Anderlecht *Adoration of the Magi* (Cat. 24), such as the naturalistic plants serving as repoussoir motifs in the immediate foreground, the plasticity and three-quarter view of some of the figures, and the haptic quality and damaged bark of the tree trunks.
In addition to these illusionistic features, further arguments against Bosch's authorship can be found in the layout of the landscape, the abrupt contrasts in palette between foreground, middle ground and background, and the marked rise in height towards the background. This last feature was, however, evidently introduced by a later hand during the overpainting of the upper third of the panel, since the underlying paint layers indicate a luminous and flat background. Conventional methods of investigation have revealed underdrawing in only some parts of the panel, which is not the case in other pictures attributed to Bosch. Apart from minor damage within and below the paint layer of the figure of St Anthony, the painting is in good condition.
The panel was originally arched. The upper corners were built out at a later date – pre-

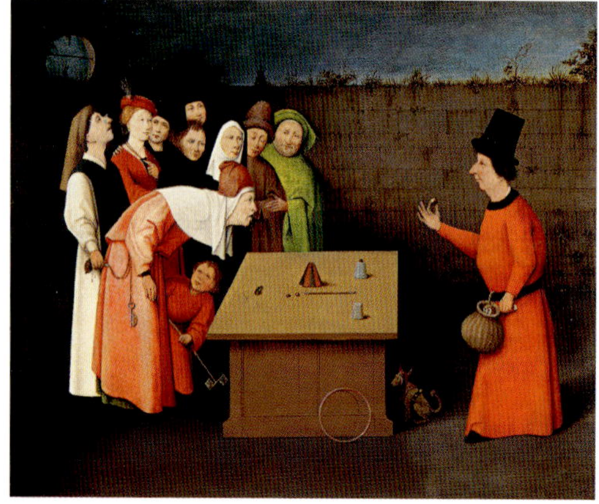

28

cisely when, we do not know – and the upper third extensively overpainted, so that the picture is today rectangular and fractionally taller than before. It probably entered the Escorial in 1574 as "another painted panel, rounded at the top, with St Anthony, by the hand of Hieronymus Bosch, three feet high and two wide". These dimensions, which convert to approximately 84 x 56 cm / 33 x 22 in., are slightly larger than those of the present work, something more likely to be explained by very approximate measuring than by the inclusion of a frame.

LITERATURE: 's-Hertogenbosch 1967, p. 65, no. 3; Unverfehrt 1980, pp. 158–160; Marijnissen 1987, pp. 436–439; Garrido/van Schoute 2001, pp. 58–67; Klein 2001, p. 123.

28
Member of the workshop or follower of Hieronymus Bosch
The Conjuror, *c.* 1510–1520
Oil on panel (oak), 53 x 65 cm / 20¾ x 25⅝ in.
Saint-Germain-en-Laye, Musée Municipal, inv. no. 872/1/87

With its themes of folly and deceit, it is almost inevitable that *The Conjuror* should have attracted an attribution to Bosch. We see a conjuror performing the cup-and-ball trick, the victim he has conned and who is simultaneously being robbed from behind, and a number of curious onlookers, including a pair of young lovers. The panel, which dendrochronological analysis shows to have been painted after 1496–1502, was long considered an original Bosch or a faithful copy.

Whether the painting is an original or a copy is hard to determine. On the one hand, it contains a number of pentimenti that testify to the repositioning of certain pictorial motifs. Thus in the underdrawing the dog sits beside the table, and the conjuror's props are laid out differently on a somewhat longer table. On the other hand the outlines of the underdrawing are in places barely perceptible and the figures

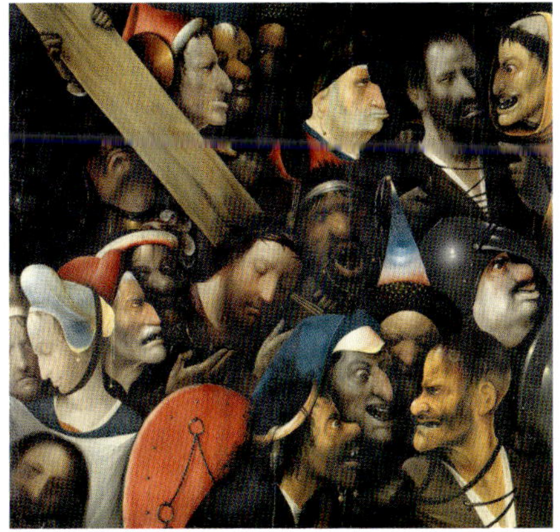

29

are modelled with only light hatching here and there. Instead, the uppermost paint layer is laid down in many places in fine brushstrokes. As a synthesis of these findings, we may assume that *The Conjuror* was based on an existing drawn or painted original, which its artist has adopted wholly or in part, while at the same time modifying certain details. This original might have been the sheet *The Conjuror* (Cat. D10), whose composition and inventory of motifs reveal certain parallels with the painting here under discussion here but which is of a superior artistic quality.

The artist who painted this genre-like figural scene was probably not its original creator *per se*. Neither this painting nor the original was made by Bosch. It is true that the owl (in the basket on the right) and the toy windmill held by the boy on the left are typical Bosch accessories, and that the little brown dog behind the table, dressed in a red hood without a peak like a sort of fool's cap, is found in reverse on the back of a horse in the *Retinue* fragment of an *Adoration of the Magi* in Philadelphia (Cat. 23.2). But the palette, the lack of background landscape or indeed any attempt to convey spatial depth, the hard outlines and linearity of the figures and the limited range of their gestures, faces and poses – all of these argue against tracing the work back to the hand of the 's-Hertogenbosch master. Striking stylistic features of *The Conjuror* include almond-shaped eyes and eyelids, and rosebud lips, its linearity and its treatment of space, in which it resembles the New York *Adoration of the Magi* (Cat. 25). This representation of a trickster, found its supreme expression in the 17th century in the thematic variant of the crooked card-sharps, as treated by Caravaggio (1571–1610) and Georges de la Tour (1593–1652). In the 19th century the painting was in a private collection in Saint-Germain-en-Laye before passing to the municipal museum.

LITERATURE: 's-Hertogenbosch 1967, p. 130, no. 33; Unverfehrt 1980, pp. 114–117, 247, no.

21; Hamburger 1984; Stein-Schneider 1985; Marijnissen 1987, pp. 446–450; Darriulat 1995; van Schoute/Verboomen 2000, pp. 42–43, 189–191; Klein 2001, p. 126; Willemsen 2001; Le Chanu/Mottin 2003; Gertsman 2004.

29

Antwerp-based follower of Hieronymus Bosch
Christ Carrying the Cross, *c.* 1515–1520
76.7 x 83.5 cm / 30¼ x 32⅞ in.
Ghent, Museum voor Schone Kunsten, inv. no. 1902 H

While some scholars consider this work to be an original by Bosch (Marijnissen 1987; Koreny 2002/03; Elsig 2004), others are sceptical (Koldeweij/Vermet/Vandenbroeck 2001). The Ghent *Christ Carrying the Cross* offers a case study in what, from a stylistic and technical point of view, can be considered a genuine Bosch. It is my opinion that, other than falling into the blanket category of "grotesque", the work is wholly unconnected with Bosch's œuvre.

Bosch's realistic conception of ugliness can be clearly distinguished from the exaggerated facial features of the Ghent picture, whose caricature-like leanings carry it closer to the Renaissance or to the work of Netherlandish painters such as Quentin Massys. Such extreme faces are found in Bosch only on rare occasions, for instance that of the old woman with the protruding lower lip begging at St Bavo's feet in the right outer wing of the Vienna *Last Judgement* (Cat. 13.2), or that of the foreground figure of Peter, his demonic eyes in their black sockets fixed upon the guard Malchus, in the left outer wing of the Lisbon *Temptation of St Anthony* (Cat. 10.1). Bosch's physiognomy is tempered: even if it is often hideous or comical, it remains anatomically realistic.

The figure of Christ in the Ghent picture, with his emphatically closed eyes and above all his crown of thorns, also departs from Bosch's usual treatment of the motif. The crown is not twisted as taut as a rope with no gaps, as in Bosch, but loosely woven. The most recent technical investigation has also revealed more differences than similarities (Spronk 2011). In comparison with *Christ Mocked* (Cat. 5), the underdrawing is economical and chiefly executed in short, uniformly fine strokes. The lower paint layers are also built up in a manner uncharacteristic of Bosch. On the evidence of its strong colour contrasts and occasionally shimmering hues, its linear underdrawing and its large-scale use of lead white (clearly visible in the photographs in Marijnissen and van Schoute/Verboomen), it is most unlikely that this picture was produced by the painter from 's-Hertogenbosch. The extreme density with which the figures are grouped above and behind each other, their relief-style presentation against a dark-as-night background, their sharp outlines and the hard interior drawing of the faces together with the pronounced sense of plasticity conveyed by the forceful play of light and shadow, are all equally untypical of Bosch.

The Ghent *Christ Carrying the Cross* belongs to a group of works treating scenes from the Passion that were produced in Antwerp by followers of Bosch. Other paintings in the same group include *Christ Before Pilate* in Princeton (*c.* 1520–1525), *Christ Before Pilate* in Rotterdam (after 1506/12, *c.* 1520), *Christ before Annas* in São Paulo (*c.* 1525/30) and two largely identical *Arrest of Christ* (*c.* 1515/20) panels (Unverfehrt). Even if not all produced by the same hand, these works are very similar in terms of composition, motifs and technique, and they are indebted to the same Antwerp workshop.

Literature: Ringbom 1965, pp. 168–169; Unverfehrt 1980, pp. 127–129; Marijnissen 1987, pp. 378–387; Venice 1992, pp. 51–52; van Schoute/Verboomen 2000, pp. 172–175, 206; Koreny 2002/03; Elsig 2004, pp. 88–91; Spronk 2011.

Detail from: **Hermit Saints Triptych**, *c.* 1504
Central panel: **St Jerome** (see ill. pp. 304/305)

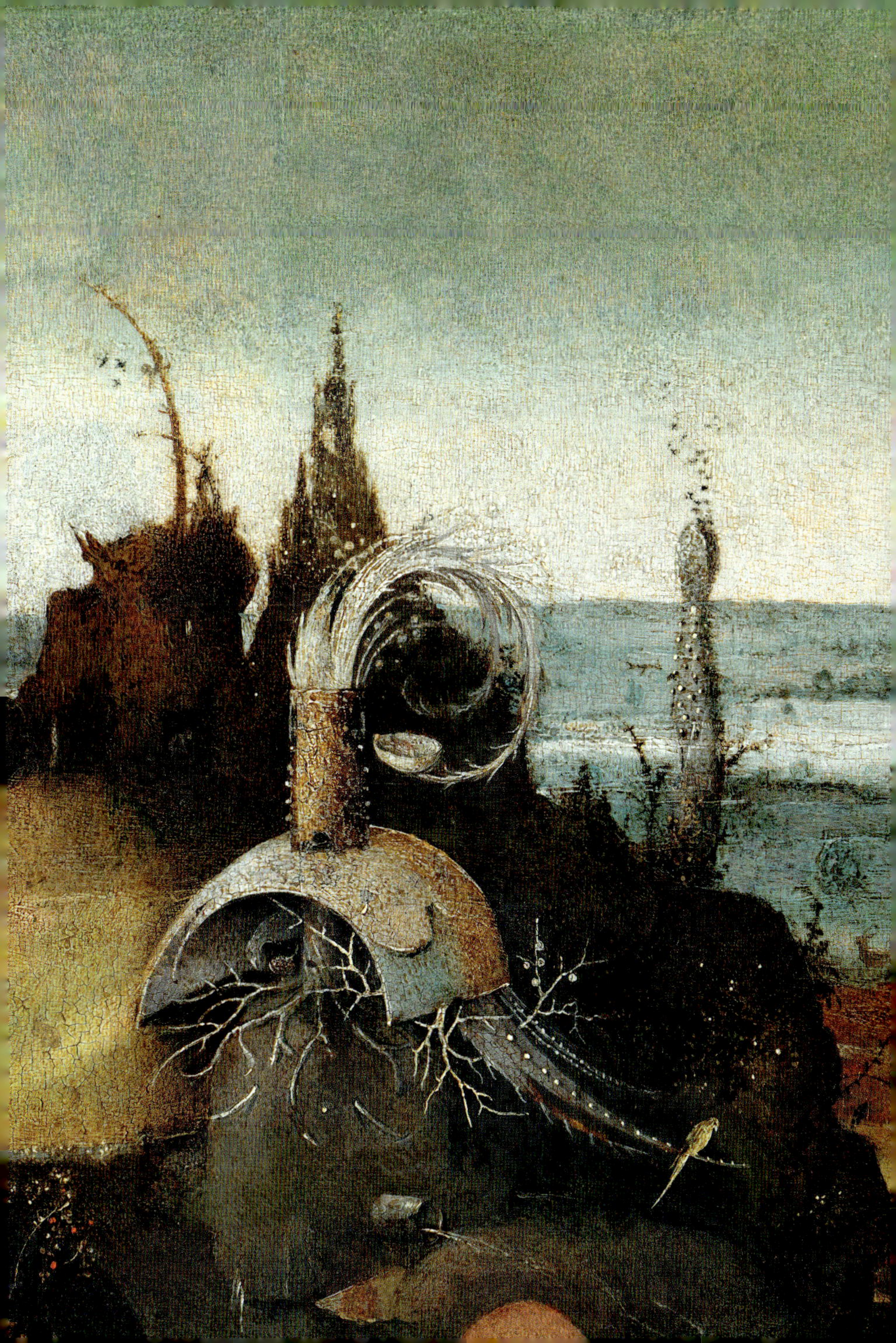

Catalogue of drawings

"For poor is the mind that always uses the ideas of others and invents none of its own."

HIERONYMUS BOSCH IN HIS DRAWING
THE WOOD HAS EARS, THE FIELD EYES, 1502–1505

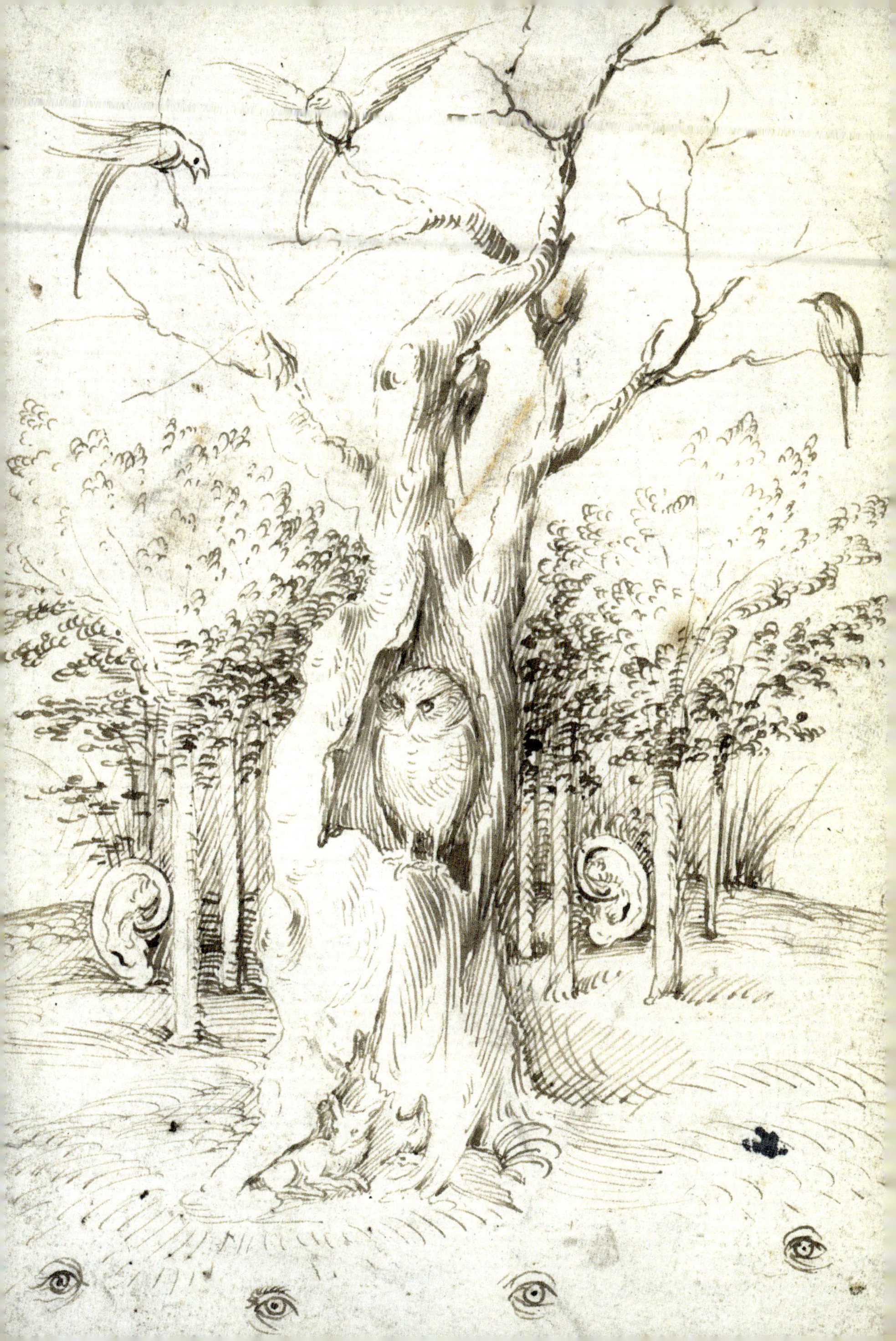

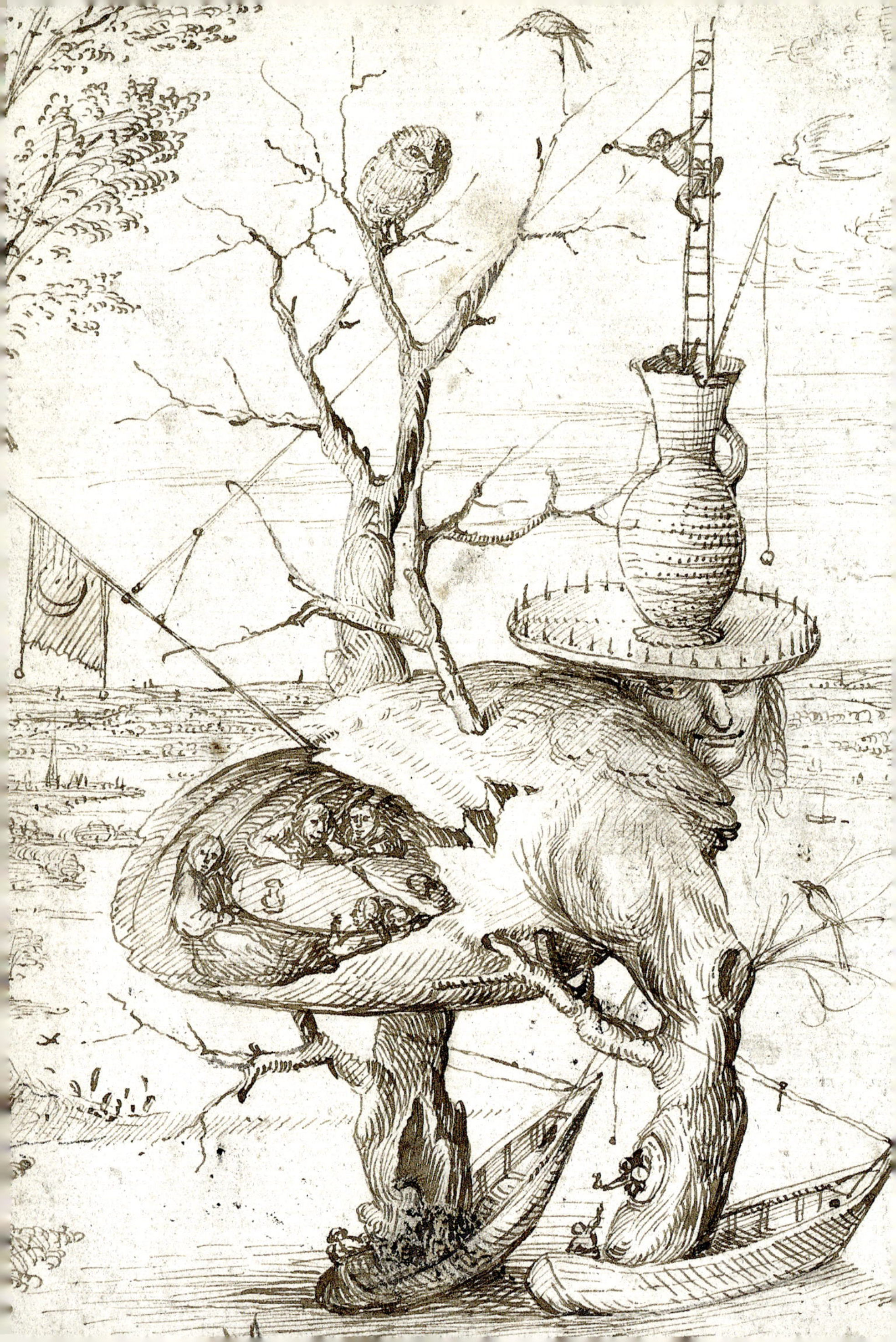

Catalogue of drawings – autograph works

Of all the questions surrounding Hieronymus Bosch and his art, those relating to his drawings remain the least resolved. Scholarship in this sphere has focused primarily on attribution, style and technique, at times on iconography, seldom on function. The sheets confidently attributed to Bosch (Cat. D1–Cat. D8) are not overall designs for pictures in the conventional sense. Although a number show complete compositions with a landscape background (Cat. D2–Cat. D6), they include no traditional main figures such as saints. Three (Cat. D1, Cat. D7, Cat. D8) feature just two or three grotesque pictorial motifs in isolation, in the manner of pattern drawings, one (Cat. D8) also being reused in a painting (Cat. 19). Another drawing (Cat. D4) is directly related to one of Bosch's major works, the *Garden of Earthly Delights* (Cat. 11). It is clear, then, that Bosch's grotesque figures were not invented spontaneously as whims on the part of the artist, but were carefully planned and designed with painting in mind. Identifying different hands in these drawings is even more fraught than is the equivalent task in the case of Bosch's paintings. Of the several dozen drawings that have been linked with Bosch, eight were executed by members of his workshop or his immediate followers (Cat. D9–Cat. D16).

Two Witches: Woman Spinning and Old Woman

The Rotterdam sheet, which shows *Two Witches* (Cat. D1r) on the recto and a *Fox and Cockerel* on the verso (Cat. D1v), resembles Cat. D5 in its technique. It does not, however, display quite the same degree of sculptural modelling as found in Cat. D2–Cat. D4, Cat. D7 and Cat. D8. It comes closer to the drawing of the beggar – attributable to Bosch – found at lower left on the verso of Cat. D3.

The two figures on the recto of the sheet are characterised by their poses as older women. The woman on the left is holding a spindle and distaff, while the woman standing further back on the right is leaning on a stick. Each wears a headscarf, a dress and an apron, with the clothes of the woman on the left ragged and her bare feet left exposed.

Page 431
Detail from **The Wood Has Ears, the Field Eyes**, *c.* 1502–1505 (see p. 444)

Page 432
Detail from **The Tree-Man**, *c.* 1503–1506 (see p. 447)

The verso shows a fox, its head somewhat reminiscent of a wild boar's, lying hidden and waiting in ambush inside its den, while a cockerel comes walking into view from behind the hillock. The pictorial motif of the fox and the cockerel is also found in Cat. D3 and in the left inner wing of the Vienna *Last Judgement* (Cat. 13.3). Below the fox, in the foreground, it is also possible to make out at least one swan's head, resembling those of the swans or geese in the left-hand foreground of Cat. D5. Its presence is an indicator of the sheet's character as a page of studies.

Nest of Owls

The drawing *Nest of Owls* (Cat. D2) gives the impression of a nature study, but it is more probably a study of a motif than the finished design for a painting. Owls are a feature of Bosch's œuvre, being found in most of his paintings and in four drawings. In this sheet the owls are not shown hunting the songbirds, their potential prey, or as a symbol of folly and evil, but simply in their natural habitat.

The sheet (which has been trimmed – probably quite a lot – along the top and bottom) has been affixed to a permanent support, with the result that the original verso, with its drawing of a *Rod with a Sphere and a Disc*, is no longer visible. The recto exhibits the slightly sketch-like manner typical of Bosch's drawing technique, employing dashed and broken contours and an airy hatching to model sculptural forms. The hatching intensifies, in places with the addition of cross-hatching, towards the areas of deepest shade, wherein shadows are also broken up by highlights. The effect is an almost impressionistic capturing of light. The same drawing technique is found in Cat. D3, Cat. D7 and Cat. D8.

The central pictorial motif is the crown of a crooked, almost leafless deciduous tree, which is home to a number of owls and songbirds. A small owl has found shelter, and perhaps indeed a nest, in a hole or crack in the bulging tree trunk with its thick, scaly bark. A larger owl with outspread wings leans down towards it. A third owl stares out from its perch just below the top of the sheet. Near the owls, unheeded, are a total of four small songbirds (magpies? jays?): two at lower left, of which one is perched on a slender branch while the other hangs upside down from a different branch, a third is shown flying across the top of the sheet, and a fourth peering down, from a branch on the right at a spider in its web. In the background a detailed landscape rises towards the right from a low horizon. On the left, between a gallows wheel and a distant town with a church spire and windmills, a group of riders is approaching, comparable with the mounted company in Bosch's *Adoration of the Magi* (Cat. 6.3). Scattered among hills and trees on the right are small settlements, a wayside calvary and a windmill, with more birds flying overhead. A tall, slender tree on the far right recalls the one in *St John on Patmos* (Cat. 3.2.1). See also p. 85, 86.

The Wood Has Ears, the Field Eyes

The drawing *The Wood has Ears, the Field Eyes* (Cat. D3) was executed by Bosch himself. By contrast, the figural studies on the back – with the exception of the beggar at lower left – were made by members of his workshop. The drawing exhibits the same technique as Cat. D2, Cat. D7 and Cat. D8. The inscription at the top, which was researched by Vandenbroeck (1981), goes back to a 13th-century religious text and reads:"*Miserrimi quippe est ingenii semper uti inventis et nunquam inveniendis*" ("For poor is the mind that always uses the ideas of others and invents none of its own"). This was written on the sheet in the first decade of the 16th century – possibly by Bosch himself – and has been cited in various literary contexts over the centuries. The verso of the sheet carries further Latin inscriptions, which are attempts at phrases, reminders and formulations. Buck deciphers them as follows: *Dicu(n)t ad* or *Dicu(n)t advenit X* and *Dicu(n)t m(ilesim) o anno venit plen(um)* [They say that the end is coming in the year one thousand (the millennium)]. This anticipation of the end of the world corresponds to the eschatological components that are frequently to be found in Bosch's paintings. The inscription of the name "Gero: Bosch" on the front dates from the 17th century, as do the inscriptions on Cat. D7 and Cat. D8.

Owing to its complexity, the sheet is undoubtedly the most important Bosch drawing to have come down to us (overview of research in: Buck 2001, pp. 197–199 and pp. 201–203). The iconography has been explored in depth in two outstanding studies. These situate the owl, in particular, within the tradition of Christian symbolism, where it represents folly, uncleanliness and temptation by evil (Vandenbroeck 1985; Bambeck 1987; on the fox, also de Bruyn 2000).

Earlier art historians attempted to interpret the drawing as a self-portrait (Benesch 1937). Koldeweij expanded this idea by proposing that it was intended as the portrait of a place. He thereby interpreted a number of pictorial elements as parts of a toponymic rebus whose sounds, when placed one after the other, produce the name –"'s-Hertogenbosch". Indeed, if we separate the picture into words –"ears" (in Dutch: *oren*),"to hear" (*horen*) and more specifically "hears" (*hoort*), eyes (*ogen*) and wood (*bos*) – it is possible to construct something resembling 's-Hertogenbosch. A corresponding reference to the artist Hieronymus Bosch is absent, however. The picture is too unspecific to be a self-portrait. Koldeweij's student Ilsink has nevertheless revived this idea. See also pp. 86, 87.

The Tree-Man

The magnificent drawing *The Tree-Man* (Cat. D4) exhibits the same graphic technique as Cat. D2 and Cat. D3, even surpassing these latter in the variety of its handling of line and in the minute detailing of the landscape.

In the centre of the portrait-format sheet, a tree-man rises above a river. His egg-shaped body, covered in part with bark and/or feathers, supports itself on two crooked, partly hollow tree trunks that at the same time resemble arms, and which are standing in boats as if they were shoes. His head, which is turned back over one shoulder towards the viewer, is crowned by a flat disc carrying an enormous jug. Inside his torso a convivial company is gathered around a table with a jug. They include at least two men and a woman, and one or two other people. A flag with a crescent moon flies from a long slanting pole, recalling an inn sign. Higher up, an owl perches in the leafless crown of the tree that rises skywards from the giant's left foot. The plant motifs in the drawing can be summed up in terms of "flourishing/living" versus "dying". Near a tall, slender tree in the lower left corner a deer is poised on the sloping bank, opposite a stork standing on one leg on the right. Birds are flying around the middle ground and mobbing an owl on the right. In the background, beneath banks of clouds, a harbour with a large number of boats extends along the irregular shoreline, and several villages or small towns are clustered around church spires.

The drawing is executed in such painstaking detail that it seems to have an autonomous character. In view of its great resemblance, however, to the tree-man in the *Hell* scene in the right inner panel of the *Garden of Earthly Delights* (Cat. 11.4), the question arises as to whether it forms part of the preparation for the painting or is a copy of it. In addition to the similarity in their general physiognomy, the cracked and jagged outline of the opening at the rear is identical to such an extent that one must be the copy of the other or must have been developed out of the other. This becomes even clearer if we rotate the drawing slightly to the right.

A connection with another Bosch triptych is present in the motif of the rocky cliff rising at the left of the sheet, topped by a few trees and a small figure, which resembles the formation seen behind St James on the left-hand exterior wing of the Vienna *Last Judgement* (Cat. 13.1). Similar cliffs border the scenes in the interior of the triptych, too, in a manner found nowhere else in Bosch's œuvre.

The sheet was used as the basis for a copper engraving (*c.* 1530–1550), which reproduced the drawing in great detail and introduced a few more figures into the foreground ('s-Hertogenbosch 1990, p. 263). See also pp. 167, *212*.

The Birds and the Mammals

The sheet *The Birds and the Mammals Go to War* (Cat. D5), which is also known as *The Gathering of the Birds*, is executed in a hand that closely resembles that responsible for Cat. D2–Cat. D4, but is more rapid and more dynamic. While the shading on the bodies is conveyed simply by closely made strokes of the pen, the shadows on the ground are more carefully delineated. Overall, however, the animals are less three-dimensional in effect than in Cat. D2–Cat. D4, Cat. D7 and Cat. D8. The right background, in particular, resembles the left background in Cat. D2.

In the left foreground the birds have assembled beneath the banner of the Holy Roman Empire with its double-headed eagle. The leaders – a gryphon and two eagles (or an eagle and an ostrich?) – are gathered at the centre as if to discuss the situation. Further birds of prey, including eagles and owls, stand ready around them, along with a cockerel, two peacocks, geese or swans, and ducks. In the right foreground three storks bearing "flags" with earthworm banners have formed a line opposite four spoonbills with bird's-head flags. Between them a bird is beating two drums. In the background, the mammals are marching past a bare and deserted rocky cliff. A unicorn and an elephant stand out prominently within their tight-knit ranks, which also include a number of hoofed animals. On top of a rock, a magnificent stag displays its antlers. A gallows wheel to its left refers to the looming threat of death. An empty middle ground, soon to become a battlefield, yawns between the two groups of animals.

Although at first sight unusual, the iconography nevertheless takes up a traditional topos: the battle between the birds and the beasts from Aesop's *Fables*, which were available in print editions by the 15th century. The present sheet, like its companion Cat. D6, may be understood less in terms of a design for a painting than as a drawing with its own autonomous value. More than simply playful illustrations, the two sheets testify to Bosch's unusual iconographic repertoire, his erudition and education and his aim to master many compositional themes rather than to perfect an elegant or beautiful style and to transmit this to his workshop.

The sheet *The Battle of the Birds and the Mammals* (Cat. D6), like its companion Cat. D5, was long disregarded by Bosch scholarship. In line with the dynamism of the events depicted, the drawing is here executed in a noticeably looser and more rapid hand. The lines and strokes of the pen are correspondingly thinner and the shadows cast by the animals are now only occasionally indicated.

The battle is being fought with extreme ferocity and dead or seriously wounded animals and severed limbs lie all around. Chaos reigns; the rules of perspective seem to have been abandoned and the animals are scattered across the picture plane. Just as the animals lose their orientation in the merciless fray, so too does the viewer struggle to find a bearing. One is provided by the distant hills set against a high horizon, from beyond which more birds are approaching.

The animals in this drawing are those frequently to be found in Bosch's landscapes, such as bears, foxes and owls, joined here by a number of fabulous and fantastical beasts. Bosch has also drawn a horse seen in rear view – a demonstration of artistic skill that had become part of the repertoire in the 15th century. Certain pictorial motifs also correspond in stylistic terms to those in other Bosch drawings, as in the case of the crouching fox in the left foreground, which resembles that in Cat. D3.

Fantasy Creatures

In the Berlin Kupferstichkabinett catalogue, the drawing *Bird Monster and Snarling Dragon* (Cat. D7r) and its verso, *Skull–Turtle Monster and Winged Gnome* (Cat. D7v), are both described as representing "Two Fantasy Creatures" (*Zwei Fantasiegeschöpfe*). Here and in the sketches on the verso, the technique is the same as in Cat. D2–Cat. D4 and Cat. D8. A monster standing upright on two legs occupies the upper two-thirds of the portrait-format sheet. On its left foot it wears a boot with an arrow tucked inside it – a frequent motif in Bosch. The creature balances an enormous arrow like a spear across its short arms. Its neck and head are like those of a goose, and a plume of feathers sweeps back from its forehead. In the bottom third of the sheet a second beast is crouching and snarling. Its body parts – its powerful back legs, for example – resemble those of no specific animal. Thick hair or feathers sprout back from its head in a prominent display. Its long tail snakes and almost coils. The fearful impression created by these two creatures is partly due also to the fact that they are both looking behind them. The decorative hair and feathers on the creatures' heads, and the fur, plumage and scales suggested on their bodies, here serve no function and probably symbolize vanity.

The other side of the sheet is dominated by the skull of an animal or a monster, the nearer, left-hand end most closely reminiscent of the skull of a horse. Towards the right end, two feet and a neck call to mind a turtle, its head reaching right to the edge of the sheet. Rapidly drawn underneath it, with no shading but within a closed silhouette, is a squat humanoid creature with bat-like wings, a thick torso and thin extremities, wearing an inverted funnel on its head and sticking its legs into a sack or a pipe.

That the drawings served as design samples is attested by the fact that all four monsters from the sheet, together with other monster drawings that cannot confidently be attributed to Bosch, were copied on to a sheet of such specimen figures today in Providence (Rhode Island School of Design, Museum of Art).

The drawing *Two Beetle-like Monsters* (Cat. D8r) and its verso, *Two Cephalopods* (Cat. D8v), are again both described, in the Berlin catalogue, as representing "Two Fantasy Creatures" (*Zwei Fantasiegeschöpfe*). The sheet exhibits a similar drawing technique to Cat. D2–Cat. D4 and Cat. D7. The recto shows, on the left, a beetle-like monster in front view, and on the right a cat-beetle monster seen diagonally from the rear. This last was transferred to the upper right tondo on the exterior of the *Fragments of a representation of The Flood* (Cat. 19.1), which establishes a *terminus ante quem* for the drawing. The present sheet thus not only testifies to the traditional function of Bosch's drawings as the forum within which the artist elaborated designs, samples and models for his paintings. It also provides technical and stylistic evidence that the *Flood* fragments may safely be attributed to Bosch. This direct link between drawing and painting simultaneously removes any doubt as to the connection between the drawings whose technique and style is the same (Cat. D2–Cat. D4, Cat. D7 and Cat. D8), or similar (Cat. D1, Cat. D5 and Cat. D6), and the paintings by Bosch (Cat. 1–20). For Cat. D8r see also p. 293.

LITERATURE

On the drawings in general: 's-Hertogenbosch 1967, pp. 168–203;
Filedt Kok 1972/73; Marijnissen 1987, pp. 452–463; Koreny/Pokorny 2001; Antwerp 2002; Silver 2006, pp. 274–303; Koreny 2012.
D1: 's-Hertogenbosch 1967, p. 168, no. 48; Antwerp 2002, pp. 182–184; Koreny 2012, pp. 152–155.
D2: Rosenberg 1961; Antwerp 2002, pp. 185–187; Koreny 2012, pp. 190–195.
D3: 's-Hertogenbosch 1967, p. 188, no. 57; Vandenbroeck 1981, 1985; Bambeck 1987; Lammertse 1994, p. 99; de Bruyn 2000; Buck 2001, pp. 197–206; Koldeweij/Vermet/Vandenbroeck 2001; Fischer 2009, pp. 165–172; Ilsink 2010; Koreny 2012, pp. 170–177.
D4: Koreny/Pokorny 2001, pp. 6–15; Antwerp 2002, pp. 168–172; Gibson 2008; Koreny 2012, pp. 184–189.
D5: Buck 2001, pp. 230–234; Antwerp 2002, pp. 177–181; Koreny 2012, pp. 162–169.
D6: Buck 2001, pp. 230–234; Antwerp 2002, pp. 177–181; Koreny 2012, pp. 162–169.
D7: 's-Hertogenbosch 1967, p. 196, no. 61; Buck 2001, pp. 211–215; Antwerp 2002, pp. 173–176; Koreny 2012, pp. 178–183.
D8: Buck 2001, pp. 207–211; Antwerp 2002, pp. 173–175; Koreny 2012, pp. 196–199.

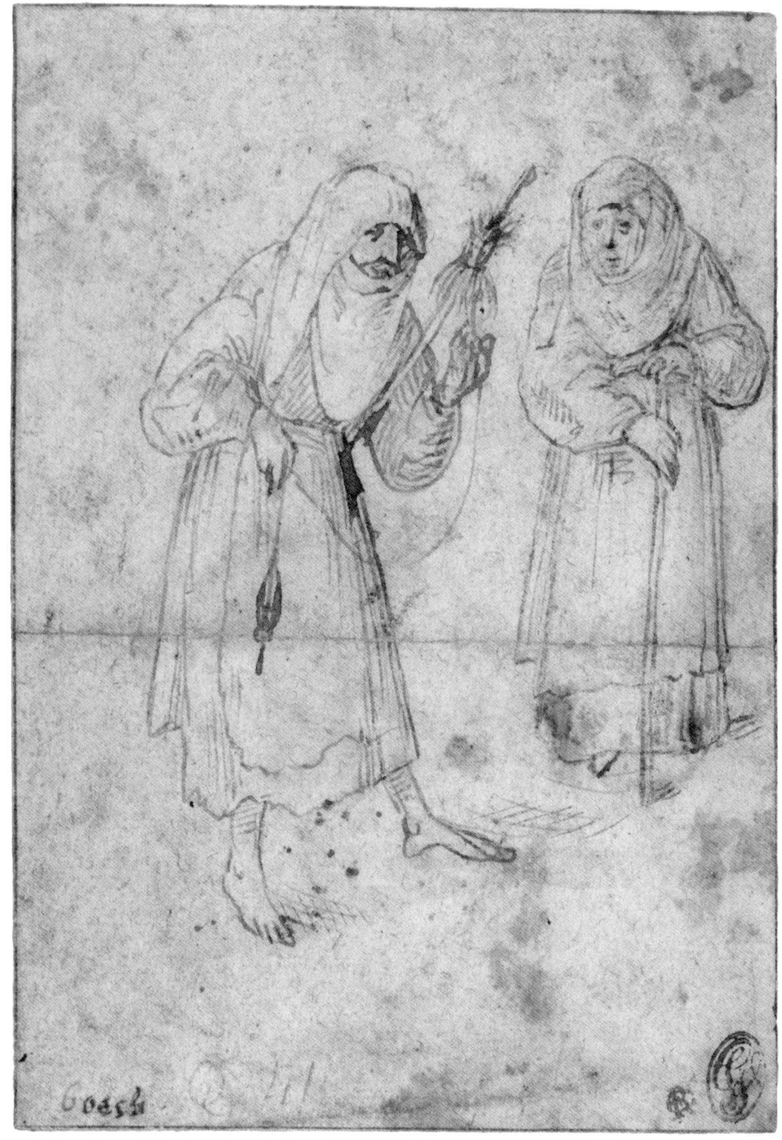

D1 (r) **Two Witches (Woman Spinning and Old Woman)**
Pen and brown and greyish-brown ink on paper, 120 x 85 mm / approx. 4¾ x 3⅜ in.
Rotterdam, Museum Boijmans Van Beuningen, inv. no. N 190

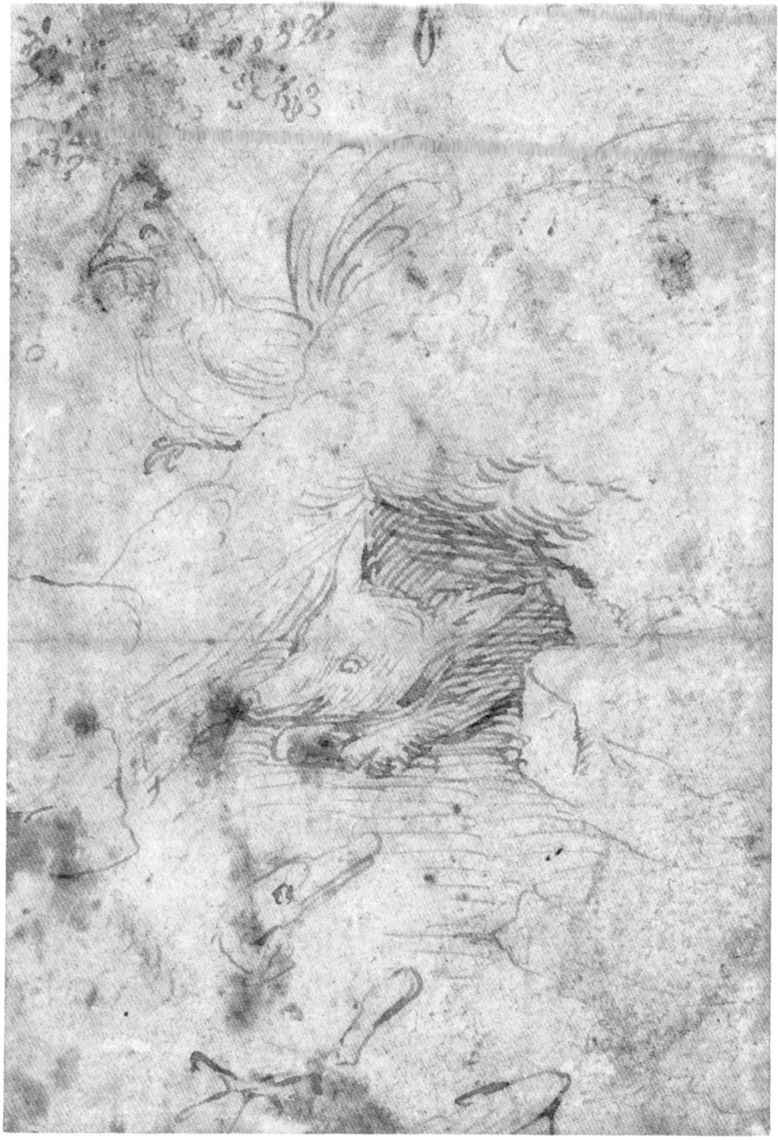

Z1 (v) **Fox and Cockerel**, *c.* 1490–1505
Pen and brown and greyish-brown ink on paper, 120 x 85 mm / approx. 4¾ x 3⅜ in.
Rotterdam, Museum Boijmans Van Beuningen, inv. no. N 190

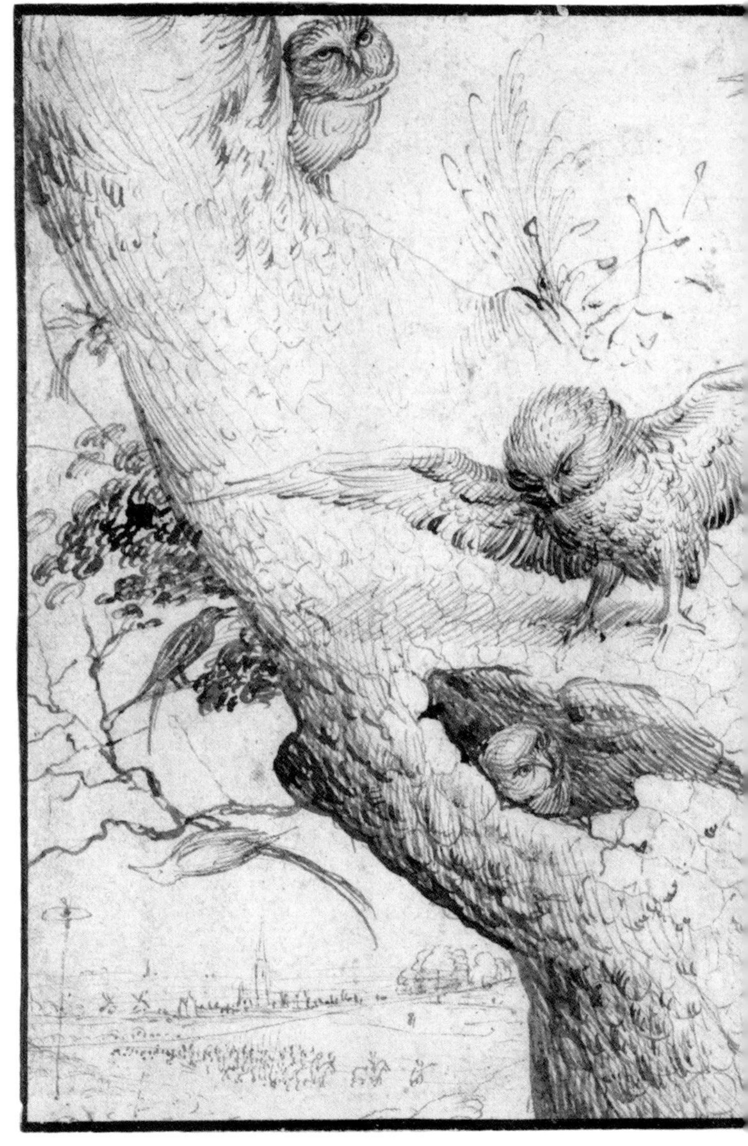

D2 Nest of Owls, *c.* 1500
Pen and brown ink on paper, 140 x 196 mm / approx. 5½ x 7¾ in.
Rotterdam, Museum Boijmans Van Beuningen, inv. no. N 175

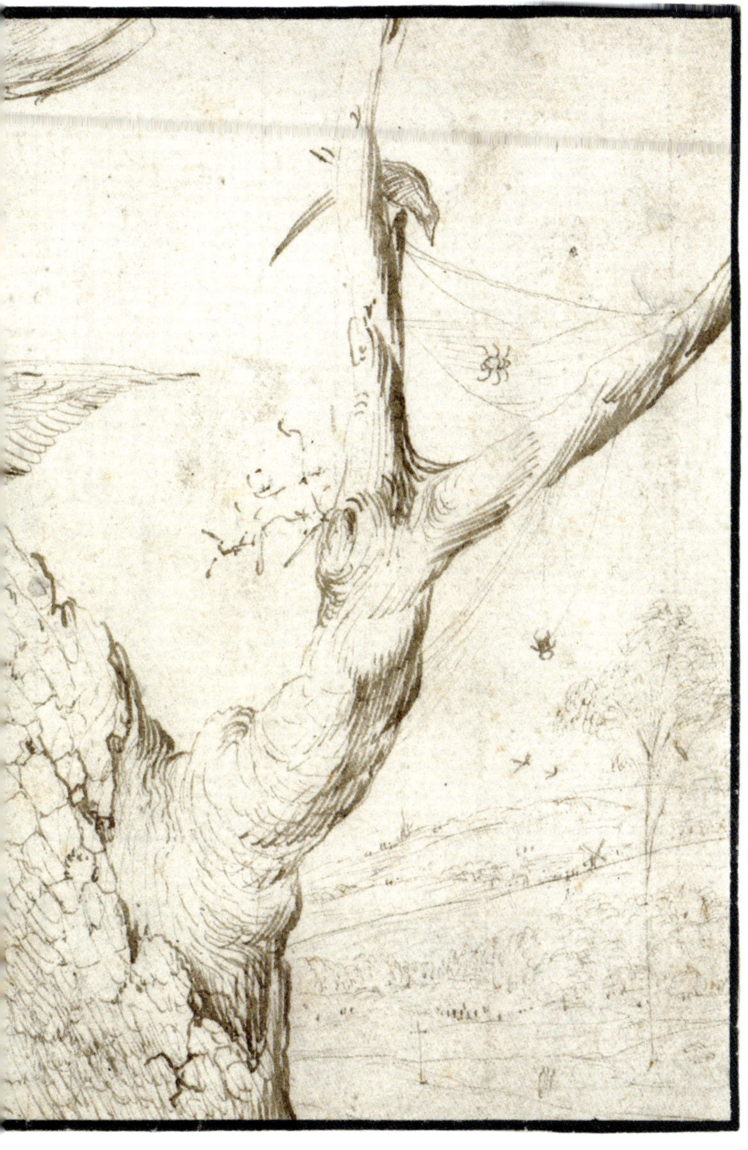

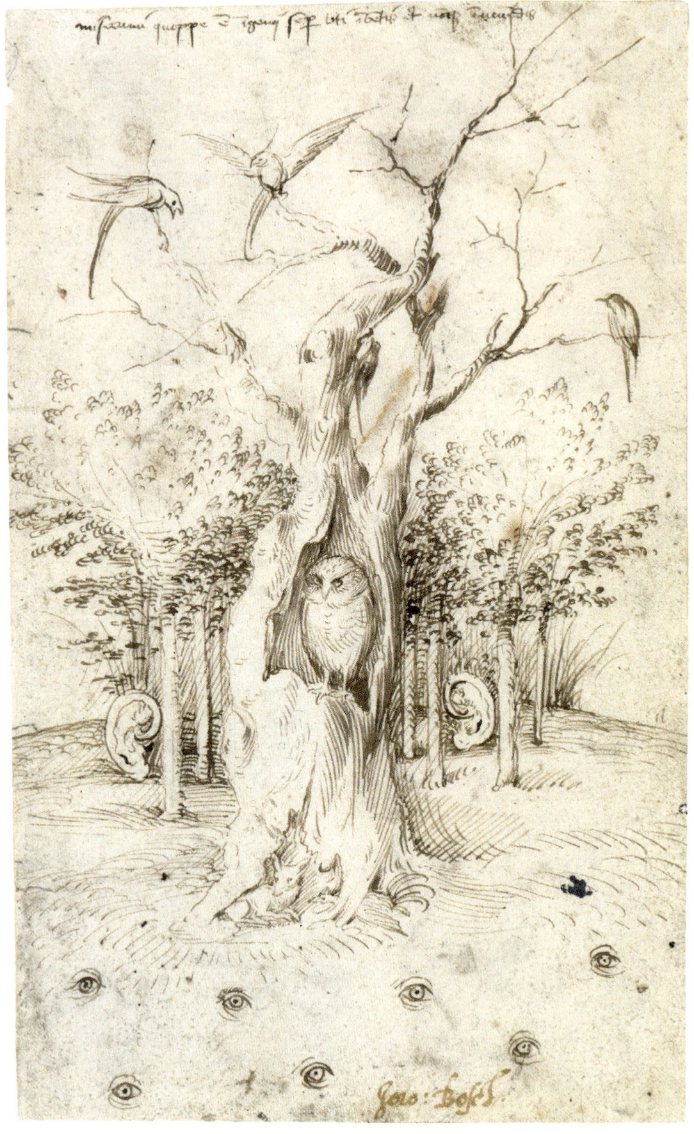

D3 (r) **The Wood Has Ears, the Field Eyes**, *c.* 1502–1505
Pen and brown ink on paper, 202 x 127 mm / approx. 8 x 5 in.
Berlin, Staatliche Museen zu Berlin, Kupferstichkabinett, KdZ 549

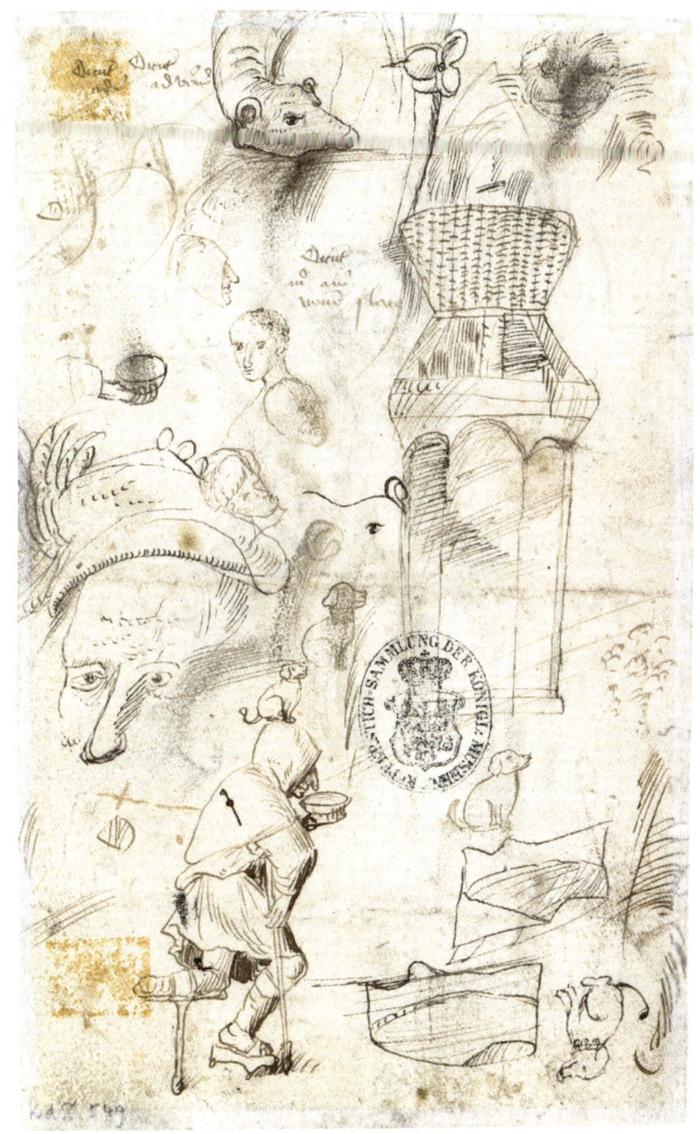

D3 (v) **Figural Studies**, *c.* 1502–1505
Pen and brown ink on paper, 202 x 127 mm / approx. 8 x 5 in.
Berlin, Staatliche Museen zu Berlin, Kupferstichkabinett, KdZ 549

D4 The Tree-Man, *c.* 1503–1506
Pen and brown ink on paper, 277 x 211 mm / approx. 10⅞ x 8¼ in.
Vienna, Albertina, inv. no. 7876

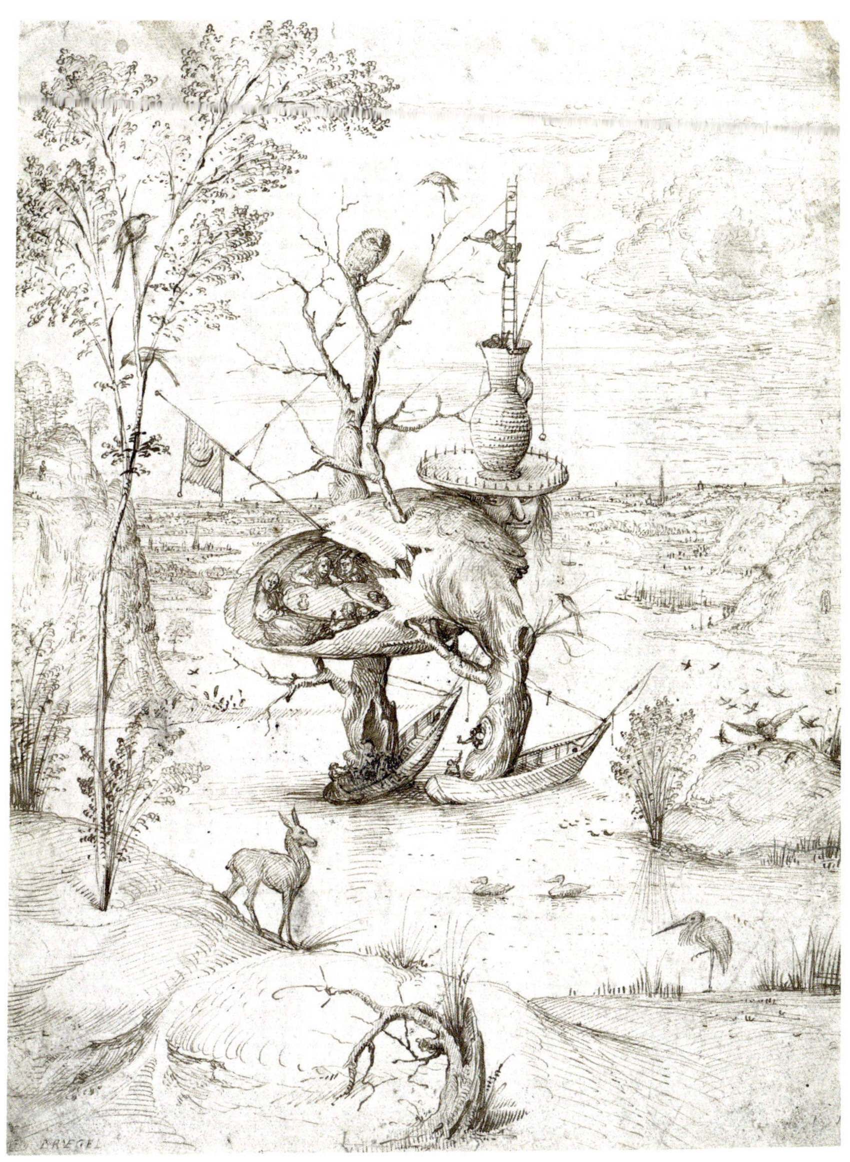
BRVEGEL

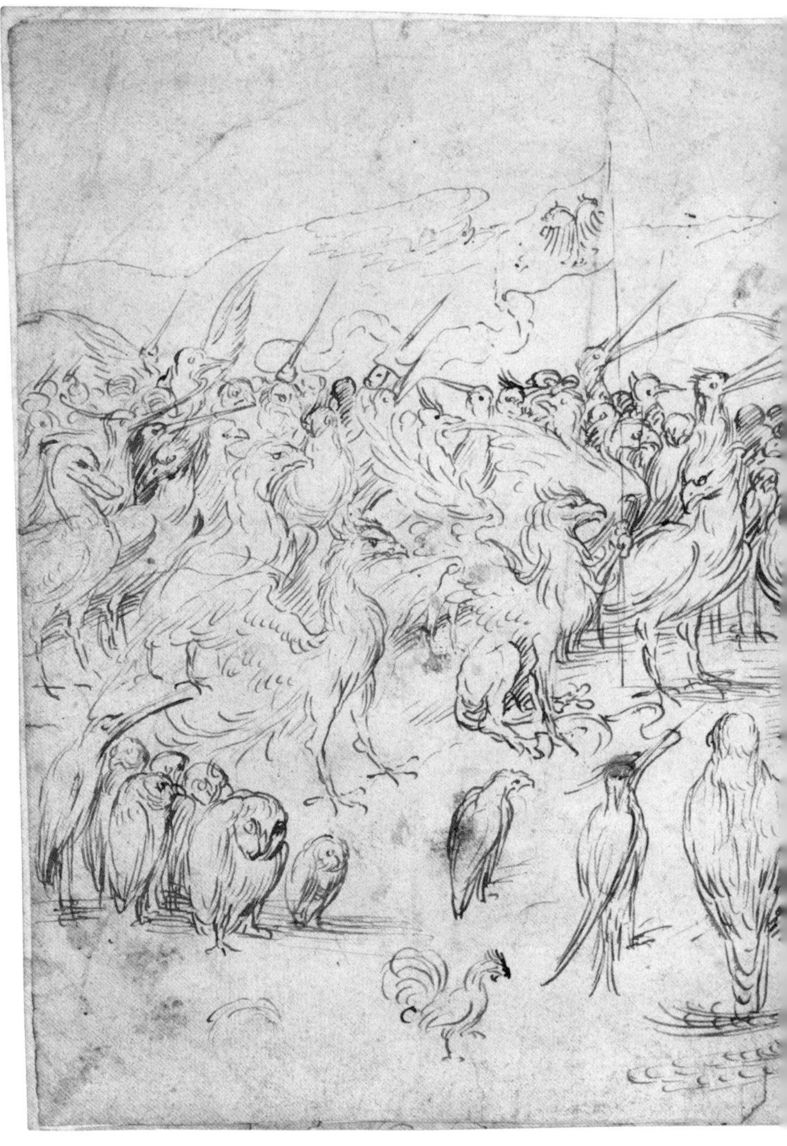

D5 The Birds and the Mammals Go to War, *c.* 1505–1510
Pen and brown ink on paper, 195 x 284 mm / approx. 7⅝ x 11⅛ in.
Berlin, Staatliche Museen zu Berlin, Kupferstichkabinett, KdZ 13136

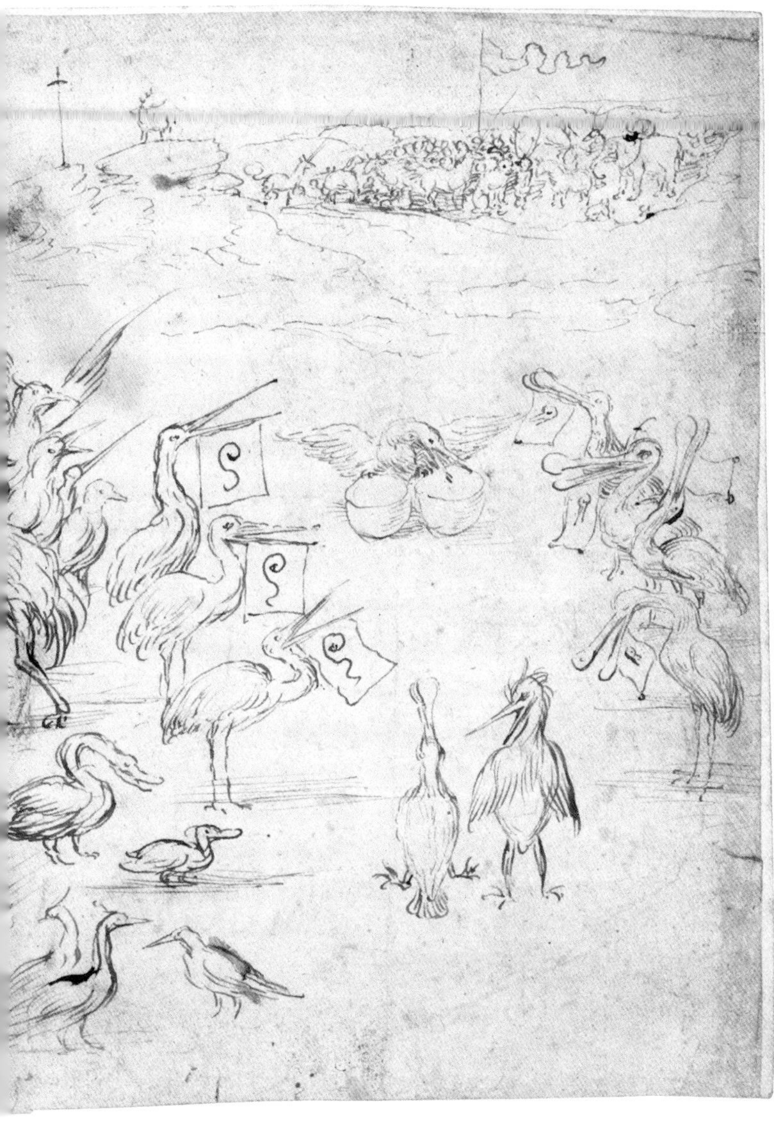

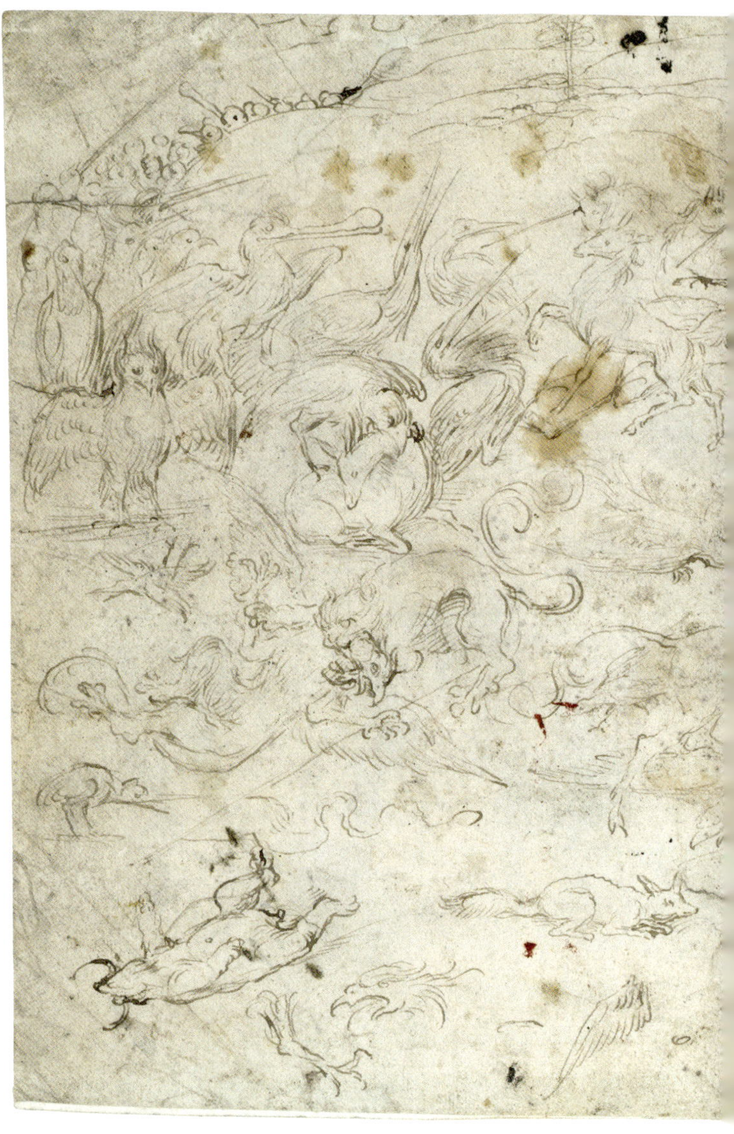

D6 The Battle of the Birds and the Mammals, *c.* 1505–1510
Pen and brown ink on paper, 203 x 290 mm / approx. 8 x 11½ in.
Berlin, Staatliche Museen zu Berlin, Kupferstichkabinett, KdZ 14715

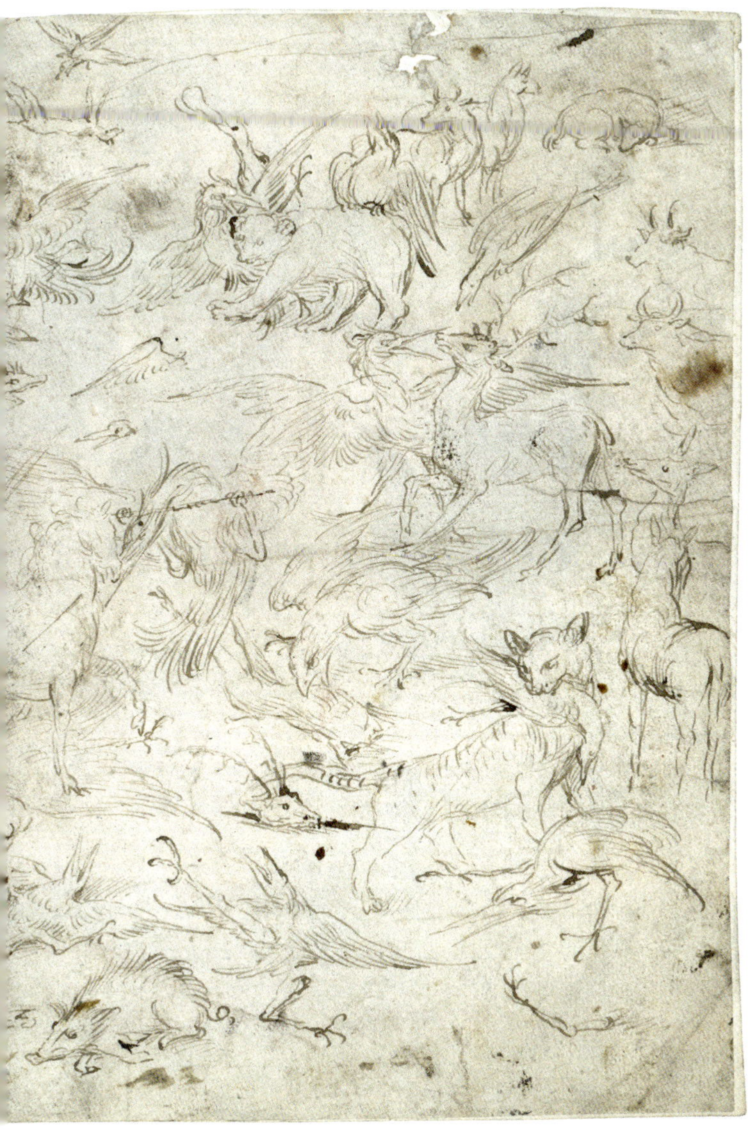

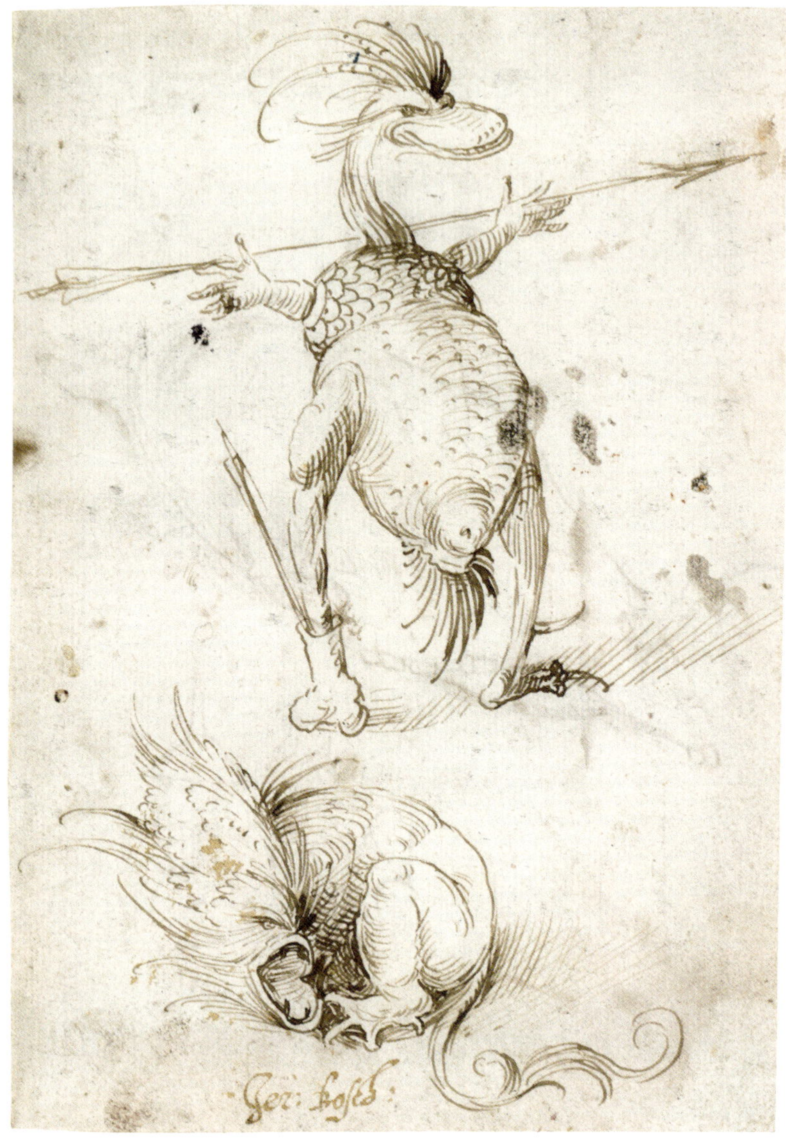

D7 (r) **Bird Monster and Snarling Dragon**, *c.* 1505–1515
Pen and brown ink on paper, 164 x 116–119 mm / approx. 6½ x 4½–4⅝ in.
Berlin, Staatliche Museen zu Berlin, Kupferstichkabinett, KdZ 547

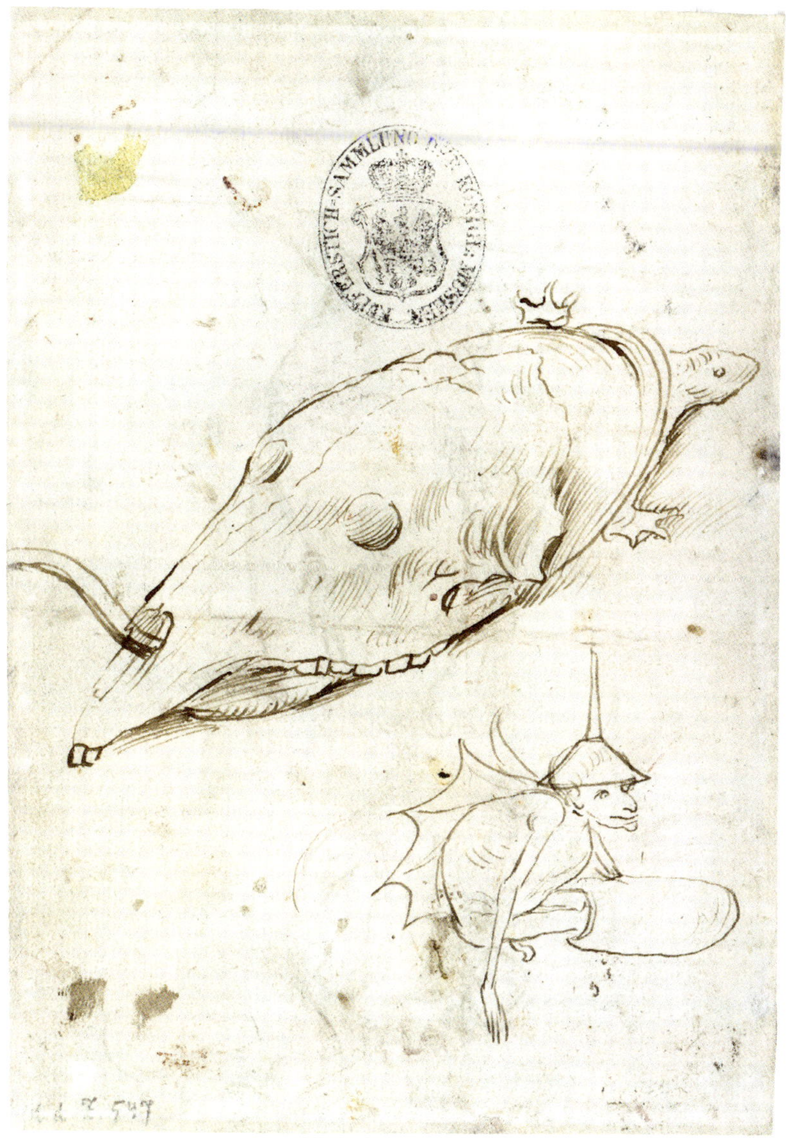

D7 (v) **Skull-Turtle Monster and Winged Gnome**, *c.* 1505–1515
Pen and brown ink on paper, 164 x 116–119 mm / approx. 6½ x 4½–4⅝ in.
Berlin, Staatliche Museen zu Berlin, Kupferstichkabinett, KdZ 547

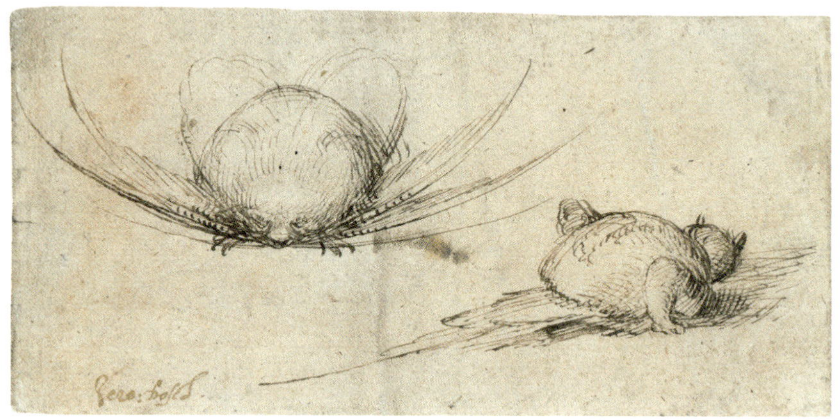

D8 (r) **Two Beetle-like Monsters**, *c.* 1505–1515
Pen and brown ink on paper, 86 x 182 mm / approx. 3⅜ x 7⅛ in.
Berlin, Staatliche Museen zu Berlin, Kupferstichkabinett, KdZ 550

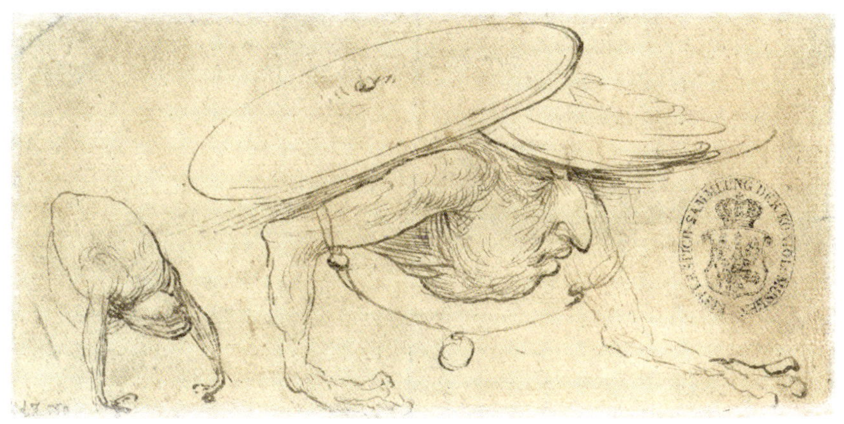

D8 (v) **Two Cephalopods**, *c.* 1505–1515
Pen and brown ink on paper, 86 x 182 mm / approx. 3⅜ x 7⅛ in.
Berlin, Staatliche Museen zu Berlin, Kupferstichkabinett, KdZ 550

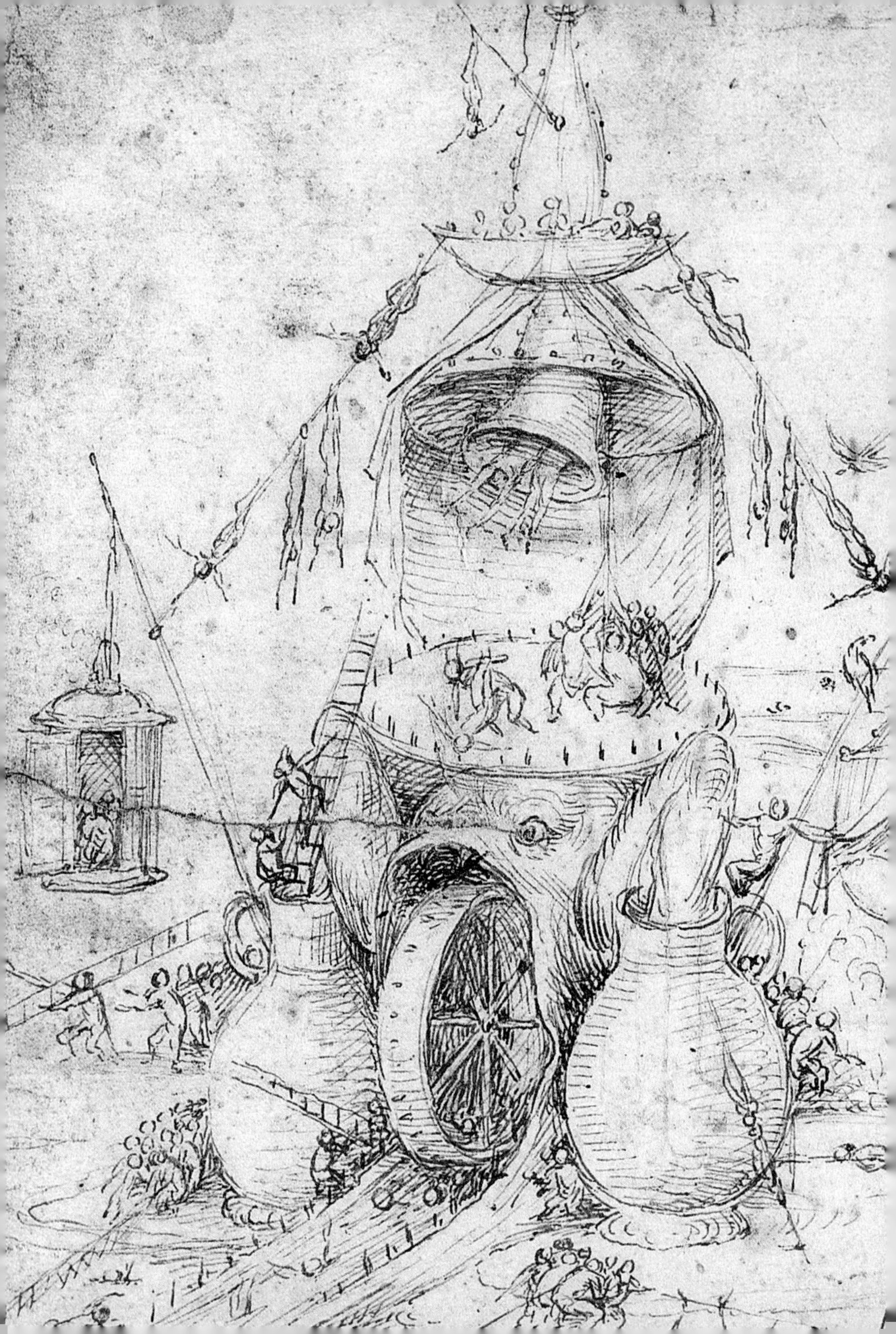

Catalogue of drawings – workshop and followers

Drollery with Beehive

The drawing *Drollery with Beehive* (Cat. D9r) is attributed to the workshop or followers of Hieronymus Bosch. A man with the seat of his leggings pulled down is kneeling on all fours inside a man-size beehive, while birds (swallows?) fly out of his backside. A manikin squatting on top of the hive has raised his lute with both hands over his head, ready to bring it down on the bare backside or the birds emerging. A woman in long robes and with her head covered crouches on the left, a pair of tongs hovering over her head. Distributed across the remaining areas of the sheet are a number of small, naked figures like infant boys, strongly reminiscent of Renaissance putti. They are hunting and catching birds. The sheet's individual motifs are thereby linked into a whole. The central motif of the beehive is found in a similar manner, as a relief decoration, in the central panel of the *Hermit Saints* triptych (Cat. 12.2) and also in *St Christopher* (Cat. 7). The verso (Cat. D9v) carries a variation of the recto, executed as a rapid sketch in which the beehive and the woman with her head covered fuse into a single motif. Appearing beside them is a tree-man based on Cat. 11.4 and Cat. D4. It is thus clear that we are looking at a sheet of ideas and exercises. See also p. 262.

The Conjuror

The drawing of *The Conjuror* (Cat. D10r) features pictorial motifs typical of Bosch, such as the sleeping dog (cf. Cat. 15, Cat. 20.3), the two children seated in the left foreground and the whirligig (Cat. 9.2), as well as characteristic aspects of style such as delicate facial features with eyes like dots and pointed chins. The large, dark shadow in the group of people on the left, however, has been roughly drawn, without any modelling of the individual figures. The drawing appears somewhat careless and summary, and as a whole to have been executed at speed, but is nonetheless of high quality. It seems too exploratory to be a copy, yet almost too rapidly sketched to be a design. It is possible that it represents a variant of a painted or drawn original by Bosch. The *Company at Table* on the verso of the sheet (Cat. D10v) is slightly more recent and corresponds in stylistic terms to the Dutch Renaissance. See also Cat. 28.

Page 456
Detail from: **Hell scene for a Last Judgement**, *c.* 1515? (see p. 469)

The Entombment

The Entombment (Cat. D11) came to light only in 1952. Although at first seen as the work of Bosch, most authors have subsequently attributed it to his workshop. The subject is also represented on the exterior of *St John on Patmos* (Cat. 3.2.2), where the story of the Passion reaches its (provisional) conclusion with the Entombment at the upper right. There, as in the present drawing, the work is symmetrical in composition: the Virgin and St John, standing behind the tomb exactly half-way along its length and with their bodies angled towards the left, form a slightly lopsided triangle. Joseph of Arimathea and Nicodemus stand respectively, at the head and foot of the tomb. Although technically the sheet is more detailed and forceful than drawings by Bosch's own hand, Koreny nonetheless identifies similarities with the manner and style of figural representation in paintings by Bosch. He points in particular to the figures in the outer wings of the *Temptation of St Anthony* (Cat. 10.1 and 10.2) – with which the London sheet shows the broadest similarity as a whole – to the poses and the execution of details like the pointed noses. He also compares the dead Christ in the drawing with the sinner on the ground in the Hell wing of *The Haywain* (Cat. 20.4). We might also draw attention to further similarities, such as the bearded man on the far right, and the crown of thorns, which is not loosely woven but is tightly wound like a rope, with no gaps, as is the case in all Bosch paintings featuring this motif (see Cat. 1, Cat. 4–8, Cat. 10, Cat. 18 and Cat. 21).

Ship of Hell and Infernal Scenes

Ship of Hell (Cat. D12), an armless giant in armour is carrying a boat on his shoulders, his head sticking up through its hull and the ship's mast rising out of the top of his head. The giant is girded with an oriental sabre and also has a hat or helmet, spurs and clogs. Numerous figures – a mixture of devils and damned souls – occupy the boat and its rigging. A figure shot through by an arrow dangles from the prow, another hangs over the stern, birds are escaping from his backside (cf. *The Garden of Earthly Delights*, Cat. 11.4). Flames leap up from the body of the ship. There is no background landscape. The paper carries the same watermark as the Dresden sheet (Cat. D14) and there are also stylistic similarities between these two drawings. With its highly detailed inventory of motifs, the sheet *Hell scene for a Last Judgement* (Cat. D13) comes very close to the Bruges *Last Judgement* (Cat. 26). Parallels with the latter can also be found in the atmospheric landscape and the skilful handling of perspective evident in the diminishing scale of the objects towards the background. It thus seems likely that the drawing is the work of the same artist.

The drawing *Hell scenes, Tree-Man Monster* (Cat. D14), now in Dresden, may stem from the same hand as the sheet *Concert in an Egg* in Berlin (KdZ 711), although the latter's motif cannot be traced to any of Bosch's surviving works. The Dresden drawing shows a variation of the tree-man in the *Garden of Earthly Delights* (Cat. 11.4) and in the Vienna drawing (Cat. D4), set in a landscape. In the hilly left foreground a man standing in the mouth of a jug is pulling towards him another man, seated on a giant lower-leg clad in jousting armour. A throng of people is massing behind. Opposite, on the right, a savage giant with a bow has made two men his prey. The pictorial motifs at upper left and right – an enormous helmet with raised visor besieged by people, and a fish-like monster on a round platform – seem like unrelated studies, but are in fact integrated, with a rapid hand, into the rest of the composition. The sheet carries the same watermark as the Vienna drawing (Cat. D12) and exhibits a similar style. The verso shows a *Standing Rabbi* (Cat. D14v).

Fantasy creatures and figure studies

The folio of fantasy creatures (Cat. D15), more a personal compilation than a specimen sheet of monsters for Hell scenes, has features in common with both Bosch's œuvre and the output of a member of his workshop as well as other Bosch followers (Buck). In the *Five Fantasy Creatures* on the recto (Cat. D15r), the anvil scene recalls the punishment of Sloth in the *Last Judgement* (Cat. 13.4), the *Seven Deadly Sins* (Cat. 15) and the Bruges *Last Judgement* (Cat. 26). Stylistically, the draughtsman uses emphatic outlines, with little sculptural modelling, and works in a fast and confident hand, so that the figures appear more dynamic than in Bosch's drawings and underdrawings. The *Seven Fantasy Creatures* on the verso (Cat. 15v) differ so markedly from those on the recto that recto and not necessarily be by the same artist. The drawing *Study for two figures for a Passion scene* (Cat. D16r), presented by Koreny (Antwerp 2002) as a "Shady-looking Pair in Conversation" (*Zwielichtiges Paar im Gespräch*), shares an affinity first and foremost with the Ghent *Christ Carrying the Cross* (Cat. 29), since the physiognomies in autograph Bosch works – witnessed by *Christ Mocked* (Cat. 5), for example – are more realistic and less distorted or mask-like. Only the beggar woman next to St Bavo in the right outer wing of the Vienna *Last Judgement* (Cat. 13.2) seems to come very close to the drawing. The verso shows *The Temptation of Eve* (Cat. D16v).

LITERATURE

D9: 's-Hertogenbosch 1967, p. 192, no. 59; Koreny/Pokorny 2001, pp. 16–21; Antwerp 2002, pp. 194–198; Fischer 2009, pp. 113, 162; Koreny 2012, pp. 230–235.

D10: Cinotti 1966, p. 89; Unverfehrt 1980, pp. 114–117; van Schoute/Verboomen 2000, p. 191; Koreny 2012, pp. 278–285.

D11: 's-Hertogenbosch 1967, p. 187, no. 56; Antwerp 2002, pp. 191–193; Koreny 2012, pp. 224–229.

D12: 's-Hertogenbosch 1967, p. 180, no. 53; Koreny/Pokorny 2001, pp. 32–37; Antwerp 2002, pp. 199–201; Koreny 2012, pp. 214–217.

D13: Koreny 2012, pp. 218–220.

D14: Buck 2001, p. 228; *Ketelsen/Neidhardt 2005*, p. 106; Koreny 2012, pp. 261–265.

D15: Buck 2001, pp. 216–223; Koreny 2012, pp. 248–253.

D16: Antwerp 2002, pp. 188–190; Koreny 2012, pp. 200–203.

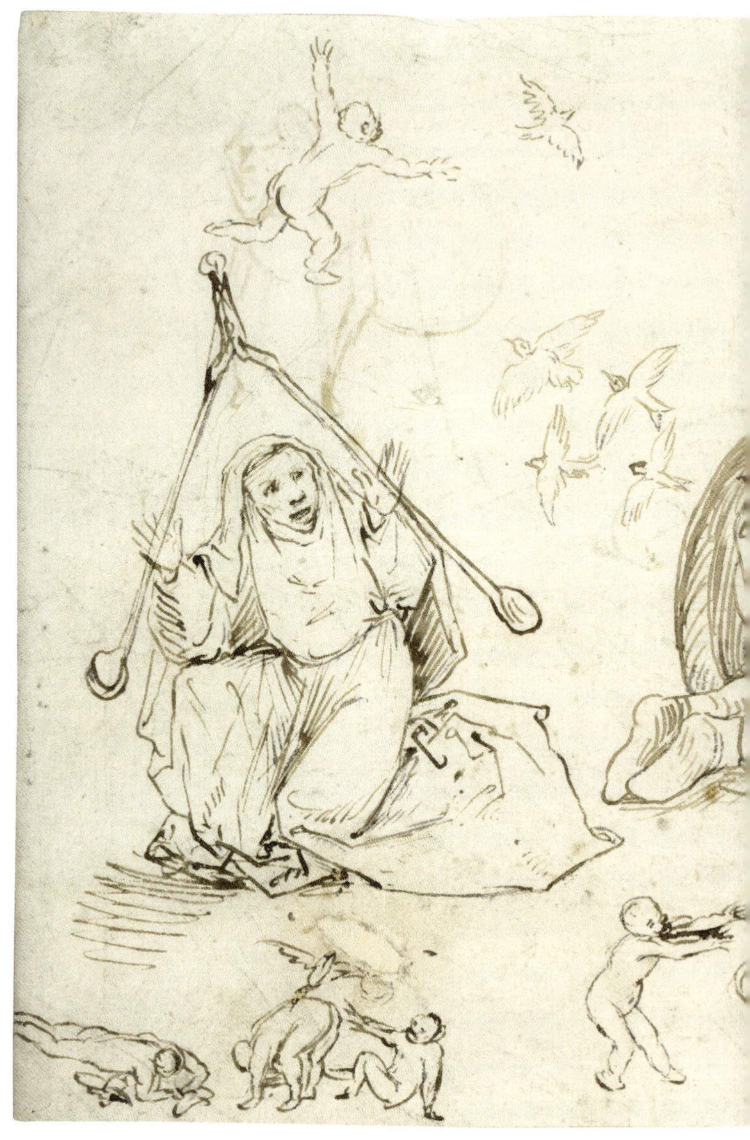

D9 (r) Workshop or follower of Hieronymus Bosch **Drollery with Beehive**, *c.* 1510–1515
Pen and brown ink on paper, watermark, 192 x 270 mm / approx. 7½ x 10⅝ in.
Vienna, Albertina, inv. no. 7797

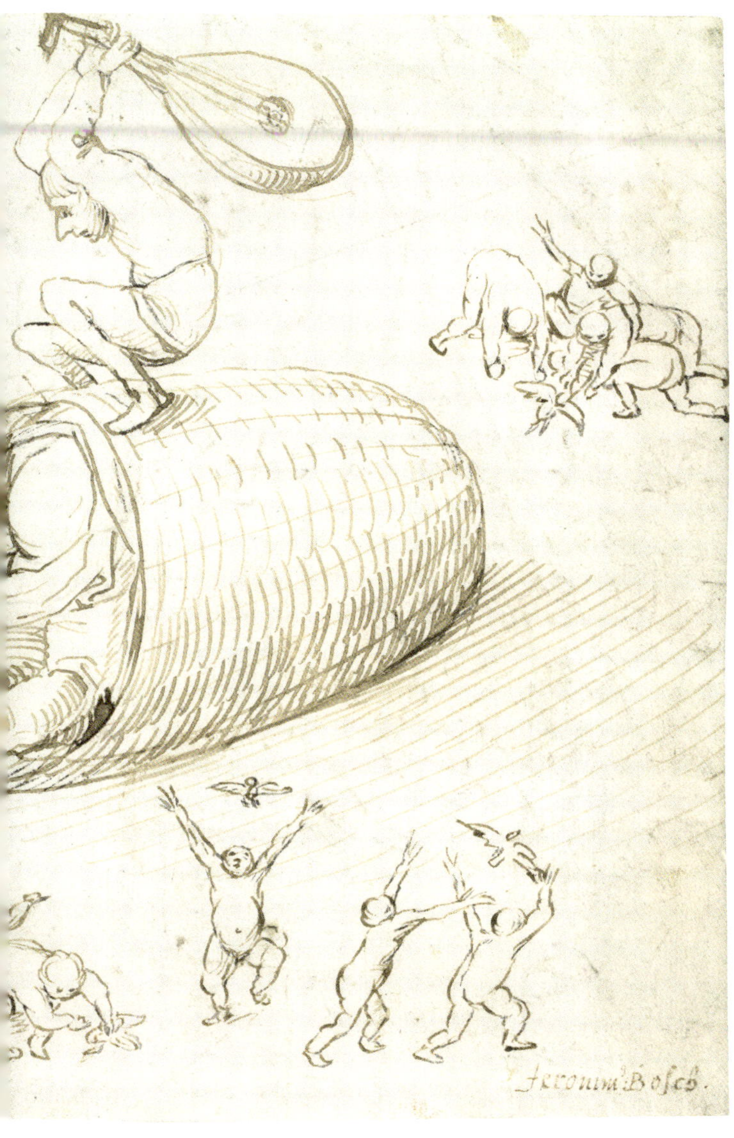

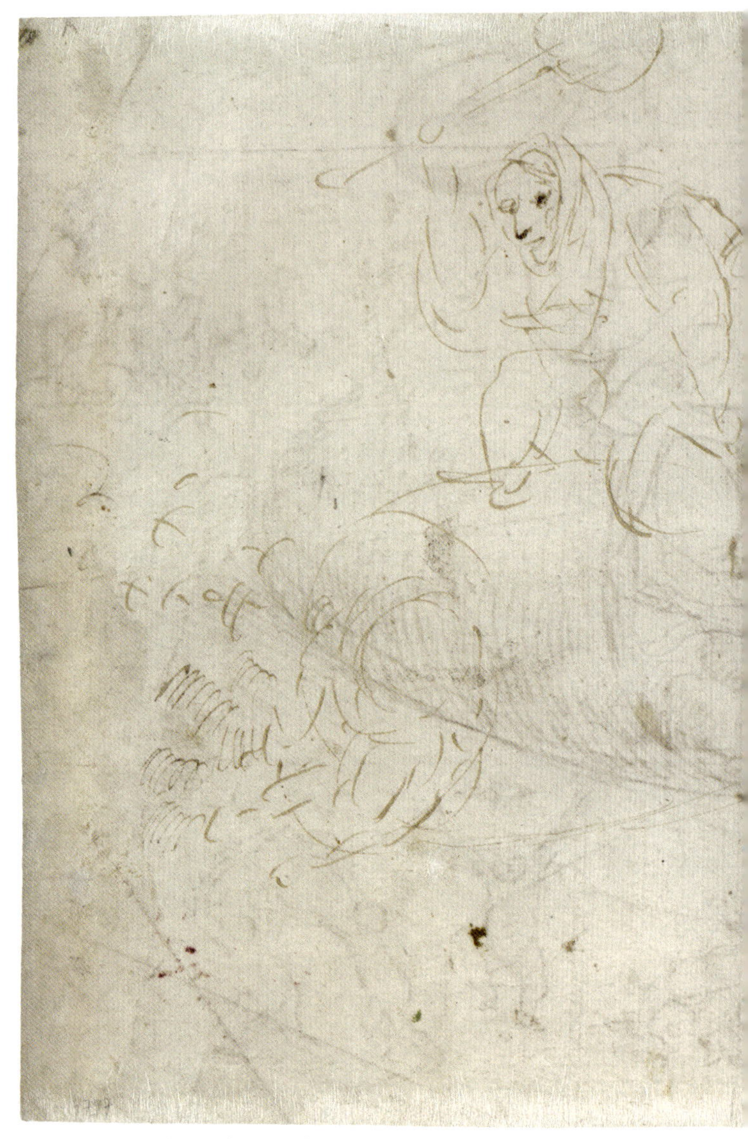

D9 (v) Workshop or follower of Hieronymus Bosch
Drollery with Beehive and Crutches Monster, um 1510–1515
Pen and brown ink on paper, watermark, 192 x 270 mm / approx. 7½ x 10⅝ in.
Vienna, Albertina, inv. no. 7797

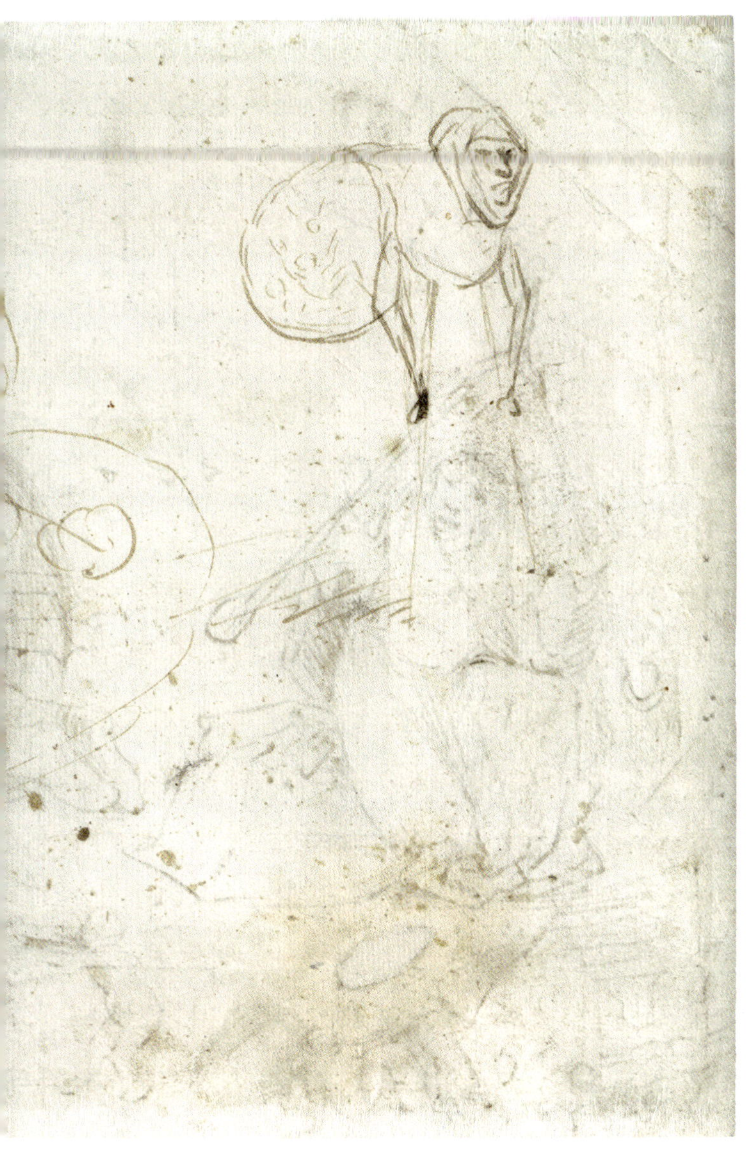

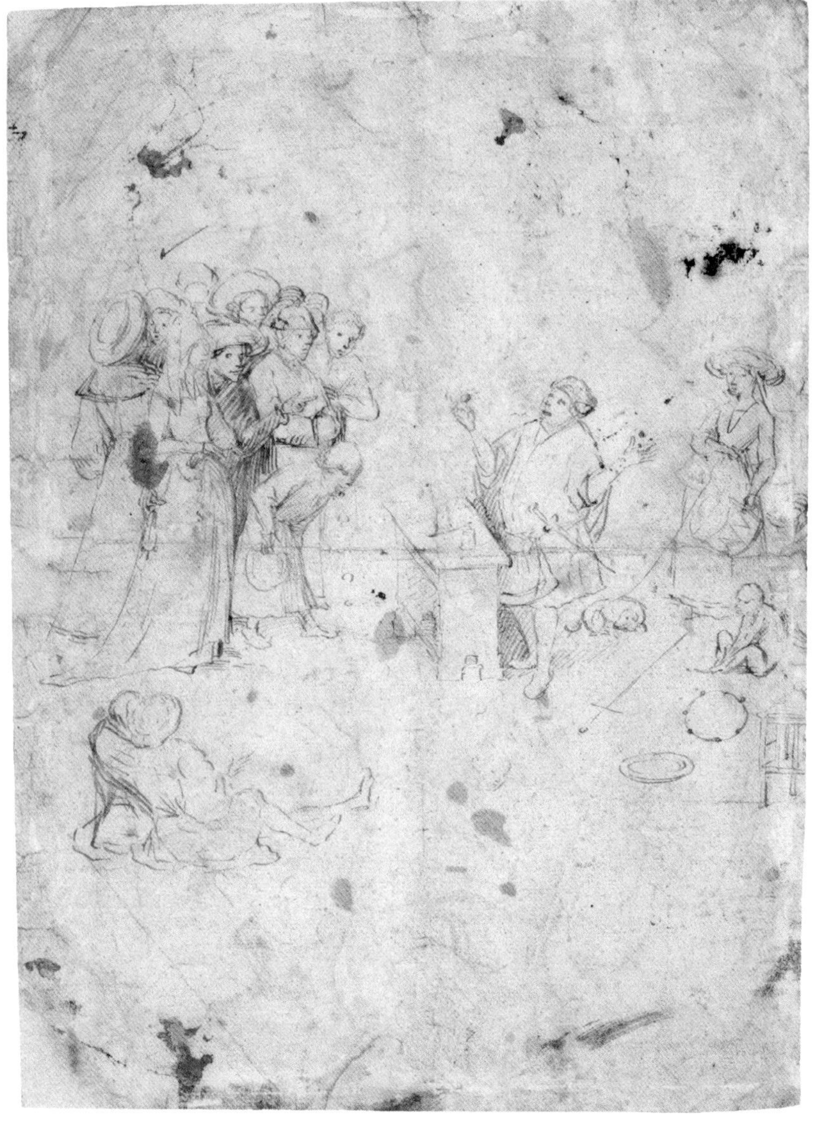

D10 (r) Member of the workshop or follower, **The Conjuror**, *c.* 1505–1515
Pen and brown ink, 278 x 206 mm / approx. 10⅞ x 8⅛ in.
Paris, Musée du Louvre, inv. no. 19197

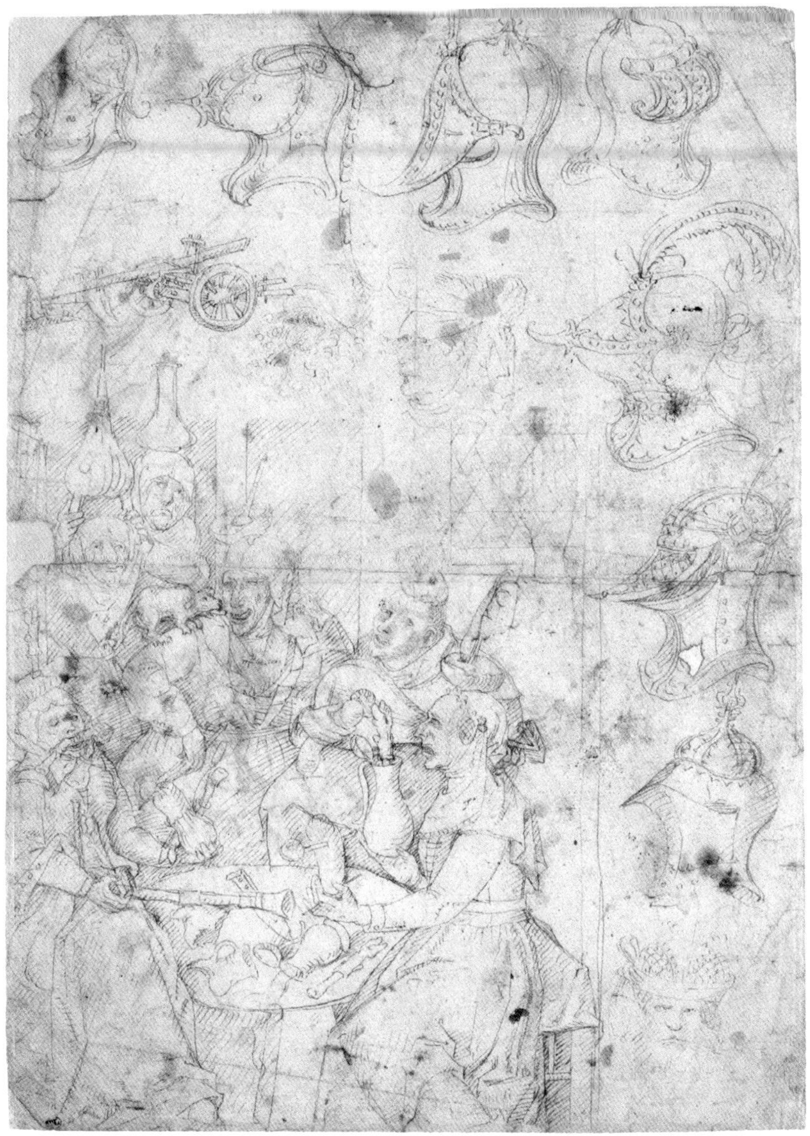

D10 (v) Follower of Hieronymus Bosch (variant after Bosch?), **Company at Table**, *c.* 1520–1545
Pen and brown ink, 278 x 206 mm / approx. 10⅞ x 8⅛ in.
Paris, Musée du Louvre, inv. no. 19197

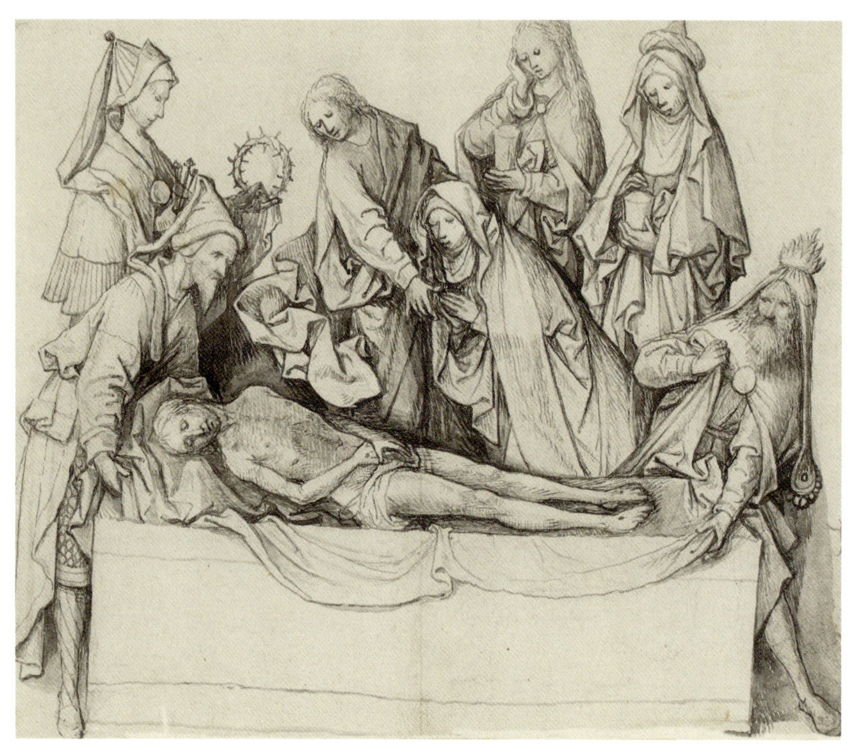

D11 Member of the workshop or follower of Hieronymus Bosch
The Entombment, *c.* 1500–1515
Brush drawing in black and grey ink, with grey wash, over black chalk, on paper, 252 x 304 mm / approx. 10 x 12 in. London, The British Museum, Department of Prints & Drawings, inv. no. 1952-4-5-9

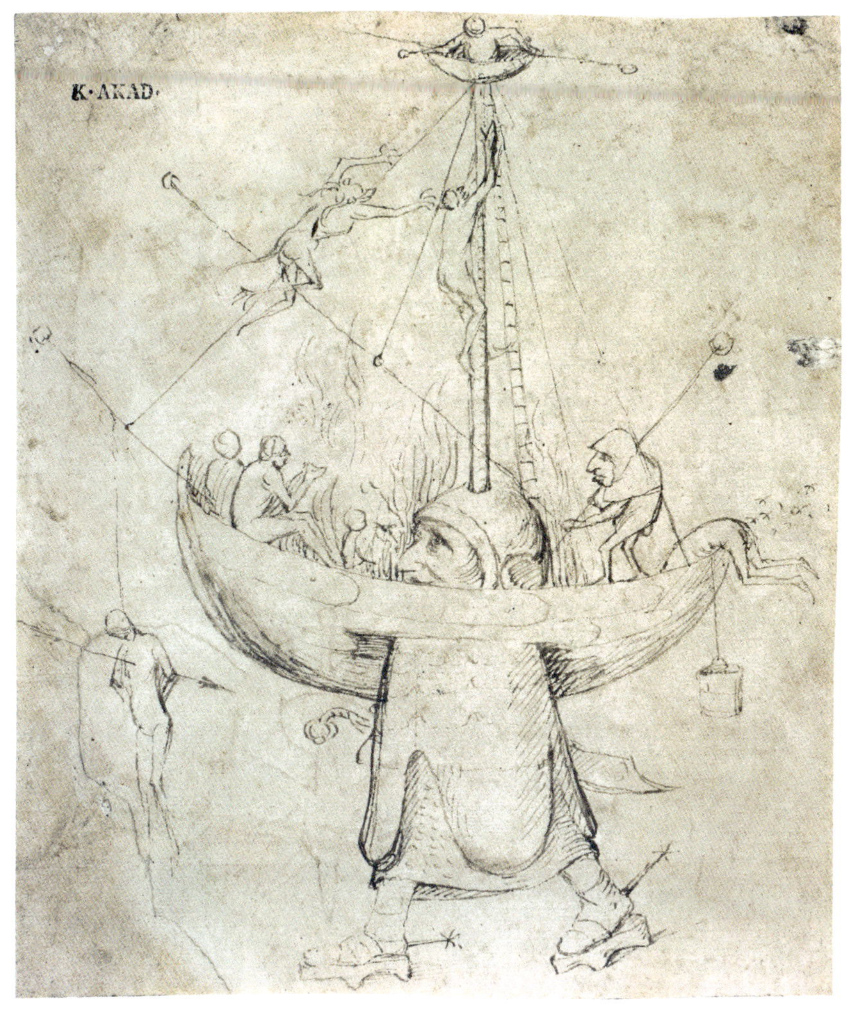

D12 Workshop of Hieronymus Bosch ('Pupil of Hieronymus Bosch'?)
Ship of Hell, *c.* 1505–1510
Pen and greyish-brown ink on paper, watermark, 175 x 154 mm / approx. 6⅞ x 6 in.
Vienna, Akademie der bildenden Künste, inv. no. 2554

D13 Member of the workshop of Hieronymus Bosch ('Pupil of Hieronymus Bosch'?)
Hell scene for a Last Judgement, *c.* 1515?
Pen and brown ink, 259 x 197 mm / 10¼ x 7¾ in.
Whereabouts unknown (last at Sotheby's, New York, 21. 1. 2003, sale no. N07870, lot 20)

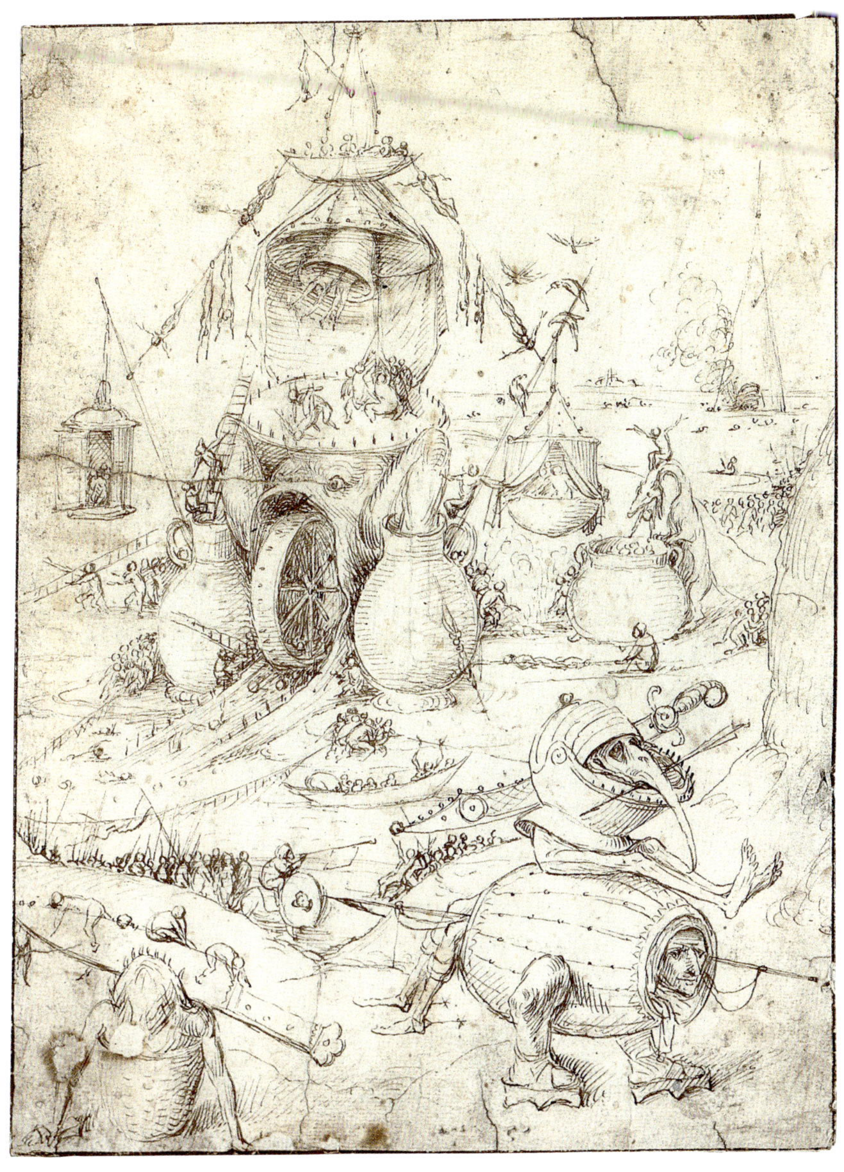

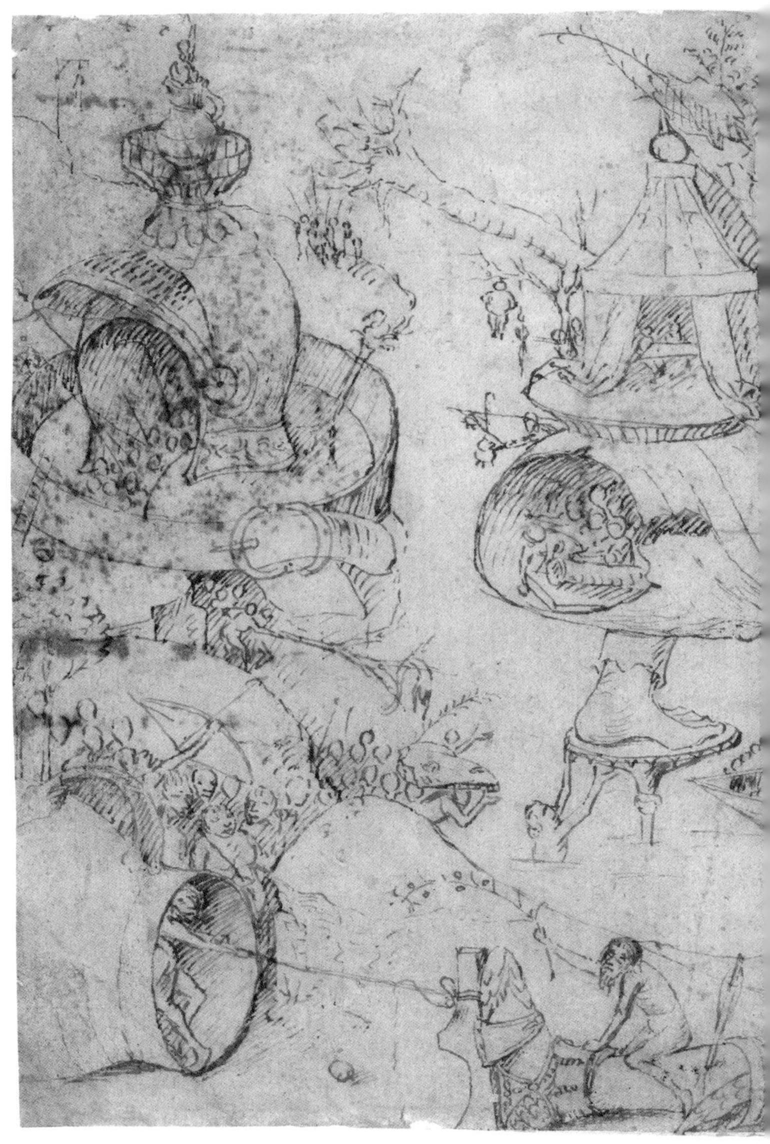

D14 (r) Member of the workshop or follower of Hieronymus Bosch
('Pupil of Hieronymus Bosch'?) **Hell scenes, Tree-Man Monster**, *c.* 1505–1515
Pen and brown ink, watermark, 199 x 277 mm / 7¾ x 10⅞ in. Dresden, Kupferstichkabinett, inv. no. C 1875

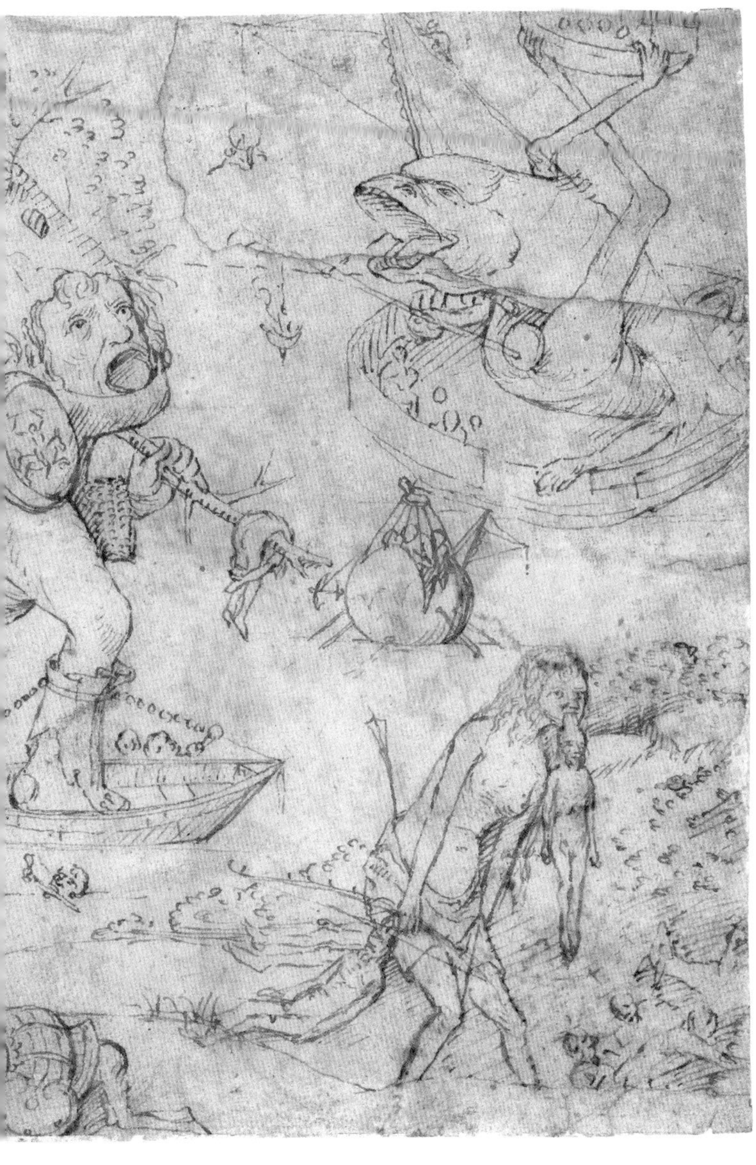

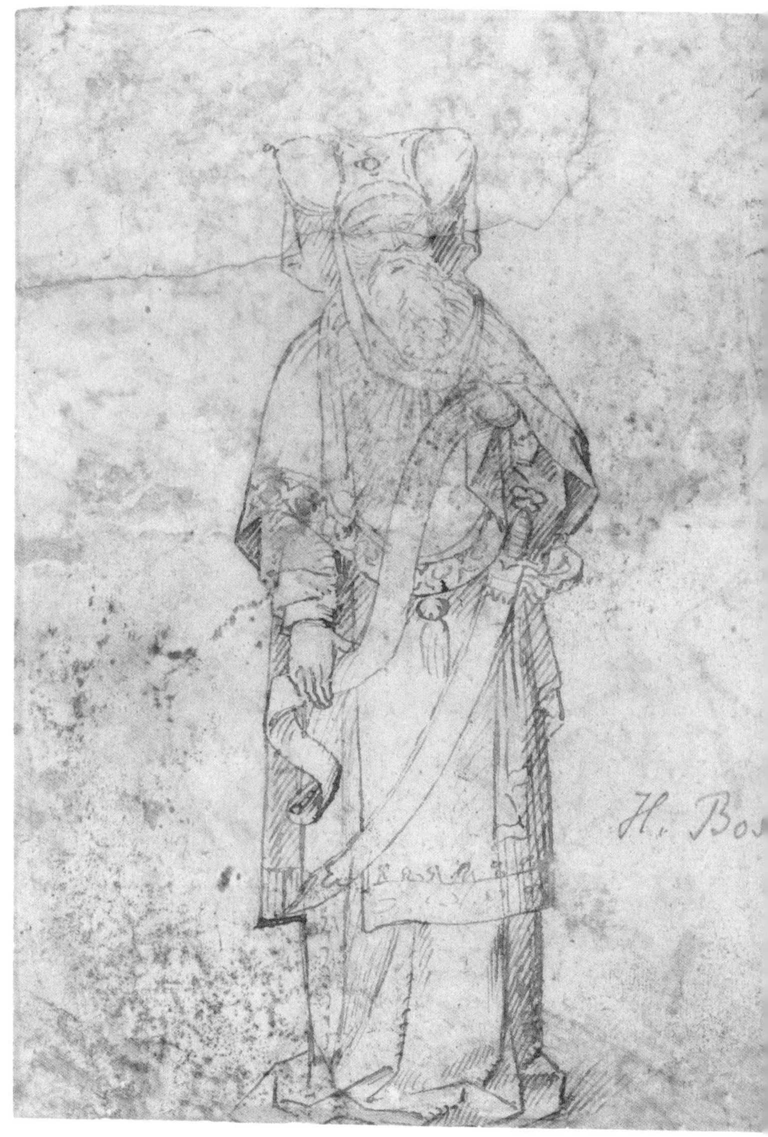

D14 (v) Member of the workshop or follower of Hieronymus Bosch
('Pupil of Hieronymus Bosch'?) **Standing Rabbi**, *c.* 1505–1515
Pen and brown ink, watermark, 199 x 277 mm / 7¾ x 10⅞ in. Dresden, Kupferstichkabinett, inv. no. C 1875

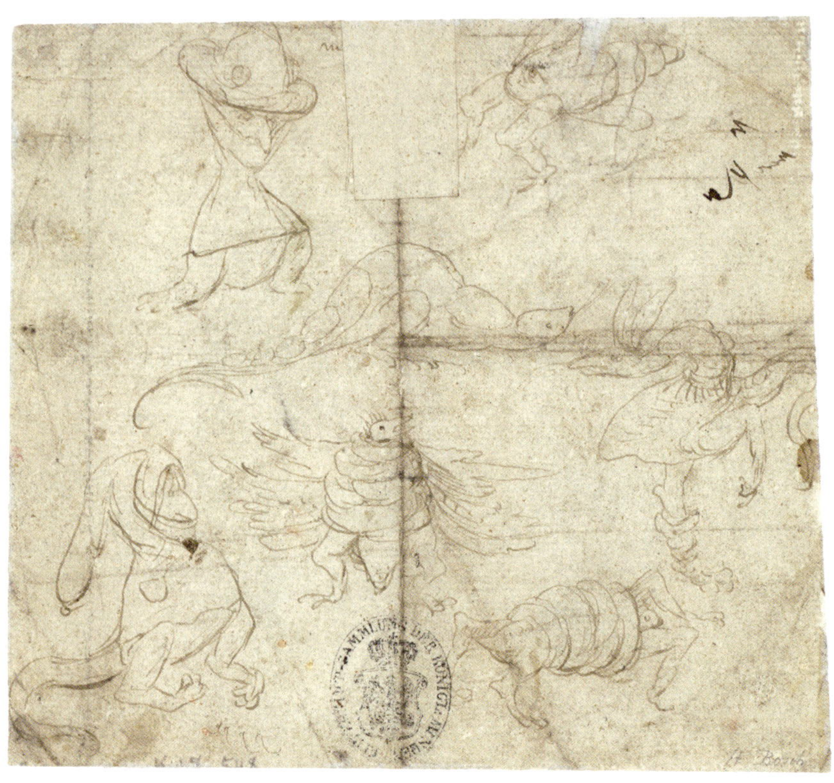

D15 (r) Member of the workshop or follower of Hieronymus Bosch ('Pupil of Hieronymus Bosch'?), **Five Fantasy Creatures; figural scene**, *c.* 1510–1515
Pen and brown ink on paper, 154/157 x 171/177 mm / approx. 6–6¼ x 6¾-7 in.
Berlin, Staatliche Museen zu Berlin, Kupferstichkabinett, KdZ 548

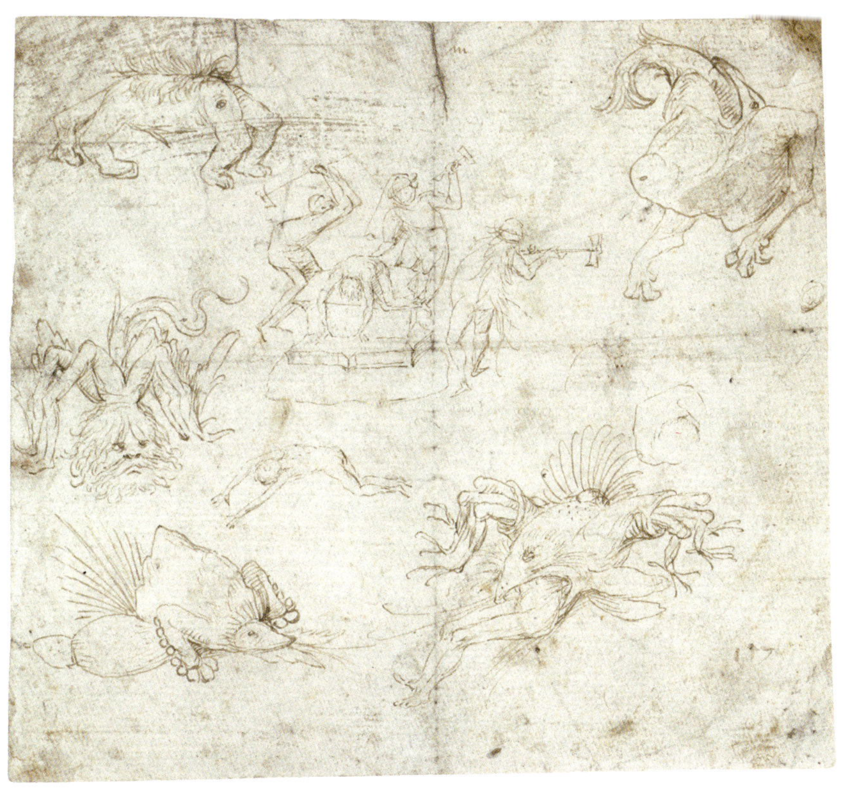

D15 (v) Member of the workshop or follower of Hieronymus Bosch ('Pupil of Hieronymus Bosch'?), **Seven Fantasy Creatures**, *c.* 1510–1515
Pen and brown ink on paper, 154/157 x 171/177 mm / approx. 6–6¼ x 6¾-7 in.
Berlin, Staatliche Museen zu Berlin, Kupferstichkabinett, KdZ 548

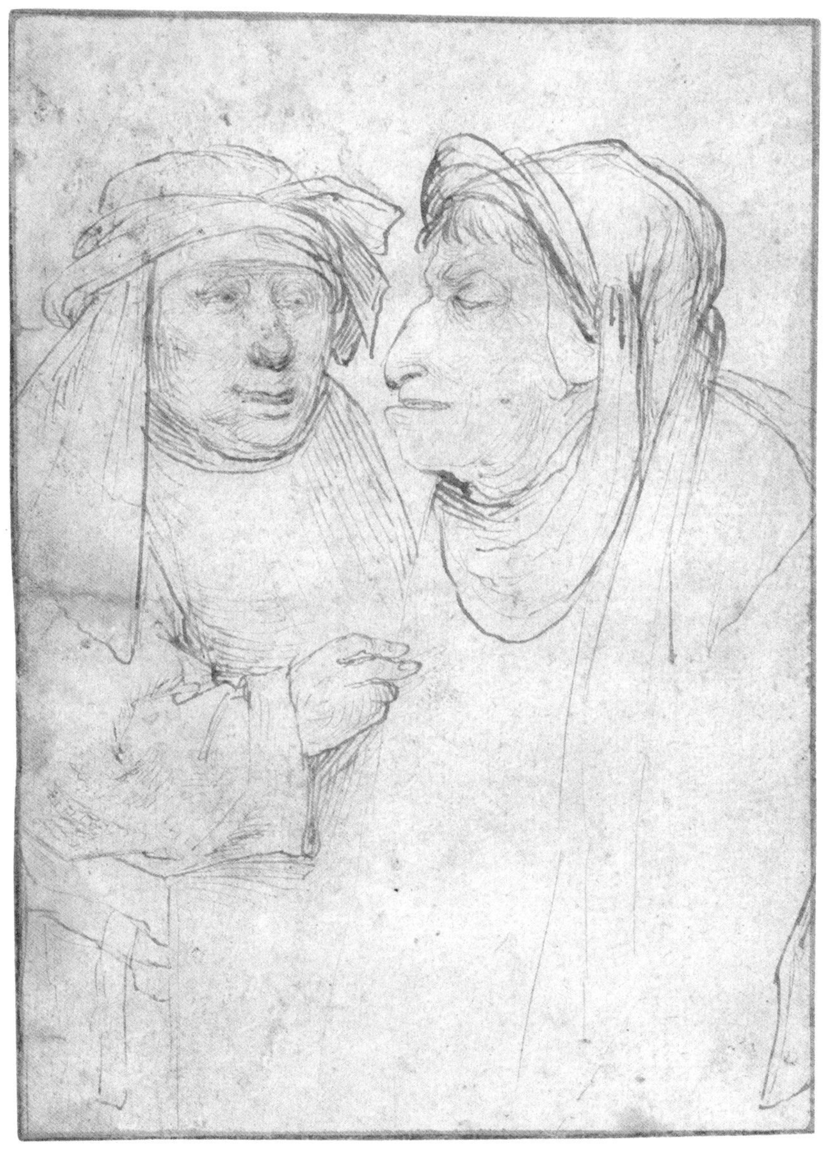

D16 (r) Workshop or follower of Hieronymus Bosch
Study for two figures for a Passion scene, *c.* 1510–1515
Pen and brown ink on paper, 137 x 103 mm / approx. 5⅜ x 4 in. Private collection

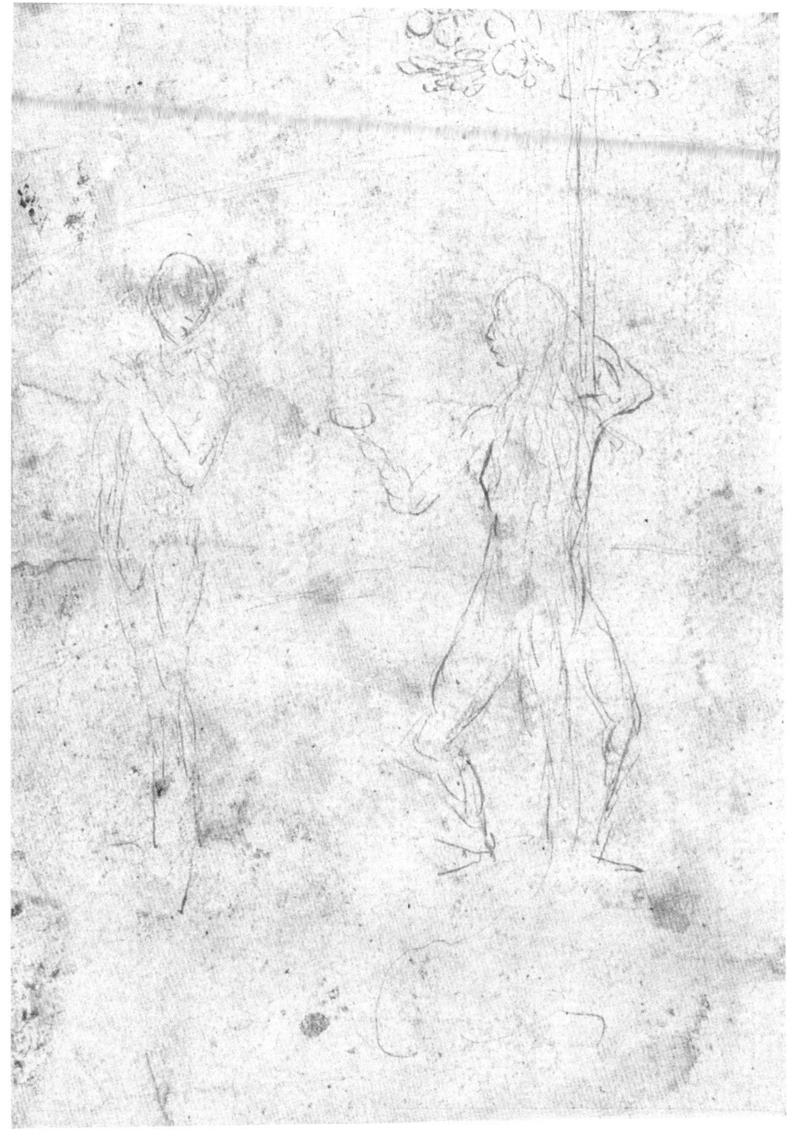

D16 (v) Workshop or follower of Hieronymus Bosch
The Temptation of Eve, *c.* 1510–1515
Pen and brown ink on paper, 137 x 103 mm / approx. 5⅜ x 4 in. Private collection

Documentary sources on Bosch's life and work

Prologue: Perspectives on Bosch

Albrecht Dürer on combining different elements within a picture:

"Doch höt sich ein jtlicher, das er nichtz vnmuglichs mach, das dy natur nitt leid, es wer dan sach, das einer trawm werg wolt machn. In solchem mag einer alle ding durch ein ander mischen."(Dürer, Albrecht, *Vier Bücher von menschlicher Proportion*, 1528, in: idem, Schriftlicher Nachlass, ed. by Hans Rupprich, 3 vols., Berlin 1956–1969, vol. 3, p. 283)

I. Family origins and first works, 1474–1487

Dominicus Lampsonius in his introduction to the set of 23 portrait engravings of famous Netherlandish painters, published posthumously by Hieronymus Cock:

"Quid sibi vult, Hieronyme Boschi, / Ille oculus tuus attonitus? quid / Pallor in ore? Velut lemures si, / Spectra Erebi volitantia coràm / Aspiceres? Tibi Ditis auari / Crediderim patuisse receſsus, / Tartareasque domos: tua quando / Quicquid habet sinus imus Auerni / Tam potuit bene pingere dextra ..."

(Lampsonius, Dominicus, Pictorium aliquot celebrium Germaniae inferioris effigies, Antwerp: Hieronymus Cock/Volcxken Diercx 1572, no. 3)

Further documents not listed below pertaining to Hieronymus Bosch's legal affairs (up to 1494) can be found in Gorissen 1973, pp. 1131–1138; pertaining to the van Aken family, *ibid.* p. 1129–1165 and *inter alia* van Dijck 2001a. Currently the largest collection of extracts from official documents relating to Bosch up to the 17th century can be found at http:// nl.wikisource.org/wiki/Thema:Jheronimus_Bosch and at the Brabants Historisch Informatie Centrum (BHIC) with digital copies.

Talks between the Brotherhood and the sculptor Adriaen van Wesel, at which Antonius van Aken and his sons were present, in the accounting year 1475/76:

"Item die proesten mit sommigen van der bruederscappen / thonyſs den maelder ende syn zoenen mit meister / ariaen van wesel den tafelmaker vergadert tot Jan / maeſs int wynhuyſs, om te spreken ende te ordineren / die patronen ende manieren hoemen die taeffel soude / verdingen ende aldair ter selver tijt verteert, xxv st[uver] xxii pl[acken]" (Brabants Historisch Informatie Centrum [BHIC]/Illustre Lieve Vrouwe Broederschap [ILVB]/Register 1469–1478/fol. 208r/ll. 9–14; Marijnissen 1987, p. 11; Gerlach 1988, p. 43; van Dijck 2001a, p. 167)

In the accounting year 1480/81 Hieronymus Bosch pays money to the Brotherhood of Our Blessed Lady for the wings of the latter's old altarpiece (dating from *c.* 1460):

"Item van Jeroen die maelre, voer die doeren van / onser liever vrouwen alde taeffel, die de voirs [creven] / proesten den selven vercoft hebben voer v Rijns gul[den] viij st[uver]" (BHIC/ILVB/Register 1478–1485/fol. 113v/ll. 13–15; Marijnissen 1987, p. 11; Gerlach 1988, p. 44; van Dijck 2001a, p. 170)

On 7. July 1484 Bosch's wife Aleid inherits the estate of Ten Roedeken in the parish of Oirschot from her deceased brother Goyaert:

"Ontfanghen van juffrouw Aliten van Mervenne die met Jeronimus van Aken hueren man ontfinc by doode wylen Godewaerts van Meervenne huers broeders 't goet Ten Roedeken in de prochie van Oirschot gelegen, behoudelijk Jeronimus zyn tocht indien hy syn gesellinne overleefde zyn leven lang"(Brussels, Algemeen Rijksarchief, rekenkamer, inv. no. 17 149; Marijnissen 1987, p. 11; van Dijck 2001a, p. 173)

In the accounting year 1486/87, a list of persons who paid their Brotherhood joining fee includes Hieronymus Bosch:

[...] / Wilhelma aerts doegter vanden ven / [...] /

[...] / Aleyt aerts doegter van uden / [...] / Jheronimus anthonissoen van aken / [...] / [...] / [...] // x Liv[res]
(BHIC/ILVB/Register 1485–1495/fol. 42v/ll. 26–35; Marijnissen 1987, p. 12; Gerlach 1988, p. 44; van Dijck 2001a, p. 175)

In 1487 Bosch is commissioned to produce a new wall hanging, probably a painting on cloth, and to create a decorative mounting for a set of antlers for the *Tafel van de Heilige Geest* alms-house, for just under two Rhenish guilders:
"Jonen den maelder van enen nyeuwen clede ende van enen hertshoren te stofferen, gegeven I Rijnsgulden XV stuver"
After 2 September 1487:
"Item inden ersten Jonen den maelder van enen nyewen clede hangende inder zalen met enen hertshoren aen hem te samen verdingt te stoffeeren voir I Rijnsgulden 15 stuvers datum des zaterdages post festum Johannes Baptist anno 87" (Archief van de Tafel van de H. Geest [THG], 's-Hertogenbosch, inv. no. 412 and THG, inv. no. 636; van Dijck 2001a, p. 174)

II. Social and artistic ascent, 1488–1501

Bosch is mentioned in 1488 in connection with a Brotherhood meal marking the admission to the sworn membership and the rise in status of various brothers:
"Ter selve tyt boven x scilling payment ende vij½ stuver die comen syn / van x smael hoender, die Coel Screynmeker totte selve maeltyt / beset heeft, ende bovendien heer Jan van Boexstel gesworen / bruer worden is, Goert Grotert scepen worden is, mester Vranc / van Gunterslaer priester, Jan van Achel bruer, mester / Jan van Vladeracken syn huuysvrou genomen is, mester Zijmon / scoelmester, [in the margin:] *Jeroen maeld[er] elken van hem gegeven x scilling autß verteert, ende / de mechde inde coken 3 st[uver] te verdrincken, ende den selven ende ons dyenaren iij quarten wyns tot ix st[uver], daertoe gedroncken waren xlviii quarten elc iii st [...] ij Rijnsgulden vij st[uver]"*
(BHIC/ILVB/Register 1485–1495/fol. 95r/ll. 21–31; Gerlach 1988, pp. 44–45; van Dijck 2001a, p. 174)

On 29 December 1487 three people promise to pay money to Hieronymus Bosch upon delivery of five *mud* (approx. 100 litres) of rye.
(Marijnissen 1987, p. 12; van Dijck 2001a, S. 174)

Accounting entry relating to the meal given by Hieronymus Bosch in autumn 1488:
"Item ter ierster vergaderingen tot Jeronimus die scilder / voer xxiiij pont runtvlees tpont enen ph[ilip]s penn[inc]; / item voer iiij loet gengbers, ij loet pepers, ½ loet sofferaens / v st[uver]; item voer wortelen ij st[uver]; item den weert een mengelen / wyns 1½ s[tuver]; item des weerts gesynne in de koecken iij st[uver]; / item onsen basternieren, coster ende dienaers iij quarten wyns / ix st[uver], ende heren Ghysbrecht van Rode onsen provisoir tot / Colen ende Lucas secretaris ons genedigen heren Roems conincs / voer elcken een mengelen wyns iij st[uver] maken tsamen xliij½ st[uver] "
(BHIC/ILVB/Register 1485–1495/fol. 126v/ll. 18–26; Marijnissen 1987, p. 12; Gerlach 1988, p. 45)

In the preface to his epistle *Ad Pisonem*, better known as *Ars poetica*, Horace (Quintus Horatius Flaccus) invokes, in the form of ekphrasis, an off-putting and ridiculous sounding image as the opposite of the coherent, harmonious concept of poetry:
"Humano capiti cervicem pictor equinam iungere si velit et varias inducere plumas undique collatis membris, ut turpiter atrum desinat in piscem mulier formosa superne, spectatum admissi risum teneatis, amici? credite, Pisones, isti tabulae fore librum persimilem, cuius, velut aegri somnia, vanae fingentur species, ut nec pes nec caput uni reddatur formae." (Quintus Horatius Flaccus, *Epistula ad Pisonem: De Arte Poetica [Ars Poetica]*, Lat. and Ger., ed., trans. and with an afterword by Eckart Schäfer, Stuttgart 1994, ll. 1–9)

Accounting entry of 1491/92 relating to the production, by Hieronymus Bosch, of a new, second panel listing the names of the past and present members of the Brotherhood of Our Blessed Lady. Although Bosch wanted to make a gift of this panel to the Brotherhood, he was paid the (symbolic) sum of 18 stuivers:
"Item want die taefel ons gezwoeren bruederen levende ende do- / de al vol was, dat men dair niemant meer in scriven en / mocht, om die te vermaken ende te verscriven, boven dat Joen der / op gemaeckt heeft, dair hy niet af en nam en der voirs[creven] / scencken woude, gegeven xviij stuvers"
(BHIC/ILVB/Register 1485–1495/fol. 224r/ll. 24–28; Marijnissen 1987, p. 12; Gerlach 1988, p. 45; van Dijck 2001a, p. 175)

In 1493/94 the stained-glass artist Willem Lombart is commissioned to paint a stained-glass window for the Brotherhood's chapel. Bosch is tasked with overseeing the project and is paid 2½ stuivers:
"Willemen Lombart gelaesmeker iij ort stuvers voer een gotspenninck hem gegeven / by den proesten doe zy met hem oeverquamen van eenen nyewen ghelaesse / dat hy maken sal, nae den proeven dat Joen die maelder hem soude maken / dwelck staen soude in ons nyewe capelle daer om hier // iij ort stuvers // Joenen den maelder gescenckt ij½ stuver tot dyen eynde dat hy den selven / Willemen Lombart soude willen te wege helpen, dat tvoirscreven gelaes mucht wael / wesen gemaeckt, daerom hier // ij½ stuver"
(BHIC/ILVB/Register 1485–1495/fol. 294r/ll. 173; Marijnissen 1987, p. 12; Gerlach 1988, p. 45; van Dijck 2001a, pp. 176–177)

Hieronymus Bosch receives 20 stuivers for the window design:
"*Voer een paer aulder slaeplakens daer Joen die maelder op soude maken / een patroen van eenen gelaes, twelck Willem Lombart soude maken in die / Thoerenstraet, // xx stuvers*" (BHIC/ILVB/Register 1485–1495/fol. 295r/ll. 1–3; Marijnissen 1987, p. 12; Gerlach 1988, p. 45; van Dijck 2001a, p. 177)

On 6. 3. 1494 several people promise to pay 51 guilders to Hieronymus Bosch on All Saints' Day, probably for a delivery of wood.
(Marijnissen 1987, p. 13; van Dijck 2001a, p. 177)

In the accounting year 1498/99, total costs of 10 ½ stuivers are recorded for a swan meal for the Brotherhood, hosted by Hieronymus Bosch at the house of Wouter van der Rullen:
"Item te vter vergaderinge, doemen den swaen / att, tot Wouter van der Rullen daer Jhero / nimus van Aken scilder dat laken lede, behalven / den swaen gecomen ende gescenct vanden / rentmeester van wegen ons genedigen heren daer / toe noch gecocht tegen Rutger van Erpe enen / anderen swaen voir acht stuvers [...] / [...] / [...] tsamen // x½ st"
(BHIC/ILVB/Register 1495–1501/fol. 298v/ll. 15–23; Marijnissen 1987, p. 12; Gerlach 1988, p. 47; van Dijck 2001a, p. 178)

Extracts from the Regulations of the 's-Hertogenbosch Brotherhood of Our Blessed Lady, 1518:
"[...] gildebroeders ende susteren alle dijnxdagen met discanteerders Vesper singhet van onse liever vrouwen. Ende alle woensdagen daer nae een loeflicke Misse van Maria ende dat met dienders ende intoneerders met costelijcke dientrocken ende cappen bedert." (*Reglement*, fol. 3r.)
"Item op dat dese ordinantie met meer andere oock die broederlike liefde der ghelederen so vergaderen aldie geswooren broeders in die stadt wonende tot allen ses weken eens ooc op die iiij principael spijndagen ende eten met malcanderen in eerlichheyt, stillicheyt ende blijtschappen. In welcke maeltijde die Benedicite ende Oracie [Oratie] woorden solenlijc gesongen in discant ende des gelijcx tusschen alle gherichten een genoechlich carmen oft loffsanc: ende nader maeltijt leest men Miserere mei Deus ende De profundis voir die dooden. Ende op dat dese maeltijde in gheen overdadighe weerschap verandert solde woorden So ist verboden dat niemant meer mach drinken dan een half kanne wijns inder maeltijt voirscreven" (*Reglement*, fol. 6v)
(*Reglement van de Illustre Lieve Vrouwe Broederschap te 's-Hertogenbosch*, 's-Hertogenbosch: Laurens Hayen 1518, 32 pp., edn. of 2000 "briefkens", copy in the collection of the Ruusbroec-Genootschap, Antwerp)

III. In the labyrinth of images: *The Temptation of St Anthony*, c. 1502

See below, at the start of the documentary sources relating to the Catalogue of Works, the extended text from José de Sigüenza, *Historia de la Orden de San Jerónimo.*

IV. Nuptial art: *The Garden of Earthly Delights*, c. 1503

Description of the *Garden of Earthly Delights* (Cat. 11) recorded by Antonio de Beatis in his travel journal, July 1517:
"Tiene un spatioso cortile, di stantie è copiosissimo et di bella / facciata; per tucto è intavolato; dentro vi a tanto camere come sale che son gran- / dissime etiam in fine alle volte, et de tavole de rovere che son vaghissime un- / date in modo di ciambellocto, come si dirà appresso. In quello sono bellissime picture, et tra le altre uno Hercule con Dehyanira nudi di bona statura, et la historia di Paris con le tre dee perfectissimamente lavorate. Ce son poi alcune tavole de diverse bizzerie, dove se contrafanno mari, aeri, boschi, campagne et molte altre cose, tali che escono da una cozza marina,

altri que cacano grue, donne et homini et bianchi et negri de diversi acti et modi, ucelli, animali, de ogni sorte et con molta naturalità, cose tanto piacevole et fantastiche che ad quelli, che non ne hanno cognitione in nullo modo se li potriano ben descrivere. / Vi sono alcune camere, dove ce notaimo un secreto et artificio molto ingenioso, / zo è un reposto in un cantone bene ornato et lavorato del medesmo legnamo che / è decto di sopra, che servea anche per serrare una porta che intrava in l'altra / camera, de modo che chi non ne fusse stato advertito, non se haria mai pensato / vi fusse stata porta alcuna. Vi è anche una gran camera dove è un lecto di / larghezza di palmi XXXIII di canna et di longhezza XXVI ad ordine, con soi / capezzalo di capo et di piedi, con linzoli et una cultra biancha, quale intesimo / chel predicto signore fe fare ad effecto che delectandose di stare spesso in ban-/checti, et havere piacere di vedere inbriachi li convitati, come erano tanto pieni / che non possevano stare più in piedi, li facea buctare sopra il dicto lecto."
(Beatis, Antonio de, *Die Reise des Kardinals Luigi d'Aragona durch Deutschland, die Niederlande, Frankreich und Oberitalien, 1517–1518*, ed. by. Ludwig Pastor (Erläuterungen und Ergänzungen zu Janssens Geschichte des deutschen Volkes; vol. 4, no. 4), Freiburg im Breisgau 1905, p. 116, l. 27 – p. 117, l. 5)

Albrecht Dürer describes his visit to Brussels and the Nassau palace, where the *Garden of Earthly Delights* (Cat. 11) also hung:
"Jtem madonna Margaretha, die hat zu Prüssel nach mir geschickt und mir zugesagt, sie woll meine fürderin sein gegen könig Carl, und hat sich sonderlich gancz tugentlich gegen mir erzeugt. Hab jhr mein gestochnen Passion geschenckt, deßgleichen ein solchen jrm pfenning maister mit namen Jan Marnix, und hab jn auch mit dem kohln conterfet. Jch hab zwey stüber für ein büffelringlein geben. Mehr 2 stüber geben, von Sanct Lucas tafel auf zu sperren. Jtem als jch bin gewest in des von Nasau hauß, do hab ich gesehen das gut gemähl in der capellen, das meister Hugo gemacht hat. Und hab gesehen die zween hübschen grosen sall und alle köstlichkeit jn dem hauß allenthalben, auch das groß beth, do 50 menschen mügen jnnen liegen. Und ich hab auch den grossen stain gesehen, den das wetter neben dem herrn von Nassau jn dem feld hat nieder geschlagen. Diß hauß leit hoch, darauß ist das schönst aussehen, darob sich zu verwundern ist. Und ich glaub nit, das in allen teutschen landen des gleichen sey."
(Dürer, Albrecht, *Schriftlicher Nachlass*, ed. by Hans Rupprich, 3 vols., Berlin 1956–1969, vol. 1, p. 155)

The pre-Delugian iconography found in the central and right inner panel is also described in Dirc van Delf's widely read treatise, *Tafel van den Kersten Ghelove* (Table of Christian Faith), ll. 20–301
"Die eerste ouderdoem is van Adam an tot Noes tiden ende / ‹stont› nader hebreeusschen croniken: dusent seshondert / ende ses ende vijftich iaren lanck. In welcken tijt der werelt / regnierde die dootsonde Luxuria, die hiet oncuuscheit. Want / die kinder Abels saghen die dochteren Cayns, dat sij suverlic / waren, so naem sise te wive [Gen. 6:2] *ende wonnen dair-an roessen, / datmen hiet gyganten. In dier tijt deedmen so groot overspil / ende lelike dinghen van oncuuscheit, die ic mi scaem gueden, / edelen herten te scriven. Die sonde wert so ghemeen, dat God* [Gen. 6:13] */ seide: si was inden hemel gheraect ende dair om dede God / op Catharactas celi, dat sijn die hemelsche veynsters [...]"*
(Dirc van Delf, *Tafel van den Kersten Ghelove*, naar de handschriften uitgegeven, ingeleid en van aanteekeningen voorzien, ed by L. M. Daniels [Tekstuitgaven van Ons Geestelijk Erf], Antwerp/Nimwegen/Utrecht 1937–1939, vol. II, Ch. XVI)

In 1503/04 Bosch's assistants are given 6 stuivers for three escutcheons bearing the arms of Jan Back, Hendrick Masscherels and Lucas van Erpe for the choir of the Brotherhood's chapel:
"Item gegeven Jheronimus knechten schilder / vanden drie schilden te makenen te wetenen / heren Jannen van Baex, ridder, Henrick Masscherels / ende Lucas van Erpe, hangende aen die / metalen pylernen, tsamen vj stuvers"
(BHIC/ILVB/Register 1501–1507/fol.190v/ll. 11–15; Marijnissen 1987, p. 13; Gerlach 1988, p. 55; van Dijck 2001a, p. 180)

V. Art for the king:
***The Last Judgement*, c. 1506**
Record of the deposit of 36 *livres* for a *Last Judgement* (Cat. 13) for Philip the Handsome, paid to Hieronymus Bosch by counsellor and senior treasurer Simon Longin in September 1504:
"Septembre l'an xvc quatre A Jeronimus van Aeken dit Bosch paintre de[meurant] au Bois le Duc la somme de trente six livres dudict pris en prest et paiement à bon compte sur ce qu'il lui povoit et pourroit estre deu sur ung grant tableau de paincture de neuf pietz de hault

et onze pietz de long, où doit estre le Jugement de Dieu assavoir paradis et infer que icellui S[eigneur] lui avoit ordonné faire pour son tres noble plaisir. Pour ce icy par sa quictancy rend[ue] ladicte somme de xxxvj l[ivres]." (In the margin:) *"Soit ce prest rabatu a la parpaye."* (Archives départementales du Nord, Lille, Register B. 2185, fol. 230v; van Dijck 2001a, p. 91; cf. Steppe 1967, p. 35, note 4; Onghena 1959, p. 27 f.; Plafond 1914, p. 7)

Marcantonio Michiel (1484–1552) on *Paradise and Hell* (Cat. 16):
"La tela del inferno cun la gran diversità de monstri fo de mano de Hieronimo Bosch. / La tela delle sogni fo de man de l'istesso. / [...]"
(Michiel, Marcantonio, *Der Anonimo Morelliano [Marcanton Michiel's Notizia d'opere del disegno]*, transl. by Theodor von Frimmel, 2 vols., Vienna 1888/89 [reprint Hildesheim 1974]; van Dijck 2001a, p. 93; Aikema 2001a, p. 25)

In 1517 *Extracting the Stone of Folly* (Cat. 18) is described in the inventory of Philip of Burgundy's palace at Wijk bij Duurstede as *"een taeffereel van Lubbertas die men die keye snijt"* and in 1524 as "*een tafreel van Lubbert Tas die men die keye uyt snyt*". (Koldeweij 1991, p. 7; van Dijck 2001a, p. 94)

Accounting entry of 1508/09 relating to a meeting in the house of Wouter van der Rullen, where a group of sworn members consulted Hieronymus Bosch and the architect Jan Heyns regarding the question of how and where to carry out the still outstanding task of painting and gilding van Wesel's altarpiece for the Brotherhood:
"In den yersten tot Wouters van der Rullen by een deel / gezworen bruders omme Jheronimum ende meester / Jan Heyns te willigen ende raet te nemen // omme onser liever Vrouwen tafel te stofferen / ende aff te nemen ende waer men die best stofferen / ßal iij wijn vertert // xiiij st" (BHIC/ILVB/Register 1507–1513/ fol. 121v–122r; Marijnissen 1987, p. 13; Gerlach 1988, p. 48; van Dijck 2001a, p. 182)

VI. *Exemplum docet*: Late works, 1504–1516

On Sunday 10. 3. 1510, after Mass, the sworn members proceeded to the house of Hieronymus Bosch for a communal meal:
"Den audsten proest nu zynde te weten Henryken van Uden j st[uver] want / hy besorgt heeft, dat die voirs[creven] misse op den voirs[creven] dach ende aultaer / gedaen is geweest, dat die gezworen bruderen twee ende twee, paer / ende paer gegaen zyn vuyt der kercke inden huise ons medebruders / Jheronimi van aken scilder ofte maelder, die hem selver scrift Jheronimus / bosch, Ende oeck doen imponeren silentium oever maltyt voir ende eer men wyn gescenkt heeft ende gedroncken, gedacht der zyele wylner Heeren Jannen Backx ridder, doen hy leefden heere tot Asten, met eenen miserere mei deus [...] / j st"
(BHIC/ILVB/Register 1507–1513/fol. 186r–186v; Marijnissen 1987, p. 13; Gerlach 1988, p. 48; van Dijck 2001a, p. 182)

Details of the meal that was served on 10. 3. 1510 (including the lavish dishes and the costs):
"Tder sevender vergaderinge ende maeltyde die gehouden is geweest / op de voirs[creven] sondach Letare Jherusalem nu lestleden, in den huise Jheronimi / van aken, scilder, die hem scrift Bosch. welke sondach quam op / den xden dach van mert nu lest leden, die deze yerste maeltyt heeft gehadt. Ende is geweest die yerste maeltyt die in die vasten / op den sondach Letare Jherusalem, die gezworen bruderen gehouden ende / gefesteerd hebben. [...] tsaemen vi g[u]l[den] Xiii ½ st[uiver]"
(BHIC/ILVB/Register 1507–1513/fol. 186v–187r; Marijnissen 1987, p. 13; Gerlach 1988, pp. 48–49; van Dijck 2001a, p. 182)

Payment of 20 stuivers made to Bosch in the accounting year 1511/12 for the design of a chasuble (a liturgical vestment):
"Jeronimo die maelder want hy tpatroen vanden / cruce heeft gemaect xx st[uver]"
(BHIC/ILVB/Register 1507–1513/fol. 295v/ll. 16–17; Marijnissen 1987, p. 14; Gerlach 1988, p. 49; van Dijck 2001a, p. 183)

In the accounting year 1512/13 Bosch is offered almost five guilders for a design for a candelabrum:
"Van Willemen van Achel op condicien datmen / Jeronimo den maelder betalen soude het patroen / vanden croenen twelcke hy gemaect heeft, alsoe- / verre hy dat begerende is // iiij gulden xix stuver i½ oert" (BHIC/ILVB/Register 1507–1513/fol. 325r/ ll. 13–16; Marijnissen 1987, p. 13; Gerlach 1988, p. 49; van Dijck 2001a, p. 183)

Accounting entry relating to the first requiem mass for Hieronymus Bosch on 9.8.1516:
"Ter ierster exequie van Jeronimus van aken maelder / ixa augusti, heren Willem hameker deken i/6 st[uver] / want hy die misse gesongen heeft ende voer zyn / presentie ½ st[uver] diaken ende subdiaken elcken i st[uver] / allen anderen priesteren sengheren costeren bastonieren / graftmekeren, beyerman orgenbleeser elcken / ½ st[uver], den choralen elcken i oert ende den / armen voer tchoer elcken lid tot iij st[uver] toe / v[idelicet] xxvij st[uver] die de vrienden bet[aelt] hebben daer / om hier niet"
(BHIC/ILVB/Register 1513–1519/fol. 166v/ll. 15–24; Marijnissen 1987, p. 14; Gerlach 1988, p. 49)

Catalogue of works
Documents available in digital form are listed at http://nl.wikisource.org/wiki/Thema:Jheronimus_Bosch
Alongside general statements on Bosch's art, the following works are described and interpreted by José de Sigüenza in his history of the Order of St Jerome, *Historia de la Orden de San Jerónimo*, 1605 (pp. 837–841): *The Garden of Earthly Delights* (Cat. 11), *The Seven Deadly Sins and the Four Last Things* (Cat. 15) and *The Haywain* (Cat. 20). Sigüenza also writes about Bosch's *St Anthony* compositions as a group.

837

"[…] ***[[On Bosch's art]]*** *Entre las pinturas destos Alemanes, y Flamencos, que como digo son muchas, estan repartidas por toda la casa muchas de un Geronimo Bosco, de que quiero hablar un poco mas largo por algunas razones: porque lo merece su grande ingenio, porque comunmente las llaman los disparates de Geronimo Bosque, gente que repara poco en lo que mira, y porque pienso que sin razon le tienen infamado de herege, tengo tanto concepto (por empeçar desto postrero) de la piedad y zelo del Rey nuestro fundador, que si supiera era esto assi, no admitiera sus pinturas dentro de su casa, de sus claustros, de su aposento, de los capitulos y de la sacristia, todos estos lugares estan adornados con ellas: sin esta razon que para mi es grande, ay otra que se toma de sus pinturas, veense en ellas casi todos los Sacramentos y estados y grados de la Iglesia, desde el Papa hasta el mas infimo, dos puntos en que todos los hereges estropieçan, y los pintò en muchas veras y con gran consideracion, que si fuera herege no lo hiziera, y de los mysterios de nuestra redencion hizo lo mismo. Quiero mostrar agora que sus pinturas no son disparates, sino unos libros de gran prudencia y artificio, y si disparates son, son los nuestros, no los suyos, y por dezirlo de una vez, es una satyra pintada, de los pecados y desvarios de los hombres. Pudierase poner por argumento de muchas de sus pinturas, los versos de aquel gran censor de los vicios de los Romanos, que cantò al principio diziendo: Quidquid agunt homines, votum, timor, ira, voluptas: Gaudia, discursus nostri est farrago libelli. Et quando uberior vitiorum copia, &c. que bueltos en Castellano, pudiera dezir assi Bosco. Quanto los hombres hazen, sus desseos, sus miedos, furias, apetitos vanos, sus gozos, sus contentos, sus discursos, de toda mi pintura es el sugeto. / Mas quando huvo de vicios tanta copia. La diferencia que a mi parecer ay de las pinturas deste hombre a las de los otros, es, que los demas procuraron pintar al hombre qual parece por de fuera, este solo se atrevio a pintarlo qual es dentro: procedio para esto con un singular motivo, que declarè con este exemplo: los poetas y los pintores son muy vecinos a juyzio de todos: las facultades tan hermanas, que no distan mas que el pinzel y la pluma, que casi son una cosa, los sugetos, los fines, los colores, las licencias y otras partes son tan unas, que apenas se distinguen, sino con las formalidades de nuestros metafisicos. Entre los poetas Latinos, se halla de uno (y no de otro que merezca nombre) que pareciendole no podia ygualar en lo heroyco con Virgilio, ni en lo comico ò tragico llegar à Terencio, ò Seneca, ni en lo lyrico à Oracio, y aunque mas excelente fuesse, y su espiritu le prometiesse mucho, avian de ser estos los primeros acordò hazer camino nuevo, inventò una poesia ridicula, que llamò Macarronica: junto con ser assi, que tuviesse tanto primor, tanta invencion è ingenio, que fuesse siempre principe y cabeça deste estilo, y assi le leyessen todos los buenos ingenios, y no le desechasen los no tales, y como el dixo: Me legat quisquis legit omnia. Y porque su estado y profession no parece admitia bien esta ocupacion (era religioso, no dire su nombre pues el le callò) fingio un vocablo ridículo, y llamose, Merlin Cocayo, que quadra bien con la [super-]*

838

superficie de la obra, como el otro que llamon Ysopo; en sus poemas descubre con singular artificio quanto bueno se puede dessear y coger en los mas preciados poetas, assi en cosas morales como en las de la naturaleza, y si huviera de hazer aqui oficio de Crytico, mostrarà la verdad desto, con el cotejo y contraposicion de muchos lugares. A este poeta tengo por cierto quiso parecerse el pintor Geronimo Bosco, no porque le vio, porque creo pintó primero que estotro tocase, sino que le tocò el mismo pensamiento y motivo: conocio tener gran natural para la pintura, y que por mucho que hiziesse le avian de yr delante Alberto Durero, Micael Angel, Urbino y otros, hizo un camino nuevo, con que los demas fuessen tras el, y el no tras ninguno, y bolviesse los ojos de todos assi: una pintura como de burla y macarronica, poniendo en medio de aquellas burlas muchos primores y estrañezas, assi en la invencion como en la execucion y pintura, descubriendo algunas vezes quanto valia en aquel arte, como tambien lo hazia Cocayo hablando de veras. Las tablas y quadros que aqui ay son tres diferencias. O pinta cosas devotas, como son passos de la vida de Christo y su passion: la adoracion de los Reyes y quando lleva la Cruz a cuestas: en la primera exprime el efecto pio y sincero de los sabios y virtuosos, donde no se vee ninguna monstruosidad ni disparate: en la otra muestra la invidia y rabia de la falsa sabiduria, que no descansa hasta que quita la vida a la inocencia, que es Christo; assi se veen los Fariseos y Escribas con rostros furiosos, fieros, regañados, que en los habitos y acciones se les lee la furia destos afectos. **[[St Anthony pictures]]** Pintò per vezes las tentaciones de san Anton (que es el segundo genero de pintura) por ser un sugeto donde podia descubrir estraños efectos. De una parte se vee a aquel santo principe de los Eremitas, con rostro sereno, devoto, contemplativo, sosegado y llena de paz el alma: de otra las infinitas fantasias y monstruos que el enemigo forma, para trastornar, inquietar, y turbar aquella alma pia y aquel amor firme: para esto finge animales, fieras, chimeras, monstruos, fuegos, muertes, gritos, amenazas, vivoras, leones, dragones y aves espantosas y de tantas suertes, que pone admiracion como pudo formar tantas ideas y todo esto para mostrar que una alma ayudada de la divina gracia, y llevada de su mano a semejante manera de vida, aunque en la fantasia y a los ojos de fuera y dentro represente el enemigo lo que puede mover a risa ò deleyte vano, ò yra y otras dessordenadas passiones, no seran parte para derribarle ni moverle de su proposita. Variò este sugeto y pensamiento tantas vezes y con tan nuevas invenciones, que me pone admiracion como pudo hallar tanto, y me detiene a considerar mi propia miseria y flaqueza, y quan lexos estoy de aquella perfeccion, pues con tan faciles musarañas y poquedades me turbo y descompongo, pierdo la celda, el silencio, el recogimiento y aun la paciencia, y en este santo pudo tan poco todo el ingenio del demonio y del infierno para derribarle en esto: y tan aparejado està el Señor para socorrerme a mi como a el, si me pongo animosamente en la pelea. **[[The Seven Deadly Sins and the Four Last Things, Cat. 15]]** Encuentrase esta pintura en hartas partes en el capitulo ay una tabla, en la celda del Prior otra, en la galeria de la Infanta dos, en mi celda otra harto buena, en que algunas vezes leo y me confundo en el aposento de su Magestad donde tiene un caxon con libros como el de los religiosos, està una tabla y quadro excelente, tiene en medio y como en el centro, en una circunferencia de [luz]

839

Luz y de gloria, puesto a nuestro Redentor en el contorno estan otros siete circulos en que se veen los siete pecados capitales con que le ofenden todas las criaturas que el redimio, sin considerar que los està mirando y que lo vee todo. En otros siete cercos puso luego los siete sacramentos con que enriquezio su Iglesia, y donde como en precio sos vasos puso el remedio de tantas culpas y dolencias en que se dexan caer los hombres, que cierto es consideracion de hombre pio, y buena para que todos nos mirassemos en ella, pues la pinto como espejos donde se ha de componer el Christiano; quien esto pintava no sentia mal de nuestra fè. Alli se vee el Papa, los Obispos y Sacerdotes, unos haziendo ordenes, otros bautizando, otros confesando y administrando otros sacramentos. Sin estos quadros ay otros de grandissimo ingenio, y no de menor provecho, aunque parecen mas macarronicos, que es el tercero genero de sus invenciones. **[[The Haywain, Cat. 20]]** El pensamiento y artificio dellos està fundado en aquel lugar de Esayas (Esai. 41), en que por mandado de Dios dize a vozes: Toda carne es heno, y toda su gloria como flor del campo. Y sobre lo que dize David (Pal. 102): El hombre es como heno, y sus glorias como la flor del campo. El uno de estos dos quadros tiene como por fundamento o sugeto principal, lo primero, que es un carro de heno cargado, y encima assentados los deleytes de la carne, la fama y la ostentacion de su gloria y alteza, figurado en unas mugeres desnudas, tañendo y cantando, y la fama en figura de demonio alli junto, con sus alas y trompeta, que publica su grandeza y sus regalos. **[[The Garden of Earthly Delights, Cat. 11]]** El otro tiene por sugeto y fundamento una florecilla y frutilla de estas que llamamos fresas, que son como unos madroñuelos, que en algunas partes llaman maiotas, cosa que apenas se gusta, *quando es acabada.* ***[[The Haywain, Cat. 20]]*** *Para que se entienda su discurso, pondrelo por el orden que lo tiene dispuesto. Entrambos tableros son un quadro grande, y dos puertas con que se cierran. En la primera de estas puertas pinta la creacion del hombre, y como le pone Dios en el Parayso, y en un lugar ameno lleno de verdura y deleytable, señor de todos los animales de la tierra, y de las aves del cielo, y como le manda para exercicio de su obediencia y de su fè, que no coma de un arbol y despues como le engaña el demonio en figura de serpiente, come y traspassa el precepto de Dios y le destierra de aquel lugar deleytable, y de aquella alta dignidad en que estava criado y puesto. En el quadro que se llama carro de heno, esta esto mas senzillamente pintado, en el del madroño està con mil fantasias y consideraciones, que tienen mucho que advertir, esto està en la primera parte y puerta. En el quadro grande que luego se signa, està pintado en que se ocupa el hombre, desterrado del Parayso y puesto en este mundo y declara que en buscar una gloria de heno y de paja o yerva sin fruto, que oy es, y mañana se echa en el horno, como dixo el mismo Dios; y ansi descubre las vidas, los exercicios y discursos con que estos hijos de pecado y de yra, olvidados de lo que Dios les manda, que es hazer penitencia de sus pecados, y levantar los ojos de la fè a un Salvador que los ha de remediar, convertirse todos a buscar y pretender la gloria de la carne, que es como heno breve, finito, inutil, que tales son los regalos de la sensualidad, los estados, la ambicion y fama. Este carro de heno en que va esta gloria, le tiran siete bestias fieras y monstruos espantables, donde se veen pintados hombres medio leones, otros medio perros, otros medio osos, medio pezes, medio lobos, simbolos todos y figura de la sobervia, de la luxuria, [avari-]*

840

avaricia, ambicion, bestialidad, tirania, sagacidad y brutalidad. Al derredor de este corro van todos los estados de los hombres, desde el Papa y Emperador y otros Principes, hasta los que tienen el estado mas baxo y mas viles oficios de la tierra, porque toda carne es heno, y todo lo endereçan los hijos de la carne, y de todo usan para alcançar esta gloria vana y caduca; y todo es dar traças como subir a la gloria deste carro, unos ponen escaleras, otros garabatos, otros trepan, otros faltan, y buscan quantos medios y instrumentos pueden para llegar alli arriba: unos ya que estavan en lo alto, caen de alli abaxo, otros atropellan las ruedas, otros estan gozando de aquel nombre y ayre vano. De suerte que no ay estado ni exercicio ni oficio, sea baxo, ò sea alto, sea divino, o sea humano, que los hijos de este siglo no lo conuiertan o abusen del, para alcançar y gozar de esta gloria de heno. Bien se que van todos caminando a prisa, y los animales que tiran el carro, forcejan porque va muy cargado, y tiran para acabar presto la jornada, descargar aquel camino, y bolver por otro, con que se sinifica harto bien la brevedad de este miserable siglo, y lo poco que tarda en passar, y quan semejantes son todos los tiempos en la malicia. El fin y paradero de todo esto està pintado en la puerta postrera, donde se vee un infierno espantosissimo, con tormentos estraños, monstruos espantosos, embueltos todos en obscuridad y fuego eterno. Y para dar a entender la muchedumbre de los que alli entran y que ya no caben, finge que se edifican aposentos y quartos nuevos: y las piedras que suben para assentar en el edificio, son las almas de los miserables condenados, convertidos tambien alli en instrumentos de su pena, los mismos medios que pusieron para alcançar aquella gloria. Y porque se entendiesse tambien que nunca en esta vida desampara de todo punto el auxilio y piedad divina, aun a los muy pecadores: y aun quando estan en medio de sus pecados: se vee al Angel Custodio, junto al que està encima del carro de heno, en medio de sus vicios torpes, rogando a Dios por el: y el Señor Iesu Christo los braços abiertos, y con las llagas manifiestas, aguardando a los que se conuierten. Yo confiesso que leo mas cosas en esta tabla, en un breve mirar de ojos, que en otros libros en muchos dias. ***[[The Garden of Earthly Delights, Cat. 11]]*** *La otra tabla de la gloria vana, y breve gusto de la fresa o madroño, y su olorcillo, que apenas se siente, quando ya es pasado: esta cosa mas ingeniosa y de mayor artificio que se puede imaginar. Y digo verdad, que si se tomara de proposito y algun grande ingenio quisiera declararla, hiziera un muy provechoso libro, porque en ella se veen, como vivos y claros, infinitos lugares de Escritura de los que tocan a la malicia del hombre, porque cuantas alegorias o metaforas ay en ella para sinificar esto, en los Profetas y Psalmos, debaxo de animales mansos, bravos, fieros, perezosos, sagazes, crueles, carnizeros, para carga y trabajo, para gusto y recreaciones, y ostentaciones, buscados de los hombres y convertidos en ellos por sus inclinaciones y costumbres, y la mezcla que se haze de unos y de otros, todos estan puestos aqui con admirable propiedad. Lo mismo de las aves, y pezes, y animales reptiles, que de todo esto esta llenas las divinas letras. Aqui tambien – se entiende aquella transmigracion de las almas que fingieron Pitagoras, Platon y otros Poetas* *que hizieron fabulas doctas de estos Metamorfosis y transformaciones, que no pretendian otra cosa sino mostrarnos las malas costumbres, habitos o siniestros avisos, de que se visten las almas de los miserables hombres, que por sobervia son leones, por vengança, tigres, por luxuria, [mulos]*

841

mulos, cavallos, puercos: por tirania, pezes; por vanagloria, pavones: por sagazidad y mañas diabolicas, raposas: por gula, gimios y lobos: por insensibilidad y malicia, asnos: por simplicidad bruta, ovejas: por travessura, cabritos, y otros tales accidentes y formas, que sobreponen y edifican sobre este ser humano: y ansi se hazen estos monstruos y disparates, y todo para un fin tan apocado y tan vil, como es el gusto de una vengança, de una sensualidad, de una honrilla, de una apariencia y estima: y otras tales que no llegan a penas al paladar, ni a mojar la boca, qual es el gusto y saborcillo de una fresa o madroño, y el olor de sus flores, que aun muchos con el olor se sustentan.

Quisiera que todo el mundo estuviera tan lleno de los traslados de esta pintura, como lo està de la verdad y del original, de donde retratò sus disparates Geronimo Bosque: porque dexado a parte el gran primor, el ingenio y las estrañezas y consideraciones que ay en cada cosa (causa admiración, como pudo dar en tantas una sola cabeça) se sacara grande fruto, viendose alli cada uno tan retirado al vivo en lo de dentro, sino es que no advierte lo que està dentro de si y està tan ciego que no conoce las passiones y vicios que le tienen tan desfigurado en bestia, o en tantas bestias. Y viera tambien en la postrera tabla el miserable fin y paradero de sus estudios, exercicios y ocupaciones, y en que se truecan en aquellas moradas infernales. El que toda su felicidad ponia en la musica y cantos vanos y lasciuos, en dانças, en juegos, en caças, en galas, en riquezas, en mandos, en vengança, en estimacion de santidad y hypocresia, vera una contraposicion en el mismo genero, y aquel gustillo breve, convertido en rabia eterna, irremediable, implacable. ***[[On Bosch's art]]*** *No quiero dezir mas de los disparates de Geronimo Bosque; solo se advierta, que casi en todas sus pinturas, digo en los que tienen este ingenio (que como vimos otros ay senzillos y santos), siempre pone fuego y lechuza. Con lo primero nos dà a entender, que importa tener memoria de aquel fuego eterno, que con esto qualquier trabajo se harà facil, como se vee en todas las tablas que pintò de san Anton. Y con lo segundo dize, que sus pinturas son de cuydado y estudio, y con estudio se han de mirar. La lechuza es ave nocturna, dedicada a Minerva y al estudio, simbolo de los Atenienses, donde florecio tanto la Filosofia, que se alcança con la quietud y silencio de la noche, gastando mas aceite que vino."*

(Sigüenza, José de, *Tercera parte de la Historia de la Orden de San Geronimo Doctor de la Iglesia*, Madrid 1605, [2]1909, pp. 837–841; facsimile repro.: Marijnissen/Seidel 1972, pp. 30–34; text edition: Sanchez Cantón, Francisco Javier, *Fuentes literarias para la historia del arte espanol* I, Madrid 1923, p. 425 ff.; excerpts: Madrid 2000, pp. 23–24; van Dijck 2001a, pp. 116–118; German translations [excerpts]: de Tolnay 1965, pp. 401–405; Belting/Kruse 1994, pp. 271–272; English translation: Snyder 1973, pp. 34–41)

1.

Crucifixion with Saints and Donor (Cat. 1) is possibly mentioned in 1664 in 's-Hertogenbosch:

"een schilderije op paneel wesende de kruijssinghe Christi, gedaen door Jeronimus Bos met den houte lijst" (Koldeweij 2001, p. 81)

6.

Adoration of the Magi with Donors (Cat. 6) is listed among the pictures delivered to the Escorial in 1574 at Philip II's behest, in order to furnish his new palace, at that time still under construction:

"Otra tabla con dos puertas: en la de en medio pintado el Nascimiento de Christo nuestro Señor, de mano de Gerónimo Bosqui, que tiene cinco pies de alto y tres de ancho sin las puertas"

(Vandenbroeck 2001, pp. 50–51, with English translation)

8.

Large Christ Carrying the Cross (Cat. 8) appears in the 1574 inventory of the first delivery of pictures ordered by Philip II for the decoration of the Escorial:

"Una tabla en que está pintado Christo nuestro Señor con la cruz a cuestas con Simón Cyreneo vestido de blanco otras figuras, de mano de Gerónimo Bosqui, que tiene seys pies de alto y de ancho quarto y tres quartas"

(Vandenbroeck 2001, p. 50, with English translation)

11.

In 1567/68, under the Duke of Alba, the *Garden of Earthly Delights* (Cat. 11) was confiscated from the

Nassau palace along with other items of value. The inventory of 20.12.1567 mentions:
"ung grand tableau devant la cheminee de Jeronimus Bosch"
(Brussels, Algemeen Rijksarchief, rekenkamer, inv. no. 593, fol. 249r; van Dijck 2001a, p. 101; Vandenbroeck 2001b, p. 88, note 7)

The Garden of Earthly Delights (Cat. 11) is listed in the 1593 inventory of the final batch of paintings sent to Spain to decorate the Escorial:
"Una pintura en tabla al ollio, con dos puertas, de la bariedad del mundo, cifrada con diuersos disparates de Hierónimo Bosco, que llaman del Madroño, con molduras doradas: tiene de alto, çerradas las puertas, dos varas y media y de ancho dos y terçia, que se compró del almoneda del Prior Don Fernando"
(Vandenbroeck 2001a, pp. 52–53, with English translation)
See also sources relating to Chapter IV.

13.
See sources relating to Chapter V.

14.
The *Triptych of the Crucified Female Martyr* (Cat. 14) is mentioned as hanging in the corridors of the Doge's Palace in the Venice travel guide *Le minere della pittura* (1664) by Marco Boschini:
"[...] quadro in tre comparti, ove si vede il martirio d'una santa in croce, [...] e è depinto da Girolamo Basi"
(van Dijck 2001a, p. 130; Aikema 2001a, p. 26)

15.
Defence and art-theoretical appraisal of the painting *The Seven Deadly Sins and the Four Last Things* (Cat. 15) and of Bosch in general, with reference to forerunners amongst the Greek painters of Antiquity, by Felipe de Guevara in his *Comentarios de la Pintura*, *c.* 1560:
"Ovo antiguamente otro género de pintura que llamaban Grillo. Dioles este nombre Antífilo, pintando un hombre, al qual por donayre llamó Grillo. De aquí quedó que este género de pintura se llamáse Grillo. Nació Antítilo en Egypto, y aprendió de Ctesideno este género de pintura, que á mi parecer fué semejante á la que nuestra edad tanto celebra de Hyeronimo Bosch, ó Bosco, como decimos, el qual siempre se extrañó en buscar talles de hombres donosos, y de raras composturas que pintar. / Y pues Hyerónimo Bosco se nos ha puesto delante, razon será desengañar al vulgo, y á otros mas que vulgo de un error que de sus pinturas tienen concebido, y es, que qualquiera monstruosidad, y fuera de órden de naturaleza que ven, luego la atribuyen á Hyerónimo Bosco, haciéndole inventor de monstruos y quimeras. No niego que no pintase extrañas efigies de cosas, pero esto tan solamente á un propósito que fué tratando del infierno, en la qual materia, quiriendo figurar diablos, imaginó composiciones de cosas admirables. / Esto que Hyerónimo Bosco hizo con prudencia y decoro, han hecho y hacen // otros sin discrecion y juicio ninguno; porque habiendo visto en Flandes quan accepto fuese aquel género de pintura de Hyerónimo Bosco, acordaron de imitarle, pintando monstruos y desvariadas imaginaciones, dándose á entender que en esto solo consistia la imitacion del Bosco. / Ansi vienen á ser infinitas las pinturas de este género, selladas con el nombre de Hyerónimo Bosco, falsamente inscripto; en las quales á él nunca le pasó par el pensamiento poner las manos, sino el humo y cortos ingenios, ahumandolas á las chimeneas para dalles autoridad y antigüedad; / Una cosa oso afirmar de Bosco, que nunca pintó cosa fuera del natural en su vida, sino fuese en materia de infierno, ó purgatorio, como dicho tengo. Sus invenciones estrivaron en buscar cosas rarisimas pero naturales: de manera, que puede ser // regla universal, que qualquiera pintura, aunque firmada de Bosco, en que hubiera monstruosidad alguna, ó cosa que pase los límites de la naturaleza, que es adulterada y fingida, sino es, como digo, que la Pintura contenga en sí infierno, ó materia de él. / Es cierto, y á qualquiera que con diligencia observáre las cosas de Bosco le será manifiesto haber sido observantisimo del decoro, y haber guardado los límites de naturaleza cuidadosísimamente, tanto y mas que otro ninguno de su arte; pero es justo dar aviso que entre estos imitadores de Hyerónimo Bosco, hay uno que fué su discipulo, el qual por devocion de su maestro, ó por acreditar sus obras, inscribió en sus pinturas el nombre de Bosch, y no el suyo. Esto, aunque sea así, son pinturas muy de estimar, y el que las tiene debe tenellas en mucho, porque en las invenciones y moralidades, fué rastreando tras su maestro, y en el labor fué mas diligente y paciente que Bosco, no se apartando del ayre y galania, y del colorir del maestro. Exemplo de este género de pintura es una mesa que V. M. tiene, en la qual en circulo estan pintados los siete pecados mortales, mostrados en figuras y exem-//plos, y aunque toda la pintura

en sí sea maravillosa, el quadro de la invidia á mi juicio es tan raro y ingenioso, y tan exprimido el efecto de ella, que puede competir con Aristides, inventor de estas pinturas, que los Griegos llamaron Ethice, lo qual en nuestro castellano suena, Pinturas que muestran las costumbres y afectos de los ánimos de los hombres [...]." (Guevara, Felipe de, *Comentarios de la Pintura, Con un discurso preliminar y algunas notas de Antonio Ponz,* Madrid: Gerónimo Ortega, hijos ele Ibarra y Compañía, 1788 [written *c.* 1560], pp. 41–44, copies in the Bodleian Library, Oxford and the Complutense University, Madrid; German translations (excerpts): Tolnay 1965, p. 401; Unverfehrt 1980, p. 67–72; English translation: Snyder 1973, pp. 28–30)

The Seven Deadly Sins and the Four Last Things (Cat. 15) appears in the 1574 inventory of the first delivery of pictures ordered by Philip II for the decoration of the Escorial:

"Una tabla en que está pintado los Siete pecados mortales, con un cerco redondo, y en medio dél la figura de Christo nuestro Señor; y a las quatro esquinas de la tabla otros quatro circulos en que está pintado: en uno la muerte, en otro el juycio, en otro el infierno, en el otro el parayso; de mano de Géronimo Bosqui, que tiene quatro pies de alto y cinco de ancho"

(Vandenbroeck 2001a, p. 52, with English translation)

16.

The inventory of paintings belonging to Cardinal Marino Grimani (*c.* 1489–1546) mentions

"Uno quadro fiandrese con lo inferno a oglio"

(Vandenbroeck 1987, p. 433, note 1325; Aikema 2001a, p. 26)

See also sources relating to Chapter V.

18.

Extracting the Stone of Folly was in the possession of Beatriz de Haro, as emerges from an inventory of January 1570:

"Otro lienzo quadrado donde se cura de la locura, por guarnescer, porque todos los demás estan guarnescidos"

(Vandenbroeck 2001a, p. 50, with English translation)

See also sources relating to Chapter V.

20.

Ambrosio de Morales on *The Haywain* (Cat. 20), *c.* 1544/45:

"Con esto que assi hemos declarado se podra entender todo lo de mas en la tabla, pues el author lo va declarando en particular. Assi yo lo dexo con solo dar cuenta aqui de otra pintura, con que en nuestros tiempos, quasi a imitacion de Cebes, se ha representando con mucha agudeza y doctrina la vida humana. Tiene esta Tabla el Rey nuestro Señor, y fue el que la invento y pinto Geronimo Bosco, pintor ingenionissimo en // Flandes. Este con gentil aviso y primor muy agudo figuro bien, y puso al propio en aquella Tabla todo nuestro vivir miserable, y el grande embebecimiento que en sus vanidades traemos. Y servira el ponerla aqui, para que quien no ha la visto lo goze en alguna manera con leerla. Es una tabla grande que tiene tres apartamientos, uno mayor en medio, y dos pequeños a los lados. En el primero de los pequeños a la mano derecha, donde comiença la pintura, esta primero la creacion del mundo y del hombre, el pecado de Adan, y el Angel como echa con la espada de fuego a el y a su muger del parayso terrenal, y parece les haze salir de aquel quadro (que representa la entrada de los hombres en la vida) hazia el otro mayor de en medio, en el qual se contiene y se muestra lo que los hombres venidos al mundo con la mala inclinacion del pecado original hazen. Para bien representar esto a y en lo alto deste quadro mayor de en medio un carro muy grande lleno de heno, con tanta muchedumbre del, que haze una como torre. Y ha se entender como carro de heno en Flamenco tanto quiere decir, como carro de nonada en Castellano. Assi, aquel carro siendo // de heno, es verdaderamente carro de nonada, y assi tiene su nombre, al propio de lo que significa. Tiran este carro algunos demonios, y otro principal, como carretero va en el yugo, y todos lo guian hazia el tercero quadro, que es la salida del mundo y de la vida. En lo alto del gran cargo de heno o de no nada, o de vanidad van muchos mancebos y damas sentados a plazer, de los quales unos tañen, otros baylan, comen y beven otros, y de diversas maneras toman plazer. A todos les haze el son el demonio con una gayta, yendo delante dellos como por guia, y detras está de rodillas un Angel muy lloroso y triste, levantados los ojos y las manos al cielo, con lastima que le haze tanta grande perdicion, y como suplicando a Dios con lagrimas, se duela de tan grande miseria. Mas abaxo al derredor del carro va infinita y muy diversa muchedumbre de gente, que non increyble ansia y porfia se trabajaban, por tomar mas heno y mas vanidad de la carga. Unos

con garfios, otros con palas y con otros generos de instrumentos se fatigan, por tomar del heno, y otros con escaleras suben muy apriessa por alcançarlo, sin otros muchos que por lo baxo llegan, y quieren abarcar // tanto, que se impossible llevarlo. Tal ay que cae con lo mucho que lleva, tal que arrebata al otro por hurto o por fuerça de lo que ha avido, y tal que le mata por tomarselo, y van contentissimos estos, como si vuiessen avido un rico despojo. Al tomar del heno es la priessa, de estorvarse unos a otros, por llegar primero. Rémpuxan algunos como mas valientes, y por feurça se hazen camino: sin otros muchos, que estan por el suelo caydos, derribada y hollada la furia que tuvieron por llegar, de otra mayor violencia de los que sotrevinieron. Detras del carro, como en lugar mas principal y mas honrado, van a cavallo los Reyes y príncipes: y estos aunque por muy linda advertencia del pintor estan puestos junto el carro, mas por su autoridad y grandeza no estienden ellos las manos, para tomar su buena parte del heno y vanidad: antes, con una gravedad muy entonada hazen señal con la mano a sus criados, que lleguen, y tomen, y traygan mucho para todos. Un poco mas abaxo estan pintados, los que buelven ya con sus hazes muy alegres y contentos, aunque con infinito sudor y fatiga los ayan avido. Estos son differentes estados y maneras de hombres, y aqui es el reñir bravamente, y matarse, por quitarse unos a // otros aun un poquillo que del heno, de la vanidad, de la nonada les ha cabido. Aqui también van muchos corriendo hazia el carro con grande agonia, para alcançar al carro, como se vuiesse de huyr, o el heno se hubiese de acabar. Los padres llevan de la mano sus hijuelos pequeños, y con grande ahinco les muestran el carro con el dedo, como si les mostrassen una grande riqueza, y los incitan para que aguijen, y traygan ellos también su hacezillo, no contentos con el grande, que ellos trayran. Otros compran de otros por mucha dinero lo que traen: y ay tantas particularidades destas, que ni yo las puedo referir todas, ni tan poco ay para que se digan. Todo esto va a parar, segun los demonios guian el carro, al quadro postrero, donde se representa, lo que despues de la vida succede. Assi esta alli pintado el infierno, y diversos generos de tormentos, que padecen las miserables almas, cuya vida se passo toda en vanidad de pecados, y fue como heno que se seco, y perecio sin dar fruto de virtud."
(Morales, Ambrosio de, *Las obras del maestro Fernán Pérez de Oliva*, Cordoba 1586; Dutch translation: de Bruyn 2001a, p. 57 f.; English translation: Snyder 1973, pp. 31–33; Salazar, 1955, pp. 124–126, cf. (with errors) van Dijck 2001a, pp. 108–109)

A deed of 1570 shows that Philip II purchased a *Haywain* from the collection of the deceased Felipe de Guevara:
"Una tabla de vara y dos terçias de alto, con dos puertas, que abierto todo él tiene de ancho tres varas, y es el Carro de Heno, de Gerónimo Bosco, de su propia mano"
(Vandenbroeck 2001a, p. 49, with English translation)

Description of *The Haywain* (Cat. 20) in the inventory of the works delivered to the Escorial in 1574 as furnishings for the new palace:
"Una tabla de pintura con dos puertas, en que está pintado de pinzel un Carro de heno que toman dél todos los estados, que denota la vanidad tras que anda; y encima del heno una figura del Angel de la Guarda y el demonio y otras figuras; y en lo alto de la tabla Dios Padre; y en la tabla de mano derecha la Créación de Adán y otras figuras de la misma historia; y en la de mano yzquierda el Infierno y las penas de los pecados mortales, que tiene cinco pies de alto y quatro de ancho, sin las puertas: es de Géronimo Bosqui"
(Vandenbroeck 2001a, p. 52, with English translation)

27.
The Temptation of St Anthony (Cat. 27), from the inventory of pictures delivered to the Escorial in 1574:
"Otra tabla de pintura en redondo por lo alto, de Sant Antón, de mano de Géronimo Bosqui, que tiene tres pies de alto y dos de ancho"
(Vandenbroeck 2001a, p. 52, with English translation)

Bibliography

Adriaenssen, Leo F. W., "Een aanslag op de calculerende clerus: De amortisatie van de geestelijke goederen in stad en meierij van 's-Hertogenbosch in 1516", in: *Noordbrabants Historisch Jaarboek* 15, 1998, pp. 81–117.

Aikema 2001a: Aikema, Bernard, "Hieronymus Bosch and Italy?", in: Koldeweij/Vermet/Kooij 2001, pp. 25–32.

Aikema 2001b: Aikema, Bernard, "'Stravaganze e bizarie de chimere, de mostri, e d'animali': Over het beeld van Hieronymus Bosch in de italiaanse kunst", in: *Desipientia* 8, 2001, no. 2, Sept., pp. 48–57.

Aikema 2001c: Aikema, Bernard, "'Stravaganze e bizarie de chimere, de mostri, e d'animali'", in: *Venezia Cinquecento* 11, 2001, 22, pp. 111–135.

Ainsworth, Maryan W., "Implications of revised attributions in Netherlandish painting", in: *Metropolitan Museum Journal* 27, 1992, pp. 59–76.

Ainsworth, Maryan W./Christiansen, Keith (eds.), *From Van Eyck to Bruegel: Early Netherlandish Painting in the Metropolitan Museum of Art*, New York 1998.

Albertanus Causidicus Brixiensis, *De arte loquendi et tacendi: Van die konste van spreken ende van swighen [Dat is een konste om te leren spreken ende swighen alst tijt is]*, 's-Hertogenbosch: Gerardus de Leempt 1484/85, copy in Koninklijke Bibliotheek, The Hague 150 C 30.

Anfam, David, "De Kooning, Bosch and Bruegel: Some fundamental themes", in: *The Burlington Magazine* 145, 2003, 1207, pp. 705–715.

Antwerp 2002: *Altniederländische Zeichnungen von Jan van Eyck bis Hieronymus Bosch*, exhibition catalogue, Antwerp, Rubenshuis, ed. Fritz Koreny, Antwerp 2002.

Asmus, Gesine/Grosshans, Rainald (eds.), *Gemäldegalerie Berlin: 200 Meisterwerke*, Berlin 1998.

Asperen de Boer, J[ohan] R[udolph] J[ustus] van/Faries, Molly, "Covering-over and covering-up: Some instances in the re-use of panels in paintings after Hieronymus Bosch", in: *Le dessin sous-jacent dans la peinture*, colloque XI, 14.–16.9.1995, ed. Hélène Verougstraete and Roger van Schoute, Louvain-la-Neuve 1997.

Athanasius, *Ausgewählte Schriften*, vol. 2, trans. from the Greek by Anton Stegmann and Hans Mertel (Bibliothek der Kirchenväter, series 1, vol. 31), Munich 1917.

Athanasius, *Select Writings of Athanasius*, in: Schaff, Philip/Wace, Henry (eds.), *Nicene and Post-Nicene Fathers*, 2nd series, vol. 6, trans. by H. Ellershaw, New York 1924, pp. 195–221.

Aurelius Augustinus, *Vom Gottesstaat*, trans. by Wilhelm Thimme, introd. and annot. by Carl Andresen (Bibliothek der Alten Welt, Reihe Antike und Christentum), 2 vols., 2nd fully rev. edn. Zurich/Munich 1978.

Axters, Stephan, *Geschiedenis van de vroomheid in de Nederlanden*, Antwerp 1950 ff., vol. 2, 1953: *De eeuw van Ruusbroec*, and vol. 3, 1956: De moderne devotie 1380–1550.

Axters, Stephanus G., *Bibliotheca Dominicana Neerlandica manuscripta 1224–1500* (Bibliothèque de la revue d'histoire ecclésiastique, 49), Leuven 1970.

Baaren, T. P. van, "The significance of gestures in the paintings of Hieronymus Bosch", in: *Genres in Visual Representation: Proceedings of a conference held in 1986* (Visible Religion, 7), ed. Hans G. Kippenberg, L. P. Van Den Bosch and L. Leertouwer, Leiden 1990, pp. 21–30.

Baert, Barbara/Fraeters, Veerle (eds.), *Aan de vruchten kent men de boom: De boom in tekst in beeld in de middeleeuwse Nederlanden* (Symbolae Facultatis Litterarum Lovaniensis, series B, vol. 25), Leuven 2001.

Baldass, Ludwig, *Jheronimus Bosch*, 2nd rev. edn. Vienna/Munich 1959 (Vienna [1]1943).

Baltrusaitis, Jurgis, *Réveils et*

Prodiges: Le gothique fantastique, Paris 1960.

Bambeck, Manfred, *Das Sprichwort im Bild: "Der Wald hat Ohren, das Feld hat Augen": Zu einer Zeichnung von Hieronymus Bosch* (Abhandlungen der Geistes- und sozialwissenschaftlichen Klasse, 1987, 10), Stuttgart 1987.

Bange, Petty, *Spiegels der christenen: Zelfreflectie en ideaalbeeld in laat-middeleeuwse moralistisch-didactische traktaten* (Middeleeuwse Studies, 2), Nijmegen 1986.

Bange, Petty, "Soziale Prägung von Dekalogerklärungen in den Niederlanden im späten Mittelalter", in: Schreiner 1992, pp. 253–262.

Bango Torviso, Isidro Gonzalo/ Marías, Fernando, *Bosch: Realidad, símbolo y fantasía*, Madrid 1982.

Bango Torviso 2006a: Bango Torviso, Isidro Gonzalo [et al.], *El Bosco y la tradición pictórica de lo fantástico* (Fundación Amigos del Museo del Prado), Barcelona 2006.

Bango Torviso 2006b: Bango Torviso, Isidro Gonzalo, "Las Tentaciones de San Antonio de Lisboa: Los ideólogos de la obra de El Bosco y su público", in: Bango Torviso 2006a, pp. 21–41.

Baschet, Jérôme, *Les Justices de l'au-delà: Les représentations de l'enfer en France et en Italie (XIIe–XVe siècle),* Rome 1993.

Bassegoda Hugas, Bonaventura, *El Escorial como museo: La decoración pictórica mueble en el monasterio de El Escorial desde Diego Velázquez hasta Frédéric Quilliet*, Barcelona 2002.

Bax, Dirk, *Ontcijfering van Jeroen Bosch*, The Hague 1949 [Eng. edn: *Hieronymus Bosch: His picture-writing deciphered*, trans. by M. A. Bax-Botha, Rotterdam 1979].

Bax, Dirk, "Bosschiana: Verloren Zoon – Johannes op Patmos – Wellusttuin – Doornenkroning", in: *Oud Holland* 68, 1953, 4, pp. 200–208.

Bax, Dirk, *Beschrijving en poging tot verklaring van het tuin der onkuisheidsdrieluik van Jeroen Bosch: Gevolgd door kritiek op Fraenger* (Verhandelingen der Koninklijke Nederlandse Akademie van Wetenschappen, Afdeling Letterkunde, new series, 63, 2), Amsterdam 1956.

Bax, Dirk, *Jeroen Bosch' drieluik met de gekruisigde martelares* (Verhandelingen der Nederlandse Akademie van Wetenschappen, Afdeling Letterkunde, new series, 68, 5), Amsterdam 1961.

Bax, Dirk, "Jeroen Bosch en de Nederlandse Taal", in: 's-Hertogenbosch 1967, pp. 61–71.

Bax, Dirk, *Hieronymus Bosch and Lucas Cranach: Two Last Judgement triptychs, description and exposition*, trans. by M. A. Bax-Botha (Verhandelingen der Koninklijke Nederlandse Akademie van Wetenschappen, Afdeling Letterkunde, new series, 117), Amsterdam/Oxford/ New York 1983.

Baxandall, Michael, *Giotto and the Orators: Humanist observers of painting in Italy and the discovery of pictorial composition 1350–1450*, Oxford 1971.

Baxandall, Michael, *Painting and Experience in Fifteenth-Century Italy: A primer in the social history of pictorial style*, Oxford 1972.

Baxandall, Michael, *The limewood sculptors of Renaissance Germany*, New Haven and London 1980 [Ger. Edn.: *Die Kunst der Bildschnitzer: Tilman Riemenschneider, Veit Stoß und ihre Zeitgenossen*, Munich 1984].

Bayless, Martha, *Parody in the Middle Ages: The Latin tradition*, Ann Arbor (Michigan) 1996.

Beatis, Antonio de, *Die Reise des Kardinals Luigi d'Aragona durch Deutschland, die Niederlande, Frankreich und Oberitalien, 1517–1518*, ed. Ludwig Pastor (Erläuterungen und Ergänzungen zu Janssens Geschichte des deutschen Volkes, vol. 4, no. 4), Freiburg im Breisgau 1905.

Béguin, Silvie/Cassanelli, Roberto (eds.), *Künstlerwerkstätten der Renaissance*, Zurich/Düsseldorf 1998.

Belting, Hans, *Hieronymus Bosch: Garten der Lüste*, Munich/Berlin 2002 [Eng. edn: *Hieronymus Bosch: Garden of Earthly Delights*, Munich/London 2002; rev. edn 2005].

Belting, Hans/Kruse, Christiane, *Die Erfindung des Gemäldes: Das erste Jahrhundert der niederländischen Malerei*, Munich 1994.

Benesch, Otto, "Der Wald, der sieht und hört: Zur Erklärung einer Zeichnung von Bosch", in: *Jahrbuch der preußischen Kunstsammlungen* 58, 1937, pp. 258–266.

Benz, Ernst, Die Vision: Erfahrungsformen und Bilderwelt, Stuttgart 1969.

Bichelaer, Alphons van den, *Het notariaat in stad en Meierij van 's-Hertogenbosch tijdens de Late Mid deleeuwen (1306–1531)*, Amsterdam 1998 [+ CD-ROM with biographies (suppl. 1) and texts of documents (suppl. 2).]

Blank, Walter, "Zur Entstehung des Grotesken", in: *Deutsche Literatur des späten Mittelalters* (Hamburger Kolloquium 1973), ed. Wolfgang Harms and L. Peter Johnson, Berlin 1975, pp. 35–46 (simult. in Publications of the Institute of Germanic Studies, University of London, 22).

Blockmans, Wim, "Institutionelle Rahmenbedingungen der Kunstproduktion in den burgundischen Niederlanden", in: Franke/Welzel 1997, pp. 11–27.

Blockmans, Wim/Prevenier, Walter, *Promised Lands: The Low Countries under Burgundian rule, 1369–1530*, transl., rev. and ed. by Edward Peters, Philadelphia (Pennsylvania) 1999.

Blondé, Bruno, *De sociale structuren en economische dynamiek van 's-Hertogenbosch: 1500–1550* (Bijdragen tot de geschiedenis van het zuiden van Nederland, 74), Tilburg 1987.

Blondé, Bruno/Vlieghe, Hans, "The social statue of Hieronymus Bosch", in: *The Burlington Magazine* 131, 1989, 1039, pp. 699–700.

Bock, Henning, *Gemäldegalerie Berlin: Gesamtverzeichnis*, Staatliche Museen Preußischer Kulturbesitz, Berlin 1996.

Boczkowska, Anna, "The lunar symbolism of 'The Ship of Fools' by Hieronymus Bosch", in: *Oud Holland* 86, 1971, pp. 47–69.

Boczkowska, Anna, "The Crab, the Sun, the Moon and Venus: Studies in the iconology of Hieronymus Bosch's triptych 'Garden of Earthly Delights'", in: *Oud Holland* 91, 1977, no. 4, pp. 197–231 [see also Spychalska-Boczkowska 1966].

Boendale, Jan van, *Der leken spieghel*, ed. M. de Vries, 3 vols., Leiden 1844–1848.

Boockmann, Hartmut, "Belehrung durch Bilder? Ein unbekannter Typus spätmittelalterlichen Tafelbilder", in: *Zeitschrift für Kunstgeschichte* 57, 1994, pp. 1–22.

Borinski, Karl, *Die Antike in Poetik und Kunsttheorie*, vol. 1: *Mittelalter, Renaissance, Barock*, Darmstadt 1965 ([1]1914).

Braekman, Willy Louis, "Middelnederlandse didactische gedichten en rijmspreuken", in: *Verslagen en Mededelingen der Koninklijke Vlaamse Academie voor Taal- en Letterkunde*, 1969, pp. 79–111.

Braekman, Willy Louis, "'Den Mensche te bekennen bi vele tekenen': Het Mnl. Prozatraktaatje over Fysiognomie en zijn brau", in: *Scientiarum Historia* 12, 1970, 3, pp. 113–142.

Brand Philip, Lotte, "The Prado 'Epiphany' by Jerome Bosch", in: *Art Bulletin* 35, 1953, pp. 267–293.

Brand Philip, Lotte, *Hieronymus Bosch*, New York 1955.

Brand Philip, Lotte, "The Peddler by Hieronymus Bosch: A study in detection", in: *Nederlands Kunsthistorisch Jaarboek* 9, 1958, pp. 1–81.

Brandt, Rüdiger, *Kleine Einführung in die mittelalterliche Poetik und Rhetorik* (Göppinger Arbeiten zur Germanistik, 460), Göppingen 1986.

Bray, Xavier, "The Crowning of Thorns", in: London 2000, pp. 114–115.

Breton, André, in collaboration with Gérard Legrand, *L'art magique*, Paris 1957.

Brinker-von der Heyde, Claudia, "Der 'Welsche Gast' des Thomasin von Zerclaere: Eine (Vor-) Bildgeschichte", in: Wenzel/Lechtermann 2002, pp. 9–32.

Brugman, Jan, *Onuitgegeven Sermoenen*, ingeleid en bezorgd door Dr. P Grootens S. J. (Studien en Tekstuitgaven van Ons Geestelijk Erf, 8), Tielt 1948.

Brugman, Jan, *Verspreide Sermoenen*, ed. A. van Dijk (Klassieke Galerij, 41), Antwerp 1948.

Bruyn, Eric de, "Het Madrilense Tafelblad: Een ikonographisch benadering", in: *Jaarboek Koninklijk Museum voor schone Kunsten*, Antwerp 1991, pp. 9–60.

Bruyn, Eric de, "De vos als allegorisch motief in het geschilderde oeuvre van Jheronimus Bosch", in: *Tiecelijn* 13, 2000, 3, pp. 107–119.

de Bruyn 2001a: Bruyn, Eric de, *De vergeten beeldtaal van Jheronimus Bosch: De symboliek van de Hooiwagen-Triptiek en de Rotterdamse Marskramer-Tondo verklaard vanuit middelnederlandse teksten*, 's-Hertogenbosch 2001 (doctoral thesis Brussels 2000).

de Bruyn 2001b: Bruyn, Eric de, "De betekenis van de gebroken kruik op Jheroniums Bosch' Sint Christoffel-paneel te Rotterdam", in: *Desipientia* 8, 2001, 2, Sept., pp. 4–9.

de Bruyn 2001c: Bruyn, Eric de, "The cat and the mouse (or rat) on the left panel of Bosch's

Garden of Earthly Delights triptych: An iconological approach", in: *Jaarboek Koninklijk Museum voor Schone Kunsten Antwerpen* 2001, pp. 7–57.

de Bruyn 2001d: Bruyn, Eric de, "Hieronymus Bosch's so-called Prodigal Son tondo: The pedlar as a repentant sinner", in: Koldeweij/Vermet/Kooij 2001, pp. 132–143.

Bruyn, Eric de, "Boommens en vogelduivel Jheronimus Bosch en de Middelnederlandse visioenenliteratuur", in: *Literatuur* 20, 2003, pp. 25–27.

Bruyn, Eric de, "The iconography of Hieronymus Bosch's 'St Christopher carrying the Christ Child' (Rotterdam)", in: *Oud Holland* 118, 2005, 1/2, pp. 28–37.

Bruyn, Eric de, "The Garden of Delights: the eroticism of its central panel and Middle Dutch", in: de Bruyn/Koldeweij 2010, pp. 94–106.

Bruyn, Eric de/Koldeweij, Adrianus Maria [Jos] (eds.), *Jheronimus Bosch: His sources*, 2nd International Jheronimus Bosch Conference, 's-Hertogenbosch 22.–25.5.2007, 's-Hertogenbosch 2010.

Bruyn, Josua, "Mittelalterliche 'doctrina exemplaris' und Allegorie als Komponente des sog. Genrebildes", in: *Holländische Genremalerei im 17. Jahrhundert*, symposium, Berlin, 1984 (Jahrbuch preussischer Kulturbesitz: special vol. 4), Berlin 1987, pp. 33–60.

Buck, Stephanie, *Die niederländischen Zeichnungen des 15. Jahrhunderts im Berliner Kupferstichkabinett: Kritischer Katalog*, Turnhout 2001.

Büchse, Angelika, *Die Anbetung der Könige von Hieronymus Bosch*, doctoral thesis Bochum 2006; online: http://www-brs.ub.ruhr-uni-bochum.de/netahtml/HSS/Diss/BuechseAngelika/diss.pdf].

Büttner, Frank, "'Argumentatio' in Bildern der Reformationszeit: Ein Beitrag zur Bestimmung argumentativer Strukturen in der Bildkunst", in: *Zeitschrift für Kunstgeschichte* 57, 1994, pp. 23–44.

Büttner, Nils, *Hieronymus Bosch*, Munich 2012.

Butzbach, Johannes, *Von den berühmten Malern [Libellus de praeclaris picturae professoribus] 1505*, with reproduction of the original text, ed. and trans. by Otto Pelka, Heidelberg 1925.

Calas, Elena, "Bosch's Garden of Delights: A theological rebus", in: *Art Journal* 29, 2, Winter 1969/70, pp. 184–199.

Campbell, Lorne, "Bosch: Christ Mocked (The Crowning with Thorns) NG. 474", in: *La Peinture dans les Pays-Bas au 16e Siècle: Pratiques d'Ateliers Infrarouges et autres Méthodes d'Investigation: Le dessin sous-jacent et la technologie dans la peinture*, colloque XII, 11.–13.9.1997, ed. Hélène Verougstraete and Roger van Schoute, Leuven 1999, pp. 29–35.

Cauchies, Jean-Marie (ed.), *La Dévotion moderne dans les pays bourguignons et rhénans des origines à la fin du XVIe siècle* (Publication du Centre Européen d'Etudes Bourguignonnes, 29), Neuchâtel 1989.

Cauchies, Jean-Marie, *Philippe le Beau: Le dernier duc de Bourgogne* (Burgundica, 6), Turnhout 2003.

Chailley, Jacques, *Jérôme Bosch et ses symboles: Essai de décryptage*, Brussels 1978.

Cheyns-Condé, Myriam, "Expression de la piété des duchesses de Bourgogne au XVe siècle dans la vie quotidienne et dans l'art: Essai de synthèse", in: Cauchies 1989, pp. 47–68.

Cinotti, Mia/Schlégl, István, *Das Gesamtwerk von Hieronymus Bosch*, Stuttgart 1966.

Clark, Gregory T., "Bosch's Saint John the Baptist in the Wilderness and the artist's 'Fleurs du Mal'", in: *A Tribute to Robert A. Koch: Studies in the Northern Renaissance*, Princeton 1994, pp. 3–11.

Coburg 2010: *Apelles am Fürstenhof: Facetten der Hofkunst um 1500 im Alten Reich*, exhibition catalogue, Coburg, Kunstsammlungen der Veste Coburg, ed. Matthias Müller, Klaus Weschenfelder and Beate Böckem, Berlin 2010.

Colenbrander, Herman T., "Avare vixisti: 'Death and the Miser' by Hieronymus Bosch, drawings, underdrawing, painting and meaning", in: Verougstraete/Schoute 2003, pp. 22–32.

Combe, Jacques, *Jerôme Bosch*, Paris 11946 [Eng. edn.: *Iheronimus Bosch*, trans. by. Ethel Duncan, London 1946].

Cook, Albert, "Change of signification in Bosch's Garden of Earthly Delights", in: *Oud Holland* 98, 1984, pp. 76–98.

Cools, Carl H. L. I., *Mannen met macht: Edellieden en de moderne staat in de Bourgondisch-Habsburgse landen, ca. 1475 – ca. 1530*, n.p. 2000.

Cramer, Thomas, *Geschichte der*

deutschen Literatur im späteren Mittelalter, 3rd rev. edn. Munich 2000.

Cuttler, Charles D., *Hieronymus Bosch: Late Work*, London 2007.

Damen, Mario, "Memoria y propaganda: Las vidrieras de Felipe el Hermoso en los Países Bajos", in: Zalama/Vandenbroeck 2006, pp. 165–184.

Darriulat, Jacques, *Jérôme Bosch et la fable populaire: Une légende médiévale aux sources de l'escamoteur de Saint-Germain-en-Laye*, Paris 1995.

Dempsey, Charles, "Sicut in utrem aquas maris: Jerome Bosch's prolegomenon to the Garden of Earthly Delights", in: *MLN [Modern Language Notes]* 119, suppl. 1, January 2004 (Italian Issue), pp. 247–270.

Deneke, Bernward, *Hochzeit* (Bibliothek des Germanischen Nationalmuseums Nürnberg zur deutschen Kunst- und Kulturgeschichte, 31), Munich 1971.

Dijck, [Lucas] Godfried Christiaan Maria van, *De Bossche optimaten: Geschiedenis van de Illustere Lieve Vrouwebroederschap te 's-Hertogenbosch 1318–1973* (Bijdragen tot de geschiedenis van het Zuiden van Nederland, 27), Tilburg 1973.

van Dijck 1998a: Dijck, Godfried Christiaan Maria van, "Peter van Os ontmaskerd", in: *De Brabantse Leeuw* 47, 1998, pp. 116–124.

van Dijck 1998b: Dijck, Godfried Christiaan Maria van, "Joos van Cleve en Jeroen Bosch in huize Vezelaer", in: *De Brabantse Leeuw* 47, 1998, pp. 13–18.

van Dijck 2001a: Dijck, [Lucas] Godfried Christiaan Maria van, *Op zoek naar Jheronimus van Aken alias Bosch: De feiten*, Zaltbommel 2001.

van Dijck 2001b: Dijck, [Lucas] Godfried Christiaan Maria van, "Hieronymus Bosch: His life and 'portraits'", in: Koldeweij/Vermet/Kooij 2001, pp. 9–16.

Dijck, Lucas [Godfried Christiaan Maria] van, "Jheronimus Bosch inspired by people in his environment: Research from the archival sources", in: de Bruyn/Koldeweij 2010, pp. 112–122.

Dinzelbacher, Peter, *Die Jenseitsbrücke im Mittelalter*, Vienna 1973.

Dinzelbacher, Peter, *Mittelalterliche Visionsliteratur: Eine Anthologie*, sel., trans., introd. and annot., Darmstadt 1989.

Dinzelbacher, Peter, *Himmel, Hölle, Heilige: Visionen und Kunst im Mittelalter*, Darmstadt 2002.

Dionysius Areopagita, *Über die mystische Theologie* und *Briefe*, Pseudo-Dionysius Areopagita, introd., trans. and annot. by Adolf Martin Ritter (Bibliothek der griechischen Literatur, 40: Patristik), Stuttgart 1994.

Dirc van Delf, *Tafel van den Kersten Ghelove, naar de handschriften uitgegeven, ingeleid en van aanteekeningen voorzien*, ed. L. M. Daniels (Tekstuitgaven van Ons Geestelijk Erf), Antwerp/Nijmegen/Utrecht 1937–1939.

Dittrich, Sigrid/Dittrich, Lothar, *Lexikon der Tiersymbole: Tiere als Sinnbilder in der Malerei des 14.–17. Jahrhunderts* (Studien zur internationalen Architektur- und Kunstgeschichte, 22), 2nd rev. edn. Petersberg 2005.

Dixon, Laurinda S., "Water, wine, and blood: Science and liturgy in the Marriage at Cana by Hieronymus Bosch", in: *Oud Holland* 96, 1982, pp. 73–96.

Dixon, Laurinda S., *Bosch*, New York 2003.

Dollmayr, Herrmann, "Hieronymus Bosch und die Darstellung der Vier letzten Dinge", in: *Jahrbuch der kunsthistorischen Sammlungen des allerhöchsten Kaiserhauses* 19, 1898, pp. 284–343.

Dresen-Coenders, Lène, "De demonen bij Jeroen Bosch: Zoektocht naar bronnen en betekenis", in: *Duivelsbeelden: Een cultuurhistorische speurtocht door de Lage Landen*, ed. Gerard Rooijakkers, Lène Dresen-Coenders and Margreet Geerdes, Baarn 1994, pp. 168–197.

Duquenne, Xavier, "Peeter Scheyfve représenté par Jérôme Bosch", in: *L'intermédiaire des généalogistes* 249, 2004, 1, pp. 11–19.

Duquenne, Xavier, "Peeter Scheyfve et Agnès de Gramme, donateurs du triptyque de l'Adoration des Mages de Jérôme Bosch (vers 1494) conservé au Prado", in: *The Quest for the Original: Underdrawing and technology in painting*, Symposium XVI, Bruges, 21.–23.9.2006, ed. Hélène Verougstraete and Colombe Janssens de Bisthoven (Le Dessin sous-jacent et la technologie dans la peinture, 16), Leuven [et al.] 2009, pp. 27–33.

Dürer, Albrecht, *Schriftlicher Nachlass*, ed. Hans Rupprich, 3 vols., Berlin 1956–1969.

Dürer, Albrecht, *Schriften und Briefe*, ed. Ernst Ullmann, text editing by Elvira Pradel, Leipzig 1993.

Dworschak, Helmut, "Der Gebrauch des Körpers beim Gebet", in: *Schwierige Frauen – schwierige Männer in der Literatur des Mittelalters*, ed. Alois M. Haas, Bern 1999, pp. 177–199.

Eco, Umberto, *Arte e bellezza nell'estetica medievale, Milan 1987 [Eng. edn.: Art and Beauty in the Middle Ages, trans. by Hugh Bredin, New Haven/London 1985]* Munich/Vienna 1991.

Eichberger, Dagmar, *Leben mit Kunst, Wirken durch Kunst: Sammelwesen und Hofkunst unter Margarete von Österreich, Regentin der Niederlande* (Burgundica, 5), Turnhout 2002.

Elsig, Frédéric, "Hieronymus Bosch's workshop and the issue of chronology", in: Koldeweij/Vermet/Kooij 2001, pp. 96–101.

Elsig, Frédéric, *Jheronimus Bosch: La question de la chronologie* (Travaux d'Humanisme et Renaissance, 392), Geneva 2004 (doctoral thesis Geneva 2003).

Erasmus von Rotterdam, *Ausgewählte Schriften*, ed. Werner Welzig, Latin and German, 8 vols., Darmstadt 1967–1980.

Erffa, Hans M. von, *Ikonologie der Genesis: Die christlichen Bildthemen aus dem Alten Testament und ihre Quellen*, vol. 1, Munich 1989.

Esser, Dorothee, *"Ubique Diabolus – der Teufel ist überall": Aspekte mittelalterlicher Moralvorstellungen und die Kulmination moralisierender Tendenzen in deutschen und niederländischen Weltgerichtsbildern des 15. Jahrhunderts*, Erlangen 1991 (doctoral thesis Aachen 1990).

Fagel, Raymond/Geurts, Jac/Limberger, Michael (eds.), *Filips de Schone: Een vergeten vorst (1478–1506)*, Maastricht 2008.

Falkenburg, Reindert L., *Joachim Patinir: Het landschap als beeld van de levenspelgrimage*, Nijmegen 1985 [Eng. edn.: Joachim Patinir: *Landscape as an image of the pilgrimage of life*, Amsterdam/Philadelphia (Pennsylvania) 1988].

Falkenburg 2007a: Falkenburg, Reindert L., "Black holes in Bosch: Visual typology in the 'Garden of Earthly Delights'", in: *Image and Imagination of the Religious Self in Late Medieval and Early Modern Europe*, Emory University, Lovis Corinth Colloquia 1 (Proteus, 1), ed. Reindert L. Falkenburg and Walter S. Melion, Turnhout 2007, pp. 105–131.

Falkenburg 2007b: Falkenburg, Reindert L., "Hieronymus Bosch's Mass of St. Gregory and 'sacramental vision'", in: *Das Bild der Erscheinung: Die Gregorsmesse im Mittelalter* (KultBild, 3), ed. Andreas Gormans and Thomas Lentes, Berlin 2007, pp. 179–206.

Falkenburg, Reindert L., *The Land of Unlikeness. Hieronymus Bosch: The Garden of Earthly Delights*, Zwolle 2011.

Feist Hirsch, Elisabeth, *Damião de Gois: The life and thought of a Portuguese Humanist, 1502–1574*, The Hague 1967.

Filedt Kok, Jan Piet, "Underdrawing and drawing in the work of Hieronymus Bosch: A provisional survey in connection with the paintings by him in Rotterdam", in: *Simiolus* 6, 1972/73, 3/4, pp. 133–162.

Fischer 2002a: Fischer, Stefan, "[Rezension von] Bruyn, Eric de, De vergeten beeldentaal van Jheronimus Bosch, 's-Hertogenbosch 2001", in: *Millennium* [Nijmegen] 16, 2002, 2, pp. 157–160.

Fischer 2002b: Fischer, Stefan, *"Der Garten der Lüste" von Hieronymus Bosch: Ansätze und Methoden der Forschung*, n.p. 2002.

Fischer, Stefan, "'Der unverschmutzte Spiegel, in dem stets das Bild erhalten bleibt': Der Maler Hieronymus Bosch und die niederländische Mystik des Spätmittelalters um Jan van Ruusbroec", in: *Das unsichtbare Sehen: Bild–Mystik–Kunst*, ed. Marco Sorace and Peter Zimmerling, Mannheim 2005, pp. 49–66.

Fischer, Stefan, "Hieronymus Bosch", in: *Biographisch-Bibliographisches Kirchenlexikon*, ed. Friedrich-Wilhelm Bautz, cont. by Traugott Bautz, Nordhausen 2007, vol. 27 (2007), col. 161–172.

Fischer, Stefan, "Die Gewalttätigkeit alles Irdischen und die Bewältigung der Welt bei Hieronymus Bosch", in: *Terminator – Die Möglichkeit des Endes: Bewältigung und Zerstörung als kreative Prozesse in Bildender Kunst, Literatur und Musik*, ed. Sebastian Baden, Karlsruhe 2008, pp. 138–150.

Fischer, Stefan, *Hieronymus Bosch: Malerei als Vision, Lehrbild und Kunstwerk*, Cologne 2009 (doctoral thesis Bonn 2007).

Fischer, Stefan, "Jheronimus Bosch's works of art as allegorical and grotesque moral satire: Theological, pastoral and didactic sources", in: Bruyn/Koldeweij 2010, pp. 145–156.

Fraenger, Wilhelm, *Hieronymus Bosch: Das Tausendjährige Reich*, Coburg 1947 (Amsterdam ²1969).

Franke, Birgit/Welzel, Barbara (eds.), *Die Kunst der burgundischen Niederlande: Eine Einführung*, Berlin 1997.

Frankfurt 1995: *Die Entdeckung der Kunst: Niederländische Kunst des 15. und 16. Jahrhunderts in Frankfurt*, exhibition catalogue, Frankfurt am Main, Städelsches Kunstinstitut and Städtische Galerie, ed. Jochen Sander, Mainz 1995.

Fransen, Bart, "Les Copies du Jardin des délices dans les collections royales espagnoles", in: Verougstraete/Schoute 2003, pp. 75–80.

Friedländer, Max J., *Early Netherlandish Painting*, vol. 5: *Geertgen tot Sint Jans and Jerome Bosch*, Leiden 1969.

Fúster Sabater, M. Dolores, "Estudio técnico y tratamiento de restauración aplicado al San Juan Bautista en el desierto de Jeronimus Bosch-el Bosco", in: *Goya* 253/254, 1996, July–Oct., pp. 77–86.

Gachard, M. (ed.), *Collection de Voyage des Souverains des Pays-Bas*, Brussels 1876.

Gaignebet, Claude/Lajoux, Jean-Dominique, *Art profane et religion populaire au Moyen Age*, Paris 1985.

Garrido, Maria del Carmen/Schoute, Roger van, "El tríptico de la Adoración de los Magos de Hieronymus van Aeken Bosch: Estudio técnico", in: *Boletín del Museo del Prado* 6, 1985, 17, pp. 59–77.

Garrido, Maria del Carmen/Schoute, Roger van, *Bosch at the Museo del Prado: Technical study*, Madrid 2001.

Garzelli, Beatrice, "Pinturas infernales y retratos grotescos: Viaje por la iconografía de los Sueños", in: *La Perinola* 10, 2006, pp. 133–147.

Gelder, Jan Gerrit van, "Der Teufel stiehlt das Tintenfass", in: *Kunsthistorische Forschungen, Otto Pächt zu seinem 70. Geburtstag*, ed. Artur Rosenauer and Gerold Weber, Salzburg 1972, pp. 173–188.

Gelfand, Laura D., "Class, gender, and the influence of penitential literature in Bosch's depictions of sin", in: de Bruyn/Koldeweij 2010, pp. 159–173.

Gerlach, Pater, "Jeronimus van Aken alias Bosch en de Onze Lieve Vrouwe-Broederschap", in: 's-Hertogenbosch 1967, pp. 48–60.

Gerlach, Pater, *Jheronimus Bosch: Opstellen over leven en werk*, The Hague 1988 [new coll. edn. of earlier articles].

Gertsman, Elina, "Illusion and deception: Construction of a proverb in Hieronymus Bosch's The Conjurer", in: *Athanor* 22, 2004, pp. 31–37.

Gessler, Jean, *De Vlaamsche baardheilige Wilgefortis of Ontcommer*, Antwerp/'s-Gravenhage 1937.

Gibson, Walter S., "'Imitatio Christi': The Passion scenes of Hieronymus Bosch", in: *Simiolus* 6, 1972/73, pp. 83–93.

Gibson 1973a: Gibson, Walter S., "The Garden of Earthly Delights by Hieronymus Bosch: The iconography of the central panel", in: *Nederlands Kunsthistorisch Jaarboek* 24, 1973, pp. 1–26.

Gibson 1973b: Gibson, Walter S., "Hieronymus Bosch and the mirror of man: The authorship and iconography of the tabletop of the Seven Deadly Sins", in: *Oud Holland* 87, 1973, 4, pp. 205–226.

Gibson 1973c: Gibson, Walter S., *Hieronymus Bosch*, London 1973.

Gibson, Walter S., "Bosch's boy with a whirligig: Some iconographical speculations", in: *Simiolus* 8, 1975/76, pp. 9–15.

Gibson, Walter S., *Hieronymus Bosch: An annotated bibliography*, Boston 1983.

Gibson, Walter S., "Bosch's dreams: A response to the art of Bosch in the Sixteenth Century", in: *Art Bulletin* 74, 1992, pp. 205–218.

Gibson, Walter S., "The strawberries of Hieronymus Bosch", in: *Cleveland Studies in the History of Arts* 8, 2003, pp. 24–33.

Gibson, Walter S., "La Mesa de los pecados capitales: Muerte, juicio y eternidad", in: Bango Torviso 2006a, pp. 167–183.

Gibson, Walter S., "An infernal invention: Bosch's tree-man", in: *Invention: Northern Renaissance studies in honor of Molly Faries* (Me Fecit, 5), ed. Julien Chapuis, Turnhout 2008, pp. 162–173.

Gielis, M.A.M.E. [Marcel], "Jheronimus Bosch: De natuur van de mens en de hoofdzonden", in: *Noordbrabants Jaarboek* 20, 2003, pp. 93–117.

Glanemans, Ronald/Oudheusden, Jan van, *De Wereld van Bosch*, 's-Hertogenbosch 2001.

Glum, Peter, "Divine judgement in Bosch's 'Garden of Earthly Delights'", in: *Art Bulletin* 58, 1976, pp. 45–54.

Gombrich, Ernst H., "The earliest description of Bosch's 'Garden of Delight'", in: *Journal of the Warburg and Courtauld Institutes* 30, 1967, pp. 403–406.

Gombrich, Ernst H., "Bosch's 'Garden of Earthly Delights': A progress report", in: *Journal of the Warburg and Courtauld Institutes* 32, 1969, pp. 162–170.

Gorissen, Friedrich, *Das Stundenbuch der Katharina von Kleve: Analyse und Kommentar*, Berlin 1973.

Gossart, Maurice, *La Peinture de diableries à la fin du moyen-âge: Jérôme Bosch. Le "faizeur de Dyables" de Bois-le-Duc*, Lille 1907.

Graziani, René, "La planta del 'San Juan en el desierto' del Bosco", in: *Archivo español de arte* 56, 1983, pp. 379–382.

Gruber, Hans-Günter, *Christliches Eheverständnis im 15. Jahrhundert: Eine moralgeschichtliche Untersuchung zur Ehelehre Dionysius' des Kartäusers* (Studien zur Geschichte der katholischen Moraltheologie, 29), Regensburg 1989.

Guevara, Felipe de, *Comentarios de la Pintura. Con un discurso preliminar y algunas notas de Antonio Ponz,* Madrid: Gerónimo Ortega, hijos ele Ibarra y Compañía, 1788 [written *c.* 1560],

Guevara, Felipe de, *Comentarios de la Pintura, c.* 1560, printed Madrid 1788, reprinted in: Sánchez Cantón, 1923.

Halsema-Kubes, Willy, "Adriaen van Wesels Altar in 's-Hertogenbosch: Rekonstruktion und kunstgeschichtliche Bedeutung", in: *Flügelaltäre des späten Mittelalters*, ed. Hartmut Krohm and Eike Oellermann, Berlin 1992, pp. 144–155.

Halsema-Kubes, Willy/Lemmens, Gerard/Werd, *Guido de, Adriaen van Wesel (ca. 1417 – ca. 1490): Een Utrechtse beeldhouwer uit de late middeleeuwen*, Amsterdam 1980.

Hamburger, Jeffrey, "Bosch's conjuror: An attack on magic and sacramental heresy", in: *Simiolus* 14, 1984, pp. 4–23.

Hamm, Berndt, "Frömmigkeit als Gegenstand theologiegeschichtlicher Forschung: Methodisch-historische Überlegungen am Beispiel von Spätmittelalter und Reformation", in: *Zeitschrift für Theologie und Kirche* 74, 1977, pp. 464–497.

Hammer-Tugendhat, Daniela, *Hieronymus Bosch: Eine historische Interpretation seiner Gestaltungsprinzipien* (Theorie und Geschichte der Literatur und der schönen Künste, 58), Munich 1981.

Hammer-Tugendhat, Daniela, "Erotik und Inquisition", in: *Der Garten der Lüste: Zur Deutung des Erotischen und Sexuellen bei Künstlern und ihren Interpreten*, ed. Renate Berger and Daniela Hammer-Tugendhat, Cologne 1985, pp. 10–47.

Hammerstein, Reinhold, *Diabolus in Musica: Studien zur Ikonographie der Musik des Mittelalters*, Bern/Munich/Frankfurt am Main 1974.

Hand, John Oliver, *National Gallery of Art: Master Paintings from the Collection*, Washington DC/New York 2004.

Hansen, Monika, *Der Aufbau der mittelalterlichen Predigt unter besonderer Berücksichtigung der Mystiker Eckhart und Tauler*, Hamburg 1972.

Harms, Wolfgang (ed.), *Text und Bild, Bild und Text*, Deutsche Forschungsgemeinschaft symposium 1988 (Germanistische Symposien Berichtsbände, 11), Stuttgart 1990.

Hartau 2001a: Hartau, Johannes, "Suche nach Glück bei nahem Untergang", in: *Frankfurter Allgemeine Zeitung* 182, 8.8.2001, p. 6.

Hartau 2001b: Hartau, Johannes, "Zur Allegorie des Müßiggangs: Bildquellen für das Motiv des Narrenschiffs bei Sebastian Brant und Hieronymus Bosch", in: *Liber Amicorum Raphael de Smedt*, vol. 2: *Artium historia*, ed. Joost van der Auwera, Leuven 2001, pp. 63–84.

Hartau, Johannes, "A newly established triptych by Hieronymus Bosch", in: Verougstraete/Schoute 2003, pp. 33–38.

Hartau, Johannes, "Das neue Triptychon von Hieronymus Bosch als Allegorie über den 'unnützen Reichtum'", in: *Zeitschrift für Kunstgeschichte* 68, 2005, pp. 305–338.

Hartlaub, Gustav Friedrich, "Hieronymus Bosch: Wege und Abwege seiner Deutung", in: *Das Münster* 10, 1957, pp. 374–377.

Heene, Katrien, "Aan de vruchten kent men de boom: De boom in tekst in beeld in de middeleeuwse Nederlanden", in: Baert/Fraeters 2001, pp. 97–119.

Heidenreich, Helmut, "Hieronymus Bosch in some literary contexts", in: *Journal of the Warburg and Courtauld Institutes* 33, 1970, pp. 171–199.

Heijting, W., "De boeken uit het klooster van de Wilhelmiten te 's-Hertogenbosch", in: *Hellinga Festschrift, feestbundel, mélanges: Forty-three studies in bibliography presented to Prof. Dr. Wytze Hellinga*, ed. Ton Croiset van Uchelen, Amsterdam 1980, pp. 289–301.

Herp, Hendrik, *Spieghel der volcomenheit*, opnieuw uitgegeven door L. Verschueren (Tekstuitgaven van Ons Geestelijk Erf), 2 vols., Antwerp 1931.

's-Hertogenbosch 1967: *Jheronimus Bosch: Bijdragen bij gelegenheid van de herdenkingstentoonstelling te 's-Hertogenbosch*, exhibition catalogue, 's-Hertogenbosch, Noordbrabants Museum, 's-Hertogenbosch 1967.

's-Hertogenbosch 1990: *In Buscoducis 1450–1629: Kunst uit de Bourgondische tijd te 's-Hertogenbosch, de cultuur van late middeleeuwen en renaissance*, exhibition catalogue, 's-Hertogenbosch, Noordbrabants Museum, 2 vols., ed. Adrianus Maria Koldeweij, Maarssen/The Hague/'s-Hertogenbosch 1990.

Heuvel, Nicolaas H. L. van den, *De ambachtsgilden van 's-Hertogenbosch vóór 1629: Rechtsbronnen van het bedrijfsleven en het gildewezen*, Utrecht 1946.

Hezenmans, J[oannes] C[ornelius] A[ntonius], *De St. Jans-kerk te 's-Hertogenbosch en hare Geschiedenis*, 's-Hertogenbosch 1866.

Higgs Strickland, Debra, "Picturing Antichrist and others in the Prado Epiphany by Hieronymus Bosch", in: *Others and Outcasts in Early Modern Europe: Picturing the social margins*, ed. Tom Nichols, Aldershot 2007, pp. 11–35.

Hildebrandt, Hans-Hagen, "Rabelais' Destruktionsarbeit am Mechanismus der Repräsentation des Mittelalters", in: *Höfische Repräsentation: Das Zeremoniell und die Zeichen*, ed. Hedda Ragotzky and Horst Wenzel, Tübingen 1990, pp. 333–350.

Hoffman, Ed, "Raadsels rond werk Jheronimus Bosch: Het altaar van de Lieve Vrouwebroederschap", in: *Bossche Bladen* 1, 2008, pp. 26–31.

Höfler, Constantin R. von, "Kritische Untersuchungen über die Quellen der Geschichte Philipps des Schönen, Erzherzogs von Österreich, Herzogs von Burgund, Königs von Castilien", in: *Sitzungsberichte der Philosophisch-Historischen Classe der Kaiserlichen Akademie der Wissenschaften* 104, 3, 1883, pp. 433–510.

Holten, Ragnar von, "Hieronymus Bosch und die Vision des Tondalus", in: *Konsthistoriek Tidskrift* 28, 1959, pp. 99–109.

Hombergh, Frederik A. H. van den, "Ein unbekannter Brief des Jan Brugman", in: *Archivum Franciscanum Historicum* 64, 1971, pp. 337–366.

Homolka, Anita, *Die Tischzuchten von Sebastian Brant, Thomas Murner und Hans Sachs und ihr realer Hintergrund in Basel, Strassburg und Nürnberg*, Munich 1983.

Horace: Quintus Horatius Flaccus, *Epistula ad Pisonem: De Arte Poetica [Ars Poetica]*, Latin and German, ed., trans. and with afterword by Eckart Schäfer, Stuttgart 1994.

Huys Janssen, Paul, "Jeroen Bosch en de familie Scheyfve: Portretten geïdentificeerd", in: *Bossche Bladen* 4, 2005, pp. 131–133.

Huys Janssen, Paul, "Hieronymus Bosch: Facts and records concerning his life and works of art", in: *Wallraf-Richartz-Jahrbuch* 68, 2007, pp. 239–254.

Ilsink, Matthijs, *Bosch en Bruegel als Bosch: Kunst over kunst bij Pieter Bruegel (c. 1528–1569) en Jheronimus Bosch (c. 1450–1516)* (Nijmeegse Kunsthistorische Studies, 17), Edam 2009.

Ilsink, Matthijs, "On three drawings by Jheronimus Bosch: The Field has Eyes and the Wood has Ears, The Treeman, The Owls' Nest", in: Bruyn/Koldeweij 2010, pp. 173–188.

Jacobs, Lynn F., "The triptychs of Hieronymus Bosch", in: *Sixteenth Century Journal* 31, 2000, pp. 1009–1041.

Jacobus de Voragine, *The Golden Legend. Readings on the Saints*, 2 vols., trans. and ed. by William Granger Ryan, Princeton 1993.

Jan van Leeuwen, *Een bloemlezing uit zijn werken*, ed. Stephanus Axters, Antwerp 1943.

Janssen, Hans/Goubitz, Olaf/Kottman, Jaap, "Everyday objects in the paintings of Hieronymus Bosch", in: Koldeweij/Vermet/Kooij 2001, pp. 171–192.

Jerome: Eusebius Hieronymus, "Letter to Eustochium", in: Schaff, Philip/Wace, Henry (eds.), *Nicene and Post-Nicene Fathers*, 2nd series, vol. 6, trans. from the Latin by W. H. Fremantle, G. Lewis and W. G. Martley, Buffalo 1893.

Jung, Vera, *Körperlust und Disziplin: Studien zur Fest- und Tanzkultur im 16. und 17.*

Jahrhundert, Cologne/Weimar/ Vienna 2001.

Justi, Carl, "Die Werke des Hieronymus Bosch in Spanien", in: *Jahrbuch der königlichen Preuszischen Kunstsammlungen* 10, 1889, pp. 121–144.

Kanz, Roland, *Die Kunst des Capriccio: Kreativer Eigensinn in Renaissance und Barock*, Munich 2002.

Kappelhof, Antonius Cornelis Marie, *Het archief van de Tafel van de H. Geest van 's-Hertogenbosch*, 's-Hertogenbosch 1980.

Kappler, Claude, *Monstres, démons et merveilles à la fin du moyen age*, Paris 1980.

Karlowska-Kamzowa, Alicja, "Painted and graphic decorations of prayer-books and the works of Hieronymus Bosch", in: *Polish Art Studies* 13, 1992, pp. 17–29.

Kayser, Wolfgang, *Das Groteske in Malerei und Dichtung*, Reinbek bei Hamburg 1960 [*Das Groteske: Seine Gestaltung in Malerei und Dichtung, Oldenburg 1957*].

Kessler, Erwin, *Ymago Sophystica: Around the Marriage at Cana by Hieronymus Bosch, some furniture, vessels and guests*, Maastricht 2001.

Ketelsen, Thomas (ed.), *Die Erfindung der Landschaft um 1500: Einem Zeitgenossen von Hieronymus Bosch auf der Spur* (Der ungewisse Blick, 9), Cologne 2013.

Ketelsen, Thomas/Neidhardt, Uta (eds.), *Das Geheimnis des Jan van Eyck: Die frühen niederländischen Zeichnungen und Gemälde in Dresden*, Berlin/ Munich 2005.

Kibedi Varga, Aron, "Visuelle Argumentation und visuelle Narrativität", in: Harms 1990, pp. 356–367.

King, David A., "The Cult of St. Wilgefortis in Flanders, Holland, England and France", in: *Am Kreuz – eine Frau: Anfänge – Abhängigkeiten – Aktualisierungen*, ed. Sigrid Glockzin-Bever and Martin Kraatz, Münster 2003, pp. 55–97.

Klein, Peter, "Dendrochronological analysis of works by Hieronymus Bosch and his followers", in: Koldeweij/Vermet/Kooij 2001, pp. 121–131.

Klemm, Elisabeth, "Zwischen Didaktik, Moral und Satire: Beobachtungen zu Tieren und Monstren in der Buchmalerei", in: *Wiener Jahrbuch für Kunstgeschichte* 46/47, 1993/94, pp. 287–301.

Koch, Robert A. M., "Schongauer's Dragon Tree", in: *Print Review* 5, 1976, pp. 114–119.

Koch, Thomas, "Lektüre und Meditation der Laienbrüder in der Devotio Moderna", in: *Ons Geestelijk Erf* 76, 2002, pp. 15–63.

Koerner, Joseph Leo, "Wirklichkeit bei Hieronymus Bosch", in: *Realität und Projektion: Realistische Darstellungen in Antike und Mittelalter*, ed. Martin Büchsel and Peter Schmidt, Berlin 2005, pp. 227–238.

Koldeweij, A[drianus] M[aria] [Jos], *De 'Keisnijding' van Hieronymus Bosch*, Zutphen 1991.

Koldeweij, Adrianus Maria [Jos], "Was Jeroen Bosch wat jaren vóór Erasmus leerling van de Latijnse School te 's-Hertogenbosch?", in: *Scolae de Buscho 1274–1999: Fragmenten uit de historie van de Latijnse School van 's-Hertogenbosch ter gelegenheid van het 725-jarig bestaan*, ed. Kees van den Oord, Vlijmen 1999, pp. 3–12.

Koldeweij, Jos [Adrianus Maria], "Jheronimus Bosch in zijn stad 's-Hertogenbosch", in: Koldeweij/Vermet/Vandenbroeck 2001, pp. 20–83.

Koldeweij, Jos [Adrianus Maria], "Jheronimus Bosch", in: *De schilderkunst der Lage Landen*, Part 1: *De Middeleeuwen en de zestiende eeuw*, ed. Jos Koldeweij, Alexandra Hermesdorf and Paul Huvenne, Amsterdam 2006, pp. 129–147.

Koldeweij, Jos [Adrianus Maria], "A man like Bosch...", in: Bruyn/Koldeweij 2010, pp. 16–33.

Koldeweij, Jos [Adrianus Maria]/ Vermet, Bernard/Kooij, Barbera van, *Hieronymus Bosch: New insights into his life and work*, Rotterdam 2001.

Koldeweij, Jos [Adrianus Maria]/ Vermet, Bernard/Vandenbroeck, Paul, *Jheronimus Bosch: Alle schilderijen en tekeningen*, Ghent/Amsterdam 2001 [Eng. edn.: *Hieronymus Bosch. The Complete Paintings and Drawings*, New York 2001].

Könneker, Barbara, *Satire im 16. Jahrhundert: Epoche, Werke, Wirkung*, Munich 1991.

Koreny, Fritz, "Hieronymus Bosch – Überlegungen zu Stil und Chronologie: Prolegomena zu einer Sichtung des Œuvres", in: *Jahrbuch des Kunsthistorischen Museums Wien* 4/5, 2002/03, pp. 46–75.

Koreny, Fritz, *Hieronymus Bosch: Die Zeichnungen, Werkstatt und Nachfolge bis zum Ende des 16. Jahrhunderts*, Turnhout 2012.

Koreny, Fritz/Pokorny, Erwin, *Hieronymus Bosch: Die Zeich-*

nungen in Brussels und Vienna (Delineavit et Sculpsit: Tijdschrift voor Nederlandse prent- en tekenkunst tot omstreeks 1850, 24), Leiden 2001.

Kotková, Olga (ed.), *Hieronymus Bosch – Následovník* Dvanáctiletý Ježíš *v* chrámu: *obraz po zrestaurování/Hieronymus Bosch , follower Christ among the Doctors: the painting after restoration*, Prague 1996.

Krause, Katharina, "'Sehet, welch ein Mensch!': Geschichte oder geistliche Auslegung des Lebens Jesu in der deutschen Malerei und Graphik um 1500", in: *Zeitschrift für Kunstgeschichte* 64, 2001, pp. 475–500.

Kröll, Katrin, "Die Komik des grotesken Körpers in der christlichen Bildkunst des Mittelalters (Einführung)", in: Kröll/Steger 1994, pp. 11–93.

Kröll, Katrin/Steger, Hugo (eds.), *Mein ganzer Körper ist Gesicht: Groteske Darstellungen in der europäischen Kunst und Literatur des Mittelalters*, Freiburg im Breisgau 1994.

Kruse, Britta-Juliane, "Neufunde zur Überlieferung der 'Predigt vom ehelichen Leben'/'Sermo de Matrimonio' im Zusammenhang mit einer 'Predigt auf die Hochzeit zu Kana'", in: *Speculum Medii Aevi: Zeitschrift für Geschichte und Literatur des Mittelalters* 1, 1995, pp. 37–62 [text edition: pp. 45–62].

Kuijer, P. T. J., *'s-Hertogenbosch: Stad in het hertogdom Brabant ca. 1185–1629*, Zwolle/'s-Hertogenbosch 2000.

Kulli, Rolf Max, *Die Ständesatire in den deutschen geistlichen Schauspielen des ausgehenden Mittelalters*, Bern 1966.

Kursawe, Barbara, *Docere – delectare – movere: Die officia oratoris bei Augustinus in Rhetorik und Gnadenlehre* (Studien zur Geschichte und Kultur des Altertums: series 1, Monographien, 15), Paderborn 2000.

Kurz, Otto, "Four tapestries after Hieronymus Bosch", in: *Journal of the Warburg and Courtauld Institutes* 30, 1967, pp. 150–162.

Laemers, Suzanne, "Hieronymus Bosch and the tradition of the Early Netherlandish triptych", in: Koldeweij/Vermet/Kooij 2001, pp. 77–85.

Lammertse, Friso (ed.), *Van Eyck to Bruegel, 1400–1550: Dutch and Flemish painting in the collection of the Museum Boymans-van Beuningen*, Rotterdam 1994.

Lammertse, Friso/Roorda Boersma, Annetje, "Jheronimus Bosch. The Pedlar: Reconstruction, restoration and painting technique", in: Verougstraete/Schoute 2003, pp. 102–118.

Lampsonius, Dominicus, *Pictorium aliquot celebrium Germaniae inferioris effigies*, Antwerp: Hieronymus Cock/Volcxken Diercx 1572.

Landau, Blandine, "Sins of the flesh and human folly: A study of The Ship of Fools by Jheronimus Bosch", in: Bruyn/Koldeweij 2010, pp. 210–229.

Lane, Barbara, "Bosch's tabletop of the Seven Deadly Sins and the Cordiale quattuor novissimorum", in: *Tribute to Lotte Brand Philip: Art historian and detective*, New York 1985, pp. 88–94.

Le Chanu, Patrick/Mottin, Bruno, "L'Escamoteur du Musée Municipal de Saint-Germain-en-Laye", in: Verougstraete/Schoute 2003, pp. 119–129.

Lentes, Thomas, "Der göttliche Blick: Hieronymus Boschs Todsündentafel – eine Einübung ins Sehen", in: *Sehen und Sakralität in der Vormoderne* (KultBild, 4), ed. David Ganz and Thomas Lentes, Berlin 2011, pp. 20–34.

Liano, Ignacio Gómez de, "La variedad del mundo o el tríptico de la Creación", in: Bango Torviso 2006a, pp. 185–216.

Limentani Virdis, Caterina, "The crucified female Saint in Venice", in: de Bruyn/Koldeweij 2010, pp. 232–242.

Lisbon 1972: *Tentações de Santo Antão: Jheronimus Bosch, exposição, documentação do tratamento, exame da pintura*, exhibition catalogue, Lisbon, Museu Nacional de Arte Antiga, Lisbon 1972.

Lisbon 1994: *Les Tentations de Bosch ou l'éternel retour (As tentaçoes de Bosch ou o eterno retorno),* exhibition catalogue, Lisbon, Museu Nacional de Arte Antiga, Milan 1994.

London 2000: *The Image of Christ*, exhibition catalogue, London, National Gallery, ed. Gabriele Finaldi, London 2000.

Lütke Notarp, Gerlinde, *Von Heiterkeit, Zorn, Schwermut und Lethargie: Studien zur Ikonographie der vier Temperamente in der niederländischen Serien- und Genregraphik des 16. und 17. Jahrhunderts* (Niederlande-Studien, 19), Münster 1998, pp. 47–70.

Macropedius, Georgius, *Georgius Macropedius' Asotus: Een neolatijns drama over de verloren zoon door Joris van Lanckvelt ['s-Hertogenbosch 1537]*, ed. [and trans. into Dutch] by Henricus

P. M. Puttiger, Nieuwkoop 1988 (doctoral thesis Nijmegen 1988).

Madrid 2000: *El jardín de las delicias de El Bosco: Copias, estudio técnico y restauracion*, exhibition catalogue, Madrid, Museo Nacional del Prado, with essays by Pilar Silva Maroto et al., Madrid 2000.

Mandabach, Marisa, "Holy shit: Bosch's bluebird and the junction of the scatological and the eschatological in Late Medieval Art", in: *Marginalia*, Oct. 2010, pp. 28–49.

Mander, Karel van, *Schilder-Boeck*, Haarlem 1604 [original text in van Dijck 2001a, pp. 115f.; Eng. trans. in Snyder 1973, pp. 42f.].

Marías, Fernando, "Bosch and Dracontius' De creatione mundi Hexameron", in: de Bruyn/Koldeweij 2010, pp. 246–263.

Marijnissen, Roger H., *Das Problem Hieronymus Bosch*, Geneva 1972.

Marijnissen, Roger H., *Laat-middeleeuwse symboliek en de beeldentaal van Hiëronymus Bosch* (Mededelingen van de Koninklijke Academie voor Wetenschappen, Letteren en Schone Kunsten van België, Klasse der Schone Kunsten, 39, 1), Brussels 1977.

Marijnissen, Roger H., *Hieronymus Bosch: The Complete Works*, with the assistance of Peter Ruyffelaere, Antwerp 1987 [Dutch edn: *Hiëronymus Bosch: Het volledig oeuvre*, Antwerp 1987].

Marrow, James H., "Circumdederunt me canes multi: Christ's tormentors in Northern European Art of the Late Middle Ages and Early Renaissance", in: *Art Bulletin* 59, 1977, pp. 167–181.

Marrow, James H., *Passion Iconography in Northern European Art of the Late Middle Ages and the Early Renaissance* (Ars Neerlandica, 1), Kortrijk 1979.

Martin, Hervé, *Le Métier du prédicateur en France septentrionale à la fin du Moyen Age (1350–1520)*, Paris 1988.

Massing, Jean-Michel, "Sicut erat in diebus Antonii: The devils under the bridge in the 'Tribulations of St Anthony' by Hieronymus Bosch in Lisbon", in: *Sight and Insight: Essays on art and culture in honour of E. H. Gombrich*, London 1994, pp. 108–127.

Mateo Gómez, Isabel, "El conejo cazador del 'Jardín de las Delicias' del Bosco y una miniatura del siglo XIV", in: *Archivo español de arte* 178, 1972, pp. 166–167.

Mateo Gómez, Isabel, "Apostillas iconográficas al Bosco y Rodrigo Alemán", in: *Boletín del Museo del Prado* 6, 1985, 18, pp. 129–133.

Mateo Gómez, Isabel, "Analyse du triptyque", in: *Jérôme Bosch: Le Jardin des Délices*, ed. Maurice Guillaud, Paris 1988, pp. 255–289.

Matilla Tascon, Antonio, "Felipe II adquiere pinturas del Bosco y Patinir", in: *Goya* 203, 1987/88, pp. 258–261.

McAlister, Neil H., "The cure of folly", in: *Canadian Medical Association Journal*, 22.6.1974/110, pp. 1382–1383.

McGrath, Robert L., "Satan and Bosch: The 'Visio Tundali' and the monastic vices", in: *Gazette des Beaux-Arts* 71, 1968, pp. 45–50.

McNamee, Maurice B., *Vested Angels: Eucharistic Allusions in Early Netherlandish Paintings*, Leuven 1988.

Mechelen 2003: *De zotte schilders: Moraalridders van het penseel rond Bosch, Bruegel en Brouwer*, exhibition catalogue, Mechelen, Centrum voor Oude Kunst, ed. Eric de Bruyn and Jan Op de Beeck, Ghent 2003.

Meier, Christel, "Malerei des Unsichtbaren: Über den Zusammenhang von Erkenntnistheorie und Bildstruktur im Mittelalter", in: Harms 1990, pp. 35–65.

Meier, Christel, "Ut rebus apta sint verba: Überlegungen zu einer Poetik des Wunderbaren im Mittelalter", in: *Das Wunderbare in der mittelalterlichen Literatur*, ed. Dietrich Schmidtke (Göppinger Arbeiten zur Germanistik, 606) Göppingen 1994, pp. 37–83.

Meijer, Gerardus Augustinus, *De Predikheeren te 's-Hertogenbosch 1296–1770*, Nijmegen 1897.

Menzel, Michael, "Predigt und Predigtorganisation im Mittelalter", in: *Historisches Jahrbuch* 111, 1991, pp. 337–384.

Mertens, Thom (ed.), *Boeken voor de eeuwigheid: Middelnederlands geestelijk proza* (Nederlands literatuur en cultuur in de middeleeuwen, 8), Amsterdam 1993.

Mesquita e Carmo, Ana Maria/Antunes de Sousa, Pedro, "Le Triptyque de la tentation de Saint Antoine de Jheronimus Bosch: La photographie et la réflectographie infrarouges dans la détection du dessin sous-jacent", in: Verougstraete/Schoute 2003, pp. 9–15.

Metzger, Catherine A., "Death

and the Miser: Alterations and implications", in: Verougstraete/Schoute 2003, pp. 39–44.

Michaelis, Rainer, "Studien zum Berliner Weltgerichtsaltar des Lucas Cranach", in: *Aachener Kunstblätter* 58, 1989/90, pp. 115–132.

Michiel, Marcantonio, *Der Anonimo Morelliano (Marcanton Michiel's Notizia d'opere del disegno)*, transl. by Theodor von Frimmel, 2 vols., Vienna 1888/89 [reprint Hildesheim 1974].

Migne, Jacques Paul (ed.), "Vitae patrum", in: *Patrologia Latina* 73, 1849, col. 132.

Miller, Henry, *Big Sur and the Oranges of Hieronymus Bosch*, New York 1957.

Molius-Chronik: *Kroniek van Molius: Een zestiende-eeuwse Bossche priester over de geschiedenis van zijn stad [von ca.1555]*, ed. [and annot.] by J. A. M. Hoekx, 's-Hertogenbosch 2004.

Morales, Ambrosio de, *Las obras del maestro Fernán Pérez de Oliva*, Cordoba 1586.

Morganstern, Anne MacGee, "The pawns in Bosch's 'Death and the Miser'", in: *Studies in the History of Art*, National Gallery of Art Washington 12, 1982, pp. 33–41.

Morganstern, Anne MacGee, "The rest of Bosch's 'Ship of Fools'", in: *Art Bulletin* 66, 1984, pp. 295–302.

Moser, Dietz-Rüdiger, "'Cave, cave, Dominus videt': Die Madrider Tischplatte des Hieronymus Bosch. Versuch einer Interpretation", in: *Durch aubenteuer muess man wagen vil: Festschrift Anton Schwob*, ed. Wernfried von Hofmeister and Bernd Steinbauer, Innsbruck 1997, pp. 299–322.

Mosmans, Jan, *Jheronimus Anthonis-zoon van Aken alias Hieronymus Bosch: Zijn leven en zijn werk*, 's-Hertogenbosch 1947.

Moxey, Keith, "Hieronymus Bosch and the 'World Upside Down': The case of The Garden of Earthly Delights", in: *Visual Culture: Images and interpretations*, ed. Norman Bryson, Michael A. Holly and Keith Moxey, Hanover (New Hampshire) 1994, pp. 104–140.

Nauwelaerts, Marcel A. M., *Latijnse school en onderwijs te 's-Hertogenbosch tot 1629* (Bijdragen tot de geschiedenis van het zuiden van Nederland, 30), Tilburg 1974.

Neuner, Antje Maria, *Das Triptychon in der frühen altniederländischen Malerei: Bildsprache und Aussagekraft einer Kompositionsform*, Frankfurt am Main 1995.

Onghena, M. J., *De iconografie van Philips de Schone* (Académie Royale de Belgique, Classe des beaux-arts, 10, fasc. 5), Brussels 1959.

Oord, Cornelis Johannes Antonius van den, *Twee eeuwen Bosch' boekbedrijf 1450–1650* (Bijdragen tot de Geschiedenis van het Zuiden van Nederland, 62), Tilburg 1984.

Oostrom, Frits P. van, *Het woord van eer: literatuur aan het Hollandse hof omstreks 1400*, Amsterdam 1987.

Oostrom, Frits P. van/Willaert, Frank (eds.), *De studie van de Middelnederlandse letterkunde: Stand en toekomst*, symposium, Antwerp, 22.–24.9.1988 (Middeleeuwse studies en bronnen, 14), Hilversum 1989.

Os Chronicle: *Kroniek van Peter van Os. Geschiedenis van 's Hertogenbosch en Brabant van Adam tot 1523* (Rijks Geschiedkundige Publicatiën, small series, 87), ed. A. M. van Lith-Droogleever Fortuijn, J. G. M. Sanders and G. A. M. van Synghel, The Hague 1997.

Panofsky, Erwin, *Early Netherlandish Painting*, Cambridge (Massachusetts) 1953.

Pauvert, Dominique, "Le vin dans l'œuvre de Jérôme Bosch et Pieter Bruegel l'Ancien", in: *Le Vin dans les œuvres*, colloque pluridisciplinaire de Libourne-Montagne Saint-Emilion, 17.–19.5.2001, ed. Amancio Tenaguillo y Cortázar, Talence 2004, pp. 125–141.

Peacock, Martha Moffitt, "Hieronymus Bosch's Venetian St Jerome", in: *Konsthistorisk tidskrift* 64, 1995, 2, pp. 71–85.

Pearsall, Derek/Salter, Elizabeth, *Landscapes and Seasons of the Medieval World*, London 1973.

Peeters, Cornelius J. A. C., *De Sint Janskathedraal te 's-Hertogenbosch* (De Nederlandse Monumenten van Geschiedenis en Kunst), 's-Gravenhage 1985.

Pinson, Yona, "Fall of the Angels and Creation in Bosch's Eden: Meaning and iconographical sources", in: *Flanders in a European Perspective: Manuscript illumination around 1400 in Flanders and abroad*, ed. Bert Cardon and Maurita Smeyers, Leuven 1995, pp. 693–707.

Pinson, Yona, "Folly and vanity in Bruegel's Dulle Griet: Proverbial metaphors and their relationship to Bosch's imagery", in: *Studies in Iconography* 20, 1999, pp. 185–213.

Pinson, Yona, "Hieronymus Bosch: Marginal imagery shifted into the center and the notion of upside down", in: *The Metamorphosis of Marginal Images: From Antiquity to the Present Time, ed.* Nurith Kenaan – Kedar Asher Ovadiah, Tel Aviv 2001, pp. 203–212.

Pinson, Yona, "Hieronymus Bosch – 'Homo viator' at a crossroads: A new reading of the Rotterdam tondo", in: *Artibus et historiae* 26, 2005, 52, pp. 57–84.

Pinson, Yona, "A moralized semi-secular triptych by Jheronimus Bosch", in: Bruyn/Koldeweij 2010, pp. 265–277.

Pita Andrade, José Manuel, "Pinturas y pintores de Isabel la Católica", in: *Isabel la Católica y el Arte*, ed. Gonzalo Anes Alvarez, Madrid 2006, pp. 13–71.

Plafond, Paul, Hieronymus Bosch*: Son art, son influence, ses disciples*, Brussels 1914.

Pleij, Herman, *Het gilde van de Blauwe Schuit: Literatur, volksfeest en burgermoraal in de late middeleeuwen*, 2nd expanded edn. Amsterdam 1983 (doctoral thesis Amsterdam 1979).

Pleij, Herman, *De sneeuwpoppen van 1511: Stadscultuur in de late middeleeuwen*, Amsterdam 1988.

Pleij, Herman, "Lekenethiek en burgermoraal" [review of Reynaert, J. (ed.), *Wat is wijsheid? Lekenethiek in de Middelnederlandse letterkunde*, Amsterdam 1994], in: *Queeste* 2, 1995, 2, pp. 170–180.

Pleij, Herman, *Der Traum vom Schlaraffenland*, Frankfurt am Main 2000.

Pleij, Herman, *Colors Demonic and Divine: Shades of meaning in the Middle Ages and after*, New York 2004.

Pokorny, Erwin, "Bosch's cripples and drawings by his imitators", in: *Master Drawings* 41, 2003, 3, pp. 293–304.

Pokorny, Erwin, "Hieronymus Bosch hält sich bedeckt: Zu Forschungsstand und rezenter Literatur", in: *Kunstchronik* 2007, 3, pp. 129–133.

Pokorny, Erwin, *Hexen und Magier in der Kunst des Hieronymus Bosch* (Lexikon zur Geschichte der Hexenverfolgung, ed. Gudrun Gersmann, Katrin Moeller and Jürgen-Michael Schmidt), 2009, online: historicum.net. URL: http://www.historicum.net/no_cache/persistent/artikel/6751/4.4.2013.

Pokorny 2010a: Pokorny, Erwin, "Hieronymus Bosch und das Paradies der Wollust", in: *Frühneuzeit-Info* 21, 2010, 1/2 (special issue "Die Sieben Todsünden in der Frühen Neuzeit"), pp. 22–34.

Pokorny 2010b: Pokorny, Erwin, "Die sogenannte Tischplatte mit den Sieben Todsünden und den vier letzten Dingen", in: *Frühneuzeit-Info* 21, 2010, 1/2 (special issue "Die Sieben Todsünden in der Frühen Neuzeit"), pp. 35–43.

Pokorny 2010c: Pokorny, Erwin, "Bosch and the influence of Flemish book illumination", in: de Bruyn/Koldeweij 2010, pp. 281–292.

Prevenier, Walter/Blockmans, Wim, *The Burgundian Netherlands*, Cambridge 1986.

Randall, Lilian M. C., "Exempla in Gothic Marginal Illumination", in: *Art Bulletin* 39, 1957, pp. 97–107.

Randall, Lilian M. C., *Images in the Margins of Gothic Manuscripts*, Berkeley/Los Angeles 1966

Raupp, Hans-Joachim, *Bauernsatiren: Entstehung und Entwicklung des bäuerlichen Genres in der deutschen und niederländischen Kunst ca. 1470–1570*, Niederzier 1986.

Reglement van de Illustre Lieve Vrouwe Broederschap te 's-Hertogenbosch, 's-Hertogenbosch: Laurens Hayen 1518, 32 pp., edn. of 2000 "briefkens", copy owned by the Antwerp Ruusbroec-Genootschap [Oord 1984, p. 81, no. 38].

Reißer, Ulrich, *Physiognomik und Ausdruckstheorie der Renaissance: Der Einfluss charakterologischer Lehren auf Kunst und Kunsttheorie des 15. und 16. Jahrhunderts*, Munich 1997.

Renger, Konrad, "Versuch einer neuen Deutung von Hieronymus Boschs Rotterdamer Tondo", in: *Oud Holland* 84, 1969, pp. 67–76.

Renson, Marianne, "Genealogical information concerning the Bronchorst-Bosschuysen triptych", in: Koldeweij/Vermet/Kooij 2001, pp. 93–95.

Reutersward, Patrick, *Hieronymus Bosch*, Uppsala 1970.

Reynaert, Jos (ed.), *Wat is wijsheid? Lekenethiek in de Middelnederlandse letterkunde* (Nederlandse literatuur en cultuur in de middeleeuwen, 9). Amsterdam 1994.

Richter, Konrad, *Der deutsche S. Christoph: Eine historisch-kritische Untersuchung* (Acta Germanica, 5, 1) Berlin 1896.

Ringbom, Sixten, *Icon to Narrative: The rise of the dramatic close-up in fifteenth-century devotional painting*, Åbo 1965.

Rivière, J., "Réévaluation du mécénat de Philippe le Beau et de Marguerite d'Autriche en matière de peinture", in: *Publications du Centre européen d'études bourguignonnes* 25, 1985, pp. 103–117.

Roggen, Domien, "J. Bosch: Literatuur en folklore", in: *Gentsche Bijdragen tot de Kunstgeschiedenis* 6, 1939/40, pp. 107–126.

Röhrich, Lutz, *Lexikon der sprichwörtlichen Redensarten*, 2 vols., Freiburg im Breisgau 1973.

Rome 1996: *Vedere i classici: L'illustrazione libraria dei testi antichi dall'età romana al tardo medioevo*, exhibition catalogue, Rome, Musei Vaticani, ed. Marcus Buonocore, Rome 1996.

Rooth, Anna Birgitta, *Exploring the Garden of Delights: Essays in Bosch's paintings and the medieval mental culture*, Helsinki 1992.

Rosenberg, Jakob, "On the meaning of a Bosch drawing", in: *De artibus opuscula 40: Essays in Honor of Erwin Panofsky*, ed. Millard Meiss, New York 1961, pp. 422–426.

Ruppel, Wendy, "Salvation through imitation: The meaning of Bosch's St Jerome in the Wilderness", in: *Simiolus* 18, 1988, 1/2, pp. 4–12.

Salazar, Abdon M., "El Bosco y Ambrosio de Morales", in: *Archivo español de arte* 28, 1955, 110, pp. 117–138.

Sánchez Cantón, Francisco Javier, *Fuentes literarias para la historia del arte español* I, Madrid 1923

Sánchez Cantón, Francisco Javier, *Libros, tapices y cuadros que coleccionó Isabel la Católica*, Madrid 1950.

Sander, Jochen, *Niederländische Gemälde im Städel 1400–1550*, Mainz 1993.

Schade, Herbert, "Der 'Traum Adams' – Das 'Grosse Geheimnis' (Ephes. 5:32) von Liebe und Tod und die Erkenntnis des Guten und Bösen in der mittelalterlichen Kunst", in: *Die Mächte des Guten und Bösen: Vorstellungen im XII. und XIII. Jh. über ihr Wirken in der Heilsgeschichte* (Miscellanea mediaevalia), ed. Albert Zimmermann, Berlin/New York 1977, pp. 453–488.

Schade, Karl, *Ad Excitandum devotionis affectum: Kleine Triptychen in der altniederländischen Malerei*, Weimar 2001.

Scher, Stephen K., "Hieronymus Bosch: An exercise in attribution", in: *Bulletin of the Rhode Island School of Design* 53, 1967, pp. 1–25.

Schiewer, Hans-Jochen, "German sermons in the Middle Ages", in: *The Sermon* (Typologie des sources du moyen âge occidental, 81–83), ed. Beverly Mayne Kienzle, Turnhout 2000, pp. 861–961.

Schlie, Heike, *Sakramentaler Realismus von Jan van Eyck bis Hieronymus Bosch*, Berlin 2002.

Schmidt, Leopold, "Das Stachelhalsband des Hirtenhundes", in: *Deutsches Jahrbuch für Volkskunde* 6, 1960, pp. 154–181.

Schnürer, Gustav/Ritz, Joseph M., *Sankt Kümmernis und Volto Santo*, Düsseldorf 1934.

Schönbach, Anton E., "Sanct Christophorus", in: *Zeitschrift für deutsches Altertum und deutsche Literatur* 17, new series 5, 1874, pp. 85–141.

Schoute, Roger van/Garrido, Maria del Carmen/Cabrera, José Maria, "Le Dessin sous-jacent chez Jérôme Bosch: L'Adoration des Mages du Musée du Prado à Madrid", in: *Le Dessin sous-jacent dans la peinture*, colloque V, 29.9.–1.10.1983, ed. Roger van Schoute and Dominique Hollanders-Favart, Louvain-la-Neuve 1985, pp. 211–215.

Schoute, Roger van/Verboomen, Monique, *Jérôme Bosch*, Tournai 2000.

Schoute, Roger van/Verougstraete, Hélène/Garrido, Maria del Carmen, "Bosch and his sphere: Technique", in: Koldeweij/Vermet/Kooij 2001, pp. 102–119.

Schreiner, Klaus, "Laienfrömmigkeit: Frömmigkeit von Eliten oder Frömmigkeit des Volkes? Zur sozialen Verfassheit laikaler Frömmigkeitspraxis im späten Mittelalter", in: *Laienfrömmigkeit im späten Mittelalter: Formen, Funktionen, politisch-soziale Zusammenhänge* (Schriften des Historischen Kollegs, 20), ed. Klaus Schreiner, Munich 1992, pp. 1–78.

Schuder, Rosemarie, *Hieronymus Bosch: Das Zeitalter – das Werk*, Berlin 1998.

Schüssler, Gisbert, "Das göttliche Sonnenauge über den Sünden: Zur Deutung der 'mesa de los pecados mortales' des Hieronymus Bosch", in: *Münchner Jahrbuch der bildenden Kunst* 44, 1993, pp. 119–150.

Schuttelaars, Antonius H., *Heren van de Raad: Bestuurlijke elite van 's-Hertogenbosch in de*

stedelijke samenleving, 1500–1580, Nijmegen 1998.
Schwartz, Gary, *Hieronymus Bosch*, New York 1997.
Schwartz, Heinrich, "The mirror of the artist and the mirror of the devout", in: *Studies in the History of Art Dedicated to William E. Suida on His Eightieth Birthday*, London 1959, pp. 90–105.
Schweizer-Vüllers, Regine, *Die Heilige am Kreuz: Studien zum weiblichen Gottesbild im späten Mittelalter und in der Barockzeit*, Bern 1997.
Scott-Robinson, Richard A., *A Vision of Tundale* (a modern rendering of the 15th-century Middle English transcription by Richard Heeg), 2008; online http://www.eleusinianm.co.uk/blueWellow/bof6tundale.html (last visited 15 May 2013).
Sedlmayr, Hans, "Die 'macchia' Bruegels", in: *Jahrbuch der kunsthistorischen Sammlungen in Vienna* 8, 1934, pp. 137–160.
Sherwood-Smith, Maria, *Repertorium van Middelnederlandse preken in handschriften tot en met 1550/Repertorium of Middle Dutch Sermons Preserved in Manuscripts from before 1550* (Miscellanea neerlandica, 29), Leuven 2003.
Sigüenza, José de, *Tercera parte de la Historia de la Orden de San Geronimo Doctor de la Iglesia, Madrid 1605, ²1909, cited from: Sánchez Cantón,* 1923, pp. 425ff. [extract of the original text in van Dijck 2001a, pp. 116ff.; extract in English trans. in Snyder 1973, pp. 34–41].
Silva Maroto, Pilar, "Bosch in Spain: On the works recorded in the Royal Inventories", in: Koldeweij/Vermet/Kooij 2001, pp. 41–46.
Silver, Larry, "God in the details: Bosch and judgement(s)", in: *Art Bulletin* 83, 2001, pp. 626–650.
Silver, Larry, *Hieronymus Bosch*, New York 2006.
Simonson, Anne, "On spiritual creativity in Hieronymus Bosch", in: *Fifteenth-century Studies* 18, 1991, pp. 221–258.
Slenczka, Ruth, *Lehrhafte Bildtafeln in spätmittelalterlichen Kirchen* (Pictura et Poesis, 10), Cologne/Weimar/Vienna 1998.
Snyder, James, *Bosch in Perspective*, Englewood Cliffs (New Jersey) 1973.
Spronk, Ron, *Eigenhandig? (All by himself?): Opmerkingen bij de schildertechniek en toeschrijvingsproblematiek bij Jheronimus Bosch/Remarks on Painting Techniques and Attributions in Regard to Hieronymus Bosch*, Nijmegen 2011.
Spychalska-Boczkowska, Anna, "Material for the iconography of Hieronymus Bosch's triptych The Garden of Delights", in: *Studia Muzealne/Muzeum Narodowe w Poznaniu* 5, 1966, pp. 49–86 [see also Boczkowska, Anna].
Stahl, Ernst Konrad, *Die Legende vom heiligen Riesen Christophorus in der Graphik des 15. und 16. Jahrhunderts: Ein entwicklungsgeschichtlicher Versuch*, Munich 1920.
Stark, Brigitte, *Das Groteske in der altfranzösischen geistlichen Literatur mit einem Überblick über das Groteske in den weltlichen Literaturgattungen*, Hamburg 1977.
Stechow, Wolfgang, "Hieronymus Bosch: The grotesque and we", in: *The Grotesque in Art and Literature: Theological reflections*, ed. James Luther Adams and Wilson Yates, Grand Rapids (Michigan) 1997, pp. 113–124.
Steemers, H.W., *Hieronymus Bosch: Een interpretatie van zijn laatste oordeel's triptiek te Wenen aan de hand van middelnederlandse literaire bronnen*, Nijmegen 1979.
Stein-Schneider, Herbert, "Le Charlatan de Hieronymus Bosch du Musée Municipal de Saint-Germain-en-Laye: Une étude iconographique", in: *Gazette des beaux-arts* 106, 1985, 6, pp. 47–51.
Steppe, Jan Karel, "Jheronimus Bosch: Bijdrage tot de historische en ikonographische studie van zijn werk", in: 's-Hertogenbosch 1967, pp. 5–41.
Sterk, Jozef, *Philips van Bourgondie (1465–1524) bisschop van Utrecht als protagonist van de Renaissance: Zijn leven en maecenaat*, Zutphen 1980.
Stroo, Cyriel/Syfer-d'Olne, Pascale, "Hieronymus Bosch: Crucifixion with a Donor and Saint Peter", in: Cyriel Stroo/Pascale Syfer-d'Olne/Anne Dubois, *The Flemish Primitives*, vol. 3: *The Hieronymus Bosch, Albrecht Bouts, Gerard David, Colijn de Coter, Goossen van der Weyden Groups* (Catalogue of Early Netherlandish Painting: Royal Museums of Fine Arts of Belgium, 3), Turnhout 2001, pp. 71–83.
Stuip, René E.V./Vellekoop, Cornelis (eds.), *Scholing in de middeleeuwen*, Hilversum 1995.
Suckale, Robert, "Süddeutsche szenische Tafelbilder um 1420–1450: Erzählung im Span-

nungsfeld zwischen Kult- und Andachtsbild", in: Harms 1990, pp. 15–34.
Suckale, Robert, *Rogier van der Weyden: Die Johannestafel, das Bild als stumme Predigt*, Frankfurt am Main 1995.
Suckale, Robert, *Stil und Funktion: Ausgewählte Schriften zur Kunst des Mittelalters*, ed. Peter Schmidt and Gregor Wedekind, Berlin 2008.
Sullivan, Margaret A., "Bosch, Bruegel, Everyman and the Northern Renaissance", in: *Oud Holland* 121, 2008, 2/3, pp. 117–146.
Sund, Horst (ed.), *Fas(t)nacht in Geschichte, Kunst und Literatur*, Konstanz 1984.
Tacke, Andreas/Irsigler, Franz (eds.), *Der Künstler in der Gesellschaft: Einführungen zur Künstlersozialgeschichte des Mittelalters und der Frühen Neuzeit*, Darmstadt 2011.
Taylor, Larissa J., *Soldiers of Christ: Preaching in late medieval and early modern France*, Oxford 1992.
The Hague 1998: *Boeken van Oranje-Nassau: De bibliotheek van de graven van Nassau en prinsen van Oranje in de vijftiende en zestiende eeuw*, exhibition catalogue, The Hague, Museum Mermanno-Westreenianum, ed. Anne S. Korteweg, The Hague 1998.
Tholen, Sybille, *Moraltheologische und moralpädagogische Allegorien (Pierter Aertsen und Joachim Beuckelaer) mit einem vorläufigen Œuvre-Verzeichnis*, Cologne 1987.
Thürlemann, Felix, *Vom Bild zum Raum: Beiträge zu einer semiotischen Kunstwissenschaft*, Cologne 1990.
Tolnay, Charles de, *Hieronymus Bosch*, 2. expanded edn. Baden-Baden 1965 ([1]1937).
Trnek, Renate, *Das Weltgerichtstriptychon von Hieronymus Bosch*, Vienna 1988.
Troeyer, Benjamin de, *Bio-bibliographia Franciscana Neerlandica saeculi XVI*, 3 vols., Nieuwkoop 1969/70, 1974.
Tuttle, Virginia G., "Bosch's image of poverty", in: *Art Bulletin* 63, 1981, pp. 88–95.
Uhrig, Sandra, *Die Versuchung des Heiligen Antonius: Eine Vision des ausgehenden Mittelalters*, Munich 1998 (doctoral thesis Munich 1998).
Unverfehrt, Gerd, *Hieronymus Bosch: Studien zu seiner Rezeption im 16. Jahrhundert*, Berlin 1980 (doctoral thesis Göttingen 1974).
Unverfehrt, Gerd, *Wein statt Wasser: Essen und Trinken bei Jheronimus Bosch*, Göttingen 2003.
Urbach, Zsuzsa/Garrido Perez, Maria del Carmen, "The copy of the Garden of Delights in Budapest revisited", in: Verougstraete/Schoute 2003, pp. 64–74.
Vandenbroeck, Paul, "Over Jheronimus Bosch: Met een toelichting bij de tekst op tekening KdZ 549 in het Berlijnse Kupferstichkabinett", in: *Archivum Artis Lovaniense: Bijdragen tot de geschiedenis van de kunst der Nederlanden*, opgedragen aan Prof Em. Dr. L. K. Steppe, ed. Maurits Smeyers, Leuven 1981, pp. 151–190.
Vandenbroeck, Paul, "Problèmes concernant l'œuvre de Jheronimus Bosch: Le dessin sous-jacent en relation avec l'authenticité et la chronologie", in: *Le Dessin sous-jacent dans la peinture*, colloque IV, 29.–31.10.1981, ed. Roger van Schoute and Dominique Hollanders-Favart, Louvain-la-Neuve 1982, pp. 107–120.
Vandenbroeck, Paul, "Bubo Significans: Die Eule als Sinnbild von Schlechtigkeit und Torheit, vor allem in der niederländischen und deutschen Bilddarstellung und bei Jheronimus Bosch", in: *Jaarboek Koninklijk Museum voor Schone Kunsten Antwerpen* 1985, pp. 19–135.
Vandenbroeck 1986a: Vandenbroeck, Paul, "'Kommen die Adepten wieder?': Über Bosch, Alchimie und esoterische Kunstwissenschaften", in: *Kunstchronik* 39, Nov. 1986, pp. 477–481.
Vandenbroeck 1986b: Vandenbroeck, Paul, "Über neuere Bosch-Literatur", in: *Kritische Berichte* 14, 1986, 2, pp. 36–47.
Vandenbroeck 1987a: Vandenbroeck, Paul, *Jheronimus Bosch: Tussen stadscultuur en volksleven*, Berchem 1987.
Vandenbroeck 1987b: Vandenbroeck, Paul, "Herkunft und Verwurzelung der 'Grillen': Vom Volksmythos zum kunst- und literaturtheoretischen Begriff, 15.–17. Jahrhundert", in: *De zeventiende eeuw* 3-1, 1987, pp. 52–84.
Vandenbroeck, Paul, "Jheronimus Bosch' zogenaamde Tuin der Lusten I.", in: *Jaarboek Koninklijk Museum voor Schone Kunsten Antwerpen* 1989, pp. 9–201.
Vandenbroeck, Paul, "Jheronimus Bosch' zogenaamde Tuin der Lusten II.: De Graal of het Valse Liefdespradijs", in: *Jaarboek Koninklijk Museum voor*

Schone Kunsten Antwerpen 1990, pp. 9–193.

Vandenbroeck 2001a: Vandenbroeck, Paul, "The Spanish *inventarios reales* and Hieronymus Bosch", in: Koldeweij/Vermet/Kooij 2001, pp. 49–63.

Vandenbroeck 2001b: Vandenbroeck, Paul, "High stakes in Brussels, 1567: The Garden of Earthly Delights as the crux of the conflict between William the Silent and the Duke of Alva", in: Koldeweij/Vermet/Kooij 2001, pp. 86–95.

Vandenbroeck, Paul, *De verlossing van de wereld*, Ghent/Amsterdam 2003.

Vandenbroeck 2006a: Vandenbroeck, Paul, "En compañía de extraños comensales: Idea del hombre, códigos de conducta y alteridad en los tapices de Felipe el Hermoso", in: Zalama/Vandenbroeck 2006, pp. 117–142.

Vandenbroeck 2006b: Vandenbroeck, Paul, "La belleza y/desde la locura: Una vinculación existencial y estética hacia 1500", in: Zalama/Vandenbroeck 2006, pp. 213–240.

Vandenbroeck, Paul, "Meaningful caprices: Folk culture, middle-class ideology (*c.* 1480–1510) and aristocratic recuperation (*c.* 1530–1570): A series of Brussels tapestries after Hieronymus Bosch," in: *Jaarboek Koninklijk Museum voor Schone Kunsten* 2009, pp. 212–269.

Vavra, Elisabeth, "Hieronymus Bosch: Teufelsbildner oder Maler der Fiktion", in: *Künstler, Dichter, Gelehrte* (Mittelaltermythen, 4), ed. Ulrich Müller, Konstanz 2005, pp. 97–114.

Vázquez Dueñas, Elena, "Felipe de Guevara: Algunas aportaciones biográficas/Felipe de Guevara: Some biographical contributions", in: *Anales de Historia del Arte* 18, 2000, pp. 95–110.

Vellekoop, Kees, "Music and dance in the paintings of Hieronymus Bosch", in: Koldeweij/Vermet/Kooij 2001, pp. 199–205.

Venice 1992: *Le delizie dell'inferno: Dipinti di Jheronimus Bosch e altri fiamminghi restaurati*, exhibition catalogue, Venice, Palazzo Ducale, ed. Caterina Limentani Virdis, Venice 1992.

Venice 2010: *Bosch a Palazzo Grimani*, exhibition catalogue, Venice, Palazzo Grimani, ed. Vittorio Sgarbi, Milan 2010.

Vermet, Bernard, "Jheronimus Bosch: Schilder, atelier of stijl?", in: Koldeweij/Vermet/Vandenbroeck 2001, pp. 84–99.

Verougstraete, Hélène/Schoute, Roger van (eds.), *Jérôme Bosch et son entourage et autres études: Le dessin sous-jacent et la technologie dans la peinture*, colloque XIV, 13.–15.9.2001, Leuven 2003.

Verschueren, Leonard Herman Hubert, "De bibliotheek der Kartuize S. Sophia te Vught", in: *Historisch Tijdschrift* 14, 1935, pp. 372–402 and 15, 1936, pp. 9–58.

Vieira Santos, Armando, "Subsidios para um estudo sobre o triptico 'Tentações de Santo Antao' do Museu de Lisboa", in: *Boletim do Museu Nacional de Arte Antiga* III, 1958, 4, pp. 19–24.

Vink 2001a: Vink, Ester, *Jeroen Bosch in Den Bosch*, Nijmegen 2001.

Vink 2001b: Vink, Ester, "Hieronymus Bosch's life in 's-Hertogenbosch", in: Koldeweij/Vermet/Kooij 2001, pp. 17–23.

Vinken, Pierre/Schlüter, Lucy, "The foreground of Bosch's Death and the Miser", in: *Oud Holland* 114, 2000, 2/4, pp. 69–78.

Vos, Dirk de, *Catalogus schilderijen 15de en 16de eeuw*, Bruges 1979.

Waadenoijen, Jeanne van, "The Lisbon Triptych by Jeroen Bosch: An annotation", in: Verougstraete/Schoute 2003, pp. 16–21.

Wachinger, Burghart, "Passion Christi und die Literatur: Beobachtungen an den Rändern der Passionsliteratur", in: *Kleinere Erzählformen des 15. und 16. Jahrhunderts* (Fortuna vitrea, 8), ed. Walter Haug and Burghart Wachinger, Tübingen 1993, pp. 1–20.

Walsh, Martin W., "Martín y muchos pobres: The grotesque image of the 'Charity of St. Martin' in the Bosch and Breughel schools", in: *Essays in Medieval studies* 14, 1997, pp. 107–120.

Warncke, Carsten-Peter, *Sprechende Bilder – sichtbare Worte: Das Bildverständnis in der frühen Neuzeit* (Wolfenbütteler Forschungen, 33), Wiesbaden 1987.

Wattel, B. D. Arvi, "Stichterportretten bij Jheronimus Bosch", in: *Desipientia* 8, 2001, 2, Sept., pp. 10–17.

Weiler, Antonius G., Volgens de norm van de vroege kerk: De geschiedenis van de huizen van de broeders van het gemene leven in Nederland (Middeleeuwse studies, 13), Nijmegen 1997.

Welzel 1997a: Welzel, Barbara, "Anmerkungen zu Kunstproduktion und Kunsthandel", in: Franke/Welzel 1997, pp. 141–157.

Welzel 1997b: Welzel, Barbara, "Niederländische Kupferstiche des 15. Jahrhunderts", in: Franke/Welzel 1997, pp. 211–227.

Welzel, Barbara, "Sichtbare Herrschaft: Paradigmen höfischer Kunst", in: *Principes: Dynastien und Höfe im späten Mittelalter*, ed. Karl-Heinz Spiess, Cordula Nolte and Gunnar Werlich, Stuttgart 2002, pp. 87–106.

Wenzel, Horst, *Hören und Sehen, Schrift und Bild: Kultur und Gedächtnis im Mittelalter*, Munich 1995.

Wenzel, Horst/Lechtermann, Christina, *Beweglichkeit der Bilder: Text und Imagination in den illustrierten Handschriften des "Welschen Gastes" von Thomas von Zerclaere*, Cologne/Weimar/Vienna 2002.

Wertheim-Aymès, Clément A., *Hieronymus Bosch: Eine Einführung in seine geheime Symbolik, dargestellt am "Garten der himmlischen Freuden"*, Amsterdam 1957.

Wezel, G. W. C. van, *Het palais van Hendrik III graaf van Nassau te Breda* (De Nederlandse Monumenten van Geschiedenis en Kunst), Zwolle 1999.

Wiebel, Christiane, *Askese und Endlichkeitsdemut in der italienischen Renaissance: Ikonologische Studien zum Bild des heiligen Hieronymus*, Weinheim 1988.

Wiesflecker, Hermann, *Kaiser Maximilian I.: Das Reich, Österreich und Europa an der Wende zur Neuzeit*, vol. 3: *Auf der Höhe des Lebens 1500–1508*, vol. 5: *Der Kaiser und seine Umwelt: Hof, Staat, Wirtschaft, Gesellschaft und Kultur*, Munich 1977 and 1986.

Will, Chris, *Jeroen Bosch: Tussen Hemel & Hel*, Amsterdam 2001.

Willemsen, Annemarieke, "Playing with reality: Games and toys in the oeuvre of Hieronymus Bosch", in: Koldeweij/Vermet/Kooij 2001, pp. 193–199.

Williams, Ulla, *Die "Alemannischen Vitaspatrum": Untersuchungen und Edition* (Texte und Textgeschichte, 45), Tübingen 1996.

Williams, Ulla/Kunze, Konrad/Kaiser, Philipp, "Information und innere Formung: Zur Rezeption der 'Vitaspatrum'", in: *Wissensorganisierende und wissensvermittelnde Literatur im Mittelalter: Perspektiven ihrer Erforschung*, colloquium, 5.–7.12.1985, ed. Norbert Richard Wolf, Wiesbaden 1987, pp. 123–142.

Win, Paul de, "Engelbert (Engelbrecht) II, Graaf van Nassau-Dillenburg en Vianden, Heer van Breda", in: *Handelingen van de Koninklijke Kring voor Oudheidkunde, Letteren en Kunst van Mechelen* 95, 1991, pp. 85–115.

Wirth, Jean, "Le Jardin des Délices de Jérôme Bosch", in: *Bibliothèque d'Humanisme et Renaissance* 50, 1988, pp. 545–585.

Wirth, Jean, *Hieronymus Bosch. Garten der Lüste: Das Paradies als Utopie*, Frankfurt am Main 2000.

Wisby, Roy A., "Die Darstellung des Hässlichen im Hoch- und Spätmittelalter", in: *Deutsche Literatur des späten Mittelalters* (Hamburger Kolloquium 1973) ed. Wolfgang Harms and L. Peter Johnson, Berlin 1975, pp. 9–34 (simult. in Publications of the Institute of Germanic Studies, University of London, 22).

Wittrock, Irma, "Die sogenannten Sintflutflügel des Hieronymus Bosch: Ein Versuch zur Interpretation der drei ersten Medaillons der Aussenflügel", in: *Oud Holland* 93, 1979, pp. 52–60.

Wuhrmann, Sylvie, "Une étude en gris: Le triptyque du Déluge de Jérôme Bosch", in: *Artibus et historiae* 38, 1998, pp. 61–136.

Wuyts, Leo, "Beschouwingen bij een Doornenkroning toegeschreven aan Bosch", in: *Jaarboek Koninklijk Museum voor Schone Kunsten Antwerpen*, 1968, pp. 35–66.

Yarza Luaces, Joaquín, *El Jardín de las Delicias de El Bosco*, Madrid 1998.

Yarza Luaces, Joaquín, "La Adoración de los Magos, Museo del Prado", in: Bango Torviso 2006a, pp. 359–374.

Zalama Rodríguez, Miguel Angel/Vandenbroeck, Paul, *Felipe I el Hermoso: La belleza y la locura*, Madrid 2006.

Index

A
Aesop
– Fables 437
Aken, Anthonis Goessens van 334, 409
Aken, Antonius van 22, 23, 24, 478
Aken, Goessen van 22, 23, 27, 409
Aken, Hubert van 22
Aken, Jan Anthonis van 408
Aken, Jan Goessens van 260
Aken, Johannes Thomaszoon van 22, 27
[Aken], Katelijn (Katharina) van 409
Aken, Katharina van 20
Aken, Thomas van 22, 23
Aken: van Aken workshop (Johannes Thomaszoon or Goessen)
– Crucifixion with Donors 23, 27, *27*
Alba, Fernando Álvarez de Toledo Alba, 3rd Duke of Alba 370
Albert I, Duke of Bavaria 180
Anonymous artist
– Elemental Chaos (*c.* 1420, from: Aurora Consurgens, watercolour on parchment) *46*
– Siebenlasterweib (*c.* 1414, from: Metten Biblia pauperum, pen and ink on parchment) *46*
Anonymous artist after Hieronymus Bosch
– *The Haywain 294*
Anonymous artist at the convent of St Bridget at Koudewater, near 's-Hertogenbosch
– St Barbara (*c.* 1480, from: The Life of St Barbara, parchment) *93*
Antiphilos of Naucratis 385
Antonello da Messina 346
Aragon, Louis d' 143
Aristides of Thebes 385
Aristotle 153
Athanasius of Alexandria 99
Augustine 147
– City of God 179, 295
Aurora Consurgens
– Elemental Chaos (*c.* 1420, watercolour on parchment; anonymous artist) *46*

B
Back, Jan 288, 348, 481
Baldung Grien, Hans
– Aschaffenburg Virgin with a Dagger 387
Barbari, Jacopo de' 276
Barendsz, Dirck
– Sicut autem erat in diebus Noe (engraving by Jan Sadeler the Elder after Dirck Barendsz) *154*, 156
Bartholomeus Anglicus
– Liber de proprietatibus rerum 153
Beatis, Antonio de 143, 144, 145, 155, 175, 259, 370, 480
Bella, Gabriel 383
Benoît, Camille 394
Beys, Lodewijk 260
Boccaccio, Giovanni
– Decamerone 180
Bomberghen, Daniel van (Daniel Bomberg) 260

Bosch, Hieronymus Paintings (with associated copies)
Adoration of the Magi with Donors 63–79, *65–70*, *74/75*, 259, 267, 350, 354, 355, 355–357, 414, 415, 417, 419, 458, 486
– Outer wings: Mass of St Gregory with Scenes from the Passion and Donor's Family *65*, 229, 354, *354*, 355–357, 360
– Left inner wing: St Peter with Male Donor 30, *66*, 80, *355*, 355–357, 412, 419
– Central panel: Adoration of the Magi 30, 32, *66/67*, *68/69*, *74/75*, 159, 170, 225, *355*, 355–357, 434
– Right inner wing: St Agnes with Female Donor 30, *67*, *70*, 83, *355*, 355–357
Allegory of Intemperance *see* Wedding at Cana with Exempla
Arrest of Christ *see* Temptation of St Anthony
Christ Carrying the Cross, Large (Madrid) *77*, 82, 94, *358*, 359–360, 361, 458, 486
Christ Carrying the Cross, Small (Vienna) 83, 85, *91*, 343, *360*, 360–363, 415
– Exterior: Christ Child with Walking Frame and Whirligig 83, *84*, *360*, 360–363, 457
Christ Carrying the Cross *see* Temptation of St Anthony
Christ Child with Walking Frame and Whirligig *see* Christ Carrying the Cross, Small (Vienna)
Christ Mocked (The Crowning with Thorns) 30, *59*, 60–62, 295, 427, 458
Creation of the World up to

the Third Day *see* Garden of Earthly Delights
Crucified Female Martyr, triptych (Sint-Ontcommer) 30, 32, 99, 259, 260, 264, 267–270, 297, *300*, *310/311*, 352, 276, *380*, 381–383, 389, 418, 487
Crucifixion with Saints and Donor *21*, 22, 26, 32, 60, *344*, 344, 412, 420, 439, 458, 486
Death and the Miser *see* Wedding at Cana with Exempla
Ecce Homo with Donors (Frankfurt am Main) 32, *49–54*, 56, 80, 343, *351*, 351–353, 412, 419, 458
Eye of God with Scenes from the Passion *see* St John on Patmos
Extracting the Stone of Folly 28, 83, 275, 288, 259, 294, *315*, *397*, 397–399, 458, 482
Fragments of a representation of The Flood 30, 156, 259, 293–295, *316/317*, *398*, *399*, 399–401, 407, 433
– Outer wings: four tondi showing the Temptation and Deliverance of Job 293, *316*, *398*, 399–401, 438
– Left inner wing: The World before the Flood 293, *317*, *399*, 399–401
– Right inner wing: The Animals leaving Noah's Ark 293, *317*, *399*, 399–401
The Garden of Earthly Delights 28, 30, 32, 48, 86, 122, 140–221, *141*, *149*, *150*, *157*, *158*, *165*, *166*, *171*, *172*, *176/177*, *181*, *182*, *184–197*, *199–202*, *204*, *207–211*, *213/214*, *217/218*, *221*, 249, 259, 281, 283, 294, 334, *339*, 342, 356, *366*, *367*, 368–374, 378, 400, 405, 422, 433, 480, 481, 483–485, 486, 487
– Outer wings: Creation of the World up to the Third Day 30, 145, *182*, *185–187*, 351, *366*, 368–374
– Left inner wing: Paradise and the Creation of Eve 146, *184*, *188*, *339*, *367*, 368–374
– Central panel: Humankind before the Flood 41, 92, 155, *157*, *158*, *165*, *166*, *171*, *172*, *176/177*, *181*, *190–193*, *195–197*, *198*, *202*, *204*, *207*, 234, *367*, 368–374
– Right inner wing: Hell 28, 156, *189*, *208–211*, *213/214*, *217/218*, *221*, 274, 296, *367*, 368–374, 436, 457, 458, 459
The Garden of Earthly Delights (tapestry) 335, 371
The Haywain 28, 30, 83, 95, 294, 295–331, *319–323*, *325–328*, *330/331*, *333*, 334, 382, *400*, 400, *401*, 401–407, 417, 422, 483, 484, 488, 489
– Outer wings: The Pedlar 61, 228, 295, *303*, *319*, 393, *400*, 401–407
– Left inner wing: The Genesis of Evil and the Loss of Paradise 41, 147, 155, 248, *320*, *333*, 349, *401*, 401–407
– Central panel: The Haywain 32, 86, 155, 279, 292, *320/321*, *325*, *401*, 401–407, 457
– Right inner wing: Hell 296, *321*, *326–328*, *330/331*, *401*, 401–407, 458
The Haywain (copy) 248, *294*, 295
Haywain in the Terrestrial Globe (tapestry) 335, *336*
Hermit Saints triptych (with Sts Jerome, Anthony and Giles) 30, 99, 259, 260–267, *271–273*, *277*, *278*, *285*, *304/305*, 334, 365, *374*, 374–377, 382, 383, 389, 418, *428*
– Left inner wing: St Anthony 263, 270, *271*, *304*, *374*, 374–377
– Central panel: St Jerome 31, 32, 86, 163, 261, *277*, *278*, *285*, *304/305*, *374*, 374–377, 414, 457
– Right inner wing: St Giles 264, *305*, *374*, 374–377, 418
The Last Judgement 30, 55, 179, 222–255, *223*, *224*, *231*, *232*, *236/237*, *241*, *242*, *246/247*, *251*, *253–255*, 259, 281, 294, 343, *376*, *377*, 377–381, 400, 422, 481
– Left outer wing: St James 32, 86, 94, 228, 352, *253*, *376*, 377–381, 436
– Right outer wing: St Bavo 85, 229, *253*, 363, *376*, 377–381, 426, 468
– Left inner wing: Fall of the Rebel Angels, The Fall and The Expulsion from Paradise 30, 147, 155, *223*, *224*, 234, *254/255*, 276, 296, *377*, 377–381, 434
– Central panel: The Last Judgement 30, 155, 170, 231, *232*, *236/237*, *238*, *241*, *242*, *246/247*, *254/255*, 274, 276, 280, *377*, 377–381, 388, 459
– Right inner wing: Hell 12, 17, 30, *251*, *254/255*, 274, 276, *377*, 377–381
– Last Judgement (copy by Lucas Cranach the Elder after Hieronymus Bosch) *245*, 248, 250, 343
Mass of St Gregory with Scenes from the Passion and Donor's Family *see* Adoration of the Magi
Paradise and Hell 30, *257/258*, 259, *265/266*, 270–276, *312/313*, 376, 382, *386*, *387*, 388–389, 400, 482
– Left inner wing, left: Heavenly Paradise *257/258*, *312/313*, *386*, 388–389
– Left inner wing, right: Earthly Paradise *257/258*, *312/313*, *386*, 388–389
– Right inner wing, left: Fall of the Damned *265*, 270, *312/313*, *387*, 388–389
– Right inner wing, right: The

Damned in Hell *266*, 270, *387*, 388–389
The Pedlar *see* Haywain, Wedding at Cana with Exempla
The Seven Deadly Sins and the Four Last Things 30, 85, 93, 95, 110, 159, 170, 240, 243, 259, 276, 280, 283, 284, 294, *308/309*, 359, 363, *382*, 383–388, 457, 459, 483, 484, 487, 488
Ship of Fools *see* Wedding at Cana with Exempla
Sint-Ontcommer *see* Crucified Female Martyr
St Bavo *see* Last Judgement
St Christopher 28, 41, 76, *78*, 89, 112, 163, 228, *357*, 357–359, 398, 418, 420, 457
St James *see* Last Judgement
St Jerome in the Wilderness (in Penitence) *19*, *29*, 31, 32, 60, 71, 76, 86, 263, *345*, 345–347, 414, 418
St John on Patmos 31, *35*, 40, *45*, 43, 225, 335, 347–351, *350*, 418, 420, 434
– Exterior: The Eye of God with Scenes from the Passion *42*, *45*, 47, 79, 280, 347–351, *350*, 412, 418, 458
St John the Baptist (in Meditation) *25*, 31, *37*, 40, 347–351, *348*, 352, 418, 420
Temptation and Deliverance of Job *see* Fragments of a representation of The Flood
Temptation of St Anthony, triptych of the 28, 30, 96–139, 179, 259, 342, *362/363*, 363–368, 370, 414, 418, 458
– Left outer wing: The Arrest of Christ 30, 112, *117*, *362*, 363–368, 426, 458
– Right outer wing: Christ Carrying the Cross 30, 83, 85, 112, *117*, *362*, 362, 363–368, 458
– Left inner wing: St Anthony Accused by Devils 30, 32, 83, *97/98*, 100, *118–121*, *123–125*, 170, 296, *363*, 363–368
– Central panel: The Temptation of St Anthony 30, 41, *102/103*, *105*, *106*, 107, *113*, *118/119*, *126–128*, *131–134*, *136/137*, *139*, 230, 262, 263, 264, 270, 335, *363*, 363–368, 375
– Right inner wing: St Anthony in Meditation 30, *97/98*, 111, *118/119*, *136/137*, *139*, 159, 264, *363*, 363–368, 375, 382
The Wedding at Cana with Exempla ("The Cana Triptych") 28, 30, 281–288, *289/290*, *306/307*, 389–397, 402, 407
– Outer wings: The Pedlar 32, 61, 71, 76, 83, 86, 170, 228, 282, 295, 296, *303*, *392*, 392–393
– Left inner wing, above: The Ship of Fools 282, *289*, *306/307*, *393*, 393–394, 395
– Left inner wing, below: Allegory of Intemperance 282, 283, *306/307*, *394*, 394–395
– Central panel: The Wedding at Cana (copy, drawing, Paris) 282, 284, *287*, 287, 390, 395, 396
– Central panel: The Wedding at Cana (copy, painting, Rotterdam) 282, *306/307*, 284, 390, 395, 396
– Central panel: The Wedding at Cana (copy, painting, Huis Bergh) 284, *286*
– Right inner wing: Death and the Miser 30, 280, 282, 283, *290*, *307*, 394, *396*, 396–397, 419
– Right inner wing: Death and the Miser (copy, drawing, Paris) 394, 397

Paintings by the workshop and paintings attributed to Bosch

Adoration of the Magi (Anderlecht) 71, 267, 337, 410, 415, *416*, *417*, 416–418, 419, 423
Adoration of the Magi (New York) 337, 410, *418*, 419–420, 425
Adoration of the Magi, fragments of the inner wings of a triptych (Philadelphia) 337, 362, 410, *414*, 414–416, 417, 425
The Conjuror 288, 337, 410, 415, 420, *424*, 424–426, 457
Ecce Homo with Saints and Donors (Boston) 38, 80, 259, 267, 337, 345, 350, 351, 352, 356, 409, *410*, *411*, 410–412, 419, 458
The Last Judgement (Bruges) 334, 337, 382, 410, *420*, *421*, 421–423, 458, 459
Sts Job, Anthony and Jerome, triptych with 32, 63, 99, 259, 270, 293, 334, 337, 346, 365, 375, 410, *412*, *413*, 412–414, 415, 417, 418
The Temptation of St Anthony (Madrid) 337, 410, *422*, 423–424, 489

Paintings by Antwerp followers

Arrest of Christ 427
Christ Before Annas (São Paulo) 427
Christ Before Pilate (Princeton) 427
Christ Before Pilate (Rotterdam) 427
Christ Carrying the Cross (Ghent) 62, *425*, 426–427, 468

Drawings, autograph

The Battle of the Birds and the Mammals 437, *450/451*
Bird Monster and Snarling Dragon (Two Fantasy Creatures) 438, *452*
The Birds and the Mammals

Go to War (Gathering of the Birds) 436, 437, *448/449*
Fox and Cockerel 433, *441*
Nest of Owls 86, 89, 434, *442/443*
Rod with a Sphere and a Disc 434
Skull-Turtle Monster and Winged Gnome (Two Fantasy Creatures) 438, *453*
The Tree-Man *212*, *433*, 435, *447*
Two Beetle-like Monsters (Two Fantasy Creatures) 438, *454*
Two Cephalopods (Two Fantasy Creatures) 438, *455*
Two Witches 433, *440*
The Wood Has Ears, the Field Eyes 86, 89, 151, *431*, 435, *444*

Drawings by the workshop or followers
Company at Table 457, *465*
The Conjuror 425, 457, *464*
Drollery with Beehive 457, *460/461*
Drollery with Beehive and Crutches Monster 457, *462/463*
The Entombment 458, *466*
Figural studies (Cat. D3v) 89, 433, *445*
Five Fantasy Creatures; figural scene 459, *474*
Hell scene for a Last Judgement 458, *469*
Hell scenes, Tree-Man Monster 459, *470/471*
Seven Fantasy Creatures 459, *475*
Ship of Hell 458, *467*
Standing Rabbi 459, *472/473*
Study for Two Figures for a Passion scene (Shady-looking Pair in Conversation) 468, *476*
The Temptation of Eve 468, *477*

Bosch, Hieronymus (portrait) *23*
Boschini, Marco
– Le minere della pittura 383, 487
Botticelli, Sandro 180
– Episode from the Life of Nastagio degli Onesti *178*, 180
– Minerva and the Centaur 180
– Primavera *175*, 180
Boucicaut Master
– God Presents Eve to Adam (from: Des proprietez des choses) *163*
Bouts, Dirk
– Earthly Paradise 248, *261*, 274
Breton, André 18
Breviarium Grimani 260
Bronchorst, Wilhelmina 243
Bronckhorst en Batenburg, Herbrech van 356
Bronckhorst en Batenburg, Theodoricus van 356
Bruegel, Jan the Elder 356
Bruegel, Pieter the Elder 15, 83, 95, 335
– The Ass at School (drawing) 262, *275*
– Children's Games 301
– Netherlandish Proverbs *299*, 301
– Way to Calvary (Vienna) 83
Brugman, Jan 43
– Onuitgegeven Sermoenen 43
– Verspreide Sermoenen 104, 151

C
Caravaggio, Michelangelo Merisi da 425
Cebes of Thebes
– Tabula Cebetis (Pinax) 403
Charlemagne, Emperor 264
Charles V, Emperor 250, 302, 334, 379, 405, 409
Charles of Egmond, Duke of Guelders 226
Charles the Bold, Duke of Burgundy 36, 183, 226
Chiloeches, Marquis de 401
Cimburga of Baden 175
Cock, Hieronymus 422, 478
Cock, Jan Wellens de 358
Coffermans, Marcellus 335
Cologne Master *see* Master of the Holy Kinship (the Younger)
Concert in an Egg (drawing) 459
Cort, Cornelis
– Hieronymus Bosch (engraving, from: Dominicus Lampsonius, Pictorium aliquot celebrium Germaniae inferioris effigies) 20, *23*
Couderborch, Simon van 39
Coxie, Michiel 335
Cranach, Lucas the Elder 286, 387
– The Judgement of Paris 144, *147*
– Last Judgement (copy after Hieronymus Bosch) *245*, 248, 250, 343
– The Penitence of St Jerome 263, *269*
– Temptation of St Anthony (woodcut) 100, *110*
Crul, Cornelis
– Mot toe, borse toe 87, 88
Ctesideno *see* Ktesideno

D
Dalí, Salvador
– The Great Masturbator 152
Dante Alighieri
– Divine Comedy 173, 274
David, Gerard 55, 389
Delf, Dirc van 109, 148
– Tafel van den Kersten Ghelove 109, 156, 481
Demoulin, François 170
Denis the Carthusian 394
Driel, Katharina van 22
Driele, Jacob van 413
Du Hamel, Alart 358
– St Christopher *80*, 94
Dürer, Albrecht 13, 34, 145, 338, 478, 481, 484
– Christ among the Doctors 62, *63*
– Little Owl (watercolour) 86
– St Jerome in his Study (engraving) 346

E
Eleanor of Castile 335
Engelbert II, Count of Nassau

and Lord of Breda 26, 161, 175, 178, 179, 369
English artist
– Pedlar (*c.* 1325–1335, from: Luttrell Psalter, parchment) *302*
Erasmus of Rotterdam 170
– Enchiridion militis Christiani 93
Ernst [III] of Habsburg, Archduke of Austria 371
Eustochium 32, 261, 262
Eyb, Albrecht von
– Ob einem manne sey zu nehmen ein eeliches weib oder niet 180
Eyck, Jan van
– Madonna of Chancellor Rolin *56*, *60*, 379
– Portrait of Giovanni Arnolfini and his Wife (The Arnolfini Portrait) 153

F
Ferdinand II, King of Portugal 368
Fernando de Toledo, Don 370
The Field Has Eyes, the Wood Ears (Netherlandish woodcut, 1546) *72*, 87
Folengo, Teofilo
– Baldus 337
François I, King of France 170, 335
Frederick III, the Wise, Elector of Saxony 250
French artist
– The Hare as Hunter (1338–1344, from: Romance of Alexander the Great, parchment) *169*
Friedländer, Max Jakob 255

G
Geertgen tot Sint Jans
– St John the Baptist *39*, 43
Ghirlandaio, Domenico 346
Goethe, Johann Wolfgang von
– Faust I 111
Góis, Damião de (Damian de Goes) 367
Gossaert, Jan (Jan Mabuse) 275, 419
– Doria Pamphilj diptych 419
– Henry III of Nassau-Breda *144*
– Hercules and Deianira 144, *146*
Goya y Lucientes, Francisco José de 15
Grameye, Jacques 372
Gramme, Agnes de 63, 355
Grimani, Domenico 260, 270, 376, 383, 388, 389
Grimani, Marino 259, 376, 488
Grünewald, Matthias
– Temptation of St Anthony 107, *109*
Guevara, Diego de (before 1442–1520) 225, *227*, 259, 337, 364, 371
Guevara, Diego de (1537/38–1566) 403
Guevara, Felipe de 287, 384, 385, 398, 401, 403, 405, 406, 408, 413, 489
– Comentarios de la pintura 13, 276, 280, 384–386, 487

H
Hadrian VI, Pope 260
Haro, Beatriz de 398, 403, 405, 413, 488
Haro, Diego de 413
Haro, Jacob de 413
Heessel, Gerardus de 81
Heiligen Leben, Der 99
Henry III, Count of Nassau and Lord of Breda 26, 143, 144, *144*, 170, 175, 179, 226, 275, 276, 291, 356, 369, 370, 406
Herri met de Blees 260, 335, 376
Heyns, Jan 39, 55, 301, 482
Hieronymus, Eusebius Sophronius of Stridon 31, 261, 263, 267, 346
– Ad Eustochium de custodia virginitatis 32, 261, 262
Hildegaertsberge, Willem van 180
Holbein, Hans the Elder 379
Horace (Quintus Horatius Flaccus)
– Ars poetica 47, 143, 479
Hours of Sophia von Bylant
– Christ before Pilate (*c.* 1475, parchment; Netherlandish artist) *92*
Hutter, Blasius 372
Huys, Pieter 335

I/J/K
Isabella I, the Catholic, Queen of Castile 225, 364, 418
Jacobus de Voragine
– Golden Legend 90, 99
Jean de Meung
– Roman de la Rose, part 2 161, 179
Joanna I, the Mad, Queen of Castile 225, 233, *235*, 239, 250, 379
John III, King of Portugal 367
John of Aragon and Castile, Prince of Asturia 233
Ktesideno 385, 487

L
Lamberg-Sprinzenstein, Anton von 380
Lampsonius, Dominicus
– Pictorium aliquot celebrium Germaniae inferioris effigies 20, *23*, 478
Langhel, Hendrixke van 411
Langhel, Vranck van (Franco van Langel) 80, 81, 411
Lathem, Jacob van 227
Lathem, Lieven van the Elder 95, 227
Lathem, Lieven van the Younger 227
Lázaro Galdiano, José 350
Leempt, Gerardus 173
Leeuwen, Jan van
– Bloemlezing 76
Leonardo da Vinci
– Five Grotesque Heads (drawing) 62

– St Jerome 346
Leopold William of Austria, Archduke 380
Letter of Lentulus 60
Leyden, Lucas van
– Judith and Holofernes (engraving by Jan Pietersz Saenredam after Lucas van Leyden) *262*
The Life of St Barbara
– St Barbara (*c.* 1480, parchment; anonymous artist at the convent of St Bridget at Koudewater, near 's-Hertogenbosch) *93*
Limbourg, brothers 22
– Très Riches Heures de Duc de Berry 60
Lomazzo, Giovanni Paolo 332
Lochner, Stephan
– Last Judgement 239, 248, *248*
Lombart, Willem 32, 288
Longin, Simon 378, 481
Lorris, Guillaume de
– Roman de la Rose, part I 161, 179
Louise-Françoise, Duchess of Savoy 178, 180, 370
Lucas van Leyden *see* Leyden, Lucas van
Luttrell Psalter
– Pedlar (*c.* 1325–1335, parchment; English artist) *302*
Lutzenborch, Bernt von 179

M

Maelwael, Jan 22
Maerlant, Jacob van
– Spiegel Historiael 156
Maess, Jan 24
Mandijn, Jan 225
Marcus, Irish monk 173
Margaret of Austria 225, 233, 275, 276, 335, 380
Margaret of Cleves 180
Margaret of York 183, 226
Mary of Burgundy 36, 226
Marmion, Simon
– Last Judgement (from: Book of Hours) *238*
– The Torment of Unchaste Priests and Nuns (from: The Vision of Tundale for Margaret of York) *220*
Masscherel, Hendrik 179, 481
Massys, Quentin 420, 426
Master ES
– Consolation through Confidence (from: Ars moriendi) 280, 283, *291*
– The Holy Saviour: sanctus salffidor (engraving) *58*, 61
– Large Garden of Love with Chess-players (engraving) 159, *160*
Master of Frankfurt
– St Christopher 94
Master of Mary of Burgundy 95
Master of the Brunswick Diptych
– St Bavo *228*
Master of the Gardens of Love
– Small Garden of Love (engraving) 159
Master of the Holy Kinship (the Younger)
– Legend of St Anthony 65, *65*
Master of the Joseph Legend
– Last Judgement with Philip and Joanna as Donors (for Zierikzee Town Hall) 100, *101*
Master of the Magdalene Legend
– Philip I of Habsburg, called the Handsome *252*
Matham, Jacob
– The Consequences of Alcoholism (engraving) *219*
Maximilian I, Emperor 26, 36, 226, 260, 275, 364
Meckenem, Israhel van the Younger
– Christ and St John as children, jousting with windmills *87*, 362
– Christ Carrying the Cross (engraving) *76*, 82, 83
– Ecce Homo (engraving) *48*, 58
– Morris Dancers (engraving) *104*, 262
Memling, Hans 261
– Last Judgement 248, 274, 280, *281*, 286
– St Wilgefortis and Mary of Egypt 268
Mendoza, Mencia de 406
Mervenne, Aleid van der 25, 301, 478
Mervenne, Goyaert van der 25, 478
Metten Biblia pauperum
– Siebenlasterweib (*c.* 1414, pen and ink on parchment; anonymous artist) *46*, 47
Michelangelo Buonarroti 34
Michiel, Marcantonio 259, 270, 376, 383, 388, 482
Mierlo, Johannes Dicbier, Sir van 356
Miller, Henry 140
Moelen, Victor vander 81
Morales, Ambrosio de 402, 403, 488, 489
Murner, Thomas 337
Mynnen, Aleid van der 25

N

Netherlandish artist
– Christ before Pilate (*c.* 1475, from: Hours of Sophia von Bylant, parchment) *92*
– The Field Has Eyes, the Wood Ears (1546, woodcut) *72*, 87

O/P

Os, Peter van 80, 81, 350, 411, 412
Panofsky, Erwin 222
Patinir, Joachim 260, 335, 358, 376, 420
– St Catherine 383
Pérez de Oliva, Fernán 402, 489
Petrus Comestor
– Historia Scholastica 156
Philip II, King of Spain 114, 276, 342, 356, 360, 367, 370, 387, 399, 403, 406, 486, 488, 489

Philip III, the Good, Duke of Burgundy (1396–1467) 227, 291
Philip I, the Handsome, of Habsburg, Duke of Burgundy (1478–1506) 26, 170, 178, 179, 225, 226, 227, 230, 233, 239, 240, 249, 275, 276, 291, 364, 370, 379, 380, 418, 481
Philip of Burgundy (1464–1524) 275, 288, 291, 292, 398, 482
Physiologus 48, 86
Pijnappel, Johanna 413
Pizan, Christine de 161
Pontheniers, Gertrudis 409
Pseudo-Boethius
– De disciplina scholarium 89
Pucelle, Jean 59

R
Rabelais, François
– Gargantua and Pantagruel 337
Raphael (Raffaello Sanzio) 34
René of Châlon, Prince of Orange, Count of Nassau 370
Ricci, Giovanni 367
Rolin, Nicolas *56*, 60, 240, 379
Romance of Alexander the Great
– The Hare as Hunter (1338–1344, parchment; French artist) *169*
Roman de la Rose 161, 179
Roovere, Anthonis de 183
Rudolf II, Emperor 372
Rullen, Heilwig van der 411
Rullen, Wouter van der 81, 301, 480, 482
Ruysbroeck, John of 41, 76

S
Sadeler, Jan the Elder
– Sicut autem erat in diebus Noe (engraving after Dirc Barendsz) *154*
Saenredam, Jan Pietersz
– Judith and Holofernes (engraving after Lucas van Leyden) *262*
Salins, Guigone de 379
Sanders van Hemessen, Jan
– Extracting the Stone of Folly *314*
Schedel, Hartmann
– Chronicle of the World 146, 174
– The Fall and the Expulsion from Paradise (from: Chronicle of the World) *153*
– God the Father as Creator of the World (from: Chronicle of the World) *183*
Scheyve, Peeter 63, 350, 355
Schongauer, Martin
– St John on Patmos (engraving) *38*, 44
– Temptation of St Anthony (engraving) 100, *110*
Scorel, Jan van
– The Flood 166
Sforza, Maria Bianca 260
's-Greven, Johannes 81
Siciliano, Antonio 419
Sigüenza, José de
– History of the Order of St Jerome 13, 14, 34, 114, 115, 145, 259, 296, 301, 360, 365, 371, 387, 480, 483, 486
Sittow, Michiel
– Diego de Guevara *227*
St Martin (tapestry) 335
St Uncumber (wall painting, Rostock) 381

T
Temptation of St Anthony (tapestry) 335
Thomas à Kempis
– De Imitatione Christi 168
Thomas Aquinas 152
tom Ring, Ludger the Younger 387
Tour, Georges de la 425

V
Verbeeck, family 335
Vision of Tundale (Visio Tnugdali) 173, *220*, 371
Vitas patrum (Lives of the Desert Fathers, correctly speaking Vitae patrum, Netherlandish edn. "Vater boeck, Leven der heiligen vaderen", French edn. "Vie des anciens Saints Père Hermites") 99, 100, 104, 107–109, 111, 112, 365, 367
Vrelant, Willem van 95

W/Z
War Elephant (tapestry, print, painting) 335
Wesel, Adriaen van 478
– Altarpiece for Delft 24
– Altarpiece for the Brotherhood of Our Blessed Lady in 's-Hertogenbosch 24, 28, 302, 347
– The Deposition *24*
– St John the Evangelist on Patmos *38*
– The Tiburtine Sibyl showing Emperor Augustus a Vision 108
Weyden, Rogier van der 27
– Crucifixion (central panel of the Crucifixion altarpiece; Vienna) 27, *31*
– Last Judgement (Beaune) 240
– St Luke Drawing the Virgin 55, 60
– St Jerome 346
Wijck, Willem Jacobs van (Willem Jacobs van der Wyel) 22
William I, Prince of Orange-Nassau (William of Orange) 370
Wittenwiler, Heinrich
– Der Ring 235
Wylic, Adriana van 348
Zanetti, A. M.
– Descrizione di tutte le pubbliche pitture della città di Venezia 268, 377, 383

Photo credits

Abbreviations used in the credits: r. = right, l. = left, t. = top, t. l. = top left, t. r. = top right, b. = below, b. l. = below left, b. r. = below right, c. = centre, c. l. = centre left, c. r. = centre right.v

Agenzia Fotografica Scala, Antella, Florence. © 2016 Photo Scala, Florence: p. 422; Archives of the publisher, authors or collectors: p. 27; © ARTOTHEK – Blauel/Gnamm: p. 101; Ashmolean Museum, University of Oxford: p. 291; Bayerische Staatsbibliothek, Munich: p. 46 r.; © bpk, Berlin: p. 248; bpk | British Library Board / Robana: p. 302; bpk | Gemäldegalerie, SMB / Jörg P. Anders: pp. 39, 245, 299; bpk | Gemäldegalerie, SMB / Volker-H. Schneider: pp. 35, 42, 45, 350; bpk | Kupferstichkabinett, SMB / Jörg P. Anders: pp. 38 r., 72, 160, 275, 431, 444/45, 448/49, 450/51, 452–455, 474, 475; bpk | Kupferstichkabinett, SMB / Volker-H. Schneider: pp. 104, 110; bpk | The Metropolitan Museum of Art: pp. 147, 418; bpk | Scala: p. 281; bpk | Skulpturensammlung und Museum für Byzantinische Kunst, SMB / Antje Voigt: p. 24; bpk | The Trustees of the British Museum: pp. 76, 87, 219, 466; Courtesy of Sotheby's Picture Library, London: p. 469; Erasmus House (on loan from the Collegiate Church of Saints Peter and Guido, Anderlecht) © Lukas – Art in Flanders VZW: pp. 416, 417; © Fitzwilliam Museum, University of Cambridge / The Bridgeman Art Library: p. 163; Foundation Huis Bergh, Collection Dr. J. H. van Heek, 's-Heerenberg, The Netherlands: p. 286; © Fundación Lázaro Galdiano, Madrid: pp. 37, 348 Galleria degli Uffizi / Raffaelo Bencini, Florence: p. 175; Gemäldegalerie der Akademie der bildenden Künste, Vienna: pp. 1–12, 17, 223/24, 231/32, 236/37, 241/42, 246/47, 251, 253–255, 376/77; Grafische Sammlung Albertina, Vienna: pp. 432, 447, 456, 460–463, 276, 282; Herzog Anton Ulrich-Museum, Braunschweig: pp. 58, 228; © 2013 Kimbell Art Museum, Fort Worth, Texas / Art Resource, NY / Scala, Florence: p. 144; Koninklijke Bibliotheek, The Hague: p. 93; Kunsthistorisches Museum, Vienna: pp. 31, 84, 91, 269, 360; Kupferstichkabinett der Akademie der bildenden Künste, Vienna: p. 467; Musea Brugge © Lukas – Art in Flanders VZW, Photo Hugo Maertens: pp. 412/13, 420/21; © Musée d'Unterlinden, Colmar: p. 109; © Musée municipal, Saint-Germain-en-Laye / Photo Laurent Sully-Jaulmes: p. 424; © Museu Nacional de Arte Antiga, Lisbon / Photo Luísa Oliveira, Arquivo de Documentação Fotográfica – DGPC: pp. 97/8, 102/03, 105/06, 113, 117–121, 123–128, 131–134, 136/37, 139, 362, 363; © Museo Nacional del Prado, Madrid: pp. 65–70, 74/5, 141/42, 149/50, 157/58, 165/66, 171/72, 176–182, 184, 186–193, 195–97, 199–202, 207–211, 213/14, 217/18, 149/50, 221, 308/09, 314/15, 319–323, 325–328, 330/31, 333, 339, 354/55, 368/69, 382, 397, 400/01; © Museo Thyssen-Bornemisza, Madrid: p. 63; Museum Boijmans Van Beuningen, Rotterdam / Photo Studio Tromp, Rotterdam: pp. 23, 78, 303, 306/07 c., 316/17, 357, 392, 398/99, 440–443; Museum of Fine Arts, Boston / The Bridgeman Art Library: pp. 410/11; Museum of Fine Arts, Ghent © Lukas – Art in Flanders VZW, Photo Hugo Maertens: pp. 19, 29, 345, 425; © Museum het Zwanenbroedershuis, 's-Hertogenbosch: p. 38 l.; © Patrimonio Nacional, Madrid: pp. 77, 294, 336, 358; Philadelphia Museum of Art / The Bridgeman Art Library: p. 414; Private Collection, Photo © The Metropolitan Museum of Art: pp. 476/77; Réunion des Musées Nationaux, Paris. © RMN-Grand Palais (musée du Louvre) / Michèle Bellot: pp. 464/65; © RMN–Grand Palais (musée du Louvre) / Jean-Gilles Berizzi: p. 261; © RMN–Grand Palais (musée du Louvre) / Gérard Blot: p. 252; © RMN / Christian Jean: p. 56; © RMN / Thierry Le Mage: p. 287; © RMN / René-Gabriel Ojéda: pp. 289, 306 t. l., 393; © Rheinisches Bildarchiv / Rolf Zimmermann, Cologne: p. 92; Rijksmuseum, Amsterdam: pp. 48, 80, 154; © Royal Museums of Fine Arts of Belgium,

Brussels / Photo d'art Speltdoorn & Fils, Brussels: pp. 21, 235, 344; © SSPSAE-VE e polo museale veneziano, Venice / Photo Luciano Romano, Naples: pp. 257, 258, 265, 266, 271, 272/73, 277, 278, 285, 297, 300, 304/05, 310/11, 312, 313, 374, 380, 386/87, 429; Staatliche Kunstsammlungen Dresden: pp. 262, 470–473; © Städel Museum – ARTOTHEK: pp. 49–54, 57, 351; Stiftung Weimarer Klassik / Herzogin Anna Amalia Bibliothek, Weimar: pp. 153, 183; The Barber Institute of Fine Arts, University of Birmingham / The Bridgeman Art Library: p. 146; The Bodleian Libraries, The University of Oxford: p. 169; The J. Paul Getty Museum, Los Angeles: p. 220; The National Gallery London / Scala, Florence: pp. 59, 352; The National Gallery of Art, Washington: pp. 227, 290, 307 r., 296; Victoria and Albert Museum, London: p. 238; Yale University Art Gallery / Art Resource, NY / Scala, Florence: pp. 306 b. l., 394; Zentralbibliothek, Zurich: p. 46 l.

Acknowledgements

The publisher would like to thank all the museums, libraries, private collections, archives and institutions named in the picture captions and the photo credits for their kind assistance in the publication of this book. A great many curators and collectors, and likewise photographers and photo agencies, have played a vital role in ensuring the success of the project through their energetic and personal commitment. Our grateful thanks go to Cristina Alovisetti (Museo Nacional del Prado, Madrid), Till-Holger Borchert (Musea Brugge – Groeningemuseum, Bruges), Bart De Sitter (LUKAS – Art in Flanders, Ghent), Andrea Domanig (Gemäldegalerie der Akademie der bildenden Künste, Vienna), Alexandra Encarnação (Museu Nacional de Arte Antiga, Lisbon), Martina Fleischer (Gemäldegalerie der Akademie der bildenden Künste, Vienna), Carmen Huerta (Museo Nacional del Prado, Madrid), Ilse Jung (Kunsthistorisches Museum, Vienna), Stephan Kemperdick (Gemäldegalerie, Berlin), Claudia Koch (Gemäldegalerie der Akademie der bildenden Künste, Vienna), Katja Lehmann (Scala, Florence), Giulio Manieri Elia (SSPSAE-VE e polo museale veneziano, Venice), Maureen Alexandra Ogrocki (Städel Museum, Frankfurt), Tânia Olim (Museu Nacional de Arte Antiga, Lisbon), Luísa Oliveira (Museu Nacional de Arte Antiga, Lisbon), Luciano Romano (Grafiluce, Naples), Anne Schulte (bpk, Berlin). We would also like to thank lithographers Giuseppe Brisotto and Silverio Zanotto (Fotolito Brisotto, Tezze di Piave) for all their efforts.

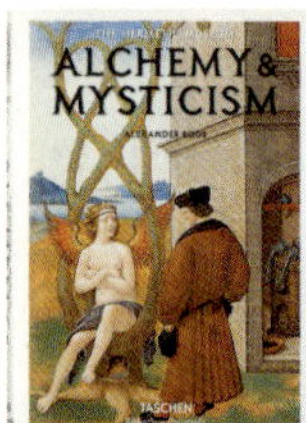

Alchemy & Mysticism

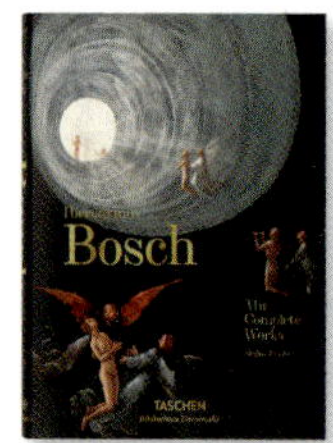

Hieronymus Bosch. Complete Works

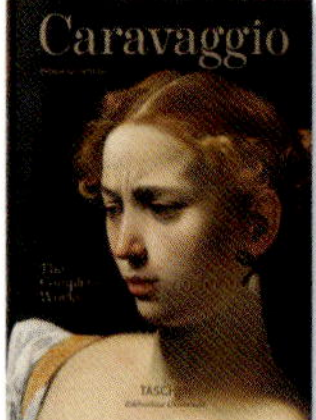

Caravaggio. Complete Works

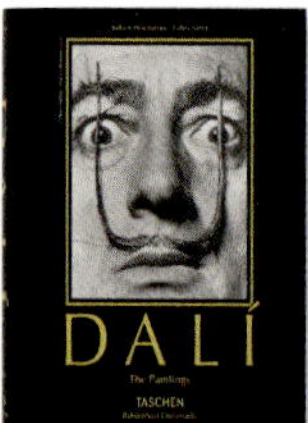

Dalí. The Paintings

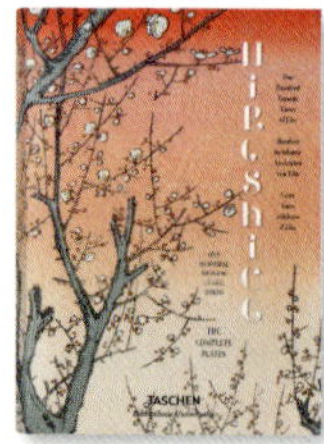

Hiroshige

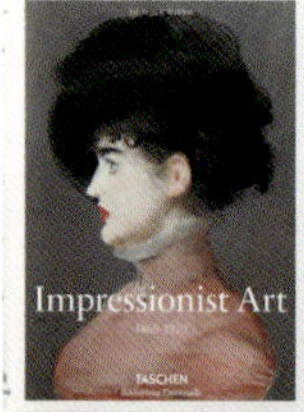

Impressionist Art

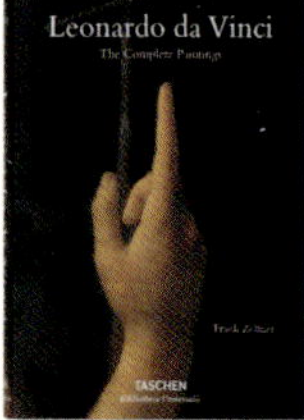

Leonardo da Vinci. Complete Paintings

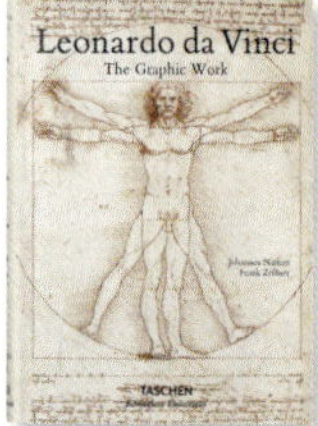

Leonardo da Vinci. The Graphic Work

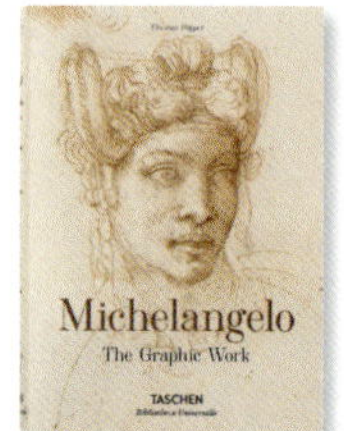

Michelangelo. The Graphic Work

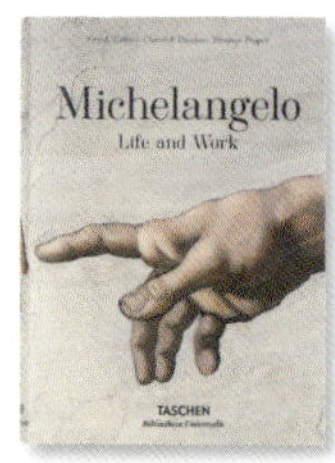

Michelangelo. Life and Work

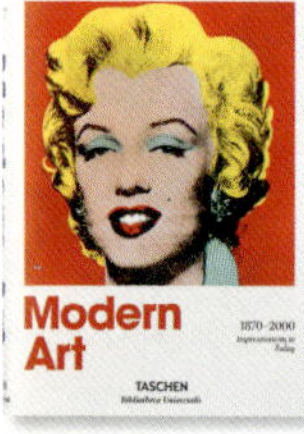

Modern Art

Bookworm's delight: never bore, always excite!

TASCHEN

Bibliotheca Universalis

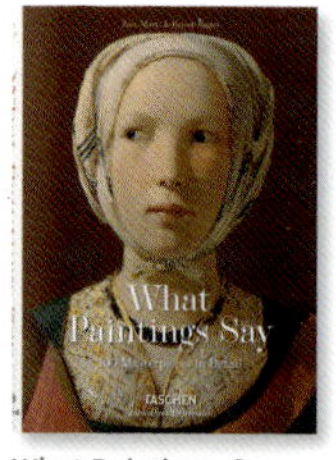

What Paintings Say

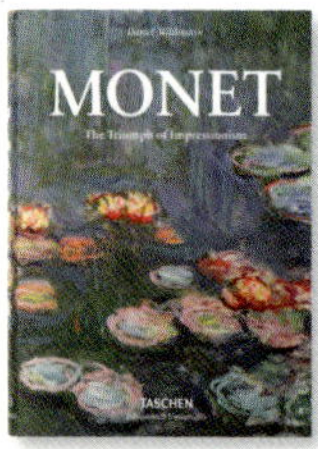

Monet

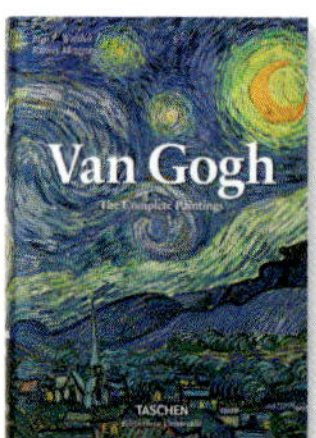

Van Gogh

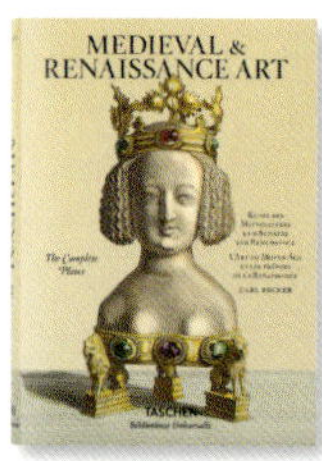

Becker. Medieval & Renaissance Art

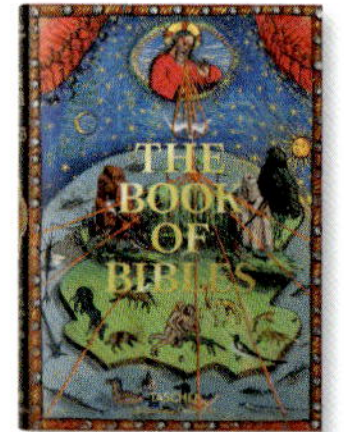

The Book of Bibles

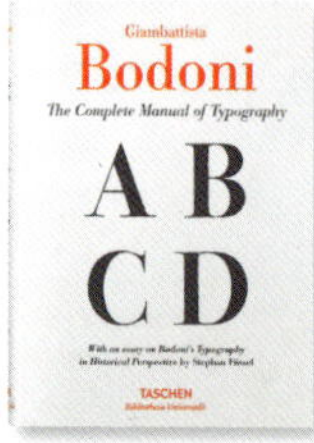

Bodoni. Manual of Typography

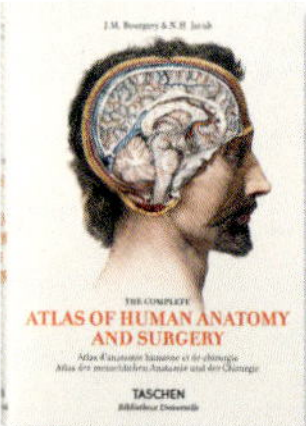

Bourgery. Atlas of Anatomy & Surgery

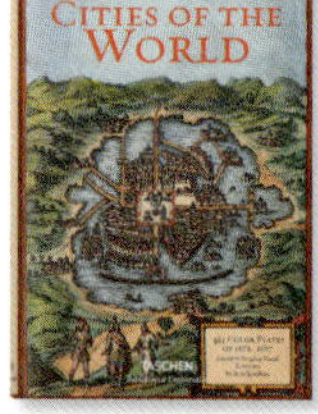

Braun/Hogenberg. Cities of the World

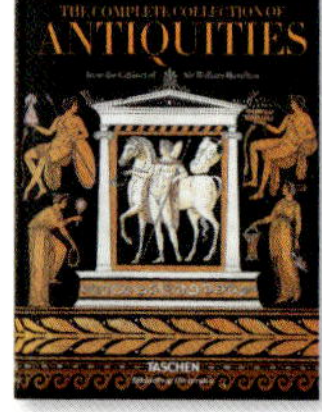

D'Hancarville. Antiquities

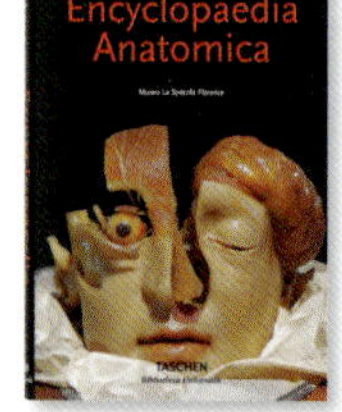

Encyclopaedia Anatomica

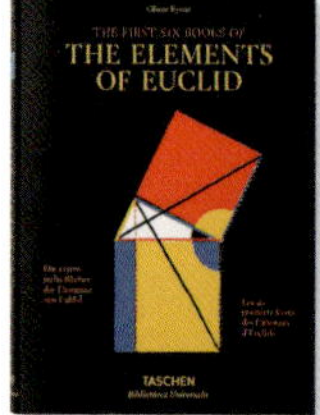

Six Books of Euclid

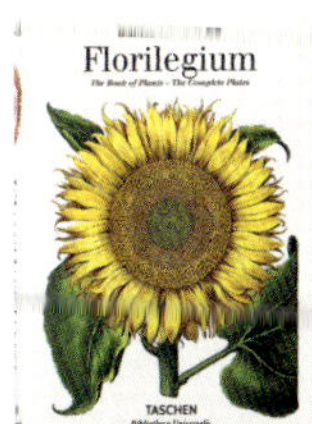

Basilius Besler's Florilegium

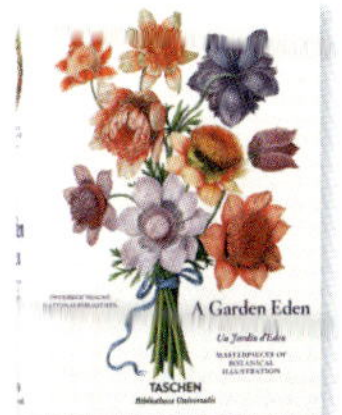

A Garden Eden

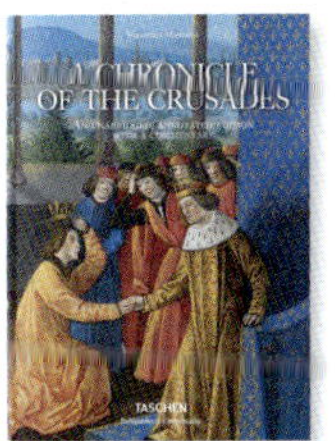

Mamerot. A Chronicle of the Crusades

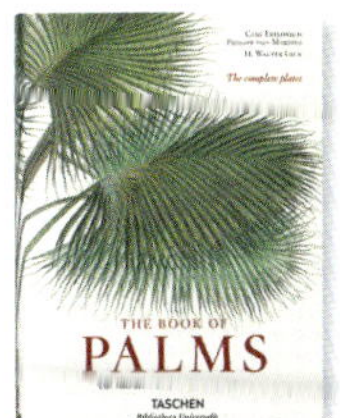

Martius. The Book of Palms

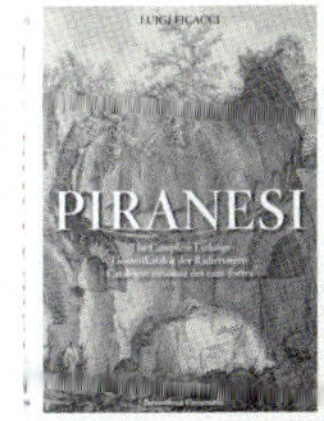

Piranesi. Complete Etchings

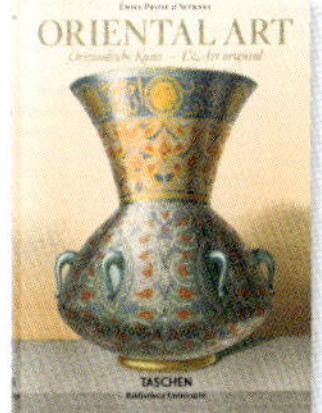

Prisse d'Avennes. Oriental Art

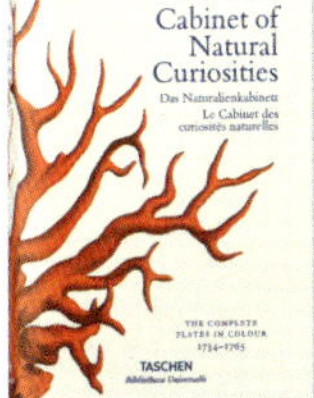

Seba. Cabinet of Natural Curiosities

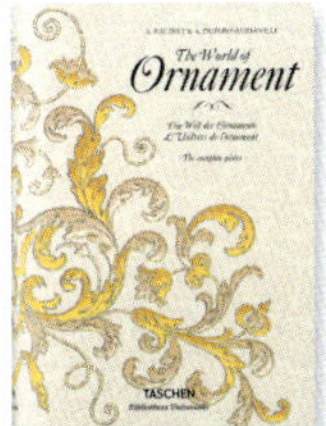

The World of Ornament

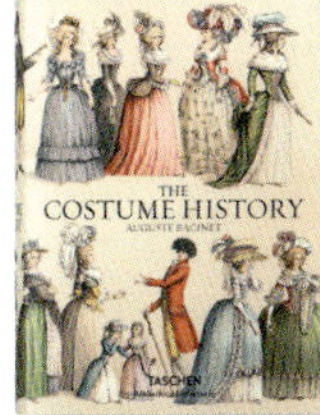

Racinet. The Costume History

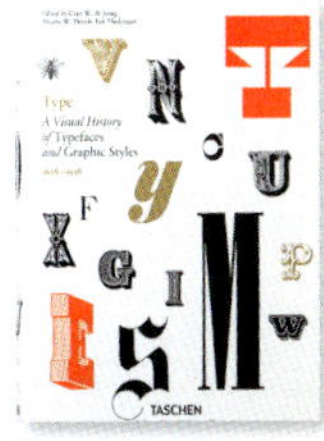

Type. A Visual History

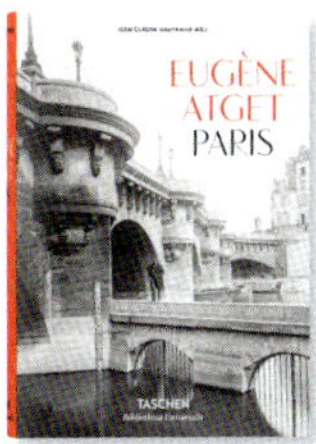

Eugène Atget. Paris

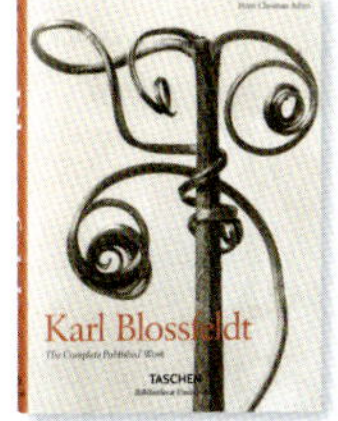

Karl Blossfeldt

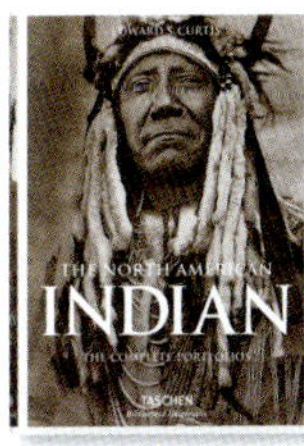

Curtis. The North American Indian

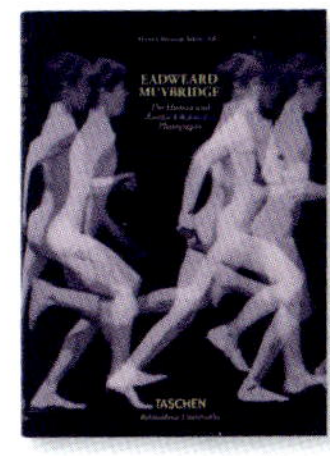

Eadweard Muybridge

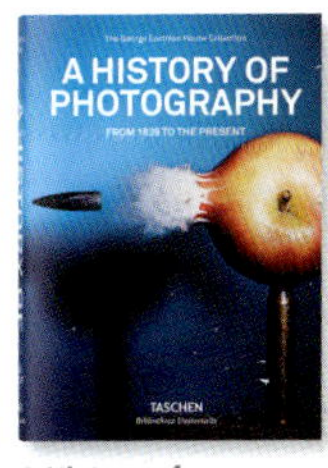

A History of Photography

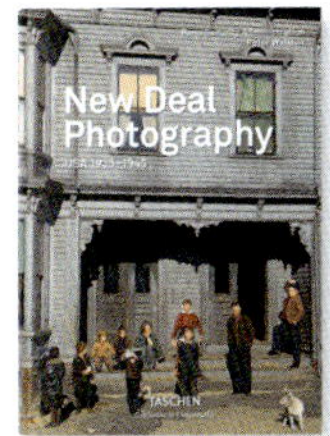

New Deal Photography

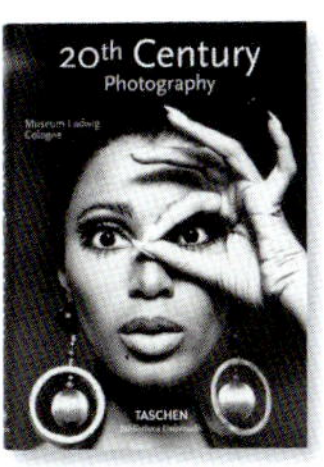

20th Century Photography

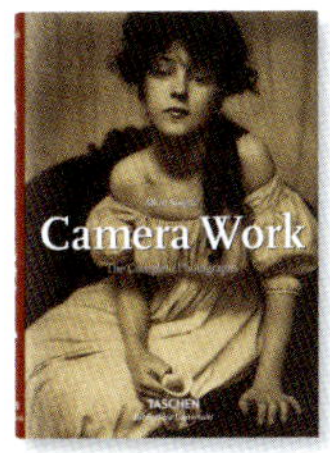

Stieglitz. Camera Work

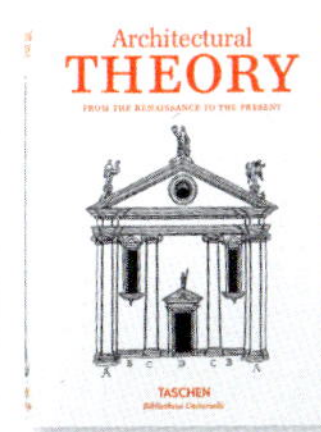

Architectural Theory

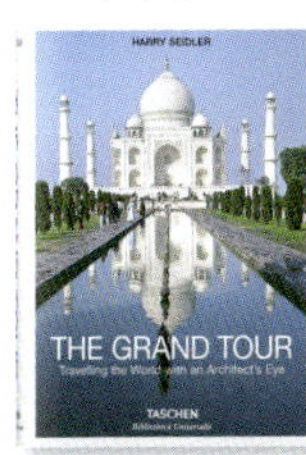

The Grand Tour

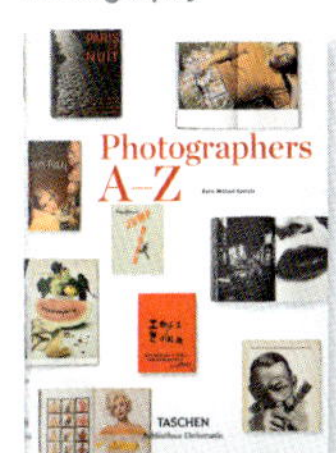

Photographers A–Z

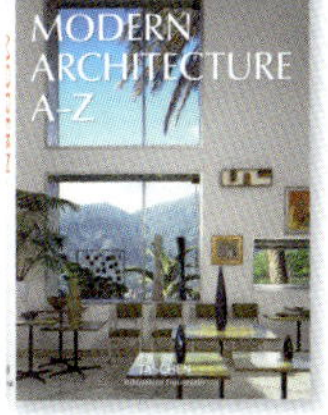

Modern Architecture A-Z

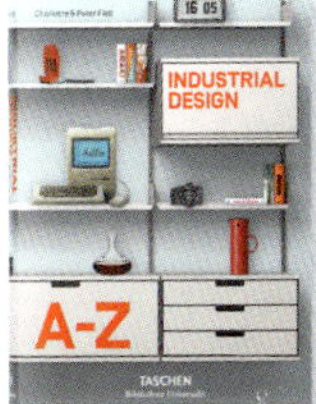

Industrial Design A–Z

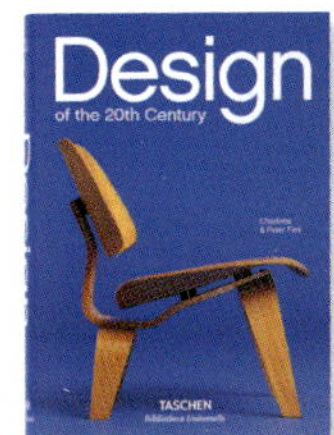

Design of the 20th Century

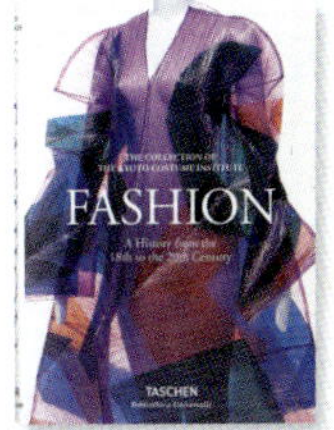

Fashion. A History from 18th–20th Century

Imprint

TASCHEN IS A CARBON NEUTRAL PUBLISHER.
Each year, we offset our annual carbon emissions with carbon credits at the Instituto Terra, a reforestation program in Minas Gerais, Brazil, founded by Lélia and Sebastião Salgado. To find out more about this ecological partnership, please check: www.taschen.com/zerocarbon
Inspiration: unlimited. Carbon footprint: zero.

To stay informed about TASCHEN and our upcoming titles, please subscribe to our free magazine at www.taschen.com/magazine, follow us on Twitter, Instagram, and Facebook, or e-mail your questions to contact@taschen.com.

Pages 1–9, 11 and endpapers:
The Last Judgement (details), around 1506
Oil and tempera on panel (oak),
163 x 127.5 cm / 64 ¼ x 50 ¼ in. (central panel),
167 x 60 cm / 65 ¾ x 23 ⅝ in. (wings)
Vienna, Gemäldegalerie der Akademie der bildenden Künste

Hohenzollernring 53, D–50672 Köln
www.taschen.com

Project management: Ute Kieseyer, Cologne
Editing: Mahros Allamezade, Cologne; Brigitte Beier, Hamburg
English translation: Karen Williams, Rennes-le-Château
English copy-editing: Chris Allen, London; Elizabeth Clegg, London
Design: Birgit Eichwede, Cologne
Cover design: Sense/Net Art Direction / Andy Disl, www.sense-net.net
Production: Ute Wachendorf, Cologne

Printed in Slovakia
ISBN 978-3-8365-3850-3

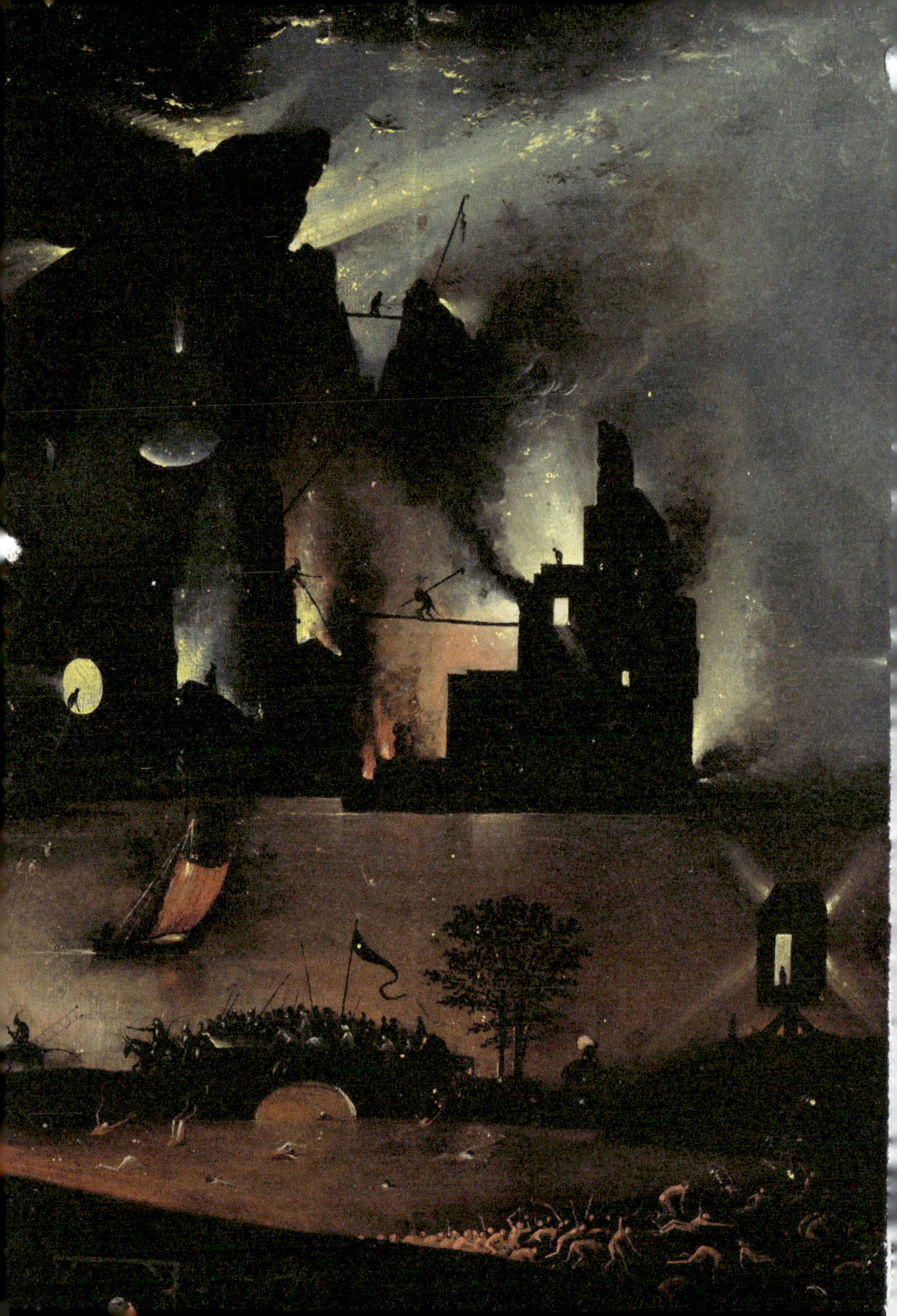